THE EUROPEAN ECONOMY

Growth and Crisis

Edited by
ANDREA BOLTHO

OXFORD UNIVERSITY PRESS

Oxford University Press, Walton Street, Oxford OX2 6DP
Oxford New York Toronto
Delhi Bombay Calcutta Madras Karachi
Kuala Lumpur Singapore Hong Kong Tokyo
Nairobi Dar es Salaam Cape Town
Melbourne Auckland
and associated companies in
Beirut Berlin Ibadan Mexico City Nicosia

Published in the United States by
Oxford University Press, New York

First published 1982
Reprinted 1985

British Library Cataloguing in Publication Data
The European economy.
1. Europe, Western—Economic conditions—
20th century
I. Boltho, Andrea
330.941'085   HC240
ISBN 0 19 877118 5
ISBN 0 19 877119 3 Pbk

Library of Congress Cataloging in Publication Data
Main entry under title:
The European economy.
Includes bibliographies and indexes.
1. Europe—Economic conditions—1945- —Ad-
dresses, essays, lectures.   2. Europe—Economic
policy—Addresses, essays, lectures.   I. Boltho,
Andrea.
HC240.E8363 1982   330.94'055   82 7909
ISBN 0 19 877118 5   AACR2
ISBN 0 19 877119 3 (pbk.)

Typeset by Hope Services, Abingdon
Printed in Great Britain
at the University Press, Oxford
by David Stanford
Printer to the University

THE EUROPEAN ECONOMY

Growth and Crisis

Preface

This book is designed to fill a gap in the economic literature on Western Europe. Despite the area's increasing integration and interdependence, applied economic research has, on the whole, shied away from cross-country comparative work. Valuable monographs have been written on particular subjects (e.g. growth or inflation), or particular countries, while short-run developments have been (and are) covered by various international organizations: but broad surveys of Europe's post-war experience have seldom appeared. Yet there would seem to be a need for such a survey in the light of the increasing interest shown by academics, students, businessmen, and journalists in the comparative experience of the European economies.

The chapters that follow try to meet this need. They were written by a group of authors who have had experience of both comparative work and policy-making. Most, at one time or another, have served in either national or international administrations. Beyond this 'policy bias', however, there has been no attempt to impose a common view on each chapter. The contributors were asked to survey a subject, but left free to concentrate within it on those themes which they felt were most interesting. Thus, despite the similarity in outlook among many of the authors, the book presents a variety of interpretations. To ensure, however, an even greater diversity, at least in the important fields of growth and inflation, Chapters 2 and 4 put forward views which are perhaps less eclectic than those of other parts of the book.

Among those who helped in suggesting topics, in providing names of prospective authors, and in giving encouragement are Sir Alec Cairncross, Andrew Graham, and Gianni Toniolo. Particular thanks must go to all the contributors themselves, who were pressurized by a dictatorial editor to accept initial blueprints and subsequent cuts, frequent modifications, extensive redrafts, and the imposition, as far as possible, of a standardized statistical basis. For once, there is much truth in inverting the usual disclaimer − any errors that may remain in the following text are not due to the authors but to the editor.

My greatest debt is to my colleague Chris Allsopp who was with me through much of the period. He helped in laying out the book's plan, in drafting many of the suggested chapter outlines, in commenting on numerous first drafts, and in inspiring parts of the Introduction. I am sure that I would never have embarked on the project had he not been there at the outset.

Oxford,
Autumn 1981

A.B.

Contents

PART I – CROSS-COUNTRY TRENDS

PART II – ECONOMIC POLICIES

Notes and List of Abbreviations

Unless otherwise states, Europe stands for Western Europe throughout this book, Germany for West Germany, and 'the post-war period' refers to the years since World War II. Though the coverage of Western Europe is technically that of OECD Europe, most discussions do not cover the experience of the smaller and/or developing countries of the area (Iceland, Luxembourg, Greece, Portugal, and Turkey). The EEC, unless otherwise stated, refers to the Community of nine member countries (the original six plus the United Kingdom, Denmark, and Ireland) as it stood between 1973 and 1979.

Years are always calendar years except when shown in the (financial year) form 1975/6. In the tables and diagrams, constant price series, unless otherwise specified, refer to data at 1975 prices. The signs $, £, and DM refer to United States dollars, pounds sterling, and Deutschmarks; the signs . ., ( ), −, mean respectively that data are not available; that data have been partly estimated by the author; that the data are close or equal to zero. A billion equals one thousand millions. In the few econometric results reported, $\overline{R}^2$ stands for the coefficient of determination and figures in brackets are t-ratios.

Abbreviations: the most frequently used abbreviations are as follows:

BIS	Bank for International Settlements, Basle
BLEU	Belgium–Luxembourg Economic Union
CAP	Common Agricultural Policy
CMEA	Council for Mutual Economic Assistance, Moscow
CSO	Central Statistical Office, London
EEC	European Economic Community, Brussels
EFTA	European Free Trade Association, Geneva
EMS	European Monetary System
EPU	European Payments Union
GATT	General Agreement on Tariffs and Trade, Geneva
HMSO	Her Majesty's Stationery Office, London
IBRD	International Bank for Reconstruction and Development, Washington
ILO	International Labour Office, Geneva
IMF	International Monetary Fund, Washington
INSEE	Institute national de la statistique et des études économiques, Paris
ISTAT	Istituto centrale di statistica, Rome
M	Money supply
NBER	National Bureau of Economic Research, New York
NIESR	National Institute of Economic and Social Research, London
OECD	Organisation for Economic Co-operation and Development, Paris
OEEC	Organisation for European Economic Co-operation, Paris
OPEC	Organization of Petroleum Exporting Countries, Vienna
PSBR	Public Sector Borrowing Requirement
RIAA	Royal Institute of International Affairs, London
SITC	Standard International Trade Classification
UN	United Nations, New York
UNECE	United Nations Economic Commission for Europe, Geneva
VAT	Value Added Taxation
WIFO	Österreichisches Institut für Wirtschaftsvorschung, Vienna

In addition, the following abbreviations are used in some diagrams:

A	Austria	E	Spain	NL	Netherlands
B	Belgium	F	France	S	Sweden
CH	Switzerland	I	Italy	SF	Finland
D	Germany	IR	Ireland	UK	United Kingdom
DK	Denmark	N	Norway		

Notes on Contributors

Johnny Åkerholm: educated at the University of Helsinki and at the Swedish School of Economics, Helsinki. Since 1971 has held different posts in the Institute for Economic Research and in various departments of the Bank of Finland. Between 1975 and 1978 at the OECD's Department of Economics and Statistics. He has published articles in Bank of Finland publications and in various Finnish journals.

Christopher Allsopp: educated at Oxford University. In 1966-7 at HM Treasury. Since 1967 Fellow and Tutor in Economics at New College, Oxford. For one year (1973-4) Head of the Economic Prospects Division at the OECD's Department of Economics and Statistics; in 1980-1 Adviser to the Bank of England. He has published articles on economic growth and policy issues, *inter alia* in the *NIESR Review* and in *Revue économique*.

Franco Bernabè: studied at the University of Turin, where he was Assistant Professor in the Faculty of Economics between 1973 and 1976. From 1976 to 1978 at the OECD's Economics and Statistics and Manpower and Social Affairs Departments. Since 1978 Chief Economist, Economic Studies Department, FIAT. His publications include *L'offerta di lavoro in Italia*, Milan 1976 (with others), and he has edited *Struttura finanziaria e politica economica in Italia*, Milan 1976.

John Bispham: studied at Manchester University before joining the National Institute of Economic and Social Research in 1967. Became Assistant Editor of the *NIESR Review* in 1970 and Editor in 1972. Between 1975 and 1977 at the Bank of England in charge of short-term forecasting. Since 1977 at the Bank for International Settlements in Basle.

Andrea Boltho: educated in Italy and at the universities of London (LSE), Paris, and Oxford. From 1966 to 1977 at the OECD's Department of Economics and Statistics where he was, *inter alia*, Editor of the *Economic Outlook* and head of the Economic Growth Division. For one year (1973-4), Japan Foundation Fellow at the Economic Planning Agency in Tokyo. Since 1977 Fellow and Tutor in Economics at Magdalen College, Oxford. His publications include *Foreign Trade Criteria in Socialist Economies*, Cambridge 1971, and *Japan: An Economic Survey*, Oxford 1975.

Alan Budd: studied at the London School of Economics and at Cambridge University. From 1966 to 1969 he was Lecturer in Economics at the University of Southampton, and in 1969-70 Ford Foundation Visiting Professor at Carnegie-Mellon University, Pittsburgh. Between 1970 and 1974 he was Senior Economic Adviser responsible for short-term forecasting at HM Treasury. Since then he has been at the London Business School where he is Professor of Economics and Director of the Centre for Economic Forecasting. He has published widely and is the author of *The Politics of Economic Planning*, London 1979.

Michael Davenport: graduated from the universities of Edinburgh and Pennsylvania. Prior to 1973 he was lecturer in Economics and Economic Statistics at York University, and later Economic Adviser with HM Treasury. From 1973 to 1980 he worked for the Directorate for Economic and Financial Affairs of the EEC Commission where he was head of the Division for France and of the Short-term Forecasting Division. He is now Director of World Model Forecasting at Wharton Econometric Forecasting Associates, Philadelphia. He has published on a number of subjects, *inter alia* in *Economica*, the *Journal of Finance*, the *Journal of Political Economy*, and the *Bulletin of the Oxford Institute of Statistics*.

Geoffrey Dicks: educated at the universities of Reading, Cambridge, and Southampton. From 1970 to 1972 he was Economic Assistant at the Department of Employment. Since 1976 he has been at the London Business School's Centre for Economic Forecasting, where he is Senior Research Officer and joint editor of the *Economic Outlook*.

Karl-Olof Faxén: educated at the universities of Stockholm, Uppsala, and Chicago. Since 1956 he has been Economic Adviser to the Swedish Employers Confederation (SAF) and has in this capacity taken part in centralized bargaining. He has also worked in the field of industrial democracy as chairman of a tripartite joint research group, and published in 1979 *Organizational Change, Learning and Productivity* (Stockholm). He has represented SAF on the Royal Commissions for Stabilization Policy, for Taxation, for Low Incomes, and for Computer Policy, and in various ILO and OECD groups. He is SAF member in the Government Research Council for Medium Term Planning and for Industrial Policy. His scientific work includes game theory (mimeo, 1951), 'Monetary and Fiscal Policy under Uncertainty' (Ph.D., 1957), and *Wage Formation and the Economy*, London 1973 (with G. Edgren and C. -E. Odhner).

Klaus Hinrich Hennings: graduated from the University of Tübingen in economics and sociology and received a doctorate from the University of Oxford. He taught there and at the University of Reading, and has been, since 1976, Professor of Economics at the University of Hanover. In 1980–1 he was Visiting Professor of Economics at the University of Virginia. He has published in such journals as the *Economic Journal, History of Political Economy, Kyklos, Zeitschrift für die gesamte Staatswissenschaft*, and *Zeitschrift für Nationalökonomie*.

John Llewellyn: after graduating from Victoria University, Wellington, he received a doctorate at the University of Oxford. In 1970 he was appointed a Research Officer in the Department of Applied Economics, Cambridge, and, in 1974, became Assistant Director of Research in the Faculty of Economics, Cambridge University. Since 1978 he has been head of the Economic Prospects Division at the OECD's Economics and Statistics Department, responsible for the twice-yearly *Economic Outlook*. He has written on growth, trade, inflation, and forecasting in e.g. the *Economic Journal* and the *Review of Economic Studies*.

Jacques Mazier: studied at the École Polytechnique and at the University of Paris. Between 1970 and 1975 at the Direction de la Prévision of the Ministry of Economics and Finance. From 1976 to 1981 Professor of Economics at the University of Rennes: at present Chargé de Mission at the Planning Commission. He is the author of *Macroéconomie appliquée: une présentation critique*, Paris

1978, and of *Accumulation, régulation et crises*, Paris 1982 (with others), and has published in *Economie et statistique, Revue économique*, etc.

Eduardo Merigó: educated in Spain and at the University of Geneva. From 1960 to 1962 at the Research and Planning Division of the UNECE. Between 1962 and 1973 with the OECD's Department of Economics and Statistics, where he was in charge of the Balance of Payments Division and, from 1971, Deputy Director of the General Economics Branch. In 1974–5 Economic Adviser to the Spanish Minister of Finance. In 1977–8 Under-Secretary of State for Regional Planning. In 1979 Head of the National Institute for Prospective Studies, Madrid. Among his numerous publications is *Economia de la inflación*, Madrid 1974.

William Nicol: educated at the University of Glasgow. Between 1974 and 1975 Research Officer in the Department of Town and Regional Planning at the University of Strathclyde. From then to end-1981 Research Fellow in the International Institute of Management, Wissenschaftszentrum, Berlin. At present with the OECD's Division for Multinational Enterprises. His publications include *Deglomeration Policies in the European Community: A Comparative Study*, Brussels 1981.

Antonio Pedone: studied at the universities of Rome and Cambridge and taught at the universities of Ancona, Naples, and Rome. His research activities have taken him to the universities of York and Oxford and, in 1979, to the Fiscal Affairs Department of the IMF. He is at present Professor of Finance at the University of Rome and Adviser to the Prime Minister's Office on financial problems. His publications include *Il controllo dell'economia nel breve periodo*, Milan 1970 (with others), *La politica fiscale*, Bologna 1971 (ed.), and *Evasori e tartassati*, Bologna 1979.

Stephen Potter: after graduating from Cambridge University, worked at HM Treasury. Returned to Cambridge in 1965 as a Research Officer at the Department of Applied Economics, where he co-authored the Reddaway Reports on foreign direct investment; also acted as Secretary and Statistician to the London and Cambridge Economic Service. From 1968 at the OECD's Department of Economics and Statistics, where he has headed Divisions concerned with balance of payments questions, short-term forecasting, and country studies; from 1976, Deputy Director of the General Economics Branch. At the time this chapter was finalized, on leave of absence at the Bank of England as Adviser, Economics and International Divisions.

Guido M. Rey: has taught at the universities of Urbino-Ancona, at Florence, and at Rome, where he is Professor of Economic and Financial Policy. Between 1960 and 1970 he was in the Bank of Italy's Economic Research Department, where he helped develop the Bank's first econometric model of the Italian economy. Since 1980 he has been President of ISTAT. His numerous publications are in the areas of economic policy, Italian economic developments, public expenditure, and econometric modelling.

Christian Sautter: educated at the École Polytechnique, at the École nationale de la statistique et de l'administration (ENSAE), and at the Institut de sciences politiques. From 1966 to 1978 he was at INSEE where, *inter alia*, he headed the Division 'Étude des entreprises' and the Medium-term Macroeconomic Unit.

For one year (1971–2) at the Economic Research Institute of the Economic Planning Agency in Tokyo. Between 1978 and 1981 he was Director of the Centre d'études prospectives et d'informations internationales (CEPII), Paris. He has written *Japon: Le prix de la puissance*, Paris 1973; edited 'Fresque historique du système productif', *Collections de l'INSEE*, série E, No. 27, 1974; and (together with M. Baba) 'La planification en France et au Japon', *Collections de l'INSEE*, série C, No. 61, 1978; and published extensively, notably in *Revue économique* and *Economie et statistique*.

Malcolm Sawyer: educated at the Universities of Oxford and London (LSE). He has worked for the OECD's Department of Economics and Statistics on public expenditure and the distribution of income, and prepared reports for the EEC on industrial matters. He has taught at University College, London, and is now Reader in Economics at the University of York. He is the author (with S. Aaronovitch) of *Big Business*, London 1975; *Theories of the Firm*, London 1979; *The Economics of Industries and Firms*, London 1981; and *Macroeconomics in Question: Orthodoxies and the Kaleckian Alternative*, London 1982. He has published extensively, *inter alia* in *Oxford Economic Papers*, *Scottish Journal of Political Economy*, *NIESR Review*, *Manchester School*, etc., and is co-editor of the annual *Socialist Economic Review*.

Palle Schelde Andersen: educated in Denmark and the United States. Assistant Professor at the University of Aarhus, Denmark, from 1966 to 1968, Visiting Lecturer at Hamilton College in 1968–9, and Associate Professor at Aarhus in 1970–3. Since 1974 with the Department of Economics and Statistics of the OECD, where he is Head of the General Economics Division, dealing mainly with inflation and labour market problems. For one year (1979–80) Research Fellow at the University of Sydney. His earlier publications include work on fiscal and tax policy, automatic budget stabilizers, and econometric modelling (published in *Swedish Journal of Economics* and in *Nationaløkonomisk Tidsskrift*), while more recent work includes publications (by OECD) on inflation and incomes policy.

Michael Surrey: after graduating from the University of Oxford, went to the Economics Section of HM Treasury where he worked on economic forecasting between 1966 and 1968. In 1968 he joined the NIESR and helped construct the Institute's first econometric model of the British economy. Between 1970 and 1976 Fellow and Tutor in Economics at Wadham College, Oxford; between 1977 and 1978 Editor of the *NIESR Review*; since 1979 Professor of Economics at Leeds University. His publications include *The Analysis and Forecasting of the British Economy*, NIESR, Cambridge, 1971; *An Introduction to Econometrics*, Oxford 1974; and *Macroeconomic Themes*, Oxford 1976.

Niels Thygesen: studied at Copenhagen and Harvard Universities. After serving as Economic Adviser to the Government of Malaysia (1969–71), and as Head of the Monetary Division in the OECD's Department of Economics and Statistics (1971–2), he has been Professor of Political Economy at the University of Copenhagen. During that period he has also been Adviser to the Danmarks Nationalbank and member of several EEC expert groups. Author of *The Sources and the Impact of Monetary Changes*, Copenhagen 1971; *The Role of Monetary Policy in Demand Management*, OECD, Paris, 1975 (with K. Shigehara), and numerous journal articles on monetary and international economics.

Willy van Rijckeghem: educated at the universities of Ghent, Copenhagen, and Paris. Has travelled widely and undertaken government advisory work in Argentina, Brazil, Morocco, and Portugal. At present Professor of Economics at the Free University of Brussels. Has published in areas of development economics, labour market problems, and stabilization policy, and has written *A World of Inflation*, London 1976 (with G. Maynard).

Nita Watts: was between 1941 and 1955 in the Economic Section, War Cabinet Office, and, later, HM Treasury. In 1955 she joined the Research and Planning Division of the UNECE where she was Deputy Director in later years. In 1964–5 at the National Economic Development Office and at the Department of Economic Affairs, London. From 1965 to 1981 Fellow and Tutor in Economics at St. Hilda's College, Oxford, and Senior Research Officer, Oxford Institute of Economics and Statistics. Her publications include contributions to UNECE *Surveys* and *Bulletins*, journal articles, and reviews. She has edited *Economic Relations between East and West*, London 1978, and is the Editor of the OUP 'Economies of the World' series.

Douglas Yuill: a graduate of the University of Glasgow, was from 1972 to 1975 Lecturer in Applied Economics at Glasgow University, then Research Fellow at the International Institute of Management, Wissenschaftszentrum, Berlin (1975–8). Since 1978 he has been at the Centre for the Study of Public Policy, University of Strathclyde, where he is now Senior Research Fellow. He is co-author of *Regional Incentives in the European Community*, Brussels 1979, and *Regional Policy in the European Community*, London 1980, and is joint editor of the annual publication *European Regional Incentives*.

Introduction

ANDREA BOLTHO*

This book is concerned with the economic development of Western Europe from the early 1950s to the end of the 1970s. Part I presents a comparative survey of trends in a number of areas, looking in particular at those variables which have often been put forward as major goals of, or constraints on, economic policy – growth, inflation, the balance of payments, unemployment or income distribution. Part II surveys some aspects of economic policy-making, while Part III looks at the experience of the five major European countries (France, Germany, Italy, the United Kingdom, and Spain) and at that of two areas, the Benelux and Scandinavia.

Clearly, this coverage is selective and incomplete. It could be argued, for instance, that chapters should have been devoted to other macroeconomic themes, such as international monetary developments, to other policy instruments, such as economic planning, and to other countries or areas, such as Austria and Switzerland or the smaller Mediterranean countries. The major reason for these and other gaps lies in the inevitable constraint of space which imposed overall limitations from the outset.

Trends

Seen in a longer-run perspective, the thirty years here surveyed were clearly exceptional. Among the more important breaks in trends, the following stand out:

(i) The exceptionally rapid growth of living standards;
(ii) The appearance of a prolonged period of full employment;
(iii) The disappearance of the agricultural sector as a significant employer in most European economies;
(iv) The very sharp decrease in the incidence of individual economic risk.

That growth was exceptionally rapid is, of course, well known. Between 1950 and 1979 the GDP of the European OECD area rose 3½ times (or by some 4¼ per cent per annum). It had earlier taken as long as seventy years to achieve a similar increase (from 1880 to 1950). Not only was growth rapid, but income distribution improved in Europe as a whole, as those countries that were poorer at the outset grew at above average rates. And income distribution probably improved within countries as well, even if the evidence on this account is scanty. Interestingly, perhaps, Eastern Europe witnessed very similar developments despite its relative post-war isolation from the West and a very different institutional set-up.

A further exceptional and equally beneficial phenomenon was the achievement in the 1960s of full employment, at least in the north-western part of the area.

* Magdalen College, University of Oxford.

This was an unprecedented success for industrial societies.[1] Bouts of full employment for the urban labour force had occurred at cyclical peaks in the past, but a prolonged period of peace-time full employment, including the virtual disappearance of underemployment on the land, was something which the more cyclically sensitive and agriculturally dependent pre-war economies had not experienced. Here again, East European trends were very similar.

Linked to rapid growth and full employment was a third change which, in a longer-run historical perspective, was perhaps the most significant. What had for centuries, indeed thousands of years, been man's principal activity – agriculture – became, within a generation, a relatively minor sector of output and employment in most Continental European countries. The proportion of agricultural employment had already been declining before 1950, but, outside the United Kingdom, the movement had been much slower. For those countries for which data are available, employment on the land represented close to 50 per cent of the labour force in 1870 and still close to 30 per cent in 1950. By 1980 this share had declined to less than 10 per cent. It is doubtful whether the European economy ever witnessed such a sharp structural change and profound sociological mutation in so short a time-span.[2]

A fourth exceptional development within the post-war period was the very significant reduction in what was called above the 'incidence of economic risk'. In pre-industrial, agricultural societies, individuals had always been subject to economic fluctuations, if only because of the vagaries of the weather. Uncertainty was an inevitable accompaniment of a primitive agriculture. From the industrial revolution onwards, this uncertainty had been replicated in the urban sectors of the economy by a new form of fluctuation in activity – the business cycle. Both were for long viewed almost as acts of God against which man was powerless. But the rapid post-war decline in the dominance of agriculture (and the great improvements made in farm productivity) meant that the influence of climatic fluctuations on output and incomes lost much of its importance. And the apparent success of European governments in coping with business cycle fluctuations, at least until the mid-1970s, meant that most people could rely on regularly rising living standards. Climatic or macroeconomic uncertainty of the kind which, at more or less regular intervals, could throw large segments of the population into famine or, at least, poverty, became largely a thing of the past.

In parallel with the decrease in 'macroeconomic risk' went a similar decrease in 'microeconomic risk', such as individuals' losses of income arising from unemployment, accident, illness, or old age. In many ways the welfare state can be seen as an extension at the individual level of macroeconomic demand management. Just as cyclical movements in the private economy could be moderated by macroeconomic policy, so an individual's income life-cycle could be protected from the vagaries of personal economic misfortunes by, for instance, a

[1] Indeed, it may have been unprecedented for all societies given that underemployment was probably widespread in earlier largely agricultural economies, but meaningful comparisons are not really possible.

[2] Earlier phenomena, such as urbanization, industrialization, or even transatlantic migration, which could be considered to have had important economic and social consequences, had all been protracted evolutions, at least in comparison with what happened to the agricultural population in the space of a quarter century.

government-administered pooling of risk. In the early 1970s, this movement went beyond the provision of income maintenance. Not only did workers claim for (and obtain) better sickness, pension, and unemployment compensation payments – they also promoted legislation which severely diminished the traditional freedom firms had to manage, as well as dismiss, the labour force on the factory floor.

Themes

Few would have expected at the end of World War II, or even in the 1950s, that the European economy would have developed so favourably. It is true that the policy-makers of the time were hoping to restore high employment in peace-time conditions, but they were also very conscious of the difficulties of such a course of action. Memories of the hyperinflations of the 1920s and 1940s on the one hand, and of the depression and balance of payments problems of the 1930s on the other, were still too strong and vivid for public opinion to entertain overly optimistic expectations. Yet success came and bred further success. The question that may be asked in retrospect is whether this success was natural, accidental, or man-made. In other words, was the growth of post-war Europe in some sense inevitable because of the spontaneous buoyancy of market econo-mies; was it the result of a sequence of favourable but fortuitous events; or was it the outcome of purposeful policies designed to achieve it?

If a theme does emerge from this book, it is that economic policies were important in shaping Europe's post-war history and had, on the whole, bene-ficial effects. Thus, the use of demand management policies contributed to the dampening of cycles and to the acceleration in economic growth. Policy inter-vention to improve external performance, e.g. via exchange rate changes, had significant effects on trade flows, greater than those subsequently obtained by a system of floating rates under which the near-permanent nature of changes in competitiveness was no longer ensured. At a more microeconomic level, inter-vention in the social area created and strengthened welfare states and equalized income distribution patterns, while selective regional policies helped overcome, or at least alleviate, spatial imbalances. Industrial policies (though not separately treated in this book) were probably important on the supply side in facilitating reconstruction first, and rapid productivity growth later. Even the often derided incomes policy instrument may have had favourable effects, if not always in curbing inflation, then at least in diminishing the incidence of open industrial conflict and reinforcing the consensus in some of the smaller countries of the area. No doubt, achievements often fell short of the increasingly ambitious targets that were being pursued, but over a thirty-year time-span, the impression that emerges is that policy was relatively effective, if not always fully efficient.

This broad-brush conclusion would seem to run counter to many of the economics profession's recent beliefs. It became increasingly fashionable in the 1970s, especially in the United States, to criticize governmental intervention and interference. Yet, to underline the importance of government in a European con-text is almost to state the obvious. Historically, European business has very often relied on government for its initial expansion, for its prosperity, or for its survival. The links between the private and the public sectors have traditionally been very close, the understanding of mutual interest highly developed, and the belief in the virtues of free enterprise much weaker than, for instance, on the other side of the Atlantic. In such circumstances, government intervention was not only accepted but often also welcomed, something that was likely to increase the effectiveness of policy action.

This effectiveness may also have been helped by some institutional and political characteristics which the United States, for instance, does not share to the same extent. Thus, the centralization which many European countries inherited from the nineteenth-century 'Napoleonic' model of administration may have contributed to greater speed both in the formulation of policies and in their implementation. And a relative degree of political stability in the post-war period may have ensured that longer-run considerations were often emphasized in economic policy-making. This is not to imply that European politicians were less myopic than, for instance, their American counterparts or, for that matter, less ready to recommend popular short-run expedients rather than unpopular longer-term remedies. But their myopia may have been reduced to the extent that they were likely to remain in power for reasonably long periods. Despite apparent instability, many European countries have in fact been ruled by relatively stable one-party systems or coalitions (e.g. France, Germany, and Italy and many of the smaller countries). Frequent alternations between two major political parties which agree on fundamentals but fight each other on economic policy, thereby often destabilizing the private sector, have, over the period under review, really been a characteristic only of the United Kingdom. And even when continuity in economic policy could not be provided by the politicians, it was frequently ensured by a permanent civil service not subject to the 'spoils system' of the United States. In many European countries, a prestigious, often efficient, and usually highly public-spirited bureaucracy was able to moderate the politicians' demands for quick and easy solutions.

It may perhaps not be an accident that these four European characteristics — close government–business relations, administrative centralization, political continuity, and a powerful bureaucracy — are also to be found, possibly in even stronger form, in the capitalist world's most successful economy — Japan.

Crisis and response

Success, however, did not only breed success, but also over-confidence, with policy-makers, and their advisers, pursuing increasingly ambitious policies. This over-confidence may have been one of the factors lying behind the crisis of the 1970s. More importantly, rapid growth in conditions of increasing full employment and rising labour market rigidities was bound to contribute to an eventual acceleration of inflation. And this acceleration may have been accompanied, or even partly caused, by changes in attitudes towards greater acquisitiveness by various social groups, yet at the same time away from risk and entrepreneurship; and to an increasing tendency to rely on governments to provide solutions for all kinds of social and even individual problems. Though the oil shock of 1973–4 no doubt sharply worsened the existing situation, an underlying trend towards a deterioration in performance was already occurring. The earlier achievement of both full employment and relative price stability turned out to be only a temporary success.

The economic history of the 1970s reads very much as a succession of usually half-hearted attempts at controlling inflation, with only disappointing results. The problems which policy-makers had feared would stifle growth in the late 1940s or early 1950s came to the fore twenty-five years later. Lulled, perhaps, by the intervening years of success, Europe hardly came to grips with the new situation created by rapid inflation and terms of trade shifts. The later 1970s were years in which older remedies were followed by many countries (as shown by the proliferation of 'burden sharing', 'locomotive', or 'convoy' approaches), and hopes of a quick return to earlier performance were held by most governments. The year 1979 was marked not only by a second oil shock, but also by the perception that the attempt to promote concerted international expansion at the 1978 Bonn summit had failed.

While the 1970s ended in disarray, the 1980s opened with a much more determined attack on inflation than earlier restrictive experiments. One possible outcome of this could be a prolonged period of stagnation as cost–push pressures and inflationary expectations are slowly purged from the system. Such a gloomy prospect is not, however, the only possible outcome. Just as capitalism survived the 1930s depression by turning to new economic policies (and some would say by rearmament), so capitalism in the 1980s could equally turn to new solutions that could defuse the conflict over income shares which seems to have become much more pronounced in our affluent societies.

Various alternatives spring to mind. One could be the development of more instruments and institutions that would allow our economies to 'live with inflation', as other non-European countries (but perhaps also Iceland) have apparently learnt to do. Another could be an attempt to develop new forms of social consensus going beyond incomes policies and welfare states by, for instance, creating greater interdependence between labour and capital through forms of workers' shareholdings. Yet another could arise from a possible trend towards a greater decentralization of productive activity, made possible by technological developments on the one hand, and by the increasing diversification of demand patterns on the other. The ensuing break-up of mass production processes could whittle down the importance of traditional oligopolies, whether in product or labour markets. None of these trends is, of course, inevitable, nor would they provide immediate solutions to today's problems, but they could point to some of the institutional and economic directions into which Europe may move in the last two decades of the twentieth century.

PART I

CROSS-COUNTRY TRENDS

1

Growth

ANDREA BOLTHO*

Introduction

The growth of the post-war European economy is, directly or indirectly, the subject-matter of the whole of this book. Growth appears as an important explanatory variable for virtually all the phenomena looked at in Part I, figures as a major aim in the economic policy discussion of Part II, and is at the centre of the story of the country chapters presented in Part III. This inevitably means that a full understanding of the growth experience of the last thirty years can hardly be obtained from the present chapter. The aim in the pages that follows is, therefore, the more modest one of providing some quantitative background and a tentative interpretation in the light of which the rest of this book can then be read.

Three major topics are investigated:

(i) The reasons for the sharp acceleration in economic growth in the 1950s and 1960s relative to earlier trends in the economic history of Europe;

(ii) The reasons for the similarly sharp deceleration which Europe experienced in the 1970s and which brought growth rates back to earlier trends;

(iii) The reasons for inter-country disparities in growth rates in both these phases.

Table 1.1, which presents overall output growth rates for most Western European countries over a number of pre- and post-war periods, illustrates these various phenomena — the longer-run 2 to 2½ per cent trend of output growth, the jump to double that rate of expansion between 1953 and 1973,[1] the relapse into lower growth after the oil shock, and the relatively large international dispersion in growth rates (particularly marked in the post-war period).

Earlier discussions of European growth have tended to concentrate on this latter aspect. A number of authors have tried to explain 'why growth rates differ', often in the light of some national experience which was particularly noteworthy — the best example being that of the relatively disappointing performance of the United Kingdom which has called forth a large number of explanations. Europe's overall trends have, on the whole, elicited less attention (with the notable exception of Maddison[2]), particularly, perhaps, because in a high growth environment they were taken for granted and research was con-

* Magdalen College, Oxford. The author gratefully acknowledges many helpful, if not always heeded, comments from Chris Allsopp and Gianni Toniolo.

[1] 1953 was chosen rather than 1950 because Germany only regained pre-war output levels by 1952–3. But results would be little changed if 1950 were taken as a base line.

[2] See, *inter alia*, A. Maddison, *Economic Growth in the West*, London 1964, and 'Phases of Capitalist Development' and 'Long Run Dynamics of Productivity Growth', both in *Banca Nazionale del Lavoro Quarterly Review*, June 1977 and March 1979.

TABLE 1.1. *Longer-run GDP trends in Europe*
(average annual percentage changes)

	1870–1913	1922–37	1953–73	1973–79
France	1.6	1.8	5.3	3.0
Germany	2.8	3.2	5.5	2.4
Italy	1.5	2.3	5.3	2.6
United Kingdom	1.9	2.4	3.0	1.3
Spain	..	1.7[a]	6.1[b]	2.8
Austria	3.2	0.8	5.7	3.1
Belgium	2.0	1.4	4.3	2.3
Denmark	3.2	2.9	4.3	2.1
Finland	2.8	4.4	5.0	2.3
Ireland	..	1.5[c]	3.3	3.6
Netherlands	1.9	1.9	4.9	2.5
Norway	2.1	3.4	3.9	4.4
Sweden	2.8	3.5	3.9	1.8
Switzerland	2.1	2.1[d]	4.6	−0.4
Total	2.0[e]	2.5[e]	4.8[f]	2.4[f]

[a] NNP; 1922–35
[b] 1954–73
[c] 1926–39
[d] 1924–37
[e] Using 1929 GDP weights at 1970 United States prices
[f] OECD Europe.
Sources: A. Maddison, 'Phases of Capitalist Development', *Banca Nazionale del Lavoro Quarterly Review*, June 1977; B.R. Mitchell, *European Historical Statistics, 1750–1970*, London 1975; UNECE, *Some Factors in Economic Growth in Europe during the 1950s*, Geneva 1964; OECD, *National Accounts of OECD Countries, 1950–1979*.

centrated on what seemed to be more pressing issues. Yet the deceleration in the later 1970s to rates of growth not very different from those Europe had recorded in earlier periods, raises the question of why the better performance of the 1950s and 1960s was possible and whether a return to rapid growth would be feasible. Thus, a study of common features is probably at least as important as an analysis of inter-country divergences.

If there is a general theme in the text that follows, it is that there was nothing inevitable about Europe's growth in the first two decades of the period, though there may have been something inevitable about the eventual deceleration. The neo-classical belief that capitalism is a self-stabilizing system whose 'natural' growth can only be interrupted by government interference and errors (e.g. in the Great Depression or in the 1970s), seems hardly tenable in the light of the experience of this period. If anything, the opposite conclusion might well hold — it was government policies that bore an important responsibility for the acceleration in growth that took place, while it was the 'natural' difficulties of reconciling full employment and price stability in a market economy that strongly contributed to the problems and difficulties of the 1970s.

I. Acceleration

The 1950-73 acceleration in growth *vis-à-vis* the interwar period, and for that matter *vis-à-vis* the late nineteenth or early twentieth century, was both very sharp and generalized. All Western European countries took part in it and so did Eastern Europe, Japan, and, to a lesser extent, North America. One of the major reasons for the difference in performance was, of course, the absence of any serious post-war recession until the mid-1970s. The level of output did decline from time to time in several countries, but the falls were usually modest, lasted for only brief periods, and were never synchronized across the area, in contrast to the massive depression of the 1930s. But even in comparison to the less troubled 1920s (when output was rising at rates of between 3½ and 4 per cent per annum), growth in the post-World War II era was more rapid and smoother. In any case, in an explanation of why Europe was so much more successful than it had been earlier, the 1930s cannot be ignored — after all, avoidance of major recessions may have been a growth stimulating factor in its own right.

The importance of supply factors

When accounting for differences in growth, economic theory usually begins by looking at supply forces and, in particular, at the rate of technical progress and at developments in the supply of factors of production. Taking these first, the 1950s and 1960s did indeed record faster growth of both the major inputs than did the 1920s and 1930s. This would seem to have been most noticeable on the capital side, judging from the indirect evidence shown in Table 1.2. Though the data are not strictly comparable across time, the changes in investment ratios

TABLE 1.2. *Investment ratios*[a]
(percentages)

	1928–38	1950–70
France	11.8	15.6
Germany	9.7	17.7
Italy	13.6	14.8
United Kingdom	5.7	12.9
Austria	6.1[b]	18.3
Denmark	8.9	15.5
Norway	12.4	23.7
Sweden	10.5	16.4
Western Europe	9.6	16.8

[a] Non-residential gross fixed investment in per cent of GNP at current prices
[b] 1924–37
Source: A. Maddison, 'Economic Policy and Performance in Europe, 1913–1970', in C.M. Cipolla (ed.), *The Fontana Economic History of Europe*, Glasgow 1976, Vol. 5 (2), p. 487.

between the two periods are sufficiently striking to suggest that capital stock growth must have been a good deal higher in post-war years. On the labour side the change is much less pronounced. Total employment rose at some 0.6 per cent per annum between 1953 and 1973 as against a growth of perhaps

0.4–0.5 per cent in the earlier period. Turning to technical progress, it is possible that this may also have accelerated after 1945 in view of the investment backlog accumulated during the recession and the war.[3] The evidence on this account is, inevitably, even shakier, but, for the United States at least, it has been argued that the rise in 'residuals' in growth accounting calculations between pre- and post-World War II periods is prima-facie evidence of a greater contribution to growth from technical progress.[4] In so far as European technical advances were in large measure determined by United States progress, the conclusion could hold for Europe as well.

On the strength of the foregoing, it could be argued that European growth in the post-war period was rapid because employment, capital, and technological progress all grew more rapidly than in earlier years. Yet this is, of course, only a proximate and very insufficient explanation. None of these factors is necessarily exogenous to the growth process itself. In fact they may all three be at least partly endogenous, in which case the search for a real explanation has not yet begun. The rate of growth of the *capital stock* is most obviously the least auto-nomous of the three since it is a function of the level of investment. This, in turn, appears to have been largely determined by the rate of growth of output itself according to the overwhelming body of post-war econometric evidence.

The endogenous nature of *technical progress* may not be so evident, but here too a number of factors suggest that while the flow of inventions may well be autonomous, the rate at which inventions are applied is a function of demand and output growth. Simple statistical evidence in favour of this argument is forthcoming from the previously mentioned growth accounting calculations. Denison himself showed that for his sample of nine countries (later enlarged to include Japan), the size of 'residuals' was to some extent correlated with output growth rates.[5] More importantly, there are powerful economic arguments for considering that technical progress is embodied in new investment and is there-fore closely linked to economic growth: 'Without gross investment, improving technology that requires new capital simply represents a potential for higher productivity: to realise this potential requires gross investment. An economy with a slow rate of gross investment is restricted in the rate at which new tech-niques can be brought into use; an economy with a high rate of gross investment can quickly bring new methods into use, and thus realise the benefits of im-proving technology.'[6] This argument applies, of course, only to embodied technical progress. But even 'disembodied' technical progress, such as better utilization of the labour force or improved managerial efficiency, is very fre-quently triggered off by new investments which impose changes in layouts on the factory floor.

[3] R.C.O. Matthews, 'Why has Britain had Full Employment since the War?', *Economic Journal*, September 1968.

[4] M. Abramovitz, 'Rapid Growth Potential and its Realization: The Expansion of Capitalist Economies in the Postwar Period', in E. Malinvaud (ed.), *Economic Growth and Resources*, London 1979.

[5] E. F. Denison, *Why Growth Rates Differ*, Brookings Institution, Washington 1967, and E.F. Denison and W.K. Chung, 'Economic Growth and its Sources', in H. Patrick and H. Rosovsky (eds.), *Asia's New Giant*, Brookings Institution, Washington 1976.

[6] W.E.G. Salter, *Productivity and Technical Change*, Cambridge 1966, p. 63.

The endogenous nature of *labour* supply is perhaps least apparent. Demographic growth is clearly exogenous (except, perhaps, in the very long run), and so, therefore, is the growth of the population of working age.[7] But employment growth will also be a function of participation rate changes, falling structural unemployment and, for Europe as a whole, of net immigration inflows from other areas. All these are, at least partly, influenced by the growth process itself. Thus, emigration into North-West Europe seems to have been largely determined by changes in the demand for labour and so, of course, was the reduction in unemployment. More importantly, if productivity growth differs between sectors and is, in some at least, partly endogenous (i.e. the faster the growth rate of output the more rapid is the growth of productivity), then labour-shifts between sectors can be as significant for growth as overall labour supply. In Europe over the period such shifts were massive and seem to have occurred largely as a consequence of rising demand for workers in the urban sector of the economy rather than in response to supply-push.[8]

The argument so far has been that just looking at supply forces is unlikely to provide much more than a proximate and very superficial explanation of post-war growth and, in particular, of what seems to have been its most dynamic component – an extremely rapid growth of the capital stock made possible by historically exceptionally high and rising investment shares in output. There are, however, two somewhat more sophisticated supply-side arguments that could, in theory, provide a better explanation, and which stress respectively the role of technical progress and of labour.[9] Proponents of the first line of thought, while admitting that technical progress requires investment to embody it, would argue that post-war Europe was ideally placed to carry out this investment because of the presence of a vast reservoir of relatively cheap and efficient technology developed in the United States (both in the interwar years and during the war), to which European access had been limited by semi-autarkic policies in some countries after the early 1930s and by war in all after the early 1940s.[10] This abundant supply of technology was bound to stimulate investment, increase profits, and lead to an acceleration in output growth.

Though this argument is very plausible, it is not certain that it can provide an important explanation for the upward jump in Europe's growth rate shown in Table 1.1, since a technological gap probably already existed in the pre-war period as well. This is, of course, difficult to document at all precisely. On the

---

[7] The latter was, in fact, slower in the post-war period, at least until the second half of the 1960s, than it had been in the interwar years.

[8] See Ch. 6 below.

[9] A third argument would stress the availability of raw materials at relatively stable prices – something which was underlined by events in the 1970s. Yet judging from the movements in the terms of trade, this availability may well have been equally, if not more, marked in pre-war Europe. Between the early 1920s and the late 1930s Europe's total terms of trade improved by close to 20 per cent, while between 1948 and the early 1970s the improvement was of the order of 10 per cent. It is true, however, that the interwar period saw much greater and more disruptive terms of trade fluctuations.

[10] This argument has never been developed specifically by any one writer in particular, but it appears in various forms in most studies of post-war European growth as at least an important contributory factor: e.g. Maddison, *Economic Growth*, or J. Cornwall, *Modern Capitalism*, London 1977.

basis, however, of a widely used proxy — differences in manhour productivity —
it would seem that throughout the interwar years America's lead had been
almost as large as it was in the early post-war period. Thus, a weighted average
of data assembled by Maddison[11] would put Europe's manhour output at 56
per cent of the United States level in 1929, 43 per cent in 1950, and 51 per
cent in 1960. In other words, though the technological gap may have been more
pronounced in the 1950s than it had been in the 1920s and 1930s, the differences in these figures would not seem to be sufficiently large to provide a full
explanation for the spurt that took place in investment propensities. No doubt,
cheap and abundant technical innovations helped expansion, but more in the
form of a permissive factor than as a major initiator of the growth process.

A second, mainly supply-oriented, argument stresses the role of labour
abundance. Its major proponents have been Kindleberger and Kaldor.[12] Kindleberger's explanation uses a dual-economy model which follows Marx–Lewis
lines. In one sector of the economy, say agriculture, relatively abundant labour
supplies imply a marginal productivity of labour close to zero and wages at
virtually subsistence levels. This allows the economy's second sector, say industry, to grow by drawing workers from the countryside at wages just above
subsistence, but well below labour's marginal product in industry. Hence profits
rise and so does investment, leading to further increases in the demand for
labour and a continuation of the growth process. The latter stops, or decelerates,
when surplus labour in agriculture has been siphoned off into factories, marginal
productivity and, therefore, wages on the land rise, and increasing urban wage
levels make inroads into the share of profits in value added.

According to Kindleberger, this simple model can be applied to Europe's
post-war situation in which the agricultural sector initially, and the Mediterranean
countries of emigration later, provided the sources of industrial labour to North-
West Europe. Kaldor, in addition, stressed the fact that a good deal of the absorption of labour in this period took place in manufacturing. The latter is a
particularly powerful 'engine of growth', partly because of its forward and backward linkage effects (it produces, for instance, the capital equipment necessary
to investment or the fertilizers which facilitate the exodus from the land), but
more importantly because, in line with 'Verdoorn's law', it is in this sector that
scale economies are most pronounced and that productivity grows faster the
faster the growth rate of output. This, in turn, improves competitiveness and
boosts export growth.

In this modified supply approach, it is not so much the absolute growth of
the labour force or of employment that matter, but the flexibility of labour
supply to the advanced and dynamic sector of the economy. This is, in turn,
a function of urban unemployment at the beginning of the period, and (more
importantly) of agricultural and Southern European underemployment throughout the period. This thesis has some resemblance to the earlier technical progress
argument — the presence of an abundant and cheap labour supply makes investment worth while, the profits so generated are reinvested and the process

[11] Maddison, 'Phases of Capitalist Development' and 'Long Run Dynamics'.
[12] C.P. Kindleberger, *Europe's Postwar Growth*, Cambridge, Mass. 1967; N. Kaldor,
Causes of the Slow Rate of Economic Growth of the United Kingdom, Cambridge 1966.

continues until the backlog is exhausted, either because there are no more under-employed agricultural workers and/or further immigration is discouraged or even halted for fear of social discontent. The argument is again very plausible and the statistical evidence which Kindleberger and Kaldor muster (in order to show the relationship between elastic labour supply and growth, and the leading role of manufacturing), while not fully conclusive, would seem to lend support to the explanation.

The major problem, however, is that, as for the earlier technological progress thesis, one is not in the presence of a new factor. In other words, there is little in the argument that sheds light on why there was such a sharp break in growth trends before and after World War II. Abundant labour supply had, after all, been a characteristic of the European economies throughout the nineteenth and early twentieth centuries. As evidence for this one can point to the much higher unemployment rates of the interwar period or, more importantly, to the very large (transatlantic) emigration flows between 1880 and 1920 and the dominant share of agriculture in the labour force of most countries prior to World War II. If anything, the Europe of the 1960s may well have been an area which, probably for the first time in recorded human history, could boast of a situation of virtual full employment. Nor can it be argued that the 'engine of growth' role of manu-facturing was limited to this period. Industrial output had been growing more rapidly than total output in most European countries already in the interwar years when, according to some, admittedly very precarious, statistical infor-mation, a relationship like 'Verdoorn's law' might have been at work.[13]

If cheap technology and abundant labour and raw materials were not novel features of industrial Europe, something else must still explain why in the 1950s and 1960s they led to 'supergrowth', while in the earlier periods they had not. Such an explanation would seem to have to come from the demand side. The theoretical underpinnings for a demand-oriented approach to growth problems are much weaker, and the danger of circularity very clear (e.g. high investment leads to high growth which stimulates investment). A possible approach, how-ever, could start by stressing the already noted major change between the pre- and post-war periods — the sharp upward shift in investment propensities. While theories of investment differ, the major competing explanations would presumably

---

[13] For 13 European countries for which data are available (out of the fourteen shown in Table 1.1, the missing one being Ireland), the following relationships were obtained for the years 1953–73:

$$\dot{Y} = 1.72 + 0.51\ \dot{IP} \qquad \overline{R}^2 = 0.87$$
$$\quad\ (4.7)\ \ (9.0)$$

$$\dot{\Pi}_{ip} = 0.72 + 0.74\ \dot{IP} \qquad \overline{R}^2 = 0.85$$
$$\quad\ \ (1.3)\ \ (8.2)$$

where $\dot{Y}$, $\dot{IP}$, and $\dot{\Pi}_{ip}$ stand for the growth rates of total output, industrial production, and industrial productivity respectively. For the interwar period for which the years covered are not uniform and the data highly uncertain, the results for 12 countries (excluding also Switzerland for lack of data), were as follows:

$$\dot{Y} = 0.02 + 0.63\ \dot{IP} \qquad \overline{R}^2 = 0.51$$
$$\quad\ (0.1)\ \ (3.5)$$

$$\dot{\Pi}_{ip} = -1.83 + 1.23\ \dot{IP} \qquad \overline{R}^2 = 0.63$$
$$\quad\ \ (1.8)\ \ (4.5)$$

agree that a principal determinant of business investment must be expectations, be these of future profits, of future demand, or of both. The rise in post-war investment would thus suggest that, compared to the pre-war period, there must have been a change in the degree of confidence held by entrepreneurs. A major reason which might account for such greater optimism and for more favourable expectations could have been the new economic policies put into effect in the late 1940s and early 1950s. Two main and novel aspects characterized these policies:

(i) At the international level, the establishment of a new economic order which facilitated reconstruction in the 1940s and growth in the 1950s and 1960s;

(ii) At the domestic level, the adoption of a new array of policy instruments which generated a belief that cyclical fluctuations could be controlled by demand management.

The role of economic policies

The growth of output in the years 1946 to 1950 (close to 9 per cent per annum) was a good deal more rapid than that which followed World War I (some 3 per cent per annum from 1919 to 1922) (Fig. 1.1). One reason for this was, of

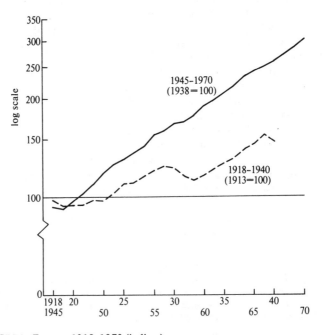

FIG. 1.1. *GDP in Europe, 1918-1970* (indices)

Sources: A. Maddison, 'Phases of Capitalist Development', *Banca Nazionale del Lavoro Quarterly Review*, June 1977; OECD, *National Accounts of OECD Countries, 1950-1979*.

course, that World War II had been much more destructive, particularly in Europe's largest single economy – Germany. To some extent, therefore, the difference between the two periods was physically almost inevitable – a rapid recovery was bound to take place (as it also did in other economies which had been severely affected by the war, such as Japan or the Soviet Union). But a second reason for the difference lay in economic policies. After World War I Britain, and particularly, France had insisted on crippling Germany with reparations, while the United States had insisted on the repayment of Europe's war debts. These two issues 'complicated and corrupted the international economy at every stage of the 1920s and during the depression'.[14] After World War II, there was much less that could be taken from Germany, while the United States not only cancelled most war debts, but also provided Europe with abundant long-term finance in the form of Marshall Aid – the first step towards the establishment of a Western economic system. Marshall Aid greatly facilitated a reconstruction process which would otherwise have been interrupted by dollar shortages. And the speed of reconstruction, which was probably unexpected to contemporary European observers, who feared a relapse into the stagnation of the 1930s (or alternatively high rates of inflation), almost certainly generated and strengthened business optimism (despite the dangers of increasing 'cold war' tensions).

The momentum of post-war recovery was perpetuated by a second international policy decision – the move to a fixed exchange rate system decided upon at Bretton Woods. Many (including Keynes) had feared at the outset that the Bretton Woods system would, on balance, impart a deflationary bias to the world economy, since deficit countries would have to bear almost exclusively the onus of adjustment via restrictive domestic policies, with little obligation on surplus countries to reflate their economies. In the event, these fears were unfounded, largely because the system was no longer on a gold, but, increasingly, on a dollar standard. Though there were dollar shortages in the early post-war years, the 1949 devaluations restored some of Europe's price competitiveness vis-à-vis the United States, and rapid growth thereafter did the same for non-price competitiveness. By the mid- to late 1950s, when the European currencies returned to full (non-resident) convertibility, not only was the dollar shortage a forgotten problem, but the opposite problem – that of a United States balance of payments deficit – was beginning to emerge. Given the reserve currency nature of the dollar, no pressures were, however, put on the United States to balance its accounts. On the contrary, European countries welcomed the addition to effective demand and to reserves which increasing United States imports and direct investment outflows were making.

Arguably, these various favourable effects were growth-promoting. The mechanism which may have been at work could have resembled that postulated in models of export-led growth.[15] In such models, a high initial level of competitiveness (achieved thanks to rapid productivity growth or an undervalued rate of exchange, or both) leads to a high demand for exports and a favourable balance of payments. The former encourages investment directly, via accelerator

[14] C.P. Kindleberger, *The World Depression, 1929-1939*, London 1973, p. 39.
[15] W. Beckerman, 'Projecting Europe's Growth', *Economic Journal*, December 1962.

effects; the latter indirectly if businessmen (plausibly) expect governments to pursue relatively expansionary policies. High investment further contributes to rapid productivity growth and hence to competitiveness and trade balance surpluses, thus initiating or reinforcing a virtuous circle. While the argument was initially developed for an individual country, *mutatis mutandis*, it can be applied to Europe as a whole. A United States economy little concerned by the balance of payments implied that European exports could expand thanks to relatively low wage costs, high productivity gains, and fixed exchange rates, while reserves could also increase, thus satisfying the mercantilist preferences of governments (Table 1.3). For Europe as a whole policies were more expansionary and confidence higher than they would otherwise have been.

TABLE 1.3. *Europe's balance of payments*[a]
(annual averages, $ billion)

	1950–54	1955–59	1960–64	1965–69	1970–73
Current balance	1.4	1.8	−0.3	2.0	4.3
Change in reserves[b]	1.3	1.1	2.4	0.3	12.7
Memorandum item: United States current balance with Western Europe	−1.0	−1.0	0.9	−0.2	−2.2[c]

[a] OECD Europe
[b] Gold and foreign exchange
[c] 1970–72
Sources: OECD, *Statistics of Balance of Payments, 1950–1961* and *1960–1977*; IMF, *International Financial Statistics* (1967/68 and 1980 Yearbooks); US Department of Commerce, *Survey of Current Business* (various issues).

Here again, there is a marked contrast with the interwar experience, during which not only did currencies fluctuate but Europe as a whole initially revalued *vis-à-vis* the dollar (Fig. 1.2). What was almost certainly the major reserve currency country at the end of World War I – the United Kingdom – only returned to a fixed parity in 1925, and then at a highly overvalued rate. Far from ignoring its balance of payments situation, the latter dominated its policy stance until the early 1930s and forced continued deflationary moves. Within Continental Europe exchange rates were often out of step with each other (e.g. the French franc's undervaluation throughout most of the 1920s) and hot-money flows abundant, in contrast to the experience of the 1950s and early 1960s at least, when capital controls were relatively effective and short-term lending much less widespread.

More importantly, economic policies may well have played a fundamental role in forming expectations and bolstering confidence at home. United States aid and balance of payments deficits would almost certainly have been insufficient in maintaining the growth momentum of the reconstruction period and in raising investment propensities in a world in which, as already mentioned, many feared a quick relapse into stagnation or runaway inflation (and some predicted

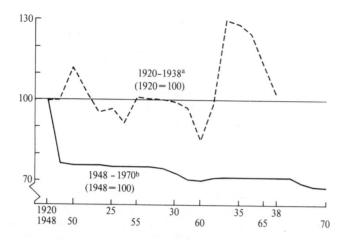

FIG. 1.2. *Europe's exchange rate vis-à-vis the dollar, 1920-1970* (indices)
a 1929 trade weights
b 1965 trade weights
Sources: League of Nations, *Monthly Bulletin of Statistics* (various issues): IMF, *International Financial Statistics* (1967/68 and 1980 Yearbooks).

a war with the Soviet Union). What probably intervened was a new confidence factor instilled by the presence of a 'bigger and better' government.

The development of Keynes's ideas had shown that full employment was not impossible in a capitalist economy. The growth in the size of the public sector, in the form of both larger automatic stabilizers and greater discretionary expenditure and tax changes, had shown that governments had the instruments to implement Keynes's theoretical propositions (and had actually succeeded in doing so in the war years). The combination of a new theory, of adequate instruments, and of a commitment, at least in some countries, to both use the theory and apply the instruments to achieve full employment and growth, must have been a powerful mechanism in maintaining the momentum of high investment rates. Business may well have felt that, in the event of a downturn, governments would and could step in to maintain the level of activity and employment. Influenced by this consideration they invested, kept up the growth of aggregate demand, and made government intervention unnecessary.[16] In a loose form such behaviour can provide an example of what modern economic theory calls 'rational expectations'. Rather than extrapolating from past behaviour, entrepreneurs used the new information at their disposal, namely a new model of how government intervention worked and in what circumstances it would be applied. By acting upon such information they, in fact, implemented the new model without much need for the intervention itself.[17]

[16] This argument is not new and can be found in various forms: first, in UNECE, *Some Factors in Economic Growth in Europe During the 1950s*, Geneva 1964, Ch. IV, p. 16; later in Maddison, *Economic Growth*, Chs. II and IV, or Matthews, 'Why has Britain had Full Employment?', and more recently in Cornwall, *Modern Capitalism*, p. 212.
[17] The major difference with the rational expectations literature of the late 1970s is the argument that private behaviour, rather than trying to offset public intervention,

It is true that the commitment to demand management and to full employment policies varied in Europe. Particularly at the beginning of the period, some
countries, for instance Germany and Italy, were much less 'Keynesian' than
others. But in these countries favourable expectations were probably sustained
by the speed of the reconstruction process – in both Germany and Italy growth
between 1946 and 1953 averaged some 8 to 12 per cent per annum.

The contrast with the 1920s and 1930s is again very marked. Though in both
those decades ample opportunities existed for profitable investment in terms of
cheap technology and labour supplies, the confidence factor was clearly much
less in evidence. It was known that capitalist economies suffered from frequent
cyclical fluctuations and, at times, also from profound depressions, and there
was little anyone could do to avoid them. In the circumstances, investment must
have been viewed as a much more risky venture than in the conditions of the
1950s when growth was rapid, full employment increasingly assured, and confidence in the stabilization and growth-promoting powers of governments rising.

The major explanation for the acceleration in growth between the interwar
and the post-war period which has been here advanced thus runs in terms of
neither neoclassical nor Marxist theory. The former, by stressing marginal
changes in supply and the self-equilibrating nature of a market system, is incapable of providing much more than a superficial and proximate explanation
for a near quadrupling of real investment and a near trebling of output over
some twenty years. The latter, by stressing the inevitability of cycles engendered
by the constant search for profits in a capitalist system, fails to account for a
quarter-of-a-century-long boom. The present explanation is theoretically much
less elegant. It stresses, in a sense, a series of man-made accidents which, by
interacting with permissive factors on the supply side, created and then perpetuated (at least for a time) an unprecedented growth process. Demand, stimulated by economic policies, created its own supply by calling forth labour from
the countryside or Southern Europe and by raising the capital stock through
high rates of investment. 'Say's law' held, but in reverse, thanks largely to a
change in the climate of ideas which, initiated by Keynes in the pre-war period,
found followers after the war in the names of, for instance, Beveridge, Monnet,
or Myrdal.

II. Deceleration

The deceleration in Europe's growth rate which set in after 1973 was sudden,
sharp, and generalized. Output growth, after running at close to 5 per cent per
annum through the late 1960s and early 1970s, fell abruptly to less than 2½
per cent between 1973 and 1979, and this deceleration occurred in virtually all
the countries here examined. Only in two (Ireland and Norway) was growth
more rapid in these years than in the 1950s and 1960s (and then only very
marginally), and both these countries were favourably influenced by special

---

reinforced it, whether in the area of short-run cyclical stabilization or longer-run growth
promotion; for a similar view applied to United States stabilization policy see M.N. Baily,
'Stabilization Policy and Private Economic Behavior', *Brookings Papers on Economic
Activity*, No. 1, 1978.

factors – Ireland by EEC and, in particular, Common Agricultural Policy membership, and Norway by the exploitation of large gas and oil reserves. One major reason for lower growth was, of course, the mid-1970s recession, just as one major reason for faster earlier growth had been the absence of any such pronounced slowdown. For the first time since 1932 (excluding war-affected years), Europe's GDP fell in 1975 by close to 1 per cent. But growth remained relatively low in the recovery years that followed – even from trough to peak (1975 to 1979) the 3¼ per cent per annum that was recorded was well below earlier rates. Nor would this seem to have been a temporary phenomenon. The early 1980s have witnessed a further deceleration and prospects for the mid-1980s at least do not look particularly encouraging.

Supply or 'accidents'?

Explanations of this deceleration couched in supply terms are, in this instance too, unsatisfactory. To begin with, a supply-induced deceleration would not have taken place abruptly but gradually and over a number of years – yet peak to peak growth rates between 1953 and 1973 hardly show much sign of a declining trend.[18] And, secondly, there seems to have been little on the supply side, in any case, that could have justified a sharp slowdown.[19] The growth of the population of working age accelerated slightly in the 1970s, and even the growth of the labour force remained close to earlier trends despite rising unemployment. It is true that increasing employment-shifts towards services (and particularly public services) may have lowered the potential for productivity gains (just as earlier labour-shifts from agriculture to manufacturing had increased it), but the direct contribution of this to lower growth was estimated by the OECD to have been extremely small and in some cases (e.g. Germany) to have actually been growth-promoting.[20] Similarly inconclusive are the arguments about technical progress. On the one hand, the gap *vis-à-vis* the United States had been closing in the 1950s and 1960s, thus progressively reducing the scope for cheap imports of technology. On the other hand, however, the technological frontier had hardly kept still and the potential for introducing new techniques in the latter 1970s might well have been accelerating.

It is true, of course, that productivity growth decelerated sharply throughout Europe (Table 1.4). But it would be hard to argue that supply influences were primarily responsible for this, if only because the deceleration was so similar across a number of countries that were, on the other hand, facing very different supply conditions. Between 1961–73 and 1973–9, ten out of the fourteen countries here considered recorded a drop in productivity growth varying between 1.7 and 2.2 percentage points per annum (Germany and Norway fared better, partly because the former could shed foreign labour while the latter had oil; Italy and Switzerland fared worse, partly because of intransigent union attitudes in Italy, largely because output actually fell in Switzerland). Moreover, productivity

[18] Taking as intermediate peaks the years 1957, 1961, 1965, and 1969, the average annual growth rates of OECD Europe are 5.0, 4.7, 4.9, 4.6, and 4.8 per cent respectively.

[19] A late 1960s projection for Europe's growth based on supply considerations saw no reason for deceleration in either the first or the second half of the 1970s: see OECD, *The Growth of Output, 1960-1980*, Paris 1970.

[20] OECD, *Economic Outlook*, July 1979, pp. 28–35.

TABLE 1.4. *Productivity*[a] *trends*
(average annual percentage changes)

	1953–79	1953–61	1961–73	1973–79
France	4.3	5.0	4.6	2.8
Germany	4.4	5.2	4.5	3.2
Italy	4.6	5.5	5.6	1.5
United Kingdom	2.2	2.0	2.9	1.2
Spain	5.0[b]	4.0[b]	6.0	4.2
Austria	4.8[c]	5.5[c]	5.1	2.9
Belgium	3.3	2.8	4.1	2.3
Denmark	2.8[d]	3.2[d]	3.1	1.3
Finland	4.2	4.8	4.4	2.5
Ireland	3.5[c]	3.4[c]	4.3	2.2
Netherlands	3.4	3.1	4.2	2.3
Norway	2.8	3.1	2.9	2.2
Sweden	2.6[d]	3.0[d]	3.2	0.6
Switzerland	2.6[d]	3.1[d]	2.9	0.9
OECD Europe	3.8	4.1	4.3	2.3

[a] GDP per employed
[b] 1954–79 and 1954–61
[c] 1951–79 and 1951–61
[d] 1950–79 and 1950–61

Sources: OECD, *National Accounts of OECD Countries, Manpower Statistics*, and *Labour Force Statistics* (various issues); B. R. Mitchell, *European Historical Statistics, 1750-1970*, London 1975.

growth had been accelerating between the 1950s and the early 1970s (in contrast, for instance, to United States experience where a longer-run underlying deceleration was almost certainly present). The most plausible explanation for what took place in Europe is in terms of output growth — productivity responded to the slowdown in activity rather than vice versa.

It has, however, been argued that the productivity story could, at least partly, be explained by a sudden large loss of capacity due to the obsolescence of energy-intensive equipment. But there is little empirical evidence which substantiates this argument. Moreover, the argument could only be true if real energy prices to final users had changed very sharply — something which, in fact, did not really happen in the years to 1979[21] — and if demand for energy intensive commodities had drastically declined — something which is unlikely to have occurred. After all, demand equivalent to over 1 per cent of Europe's GDP was shifted away from largely non-tradeables to tradeables (in the form of exports to OPEC), whose energy intensiveness was almost certainly higher. But while there was probably no sudden large loss of capacity, there was a sharp break in trend for investment. Investment ratios declined virtually everywhere in the post-1973 world (Table 1.5) (the only exceptions being, here again, Ireland and Norway), and this, no doubt, reinforced the productivity slowdown. But in either case one is in the presence of a largely cyclical reaction, the reasons for which are unlikely to be found on the supply side.

[21] OECD, *Economic Outlook*, July 1980 and July 1981.

TABLE 1.5. *Investment ratios*[a]
(percentages)

	1950–54	1955–59	1960–64	1965–69	1970–73	1974–79
France	16.5	17.2	20.8	23.3	24.3	22.5
Germany	20.5	23.4	24.5	23.6	24.4	21.2
Italy	20.2[b]	24.1	27.0	23.8	23.3	20.0
United Kingdom	13.2	15.3	17.7	20.3	20.3	18.8
Spain	..	15.9	17.6	22.6	23.0	21.9
Austria	17.6	20.3	24.2	25.5	27.3	26.0
Belgium	19.4[c]	19.7	22.8	23.9	22.3	21.9
Denmark	16.6	17.5	21.7	24.5	26.1	22.8
Finland	25.2	27.4	29.2	28.4	29.1	27.0
Ireland	17.1	15.6	17.6	22.4	26.1	26.2
Netherlands	18.7	21.1	22.2	25.2	24.3	20.8
Norway	27.2	28.4	27.7	28.0	30.3	32.0
Sweden	17.5	19.1	21.4	22.3	21.8	20.2
Switzerland	18.7	21.6	26.3	25.3	26.8	23.3
OECD Europe	17.3	19.9	22.3	23.2	23.7	21.5

[a] Gross fixed investment in per cent of GDP at constant prices
[b] 1951–54
[c] 1953–54
Sources: OECD, *National Accounts of OECD Countries* (various issues).

One possible explanation for the break in trends, put forward in particular by the 'McCracken Report',[22] runs in terms of a combination of unforeseen accidents and a number of economic policy mistakes sparking off a commodity price boom, a synchronized expansion in all the major industrialized countries, and a quadrupling of oil prices. Faced, at one and the same time, with an inflationary and deflationary shock and with record current account deficits, economic policies were forced into a restrictive direction which engineered, or strengthened, a recession and worsened expectations. 'But there is no fundamental reason why, in more favourable circumstances and with improved policies [adverse expectations] cannot be reversed.'[23]

While there is clearly some truth in this interpretation, it could be argued that something more fundamental than just a string of accidents and policy mistakes may have been behind what, by the early 1980s, appeared as a medium-term slowdown. A major and more structural reason would seem to have been the gradually accelerating rate of inflation that Europe had already witnessed through the 1960s and which exploded in 1973–4. The causes of that inflation are investigated in detail in other chapters of this book (particularly Chapters 3 and 4), but a brief account of how the earlier growth process may have impinged on price increases well before the commodity and oil price booms of 1972–4 may be warranted.

[22] P. McCracken *et al.*, *Towards Full Employment and Price Stability*, OECD, Paris 1977.
[23] Ibid., p. 14.

Growth and inflation

It was argued above that growth in the 1950s and 1960s had been made possible by a combination of buoyant entrepreneurial expectations and permissive supply factors, particularly on the labour side. Yet there is something essentially fragile and temporary about a growth process that relies on business confidence (since this can suddenly give way to pessimism), and on elastic labour supplies in the countryside (since these will eventually dry up with possible unfavourable consequences on either investment and/or inflation). To some extent this is what happened in Europe. By the mid-1960s the agricultural labour force had shrunk to some 15 per cent of total employment in the countries here considered, and the age composition of the remaining farm workers suggested that further outflows from the land were unlikely to contribute much to urban employment. And while international migration was potentially capable of supplying the needs of Europe's labour markets for many years to come, social obstacles to a continuing influx of immigrants from further and further away were growing rapidly (cf. the barriers to immigration put up by the United Kingdom and Switzerland as early as the early or mid-1960s). It was in these years that Europe also achieved the nearest to full employment conditions that it had probably ever witnessed in its history. According to EEC data, the Community's unemployment rate fell below 2 per cent in 1964-6 (and below 1 per cent in both France and Germany).

The achievement of virtual full employment conditions combined with a diminished supply elasticity of agricultural or foreign workers to the urban sectors of the European economies was bound to lead, in conditions in which the growth tempo had not slackened, to a strengthening of labour power and to a shift in income distribution away from capital. This is to some extent illustrated in Fig. 1.3, which shows the movement of two profit indicators – the gross profit share in value added in manufacturing in six countries for which data are available,[24] and the share of corporate income in national income (excluding the self-employed sector) for a somewhat larger sample of countries. Both series show a declining trend through the period, with two breaks apparent (in the early and late 1960s), neither of which would seem to be of a cyclical nature. Supporting evidence for declining profit shares can also be found in estimates prepared by Sachs of the difference between the growth of productivity and product wages (defined as nominal wages deflated by the value added deflator of the sector in question).[25] In the four major economies this difference was positive in the years 1962-9 (0.4 per cent per annum in manufacturing and 0.1 per cent in the total economy), but became negative in the years 1969-73 (−2.2 and −0.5 per cent respectively).

Not all these fluctuations can, of course, be ascribed directly to changing labour market conditions. Thus, the early 1960s deterioration in profitability, particularly marked in manufacturing, could have, in part at least, been associated with the rapid opening of Europe to international trade, which put down-

---

[24] France is the one major country missing from this sample.

[25] J.D. Sachs, 'Wages, Profits and Macroeconomic Adjustment: A Comparative Study', *Brookings Papers on Economic Activity*, No. 2, 1979.

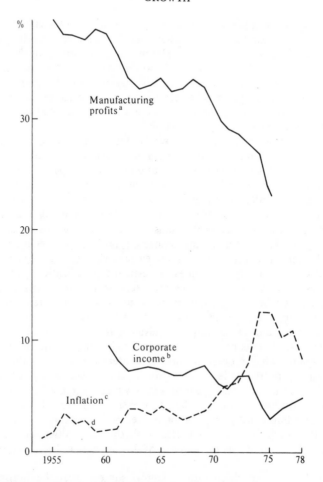

FIG. 1.3. *Indicators of profitability and inflation* (percentages)

[a] Gross operating surplus in per cent of value added in six countries (Germany, Italy, United Kingdom, Denmark, Netherlands, and Sweden)

[b] In per cent of national income at factor cost, excluding entrepreneurial income, in nine countries (France, Germany, Italy, United Kingdom, Belgium, Finland, Netherlands, Sweden, and Switzerland)

[c] Consumer prices in OECD Europe: annual percentage changes

[d] Smoothed to exclude France in 1958

Sources: T. P. Hill, *Profits and Rates of Return*, OECD, Paris 1979: OECD, *National Accounts of OECD Countries* (various issues): IMF, *International Financial Statistics* (1980 Yearbook).

ward pressures on profit margins in the tradeable sector. And the stabilization of income shares from the mid- to the late 1960s would seem to have been powerfully helped by the open or tacit incomes policies put into practice in those years by a number of governments.[26] But, increasingly, changing factor supplies

[26] D. Soskice, 'Strike Waves and Wage Explosions, 1968–70: An Economic Interpre-

were affecting factor returns and the 'wage explosions' of the late 1960s can be seen not only as a reaction to the earlier period of relative austerity but also as a belated recognition that in full employment conditions labour's power had changed. Indeed, this change in labour's power also manifested itself at the turn of the decade in legislative changes passed by (usually) social democratic governments, and designed to provide better income maintenance provisions over the life cycle and strengthen the power of trade unions in negotiations on matters of factory-floor management and dismissals.[27]

The shift from a situation of relative labour abundance to one of relative labour scarcity had a number of interrelated effects on Europe's growth performance. First, rising wage claims were, as far as possible, passed on in the form of higher prices. Thus, both the periods in which profit shares declined also saw an acceleration in inflation (if at very different rates). High and accelerating inflation, in turn, was, of course, one of the major reasons for the breakdown of 1973-4. Second, in so far as the transmission of wage increases to prices was difficult (e.g. in open sectors of the economy), profit shares declined with both direct and indirect negative effects on entrepreneurial confidence. Directly, lower profits were likely to depress investment propensities. Indirectly, diminished cash-flow meant that increasing recourse had to be made to outside finance at a time when budget deficits were also rising, and often proving more attractive in tapping household savings (for the EEC as a whole net government lending went from an average surplus equivalent to 0.3 per cent of GDP in the years 1960-4, to deficits of 0.8 per cent in 1965-9 and 0.5 in 1970-3). An increasingly complicated process of financial intermediation was thus put into effect in some countries at least. This process did not starve firms of funds, but implied rising costs and rising gearing ratios which over the longer term were bound to contribute to a diminished propensity to invest. Third, the labour market rigidity imposed by trade-union-backed legislation, while not necessarily very serious in periods of upswing, created further difficulties for the financial position of the corporate sector in years of slowdown (e.g. 1971 and, of course, 1974-5).

The combination of these various factors suggests that the Europe of the late 1960s and early 1970s was undergoing a transformation which might well have led, over the longer run, to both higher rates of inflation and lower rates of investment and, therefore, of growth, than experienced earlier. The expansionary policies of 1972-3 masked this phenomenon, and growth in those years remained at very high levels, but some indication of the underlying deterioration is provided not only by the much higher rates of price increases (though these stemmed more from commodity than from labour market pressures in those particular years), but also, and more importantly, by the worsening position of the corporate sector. For most countries for which data are available, net borrowing as a percentage of gross capital formation rose sharply between 1965-9 and 1970-3, and the share of total investment accounted for by the corporate

---

tation', in C. Crouch and A. Pizzorno (eds.), *The Resurgence of Class Conflict in Western Europe since 1968*, London 1978.
    [27] These changes are analysed in greater detail in Ch. 6 below.

sector stagnated. Though overall investment ratios were still rising in the early 1970s in a number of countries, the movement was not only less widespread and less pronounced than earlier, but at times also reflected a shift in the composition of gross capital formation towards the public or household sectors.

Even these trends, however, are unable to explain the sudden drop in overall investment shares that took place in the later 1970s. A further factor needs to be added to the forces depressing business expectations. It was argued above that an important reason for rapid and steady growth in the 1950s and 1960s had been rapid and steady growth itself, and the feeling that this would continue thanks to the ability governments now had to control cyclical fluctuations and stimulate longer-run expansion. But in the mid-1970s governments clearly failed to prevent a sharp recession: indeed, some governments were even instrumental in initiating or deepening it. And in the later 1970s governments equally clearly failed to solve the problem of stagflation and restore growth rates to previous levels. In other words, demand management policies which, until then, had been thought to be both powerful and successful, partly perhaps because they had never really been called in to tackle much more than minor slowdowns or moderate inflationary bouts, 'failed to deliver' on the first occasion on which the Western world entered into a synchronized recession. The optimism and confidence in governments that had sustained investment in the 1950s and 1960s were replaced by much greater uncertainty, and pervasive pessimism (aided and abetted by the concomitant shift in the economics profession's orthodoxy) about the ability of governments to fine-tune or even manage an economy.

The explanation advanced so far for lower growth is, in a broad sense, not very different from that put forward previously to explain rapid growth. Just as permissive supply conditions and confidence had earlier reinforced each other, so a turn in expectations, combined with somewhat less permissive supply factors, precipitated Europe into a much less favourable situation. But it is important to note that the lower elasticity of labour supply, which set in from the mid-1960s onwards, represented not so much a direct physical bottleneck to growth (since a higher rate of investment and, therefore, of productivity growth could have lifted it), as an indirect barrier working via lower profitability and higher inflation, reinforced by a relatively rigid and oligopolistic labour market. This is highlighted by the situation in the later 1970s, when, despite rapidly rising unemployment and an acceleration of the growth of the population of working age, there was little sign of a shift in income distribution back to profits, or of a deceleration in inflation.

In a sense, therefore, it can be argued that a slowdown was inevitable, but not so much because of the progressive drying-up of earlier sources of growth (American technology or farm labour), but rather because of the successful workings of the capitalist system itself. The achievement and maintenance of full employment conditions for a number of years was probably incompatible with a reasonable degree of price stability or, at least, a steady rate of inflation. Success was obtained, for a time, partly as a result of labour's lagged perception of its true position, partly as a result, at least in some countries, of social-democratic efforts designed to create welfare packages, incomes policies, and other forms of consensus. But in the longer run, such efforts might well have failed. The year 1973 represented a watershed, in the sense that the oil shock and the ensuing recession were a very sudden break with the past, but the trend towards a deteriorating performance had already set in earlier. In a way, the successes of the 1950s and 1960s had laid the preconditions for at least some of the failures of the 1970s.

III. Inter-Country Differences

Coincident acceleration or deceleration are probably easier to explain than the presence and persistence in the post-war period of significant differences in growth rates. Both in the prosperous 1950s and 1960s and in the less buoyant 1970s, Europe's economic expansion was characterized by the uneven performance of a number of countries, of which those of France and Germany on the one hand and that of the United Kingdom on the other were probably the most striking. If anything, the disparities increased in the later 1970s. While in the years 1953 to 1973 the spread between the fastest − and the slowest − growing countries (Spain and the United Kingdom respectively) had been of the order of 3 percentage points per annum, in the six years to 1979 the difference (between Norway and Switzerland on this occasion) rose to 5 percentage points,[28] and the standard deviation of average annual percentage growth rates increased from 0.9 to 1.1. Otherwise, however, there was little change in the ranking of the countries between the two sub-periods. If one excludes the two special cases of Ireland and Norway which, as mentioned earlier, achieved an acceleration of their growth following the first oil shock, the rank correlation coefficient for the position of the twelve remaining countries shown in Table 1.1 is as high as 0.85, suggesting that the impact of the crisis was relatively evenly spread − though everybody decelerated, most countries maintained their relative position in the growth league-table. In the light of this, it could be argued that any explanation for 'why growth rates differed' in the post-war period can, at least at a first approximation, encompass both periods under discussion. Special factors that may have affected the relative performance of some countries in some parts of the period will, however, be mentioned.

The literature on reasons for differential growth performances in the post-war period is relatively abundant and some reference to it has already been made in Section I above. At one end of the spectrum one finds the growth-accounting work of Denison, which concentrates almost exclusively on the supply side,[29] and at the other export-led growth models which see growth originating primarily from the demand side.[30] In between come the Kindleberger or Kaldor approaches which privilege some supply elements (the growth of the labour force or of manufacturing), but do not neglect the role of profitability or competitiveness and of demand forces,[31] or the more recent work by Cornwall, which stresses the interactions between investment, technology, and manu-

---

[28] Or to 3½ points if one excludes the two special cases of Ireland and Norway.
[29] Denison, *Why Growth Rates Differ*.
[30] Beckerman, 'Projecting Europe's Growth'.
[31] Kindleberger, *Europe's Growth*; Kaldor, *Causes of Slow Economic Growth*.

facturing.[32] Most of these works provide insights into the growth performance of the European countries in the post-war period so that an eclectic approach accepting elements from a number of these various interpretations may be best suited for the purposes at hand. In other words, the search will not be for one unique cause, but rather for those major demand and supply forces whose interaction has probably allowed some countries to develop more rapidly than others.

Backwardness

On the supply side, one element common to most explanations is what could go under the very general heading of 'starting points' or relative 'backwardness'. This in turn can be divided into two main themes. According to the first, very simple, argument, pre-war stagnation and/or war destruction meant that in some countries growth was bound to be faster, at least in the reconstruction period but probably also thereafter, if only because of the momentum imparted in the late 1940s. Thus, the three fastest-growing countries of the years 1953-61 (Germany, Italy, and Austria) had in common not only defeat in war, but also a long catch-up period on pre-war income levels (Austria and Italy recovered their pre-war GDP peak in 1950, Germany in 1952). Conversely, more slowly growing countries, such as the United Kingdom, Norway, or Sweden, had already come back to pre-war output peaks by 1945 or 1946.

More important than these relatively short-run catch-up factors, was the relative 'backwardness' or 'maturity' of the various European countries in terms of their per capita incomes, productivity levels, or employment structures. The potential for rapid growth differed, depending, *inter alia*, on the scope for importing technology from abroad and on the size of the agricultural labour force. Thus, countries with a good deal of farm employment were able to boost their growth rates simply by transferring labour from low productivity agriculture to high productivity industry. OECD estimates of the size of this effect, inevitably made under simplifying *ceteris paribus* assumptions, suggest that for the period 1955-68, resource reallocation accounted for one-third of Italian and Finnish growth, but only 5 per cent of British growth.[33]

But relative backwardness has, of course, a much more important dimension than just the purely statistical effect of boosting growth rates thanks to inter-sectoral shifts. In Kindleberger's model it allows the modern sector of the economy to grow rapidly because of the high profits which elastic labour supplies in the countryside make possible. In Kaldor's model it stimulates manufacturing growth at the sort of income levels most of Europe was at in the 1950s and 1960s. And in Cornwall's interpretation, relative backwardness facilitates, in addition, rapid technological progress since cheap technology developed elsewhere can be easily adopted.

All these explanations would seem to be able to contribute to an understanding of the post-war growth process. Taking the growth of manufacturing output first (and using industrial production as a ready-made proxy), it will be

---

[32] Cornwall, *Modern Capitalism*.
[33] OECD, *Growth of Output*, p. 39. Results obtained by Denison (*Why Growth Rates Differ*) are not very dissimilar.

seen that in general 'rates of growth of aggregate output are "high" only when the rate of growth of manufacturing output is greater than the rate of growth of total output',[34] with Spain and the United Kingdom as the most obvious extreme and opposite examples (Fig. 1.4A).

Though the Kaldorian explanation provides for reasons why overall growth should be a function of sectoral growth, in so far as manufacturing represents from 30 to 40 per cent of GDP, a relatively close relationship could be expected to exist in any case. Fig. 1.4B thus presents a somewhat different indicator of backwardness – the availability of labour supply to the industrial sector of the economy, very imperfectly proxied by the growth of non-agricultural employment. This variable is clearly influenced by more than just inter-sectoral resource shifts, since it also reflects the impact of demographic, participation rate, and migration changes. And even if these factors were of negligible importance, it would still be unable to fully catch labour's elasticity to the modern sector of the economy, since surplus labour was available in many countries outside agriculture (e.g. in handicraft or informal service activities). Yet despite its imperfect nature, it is statistically significant in an explanation of growth rate differences. Relatively rapidly growing countries (Spain, Italy, or Finland) benefited from internal migrations; relatively slowly growing ones (the United Kingdom or Ireland) did not. The explanation is, however, only very partial. Several countries stand out as glaring exceptions – Austria in particular, as already noted by Kindleberger, but also France and Germany. To some extent these exceptions are due to the different experiences of the 1950s and 1960s. Separating the two sub-periods shows that for France and Germany, at least, the relationship is closer – very rapid earlier German growth coincided with a very rapidly growing labour force, while the 1960s saw a slowdown in both, and the reverse was true in France.

Finally, a third proxy for maturity – the gap in hourly productivity *vis-à-vis* the United States at the start of the period – also provides a statistically significant variable for subsequent differences in growth rates. The relationship is somewhat closer in this instance, with only one major exception provided by Ireland. Here again, allowance for different performance in the two sub-periods would bring Ireland closer to the regression line, at least in the 1960s when Irish growth (at 4.3 per cent per annum) was more than double the 1.8 per cent average of the years 1953–61.

Demand, policies, attitudes

Any of these three variables, or indeed their combination[35] would thus seem to provide some reasons for why there were differences in growth rates in the period. Yet their explanatory power is inevitably limited. As was argued earlier on, permissive supply conditions *per se* could well be insufficient unless optimistic expectations and dynamic entrepreneurs did avail themselves of the existing opportunities. It is here that demand-side explanations come to the fore and, in particular, the role of investment and exports. Investment, in particular,

---

[34] Cornwall, *Modern Capitalism*, p. 125.

[35] Fifty per cent of the variance of growth rates can be 'explained', for instance, by the combination of elastic labour supplies and technological 'backwardness'.

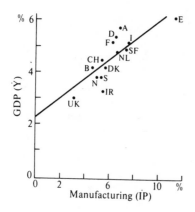

A. GDP growth and growth of manufacturing [a]

$$\dot{Y} = 2.3 + 0.39 \, \dot{IP} \qquad \bar{R}^2 = 0.62$$
$$(4.3) \quad (4.7)$$

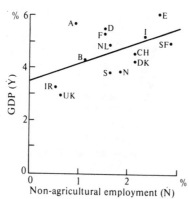

B. GDP growth and growth of non-agricultural employment

$$\dot{Y} = 3.5 + 0.69 \, \dot{N} \qquad \bar{R}^2 = 0.22$$
$$(6.2) \quad (2.1)$$

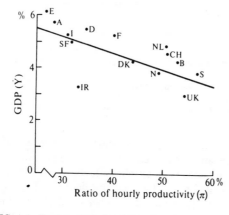

C. GDP growth and ratio of hourly productivity to United States level in 1953

$$\dot{Y} = 7.0 - 0.06\pi \qquad \bar{R}^2 = 0.38$$
$$(8.6) \quad (3.0)$$

FIG. 1.4. *'Backwardness' and growth, 1953-1973* (average annual percentage changes)
[a] Proxied by industrial production
Sources: OECD, *National Accounts of OECD Countries, 1950-1979*: OECD, *Manpower Statistics, 1950-1962*: OECD, *Labour Force Statistics* (various issues); IMF, *International Financial Statistics* (1980 Yearbook); A. Maddison, 'Long Run Dynamics of Productivity Growth', *Banca Nazionale del Lavoro Quarterly Review*, March 1979; author's estimates.

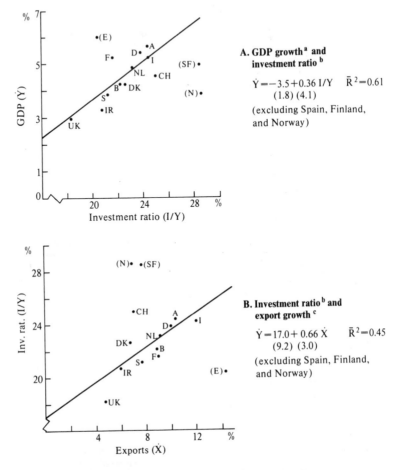

FIG. 1.5. *Growth, investment and exports, 1953-1973* (percentages)
[a] Average annual percentage changes
[b] Gross fixed investment in per cent of GDP at constant prices
[c] Goods and services; average annual percentage changes
Source: OECD, *National Accounts of OECD Countries, 1950-1979.*

would seem to be important for a number of crucial reasons. It is investment that vehicles technological progress and creates capacity; it is investment that strengthens demand and demand pressures via multiplier effects; and it is investment that allows profits to be generated since it is via investment that the availability of cheap labour and technology are exploited. In other words, investment would seem to be the real engine that drives growth through its effects on supply, on demand, and on profits. Investment, in turn, is driven by a number of elements of which, as argued earlier, the most important is probably expectations. While it is virtually impossible to proxy the latter, an indirect factor which might have influenced expectations favourably could have been the growth of exports in so far as this strengthened the balance of payments and hence entrepreneurial confidence. As proponents of export-led growth theories admit, it is difficult to determine the direction of causation between high investment and high export growth, but this does not, *per se*, diminish the importance of foreign demand as a further element in the puzzle.

The relationships between growth and investment and between investment and exports are shown in Fig. 1.5. The aggregate investment ratio in output is clearly an imperfect proxy for the contribution of business investment to growth, since it can be influenced by relative price differences between countries, the composition of output, the type and ownership of the capital goods that are installed, etc. Three countries, with very high or low incremental capital–output ratios, stand out. Finland and Norway show sharply above-average investment ratios due, on the one hand, to their very low population densities which require much higher infrastructure investment, and, on the other, to the composition of their industrial output, heavily concentrated in highly capital-intensive semi-manufactures. Spain is at the other extreme, largely because its manufacturing production is much less capital-intensive, but partly also because of a relatively low infrastructure effort. For the remaining countries of the sample, however, high investment ratios and high growth rates would seem to be fairly closely correlated. The same is clearly true for the relationship between investment ratios and growth of exports of goods and services (provided the three outlying observations of Spain, Finland, and Norway are again excluded). The major remaining exception to the general rule is Switzerland, but this country's high investment ratio is heavily influenced by a well above average share of construction investment.[36] In addition, Switzerland was the only country which in the fixed exchange rate period from 1948 to 1970 did not devalue *vis-à-vis* the dollar (and, therefore, revalued by a large margin *vis-à-vis* its European trading partners). Under such circumstances, an export-led growth process was unlikely to materialize.

The various factors looked at so far would seem to go a long way in explaining differences in economic growth over the twenty years up to the first oil shock. But they do not seem sufficient. Other factors were at work, of an even more diffuse and less quantifiable nature. One of these must have been the role of economic policies, whose importance was stressed earlier on. It is difficult to account for the role of policies in any precise way, either in their contribution to short-run demand management[37] or to longer-term growth. But some indication of their effectiveness may be provided by the evidence of those countries which recorded a marked acceleration in growth between the 1950s and the 1960s (Table 1.6). Spain, Belgium, and Ireland are cases in point. Spain, whose experience is discussed in greater detail in Chapter 19 below, benefited from a policy package in the late 1950s which included substantial liberalization of the economy and a large (30 per cent) devaluation. Both these changes were instrumental in the acceleration of growth that followed. A very similar, if less drastic, change in policies took place at roughly the same time in France, with very similar consequences.[38] Belgium and Ireland had been hampered by restrictive

---

[36] OECD, *Economic Survey of Switzerland*, 1972, p. 31.
[37] See Ch. 10 below.
[38] See Ch. 15 below.

TABLE 1.6. *GDP trends, 1953-1979*

	1953-61	1961-73	1973-79	1953-61 to 1961-73	1961-73 to 1973-79
	(average annual percentage changes)			(changes in percentage points)	
France	4.9	5.6	3.0	0.7	−2.6
Germany	7.2	4.5	2.4	−2.7	−2.1
Italy	5.8	5.1	2.6	−0.7	−2.5
United Kingdom	2.9	3.1	1.3	0.2	−1.8
Spain	4.7[a]	6.9	2.8	2.2[a]	−4.1
Austria	6.8	4.9	3.1	−1.9	−1.8
Belgium	3.4	5.0	2.3	1.6	−2.7
Denmark	3.9	4.5	2.1	0.6	−2.4
Finland	5.5	4.7	2.3	−0.8	−2.4
Ireland	1.8	4.3	3.6	2.5	−0.7
Netherlands	4.6	5.2	2.5	0.6	−2.7
Norway	3.4	4.3	4.4	0.9	0.1
Sweden	4.0	3.9	1.8	−0.1	−2.1
Switzerland	5.2	4.1	−0.4	−1.1	−4.5
OECD Europe	4.9	4.7	2.4	−0.2	−2.3

[a] 1954-61

Source: OECD, *National Accounts of OECD Countries, 1950-1979*.

policies throughout most of the 1950s, largely because of price and/or balance of payments considerations. The shift to a more expansionary stance in the late 1950s seems to have been very important in allowing a pick-up in the growth rate, helped in the Belgian case by United States direct investment and in the Irish case by a reversal in demographic and hence labour-market trends (in the 1950s both the population of working age and total employment were falling).[39] Denmark is a further example of a country which moved from a balance-of-payments-constrained policy in the 1950s to a more accommodating and growth-promoting stance in the 1960s, with clear effects on growth performance.[40]

For those countries which decelerated through the period, the role of economic policies may not be as obvious. For Germany and Austria, for instance, the slowdown would seem to have been largely due to the exhaustion of favourable catch-up factors on the supply side, and, for Switzerland, to the restrictions on foreign immigration imposed in the mid-1960s. But Italy's deceleration, at least, could in large part be explained by the shift in economic policy from an accommodating stance until the 1962-3 boom to a more restrictive position in the following decade. Similarly, relatively restrictive policies can shed light on the downward deviations from the average deceleration in the post-1973 period. While for virtually all the European countries this was remarkably similar (of the

[39] On Belgium, see Ch. 20 below: on Ireland, K.A. Kennedy and B.R. Dowling, *Economic Growth in Ireland*, Dublin 1975.
[40] See Ch. 21 below.

order of 2 to 2½ per cent per annum), it was a good deal sharper in Spain and Switzerland, two countries which for balance of payments and/or inflation reasons were forced, or chose, to follow policies of severe restraint. Finally, the United Kingdom performance throughout the thirty years may have been unfavourably influenced by a succession of 'stop–go' policies.

Lastly, no account of differences in growth rates can ignore broadly defined social factors. However homogeneous Western Europe may seem relative to the developing or socialist world, differences between European countries in attitudes and behaviour were pronounced at the beginning of the period, and were far from eliminated through the ensuing quarter of a century of rapid growth and internationalization. Indirect evidence for this can be found, for instance, in some detailed cross-country studies of productivity differentials in similar plants.[41] Even in cases in which industrial sectors, plant size, and capital endowment per worker were broadly similar, labour productivity could vary by factors going from 1 to 2 between European countries. There would seem to be little doubt that differing management and, in particular, workers' attitudes lie behind such striking divergences, attitudes which can presumably be traced back to complex historical and social trends.

While it would be generally agreed that such social forces are important, assessing, let alone quantifying, their impact is well-nigh impossible. An inkling of the sort of factors that may have been at work can, however, be gleaned from Figs. 1.4 and 1.5. It will be seen that a number of countries appear very regularly below all or most of the estimated regression lines – the United Kingdom, Denmark, Norway, and at times also Finland and Sweden (Ireland, as mentioned earlier, is somewhat exceptional because of its depressed growth in the 1950s). If there is a social factor common to these countries, this is probably the early appearance of a welfare state. Conversely, France, Germany, and Spain (but also Austria), appear consistently above the regression lines and these are countries in which welfare states developed later and income distribution patterns remained, almost certainly, fairly unequal for longer.

This argument may echo a thesis that received prominence in Britain in the later 1970s and which argued that the United Kingdom's disappointing performance could be traced to the rapid growth of the country's public sector.[42] Though there is some statistical evidence linking growth rates to changes in (but not levels of) public expenditure shares in GDP, the direction of causation is ambiguous. Public demand may well have attempted at times, particularly in the United Kingdom, to supplement sluggish private demand, rather than having been the cause of the latter. The very tentative idea here put forward is somewhat different. What is being argued is that, in a very diffuse sense, the early establishment of widespread welfare provisions, the successful attempts at reducing income inequalities, and the general preference for leisure often implicit in such choices, may have reduced the flexibility with which the economy and

---

[41] See, for instance, C.F. Pratten, *Labour Productivity Differentials within International Companies*, University of Cambridge, Department of Applied Economics, Cambridge 1976; or D.T. Jones and S.J. Prais, 'Plant-Size and Productivity in the Motor Industry: Some International Comparisons', *Oxford Bulletin of Economics and Statistics*, May 1978.

[42] R. Bacon and W. Eltis, *Britain's Economic Problem*, London 1978 (2nd edn.).

the labour market in particular reacted to new stimuli and opportunities. Though from a welfare point of view countries with very advanced social legislation at the outset clearly benefited, their record was less satisfactory from the standpoint of conventionally measured growth.

Conclusions

The foregoing pages have tried to provide a deliberately eclectic picture of Europe's post-war growth to the end of the 1970s. A major distinction was made between explanations for the generalized acceleration that took place in the 1950s and 1960s and for the subsequent deceleration in the 1970s on the one hand, and for inter-country differences in growth rates on the other. On the first issue, it was argued that the role of supply factors was permissive rather than initiating. What launched Europe on to a higher growth trend were primarily new economic policies, domestic as well as international, and the perception of this changed policy environment by entrepreneurs. Once growth was started, success bred further success as confidence strengthened and expectations proved to be self-fulfilling. Such a growth process, however, was likely to decelerate at some time or other. The gradual achievement of real full employment in Europe as a whole meant that for growth to continue at earlier rates investment had to rise and, therefore, also profitability. But while investment ratios went on increasing in the late 1960s and, to some extent, even in the early 1970s, profitability declined as labour exploited, if with a lag, its increasingly monopolistic position. The resulting upward spurt in wages was one of the factors that led to the general acceleration in inflation, to increasingly coincident fluctuations in the world economy, and, finally, to the 1973–4 watershed. After that, the momentum was broken. Not only did countries switch from permissive to restrictive economic policies, but entrepreneurial confidence, which had been so important a force in driving growth until then, collapsed.

Trying to account for individual country experiences, the main, and hardly very controversial, thesis put forward was that initial differences in levels of economic development were among the more important factors. Countries which at the outset had a relatively large agricultural labour force, a relatively small manufacturing sector, or relatively low productivity levels, were all in a more favourable position from a growth point of view than their more mature neighbours. This potential for growth was then, more or less successfully, transformed into actual growth via high levels of investment which were influenced, inter alia, by government policies, export and balance of payments performances, or even the momentum of post-war reconstruction.

The major conclusion that emerges from this brief survey is that post-war growth was not inevitable, but, in a sense, a man-made accident. Similar favourable preconditions for growth had existed on earlier occasions. What was different in the early post-war years was the climate of opinion which allowed an unprecedented upward spurt. Entrepreneurs believed that governments would maintain full employment, while workers believed that governments would preserve price stability. Neither set of expectations could necessarily last for ever, and, indeed, when governments were put to the test on inflation (in the late 1960s) and on growth (in the mid-1970s), they were unable to satisfy the high expectations that had been built up. The inflation (and therefore probably the ensuing deceleration), were probably inevitable given the existing institutional framework. As has been argued in the past, capitalism may be unable to reconcile *prolonged* full employment and *relative* price stability.

These brief comments also throw some light on what could be the problems and prospects for the 1980s. The return to very high rates of unemployment, the appearance of very large margins of spare capacity, and the economic possibilities opened up by continued technological progress, would suggest that in the early 1980s no supply constraints should inhibit faster growth (barring, of course, any crisis on the energy side). Whether growth will resume or not will then depend, as it did in the 1950s and 1960s, on policy-makers', entrepreneurs', and trade unions' reactions. If inflationary expectations quickly subside and if entrepreneurial confidence returns, prospects for a time could well be favourable. But if the inflationary momentum is more deeply ingrained in European societies (as argued in Chapter 3), if the oligopolistic nature of labour markets is not broken despite high rates of unemployment, and if entrepreneurial expectations in these circumstances remain depressed (as they were in the 1930s), the possibility of a vicious circle of declining investment pulling down potential output levels and exacerbating the struggle for income shares cannot be discounted.

Bibliography

The major works on Europe's comparative growth experience have already been mentioned in the body of this chapter. An early international survey was by the UNECE, *Some Factors in Economic Growth in Europe during the 1950s* (Economic Survey of Europe in 1961, Pt. 2), Geneva 1964, which was followed by *Structural Trends and Prospects in the European Economy* (1969 Survey, Pt. 1), New York 1970, and *The European Economy from the 1950s to the 1970s* (1971 Survey, Pt. 1), New York 1972. The OECD's directly comparative literature on the subject is limited to *The Growth of Output, 1960–1980*, Paris 1970, but abundant longer-run material can be found in its annual *Economic Surveys* for various countries.

More analytical studies are those by A. Lamfalussy, *The United Kingdom and the Six: An Essay on Economic Growth in Western Europe*, London 1963; A. Maddison, *Economic Growth in the West: Comparative Experience in Europe and North America*, London 1964; C.P. Kindleberger, *Europe's Postwar Growth: The Role of Labor Supply*, Cambridge, Mass. 1967; E. Denison, *Why Growth Rates Differ: Postwar Experience in Nine Western Countries*, Brookings Institution, Washington 1967; J. Cornwall, *Modern Capitalism: Its Growth and Transformation*, London 1977 (some of these cover not only Europe, but also Japan and/or North America). Two works primarily concerned with the United Kingdom which, however, provide insights into other countries' performance are N. Kaldor, *Causes of the Slow Rate of Economic Growth of the United Kingdom*, Cambridge 1966, and R. Bacon and W. Eltis, *Britain's Economic Problem: Too Few Producers*, London 1978 (2nd edn.).

For individual countries, indications for further reading are provided in the bibliographies attached to Chapters 15 to 21 below. C.M. Cipolla (ed.), *The Fontana Economic History of Europe* (Vol. 6, *Contemporary Economies*), Glasgow 1976, provides a perspective on the twentieth-century experience of France, Germany, Italy, the United Kingdom, Spain, the Benelux countries, Scandinavia, and Switzerland.

2

Growth and Crisis – a Marxist Interpretation

Introduction

In 1974 the capitalist world entered a deep crisis. All European countries were affected, even though there were major differences in their underlying economic situations (for example, Germany's remarkable competitive performance; Britain's almost permanent crisis; France's uneven resistance). The impact of the crisis was the more intense since it followed the long period of rapid economic growth in the 1950s and 1960s. Once again, there appeared to be a risk of long-term stagnation – a possibility which had not been seriously contemplated since the early post-war years. The spectre of the 1930s depression returned.

In this context it is natural that there should have been a resurgence of Marxist-oriented works of an applied kind. Economic discussions focused again on central issues, such as the role of the 'trade cycle' – or of crises – in the dynamic adaptation of capitalist economies; on the problems posed by profitability, or by increased pressures and claims on the distribution of income; as well as by the emergence, during the 1960s, of demands for new life-styles and work conditions. These are some of the central concerns of Marxist economics, which provides an appropriate framework for analysing their interactions.

This chapter examines the growth of the European economy from a Marxist point of view. The first section puts forward an analytical framework which is then applied to the broad features of growth and crises over the period from the early 1950s to the end of the 1970s. The remainder of the chapter distinguishes two phases. The first, 1950-73, is the period of substantial growth which sees the spread of a new form of capital accumulation and new employment relationships, but which is also marked, from the early 1960s onwards, by a slow deterioration in profitability, rising pressures on the distribution of income, accelerating inflation, and increasing problems with external constraints. The second, 1974-9, is the period of crisis, which is triggered off by the rise in oil prices, but whose origins lie further back in the progressive deterioration in economic conditions during the previous period.

I. Capitalist Growth and Crises – Some Methodological Points

The history of capitalism appears as a sequence of periods of growth and of crises which require both a theoretical and a historical explanation, which Marxist analysis would seem ideally suited to provide. For a long time, Marxist

* University of Rennes.

studies of growth and crises have, however, been subject to a number of limitations:

(i) A mechanistic interpretation of the 'law of the falling rate of profit' combined, from time to time, with a 'catastrophic' vision of the future which periodically announced the final crisis of the capitalist system;[1]
(ii) A difficulty in understanding the workings of contemporary economies which led to somewhat one-sided explanations, at times contradicting each other: e.g. the thesis of state monopoly capitalism, the works of Baran and Sweezy on the rising surplus,[2] studies of imperialism,[3] etc.;
(iii) A marked tendency on the part of the 'algebraic Marxists' to bury themselves in the debate on the transformation problem,[4] and, more generally, an inability of Marxist authors to use rigorously the labour theory of value in empirical works.

This chapter shares the approach and essential purpose of Marxist analysis, which is to discover the laws of motion of the capitalist system. Hence it places at the centre of analysis social struggles and the changes that occur in the conditions of production, in life-styles, in institutions, and in employment relationships. It also retains from the Marxist approach the basic analysis of crises. On the other hand, it parts company with orthodox Marxist analysis on the empirical and statistical side. Thus, it does not refer to the very abstract concept of labour value, but uses conventional data on prices, wages, and profits. These three points are developed below.

The lessons of history – capitalist 'regulation' and accumulation

History provides clear evidence that the processes of dynamic adjustment – or the 'regulation' of capitalist economies – do not remain invariant through time. On the contrary, structural changes and the emergence of new institutions can be observed at different stages of economic growth. Thus, the nature of competition has greatly changed in the course of one century; the links between banks and firms have been radically modified, and also differ sharply between countries, while the relationships between workers and employers have evolved under the simultaneous influence of social struggles, of changes in labour relations, and of new negotiating procedures. Similarly, the forms of government intervention (e.g. monetary policy, social policy, public investment), have clearly changed over time.

Each period in the history of capitalism is characterized by a certain institutional stability within which can be detected relatively lasting mechanisms of what will be called 'regulation', in terms, for instance, of wage, employment, profit, and price formation.[5] This crucial concept of 'regulation' can be defined

[1] P. Boccara, *Etudes sur le capitalisme monopoliste d'Etat. sa crise et son issue*, Paris 1974.

[2] P.A. Baran and P.M. Sweezy, *Monopoly Capital*, New York 1966.

[3] S. Amin, *Accumulation on a World Scale*, New York 1974.

[4] M. Morishima, *Marx's Economics*, Cambridge 1973.

[5] This approach is particularly developed by Boyer with regard to the analysis of wages and inflation: R. Boyer, 'Wage Formation in Historical Perspective: The French Experience', *Cambridge Journal of Economics*, September 1979; see also his 'La crise actuelle', *Critiques de l'économie politique*, No. 7-8, 1979.

as 'the way in which a system as a whole functions, the conjunction of economic mechanisms associated with a given set of social relationships, of institutional forms and structures'.[6] More broadly, 'the term refers to the balance of social, institutional and economic forces which characterize, at a particular time, the economic system or particular parts of it'.[7]

It is clear that there can be no perfect correlation between any given economic and social structure and the forms of 'regulation'. At any time existing economic mechanisms constitute a specific 'regulation', which need not be stable, since 'regulation' itself continually modifies the nature and state of social relationships. There are, however, certain basic forms of 'regulation' capable of effectively guaranteeing a reproduction of the whole system and of preserving existing institutions and social structures. This approach is diametrically opposed to the neo-classical one for which economic processes are taken as unchanging, are identical in all markets, and can be reduced to the interplay of supply and demand (even if neo-classical analysis has shown great flexibility in integrating the most diverse phenomena — imperfect competition, the heterogeneous nature of the labour market, racial discrimination, etc.).

Five major features describe the main characteristics of capitalist growth:

(i) The process of accumulation, which includes employment relationships, the mode of production, life-styles, and the nature of competition;
(ii) The existing institutional framework, e.g. the nature of government intervention, collective negotiation procedures, or the methods for financing accumulation;
(iii) The level of development;
(iv) The 'regulation' procedures in operation;
(v) The extent of the international division of labour;

This listing in order of importance is only put forward to structure the analysis, but the different points must not be considered in isolation, as tends to be the case in certain Marxist studies which only emphasize specific aspects (state monopoly capital, the obstruction of scientific and technical progress,[8] centre–periphery relationships, etc.).

The notion of accumulation requires expansion in view of its importance. A distinction must be made between extensive and intensive accumulation. The former implies a growth of the capital stock which does not alter existing production techniques, and which is accompanied by low productivity growth. In the latter, the technical and social organization of work is profoundly modified, the growth of investment is better planned, and productivity growth is rapid. Capital-intensive and extensive accumulation are not mutually exclusive, but over long periods of time one of them is usually predominant. This was particularly the case during the 1950s and 1960s when a regime of capital-intensive accumulation was established. Closely linked to this was the development of a new employment relationship which was characterized by an increasing division of labour, a lowering of the skill content of many jobs, increased work intensity,

[6] Boyer, 'Wage Formation', p. 100. See also. J.-P. Benassy, R. Boyer, and R.M. Gelpi, 'Régulation des économies capitalistes et inflation', *Revue économique*, May 1979.

[7] J.A. Wilson's 'Translator's Introduction' to Boyer, 'Wage Formation', p. 99.

[8] Boccara, *Etudes sur le capitalisme.*

but also a more rapid growth in the purchasing power of wage earners, the development of mass consumption and the launching of a new life-style.

'Regulation' and capitalist crisis

The major achievements of the Marxist analysis of crises should be placed within the broad framework of the 'regulation' approach. It should be noted, in particular, that forms of 'regulation' and the main features that characterize the stages of capitalist growth (the process of accumulation, institutions, the state of the international division of labour, etc.) need not always be in harmony with each other. Indeed, the form of 'regulation' can at times become incapable of ensuring the reproduction of the system. Such mismatches are then at the root of a crisis which calls into question and alters institutional forms and 'regulation' methods. Two forms of crisis should be distinguished:

(i) Mutation crises, which alter the main features of the previous period (e.g. forms of accumulation, or external constraints) and guarantee the emergence of new mechanisms of control. The crisis of the 1930s is the best-known example; the crisis of the 1970s also falls into this category (as will be seen later on);

(ii) 'Regulation' crises, in which cyclical fluctuations only appear as one mechanism of dynamic adjustment among many. An example is provided by the business cycles of the second half of the nineteenth century and right up to 1930. The spread of capital-intensive accumulation and the progressive introduction of monopolistic 'regulation' have led to the disappearance of this type of crisis since 1945 in favour of much milder cyclical fluctuations.

Such a point of view is diametrically opposed to that of some Marxist writers who use the same tools to explain all overproduction crises whatever the characteristics of the period. Thus the 1974-5 crisis is 'the twentieth over-production crisis since the formation of the world market'.[9]

It none the less remains true that the most important elements in the Marxist analysis of crises remain valid, provided they are used in a coherent fashion and placed in their historical context. The study of fluctuations of the rate of profit thus remains essential, but the traditional differences between explanations of the crisis in terms of underconsumption, sectoral imbalances, or overaccumulation, must be discarded in favour of a combined approach incorporating all these explanatory factors. The origins of crises cannot be found in a single cause (such as the exhaustion of opportunities for technical progress, increases in the organic composition of capital, the evolution of the balance of power in favour of workers, profit crises, the increasing international division of labour, etc.). On the contrary, these different approaches must be interlinked. Within this framework each economy then appears stamped by its own history and develops according to its own possibilities.

Statistical indicators and labour values

The use of Marxist concepts for statistical purposes has always presented formidable problems and the efforts made in this area have frequently lacked precision.

[9] E. Mandel, *The Second Slump*, London 1978, p. 34.

At a theoretical level, the problem of the transformation of values into prices has generated a lively controversy, but, with hindsight, this appears to have been somewhat unproductive. Numerous writers, with very varied backgrounds, agree that, except under very restrictive assumptions, there is no possibility of moving from values to prices. The labour theory of value can only be used to analyse at the most abstract level the way in which the capitalist system works, particularly by isolating the concept of exploitation. But is is of little use when trying to understand the actual problems of crisis or of inflation. In particular, the traditional approach provides for the determination of relative prices, but is silent on the determination of the general price level. It is surprising to observe the disparity which exists, in most works, between the large number of pages devoted to the transformation problem and the paucity of results obtained when questions of inflation and overaccumulation are tackled directly.

Such a situation is clearly unsatisfactory, and some authors have attempted to make their own original contributions, particularly when trying to analyse inflation, by separating values from prices,[10] or even by relying on the notion of the 'money value of the hour of abstract work'.[11] Overall, results have been far from conclusive, and the link between real and nominal values has remained weak. Special mention must be made of the 'labour time accounting' approach, which allows the determination of a set of values, distinct from that of costs and independent of the wage–profit distribution. Three methodological difficulties arise in this approach:

(i) The problem of how to incorporate changing production techniques and fixed capital;
(ii) The problem of the heterogeneous nature of work; thus, the reduction of complex work-forms into simpler forms hardly seems compatible with the segmentation of the labour market which constitutes a structural feature of capitalism;
(iii) The problem of measuring the work content of imported commodities.

It is none the less the case that a number of important results can be obtained by this method.[12] Thus the calculation of the gap between actual work and the work necessary for the reproduction of the labour force allows a proper analysis of the exploitation of labour. The links between capital accumulation, productivity, and profitability can also be seen in a new light,[13] particularly with regard to the influence of rising capital intensity. But work in this area has not yet progressed far enough to throw new light on the problems of growth and crises.

In summary, value theory helps to explain the major relationships of capital production, but it is impossible to link the labour theory of value with the traditional nominal variables (prices, wages, profits, etc.). In order to analyse the problems of growth, crisis, and inflation, this chapter will therefore use as statistical indicators the series currently used in the national accounts, e.g. labour

[10] A. Lipietz, *Crise et inflation: pourquoi?*, Paris 1978.
[11] M. Aglietta, *A Theory of Capitalist Regulation – The US Experience*, London 1979.
[12] M. Hollard, *Comptabilités sociales en temps de travail*, Paris 1978.
[13] E.N. Wolff, 'The Rate of Surplus Value, the Organic Composition, and the General Rate of Profit in the U.S. Economy, 1947–67', *American Economic Review*, June 1979.

productivity, the capital–output ratio, the wage share, and the rate of profit. The field of investigation is usually the whole economy, except for France where it is limited to the non-agricultural sector.

The statistical indicators are themselves subject to numerous deficiencies which can only be mentioned briefly in this context. Some of these concern measurement problems (lack of information on non-wage incomes, the conventions used to construct capital stock series at constant prices, changes in price bases, etc.). Others are more fundamental and relate to the concepts and definitions that are used. It should also be borne in mind that despite the attempts at harmonization made by international organizations such as the OECD or the EEC, level comparisons remain fraught with difficulties. This is particularly true in the case of ratios which incorporate capital stock series for which the national accounts data of each country have had to be used.[14]

The discussion in the sections which follow is restricted to the European economies (essentially the four major countries of the EEC), and the emphasis is primarily on the problems of capital accumulation and profitability. No claim is made to provide a complete picture of the process of accumulation, of the institutional framework, or of the procedures of 'regulation' which were at work.

II. Capital-Intensive Accumulation and Growth in the European Economies, 1950–1973

It is well known that the period of growth which began immediately after World War II was exceptional in the history of capitalism, both in extent and duration. This growth phase seems to have been largely due to a surge in capital-intensive accumulation, to the introduction of new methods of production, to a sustained growth in the purchasing power of wage earners, and to a rapid rise in mass consumption. This section begins by looking at the process of capital-intensive accumulation. It then examines the links between capital-intensive accumulation and labour productivity, as well as the distribution of income between wages and profits. This, in turn, allows an analysis of the interactions between capital accumulation and changes in employment relationships which shows that a turning-point occurred in the mid-1960s. It was then that the opportunities for growth declined, that the wage share increased, and that profitability began to be eroded. By the early 1970s, a crisis of overaccumulation had begun and inflation was accelerating. The last subsection investigates the increasing degree of internationalization which started in the 1950s.

The foundations of capital-intensive accumulation

After the uneven development of the immediate post-war years (1945–50) and the substantial 1949 devaluations, Europe experienced almost continuous growth

---

[14] An INSEE publication (Y. Barou, M. Dollé, C. Gabet, and E. Wartenberg), 'Les performances comparées de l'économie en France en R.F.A. et au Royaume-Uni', *Collections de l'INSEE*, série E, No. 69, 1979), provides some reliable comparisons between France and Germany, but it uses 'old base' national accounts series for France. The move to 'new base' data has led to significant changes in some series. In particular, the capital–output ratio, which was rising from 1965 onwards according to the earlier data, now remains stable until 1974. This strengthens the need for care when using the data.

of output, with only the United Kingdom, among the major economies, developing relatively slowly. More significant differences, however, appeared with respect to inflation – virtual price stability in Germany until the end of the 1960s, somewhat greater fluctuations in Italy and the United Kingdom, frequent inflationary pressure in France. These inter-country disparities reflect different starting-points and the greater or lesser speed with which reconstruction took place. But overall one can detect a similar accumulation process at work, which relied on marked changes in production conditions and on the rise of a new employment relationship.[15]

Changing production conditions occurred as a result of the sustained growth in investment and took the form of an increased division of labour, of a development of automation, of a lowering of the skill content of individual jobs, and of an extension of assembly line work. The need to make use of a much larger capital stock led to the adoption of continuous production methods (particularly in semi-manufacturing industries) so as to limit the increase in the organic composition of capital. As a result, the intensity of work rose but substantial productivity gains were achieved. This accumulation process was clearly linked to the appearance of new products (e.g. new consumer durables or standardized semi-manufactured goods) and new processes, for instance the progressive replacement of coal by oil.

Profound social changes occurred at the same time. In particular, the number of assembly line workers increased greatly at the expense of unskilled labourers and, above all, of the traditional craftsmen who were capable of exerting a measure of control over the work process. Artisan-like activities declined sharply or were integrated into capitalist production, particularly in the service and commercial sectors. The growth in corporate employment – which took place in all the European countries except the United Kingdom, where it had occurred at an earlier date – confirms this movement.

This capital-intensive process of accumulation can be observed in all the European economies, though each of them displayed its own individual characteristics. A first indicator of such disparities is provided by the development of investment shares (Fig. 2.1). Germany recorded a high and rapidly rising share of investment in GDP until the early 1960s. A break in trend occurred, however, in the mid-1960s, and from 1971 onwards the fall in the investment rate became more marked. France, on the other hand, experienced a more regular growth right up to 1973-4. Even so, the industrial transformation which the country underwent did not eliminate the gap with Germany. Italy achieved rapid investment growth at the beginning of the period, but 1963 represented a turning-point. The over-rapid transformation in work conditions and life-styles came up against relatively rigid social structures, and the rate of accumulation had to slow down. Lastly, the United Kingdom occupies a unique position. The country's investment ratio, though increasing slowly, remained low throughout the period – a first illustration of the obstacles confronting the British economy.

The transformations in production methods also led to important changes in the nature of employment relationships. The growth of real wages had to be sufficiently rapid and smooth to ensure rising outlets for the mass production of

[15] Y. Barou, B. Billaudot, and A. Granou, *Croissance et crise*, Paris 1979.

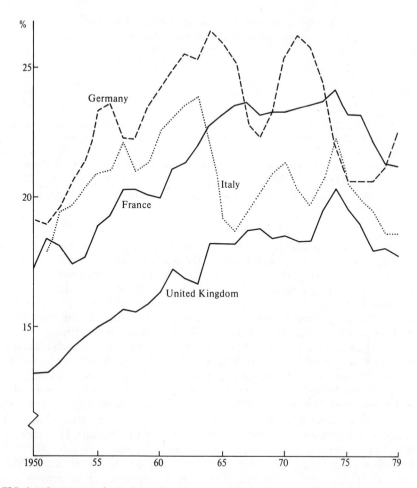

FIG. 2.1. *Investment shares* (gross fixed investment in per cent of GDP at current prices)
Source: OECD, *National Accounts of OECD Countries, 1950–1979.*

durable consumer goods industries. New wage determination mechanisms had thus to be developed. *Inter alia*, they took the form of collective bargaining procedures between the social partners, the establishment of links between rising wages and productivity gains, and, in some cases, the *de facto* indexation of wages to prices. The government also intervened in various ways, e.g. by setting up incomes policies, by encouraging the practice of collective agreements, or by the determination of minimum wages. Partly as a result, there was a very significant break with earlier periods in the rate of growth of real earnings per head. In all the European countries the purchasing power of wages rose steadily (Table 2.1).

Owing to the sustained growth of the consumer goods department, a better balance could be ensured at the macroeconomic level with the investment goods department which, in turn, was driven forward by the efforts made at modernizing

TABLE 2.1. *Growth of real wages*[a] *per employee*
(average annual percentage changes)

	1950–60	1960–73	1973–79
France	5.2	4.8	3.8
Germany	5.8	5.6	2.7
Italy	4.9[b]	6.5	1.9
United Kingdom	2.7	3.2	1.6

[a] Compensation of employees deflated by implicit private consumption deflator
[b] 1951–60

Sources: OECD, *National Accounts of OECD Countries* (various issues); OECD, *Manpower Statistics, 1950–1962*; OECD, *Labour Force Statistics* (various issues); M. Baslé, J. Mazier, and J.-F. Vidal, 'Croissance sectorielle et accumulation en longue période', *Statistiques et études financières*, No. 40, 1979; ISTAT, *Annuario di contabilità nazionale, 1978*

and extending plant and equipment. This thesis has been shown to be true for France, where data exist which divide the economy into the two producing departments.[16] During the 1960s the rapid extension of department 1 (production goods) was linked to the regular capital deepening of department 2 (consumer goods), while the latter's outlets were rooted in the growth of real wages. This was in contrast with the interwar years which witnessed, until 1930, a self-propelled growth in department 1 with little change in department 2.

Apart from these general trends, there were specific features in each economy. It was in the Northern European countries that collective bargaining and social agreements were most developed and the changes in labour practices most advanced. In the United Kingdom, the restrictive practices of the unions acted as an effective brake on the accumulation process, via, for instance, closed shop agreements, resistance to new methods of production (particularly to shift-work), or the persistence of very decentralized wage negotiations. In France and Italy, the existence of a trade-union movement with a more revolutionary tradition often made salary increases very dependent on the social and political context. Lastly, even at the end of the 1960s, important differences in consumption patterns still remained. Thus in 1970 the share of food products in total consumption was still 40 per cent in Italy as opposed to 27 per cent in France and 24 per cent in Germany, while the share of household durables was 5.7 per cent in Italy as opposed to 10.9 per cent in Germany.

Capital accumulation and productivity

The introduction of new methods of production was characterized at the macro-economic level by increasing capital intensity, as shown by the acceleration in the growth of the capital–labour ratio in those European countries for which data are available (Table 2.2).

[16] H. Bertrand, 'La croissance française analysée en sections productives (1950–1974)', *Statistiques et études financières*, No. 35, 1978; H. Bertrand, J. Mazier, Y. Picaud, G. Podevin, 'La crise des années 30 et des années 70: une analyse en sections productives', *Revue économique*, March 1982.

TABLE 2.2. *Growth of capital–labour ratio*
(average annual percentage changes)

	1950-60	1960-65	1965-70	1970-73
France[a]	2.9	3.9	5.0	5.8[b]
Germany	3.9	7.4	6.2	7.0
Italy	2.5[c]	6.2	3.5	..
United Kingdom	2.3	2.8	4.7	3.7
Sweden	–	2.5	3.2	3.9

[a] Excluding the agricultural sector
[b] 1970-72
[c] 1955-60

Sources: OECD, *Manpower Statistics, 1950-1962*, and *Labour Force Statistics* (various issues); and for the capital stock data the following publications: Y. Barou, 'Une fresque sectorielle de l'économie britannique', *Statistiques et études financières* (*SEF*), No. 33, 1978, for the United Kingdom; J. Mairesse, 'L'évaluation du capital fixe productif: méthodes et résultats,' *Collections de l'INSEE*, série C, No. 18-19, 1972 (regularly updated in INSEE, *Economie et statistique*), for France; F. Cellier, 'Déformation sectorielle et évolution économique de la RFA', *SEF*, No. 35, 1978, for Germany; M. Ward, *The Measurement of Capital*, OECD, Paris 1976, for Italy and Sweden.

In Germany during the 1950s the relative abundance of skilled labour, due to the inflow of refugees from the east, was more than compensated for by the very rapid growth in investment. During the 1960s labour became scarcer, despite massive foreign immigration, and even greater efforts were made to increase the capital intensity of production. A turning-point occurred, however, at the end of the 1960s when the rate of growth of the capital–labour ratio decelerated sharply. In France, too, the growth of capital per head accelerated in the 1950s and 1960s, particularly in sectors such as agriculture, construction, services, and commerce, whose capital stock rose significantly as the result of the introduction of a more capitalistic type of production. Even in the United Kingdom, in spite of a relatively low rate of investment, a similar movement was apparent, particularly in periods of slowdown.

Rising capital intensity led to a sharp increase in trend productivity growth in comparison with earlier periods. This was one of the essential features of the accumulation process which began in the wake of World War II. But here too significant differences between countries appear. In Germany, after the rapid gains of the 1950s, productivity growth slowed down, particularly in the 1970s (Table 2.3). A similar picture emerges for Italy after the mid-1960s. In France, on the other hand, productivity growth remained stable, at least until 1973, in industry as well as in non-industrial sectors. This point deserves attention, since the growth of capital per head was higher in Germany than in France during the 1960s. Finally, the United Kingdom's low productivity growth was linked to the difficulties encountered by British firms in introducing labour-saving investment, and, more generally, to the whole structure of the country.

Capital accumulation, by transforming the conditions of production, is one of the chief causes of productivity gains. But it also entails a rising capital intensity which can affect the capital–output ratio. When the growth of productivity falls short of the increase in the capital–labour ratio, the capital–output ratio rises,

TABLE 2.3. *Growth of labour productivity*[a]
(average annual percentage changes)

	1950-60	1960-73	1973-79
France	4.8	4.7	2.8
Germany	5.8	4.4	3.2
Italy	5.1[b]	5.9	1.5
United Kingdom	2.1	2.8	1.2

[a] GDP per employed
[b] 1951-60

Sources: OECD, *National Accounts of OECD Countries, 1950-1979*; OECD, *Manpower
Statistics, 1950-1962*; OECD, *Labour Force Statistics* (various issues); CSO,
Economic Trends Annual Supplement, 1981; Direction de la prévision,
Ministère de l'Economie, 'Croissance sectorielle et accumulation en longue
période', *Statistiques et études financières*, No. 40, 1979; ISTAT, *Annuario di
contabilità nazionale, 1978*.

which, other things being equal, tends to reduce the rate of profit. One thus
obtains from the standard national accounting aggregates one of the traditional
mechanisms at work in the 'long-term tendency for a falling rate of profit'.
The notion of a capital–output ratio is none the less fraught with ambiguities,
particularly on account of the problems raised by the definition and measurement of the capital stock. Nor can this ratio be considered as a purely technical
expression of the efficiency of production, since changes in this efficiency
depend on the whole structure of social relations and not only on exogenous
and purely technical factors. Medium-term trends in the capital–output ratio,
however, provide a useful indication of the nature of the growth process in the
different economies (Fig. 2.2).

Very broadly, the acceleration in the growth of the capital–labour ratio led
to a noticeable improvement in labour productivity and, initially, to decline in
the capital–output ratio. Such a decline also occurred, in a number of countries,
due to the extension of shift-work, and the continuous or semi-continuous use
of capital equipment (Table 2.4). In the United Kingdom, by contrast, the restrictive practices of the unions acted after the beginning of the 1960s as an
effective brake to the installation of new methods of production (e.g. closed-
shop agreements, demarcation disputes, controls on immigration, etc.). These
practices effectively prevented British management from intensifying the work
effort as other countries had done, and the capital–output ratio could not decline.

However, the constant changes in technology became more and more costly
in terms of capital. Eventually, productivity gains were more than offset by
increasing capital–labour ratios, and the capital–output ratio reached a trough
and began to rise. Very simple econometric tests[17] suggest that the change in
trend took place in 1956 in the United Kingdom, and in 1960 in Germany, while
the ratio flattened out in 1966 in France. The reasons for this change were not
simply technical or economic, such as saturation for the products of key industries which had fuelled the accumulation process, or excessive investment
relative to expected productivity gains. Social changes also played an important

[17] See J. Mazier, *Macroéconomie appliquée*, Paris 1978, p. 83.

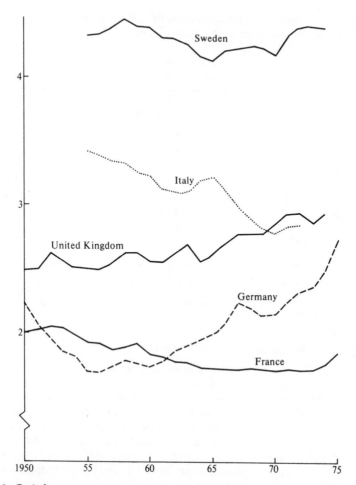

FIG. 2.2. *Capital–output ratios* (ratio of gross fixed capital stock to GDP at constant prices)
Note: figures are not strictly comparable between countries.
Sources: OECD, *National Accounts of OECD Countries, 1950–1979*, and, for capital stock
data, the sources listed under Table 2.2.

role, in particular workers' resistance in the form, for instance, of strikes by
assembly-line workers against the increase in routine tasks, struggles against lay-
offs, the development of absenteeism, or the calling into question of the power
of employers.

This brief analysis of the links between accumulation and productivity has
shown how a regime of capital-intensive accumulation was able to generate a
higher productivity trend. Initially, the capital–output ratio declined in most
European countries. But this growth strategy became increasingly capital-using,
the growth in productivity decelerated in a number of countries, tensions arose
on the social front, and the opportunities for growth declined from the mid-
1960s onwards. Rising, or even stable, capital–output ratios do not, however,

imply that profit rates will automatically decline. Much depends on the evolution of exploitation rates and changes in relative prices.

TABLE 2.4. *Indicators of shift-work*
(percentages)

| | | Share of industrial labour on shift-work | |
		Manual workers	All employees
France	1957	14.3	
	1963	20.1	
	1974	31.3	
	1975		19.6
Germany	1975		21.9
Italy	1975		22.3
United Kingdom	1954	12.5	
	1963	20.0	
	1975	20.5	18.4
Belgium	1975		24.1

Sources: Direction de la prévision, Ministère de l'Economie, 'Réduction de la durée individuelle du travail, travail en équipes et durée d'utilisation des équipements', *mimeo*, Paris 1980; Eurostat, *Working Conditions in the Community, 1975*, Brussels 1977.

Income distribution and profitability — towards a crisis of overaccumulation

The rate of profit plays a central role in the dynamics of capital accumulation as an indicator of the profitability of investment, of internal cash-flow, and also of future profit expectations. An analysis over the medium term can usefully start from a decomposition of the profit rate into its three principal determinants: the share of profits in national income (which is linked to the rate of exploitation), changes in relative prices between the GDP deflator and investment goods prices, and the inverse of the capital–output ratio, which reflects productive efficiency.[18] The latter has already been looked at above. Hence the discussion will consider the first two elements.

Rather than examining changes in the share of gross corporate profits in GDP, it may be preferable to look at its inverse, i.e. the share of labour income adjusted for the shift of workers from self-employment to the corporate sector.[19] Until the early or mid-1960s, the labour share declined gently in Germany and Italy, fell rapidly in France, but rose somewhat in the United Kingdom (Fig. 2.3). This is not in contradiction to the large increase in real wages which was noted

[18] More formally:

$$\frac{\Pi}{p_k K} = \frac{\Pi}{PY} \times \frac{P}{p_k} \times \frac{Y}{K},$$

where Π stands for profits, K for the real capital stock, Y for real income, and P and p_k for the general price level and the price level of investment goods respectively.

[19] This adjustment is made by imputing to the self-employed a fictitious labour income equal to income per employee in the corporate sector; the latter includes employers' social security contributions.

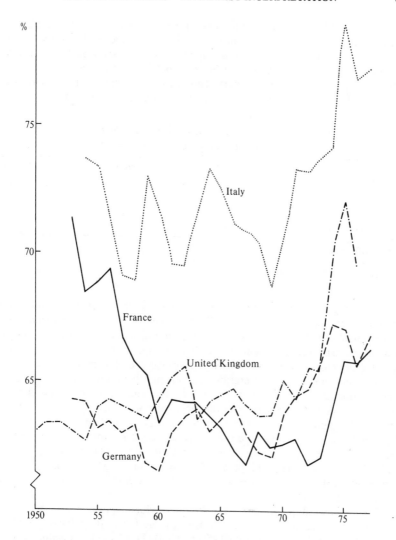

FIG. 2.3. *Labour shares* (compensation of employees and imputed labour income of self-employed in per cent of GDP at current prices)
Note: figures are not strictly comparable between countries
Sources: OECD, *National Accounts of OECD Countries* (various issues); OECD, *Manpower Statistics, 1950–1962*, and *Labour Force Statistics* (various issues)

earlier. The rising capital intensity incorporated in the new methods of production and the ensuing productivity gains allowed both rises in real wages and increases in the share of profits. This is confirmed by changes in the relationship between real per caput wages and labour productivity (Table 2.5).

In other words, the 1950s and the beginning of the 1960s were marked by a rise in the rate of exploitation, though this was both irregular and not very pronounced. Periods of decline in the labour share (1952–60 in France, 1950–60 in

Germany, 1964-9 in Italy) alternated with phases during which the balance of power shifted in favour of employees (1960-4 in France and Germany, 1962-4 in Italy). Moreover, this was not a general trend, as shown by United Kingdom experience – here the share of labour income rose through time as well as fluctuating in line with productivity. This is a further expression of the resistance of British workers to the adoption of new methods of production.

TABLE 2.5. *Ratio between real wage and productivity growth*[a]
(average annual percentage changes)

	1950–60	1960–73	1973–79
France	0.3	0.1	1.0
Germany	–	1.2	–0.5
Italy	–0.2[b]	0.5	0.4
United Kingdom	0.6	0.3	0.4

[a] For definitions, see Tables 2.1 and 2.3
[b] 1951–60
Sources: As Tables 2.1 and 2.3.

A turning-point occurred at the end of the 1960s (in Germany and Italy) or at the beginning of the 1970s (in France). The rise in the labour share at this time illustrated the growing social and technical constraints on the process of capital-intensive accumulation. The calling into question of work conditions, the development of absenteeism, the social struggles of the period, partly explain the German and Italian deceleration in productivity growth as well as the French acceleration in real wage growth. At the same time, employers found it more difficult to draw on immigrant or female labour, while surplus labour reserves in the countryside in, for instance, France or Italy were being progressively exhausted. Lastly, this was a period in which social security contributions and, more generally, indirect labour costs, rose more rapidly than the wage and salary bill. The rise in the share of labour, whose extent differed depending on country, depressed profit rates and contributed to the deceleration in growth rates which began in the mid-1960s.

The downward pressure on profitability which appeared at this time was reduced in several of the major countries by the fall in the relative price of investment goods[20] apparent from 1950 to 1970 (Fig. 2.4). This decline, however, was neither general nor lasting. It was not present in Germany, where the price of investment goods increased at roughly the same rate as the GDP deflator, while in France the decline, from 1952 onwards, partly compensated for the upward jump which had taken place during the Korean war. And throughout the 1970s the relative price of capital equipment rose in three of the four countries.

Relative price changes are no doubt an important component in the process of 'regulation' of economic systems, a component which cannot be looked at in detail within the context of this chapter. Such changes are a function of numerous factors. Thus the fall in the relative price of investment goods, as well

---

[20] This indicator is calculated relative to the GDP deflator. The use of an investment concept which includes housing no doubt introduces some bias.

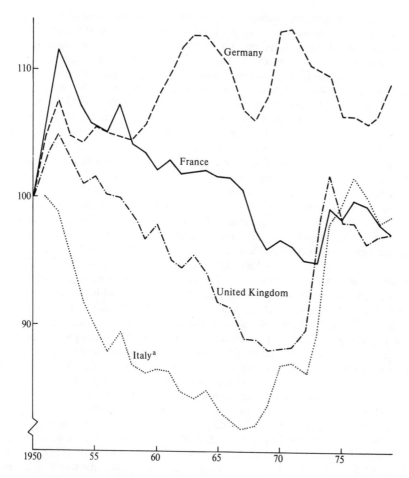

FIG. 2.4 *Relative investment prices* (ratio of gross fixed capital formation to GDP implicit national accounts deflators. Indices: 1950 = 100)
[a] 1951 = 100

Sources: OECD, *National Accounts of OECD Countries, 1950-1979*: CSO, *Economic Trends Annual Supplement, 1981*.

as of energy and transport services during the 1950s and 1960s, can be related to the productivity gains obtained in these sectors, but one must also take into account the dominant positions occupied by various industrial branches within the productive system, changes in taxation and in subsidies due to public intervention, or even the uneven pressure of national or international competition.

Turning now to the profit rate – a key concept in the analysis of accumulation – this can be expressed in various ways, e.g. gross or net, before or after tax, related to fixed or total capital, etc.[21] Detailed studies show, however, that whatever the conventions used, the results obtained are broadly similar.

[21] The profit indicator here used relates gross profits to the gross fixed capital stock at

Profit rates declined during the 1960s or at the beginning of the 1970s in most European countries[22] (Fig. 2.5). The trend was particularly pronounced in Germany, the United Kingdom, and Sweden, but can also be found in other dominant economies like the United States. This movement need not, however, have the same significance in every case. Thus, despite the difficulties of international comparisons, it would seem that profitability was, at the outset, a good deal higher in Germany than elsewhere, so that its decline may have reflected only a convergence towards the international average. France stands out as an exception in so far as it did not record a downward trend. On the contrary, the rate of profit rose until 1969 and remained stable between then and 1974.

The difficulties met in obtaining a sufficient level of profits can by and large be explained by the various factors so far examined, and in particular by the diminished efficiency of new production processes which translated itself into a rising capital–output ratio. Until the mid-1960s, a partial compensation was provided by a fall in the wage share of labour income linked to the intensification of work methods in France and Germany, but not in the United Kingdom where, because of workers' resistance, the labour share continued to grow.

From the end of the 1960s, the rate of exploitation declined, reflecting technical and social constraints on any new attempt at intensifying work pressures, and the labour share rose. A further factor which added to the erosion of profitability in the early 1970s was an increase in the relative price of investment goods. Only France remained relatively immune from these trends in so far as the labour share only increased after 1973. Moreover, taxes and subsidies were used actively in France (but also in the United Kingdom) to reduce pressures on the distribution of national income. Most of the elements for an overaccumulation crisis were thus in place in Europe at the beginning of the 1970s.

The text so far has stressed the constraints which the process of capital-intensive accumulation was bound to encounter because these appear to have been one of the major reasons for the crisis. However, a variety of methods were used to counteract the decline in profitability, and these will now be examined. A first factor was an increasing recourse to credit throughout the 1960s by firms faced with profit difficulties. Borrowing took place so that investment rates and profitability would be maintained. Secondly, the attempt to reconstitute profit margins and the pressures on income distribution largely contributed to the acceleration in inflation from the end of the 1960s. Thirdly, profound changes took place in the international economy, some of which originated in the immediate post-war period. Three, in particular, deserve consideration:

(i) The need for a large market, created by the new methods of production, led to a rapid development of international trade and to the lowering of

---

the beginning of the year measured at replacement cost (i.e. reflated with the help of the implicit national accounts deflator for gross fixed capital formation). Gross profits correspond to the operating surplus of the corporate sector as defined in the national accounts; in the case of France, an adjustment has been made which takes into account the incomes of the self-employed.

[22] This result is confirmed by other studies; see in particular A. Glyn and B. Sutcliffe, *British Capitalism. Workers and the Profits Squeeze*, London 1972, for the United Kingdom, and T.P. Hill, *Profits and Rates of Return*, OECD, Paris 1979, for international comparisons.

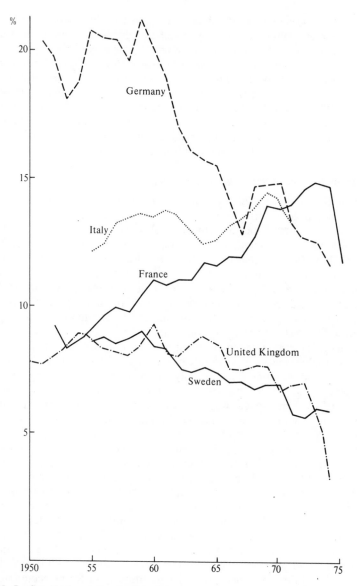

FIG. 2.5. *Profit rates* (operating surplus of corporate sector in per cent of gross fixed capital stock at beginning of year at current prices)
Note: figures are not strictly comparable between countries.
Sources: OECD, *National Accounts of OECD Countries* (various issues), and, for capital stock data, the sources listed under Table 2.2.

customs barriers, both of which acted as stimulants, especially in Europe. But the problems of competitiveness and external constraints gradually became major preoccupations for numerous European economies;

(ii) The decline in profitability and increased international competition brought about a growing internationalization of production and the emergence of multinational monopoly capitalism;

(iii) At the same time, the period of rapid growth of the 1950s and 1960s was helped by the exploitation of the resources of the Third World and especially by cheap energy supplies. The commodity price boom of 1972–3 was the first indication that this state of affairs might be in jeopardy. The sharp increase in the price of oil at the end of 1973 acted as the catalyst which unleashed the crisis of the later 1970s, the seeds of which, however, had been sown in the mid-1960s.

Falling profits, debt accumulation, and inflation

The virtually uninterrupted and generalized deterioration in the financial structure of corporations during the 1960s is striking. Thus, the (current price) ratio between debt outstanding and the capital stock increased regularly between 1955 and 1974 in France and in Germany, from 13 to approximately 30 per cent.[23] Similarly, the capacity of firms to meet debt payments declined markedly, the ratio between outstanding debts and gross profits rising from 1 to 2.9 in Germany, and from 2.3 to 3.5 in France during the same period. Even in the United Kingdom, where recourse to borrowing was traditionally limited, the fall in self-financing ratios forced corporations to accumulate debt despite the reduction of investment plans from the early 1970s.

Resort to external finance appeared to firms a means to compensate for the fall in profitability as long as the rate of return on new investment was above the cost of borrowing. More fundamentally, given limited self-financing possibilities, loans played a major role in sustaining accumulation. The preservation of a sufficiently high investment rate was in effect necessary to ensure new productivity gains, intensify work rhythms, and re-establish the rate of exploitation.

To a large extent these efforts were unsuccessful and the obstacles encountered by the process of capital-intensive accumulation were not overcome by increasing indebtedness. In some respects, the difficulties were even exacerbated. Thus, increased financial costs, linked to the rapid rise in outstanding debt and in interest rates, reduced corporate cash-flows and further depressed profitability.

According to some Marxist authors this rapid growth in indebtedness was one of the causes of the late-1960s acceleration in inflation[24] (Table 3.1). This is, however, debatable, and the acceleration in inflation would seem better explained by the growing pressures and claims on income distribution and by the progressive establishment of a new monopolistic type of 'regulation'. Thus, a number of authors have shown that the attempts by different economic agents (e.g. corporations, banks, workers, the government, the self-employed) to increase their share in national income resulted in an acceleration in inflation.[25]

[23] J. Mazier, B. Loiseau, and M.B. Winter, 'Rentabilité du capital dans les économies dominantes, *Economie et statistique*, February 1977.

[24] Aglietta, *Theory of Capitalist Regulation*; Mandel, *Second Slump*.

[25] For this purpose it is necessary to take into account all incomes (wages, profits, interest, self-employed income, taxes, and transfers); see R. Boyer and J. Mistral, *Accumulation, inflation, crises*, Paris 1978; Mazier, *Macroéconomie*.

The 1960s seem to have been characterized by such increasing conflicts over income distribution. As examples one can cite the increase in the labour share resulting from union resistance, and the limits encountered by the process of capital-intensive accumulation; the defensive behaviour of the self-employed who strived to maintain their level of income; the rises in European agricultural prices due to institutional changes; increases in financial costs resulting from growing indebtedness; or the attempts by firms to maintain profits at a level sufficient to repay the large investments made previously. This search for a minimum profit rate was made all the more difficult since productivity growth decelerated from the mid-1960s. It was only the government which was able, by means of tax concessions and subsidies, to ease some of these clashes on income distribution and thereby contribute to the reduction of inflationary pressures.

The analysis so far has not provided an explanation of why this permanent contradiction of capitalism (i.e. the conflict over income distribution) only manifested itself in the form of an acceleration in inflation at the end of the 1960s. The answer lies in the establishment, at the beginning of the 1960s, of a new form of 'monopolistic regulation', which marked a break with the methods of 'regulation' which predominated in the earlier stages of capitalism. Several original features characterized this new 'monopolistic regulation'.[26] In particular, prices were no longer very responsive to the existence of excess capacity and depended much more on firms' profit considerations. Wages were increasingly indexed to prices and real wage increases were partially generated by productivity gains in certain leading sectors. Moreover, the increasing share of 'social' wages in total wage income diminished the dependence of employees' incomes on labour market conditions. In addition, a number of structural changes took place – the strengthening of a monetary system in which the central bank was no longer constrained by the requirement of domestic gold convertibility, the consolidation of collective bargaining procedures, the extension of social policies, the movement towards a greater concentration of capital, etc.

This new form of 'monopolistic regulation' was clearly different from the older 'regulation' which had predominated until World War II and which can be described as 'competitive regulation'. Within the latter's framework, market forces played a large role. Thus, prices were sensitive to changes in demand and supply, while wages, which were the price for a particular commodity, namely labour, were largely determined by business-cycle fluctuations. Also, the workings of the gold standard imposed strict limits on the expansion of the money supply. Until the end of the nineteenth century, all the major macro-economic variables had fluctuated in the same direction, and the alternation of periods of expansion and of crisis had represented the normal functioning of an economy submitted to such a form of 'regulation'. The acceleration in inflation from the end of the 1960s would thus seem to result from growing pressure on income distribution and the take-off of a monopolistic type of 'regulation'. ·

Accelerating internationalization

International factors have always played a fundamental role in the process of

---

[26] Boyer, 'Wage Formation'.

capital accumulation, but they assumed a new dimension in the wake of World War II. Initially, there was a search for wider markets which led to the acceptance of free trade and to a rapid rise in the volume of international exchanges. This was followed by a world-wide organization of capitalist production based on the domination of developing countries and on an increasing internationalization of investment.

The movement in favour of free trade, which began in the early 1960s, was largely stimulated by the limited size of the domestic market relative to the mass-production potential of new techniques on the one hand, and by the pressures exerted by the most powerful and competitive world firms on the other. The movement was particularly strong in Europe as witnessed by the setting up of EFTA and, above all, of the EEC. Trade grew rapidly, but the world market quickly imposed certain uniform standards and divergences in competitiveness began to appear.

Thus the United Kingdom, very open to foreign trade since the early 1950s, recorded a deterioration in competitiveness and a sharp fall in the share of exports in GDP. Balance of payments constraints imposed restrictive measures at frequent intervals, and the country was trapped in a vicious circle in which the slow growth of the domestic market and the inadequacy of investment (particularly in industry) restricted productivity growth and prevented any improvement in competitiveness. In France, exports played a less important role until the mid-1960s, but a structural transformation progressively took place in the country's external trade. Thanks to a rapid expansion of the domestic market and government encouragement via, *inter alia*, large public purchases, the competitiveness of the investment goods sector improved while at the same time French exporters were able to move away from the slow-growing traditional colonial markets. The trade position remained none the less somewhat fragile in view of an above-average domestic growth rate and insufficient specialization in skill-intensive commodities.

Germany's international strategy was different. The country benefited at the outset from a dominant position in investment goods. Hence German exports were one of the more dynamic elements of demand already in the 1950s, whereas domestic growth was more subdued, in particular from the early 1960s. In Italy, too, exports played a leading role in growth from the very beginning of the period, but excessive reliance was probably put on the substantial growth of the European consumer goods market.

Several conclusions can be drawn from this sketch.[27] External constraints in a number of countries during the 1960s led to the periodic adoption of policies of austerity geared to restraining domestic growth and stimulating exports. But the competitiveness of an economy is not solely a function of the dynamism of its exports. Control of the domestic market is also crucial and is often a stepping-stone to gains in market shares abroad. Governments often followed export-promoting policies, but these were frequently insufficient since they neglected the important aspect of regaining control of the home market.

Since the 1950s, the movement towards free trade and the revival of accumulation in the major economies were also accompanied by the setting up of new

---

[27] J. Mistral, 'Competitivité et formation du capital en longue periode', *Economie et statistique*, February 1978; Barou *et al.*, 'Performances comparées'.

forms of domination on the world market. Foreign investment was concentrated in raw materials and energy extraction and the terms of trade of primary producers deteriorated steadily (Table 2.6).[28] A large inflow of immigrants into North-Western Europe provided a workforce which was poorly paid and ready to accept new methods of production. Both improving terms of trade and the use of immigrant labour substantially contributed to profits in the dominant economies, while neo-colonialism accentuated the underdevelopment of the peripheral countries.

TABLE 2.6. *Developing countries' terms of trade*[a]
(indices: 1975 = 100)

	1954–55	1960–61	1966–67	1972–73	1978–79
Non-oil developing countries	123	111	110	113	106
Oil-exporting countries	..	36	33	43	113

[a] Export unit values divided by import unit values
Source: IMF, *International Financial Statistics* (1980 Yearbook).

At a later stage, foreign investments took place in manufacturing as well, and a capitalist division of labour began to operate in the world market as a whole. At the outset, the movement was largely a prerogative of American firms which invested both in developing and developed countries – particularly in Europe. This new international economic order, which predominated during the 1950s and 1960s, was a reflection of American hegemony throughout the entire capitalist world. The latter was also symbolized by the Bretton Woods system which consecrated the position of the dollar as the international currency.

But this system generated new contradictions. From the end of the 1960s, and in response to declining profits, the internationalization of production increased and this was no longer the prerogative of American firms alone. At the cost of large structural changes at home, European and Japanese firms increasingly developed their activities abroad. This trend called into question America's hegemony, which was also undermined by the country's growing balance of payments disequilibrium, the crisis of the dollar, and the break-up of the Bretton Woods international monetary system. One of the essential factors preserving the cohesion of the system thus disappeared. It can also be argued that a contradiction arose between the international requirements of the reproduction of capital and the purely national procedures of 'regulation'.[29] This contradiction between methods of 'regulation' and basic economic conditions exacerbated the instability of the system.

The early 1970s also witnessed increasing raw-material prices (Table 2.7)

[28] The terms of trade of the developing countries are expressed as the ratio of the unit value of their exports to the unit value of their imports. Such a global indicator provides only a rough idea of the decline in the terms of trade that actually took place. Data for individual countries, particularly for countries producing only one commodity, are much more indicative.

[29] G. de Bernis, *Les firmes transnationales et la crise dans l'Occident en désarroi*, Paris 1978.

TABLE 2.7. *Raw material and oil prices*

	Raw material prices		Oil prices[a]	
	Indices: 1970 = 100	Percentage changes	$ per barrel	Percentage changes
1973	166	54.2	2.7	42.1
1974	211	27.6	9.8	261.5
1975	174	−17.8	10.7	9.8
1976	195	12.2	11.5	7.4
1977	235	20.4	12.4	7.7
1978	224	−4.7	12.7	2.4
1979	260	16.0	17.0	33.6

[a] Saudi Arabia

Source: IMF, *International Financial Statistics* (1980 Yearbook).

which compensated for the long-term deterioration in the terms of trade observed in earlier years. This trend reflected the political emergence of the countries of the Third World rather than any underlying scarcity of primary commodities, with the possible exception of oil. The problems encountered in obtaining a sufficient rate of return were accentuated by the turn-around in raw material prices. The oil shock clearly had similar effects, and finally provided the catalyst which triggered off a crisis already germinating at the end of the 1960s.

III. The European Economies in Crisis

The crisis which began in 1974 had its origin in the conjunction of two phenomena:

(i) A domestic crisis of overaccumulation linked to factors such as the diminished efficiency of new production processes, resistance to the introduction of new methods of production, and growing pressures and claims on income distribution. The size of the problem differed depending on the country − in France overaccumulation was relatively limited, while it was more pronounced in Germany and particularly marked in the United Kingdom. But, overall, the continuation of capital accumulation encountered increasing difficulties in finding a sufficient level of profits;

(ii) A reproduction crisis at the international level which reflected, *inter alia*, new contradictions in the process of the internationalization of production, external constraints which gave rise to chronic balance of payments problems, the attack on American hegemony, the breakdown of the international monetary system, and the calling into question of the exploitation of Third World countries.

From 1974 to the end of the decade, the European economies experienced a generalized slowdown, but no downward spiral. If output trends were relatively similar, this was not the case for inflation and competitiveness. The wide divergences in performance in these areas reflected the varying degrees of maturity of the different European economies and their economic and social structures.

The changes which took place also tended to cast doubt on the very basic premises of the capital-intensive accumulation process underlying economic growth after World War II. The years 1974-9 in fact marked the entry of the dominant economies into a mutation crisis.

The experience of stagflation

The oil crisis, by increasing the difficulties for the corporate sector in obtaining a sufficient rate of return, played a major role in launching the mid-1970s recession. The reduction in domestic purchasing power which followed the increase in oil prices, combined with the restrictive economic policies of the time, led to a contraction in demand and thus in output further aggravated by a pronounced stock cycle.

The two driving forces behind the capital-intensive accumulation process of the 1950s and 1960s – the growth in mass consumption and the sustained rate of investment – were both stopped in the mid-1970s. Private consumption decelerated sharply (and actually fell between 1973 and 1977 in the United Kingdom), largely because of a slowdown in the growth of real incomes rather than because of saturation (though symptoms of saturation may have appeared for a few commodities such as cars or household durables). At the same time investment fell sharply (Fig. 2.1), particularly in Italy and in the United Kingdom where this decline may have had serious consequences for future growth prospects. Faced with increasingly pessimistic projections for profits and demand, firms sharply reduced their investment plans, most notably in industrial sectors such as semi-manufactures and consumer goods. In addition, the constraint imposed by the world market and the deceleration in the growth of international trade strongly reinforced the spread of the crisis even to countries, such as France, which were originally less affected by the phenomenon of overaccumulation.

The recession that began in 1974-5 did not, however, lead to a cumulative downward spiral in activity, and the years 1976-9 saw a moderate revival (Table 2.8). Consumer demand was able to expand, if only slowly, due to continuing growth in household income made possible by employment protection and the growth of 'social' wages. Government expenditure and social policies also played a role in sustaining economic activity. And on the monetary front, central bank refinancing mechanisms as well as the development of international loans and intermediation helped to avert a financial crisis.

TABLE 2.8. *Growth of major demand components in the EEC* (average annual percentage changes)

	1970–73	1973–76	1976–79
Private consumption	4.7	2.2	3.2
Government consumption	4.3	3.5	2.4
Gross fixed capital formation	3.9	−1.6	2.7
Exports of goods and services	8.8	5.0	5.4
Imports of goods and services	8.7	3.1	6.1
GDP	4.4	1.8	3.0

Source: OECD, *National Accounts of OECD Countries, 1950–1979.*

In all the European economies, there was a certain similarity in the behaviour of real variables – growth slowed down, unemployment increased, and investment declined with no signs of an endogenous revival taking place. But major disparities appeared for nominal variables. A polarization took place between a first group of countries (among which can be found Belgium, the Netherlands, and above all Germany) which succeeded in holding down inflation, and in preserving, or even strengthening, the value of their currencies, and a second group (Italy, the United Kingdom) where inflation remained high and exchange rates depreciated sharply. France occupied an intermediate position (Tables 3.1. and 2.9). These differences were paralleled by similar differences in the way in which countries succeeded in re-establishing current balance equilibrium.

TABLE 2.9. *Changes in effective exchange rates*
(indices: beginning of each period = 100)

	1970–79	1970–73	1973–76	1976–79
French franc	100.1	106.1	97.4	96.8
DM	162.0	119.3	110.9	122.5
Lira	54.8	90.1	71.2	85.4
Pound	69.0	88.0	75.7	103.7
Dollar	77.6	83.0	106.5	87.8

Source: IMF, *International Financial Statistics* (1980 Yearbook).

Such differences in performance were not only due, as is often argued,[30] to different policy choices in favour of greater or lesser restraint in the struggle against inflation or in the defence of exchange rates. They in fact reflected underlying economic and social relationships in each country. One indicator of this was the changes which took place in employment policy and in labour productivity, changes which marked an important turning-point in the process of capital-intensive accumulation characteristic of the earlier years.

Labour market reactions and the productivity slowdown

Faced with a dramatic fall in activity, firms were forced to scale down the size of their workforce to the new growth rate. The speed with which this was possible differed across Europe depending on the nature of each country's labour market, on workers' resistance, and on the extent of government aid.

The speed of adjustment was particularly high in Germany, where no reduction was apparent in the elasticity of employment with respect to output.[31] This reflected the great flexibility of the German labour market, flexibility which was at least partly due to the large number of immigrant workers, many

---

[30] EEC, 'Changes in Industrial Structure in the European Economies since the Oil Crisis', *European Economy*, Special issue, 1979.

[31] The speed of employment adjustment a (which appears on the horizontal axis of Fig. 2.6) is determined by the rate at which actual employment (N_t) approximates desired or technically necessary employment (N_t^*), the latter being determined by output (Y), and labour productivity trends (Q*):

of whom were laid off. In France, the United Kingdom, and the Netherlands, the reductions in employment were much more limited at the beginning of the recession, reflecting the intensity of the struggles waged to protect jobs. Italy stood out as an extreme case, since employment increased more rapidly during the crisis than before. This seemingly paradoxical development reflected both a marked hardening in social attitudes in the early 1970s and a conscious choice in favour of shorter working hours combined with job preservation.

These differences in labour market flexibility led in the short run to a more or less marked slowdown of productivity growth, with inevitable consequences for inflation rates. The slowdown persisted in the medium term (Table 2.3), but varied in extent across countries and sectors. It was pronounced in Italy and in the United Kingdom, but less marked in France, in Belgium, and in the Netherlands. It was least apparent in Germany; indeed, it could even be argued that there was some acceleration in the growth of productivity in German industry after 1973. This break in the productivity trend involved a fundamental change in the process of capital-intensive accumulation, one of whose major earlier characteristics had, of course, been a medium-term acceleration in the growth rate of output per man.

How should this slowdown be interpreted? Opinions differ on this very controversial issue and only a few remarks will be ventured.[32] A decline in the 'autonomous trend' of technical progress due to a progressive exhaustion of the major innovations which marked the 1950s and 1960s seems unlikely. If there was a decline it simply reflected the impact of lower growth and investment. In any case, rationalization effects could have significant effects on productivity (Table 2.10). In Germany, for instance, 1¼ million jobs were abolished between 1973 and 1977, of which over 1 million were in industry alone (the corresponding figures in France were of 200,000 jobs created in total and 350,000 lost in industry). If the unemployment rate remained relatively low in Germany (3.4 per cent in 1978-9 as against 5.5 per cent in France, 7.3 per cent in Italy, 6.0 per cent in the United Kingdom), this was not only due to the repatriation of immigrants, but also to a relatively low rate of growth of the population of working age. A further response to the crisis came in the form of new types of employment, e.g. the resort to temporary labour, to part-time work, or to subcontracting. More generally, attempts were made to create less permanent work contracts in order to ensure a greater flexibility in the management of labour.

Employment, profits, monopolistic 'regulation', and the persistence of inflation

These various arguments on labour market flexibility and productivity can also be used to analyse the reasons for the persistence of inflation. Developments in the years 1974-9 were strongly marked by the attempts made to restore profit

---

$$N_t - N_{t-1} = a\ (N_t^* - N_{t-1});$$
$$N_t^* = N_{t-1}\ (1 + n_t^*);\ \text{and}$$
$$n_t^* = \dot{Y}_t - \dot{Q}_t^*;$$

where the dots over the variables denote percentage changes.

[32] R. Boyer and P. Petit, 'Productivité et emploi: évolution récente et perspectives', *mimeo*, CEPREMAP, Paris 1979.

TABLE 2.10. *Changes in productivity[a] and employment*

	Productivity[a] (average annual percentage changes)				Employment (changes in thousands)			
	total economy		manufacturing		total economy		manufacturing	
	1970-73	1973-79	1970-73	1973-79	1970-73	1973-79	1970-73	1973-79
France	4.8	2.8	5.2	4.1	471	313	231	−377
Germany	3.9	3.2	5.5	3.2	32	−1,160	(−590)	−748
Italy	4.2	1.5	4.7[b]	1.9[b]	−161	1,230	−121[b]	176[b]
United Kingdom	3.8	1.2	5.6	0.8	236	102	−509	−677
Belgium	4.3	2.3	7.3	5.2	80	8	−9	−217
Denmark	3.3	1.3	6.2[b]	..	70	113	−70[b]	−56[b]
Netherlands	4.6	2.2	8.5[c]	4.3[c]	−13	49	−83[c]	−164[c]

[a] Output per employed
[b] Industry
[c] Including mining

Sources: OECD, *National Accounts of OECD Countries, 1950-1979*, and *1962-1979*;
OECD, *Labour Force Statistics, 1968-1979*.

rates, which had clearly fallen from 1974 to the late 1970s. Declining demand led to the appearance of substantial excess capacity which could not be fully off-set by mothballing or accelerated scrapping of capital. In consequence, the capital–output ratio rose substantially. And though firms tried to adapt their workforce to the new rate of economic activity, this adjustment, as was seen above, could only be partial. Hence, the growth of labour productivity de-celerated sharply and the share of labour income increased (Fig. 2.3). Faced by limited demand and confronted with the impossibility of restoring profitability to earlier levels, firms tended to raise their prices.

In order to understand the differences in inflation rates within Europe two variables appear to be crucial:[33]

    (i) The speed of employment adjustment which is a function of labour market flexibility and trade-union strength;

    (ii) The elasticity of the profit share to the reduction in demand,[34] which reflects the capacity of the corporate sector to defend its profits as a function of its monopoly power or even its integration in the world market.

The behaviour of these two variables in the short run (1974-5) is shown in Fig. 2.6. The slower the employment adjustment, the greater was the pressure on costs and the more rapid the increase in prices. Thus, in France, the United Kingdom, and the Netherlands lower labour market flexibility than earlier re-sulted in strong inflationary pressures. In Germany, on the other hand, where the number of jobs was significantly reduced, the rate of adjustment in employ-ment was similar to that of the 1960s and inflation could slow down from 1975

---

[33] Boyer and Mistral, *Accumulation, inflation, crises.*

[34] The elasticity is measured by the ratio between percentage changes in the profit share and percentage changes in output.

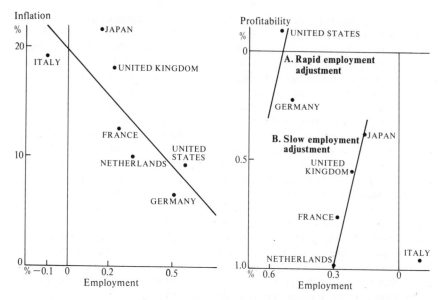

FIG. 2.6. *Short-run changes in employment,*[a] *inflation,*[b] *and profitability*[c] *in manufacturing, 1974-5.*

[a] Ratio of actual employment changes to the changes that would have resulted from an immediate adaptation of numbers employed to output changes: the higher the ratio the greater the speed of adjustment.

[b] Consumer prices excluding food products: average annual percentage changes.

[c] Elasticity of profit share with respect to changes in output: the lower the ratio, the greater the stickiness of profits.

Source: R. Boyer and J. Mistral, *Accumulation, inflation, crises*, Paris 1978.

onwards. The acceleration of Italian inflation is to be seen in the light of the very exceptional increase in employment in that country.

The second element that must be considered is the behaviour of profit shares and, in particular, of the elasticity of profit shares to changes in demand. The higher this elasticity is, the higher inflation rates are. The combination of these two parameters (speed of adjustment in employment and elasticity of the share of profits) provides a relatively satisfactory explanation for the differences in inflation rates in the major European economies.

This method of price formation – which combines labour market inflexibility with the defence of profit shares – is characteristic of the 'monopolistic regulation' which was strengthened during the 1960s and which continued during the crisis. Comparisons with the depression of the 1930s clearly show that at the time the speed and extent of the employment adjustments that were made and the elasticity of prices to the appearance of excess capacity were much greater. It is not surprising that in the circumstances prices could have fallen for several years.

The framework so far developed for 1974-5 can also be used to look at inflationary differentials for the whole 1974-9 period. Whatever its origins, the medium-term deceleration in productivity growth had clear inflationary consequences. In particular, the behaviour of both employers and workers, which had to a large extent been forged during the 1950s and 1960s, implicitly incorporated an assumption of rapid productivity growth, whether in wage negotiations, pricing behaviour, or investment planning. In these circumstances, the slowdown in productivity inevitably involved readjustments which, in part, found expression in the persistence of high inflation rates. Indeed, in the years 1974-9 it was the countries which experienced the greatest reduction in productivity growth (Italy and the United Kingdom) which also experienced the highest inflation rates; on the other hand, Germany, whose deceleration in productivity growth was modest, was able to reduce its inflation rate substantially.

The discussion so far, though it has emphasized a number of important factors, cannot, of course, exhaust the subject. The way in which each economy is slotted into the world market is also crucial. Domestic performance and international competitiveness must be examined in conjunction. At the most obvious level, it can be seen that those countries which were able to control their exchange rates (Germany and the countries belonging to the old 'snake'), benefited from a 'virtuous circle' (progressive revaluation of their currencies and limited internal inflation), while those that were not (Italy or the United Kingdom) found themselves trapped in a 'vicious circle' (depreciation leading to rising import prices and acceleration in domestic inflation).

Adaptation to external constraints and international crisis

Balance of payments constraints were an obstacle to growth in most countries, since austerity policies had to be enforced to limit imports and offset the effects of higher oil prices. The effectiveness of these policies was very variable depending on the position of the various economies within the world and on their capacity to reorganize their productive structures sufficiently rapidly. Two factors were important in this respect — the capacity to adapt to changes in world demand and the specialization of the different economies.[35]

The capacity of the European economies to adapt to the pattern of world demand constituted an important differentiating factor. Thus Germany continued to benefit from relatively favourable demand trends thanks to her specialization in investment goods which helped to compensate for a small loss in competitiveness caused by successive DM revaluations. France seems to have benefited from a favourable geographic distribution of its markets, partly linked to the growing importance of the OPEC countries, but also from currency depreciation which favourably affected its costs. At the other end of the scale Italy and the United Kingdom were no doubt handicapped by the high rate of domestic inflation, which partially offset the depreciation of their currencies, and by less favourable geographic and commodity compositions of trade.

These conclusions are strengthened by an examination of the specialization of the various European economies (Table 2.11). Germany's performance was related to its strong position in products requiring a high content of skilled labour and in 'upstream sectors', necessary for the preservation of technological independence (e.g. telecommunications, electronics, machine-tools). The fragility of Italy's export performance, on the other hand, was underlined by the country's

---

[35] EEC, 'Changes in Industrial Structure'.

specialization in products of low skilled labour and capital intensity, products which were moreover in competition with new industrializing countries. The decline in the British economy is illustrated by its growing dependence on foreign suppliers for products with a high technology and skilled labour content, and its growing specialization in areas of low capital intensity. France showed relatively favourable trends (contraction in those areas which require little skilled labour, expansion in exports of 'fundamental' products) but the results obtained appear fragile.

TABLE 2.11. *Shares in OECD exports of 'fundamental products'*[a]
(percentages)

	1963	1970	1976
France	8.0	8.2	9.2
Germany	22.0	20.6	21.3
Italy	4.7	6.0	6.8
United Kingdom	13.3	9.2	7.9
United States	22.1	18.6	15.3
Japan	7.0	12.7	15.5

[a] Defined as 'main technology-intensive products' (e.g. computers, telecommunication equipment, machine tools), 'main investment goods' (e.g. machinery, electrical equipment), and 'main intermediate goods' (those products used in all major production processes)
Source: EEC, *European Economy*, November 1979.

These disparities in the capacity of adaptation to international changes in demand underline the importance of external constraints in the development of the crisis. At the same time, ongoing trends in the internationalization of production, which strengthened after 1974, modified the forms of 'regulation' at the international level, in particular in the relations between the United States and other developed countries on the one hand and between the Third and the industrialized worlds on the other.

Though the United States remained the major world economy, it no longer occupied, in its relationship with Europe and Japan, the dominant position it had formerly held. This can be seen by looking, for instance, at trends in trade balances, at the flow of foreign investment, or even at productivity growth rates. Hence the reorganization of the international monetary system and definition of the appropriate place for the dollar within this system were made more difficult. The functioning of the floating system in this period, based on the preponderance of international financial capital, did not constitute an adequate method of 'regulation', and the capitalist world economy found itself deprived of an essential institutional structure.

A second source of disequilibrium came from the changed relationships between the countries of the Third World and the dominant economies. The competition from newly industrializing countries has often been mentioned in this context, but until the late 1970s, the size of these economies was still very small. What could happen in future, however, is an acceleration in the flow of direct investment into these countries designed to restore profitability for Western enterprises by exploiting the large differences in labour costs. Such a development, if it became generalized, could lead to an impasse, since it would imply a growth in production capacities in the dominated countries not paralleled by a similar growth in the domestic market for consumer goods, since wages would have to remain low. And in the dominant economies entire industrial sectors would be threatened; nor would the development of investment goods and new technology industries be able to provide sufficient compensation. Far from being a remedy for the crisis, such a movement would only accentuate the phenomenon of overproduction in the world at large.

Whatever the issue – be it the relations between the dominant economies or with the Third World or the conditions necessary to achieve an acceleration in productivity growth – it is clear that the very basis of the process of capital accumulation of the earlier years was called into question by the crisis.

Conclusions

The economic crisis which began in 1974 had its origins in the late 1960s, both in a domestic crisis of overaccumulation and in an international crisis of capital reproduction. This led to increasing domestic difficulties for corporations in obtaining a sufficient level of profits, and to new contradictions and clashes at the international level. The 'oil crisis' acted as the catalyst which sparked off the crisis.

Between then and the late 1970s, Europe experienced a general slowdown often accompanied by inflation. The resilience of real incomes, linked to employment protection and to the development of the 'social' wage, the support provided by government expenditure, and the role played by credit expansion, made it possible to avoid a cumulative downward trend, but no autonomous stimulating mechanism emerged. Profitability was only restored to a partial extent, and, faced with unfavourable long-term prospects, investment remained sluggish; indeed, the development of foreign investment only emphasized this phenomenon. Despite the opportunities that existed in certain areas (e.g. telecommunications, electronics, new services), no key sector grew sufficiently rapidly to offset the deceleration in the more traditional branches which had been most affected by the crisis. The slowdown in growth and the stagnation of investment led, in turn, to a sharp deceleration in productivity growth, a factor which further depressed profitability.

Economic policies appeared impotent. The acceptance of large budget deficits was clearly not a powerful enough force to stimulate growth, since these deficits were directly linked to stagnation in economic activity. External constraints and the vulnerability of the trade balance to any oil price increase prevented governments from following more stimulating policies – if anything, the opposite happened since the austerity policies designed to control wages led to an even greater contraction of the domestic market and thus to a reduction in demand.

The only countries able to follow such policies were those which could change their industrial structure sufficiently and develop their exports thanks to their dominant position in the world economy. In practice, in Europe it was only Germany that could follow such a strategy.

These various developments have led to major changes in the process of capital-intensive accumulation which had been predominant since the end of World War II – in employment relationships, in the management of the labour force, in the forms of government intervention, or in the internationalization of capital. The years 1974-9 marked the entry of the dominant economies into a period of major crisis which will eventually alter the institutional and other characteristics of the rapid growth phase of the 1950s and 1960s and which will ensure the emergence of new forms of 'regulation'. In this sense, the crisis of the late 1970s is similar to that of the 1930s even if it differs from the latter in its origins and in its development.

The attempts to transform the nature of the traditional employment relationship represented a very important change. The introduction of new forms of work intended to increase labour market uncertainty – temporary work, subcontracting, part-time work – were designed to achieve greater flexibility and mobility in the management of labour. Both governments and firms were thus trying to overcome the labour market rigidities which, in many countries, had prevented a sufficiently rapid industrial restructuring. At the same time, attempts were made, via wage policies, to impose freezes or reductions in purchasing power so as to break the earlier link between real income and productivity growth. If such wage and employment policies were to spread, they would probably have seriously unfavourable consequences on those economies which are not dominant at the world level (i.e. all the European economies except Germany), since they would contribute to a reduction in demand at home and would be unable to increase exports permanently and sufficiently.

Further changes could take place in the area of work conditions. Two avenues in particular are open, both of which are still in their infancy – increases in the skill content of individual jobs, and creation of small, independent work teams on the one hand, increasing automation in both industry and services on the other. Such changes could bring about large productivity gains and transform work conditions. But they are unlikely to be adopted on a large scale as long as a lasting revival of accumulation does not take place.

The various forms of government intervention were also subject to pressures – on the one hand the financial problems encountered by the social security systems led to demands for major reforms which could, over the medium term, call into question the size of the 'social' wage. Similarly, increasing criticism was voiced at what was considered to be too high a volume of government expenditure. These criticisms could bring about a reduction in some public services (such as health, education, or communications) and an at least partial return to the private sector. On the other hand, government intervention was increased via public investment programmes which, in several European countries, sustained demand, and via action in favour of the corporate sector, such as various encouragements to exports, public procurements, or help in industrial restructuring.

Some of the more important issues raised by the crisis were of an international nature. An increasing divergence appeared between, on the one hand, the worldwide strategy of capitalist firms, and, on the other, the purely national focus of 'regulation'. Floating exchange rates and the leading role played by international financial capital are of course methods of 'regulation', but they seem insufficient. They are very much geared to short-term problems; they can create cumulative exchange rate effects (e.g. 'virtuous' or 'vicious' circles); and they seem fairly unstable. They are in no way a substitute for an international monetary system capable of responding in the medium term to the needs of world-wide accumulation.

Turning to relations with the developing world, there is a risk that increasing direct investment in low-wage countries could aggravate the problem of over-production. Whole industrial sectors in Europe and North America could be doomed, with no assurance that the domestic markets of the dominated countries would be developed. This could only happen if there was a profound change in the latters' industrialization strategy in the form of more rapid growth in wage incomes, enabling the development of markets for consumer goods and thereby providing outlets for the new industries.

In many countries external constraints and the pressures of international competition are strengthening the position of those who favour protectionist measures, and some moves in this direction were already taken in the late.1970s, notably in the EEC. If such measures spread without agreement between trading partners, there could be serious consequences because of the high degree of interdependence achieved by the developed capitalist countries. On the other hand, the implementation of a selective and mutually agreed protectionist policy could, in the eyes of some, have beneficial effects. It would lead to a domestic-ally oriented accumulation process, and would encourage a strategy of import substitution which could progressively ease the external constraints. If this were to happen, it would modify one of the most important characteristics of the period of past growth, namely free trade.

A final issue is Europe itself. The growing disparities between the different countries of the EEC raise the possibility of a break-up of the Community. On the other hand, Europe could initiate a reorganization of the world capitalist system. It is at the European level that trade flows could most easily be regu-lated in ways that take account of the needs of the various economies and protect the interests of the Third World. Similarly, and more immediately, the installation of a real European monetary system could constitute the first step in a reorganization of the international system which would have to depend on the joint management of three currencies – the dollar, the yen, and the Euro-pean currency. For such an attempt to be successful, the exclusive role of the dollar as an international currency would have to dwindle. This would, in turn, imply a retreat of American capitalism. Such a retreat, and more generally, a redistribution of economic power in the world, will no doubt represent some of the most important issues in the period to come.

Bibliography

The major exponents of the traditional Marxist analysis of contemporary capi-talism have been P.A. Baran and P.M. Sweezy in North America and E. Mandel in Europe. The formers' major work (*Monopoly Capital*, New York 1966), attempts a reconsideration of Marxian analysis of the United States economy in the light of the shift from a competitive market structure to one dominated by monopolies. A more recent work by Sweezy on international issues is his 'The Present Stage of the Global Crisis of Capitalism', *Monthly Review*, April 1978.

Mandel has examined world and, in particular, European capitalism for a number of years. Among his more recent works are *Late Capitalism*, London 1975, *The Second Slump*, London 1978, and *Long Waves of Capitalist Development*, Cambridge 1980, which presents a Marxist reconsideration of Kondratieff cycles.

The 'new' Marxist approach which gives prominence to the concept of 'regulation' and which was developed in this chapter originates from work in France in the 1970s, of which the two most important initiators have been M. Aglietta (*A Theory of Capitalist Regulation — The US Experience*, London 1979), and R. Boyer, 'La crise actuelle', *Critiques de l'économie politique*, Nos. 7–8, 1979, and, with J. Mistral, *Accumulation, inflation, crises*, Paris 1978). Further accounts can be found in Y. Barou, B. Billaudot, and A. Granou, *Croissance et crise*, Paris 1979, and A. Lipietz, *Crise et inflation: pourquoi?*, Paris 1978.

A recent Marxist interpretation of German economic developments can be found in E. Altvater, J. Hoffmann, and W. Semmler, *Vom Wirtschaftswunder zur Wirtschaftskrise*, Berlin 1979. Italian authors not unsympathetic to Marxist themes are M. Salvati ('L'origine della crisi', *Quaderni piacentini*, March 1972, or *Il sistema economico italiano*, Bologna 1975) and A. Graziani (*L'economia italiana dal 1945 ad oggi*, Bologna 1979, 2nd edn.). A more orthodox interpretation, close to the line of the Communist Party, is provided by M. D'Antonio (*Sviluppo e crisi del capitalismo italiano, 1951–1972*, Bari 1973). For the United Kingdom, the best Marxist account of the economy's longer-run problems is A. Glyn and B. Sutcliffe, *British Capitalism, Workers and the Profits Squeeze*, London 1972.

3

Inflation

CHRISTOPHER ALLSOPP*

Introduction

In the quarter-century following World War II Europe enjoyed unprecedented economic growth. For much of this time this was achieved at rates of inflation which, though much higher than the virtual (peacetime) price stability recorded in the previous century, were commonly regarded as acceptable (Table 3.1). The situation deteriorated, however, during the 1960s, until, by the 1970s, the problem of inflation had come to dominate all others. Indeed, by the end of the period, inflation had become so intractable that growth and high employment – the foundations of the post-war consensus – themselves began to look increasingly unattainable. In the light of this experience, two major questions arise – what accounted for the relative price stability of the 1950s and 1960s (a period of very rapid growth), and what factors were responsible for the more recent deterioration?

These are wide questions and the present chapter can only attempt a sketch of some of the considerations that are relevant. Inflation remains one of the least well understood of economic phenomena. Existing models, whilst useful and suggestive, can hardly be regarded as equal to the task of explaining European inflation in all its complexity. And it goes without saying that if there is a simple, and costless, cure for inflation, then it has not yet been discovered. Thus any account of European inflation must start from a position of some modesty. By the same token, however, an account of the similarities and differences between countries may be useful if it serves to redress the balance against those who present over-simplistic accounts of the origins of inflation – and its cure.

Tempting as it is to explain the rise in European inflation as due to some single underlying cause, a study of the period suggests that such an approach would be dangerously inadequate. There are important differences between countries and between episodes within countries. A first distinction that needs to be made is between the period of approximately fixed exchange rates and the subsequent period of floating. That would be necessary for analytical purposes even if inflation were ascribed to a single cause – such as the money supply. In the more eclectic treatment attempted here, which emphasizes both institutional aspects and the diversity of experience, it is necessary in addition to recognize that there may be different types of inflation as between countries and periods.

The diversity of experience is perhaps most apparent in the policy responses of different European governments to inflation. Not only did the priority given to price stability vary, but also the preferred instruments of control differed, with various forms of incomes policies to the fore in Scandinavia, in Austria,

* New College, University of Oxford.

TABLE 3.1. *Longer-run inflation[a] trends in Europe*
(average annual percentage changes)

	1870–1913	1920–38	1948–69	1969–79
France	0.1	3.6	5.6	8.9
Germany	0.6	−0.1[b]	1.6	4.9
Italy	0.6	0.3	3.1	12.2
United Kingdom	−0.2	−2.6	3.5	12.5
Spain	..	−0.4[c]	5.9	14.0
Austria	0.1[d]	2.1[e]	5.6	6.1
Belgium	−	4.4[f]	2.0	7.1
Denmark	−0.2	−2.0	4.3	9.3
Finland	0.6	0.5	4.2	10.3
Ireland	..	−0.5[g]	3.7	12.7
Netherlands	..	−2.9	4.0	7.0
Norway	0.6	−3.1	4.0	8.4
Sweden	0.5	−2.7	3.9	8.6
Switzerland	..	−2.8	1.9	4.9
Total	0.2[h]	0.1[h]	3.4[j]	9.1[j]

[a] Consumer prices
[b] 1924–38
[c] 1920–35; Madrid only
[d] 1879–1913
[e] 1923–38
[f] 1921–38
[g] 1922–38
[h] Using 1929 GDP weights at 1970 United States prices
[j] OECD Europe

Sources: A. Maddison, 'Western Economic Performance in the 1970s: A Perspective and Assessment', and 'Phases of Capitalist Development', *Banca Nazionale del Lavoro Quarterly Review*, September 1980 and June 1977; B. R. Mitchell, *European Historical Statistics, 1750–1970,* London 1975; IMF, *International Financial Statistics* (1980 Yearbook).

and, from time to time, in the United Kingdom, while other countries relied more heavily on monetary control or more generally on the use of the demand management instruments. Much of this diversity of response seems, in broad terms, to be justified in that the causes of inflationary episodes and the effectiveness of the various policy instruments do appear to have differed between European countries.

But whilst the diversity of experience is one of the themes of this chapter, it is also necessary to bring out the common threads. In the 1950s and 1960s the relative fixity of exchange rates was a powerful unifying factor which meant that there were limits to the extent to which inflation rates in Europe could diverge. But to say that inflation rates under fixed exchange rates would have to be subject to some sort of convergence is not to say anything very interesting. Rather, the problems which 'might' have appeared as inflation appeared elsewhere — as low profitability and growth, or as unemployment, or perhaps even as pressure towards devaluation. The early 1970s move to floating made greater divergence possible. Nevertheless, in the 1970s there were also powerful forces making for a similarity of experience and response — e.g. international commodity price rises, two oil crises, and the general deterioration of expectations. There were similarities too in the underlying problems faced, of which the most important (and least quantifiable) was probably an increasing structural rigidity, especially in the labour market.

The chapter's first section briefly looks at some theoretical difficulties in accounting for inflation in Europe. It reiterates some well-known points about what is meant by 'inflationary pressure' and the circumstances in which such pressure would manifest itself as rising prices — rather than something else, such as balance of payments difficulties. Sections II and III analyse general trends in inflation over the post-war period by looking, first, at the years of relative stability bounded by the early 1950s Korean War boom and the late 1960s wage explosions, and moving then to the 'great inflation' years of the 1970s. The fourth section focuses on the major differences that appeared between countries. The contrasts — for example between Germany on the one hand, and Italy or the United Kingdom on the other — are illuminating and suggest that differences in price performance arise from deep-seated differences in attitudes and institutional structures. Policy prescriptions derived in one context are not necessarily transplantable to another. The concluding section returns to this policy issue as well as drawing together the major threads.

I. Some Theoretical Considerations

It is not the aim of this chapter to provide a theoretical explanation of the inflationary process, or even to survey the various approaches to inflation in the economic literature. It would seem useful, however, to begin with a few methodological considerations on whether a single 'cause' of inflation may exist, on the nature of the inflationary process, and on the possible policy responses to it, in the light of which Europe's actual experience can then be reviewed.

The 'explanation' of inflation

The explanation of the overall price *level* has always presented a problem for economists — even when they are concerned with the hypothetical case of a perfectly functioning economic system. One of the difficulties arises from the fundamental proposition that, in equilibrium, nothing much depends on the absolute level of prices — which means in turn that inflation, if an economy is fully adapted to it, need have few real effects. By the same token it may be hard to explain what determines the *rate* of inflation. Often it may appear that inflation feeds on itself, and that expectations of inflation are the main explanation of it.

A common way out for the theorist is to invoke the 'Quantity Theory of Money'[1] according to which the price level is 'determined' by an exogenously given stock of money and the rate of inflation by changes in it. To many it then seems a small step to argue that controlling inflation is a simple process of controlling the supply of money. Such a view is blatantly oversimplified (though perhaps because of that it has a remarkable grip over people's minds). It illustrates, however, how convenient it would be if the price level, in Europe, or in individual countries, could be explained in terms of some simple exogenous

[1] More fully discussed in Ch. 4 below.

variable, which could be taken as determined outside the economy or economies concerned. Another extremely important example of appeal being made to an 'exogenous' variable comes from those theories which 'explain' the domestic price level for an individual country under fixed exchange rates by the (exogenous) price of internationally traded goods.[2]

The problem with these approaches (or more sophisticated expectational versions of them), which, in the guise of monetarist or 'international monetarist' theories, are highly influential, is that they appear far too simplified and restricted to be useful in analysing European inflation. In practice, neither the money supply nor the exchange rate can be taken as 'exogenous' in the relevant sense (in both cases they are better seen as intermediate targets).

It is, of course, necessary to concede that if important variables such as the exchange rate or the money supply *were* fixed exogenously, there would be limitations on the scope for variation in the price level. But the interesting questions then lie further back — in the economic institutions and policies that allowed the maintenance of the exchange rate and possibly in the costs (e.g. in terms of growth forgone) in maintaining fixity of the rate. In the case of theories couched in terms of the money supply, the difficulties are, if anything, even greater. In no European economy does the money creation process even approximate the paradigm of the 'fixed quantity of outside money'of the textbooks.[3] In institutional practice, with the move towards 'monetarist' ideas in the 1970s, monetary policy has been formulated in terms of targets, implying, by the terminology itself, that it is not the money supply that is exogenous but something else. And even if the causality of the monetarist story were accepted, the important question is often what it was that led the authorities — perhaps forced them — into accommodating inflationary pressure rather than resisting it. Economic policy is not 'exogenous' either.

In fact, the search for an exogenous variable to explain the price level — and thereby inflation — may be chimerical. It may be more fruitful to try and identify the forces that lead to inflationary pressure, and to see these against the constraints imposed by policy and (for the individual economy) by the exchange rate regime and price developments in trading partners and the world economy.

The nature of inflationary pressure

The term 'inflationary pressure' has a moderately well-understood everyday meaning. It is, nevertheless, hard to define at all precisely. Broadly, what is needed is a diagnosis of the underlying cause or causes of inflation together with, for each cause, a measure of extent. In keeping with the traditional approach, the text looks first at demand-pull and then at cost-push forces.

---

[2] Such an approach achieved prominence originally for small economies in the guise of the 'Scandinavian' model of inflation (see, for instance, O. Aukrust, 'Inflation in the Open Economy: A Norwegian Model', in L.B. Krause and W.S. Salant (eds.), *Worldwide Inflation*, Brookings Institution, Washington 1977. Nowadays this set of ideas is usually described as 'international monetarist'; see Ch. 4 below.

[3] Cf. N. Kaldor, 'Memorandum', House of Commons, Treasury and Civil Service Committee, *Memoranda on Monetary Policy*, HMSO, London 1980.

The most commonly cited cause of inflationary pressure is an excess of monetary aggregate *demand* as compared with the supply potential of the economy. In certain special cases not necessarily associated with rising prices the consequences are directly observable. Generalized shortages expressed as queues or rationing (sometimes called suppressed inflation) would be one such case. Another would be an excess of imports over exports appearing as an (unsustainable) balance of payments deficit. More normally, if the generalized excess demand is not suppressed in rationed markets, nor satisfied from abroad, it is widely agreed that such a disequilibrium may be associated with rising, or even accelerating, prices. Though very little follows from the diagnosis in the way of predictions for the future rate of inflation (or for any new equilibrium) the diagnosis itself (which is well short of a model of the process of inflation) carries clear implications for policy action.

Though the concept of excess demand – and demand–pull inflation – is reasonably clear, there are severe practical difficulties in determining when excess demand exists and in measuring its extent. The normal proxies for the pressure of demand – the extent of unemployment, or the degree of capacity utilization – may, as is well known, be dangerously misleading in a European context. The degree of under-utilization of resources (especially of labour) was very large in the immediate post-war period in some countries. In such circumstances, the unemployment percentage may be no more than an approximate indicator of short-term variations in demand pressures; and apparently unchanging unemployment could conceal major secular changes in the longer-term balance between supply and demand in labour markets. Capacity utilization indices suffer from analagous difficulties of interpretation.

There are two further difficulties in identifying pressure of excess demand for European countries. The first is simply that, for most of the period, in most countries, policy actions were being taken to avoid situations of excess demand (or of balance of payments difficulty). Thus in looking at the period with hindsight one is looking, to a large extent, for mistakes and for failures of policy. The second is that it is quite possible for an individual country to be underemployed with spare capacity but for excessive demand to be a factor explaining inflation in a larger grouping, such as Europe as a whole, or the world economy.

Turning to *cost* inflationary pressures, these are even harder to pin down than demand pressures. Early attempts to define cost–push inflation tended to stress the initiating impulse – from wages, or from import prices – as its defining characteristic. Though it is often useful to discuss the initial impacts, this is not a good way of characterizing a situation that leads to a *process* of rising prices and wages. *Per se*, a rise in wages or commodity prices would lead, not to inflation, but to changes in relative prices and in income distribution, nationally or internationally. The inflationary pressure lies not so much in the initiating act but in the resistance of the economic system which turns the impulse into a spiral of rising prices and wages.

In diagnosing a cause for inflation which does not stem from excessive monetary demand, the natural candidate is, in broad terms, the struggle over income shares (as exemplified by conflicts over distribution between, for instance, capital and labour, the private and the public sector, or various organized groups in society). Such views of the inflationary process have been described as 'competing claims' theories: 'a catch-word that covers a large variety of distributional conflicts at all levels of the economy'.[4] It is important to note that such a diagnosis of an inflationary problem has two distinct elements:

(i) The conflicting interests and aspirations that are always present in any economic system;
(ii) The mechanisms (e.g. of wage bargaining) by which these lead, in a dynamic setting, to price and wage increases.

In view of this, it makes sense to ask, in looking at European inflation, whether the underlying conflicts in society intensified over the period, or whether changes in the institutional structure increased the inflationary potential. And it also makes sense — hard though it may be to give an answer — to ask the question as to whether there were or are significant differences between European countries either in the degree of conflict, or in the inflationary potential of their institutional structures. It is possible to go further and note that, in the context of counter-inflation policy, there is an important distinction to be made between those elements of policy which seek to reduce strife and promote consensus and those elements which try to improve the institutional structure, or, more directly, to limit the extent to which distributional conflicts can lead to inflation.

So far the discussion has concentrated on 'inflationary pressure' which can be taken as indicating a certain type of disequilibrium, often associated with rising prices. One of the problems is that inflation itself may do little to eliminate the source of disequilibrium — whether the origin lies in excessive demand, or in 'competing claims'. One possibility is that inflation simply continues whilst the disequilibrium persists. The difficulty then is to explain why inflation does not *accelerate* as the expectation of rising prices gets built in to the starting-point. Indeed, the recognition that there were explosive possibilities inherent in allowing inflationary disequilibria to persist (as opposed to the earlier trade-off ideas) was *the* most important change that occurred in the field of economic policy formation in post-war Europe, a change that can be dated approximately as taking place between the late 1960s and 1970s.

Implications for policy

Academic controversy over the causes of inflation and its cure tend to emphasize the differences between the various schools of thought — e.g. monetarist, demand–pull, cost–push. When it comes to policy there appears to be a similarly wide split, with those who emphasize demand (and money) propounding the view that the demand management instruments must be used to control inflation, and the cost–push school tending to put weight on 'non-conventional' policies of various kinds — such as incomes policies. In practice the dispute is less divisive than sometimes appears:

(i) There is no disagreement that excess demand and/or excessive monetary expansion is a possible cause of inflation, and that control of demand is a necessary element in any anti-inflation strategy;

[4] P. McCracken *et al.*, *Towards Full Employment and Price Stability*, OECD, Paris 1977, p. 155.

(ii) If inflation is controlled by demand policies, then monetarists and others would see the 'natural' rate of unemployment as dependent on institutional structures, i.e. on the forces that others would see as lying behind cost–push inflation. This means that in principle, there could be a role for 'non-conventional' policies in lowering *unemployment*;

(iii) The cost-push school would see the use of incomes policies and the like as necessary for the control of inflation. Only if inflation were under control could the demand management instruments be used for their traditional purposes – growth and full employment. In the absence of successful incomes policies, it would be widely agreed that the demand management instruments would, in practice, have to be used against inflation – perhaps at heavy cost in terms of unemployment.

It is apparent that in pragmatic terms, both schools end up by stressing monetary and fiscal control on the one hand, as well as the use of other 'non-conventional' policies. For 'practical' monetarists, the function of these policies is to allow a lower level of unemployment: for others the function is, in fact, the same, since they take the view that without incomes policies, very high levels of unemployment would be necessary to control inflation. The cost–push school is principally differentiated by its greater scepticism about the efficiency of demand management policy in controlling inflation at acceptable cost – hence their belief in the need for incomes policies.[5]

This broad area of consensus may even have been reinforced in the 1970s by the already mentioned perception that inflation was accelerating. Though the evidence on the 'accelerationist thesis' for European economies may not be particularly strong, the widespread acceptance of the thesis has two profound implications. Control of inflationary pressure becomes a *necessary* condition for other economic objectives, rather than one amongst several objectives. And, since at some point such control will have to be exercised – by non-accommodating policies – there is no escape from it. Indeed, it can further be argued that the quicker and more firmly the nettle is grasped, the better, in that the rate of inflation at which control is exercised will be the higher the longer it is postponed, and the greater will be the costs of subsequently reducing it. More and more reliance was thus placed towards the end of the 1970s on demand management, with the consequence that unemployment has risen. One of the great questions for the future is the extent to which this policy will succeed. If it does not, then further changes, going perhaps beyond the conventional scope of incomes policies, appear almost inevitable.

II. The General Trend of European Inflation – From the Korean War to the Wage Explosions

Post-war European inflation was high in the early years of the reconstruction period and remained high until 1951. It then decelerated through the 1950s to a

---

[5] It should be clear that the success of an incomes policy need not be in reducing measured inflation; it could lie elsewhere, e.g. in a lower level of unemployment or in greater consensus.

TABLE 3.2. *Inflation*[a] *trends, 1948-1979*
(average annual percentage changes)

	1948–52	1952–61	1961–69	1969–73	1973–79
France	14.1	3.3	4.0	6.2	10.7
Germany	0.4	1.3	2.5	5.3	4.6
Italy	3.4	2.0	4.1	6.5	16.1
United Kingdom	5.2	2.4	3.8	8.0	15.6
Spain	6.0	5.2	6.7	8.4	17.9
Austria	19.3	1.9	3.5	5.7	6.3
Belgium	1.6	1.2	3.2	5.1	8.4
Denmark	4.8	2.5	6.1	7.0	10.7
Finland	2.3	3.7	5.7	6.8	12.7
Ireland	4.6	2.6	4.6	9.3	15.0
Netherlands	7.0	2.1	4.7	6.8	7.2
Norway	7.3	2.6	4.0	7.9	8.7
Sweden	6.1	2.9	3.9	6.8	9.7
Switzerland	0.9	1.0	3.5	6.4	4.0
OECD Europe	5.1	2.3	3.7	6.4	10.9
Standard deviation	4.9	1.1	1.0	1.2	4.3
United States	2.5	1.3	2.6	4.9	8.5

[a] Consumer prices
Sources: IMF, *International Financial Statistics* (1967/68 and 1980 Yearbooks).

low point around 1958–9. It rose gently through the 1960s and then sharply at the turn of the decade as the rise in nominal wages accelerated to two-digit figures almost simultaneously in most European countries (Table 3.2). The question addressed in this section is: 'What accounts both for the relatively favourable performance through most of this period of fixed exchange rates, and for the deterioration experienced at the end of the 1960s?' Apart from looking at the course of inflation the section tries to bring out the ways in which the problems posed were looked at by policy-makers and the remedies proposed at the time.

The Korean War boom

It is sometimes not appreciated that inflation in Europe was, around 1950, high even by the standards of the 1970s. After the turmoil of the early post-war years and the runaway inflations experienced in some countries (e.g. France, Germany, Italy, Austria, or Finland), monetary reforms on the one hand and the resumption of more normal production patterns on the other had led to a sharp deceleration in European inflation (from perhaps 15 per cent in 1948 to 3 per cent in 1949 and only 1 per cent in 1950). This return to virtual price stability was, however, interrupted by the effects of three separate factors which, during 1950, brought about a sudden reacceleration of price pressures. First, most European currencies were devalued *vis-à-vis* the dollar in late 1949, usually by as much as 30 per cent (the Belgian franc and the lira devalued by less, the value of the Swiss franc remained unchanged). The effects on inflation were to some extent suppressed in 1950 by widespread subsidies and price controls, but came through in 1951.[6] Second, growth accelerated sharply in the West. GNP rose at an average rate of 8½ per cent in 1950-1 in the United States and at 7 per cent in Europe. The effects of this coincident and very rapid upswing on increasingly strained supply capacities were then compounded by a third factor – the outbreak of the Korean War – which generated a scramble for raw materials and a very sharp acceleration in defence expenditure.

The ensuing inflation was felt most strongly in 1951, when consumer prices rose by 11½ per cent in Europe (and by 8 per cent in the United States). During the year, however, prices decelerated. By 1952 inflation was down to 5 per cent, and 1953 saw virtual price stability. Though information on wages in this period is scanty, it would appear that wages and salaries followed a very similar development – a sharp acceleration in 1951 to double-digit rates in virtually all European countries (with the notable exception of Switzerland which had *de facto* revalued), a slowdown in 1952, and a sharp deceleration in 1953 to perhaps only 5 per cent.

The short-lived nature of the inflation of this period stands in sharp contrast to the lasting inflationary impact of the 1972-3 crisis. At the outset there were a number of similarities between the two episodes (Table 3.3). Both periods witnessed a coincident rapid and sharp acceleration in the growth of the Western world; both periods experienced pronounced commodity price booms and very similar terms of trade deteriorations; and though oil prices did not rise in dollar terms in the early 1950s, while they quadrupled at the turn of 1973, the 1949 devaluations imparted some upward pressure on all dollar-denominated raw material prices.

One important reason for the difference in price behaviour may lie in the climate of inflationary expectations. These were high and rising in the early 1970s as a consequence of the wage explosions of the turn of the 1960s and a decade of accelerating inflation. In the early 1950s, by contrast, the acceleration was viewed by many as purely temporary.[7] This perception was reinforced by a second factor – the behaviour of commodity prices. While in the year to March 1951 these rose by some 65 per cent, they fell rapidly in the subsequent two years. By March 1953, spot prices were only 10 per cent above their March 1950 level. In contrast, commodity prices rose not only somewhat more sharply in 1972-3, but their subsequent falls were very modest (only 5 per cent in the two years to August 1975). And the rise in import prices was, of course, much more marked in the 1970s in view of what had happened to oil.

A third reason can be found in the development of real wages. While in 1973-4 real wage growth slowed down, in 1951-2 it actually accelerated as productivity and output growth remained relatively strong. Though policies in several countries moved into a restrictive stance, the squeeze was in no way similar to the one imposed in 1974, nor was it compounded by the deflationary effects of the OPEC terms of trade improvement. Money wage growth could thus decelerate without any pronounced adverse effects on standards of living. But the most important reason for both the money wage and price slowdowns lies probably in the very different labour market conditions characterizing the two periods. The

[6] UNECE, *Economic Survey of Europe in 1951*, Geneva 1952, p. 109.
[7] W. Fellner *et al.*, *The Problem of Rising Prices*, OECD, Paris 1964, p. 9; UNECE, *Incomes in Post-war Europe*, Geneva 1967, Ch. 2, p. 1.

1973-4 price rise was superimposed on a labour market which was not only tight but had been tight for a decade, and on a strong labour movement which had shown its militancy and achieved a substantial shift in income distribution away from capital through the 1960s. In the early 1950s, on the other hand, trade union movements were much weaker and unemployment substantial in most countries.

TABLE 3.3. *Comparison of two commodity price booms*
(indices)

	OEEC Europe (1949 = 100)		OECD Europe (1972 = 100)	
	1951	1952	1974	1975
Terms of trade[a]	90	95	89	92
Import prices[a] − total	138	135	188	196
− extra-Europe	117	111	..	..
	(March 1950 = 100)		(August 1972 = 100)	
	March 1951[b]	March 1952	August 1973[b]	August 1974
Memorandum item:				
Commodity prices[c]	164	124	187	196

[a] Goods and services
[b] Peak month
[c] *The Economist*'s dollar index of spot prices
Sources: OEEC, *Statistics of National Product and Expenditure, 1938 and 1948 to 1955*, Paris 1957; OECD, *National Accounts of OECD Countries, 1950-1979; The Economist* (various issues).

From the early 1950s to the late 1960s

The period of nearly twenty years which ran from the end of the Korean War boom to the wage explosions of the turn of the 1960s was one of relatively subdued price developments, with European (consumer price) inflation averaging some 3 per cent per annum (and only 2¼ per cent in 'dollar terms' as against the United States' 2 per cent). The two major features of this period were:

(i) The apparent responsiveness of inflation to changes in demand pressures with short lags;
(ii) The gradual, mild trend acceleration of both price and, in particular, wage inflation.

Both these features are illustrated in Fig. 3.1, which presents a proxy for demand pressures in the form of tentative estimates of the gap between actual and potential output for Europe as a whole. The pro-cyclical movement of wages and prices is well in evidence, as is also the declining responsiveness of inflation to recessions (with wages, in particular, rising more rapidly in 1967 than in 1958-9 despite rather similar cyclical conditions), and its increasing elasticity with respect to booms (cf. the 1955-6 and 1962-5 experiences).

From the vantage-point of the 1970s, the inflation of this period looks very moderate. Yet this was clearly not the perception of the time. On the contrary,

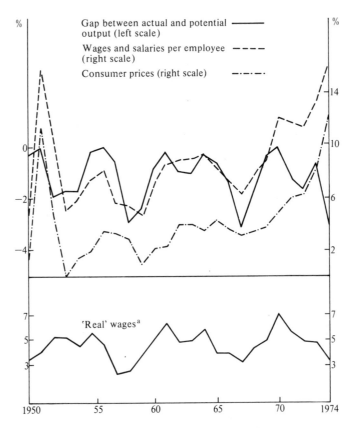

FIG. 3.1. *Wages, inflation, and the cycle in Europe* (percentages)
Note: all the 1957–9 observations exclude France.
ᵃ Nominal wages deflated by consumer prices
Sources: OECD, *National Accounts of OECD Countries, Manpower Statistics*, and *Labour Force Statistics* (various issues); OECD, 'The Measurement of Domestic Cyclical Fluctuations', *OECD Economic Outlook – Occasional Studies*, July 1973: IMF, *International Financial Statistics* (1967/68 and 1980 Yearbooks); editor's estimates.

official policy pronouncements viewed price pressures with disquiet. Indeed, the OEEC devoted a special experts' report in 1961 to 'the problem of rising prices'.[8] It is interesting to note that the concerns expressed at the time and the policy prescriptions which were advanced prefigure much of the debate that became so prominent in the 1970s. Broadly, concern stemmed from what policymakers perceived as two related difficulties:

(i) Within the general policy of high employment and growth it was felt that stabilization policy should be applied flexibly enough to avoid either recession or excessive demand pressures in the short run;

(ii) It was also felt that success in generating rapid growth and high employment could *itself* pose a threat to price stability over the longer term.

[8] Fellner, *Rising Prices*.

The first of these led to calls for better demand management and avoidance of the errors which had led to pressures of a demand-inflationary kind in the years 1955-7. But apart from any errors in policy generating excess demand, it was also felt that excessive wage increases were a powerful independent source of inflation, at least in some countries, which suggested that rising prices would continue as a problem into the 1960s.

These two views also implied a disagreement about policy. Taking again the OEEC experts' report as representative of opinion at the time, the majority was in favour of a wages policy: 'Governments cannot allow the large and powerful force that comes from the present wage negotiation machinery to remain outside the arena of stabilization policy without serious risk of having its efforts to put on a good performance inside the arena frustrated.'[9] The majority went on to discuss the consequences of exclusive reliance on demand management. 'The restraint of demand may work for a time if pushed to the point of compromising the objectives of high employment and growth, but price stability achieved this way would surely be in constant jeopardy because of its shaky political foundation.'[10] There was no denial here of the possibility of curtailing inflation by tight demand management policies, but there was a profound pessimism, characteristic of nearly all those who advocated incomes policies, about the costs of the alternative.

The dissentients[11] were against the advocacy of wage policies for reasons which are also familiar, and relevant to the continuing debate over inflation in the 1960s and 1970s. They suggested that governments were ill equipped to interfere in the wage bargaining process, that such policies of intervention would, to be successful, have to escalate, and that the microeconomic costs would be considerable. Their position also illustrates well the optimism which was later to become a characteristic of monetarist pronouncements on inflation control: 'It is true that the bargaining arrangements . . . lower the level of employment attainable at a stable general price level. But the question is whether this adverse effect will prove to be great or relatively insignificant . . . It may well turn out that the majority is unduly pessimistic . . .'[12] If the optimism were to turn out to be misplaced, they were still not in favour of incomes policies, but argued that monopolistic elements should be tackled more directly.

The differences shown in the degrees of optimism or pessimism about the ease of inflation control and the efficiency of market forces plus demand management are clearly important. But a subtler difference is apparent in the varying recommendations about how to achieve economic objectives in the presence of cost-push forces. On one side the recommendation was to use demand management policies provided an accommodation with the unions could be achieved. On the other, if the unions posed a threat, then, not to put too fine a point on it, their powers should be curtailed.

This conception of the problem of inflation continued through the 1960s. If anything, optimism over the perfectability of demand management increased through the decade. By and large it was felt that inflation would respond to restrictive policies if they were applied. And, by and large, the evidence suggested

---

[9] Ibid., p. 56.
[10] Ibid., p. 57.
[11] Professors Fellner and Lutz.
[12] Fellner, *Rising Prices*, p. 64.

that, in most countries, inflation was reactive to the pressure of demand.[13] In one form or another, the so-called 'Phillips curve' seemed to apply. This relative optimism about the existence of a trade-off was, however, combined with increasing worries over inflation of the cost–push variety at least in some countries: and there were a number of important examples of attempts at incomes policies. Significantly, these tended to be seen as a 'third instrument of policy' potentially helpful in meeting *general* economic objectives, and not necessarily as primarily to do with inflation. For example, one of the justifications for incomes policy in the United Kingdom was that it would improve competitiveness, and be a substitute for exchange rate movements.[14] In the smaller, highly open economies – especially Scandinavia and Austria – inflation tended to be seen as determined by price developments in trading partners and the world economy (via the 'Scandinavian' model of inflation), and incomes policies (or at least centralized wage formation) were an integral part of the formulation of the general stance of policy.

The 'wage explosions'

The more pessimistic view of the inflationary process appeared to be confirmed at the end of the 1960s when the normal relationship between the pressure of demand and inflation virtually broke down in most European countries. This period saw a sudden acceleration in the growth of nominal wages in the four major economies of the area, which, by the early 1970s, had spread to almost all the smaller countries. The year 1968 was one of protest movements all over the world.[15] The wage explosion in France was clearly associated with the *événements* of May which resulted in a 35 per cent increase in minimum wages, and a jump from 6 to nearly 12 per cent for average wage rises between 1967 and 1968. Strike waves then hit Germany, Italy, and the United Kingdom in the autumn of 1969. In Germany, the strikes were unofficial, and, though not very widespread, began in the crucial steel and engineering sectors. In the United Kingdom, and even more in Italy, the disputes were on a massive scale. In all three countries, as earlier in France, the strikes had for the authorities the disturbing characteristic of being triggered off by rank and file militancy rather than by pressure from the official unions. Indeed, centralized union bureaucracies seemed in many cases to be as worried by the phenomenon as governments. Elsewhere in Europe the process was perhaps less marked, though strike incidence also rose sharply in 1970 in Spain, Belgium, Ireland, and the Netherlands. Everywhere in Europe there was an acceleration in the growth of nominal wages.

Some indication of the scale of the wage increases is given in Table 3.4, which shows nominal and real wage changes as well as an indicator of strike activity. The years have been chosen to catch, as far as possible, the timing of the wage spurt. Though the rough coincidence is impressive, it is not exact. Many of the smaller countries lagged, and it is difficult to know whether the wage acceleration

---

[13] See, for instance, the evidence presented in OECD, *Inflation: The Present Problem*, Paris 1970, Annex A.

[14] R.F. Harrod, *Towards a New Economic Policy*, Manchester 1967.

[15] Not only in Europe, but also in the United States, and even in Eastern Europe.

TABLE 3.4. *The wage explosions*

		1965–67	1968–69	Change
France	(i) nominal wages[a]	5.8	11.0	5.2
	(ii) real wages[b]	2.9	5.4	2.5
	(iii) working days lost in strikes[c]	2,569	..	..
		1966–68	1969–70	Change
Germany	(i)	5.6	12.0	6.4
	(ii)	3.3	9.2	5.9
	(iii)	147	171	24
Italy	(i)	6.9	11.3	4.4
	(ii)	4.3	7.3	3.0
	(iii)	10,761	29,356	18,595
Denmark[d]	(i)	9.5	11.1	1.6
	(ii)	1.6	5.7	4.1
	(iii)	20	79	59
Ireland[d]	(i)	9.0	15.4	6.4
	(ii)	5.2	7.0	1.8
	(iii)	457	972	515
Netherlands	(i)	7.8	12.5	4.7
	(ii)	3.3	6.5	3.2
	(iii)	11	180	169
		1967–69	1970–71	Change
United Kingdom	(i)	6.9	12.0	5.1
	(ii)	2.4	3.9	1.5
	(iii)	4,774	12,265	7,491
Spain	(i)	11.3	12.2	0.9
	(ii)	6.5	4.9	−1.6
	(iii)	345	976	631
Austria[d]	(i)	9.2	11.3	2.1
	(ii)	5.6	6.5	0.9
	(iii)	14	15	1
Belgium	(i)	6.9	9.8	2.9
	(ii)	3.7	5.5	1.8
	(iii)	236	1,336	1,100
Finland	(i)	9.2	11.6	2.4
	(ii)	3.3	6.6	3.3
	(iii)	255	1,472	1,217
Norway[d]	(i)	8.4	10.8	2.2
	(ii)	4.6	2.2	−2.4
	(iii)	13	28	15
Sweden	(i)	6.6	7.7	1.1
	(ii)	3.5	0.3	−3.2
	(iii)	38	497	459
Switzerland	(i)	5.9	13.2	7.3
	(ii)	2.9	7.8	4.9
	(iii)	1	5	4

[a] Wages and salaries per employee, average annual percentage changes
[b] Nominal wages deflated by consumer prices, average annual percentage changes
[c] In thousands, annual averages
[d] Total employee compensation per employee.

Sources: OECD, *National Accounts of OECD Countries*, and *Labour Force Statistics* (various issues); ILO, *Yearbook of Labour Statistics, 1974*.

reflected an autonomous increase in militancy and cost-push pressure, or the impact of inflation 'imported' from the major countries. Yet the fact that *real* wages accelerated virtually everywhere suggests that demonstration effects and the wave of militancy were important factors behind the generalized increase in inflation. On the face of it at least, the rise in European inflation at the end of the 1960s reflected an upward shift in cost-push pressures.

The wage explosion has brought forth an abundant literature, but its causes remain controversial. One of the reasons is that the rise in European inflation at this time is part of a world-wide phenomenon, with prices rising particularly rapidly in North America. In the United States, the acceleration in inflation appears to have reflected increasing demand pressures as the 1960s boom continued, and as the Vietnam War and the 'great society' programmes swelled public expenditure. Even in the United States, however, militancy and cost-push pressures appear to have been important. In Europe, the conventional explanation in terms of demand pressures, or monetary expansion, fares much less well. Econometric investigations have usually yielded negative conclusions on the importance of the money supply or demand pressure.[16] Certainly, though growth was rapid in 1969-70 (particularly in Germany), the increase in wages went well beyond what could have been expected on the basis of past relationships. A more plausible account lays stress on the previous period of wage moderation and rationalization of work which was imposed by governments or businesses in the mid-1960s.[17] It is suggested that an accumulation of grievances (as, for example, under the incomes policy in the United Kingdom, or slow growth in Italy) led to strike actions in an environment in which labour felt, because of continuing high employment, relatively secure. This in turn led to institutional changes which reinforced union power in matters of negotiation *vis-à-vis* employers, particularly in France and Italy.[18] And individual governments usually ratified the wage increases *ex post*,[19] partly because inflation in the United States and in other European countries was accelerating, thus reducing the threat to competitiveness.

An assessment

As has been seen, the 1960s started with low inflation but with developing worries about cost-push inflationary forces, and about the longer-term compatibility of full employment and price stability. At the end of the 1960s, these fears seemed fully justified by the wage explosions and general rise in inflation that occurred. For much of the two preceding decades, however, inflationary pressure did appear to be contained. An important reason was the commitment to the Bretton Woods system of fixed (but adjustable) exchange rates. The

[16] See, for instance, W.D. Nordhaus, 'The Worldwide Wage Explosion', *Brookings Papers on Economic Activity*, No. 2, 1972; G.L. Perry, 'Determinants of Wage Inflation around the World', *Brookings Papers on Economic Activity*, No. 2, 1975.

[17] D. Soskice, 'Strike Waves and Wage Explosions, 1968-1970: An Economic Interpretation', in C. Crouch and A. Pizzorno (eds.), *The Resurgence of Class Conflict in Western Europe since 1968*, London 1978.

[18] J.D. Sachs, 'Wages, Profits and Macroeconomic Adjustment: A Comparative Study', *Brookings Papers on Economic Activity*, No. 2, 1979.

[19] Ibid.

combination of the direct effects of international competition and the discipline imposed on economic policy appeared to work — and the dispersion of inflation rates within Europe was very moderate. This was only achieved, however, at the expense of some divergence of performance on the real side — notably between Germany and the United Kingdom. Eventually Britain was forced to devalue, a move which made the whole edifice of Bretton Woods look increasingly shaky.

Of course, the strains on the Bretton Woods system and the onset of rapid inflation in the late 1960s were interrelated, and it is not possible to say what caused what. But another factor of great importance is that the fixed exchange rate system, itself, ceased to be much of a 'discipline' when both Europe and America were simultaneously inflating in the late 1960s. Governments at the time were much exercised about trends in competitiveness — the advantages of undervaluation had become apparent in many European countries, as had the disadvantages of what was seen as overvaluation of the dollar and pound — which meant they were more inclined to ratify wage agreements *ex post* if they were not too much out of line with competitors. Another way of putting the same point is to note that the 'islands of stability' — especially the United States and Germany, and earlier Italy — which were widely thought to have exerted downward pressure on international trade prices in the 1950s and most of the 1960s — disappeared. As is noted in an OECD report of the time,[20] international trade prices accelerated sharply in 1969 and 1970 to rates comparable with domestic inflation — whereas previously they had tended to be markedly lower.

Whilst the general nature of the inflation problem goes part of the way towards explaining why there was not greater pressure on individual European governments to curb inflation in the late 1960s, it does not explain the origins of the inflationary pressure itself. Even if it is ascribed to wage explosions, there still remains the difficulty of accounting for the upsurge in militancy, and the environment which allowed that militancy to be translated so easily into inflationary wage increases.

A very important question concerns the influence of demand. It was seen above that short-term pressures do not easily account for the wage explosions, nor do simplistic explanations in terms of the money supply.[21] But, as was noted in Section I, there is a general problem in assessing demand pressure in Europe. Apart from the obvious success in lowering unemployment rates in the 1950s and 1960s, the massive relocations of labour from lower productivity sectors and the international movements from Eastern Europe into Germany, and from Southern Europe into North-Western Europe, suggest that the *longer-term* balance in the labour market was tightening. So too does the changing composition of increments to the labour force. In the 1960s, a large part of the rise in labour input was due to increases in female participation rates which probably reflected both social forces and high demand for labour. It is thus possible that under-utilization of labour and concealed unemployment lay

[20] OECD, *Inflation*, pp. 23–5.

[21] It is sometimes suggested that United States balance of payments deficits and expansion of the world money supply can account for the rise in inflation at this time. It is necessary to be very sceptical of this claim since the wage settlements that led to the wage explosions occurred as a rule *before* the very large dollar outflows.

behind the good price performance of the 1950s and that high demand and the move to more genuinely full employment conditions explain the onset of inflation in the late 1960s.

This is a plausible hypothesis, but very hard to prove, one way or the other. If it is true that earlier moderation was, in effect, due to high unemployment of a concealed kind, and that the breakdown occurred as this was eliminated, then there are profoundly pessimistic implications. The hypothesis would suggest that the old fear – prominent amongst the architects of demand management policies – that high employment would turn out to be incompatible with stable prices – was justified. What is being put forward in this kind of hypothesis is not that there were technical mistakes in demand management of a minor kind, but that the whole attempt to maintain growth and full employment was doomed to failure – in the absence of specific policies to deal with inflation.

The hypothesis of a secular change in demand pressure is hard to distinguish in practice from another which stresses a secular change in expectations and aspirations.[22] Broadly, it is argued that the experience of success and the diminution of economic risk[23] would, over time, be bound to increase inflationary pressure. In the 1950s, the capacity of the European economies to deliver rising living standards exceeded expectations, and this, in itself, was a powerful factor making for moderation. As time went on, such rises came to be taken for granted, and demands increased. At the same time, productive potential may, for supply side reasons, have started to slow down – the two movements opening up a gap between aspirations and achievements that could not be filled. The result was thus inflationary pressure of a cost–push, or 'competing claims' kind. In support, it could be argued that a number of wage explosions had followed periods of slower growth and apparently frustrated expectations. And slower-growing countries such as the United Kingdom had always appeared to have had difficulties with cost–push pressure. This hypothesis too would be hard to falsify.

There is more to the 'competing claims' thesis than expectations of rising living standards. As is described elsewhere in this book, the mid- to late 1960s were marked by generally strong demands on the economic system. Welfare states were being strengthened, public expenditure had been rising rapidly, the claims of minority groups were being actively promulgated, and so on. The climate of opinion about the feasibility of economic management was itself a reason for increased political demands being put on the system. But the result was that taxes as a proportion of GDP had been rising, and 'privately financed consumption'[24] had been correspondingly squeezed, raising the possibility of what came to be called 'tax–push' inflation.[25] At the same time there is qualitative evidence that bargaining structures may have become more prone to generate inflation. Not only was there probably a trend to increasing monopolization and

---

[22] McCracken, *Towards Full Employment*, Ch. 5.

[23] See introductory chapter to this book.

[24] OECD, *Expenditure Trends in OECD Countries, 1960-1980*, Paris 1972, Ch. 3.

[25] Tax-push inflation is a misnomer. It is not the rise in taxes that leads to inflation *per se*, but the resistance and frustration that increases conflict over distributional issues in general; for some evidence on the phenomenon, see OECD, *Public Expenditure Trends*, Paris 1978, Annex B.

market power for the various groups in society, but also labour legislation – especially employment protection measures – may have increased the rigidity of the existing pattern of distribution as well as making it more likely that frustration with it would, by one route or another, turn out to be inflationary.

III. The General Trend of European Inflation – The 1970s

Both wage and, particularly, price inflation were at record levels throughout the 1970s. The period began with (mild) deflation, which proved unable to control inflationary pressures, and ended with (prolonged) stagnation which was almost equally impotent. A commodity price boom and two major oil price rises were, of course, important reasons for these unfavourable trends, but other forces were also at work to make European inflation highly resistant. If there was a trade-off at all between inflation and unemployment, it was now very adverse. In spite of this, there did not appear to be any easy alternative. Over the 1970s both monetary and fiscal policy were diverted more and more, away from their traditional role in supporting growth and high employment, to the new role of containing inflationary pressures. The brief respite in 1978 was quickly followed by rising commodity prices, and, entirely coincidentally, by the second oil crisis. The response everywhere was to tighten policy, with the inevitable result of more recession and further rises in unemployment at the beginning of the 1980s.

The early 1970s

The response of most European governments to the developing wage/price spiral of the late 1960s was to restrict demand and output. This phase can be seen as an attempt to make use of the traditional assumed trade-off between inflation and the pressure of demand to slow the rise in prices, and it led to the 'mild' recession of 1970–1. In contrast to what had happened in 1958, and to a lesser extent in 1967, wages and prices seemed almost completely insensitive to demand pressures. Consumer prices continued to accelerate (for Europe as a whole) up to the middle of 1971, despite a rise in unemployment to over 3 per cent at the trough of the recession. It began to look as if the demand management weapon for controlling inflation no longer worked – or, if it did work, the costs in terms of unemployment appeared so great as to be beyond the limits of political feasibility.

There are many reasons for the subsequent reversal of policy positions, both in Europe and in America.[26] For most European countries, the experience of the recession appeared to confirm the worst fears about cost-push pressures; and it is worth recalling that policy-making in some countries was much affected by 'the sense of unease to which the discord in labour markets – and in the streets – had given rise'.[27] If inflation is seen as arising from conflicts over distribution, then there is an obvious danger that recession and unemployment, whilst they may help to contain the pressure, may exacerbate the underlying tensions. And starting from a position of under-utilized resources, it may appear possible to

[26] See, for instance, C.J. Allsopp, 'The International Demand Management Problem', in D. Morris (ed.), *The Economic System in the UK*, Oxford 1979 (2nd edn.).

[27] McCracken, *Towards Full Employment*, p. 52.

defuse labour market pressures by the rises in real income that are possible during an upswing. As is well known, this kind of reasoning led to some spectacular 'U-turns' in policy (e.g. in the United Kingdom).

The process of policy reversal was, however, a generalized one, and its causes went beyond the failure of inflation to respond to lower demand. One important reason was the breakdown of the Bretton Woods system and the period of 'dirty' floating in the second half of 1971 prior to the Smithsonian Agreements. European governments, willing to expand for domestic reasons, and concerned that their currencies should not be pushed up too far relative to the dollar, were prepared to accept rapid monetary expansion initiated by the dollar outflows of that time.

In contrast to the situation in the late 1960s, when it was genuinely difficult to give a satisfactory account of the rise in inflation, the further rapid rise in 1972 and 1973 is only too easy to explain. In fact there are *too many* possible explanations, so that evidence from this period does not discriminate well between alternative hypotheses about inflation. On the face of it, the rise in inflation — which was initiated in *goods* markets — is an example of excess demand, coming on top of a situation which was already bad for cost–push reasons. Some qualifications to the simple story are, however, necessary. Demand was high, and the boom was highly coincident between countries. But there had been other coincident upswings in the world economy, and the level of resource utilization was not especially high — probably no higher than in 1969. What was exceptional was the speed of the upswing, with industrialized countries growing at about 7½ per cent between the first halves of 1972 and 1973. Going behind the boom itself, to its causes, there are also several — no doubt reinforcing — reasons. It can be ascribed to over-expansionary fiscal policies or to over-expansionary monetary policies, or to both. And behind these policy responses there were fears about labour market unrest, and, since 1972 was an election year in several major countries, fears about re-election.[28]

One of the consequences of over-rapid expansion was to put upward pressure on commodity prices. But again, this is not the whole story. There were important supply side shocks — especially bad harvests in 1972. And there appears to be little doubt that rapid monetary expansion contributed a speculative element to commodity price rises, and to the inflation of real estate values which occurred in several European countries. Finally, the oil price rises themselves were an exogenous factor, further raising world and European inflation in a most unfavourable way.

Rapidly expanding demand, commodity price rises, and the general climate of inflation meant that the incomes policies, introduced or strengthened in many countries as an adjunct to earlier reversal of policies, simply could not succeed. Their failure in this period, however, has little significance for any longer-term assessment of their usefulness or otherwise in dealing with inflationary problems of the 'competing claims' type. They were simply blown apart by commodity price rises and excess demand.

---

[28] France, Germany, the United States, Canada, and Japan all went to the polls in the second half of 1972 or in the first half of 1973.

The perception of inflation after the oil crisis

In early 1974 European governments were faced with a formidable array of problems – high inflation, balance of payments deficits, and the possibility of severe recession. With the effects of the commodity price boom still working through, and with the rise in oil prices, it was more or less certain that recorded inflation would rise to two-digit levels, something which was almost unthinkable only a few years earlier. But much of this dramatic rise in inflation represented once-and-for-all effects. The real problem was to make sure that when the inevitable price changes had passed through, there would be a rapid deceleration of inflation – as there had been after the Korean War boom.

Looking at the commodity price rises, it was clear that there were two rather different ways of interpreting the stimulus to inflation that they had provided:

(i) They could be seen as an indication of world excess demand (due to excessive growth and supply side shocks such as bad harvests). On this view they were important in the transmission mechanism, but ultimately reversible if world demand was brought under control (as had happened in the early 1950s);

(ii) They could be seen as a more permanent shift in the real terms of trade, an idea popularized by 'The Club of Rome' and others. If this was the case, then the movement was not reversible, and the problem was to adjust to the new relative prices in a non-inflationary way.

As far as the first of these ways of looking at the problem was concerned, most governments had introduced restrictive policies during 1973-4, and it was clear that the overall rate of expansion of the world economy was slowing down. One result was that commodity prices stabilized in the summer of 1973, and it was widely expected that this represented the peak – that is until the oil crisis led to further waves of speculative buying, prolonging the commodity price boom into 1974. As far as the second hypothesis was concerned, it was apparent that the situation varied between commodities. In the case of oil it was clear that the price rise represented a permanent change in the terms of trade and a shift in the international distribution of income towards OPEC. For other raw materials, however, it could be expected that with more normal supply and demand conditions the terms of trade shift would reverse itself (though there were, at the time, widespread fears in consumer countries that other primary producers might succeed in following the OPEC example in forming cartels).

It could thus be argued that the inflationary problems posed by the 'supply shocks' of 1973-4 were not insurmountable. Indeed, on a very speculative note, it seems probable that if an 'oil crisis' or something like it had occurred in the late 1940s or early 1950s, it would have been a relatively minor addition to the difficulties already faced (and, as noted above, in important respects the Korean War boom was like an oil crisis). In the period of maximum economic optimism – the mid-1960s – it seems highly probable that offsetting policy action would have been agreed. If in the 1970s it actually appeared to pose problems of altogether greater magnitude, the obvious reason is that the economic situation was already very bad. Cost inflation was continuing as a serious problem; there was excess demand in the world economy and in some individual countries;

commodity prices had risen exceptionally; above all, inflationary expectations had increased and were much more volatile, reflecting both recent experience and the breakdown of the international monetary system.

The policy response

In broad terms, it is useful to think of three possible responses to the problems posed by the inflation of this period:

(i) The view could be taken that monetary and fiscal deflation was the appropriate response to inflation of whatever type;

(ii) A more eclectic position would stress the need to remove any excess demand, but would then see the problem of inflation as arising from cost–push forces. Once excess demand was eliminated, inflation control would not be made easier by further rises in unemployment;

(iii) A more radical position, stressing 'target wage behaviour'[29] and the 'competing claims' approach to inflation, would suggest that the underlying problems would get worse with deflation and unemployment.

All these positions were influential after the oil crisis. Germany and Switzerland, particularly, stressed the desirability of deflation, and were prepared to risk a major recession. The second position was taken up explicitly by the United Kingdom in 1974 and implicitly by most other European countries. The final view – that deflation could make things worse, was probably most important in the Nordic countries. Not surprisingly, therefore, the initial response within Europe was very diverse. Restrictive policies were immediately instigated in Germany and Switzerland. Britain and the Netherlands both argued for offsetting policies, but in both cases the actual response was muddled. Sweden, which had carried out restrictive policies earlier, took explicit offsetting action. Italy, which had joined the world upswing late after a long period of mediocre growth, tried initially to continue growing, but was rapidly forced by international payments problems to carry out heavy deflation. Very soon (in the second half of 1974) it became apparent that a major world recession was developing and all European economies were dragged into it by international linkage effects, whatever their views about the optimal response to inflation.

The severe recession and ensuing slow growth only had a moderate effect on inflation in most countries. By the second half of 1975 it had fallen from the peak of about 15 per cent to only 10 to 11 per cent, which was not an impressive achievement given the once-and-for-all nature of the impact in 1973-4. Inflation then hovered around this mark in 1976 and 1977, before coming down to 8½ per cent in 1978. The relatively good performance in that year reflected an appreciation of European currencies against the dollar, commodity prices slowing down, stable oil prices, and the earlier marked slowdown in wage inflation in the two major inflation-prone countries (Italy and the United Kingdom). The respite was, however, short-lived. Inflation rebounded to 10 per cent in 1979 (and more in 1980) under the influence of some increase in activity (following the Bonn summit of 1978), and, especially, the renewed oil price rises following the revolution in Iran. The second oil crisis at the end of the decade had a direct price-raising effect which was almost exactly similar to that of the

[29] Mainly put forward in the United Kingdom by the so-called 'New Cambridge School'.

1973-4 crisis. Thus the decade ended with further problems of inflation and of adaptation to worsened terms of trade — problems which had, after the first oil crisis, proved to be extremely intractable in most European economies.

The diversity of experience in this period between the two oil crises is striking. For the first time since the early post-war years, inflation rates diverged greatly between countries — from 18 per cent per annum in Spain to 4 per cent in Switzerland. And within countries — especially those such as Britain, Denmark, Finland, and Norway (but also Belgium) which attempted incomes policy packages — inflation was very variable. For example, in the United Kingdom, Finland, and Ireland the difference between the peak year of 1975 and the low of 1978 was of the order of 10 to 16 percentage points (by contrast, inflation was rather stable in France, Germany, and Sweden).

Some common threads

Obviously, all European countries experienced the problems posed by oil, and they were all affected by recession, subsequent slow growth, and persistently high unemployment. Beyond this, there are other threads that need to be brought out. The first is the experience of floating exchange rates as it affected inflation and its control. In the late 1960s, floating exchange rates had usually been advocated as a system that would contribute to national economic sove-reignty by removing balance of payments constraints. They did not operate that way for European countries in the 1970s. Of course, they did allow the vast divergence in inflation performance already referred to — and given this diver-gence it was no doubt inevitable that exchange rates would have to float. But the external constraint on economic policy, especially for weaker countries, appeared actually to be increased. The reason was that with major difficulties of inflation control, the possibility of a fall in the exchange rate was a more frightening prospect than a balance of payments deficit under fixed exchange rates. There are a number of cases where fear of this possibility led to strongly restrictive domestic policies — in Italy soon after the oil crisis; in France too such reasoning was one of the factors behind the Barre Plan; and most dramatically, the reversal of policy in the United Kingdom in 1976 was a direct result of exchange rate weakness. But the idea that inflation control required at least the avoidance of exchange rate falls was more generally held. Indeed, it was widely believed that Germany and Switzerland (but also Austria and the Benelux countries) had gained from a rising exchange rate prompting a virtuous circle after the oil crisis, and there were attempts to emulate this.

In view of the priority given to exchange rate stability, it is not surprising that, as conditions stabilized somewhat in the later 1970s, there should have been moves towards greater fixity of exchange rates with the institution of the EMS. The entry of France and Italy into the EMS in 1978 — and hence the acceptance of something like parity with Germany — could be seen as a strong commitment to inflation control. But these attempts to go back to fixed ex-change rates within Europe illustrated well a point made in Section I. Even were they to succeed perfectly, the fixity of exchange rates (say *vis-à-vis* Germany) would in no sense be an explanation of the rate of inflation. Rather, it would be the success of the anti-inflation strategy *within* countries that allowed the fixity of the exchange rates.

The breakdown of the Bretton Woods system was also one of the factors behind another common strand of experience – the widespread adoption within Europe of monetary targets as an element in counter-inflation strategy. The reasons for this are fully discussed in Chapter 11. Much of the impetus in this direction came from German experience with massive monetary inflows in the early 1970s, where it was felt that neither interest rates nor the exchange rate were good or even reasonable indicators of the stance of policy in the disturbed conditions of the time. In practical terms the later adoption of monetary targets by most European governments probably owed more to the desire to set up some domestic intermediate target to replace the commitment to a fixed exchange rate than to any conversion to monetarist doctrine *per se*. This concern interacted with the pragmatic view that over-rapid monetary expansion had been at least a contributory factor in the inflationary excesses of the early 1970s boom period. But, as with external intermediate targets, the point needs to be stressed that neither the monetary targets that were adopted, nor the actual rates of growth of the money supply that ensued in European countries, constitute an adequate explanation of inflation in Europe in the 1970s. The money supply is not an exogenous instrument of policy (even under floating exchange rates), and behind European attempts to meet their monetary objectives there was active use of both monetary and fiscal instruments of policy.

Finally, one other common element is worth bringing out. For an individual country, commodity price movements appear as an exogenous influence on inflation. But Europe as a whole is large enough to have an influence on international markets – especially when it was moving in a rather similar way to the United States or Japan. Commodity prices did fall, producing some improvement to inflationary trends in 1975: with the upswing in 1976, however, commodity prices moved up again surprisingly quickly. Most disturbingly, the expansionary moves that led to an upturn in 1978–9 in Europe had an almost immediate effect on international primary product prices, raising the question – in abeyance since 1974 – as to whether any return to more rapid growth would be frustrated by rising commodity prices and the inability of European economies to adapt to them in a non-inflationary way. In the event this movement was swamped, as it had been in 1973, by an oil crisis. But unlike the situation in 1973–4, there was now no serious divergence of view on how to react to the inflationary stimulus of renewed oil price rises. All European countries adopted non-accommodating, or actively restrictive fiscal and monetary policies, precipitating a further phase of European recession. Consensus, of a sort, had been achieved.

IV. The Diversity of Experience

Under the Bretton Woods system of pegged exchange rates the diversity of inflation experience was extremely moderate. In both the 1950s and 1960s the standard deviation of inflation rates was only 1 percentage point; and the range (between Germany or Switzerland on the one hand, and Spain on the other) was about 4 percentage points. With floating exchange rates, both the range and the standard deviation rose substantially (Table 3.2). That is just what would be expected. It is very striking, however, that under the adjustable peg system, the range of performance on the 'real' side was large, and that beyond that there was an enormous diversity both in the problems that European governments appeared to face and in their responses to them. In the 1970s, moreover, though diversity increased, there were significant common elements.

The Bretton Woods period

The similarities of experience in this period have already been stressed. The small range of differences in inflation rates would seem to be 'explained' by two major causes – parity changes and labour market conditions. Most of the out-lying observations (e.g. Spain and Finland in the 1950s, or Spain, Denmark, and Finland in the 1960s) were for countries that devalued their currencies. Indeed, calculating inflation rates in 'dollar terms' leads to a standard deviation for the fixed exchange rate years of 1952–69 of only 0.8. On the labour market front, an estimate of an international Phillips curve shows on the whole a reasonable inverse relationship between unemployment and inflation, at least for the 1950s (Fig. 3.2).[30] In the 1960s, however, the relationship, though not breaking down, is much weaker. A number of observations would seem to lie along an almost vertical line, particularly if the two extreme, and opposite, German and Italian observations are excluded.

To bring out the diversity of experience, it may be useful to start with these two countries. In the early 1950s both had high unemployment and the union movements were finding their feet after only recent re-establishment. In both countries wage developments were very moderate in relation to rapidly growing productivity, and this was no doubt one factor in the rapid growth experienced. Inflation in the 1950s averaged 1¼ per cent for Germany and 2 per cent for Italy. Apart from low demand pressure and weak unions initially, it is probable that the rapid growth in living standards was, itself, a factor making for moder-ation. In the 1960s, however, the experience of the two countries diverged. In Italy, a wage explosion in 1962–3, following high pressure on capacity, led to much more restrictive demand management policies, much slower growth, and the continuation of somewhat higher inflation. In Germany, although in the early 1960s the pressure of demand was, if anything, higher (at least on a longer-term basis), a much more successful transition to lower growth was made, and inflation remained low up until the wage explosion at the end of the 1960s.

At the other extreme in terms of overall economic performance, the United Kingdom nevertheless had a rate of inflation which was almost exactly average for Europe. Nevertheless, it is clear that the authorities were concerned about inflationary pressure, though, significantly, the immediate concern was with the related problem of the balance of payments. In the 1960s, incomes policy ex-periments tended to be seen as a way of improving general economic perform-ance – including economic growth – and not solely in terms of inflation control.

---

[30] The estimates shown in the figure exclude Spain, Ireland, and Switzerland, in the first two cases for lack of data for the earlier period, and in all three cases because these coun-tries' labour markets are atypical in view of substantial agricultural underemployment through the period and/or large net migration flows. A similar relationship for the 1950s has also been shown in J. D. Smyth, 'Unemployment and Inflation: A Cross-Country Analysis of the Phillips Curve', *American Economic Review*, June 1971.

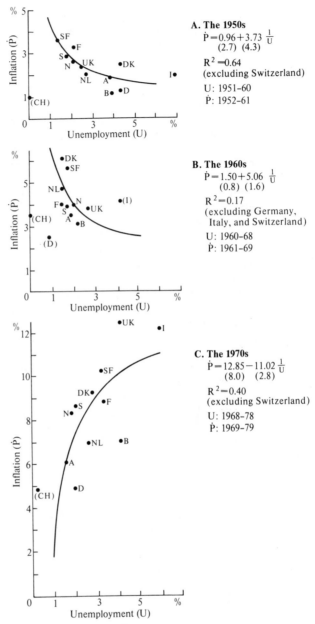

A. **The 1950s**
$$\dot{P} = 0.96 + 3.73\,\frac{1}{U}$$
$$\quad(2.7)\quad(4.3)$$
$R^2 = 0.64$
(excluding Switzerland)
U: 1951–60
$\dot{P}$: 1952–61

B. **The 1960s**
$$\dot{P} = 1.50 + 5.06\,\frac{1}{U}$$
$$\quad(0.8)\quad(1.6)$$
$R^2 = 0.17$
(excluding Germany,
Italy, and Switzerland)
U: 1960–68
$\dot{P}$: 1961–69

C. **The 1970s**
$$\dot{P} = 12.85 - 11.02\,\frac{1}{U}$$
$$\quad(8.0)\quad(2.8)$$
$R^2 = 0.40$
(excluding Switzerland)
U: 1968–78
$\dot{P}$: 1969–79

FIG. 3.2. *Unemployment*[a] *and inflation*[b]
[a] In per cent of the labour force, U.
[b] Average annual percentage changes in consumer prices, $\dot{P}$.
Sources: A. Maddison, 'Western Economic Performance in the 1970s: A Perspective and Assessment', *Banca Nazionale del Lavoro Quarterly Review*, September 1980; OECD, *Economic Outlook*, July 1981; IMF, *International Financial Statistics* (1980 Yearbook).

Nevertheless, the policies were not powerful enough to stave off devaluation in 1967.

Whilst devaluation in the United Kingdom can be understood in terms of the failure to contain inflationary pressure, which forced a reluctant and delayed accommodation to it, devaluation in France appeared to be used much more consciously as an instrument of policy. The rapid wage rises in the period of very high demand in 1956-7 obviously posed a threat to the competitiveness of the economy. Devaluation was seen as preferable, and it is notable that with the stabilization measures adopted in 1958-9 it appeared to lead to little wage reaction. The experience after the wage explosion of 1968 was rather similar: France apparently successfully offset the effects on competitiveness. Indeed, French experience is interesting from another point of view. There appeared, through the 1960s, to be considerable inertia in nominal wage rises. These were, however, high enough to give France an above average rate of inflation, the real effects of which were successfully offset by exchange rate changes. In some ways, Spain's experience was not too dissimilar.

Turning to the smaller European countries, the range of experience is even wider — though the influence of international prices was strong in all of them. In Switzerland, very low inflation was combined with no unemployment. Inflationary pressure was, apparently, in most years of the period, minimal. By contrast, Finland appeared to have high inflationary pressure during much of the 1950s and 1960s, which was unsuccessfully contained by resort to prices and incomes policies and imposed devaluations in 1957 and 1967. Denmark, too, in the 1950s, appeared to have a rather unsuccessful incomes policy.[31] There are, however, two notable examples of small countries with apparently successful incomes policies. Austria and Norway both succeeded in growing rapidly, with a high utilization of resources throughout the period. In Sweden, too, centralized wage formation was an integral part of the generally good economic performance — though on inflation the record was less impressive. An interesting feature of Sweden's experience is that even under centralized wage formation, wages appeared responsive to demand pressures. Belgium and the Netherlands provide an interesting set of parallels and contrasts. During the 1950s, Dutch incomes policy was widely credited with making a major contribution to the generally good performance of the economy. Belgium, by contrast, had heavy unemployment and slow growth — though an even better price performance than her neighbour. In the 1960s, Dutch incomes policy broke down in a period of high demand in 1964-5, with a wage explosion. Because of the incomes policy, Dutch wages had lagged behind those in neighbouring Common Market countries, and there was an element of catch-up involved. In Belgium growth accelerated, but inflation remained moderate, helped by a widespread system of indexation.

The main point that stands out from this brief description of the 'fixed' exchange rate period is that, behind the convergence of inflation rates imposed by the exchange rate system, there was a great deal of variation in the problems

---

[31] An assessment at the end of the 1950s noted that 'Danish experience shows very clearly that a high degree of centralisation and synchronisation of collective bargaining is no guarantee that money wage increases will be kept within the range consistent with the general national interest'; Fellner, *Rising Prices*, p. 313.

faced and in the policies adopted. In extreme cases, divergent performances led to devaluations – as in France, Britain, Spain, or Finland (and good performance led to upward revaluations of the DM). But even when exchange rate changes were not involved, both demand management policies and incomes policies were being used to meet overall economic objectives which included implicit targets for the exchange rate and international competitiveness. And the range of experience with incomes policies – of the 'consensus type', or of the type that sought to constrain wage and price rises – was equally broad. It is, however, difficult to resist a qualitative assessment. It appears that two countries, Germany and Switzerland, stand out as having a very low degree of inflationary 'pressure'. Not only were they successful overall, but wage rises appeared (until the late 1960s) to be unusually reactive to demand pressures. At the other end of the spectrum, Austria and Norway appeared particularly good at dealing with such wage pressures as they might have had by centralized wage formation systems. The main benefit did not appear in inflation (that could be taken as being determined by the exchange rate), but in maintaining competitiveness, growth, and high employment.

The 1970s

A notable feature of the 1970s – and especially of the post-oil-crisis period – is the extent to which good or bad performance, established in the 1950s and 1960s, persisted in dramatically changed circumstances. Thus Germany and Switzerland were, in relative terms, spectacularly successful in dealing with the inflationary shocks of the 1970s. Austria and Norway, less successful on inflation, nevertheless maintained high growth and high employment.[32] Italy and the United Kingdom, with apparently serious problems of volatile inflationary pressure in the late 1960s, stood out as especially inflation-prone in the 1970s. This observation alone suggests that very considerable caution should be exercised in drawing any conclusions about the effectiveness of the particular policies followed after the oil crisis. In particular, no strong conclusions for policy follow from the observation that Germany and Switzerland carried out restrictive policies, and got their inflation down rapidly. This does not mean that similar measures would have been similarly efficacious in other European economies. The ranking of countries was likely to be much as actually occurred, more or less whatever policies were followed.

A notable feature of the experience of Germany and Switzerland was that their exchange rates rose following their response to high inflation. This has raised the question as to whether their high exchange rate policy was, itself, a major reason for success in bringing down price pressures. There has been a tendency to draw the conclusion that the exchange rate is an important link – perhaps the principal link – in the chain of causation between tight policies and progress against inflation. A number of observations are in order:

(i) Whatever the part played in the transmission mechanism by exchange

---

[32] Norway, of course, had the benefit of energy self-sufficiency. This, however, was not a sufficient condition for a continuing good performance, as shown by the example of the United Kingdom in the later 1970s.

rate movements, success in getting down inflation depends ultimately on *domestic* forces. In the case of Germany and Switzerland, it is very unlikely that the exchange rate would have risen as it did in the absence of the widespread expectation that restrictive policies would work in those countries;

(ii) The effect of exchange rate appreciation on real competitiveness in Germany and Switzerland was fairly minor, but an even more dramatic rise in the exchange rate of the United Kingdom in the late 1970s had its chief effect on competitiveness and on output and only a muted influence on inflation;

(iii) Both Germany and Switzerland were shielded from the effects of restrictive policies (which initiated the exchange rate rises) by migrant workers who returned home.

It is thus hard to assess the part played by exchange rate movements in Germany and Switzerland. The upward tendencies may have helped to initiate a 'virtuous' circle – the obverse of the 'vicious' circle of exchange rate falls and domestic inflation feared by more inflation-prone countries. But in both cases it is the domestic situation that is really important. Unless domestic inflation is responsive downwards, no virtuous circle could be maintained; and without the fear that domestic wages would react to exchange rate falls, the vicious circle would not be a worry.

By contrast, Italy, the United Kingdom, and Spain showed tendencies to explosive wage inflation after the oil crisis. In Italy and the United Kingdom, indexation of wages (the *scala mobile* in Italy, the 'threshold' agreements in Britain) was clearly a factor, in that the adverse movement of the terms of trade meant that the implicit guarantees of real wage rises simply could not be sustained. In Spain very strong cost–push pressure reflected not only the oil crisis but also the lifting of the controls established by the Franco regime. Indexation also caused problems in a number of smaller countries. The various attempts at incomes policy packages (e.g. in Scandinavia or in the British Isles) met with varying success. In the United Kingdom, the incomes policy was associated with a very rapid deceleration of wage rises from the peak of 1975; but, as so often, the gains appeared short-lived, with wage inflation rising in 1978-9 in the 'Winter of Discontent'.

A feature of the 1970s is that – looking across countries – the Phillips curve became significantly 'perverse'. Instead of the 'trade-off' relationship that was apparent during the 1950s, high inflation and high unemployment appeared to go together; as did good performance on both these counts (Fig. 3.2). This observation – and a similar change is apparent in time-series data for some European countries – is subject to widely different interpretations.

(i) One possibility, which has been used to justify tight policies, is that high inflation caused high unemployment;

(ii) Another, diametrically opposed, would see such a relationship as the natural result of the policy response to varying degrees of inflationary pressure.

In the experience of European countries over the 1970s and earlier, it is hard to find any support for the first proposition. The evidence, qualitative as it is, suggests that some countries did in fact suffer from relatively little inflationary pressure, or were systematically good at dealing with it. It is quite natural that Germany, Austria, and Switzerland should show a relatively good performance on both counts. In other countries the persistence of inflationary pressure led to greater and greater attempts to constrain it; and greater and greater reliance on the demand management instruments to perform that role. Where incomes policies helped, they were used to bring down both inflation and unemployment.

Conclusions

In evaluating the general trend of European inflation since the war there is an understandable tendency to emphasize two very different strands of that experience. The first is the influence of commodity price rises – especially for oil – which is often put forward as sufficient explanation of the deterioration of the 1970s. The second basically sees the deterioration in price performance as due to the over-ambitious use of the instruments of monetary and fiscal policy in the 1950s and 1960s. This thesis has optimistic and pessimistic variants. To the optimists, better use of monetary and fiscal instruments would allow, after a transition period, a return to non-inflationary growth at some supply-determined rate. To the pessimists, stable prices and high employment are incompatible. The 1970s are seen as the nemesis that followed the hubris of the 1950s and 1960s.

These views are oversimplified. In looking at the influence of commodity prices, it is striking that the principal episodes of European inflation are punctuated by major shocks which are of approximately equal magnitudes. But the Korean War commodity price boom led only to a short-term rise in inflation, whereas the commodity and oil crises of the 1970s appeared to pose altogether more serious problems. One of the explanations, as was seen, was that the terms of trade deterioration in the 1950s was reversed, whereas the oil price rises of the 1970s represented a more permanent shift in international income distribution. But the important lesson is that the economic situation had changed dramatically between the 1950s and 1970s. Clearly, the pressure of demand on resources was higher in the 1970s; and in 1974–5 there was no possibility of a boost to supply comparable to the rise in productivity in the reconstruction period. Even more importantly, however, it does appear that the flexibility and adaptability of European economies had been reduced. The intractable problems of the 1970s can be seen as arising from the interaction of the major relative price changes (and their effects on international income distribution) with domestic problems of cost–push – or 'competing claims' – inflationary pressure. By the end of the 1970s these problems of adaptation threatened growth itself, as attempts to expand seemed to lead to commodity price rises, inflationary responses, and renewed restrictive action.

This raises the second question: to what extent was the underlying deterioration an inevitable consequence of the mistaken use of demand management policy? It would be idle to pretend that there is a clear-cut answer. One aspect that stands out is that, for most European countries, there is evidence for some trade-off between inflation and demand pressure during much of the period. But neither demand pressure, nor monetary or fiscal policy, can easily account for the dramatic deterioration at the end of the 1960s. On the face of it, this episode amply justifies the fears that were expressed at the beginning of the 1960s about cost–push pressure.

It remains, however, hard to discriminate between alternative hypotheses about the cause of the longer-term deterioration. It was related in a complex way to the breakdown of the Bretton Woods system, and to developments in the United States. The cost–push pressure itself could owe something to longer-term changes in the pressure of demand as European reserves of labour were used up. And the rise in aspirations and institutional changes associated with 'competing claims' explanations of inflationary pressure could themselves be a consequence of prolonged high employment and the diminution of economic risk.

What can be said, however, is that little was done to deal with the problems of inflationary pressure that were foreseen in the 1960s. There was, of course, considerable divergence of view as to whether the remedy lay in tolerating somewhat higher unemployment, or more fundamentally in some sort of wages policy, or even in curbing union power. But for most of the 1960s there was no willingness to countenance lower pressure of demand: on the contrary, the ambition of the authorities actually increased. And whilst the possible incompatibility of full employment and price stability was well recognized, the inflationary pressures perceived at the start of the 1960s were allowed to persist through the decade.

The early 1970s saw a worsening of the situation as mistakes in policy and exogenous events were superimposed on the earlier and accelerating inflationary trend. After a period of hesitation, in which countries' reactions differed, most governments in the second half of the 1970s moved to a much tighter policy stance. An important reason for the uniformity of response was the unfavourable experience of those countries which had attempted offsetting policies after the oil crisis of 1974. Eventually, external problems and the persistence of inflation meant that they were dragged into recession anyway – and in many cases forced to deflate further. It appeared that countries such as Germany and Switzerland which had deflated early on had ended up with lower inflation and lower unemployment. Although in the higher inflation countries there was little evidence that inflation was responsive to monetary targets or to the pressure of demand, international experience within Europe seemed to suggest that toughness paid off, even to the extent of reversing the normal 'trade-off'. And this view was reinforced by the 'accelerationist' thesis, that unless inflationary pressure was dealt with, then it would get worse.

There is a very important question as to whether European experience justifies the kind of lessons that were drawn from it in the late 1970s. Looking back to the Bretton Woods period, superficial examination suggested that the fixed exchange rate system had succeeded, and that European inflation rates were kept within fairly narrow bounds. In fact, however, the notable thing about that period was the wide range of experience that went with relative fixity of exchange rates. Not only did economies vary greatly in the weight they put on different types of policy (e.g. incomes policy versus demand management), but the problems faced, and the degree of overall success also differed. And from this broader perspective, what stands out is not the changes in the 1970s, but the continuity within countries of overall performance. To state the obvious, Germany and Switzerland stand out as having had little inflationary pressure in the 1960s and as having had good performance in the 1970s. But good perform-ance in both periods is a characteristic too of some of the countries which relied on incomes policy — Austria is the outstanding example. And problems of wage pressure, unresolved in the 1960s in France, Italy, and the United Kingdom, persisted in the 1970s.

This persistence suggests a strongly negative conclusion: it is highly dangerous to draw general lessons for policy from the experience of particular countries — such as Germany. There are no easy panaceas to be transplanted from one country to another. Rather, the inflationary problem appears deeply rooted in the social and institutional structures of European economies, and its control is ultimately a domestic problem. It appears self-evident that the extent of the underlying difficulty differs between countries, and that the appropriate policy response may differ also. What works in one country may not work in·another.

What, then, should be made of the trend during the 1970s towards greater reliance on demand management policy to control inflation — with, in many cases, explicit or implicit commitments to monetary or exchange rate targets? To an extent, of course, it can be explained in terms of purposeful policy in the less inflation-prone countries, and as an inevitable response in the others. But there appears more to it than that. It would be widely agreed that in the absence of other ways of dealing with inflationary pressure — such as incomes policy — a non-accommodating demand management stance is, in practice, inevitable. Consensus in Europe at the start of the 1980s appeared to reflect the absence of alternatives to demand management policy rather than genuine optimism that it would bring down inflation at acceptable cost.

Bibliography

To obtain an idea of the course of inflation over the post-war period and of the climate of ideas surrounding the various inflationary episodes, a very good starting-point is provided by the three special reports provided by the OECD: W. Fellner *et al.*, *The Problem of Rising Prices*, Paris 1964 (A Report of a Group of Experts to the OEEC originally published in 1961); *Inflation: The Present Problem*, Paris 1970 (written by the Organization's Secretariat), and P. Mc-Cracken *et al.*, *Towards Full Employment and Price Stability*, Paris 1977 (ano-ther report by a Group of Experts, concerned not only with inflation, but also with more general issues of economic policy). Another international survey of inflationary trends is contained in UNECE, *Incomes in Post-war Europe*, Geneva 1967, which looks at wage and price developments from the early 1950s to the mid-1960s.

Among more academic contributions, an important volume surveying theories and the evidence of four European countries (France, Germany, Sweden, and the United Kingdom, usually from the late 1950s to the mid-1970s) is L.B. Krause and W.S. Salant (eds.), *Worldwide Inflation*, Brookings Institution, Washington 1977. Several American studies of international inflation in a com-parative framework are: W.D. Nordhaus, 'The Worldwide Wage Explosion'; G.L. Perry, 'Determinants of Wage Inflation around the World'; and R.J. Gordon,

'World Inflation and Monetary Accommodation in Eight Countries', all in *Brookings Papers on Economic Activity* (No. 2, 1972; No. 2, 1975; and No. 2, 1977 respectively). Further, largely American, views are contained in D.I. Meiselman and A.B. Laffer (eds.), *The Phenomenon of Worldwide Inflation*, Washington 1975. A European survey is provided by G. Maynard and W. van Rijckeghem, *A World of Inflation*, London 1976. A collection of papers with greater emphasis on policy issues is E. Lundberg (ed.), *Inflation Theory and Anti-Inflation Policy*, London 1977.

The 'differential productivity growth' or 'structural' analysis of inflation was first put forward in Scandinavia by O. Aukrust (see, for instance, his contribution to the Krause and Salant volume mentioned above) and by G. Edgren, K.-O. Faxén, and C.E. Odhner, *Wage Formation and the Economy*, London 1973; it has been tested by e.g. J. Eatwell, J. Llewellyn, and R. Tarling, 'Money Wage Inflation in Industrial Countries', in *Review of Economic Studies*, No. 4, 1974, or G. Maynard and W. van Rijckeghem, 'Why Inflation Rates Differ: A Critical Examination of the Structuralist Hypothesis', in H. Frisch (ed.), *Inflation in Small Countries*, Berlin 1976. The 'tax–push' inflation hypothesis was first put forward in D. Jackson, H.A. Turner, and F. Wilkinson, *Do Trade Unions Cause Inflation*, University of Cambridge Department of Applied Economics, Cambridge 1972, and some international tests for it can be found in OECD, *Public Expenditure Trends*, Paris 1978. The monetarist interpretation has a long history (and a fuller bibliography is provided at the end of Ch. 4 below); a representative work of this approach is M. Parkin and G. Zis (eds.), *Inflation in the World Economy*, Manchester 1976.

4

Inflation – a Monetarist Interpretation

ALAN BUDD and GEOFFREY DICKS*

Introduction

The aim of this chapter is neither to praise monetarism nor to bury it. It would obviously be wrong to suggest that there has been one single or simple cause of all price developments in Europe since the war. The intention here is to examine the part played by the money supply in the history of inflation. In the three decades covered by this survey the average rate of inflation rose from about 3¼ to 3½ per cent in the 1950s and 1960s to some 8½ to 9 per cent in the 1970s. In addition, the divergence between the inflation rates of individual countries increased markedly in the more recent period. It will be shown that these broad developments can be explained by the course of monetary policy. Even where the inflationary impulse had some other cause, sustained inflation was only possible when monetary policy accommodated it.

The arrangement of the chapter is as follows. The first section sets out an eclectic monetarist theory of inflation under fixed and flexible exchange rates.[1] The second part looks at the general history of prices in Europe between 1950 and 1979. The third part explores the connection between the money supply and the experience of inflation, and the Conclusions summarize the various arguments.

I. Inflation Under Fixed and Flexible Exchange Rates

The monetary approach to inflation

It is generally recognized that two elements are sufficient to establish the link between the growth of the money supply and the rate of inflation in a *closed economy*: the 'Quantity Theory of Money' and the 'Natural Rate of Unemployment' hypothesis. The first refers to the determinants of the demand for money and the second to the determination of the level of output. The modern version of the 'Quantity Theory' states that the demand for money is a stable function of nominal income, and, in its crudest version, only of nominal income. From this it must follow that changes in the supply of money result in changes in nominal income. A more general form relates the demand for money to nominal income and interest rates. The link between changes in money supply and nominal income is then less direct and will depend on the interest elasticity of the demand for money and on the extent to which interest rates can vary. The greater the interest elasticity, the smaller the required change in nominal income

---

* London Business School.

[1] For some of the main sources of this theory, see the bibliography at the end of this chapter.

to restore equilibrium, the extreme case being that of the Keynesian 'liquidity trap' in which the interest elasticity is infinite. However, in an open economy at least, it could be argued that interest rates cannot change because, for example, of international capital movements; it then follows that the impact of changes in the money supply would again fall entirely on nominal income.

The 'Quantity Theory' on its own does not provide a theory of inflation but only of nominal income. The 'Natural Rate' hypothesis completes the picture by offering a theory of real output. The hypothesis is largely a restatement of the neo-classical view of the operation of the labour market in which the supply and demand for labour depend on real wages. In the short term, employees may confuse nominal wage changes with real wage changes and may mistakenly work for lower real wages than they intended. If employers are able to change prices rapidly there can be a period in which output and employment are raised above their equilibrium levels. During this period an increase in the money supply raises both nominal and real output. But in the longer term, employees adjust their nominal wage claims and output and unemployment are restored to their 'natural' levels. In the longer term, therefore, changes in the money supply affect prices and nominal incomes but not real incomes.

While the 'Natural Rate' hypothesis suggests that there can be a short-run real response to changes in the money supply, more recent theoretical developments, associated with the idea of 'rational expectations', object even to this.[2] The 'rational expectations' school questions whether economic agents will make mistakes in response to systematic movements in economic policy. It distinguishes between anticipated and unanticipated changes in the money supply and argues that only the latter can lead to changes in output (the former resulting entirely in changes in prices even in the short run). The distinction between the simple monetarist approach and the stronger version presented by the 'rational expectations' school relates to short-term dynamics rather than to the longer-term behaviour with which this chapter is concerned. However, the 'rational expectations' approach does have two important implications. The first is that it suggests an alternative transmission mechanism from money to prices. Economic agents will adjust their prices rapidly to changes in the money supply because they anticipate that the ultimate effect will fall on prices. This is not a question of a self-fulfilling prophecy but of rational behaviour in the light of the assumed properties of the economy. The second implication is that agents will learn from experience. Thus lags between changes in the money supply and changes in prices are likely to shorten after an episode of inflation.

Turning now to inflation in an *open economy*, a crucial distinction must be made between a system of floating and one of fixed exchange rates. For purposes of exposition it is easiest to start from the simplest monetarist case in which it is assumed that money is the only financial asset and that changes in the money supply leave all real quantities (including relative prices) unchanged.

[2] See, for instance, T.J. Sargent and N. Wallace, ' "Rational Expectations," the Optimal Monetary Instrument and the Optimal Money Supply Role', *Journal of Political Economy*, April 1975, and 'Rational Expectations and the Theory of Economic Policy', *Journal of Monetary Economics*, April 1976.

This, it should be emphasized, is not essential to the argument, but simplifies the comparison between fixed and flexible exchange rates.

In the case of *flexible exchange rates*, a change in the money supply that led to absolute but not relative price changes at home would imply that the relative prices of domestic goods and of foreign tradeable goods also remained unchanged. Since the prices of foreign goods, in terms of their own currencies, can be assumed to be unchanged, the adjustment must come through a variation in the exchange rate. Thus, under flexible rates, each country's inflation rate will depend on the growth of its money supply. The exchange rate will change to maintain constancy of relative prices with foreign goods.

Under *fixed exchange rates* there appears to be a problem. If the money supply rises, domestic prices – according to the theory – should rise. But if foreign prices are unchanged and if the exchange rate is fixed, a change in domestic prices will change relative prices. The solution to the problem, provided by the simple version of the 'monetary theory of the balance of payments', is that the domestic money supply cannot change. In other words, under fixed exchange rates an economy cannot control its own money supply. If it attempts to expand the money supply beyond the level determined by international conditions, the result will be a deficit in the balance of payments, a loss in reserves, and an eventual return of the money supply to its original level in view of the following (over-simplified) monetary identity:

Changes in money supply (ΔM) = Domestic credit expansion (DCE)
plus change in reserves (ΔR).

Though the authorities can change domestic credit expansion, the equilibrium level of the money supply is determined by the level of nominal income. Since under fixed exchange rates it is assumed that prices cannot change, and since, for the moment, output cannot change either, an increase in domestic credit expansion can only result in a loss of reserves.

There is thus an extreme contrast between flexible and fixed exchange rates. Under the former an economy can choose its own monetary growth and hence its own rate of inflation; under the latter a country loses control over its own monetary growth and its inflation rate will depend on that in the rest of the world.

This simple approach immediately suggests that any study of inflation in Europe must distinguish broadly between two periods. The first – till 1971-2 – was in principle the era of the 'adjustable peg' in which exchange rates could be changed, but only under rather exceptional circumstances. This period is, therefore, relatively close to the case of fixed exchange rates. The second period – covering most of the 1970s – was one of floating rates. Though flexibility was only occasionally complete and though there was a considerable amount of intervention as well as attempts, most notably in Europe, to re-establish some kind of adjustable peg system, these years none the less approximate the flexible exchange rate case. If the simple monetarist approach is correct, one would expect to find inflation rates in Europe clustering fairly close together in the first period, and one should be able to explain much of the inflation by developments in Europe as a whole. In the second period, however, the European dimension should be far less significant, since countries were allowed far greater freedom to pursue their own monetary policies. If they used this freedom one would expect to find much greater inter-country divergence with respect to inflation than in the 1950s and 1960s. (It does not necessarily follow, however, that inflation rates will have diverged under flexible rates, since economies could have maintained policies which were consistent with unchanged exchange rates.)

It should be noted that although the emphasis has been on the crucial difference between inflation under fixed and flexible exchange rates, the historical evidence may not distinguish between them so clearly. In the case of flexible exchange rates it has been suggested that there is a causal link between the growth of a country's money supply and its inflation. In the case of fixed exchange rates such a causal link has been denied, since the inflation rate is set by conditions in the world. However, the equilibrium conditions will look exactly the same. Under fixed rates there will be an observed relationship between money supply and inflation, although it is the money supply which (according to the monetary theory of the balance of payments) is endogenous and the inflation rate which is exogenous.

From theory to practice

The preceding brief account has relied on an extremely simple monetary theory, which has assumed, *inter alia*, that money is the only financial asset and that changes in the money supply leave real variables unchanged. Neither assumption is correct, but their relaxation does not invalidate the usefulness of the monetary approach in general as an explanation of the inflationary process.

If one introduces other financial assets which are substitutes for money, the impact of a change in the money supply need no longer fall wholly on the level of nominal income, but could also affect interest rates (provided, as mentioned earlier, that these can change). The recognition of the existence of other financial assets has two implications. First, an increase in the money supply, on its own, may not result in a proportionate increase in nominal income. Second, a change in the supply of other financial assets – for example government securities – may also cause a change in nominal income. These are important qualifications to the simple monetarist approach, but they are not crucial for a long-term study of this kind. It can be plausibly argued that there are constraints in terms of portfolio behaviour which bind the growth of the money supply and the size of public sector debt in the long term.

The second major simplification was to assume that changes in the money supply could not alter real output. Few would deny that such changes have short-run effects on output (though as mentioned earlier, the 'rational expectations' school would argue that only unexpected changes can do this). It is less clear, however, whether they can influence longer-run output levels. If, in response to money supply changes, real interest rates also changed, then the allocation of resources and the structure of output would almost certainly alter. It is possible that the level of output might also change in the long term, but such effects are highly unlikely to have been major factors in determining economic growth and can, therefore, be safely ignored.

Two further assumptions of the simple theory, which are not necessarily true in practice, affect the application of the model to the fixed exchange rate case. The theory asserts, firstly, that changes in money supply leave relative prices unchanged, yet the relationship between domestic and foreign prices, in particular, could alter so that in the short run at least a country may be able to generate its own rate of inflation. Secondly, it is argued that the money supply is not under the control of the authorities. This implication follows from the assumptions that domestic prices are determined by world prices and that the level of output depends on real conditions. But it has already been suggested that domestic prices can move independently of world prices in the short run. It is also true that output can change in the short term in response to fiscal and monetary policies. And, finally, the authorities also retain some control over the money supply since the effects of reserve changes can be 'sterilized' by appropriate open-market operations, at least in the short term. What is important to note from these various points, for the purposes of this survey, is that even under fixed rates, domestic inflation need not be tied rigidly to world inflation.

The division of the period into two stylized regimes – of fixed and flexible rates – is another oversimplification. The first period was in principle the era of the adjustable peg, and exchange rate adjustments, though rare, did occur. The second period saw considerable intervention and floating was far from 'clean'.

These various complications raise two types of difficulty. The first is that, because the monetarist approach is greatly oversimplified, it may appear to fail even though it is correct. This possibility, however, seems fairly small, particularly if monetarism is treated as a long-term theory. Most of the complications listed are short-term in their effect. The second type of difficulty is that the theory may appear to succeed even though it is false. Partly this is a question of causality, which is discussed below. More importantly, there is a basic difficulty in so far as the approach presents a theory of inflation but not one of output, apart from the hypothesis of a 'natural rate' (whose level is, in any case, not explained). It is possible that monetary expansion does cause real growth. Casual evidence suggests otherwise, since the slower growth of the 1970s was associated with higher monetary growth, but it can still be argued that real growth would have been lower if monetary growth had been lower. Though this looks improbable, it cannot be refuted.

The problem of causation is insoluble. It is fairly easy to show an empirical relationship between the rate of inflation and the growth of the money supply in the long term. The present approach sets out a theory which suggests that causation runs from money to prices. Many argue that the causation runs in the opposite direction. An alternative approach, for instance, is that inflation has some exogenous source (e.g. trade-union militancy) which raises nominal income and hence the demand for money. The money is supplied by the banking system (helped, if necessary, by the government) and the money supply rises to accommodate higher prices. In other words, the observed increase in the money supply arises from an increase in demand. By contrast, the monetary approach emphasizes that changes in the supply of money are the independent source of price changes and that governments can, in principle, control this supply. If there have been independent causes of inflation which have been accommodated, this must be seen as an implied choice by governments. As far as possible, reasons will be provided in the course of the narrative that follows for arguing either that monetary shocks have been the prime cause of inflation, or that monetary accommodation has allowed inflation to continue, but it is readily admitted that this will not fully solve the causation problem.

Before turning to this narrative, two further practical problems must be tackled:

(i) The relationship between domestic and world money supply, particularly under fixed exchange rates;

(ii) The possibility of differences in international inflation rates arising from differences in productivity growth rates.

It was argued earlier that, under fixed exchange rates, the basic simple identity:

$$\Delta M = DCE + \Delta R$$

implies that the change in the money supply is endogenous. Excess domestic credit expansion must result in a fall in reserves. But if one country is losing reserves, another country must be gaining them. Unless the gaining country (or countries) can sterilize the effect of the reserve increase, it will experience an increase in its money supply with a consequent increase in the world's money supply. It may appear from this that any country can cause an increase in the world money supply through its own credit policies and that, indeed, some of the increase will accrue to the initiating country. However, that can only be true to the extent that a country's own currency will be held as a foreign currency reserve abroad. The most important example of the latter case in the post-war period was that of the United States, which until 1971-2 provided the main source of international reserves. In other words, the United States had the power to determine the world's money supply and hence the world rate of inflation.

The special role of the United States – and hence its importance in the history of inflation in Europe – was derived from two separate but closely related factors. The first, as mentioned above, was its position as a source of international reserves. The demand for international reserves is, presumably, a demand for *real* reserves in relation to the real level of international trade. If world prices double, the demand for international reserves, in nominal terms, will more or less also double. Thus the United States was able, in principle, to adopt policies which allowed it to run a large balance of payments deficit, in the confident belief that other countries would acquire additional dollars to finance the United States-induced inflation.[3] The second factor which gave the United States its special role was that it was the dominant economy in the Bretton Woods system. As dominant economy it was able to set its credit policies towards the aim of domestic price stability and/or short-term demand stabilization, while other economies set their policies towards the objective of exchange rate stability (together, if need be, with an objective for the level of reserves). Thus, until 1971-2 the United States set the inflation rate for much of the world.

Turning to the second problem, it was suggested that under a system of fixed exchange rates domestic inflation would depend on world inflation. One might deduce from this that all linked economies would have approximately the same

---

[3] This is analogous to the power a domestic monetary authority may have simultaneously to generate inflation and ensure that the excess money which caused the inflation will be held by the public.

rate of inflation. Yet even under fixed exchange rates there may be systematic differences. The central idea is that the relative prices of traded and non-traded goods may change through time.[4] Broadly speaking, international competition will ensure that all countries will experience the same rate of inflation as far as traded goods are concerned, but that need not apply to non-traded goods nor to wages (unless there is complete international mobility of all factors).

If profit shares are constant, one would expect to see wages rise most rapidly in those countries with the most rapid growth of productivity. If it is further assumed, as a first approximation, that the rate of increase of wages is the same in all industries within an economy and that productivity growth in non-traded goods is lower than productivity growth in traded goods, it will then follow that the highest rate of inflation in the non-traded goods sector will be in the economies with the most rapid growth of productivity. Thus the *overall* rate of inflation (of traded and non-traded goods) will also tend to be highest in those economies with the most rapid productivity growth even under fixed rates of exchange. This general result should also hold under flexible exchange rates when inflation is measured in terms of a world currency.

II. Inflation in Europe, 1950–1979

This section examines the course of prices in Europe as a whole over the last three decades.[5] The second half of the 1940s, when the European economy was recovering from the war, is ignored, and the narrative begins in 1950 (a year when prices were falling) and ends with 1979 (when the rate of inflation was accelerating back into double figures). In keeping with the spirit of this chapter the analysis restricts itself to trying to answer the question: to what extent can movements in the European price level be explained by prior movements in the money supply?

Over the whole of the thirty-year period European consumer price inflation averaged close to 5 per cent per annum, with the rate rising from just under 3 per cent in the 1950s to just over 3 per cent in the 1960s and 8½ per cent in the 1970s (Table 4.1). Over the same period money supply rose at an average rate of nearly 9 per cent on a narrow definition and of over 11 per cent on a broader definition. On each definition there was an acceleration (from 6½ per cent in the 1950s to 8 per cent in the 1960s and 11¾ per cent in the 1970s on the narrow definition and from 8½ to 10½ and 14 per cent respectively on the broad definition). It is immediately clear therefore that the 1970s' inflation rate was 5½ per cent per annum higher than that of the 1950s and that this was *associated* with a 5½ per cent per annum increase in the rate of monetary growth.

Table 4.1 also shows that while the growth of nominal output accelerated in line with that of the money supply from 9–9½ per cent in the 1950s and 1960s to 12½ per cent in the 1970s, real growth declined from an average of 5 per cent

---

[4] For a further discussion see B. Balassa, 'The Purchasing-Power Parity Doctrine: A Reappraisal', *Journal of Political Economy*, December 1964; T. Burns, P.W.M. Lobban, and P.J. Warburton, 'Forecasting the Real Exchange Rate', *London Business School Economic Outlook*, October 1977.

[5] In this section 'Europe' consists of the following nine countries: France, Germany, Italy, the United Kingdom, Belgium, Denmark, the Netherlands, Norway, and Sweden.

TABLE 4.1. *Longer-run trends in Europe*[a]
(average annual percentage changes)

	1950–79	1950–59	1959–69	1961–79
Inflation[b]	4.9	2.9	3.2	8.5
Money supply – M 1[c]	8.9[d]	6.5[e]	7.7	11.8
– M 2[c]	11.2[d]	8.4[e]	10.6	13.8
GDP – nominal	10.3	9.4	9.0	12.5
– real	4.4	5.2	4.9	3.2
Excess monetary growth[f] – M 1	4.5	1.3	2.8	8.6
– M 2	6.8	3.2	5.7	10.6

Note: totals may at times differ from those provided in other chapters because of the
somewhat more restricted coverage of Europe here used. For detail on the various
series shown, see Appendix to this chapter.
[a] Sum of nine countries (the four major economies, the Benelux, Denmark, Norway, and
Sweden)
[b] Consumer prices
[c] M 1 and M 2 stand for the narrow and broader definitions of the money supply
respectively
[d] 1952–79   [e] 1952–59
[f] Growth of money supply less growth of real GDP
Source: IMF, *International Financial Statistics* (1980 Yearbook).

in the 1950s and 1960s to 3¼ per cent in the last decade. As a result, the acceleration in 'excess' monetary growth, i.e. the difference between nominal
monetary growth and the rate of growth of real output, was even more pronounced. On the narrow definition it rose from 1¼ per cent in the 1950s to
8½ per cent in the 1970s; on the broader definition from 3 to 10½ per cent. The
correlation over long periods between excess monetary growth and the rate of
inflation seems therefore particularly close.

Fixed exchange rates, 1950–71

In the first two decades of the period the world economy was by and large
operating a fixed exchange rate regime. Over the twenty years there were only a
few parity changes, of which the main ones were: the devaluation of the French
franc in 1957–8 and again in August 1969; the revaluations of the Deutschmark
and the Dutch guilder in March 1961; the DM revaluation of 1969; and the devaluations of the pound and the Danish krone in November 1967. As a result of
these parity changes, Europe's exchange rate against the dollar moved from 100
in 1950 to 93 by the early 1970s, a fall of 7 per cent or 0.3 per cent per annum
(Appendix Table 4.A2). For Europe as a whole therefore it is not inappropriate
to treat this period as one in which currencies were fixed to the dollar.

The theory set out in Section I suggests that monetary growth and inflation
in Europe should have moved broadly in line with what was happening in the
United States during the two decades. European consumer price inflation could,
however, have been somewhat more rapid, partly because productivity growth
was higher in Europe than in the United States and partly because the (small)
fall in the exchange rate would have permitted faster price increases in some
countries. In fact, over the twenty-two years United States inflation averaged
2½ per cent per annum and European inflation 3½ per cent or, when account

is taken of European devaluations, just over 3 per cent in dollar terms. Figure 4.1 also shows that on a cyclical basis, and even on a year-to-year basis, price improvements in Europe corresponded quite closely with United States price changes. In 1951, all countries experienced the rapid inflation consequent upon the Korean War. In the mid-1950s the inflation rate came down sharply, but accelerated again with demand pressures in 1956-7. In the (trough-to-trough) cycles of 1958-62, 1963-6, and 1967-71, the inflationary experience was common to both Europe and the United States. Although beyond the scope of this chapter, one could present a simple theory of the cycle in terms of the policy reactions to inflation and unemployment. At the trough, inflation is low and unemployment high. Governments relax their fiscal and monetary policies, producing first an increase in real growth and later an acceleration of inflation. They then respond to accelerating price increases by deflationary policies which reduce output and inflation. The whole process takes about four years.

Figure 4.1 also shows the ratio of European to United States prices, both measured in dollars. This ratio rose more or less steadily from 0.75 in 1950 to a peak of 0.89 in the mid-1960s. Movements around the trend line reflect the lags between exchange rate changes and price movements. Thus, the fall in the European exchange rate against the dollar in the late 1950s allowed European prices to rise relatively more rapidly in the early 1960s. From 1967 onwards, however, United States inflation was generally faster than European inflation as a result

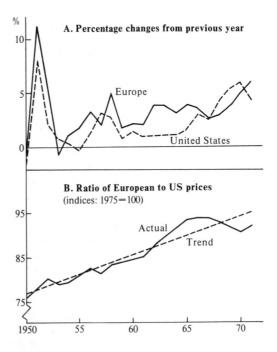

FIG. 4.1. *Inflation in Europe and in the United States* (consumer prices)
Source: IMF, *International Financial Statistics* (1980 Yearbook).

of expansionary policies associated in particular with the Vietnam War. By the end of the 1960s the strains on the fixed exchange rate regime were becoming apparent and led to the Smithsonian realignment of December 1971, which in effect ratified the United States' expansionary stance and allowed the European economies to adopt less inflationary policies. Since 1972 the world has been operating under a floating exchange rate regime.

Having seen how inflation in Europe and North America moved very much in line in the 1950s and 1960s, the text now turns to the experience of individual European countries (Table 4. A3 in the Appendix). If this experience is traced chronologically through the fixed rate period it is clear that price movements had much in common between countries. Thus in 1951 there was a generalized and major inflationary upturn as a consequence of the Korean War, with European consumer prices rising on average by 11 per cent and the range going from 7.8 per cent in Germany to 17.6 per cent in France. The rate of inflation was sharply reduced in the next two years and so was inter-country dispersion, which, in 1953, went from only −2.1 per cent (France) to 1.7 per cent (Norway). For the rest of the decade European inflation continued to move in a very narrow range. The exception was France in 1958-9, when inflation rose to over 20 per cent following a series of devaluations which, in 1957-8, had reduced the value of the franc by nearly 30 per cent against the dollar. These in turn had resulted from the policies of the government which had increased military and social expenditure in 1955-6. In the words of Hansen, the spending spree was 'probably the worst' set of budget policies he encountered in his study of European fiscal policy.[6] As a result the balance of payments moved heavily into deficit, the franc was devalued, and the money supply increased to validate the higher price level.

The cyclical growth in output in the early 1960s produced an equivalent acceleration in inflation in all countries, so that by 1962-3 European inflation had doubled from under 2 per cent in 1959 to nearly 4 per cent. Similar increases were recorded in individual countries. In Germany, for example, inflation rose from under 1 per cent in 1959 to 3 per cent in 1962, even though the DM had been revalued against the dollar by 5 per cent. For the United Kingdom, the movement was from under 1 to 4 per cent, for Italy from −½ to 7½ per cent, and so on. For the rest of the 1960s European inflation remained in the 2½-4 per cent range. There was some acceleration in Britain and Denmark due to the November 1967 devaluation, and in France, where the authorities pursued deliberately expansionary monetary policies after the May 1968 strikes in order to promote the revival of activity and to accommodate the higher wage settlements.[7] By the early 1970s the strains of the fixed exchange rate system were also becoming evident within Europe, with the move to higher and more varied inflation rates. By 1971-2 European inflation had moved up to 6 per cent and all countries had participated in this – the 1971-2 range went from the Belgian 5.4 per cent (cyclical) peak to the United Kingdom's 9.4 per cent (cyclical) peak. But it was only in the post-Smithsonian era that really marked intra-European divergences began to emerge.

[6] B. Hansen, *Fiscal Policy in Seven Countries, 1955-1965*, OECD, Paris 1969, p. 172.
[7] OECD, *Monetary Policy in France*, Paris 1974.

Floating exchange rates, 1972–79

Under a flexible exchange-rate regime the theory of Section I suggests that inter-country rates of inflation will differ according to relative rates of monetary growth, transmitted on to prices generally, but not exclusively, by way of exchange rate movements. As such there is no a priori expectation that European inflation should be related to inflation in the United States, nor indeed that prices in individual European countries should move in line with prices in other countries, since each government was free to choose its own monetary policy and hence, from a monetarist viewpoint, its own exchange and inflation rates.

TABLE 4.2. *Changes between the fixed and floating exchange rate periods*[a]
(differences in average annual percentage changes)

	M 1[b]	M 2[b]	GDP	Excess monetary growth[c]	Inflation[d]
France	−0.1	2.1	−1.3	3.4	4.0
Germany	−0.1	−3.1	−3.7	0.6	3.2
Italy	7.2	5.1	−2.6	7.7	9.0
United Kingdom	10.0	10.0	−0.6	10.6	9.0
Belgium	3.5	4.7	−0.3	5.0	4.9
Denmark	3.4	3.6	−1.4	5.0	4.8
Netherlands	4.2	5.0	−1.3	6.3	3.2
Norway	5.0	6.5	−1.1	7.6	4.2
Sweden	4.6	2.8	−2.0	4.8	4.6
Total	4.6	4.1	−1.9	6.0	5.4

[a] Defined as the years 1950–69 and 1969–79 respectively
[b] M 1 and M 2 stand for the narrow and broader definitions of the money supply respectively
[c] Growth of M 2 less growth of GDP
[d] Consumer prices
Source: IMF, *International Financial Statistics* (1980 Yearbook).

A comparison of the fixed and floating rate years is presented in Table 4.2, which shows that the change in experience of the European countries between the two periods was remarkably similar. All countries recorded higher rates of inflation in the 1970s than in the previous two decades. The increases range from 3¼ per cent per annum in the case of Germany and the Netherlands to 9 per cent for the United Kingdom and Italy. Nearly all countries also used their new freedom to expand their money supplies more rapidly than in the 1950s and 1960s. At the same time — the monetarist would argue in consequence — as Table 4.3 shows, exchange rates were also much more volatile in this period. Thus, relative to its trading partners, Germany's exchange rate appreciated by 5½ per cent per annum over the years 1970-9, while Italy's exchange rate fell by 6½ per cent per annum over the same period. All countries also experienced a slower underlying rate of economic growth in the 1970s. Compared with the 1950s and 1960s, Germany's monetary growth, for example, was 3.1 per cent lower on the broad measure in the 1970s, while output was 3.7 per cent lower,

TABLE 4.3. *Effective exchange rates*
(indices: 1970 = 100)

	France	Germany	Italy	United Kingdom	Belgium	Denmark	Netherlands	Norway	Sweden
1971	98.5	103.7	98.9	100.2	100.3	99.4	101.1	99.4	99.9
1972	101.8	107.2	98.6	96.9	103.3	100.1	102.5	100.1	102.0
1973	106.4	119.4	68.8	87.7	104.4	106.6	105.8	104.9	103.8
1974	99.4	125.6	81.1	85.0	105.5	107.4	111.8	111.1	103.7
1975	109.4	127.7	77.9	78.5	106.6	111.3	113.6	114.6	109.0
1976	103.8	132.4	63.8	66.4	107.1	113.7	115.9	116.0	109.4
1977	98.4	143.2	58.7	63.1	111.9	114.0	121.6	116.7	106.1
1978	98.7	153.3	55.9	64.0	114.9	115.0	124.6	108.4	98.5
1979	100.4	162.4	54.7	68.9	116.8	114.9	127.0	107.4	100.6
1970–79[a]	–	5.5	−6.5	−4.0	1.7	1.6	2.7	0.8	–

[a] Average annual percentage changes
Source: IMF, *International Financial Statistics* (1980 Yearbook).

so that there was a small increase in excess monetary growth. On this basis (the change in excess monetary growth) the range went from Germany with 0.6 per cent to the United Kingdom with 10.6 per cent per annum.

In the 1970s, therefore, Europe experienced higher inflation associated with more rapid monetary growth, lower output growth, and consequently even more rapid growth of excess money. The years of rapid monetary growth were the early 1970s, especially 1972-3, and the years of rapid inflation were 1974-5. Most governments responded to the acceleration of inflation by pursuing tighter monetary policies, in many cases consistently over the remainder of the decade. In other cases, notably the Scandinavian countries, monetary policy was either not significantly tightened in 1973-5 (Sweden) or tightened initially but relaxed in 1975-6 (Denmark, Norway). It was in these countries too that exchange rates fell sharply in the late 1970s (with the exception of Denmark) and where inflation accelerated in 1976-7. In all the other European countries covered here inflation was on a downward path from 1974-5 to 1979.

The next section considers how far these developments under the periods of fixed and flexible exchange rates justify the monetarist approach to inflation.

III. The Monetarist Explanation of European Inflation

The preceding section (and the Appendix) have set out the salient historical data on price movements, exchange rates, and money supplies in nine European countries and in the United States in the post-war period. These figures will now be examined from the monetarist perspective. The theoretical analysis of Section I emphasized the difference between a fixed and a flexible exchange rate regime. In the former the monetarist argument is that, given a stable demand for money, prices in a closed economy (i.e. the world economy under fixed exchange rates) depend upon the world money supply, and that, as far as an individual country is concerned, its money supply is given and any excess of domestic credit expansion merely results in a deficit in the balance of payments.

For the individual economy, therefore, the prices of traded goods depend, in the long run, on world prices. There will however be trend differences in consumer price inflation between countries as a result of differential rates of productivity growth, and short-run differences because the adjustment from world to domestic prices does not occur instantaneously. In a flexible exchange rate regime, on the other hand, the individual country regains control of its own money supply and does not therefore have to accept the world rate of inflation. By expanding its money supply relatively more slowly (quickly) than other countries it can achieve a relatively slower (faster) rate of inflation with its exchange rate rising (falling) in the process.

It is clear from this that the monetarist diagnosis of inflation subsumes a number of separate hypotheses. It requires, as a necessary condition, the existence of a well-defined, stable demand-for-money function. 'Strong evidence in support of the thesis that such a function exists' was provided by one investigation made for the world economy under fixed exchange rates.[8] Given this, a further study of the determination of wage and price inflation at the world level concluded that both of these could be explained by the excess demand-expectations model (i.e. a monetarist approach in contrast to a socio-political approach to wage determination).[9] Cross and Laidler,[10] using a methodology which Laidler had already shown to be valid for the United States[11] — a good approximation to the closed economy — and applying it to twenty industrialized countries, also found that domestic rates of inflation were sensitive to excess demand and to the expected inflation rate. These results are strengthened by an analysis of variance approach, which found no statistical difference in the rate of inflation in sixteen OECD countries.[12] Spitäller extended the period under examination to span the flexible exchange rate years to 1976, and found for the seven major industrial economies that 'money changes appear to affect the rate of inflation in all countries except Italy, but even there results are plausible, if insignificant statistically'.[13] Finally, it should also be noted that other researchers have found empirical validity in the monetary approach to the balance of payments.[14]

There is therefore a considerable body of evidence in support of the monetarist

[8] M.R. Gray, R. Ward, and G. Zis, 'The World Demand for Money Function: Some Preliminary Results', in M. Parkin and G. Zis (eds.), *Inflation in the World Economy*, Manchester 1976, p. 173.

[9] N. Duck, M. Parkin, D. Rose, and G. Zis, 'The Determination of the Rate of Change of Wages and Prices in the Fixed Exchange Rate World Economy, 1956–71', in Parkin and Zis, *Inflation in the World Economy*.

[10] R. Cross and D. Laidler, 'Inflation, Excess Demand and Expectations in Fixed Exchange Rate Open Economies: Some Preliminary Empirical Results', in Parkin and Zis, *Inflation in the World Economy*.

[11] D. Laidler, 'The Influence of Money on Real Income and Inflation — A Simple Model with some Empirical Evidence for the United States, 1953–72', *Manchester School*, December 1973.

[12] H. Genberg, 'A Note on Inflation Rates Under Fixed Exchange Rates', in Parkin and Zis, *Inflation in the World Economy*.

[13] E. Spitäller, 'A Model of Inflation and its Performance in the Seven Main Industrialised Countries, 1958–76', *IMF Staff Papers*, June 1978, p. 270.

[14] See, for instance, M.E. Kreinin and L.H. Officer, 'The Monetary Approach to the Balance of Payments: A Survey', *Princeton Studies in International Finance*, No. 43, 1978, for references both favourable and unfavourable to the monetary approach.

analysis, which is further strengthened by the movements in European prices, exchange rates, and money supplies described in this chapter. Briefly, it has already been shown that:

(i) For Europe as a whole inflation accelerated over the thirty-year period and this was associated with a faster rate of monetary growth;

(ii) In the fixed exchange rate period prices in Europe moved very much in line with prices in the United States, as did prices within Europe once devaluations were taken into account;

(iii) In the flexible exchange rate period intra-European inflation rates diverged, as did monetary growth, while exchange rates were more volatile. Further, rapid monetary growth preceded rapid inflation by about two years (Table 4.4).

TABLE 4.4. *Trends in Europe,*[a] *1970-1979*
(percentage changes from previous year)

	Inflation[b]	Money supply		GDP	
		M 1[c]	M 2[c]	nominal	real
1970	4.9	7.5	10.0	13.1	5.1
1971	6.0	12.4	13.5	11.0	3.4
1972	6.2	14.0	16.6	10.7	3.9
1973	7.9	10.8	17.1	13.6	5.8
1974	11.9	9.8	14.6	13.0	1.8
1975	12.2	13.6	13.9	12.3	−1.1
1976	10.0	11.3	13.3	14.9	5.0
1977	9.8	11.3	12.6	11.7	2.0
1978	7.3	14.7	13.2	11.8	3.2
1979	9.2	12.5	12.9	12.9	3.4
1969–79[d]	8.5	11.8	13.8	12.5	3.2
1950–69[d]	3.1	7.2	9.7	9.2	5.1

[a] Sum of nine countries (the four major economies, the Benelux, Denmark, Norway, and Sweden)
[b] Consumer prices
[c] M 1 and M 2 stand for the narrow and broader definitions of the money supply respectively
[d] Average annual percentage changes
Source: IMF, *International Financial Statistics* (1980 Yearbook).

It should also be noted that, in the 1970s, compared with the 1950s and 1960s, changes in inflation in individual countries were associated with exchange rate and excess money supply movements, and that the exchange rate movements generally followed prior movements in the money supply and preceded consumer price developments. Table 4.5 brings together the figures on inflation and on the growth of nominal incomes with movements in the money supply in a simple correlation exercise. It shows that for most European countries movements in the money supply, broadly defined, preceded changes in nominal GDP by one to two years and inflation by two to three years. Using the narrow definition, there would seem to be some evidence to suggest that money is made available on demand with no or only a very short lag on output.

TABLE 4.5. *Correlation coefficients between monetary expansion and inflation or nominal GDP growth,*[a] *1950-1979*

	Correlation between inflation and monetary expansion		Correlation between nominal GDP growth and monetary expansion	
	M 1[b]	M 2[b]	M 1[b]	M 2[b]
France	–	0.26 (2)	0.09 (1)	0.38 (1)
Germany	0.05 (1)	–	0.39 (1)	0.45 (1)
Italy	0.71 (3)	0.89 (1)	0.66 (3)	0.76 (1)
United Kingdom	0.76 (3)	0.91 (2)	0.80 (0)	0.88 (2)
Belgium	0.68 (2)	0.83 (2)	0.61 (1)	0.80 (1)
Denmark	0.51 (3)	0.61 (2)	0.67 (0)	0.70 (0)
Netherlands	0.51 (2)	0.59 (2)	0.64 (1)	0.46 (1)
Norway	0.82 (2)	0.78 (2)	0.58 (2)	0.57 (3)
Sweden	0.62 (0)	0.64 (3)	0.67 (0)	0.63 (2)
Total	0.75 (2)	0.87 (2)	0.68 (1)	0.70 (2)

[a] The figures shown are the highest correlation coefficients obtained between the variables indicated when monetary expansion is lagged 0 to 3 years. The figures in brackets show the particular lag which was chosen

[b] M 1 and M 2 stand for the narrow and broader definitions of the money supply respectively

Source: IMF, *International Financial Statistics* (1980 Yearbook).

Inflation and the monetarist approach

The text so far has suggested that there is considerable support for the monetarist approach to inflation. In the 1950s and 1960s Europe was, in effect, part of a fixed rate system and accepted the rate of inflation set by the United States. In the 1970s each country had greater freedom of choice. The result was a generally higher rate of inflation in both Europe and the United States. Some countries, for example Italy and the United Kingdom, followed monetary policies which caused them to break away completely from inflation rates in the rest of Europe.

The monetarist approach cannot and does not claim to tell the whole story. There are two important gaps. The first is the case in which inflation appears to have a non-monetarist cause. Although the data suggest that changes in monetary growth have preceded changes in inflation by about two years, it is important to consider whether there were occasions in which there were autonomous increases in the inflation rate. The second gap concerns the reasons for monetary expansion. From a historical point of view it is unsatisfactory to suggest that inflation stems from an acceleration of monetary growth, since the immediate supplementary question is, why did monetary growth accelerate? The following few pages seek to fill these two gaps.

The general picture of inflation and monetary growth in Europe is shown in Fig. 4.2. There is a peak of inflation in 1958, then a steady acceleration from 1967 to 1975 and a fall since then. The increase in inflation in 1958 appears to be an isolated incident. Since 1970, monetary growth has generally been higher than it was in the 1950s and 1960s though it has fallen from the peak of 1973. Explanations are therefore required for the brief acceleration of inflation in

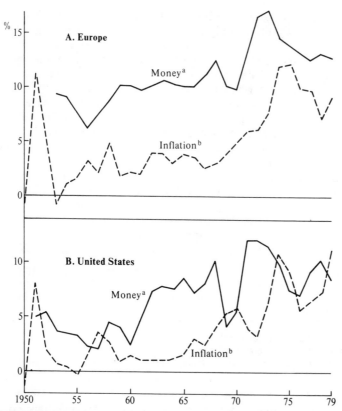

FIG. 4.2. *Monetary growth and inflation* (percentage changes from previous year)
[a] Broadly defined money supply
[b] Consumer prices
Source: IMF, *International Financial Statistics* (1980 Yearbook).

1958, and for the generally rapid growth of the money supply since 1970.

Examination of Appendix Table 4. A3 shows that the inflation of 1958 was entirely a French phenomenon. French prices actually fell slightly in 1957, then rose by over 15 per cent in 1958. The accompanying monetary growth was 10.5 per cent in 1957 and 8.2 per cent in 1958. That may appear to cast doubt on the monetary approach. However, as already explained, under fixed exchange rates

TABLE 4.6. *France – monetary growth*[a]
(percentages)

	1956	1957	1958	1959
Change in money supply[b]	11.6	10.5	8.2	9.9
of which: Domestic credit expansion	11.7	16.3	10.4	6.7
Change in reserves	0.1	−3.3	0.1	4.2
Other	−0.2	−2.5	−2.3	−1.0

[a] Broad definition of money supply
[b] Percentage changes from previous year
Source: IMF, *International Financial Statistics* (1980 Yearbook).

the adjustment to excessive credit creation is felt through the balance of payments (Table 4.6). From 1956 to 1958 DCE was excessive relative to France's normal demand for money. The result was a major reserve loss (in 1957) which was unsustainable. The cause of the excessive DCE was an attempt to boost defence expenditure without raising taxes adequately. The consequence was a series of devaluations which reduced the exchange rate against the dollar by about 30 per cent. The impact of the devaluations on prices was felt most fully in 1958. By 1959, the devaluations and the reduction in DCE had been sufficient to cause an increase in reserves. If the French franc had not been devalued, far tighter credit policies would have been required and the price spurt of 1958 could have been avoided.

A similar inflation peak was recorded in Italy in 1963. This followed two or three years of rapid monetary growth (Table 4.7). By 1963 DCE was clearly

TABLE 4.7. *Italy – monetary growth*[a]
(percentages)

	1960	1961	1962	1963	1964	1965
Change in money supply[b]	14.7	15.4	17.1	15.4	10.9	12.5
of which: Domestic credit expansion	12.1	15.0	15.5	19.7	14.0	10.2
Change in reserves	2.8	1.7	1.8	−0.3	−0.3	1.8
Other	−0.2	−1.3	−0.2	−4.0	−2.8	0.5

[a] Broad definition of money supply
[b] Percentage changes from previous year
Source: IMF, *International Financial Statistics* (1980 Yearbook).

excessive to the point at which there was some loss of reserves (though most of the DCE/money supply gap is explained by 'other' factors). Italy experienced accelerating inflation in 1962 and 1963 but after 1963 DCE was reduced and the inflation rate fell back.

Thus, under fixed exchange rates, countries had the option of devaluing the currency or of reversing their credit policies. Germany presents an example of the opposite approach. The revaluations of 1969 and 1970, for example, followed three years of reserve accumulation (Table 4.8). The relatively low rate of DCE (again in combination with 'other' factors) caused an inflow of reserves which boosted the money supply. Germany chose to revalue rather than to expand

TABLE 4.8. *Germany – monetary growth*[a]
(percentages)

	1966	1967	1968	1969	1970
Change in money supply[b]	12.1	12.9	15.3	13.6	11.4
of which: Domestic credit expansion	19.1	14.0	15.7	17.4	15.8
Change in reserves	0.2	0.7	1.7	−0.9	1.4
Other	−5.3	−1.8	−2.2	−2.9	−5.8

[a] Broad definition of money supply
[b] Percentage changes from previous year
Source: IMF, *International Financial Statistics* (1980 Yearbook).

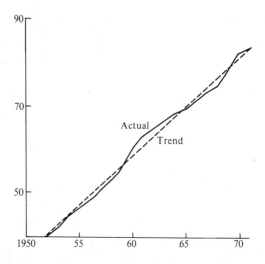

FIG. 4.3. *Relative monetary expansion* (ratio of European to United States broadly defined money supply. Indices: 1975 = 100)
Source: IMF, *International Financial Statistics* (1980 Yearbook).

DCE, and was thus able to achieve relatively low inflation in the late 1960s.

It was said above that it was not sufficient to explain the acceleration of inflation simply in monetary terms; one also needs to understand why monetary growth expanded in the 1970s. Fig. 4.2 shows that there was some acceleration in 1967 and 1968 followed by two years in which monetary growth returned to its normal rate. Then monetary growth accelerated rapidly to 17 per cent in 1973 and remained above the growth rates of the 1960s to the end of the decade. The discussion of inflation under fixed exchange rates suggests that monetary growth until the early 1970s should have been determined largely by the United States. Fig. 4.2 shows that monetary growth in the United States started to accelerate after 1961 and rose to over 10 per cent in 1968. This expansion was followed by two years of slow growth in 1969 and 1970. Fig. 4.3 shows the ratio of the money supply in Europe to that in the United States during the fixed exchange rate period. As expected, the European money supply grows more rapidly than that of the United States. From about 1964 onwards the ratio is below the trend line, broadly suggesting that America's money supply was getting out of line with Europe's. The explanation for this acceleration is to be found in the expansionary domestic policies of the Democratic administrations combined, from the mid-1960s onwards, with the escalation of the Vietnam war. Rising expenditure was financed by monetary growth rather than by taxation. The loss in reserves this induced in the United States led to an acceleration of monetary growth in Europe.

The inflationary impact was felt first in the United States, where the rate of price increases started to accelerate after 1965. Europe 'caught' the inflation from about 1967 onwards. The United States responded to its inflation by a sharp contraction of monetary growth in 1969 and 1970. Europe experienced a similar contraction. The combination of monetary restraint and the rapid inflation of 1969-71 resulted in a squeeze on real money balances which in turn led to the recession of 1970-1. The attempt by the United States to escape from that recession by a renewed and rapid acceleration of monetary growth finally placed excessive strains on the Bretton Woods system, which collapsed at the end of 1971.

This account of inflation in the late 1960s has concentrated on monetary developments in the United States and Europe. However, at the time, the emphasis was on wage developments, particularly in Europe. The growth of earnings doubled in France, the United Kingdom, and the United States between 1967 and 1968. In Germany and Italy it doubled between 1968 and 1969. It is fairly clear from Fig. 4.2 that there was nothing in the preceding years' growth of the money supply to explain a leap of that size. It is also clear that the movement of consumer prices was more modest, in 1968 and 1969, than the movement of earnings. The gap between earnings and prices could partly be accommodated by a rapid growth of output, but it must be accepted that the earnings explosion of 1968 and 1969 was at least partly autonomous.

A broad indication of the extent to which monetary policy accommodated the increase in earnings is provided by Fig. 4.4. The continuous line shows the

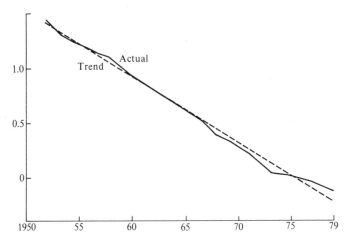

FIG. 4.4. *Price level-money supply ratio in Europe* (log of ratio of consumer prices to broadly defined money supply. Indices: 1975 = 100)
Source: IMF, *International Financial Statistics* (1980 Yearbook).

ratio of the price level to the money supply in Europe (which is downward because of the growth of real output). Points above the trend suggest that prices are higher than might be expected given monetary conditions. Since prices do not adjust instantaneously to changes in money supply, one would expect that during a period of rapid monetary expansion, prices would be low relative to money supply. If there is an exogenous shock to prices – as during an autonomous wage explosion – the ratio of prices to money supply would tend to lie above the trend. The figure does not show any exceptional movement in prices relative to money supply in 1968 and 1969. This suggests that consumer prices were no higher than would have been expected given monetary conditions; since monetary growth in Europe was reduced in 1969 and 1970, it can be said that monetary policy did not accommodate the wage increase.

Inflation in the 1970s

Since flexible exchange rates allow each economy to pursue an independent monetary policy, one cannot rely on United States policies as an explanation for monetary and price developments in the 1970s. However, the change in exchange rate regimes was by no means sudden. Since the floating system was so new, it took several years for economies to adjust to it. Not surprisingly, policies in many cases continued to be conducted as if exchange rates were still fixed. Countries had good cause to adopt a cautious approach. Flexible exchange rates tended to move rapidly in response to changes in monetary policy, with the result that real exchange rates (the effective nominal exchange rate adjusted for relative price movements) changed sharply. These changes threatened to disrupt international trade, and some economies continued to amass reserves rather than see their exchange rate rise. The consequence was a loss of monetary control, and inflation continued to be transmitted from one country to another. Thus the link between European and United States inflation rates, though weakened, was not broken completely.

It was pointed out in Section II that two things happened in the 1970s which are extremely important from the standpoint of the present approach. The first was a deceleration in the growth of real output (from the 5.1 per cent annual rate of the 1950s and 1960s to 3.2 per cent). The second was an acceleration in the growth of the broadly defined money supply (from 9.7 per cent a year to 13.8 per cent). 'Excess monetary growth' (the gap between monetary and real growth) thus increased by 6.0 per cent. This corresponds closely to the 5.4 per cent increase in the inflation rate between the two periods.

The explanation for the acceleration in monetary growth – and thus for the acceleration in inflation – would seem to have been the attempt by policy-makers to restore the growth performance of the 1960s. It appears that a fall in the underlying rate of growth of output started in all industrial economies at the beginning of the 1970s. If policy-makers extrapolated the growth rates of the 1960s into the 1970s they would have thought that, on average, about 1½ per cent of spare capacity was appearing each year. After only two years at what was in fact full capacity growth it would have appeared possible to add 3 per cent to one year's growth without hitting capacity constraints. Thus, at the beginning of 1973, policy-makers might have believed that there was 3 per cent of spare capacity to be added to the assumed underlying growth of 4½ per cent. In other words, they might have believed that a growth of output of 7½ per cent was feasible whereas only 3¼ per cent in fact was. Expansionary fiscal and monetary policies designed to achieve 'full capacity working' were, in such circumstances, bound to result in inflation. It was of course, possible to achieve a short-term response, most notably in 1973, but inflation followed rapidly as output came back to its sustainable path. Once the inflation had been generated its elimination was painful and governments adjusted their policies only slowly.

This account presents the story very much from the side of 'demand–pull', with expansionary policies causing growth in the short term and inflation in the longer term. But one cannot rule out an element of 'cost–push' which was accommodated by monetary policy. Employees sought to maintain the growth of real incomes they had come to expect in the 1960s. Employers might equally have expected that the pay increases were feasible. The bargains resulted in nominal contracts which the policy-makers validated by monetary policy. The real outcome was rather worse than expected. In either case the story of the 1970s is the story of a mistake about sustainable growth. Had the authorities – and everyone else – known what was happening, they would have reduced monetary growth. Instead they did the opposite and the inevitable result was higher inflation.

Finally, one may ask what contribution was made by the increase in oil prices in 1973-4. There was certainly a rapid acceleration of inflation in Europe in 1974-5 after the first oil price increase. But Fig. 4.2 shows that this acceleration had been preceded by rapid monetary growth in 1971-2. It is thus possible that the increase in oil prices was part of the response to that monetary expansion. That cannot be the whole story, since the oil shock involved a considerable increase in the real price of oil as well, which was made possible by the development of the OPEC cartel. Nevertheless, it can be argued that the rise in oil prices was not an independent source of inflation even in the short run. In other words, monetary growth had been so rapid in the preceding years that it was readily able to accommodate higher oil prices. Fig. 4.4 can be used to explore this argument. It shows that from 1971 onwards, the money supply was high relative to the price level. The inflation of 1974 and 1975 brought the money supply and the price level back onto their trend relationship with each other. The oil price increase was absorbed in this adjustment.

A simple analysis like this does not, of course, establish that the oil price increase had no independent effect on the price level. It is possible that the adjustment to the monetary expansion of 1971 and 1972 might have taken longer if real oil prices had not risen so dramatically. But had this rise been a major independent source of inflation one might have expected to see all European economies experiencing a similar increase in inflation in 1974 (once allowance was made for differing shares of oil in total inputs). Yet there was a wide range of reactions (Appendix Table 4. A3). In Germany, for instance, inflation rose from 6.9 to 7.0 per cent and in the Netherlands from 8.0 to 9.6 per cent (although this can partly be explained by reliance on natural gas); in France, Italy, and the United Kingdom, on the other hand, inflation nearly doubled. The Appendix figures show that the inflation experience generally corresponded to the preceding growth of the money supply. Germany, however, is something of a counter-example, since it recorded accelerating inflation during this period even though its monetary policy was relatively stable (Table 4.5 also shows that Germany's inflation could not be explained by a simple correlation with the money supply). It would appear that Germany was unable to escape the general acceleration of prices in spite of stable monetary policies combined with flexible exchange rates.

If prices are low relative to the money supply, the trend relationship can be restored either by a more rapid growth of prices or by a slower growth of the money supply. Fig. 4.2 shows that in 1974 and 1975 both processes were in operation. Monetary growth was reduced while inflation stayed high. The resulting squeeze on the real money supply produced the recession of 1975. Subsequently, inflation fell. The recession would have been more modest and the decline in inflation would have been postponed if monetary policy had been less restrictive in 1974 and 1975.

Conclusions

This chapter has set out a simple theory of inflation under fixed and flexible exchange rates. In both cases the rate of inflation depends on monetary growth but the mechanism by which this happens varies according to the exchange rate regime. Under fixed rates the rate of inflation is likely to be set by the United States; other countries adjust their fiscal and monetary policies to maintain their parities and experience the going rate of world inflation. Consumer price inflation can still differ between countries since consumption includes non-traded goods. The theory suggests that it will be most rapid in those countries which achieve the most rapid growth of productivity. Under a regime of flexible exchange rates, countries are free to pursue independent monetary policies and to achieve their own rate of inflation. Exchange rates adjust to preserve international price relativities.

Although Europe did not experience a world of either completely fixed or of completely flexible rates, the pre-1971 period is reasonably close to the former regime and the post-1971 period to the latter. Section II, accordingly, presented a broad-brush picture of inflation and monetary growth in these two periods. Events were consistent with the monetarist approach. The fixed exchange rate years saw inflation rates in Europe generally moving in line with those in the United States, while within Europe there was little inter-country divergence. In the 1970s, on the other hand, divergences were much greater. In addition (although this has no necessary connection with the move to flexible rates), monetary growth and inflation were both higher in the 1970s than they had been in the 1950s and 1960s.

Section III considered the monetarist explanation in more detail. On the question of causality the results suggested that accelerations of monetary growth preceded accelerations of inflation. Finally, the section discussed the reasons for the monetary expansion of the 1970s. It was suggested that this arose through a mistaken attempt to maintain the real growth performance of the 1960s.

No attempt was made to establish that the growth of the money supply explains the rate of inflation at all times and in all places. It is accepted that there can be shocks to the price level from wages and from raw materials (though it does not seem that the oil price increase of 1973–4 was a major independent source of inflation). However, the history of inflation in Europe surely establishes that an acceleration of monetary growth is a necessary condition for sustained inflation and that any account of inflation which ignores monetary factors is gravely incomplete.

Appendix: Supplementary Statistical Material

This Appendix presents historical data on money and inflation in Europe and in the United States from 1950 to 1979. The figures are for the most part taken from IMF, *International Financial Statistics* (1980 Yearbook). Consumer price inflation corresponds to line 64 in that publication, the narrow definition of money to line 34, the broad definition to the sum of lines 34 and 35, real output to line 99 *ar* (GNP) or line 99 *br* (GDP), and nominal output to lines 99 *a* or 99 *b*. For some of the earlier years of the 1950s, GDP data come from OEEC, *Statistics of National Product and Expenditure, 1938 and 1947 to 1955*, Paris 1957, and OECD, *National Accounts of OECD Countries, 1950–1979* and *1950–1968*.

The IMF money supply data are given for the end of each year: the figures here shown are based on annual averages taken as the mean of two end-year observations. Annual growth rates are, therefore, from mid-year to mid-year. Excess monetary growth is defined as the difference between the growth rates of the broadly defined money supply and real GDP.

TABLE 4.A1. *Inflation, monetary and GDP growth in Europe*
(percentage changes from previous year)

	Inflation	Money supply		GDP		Excess monetary growth	
		M 1	M 2	nominal	real	M 1	M 2
1950	−0.6	..	..	9.9	8.5	..	..
1951	11.1	..	..	18.3	6.0	..	..
1952	4.7	..	..	11.5	3.5	..	..
1953	−0.7	6.5	9.4	6.3	5.7	0.8	3.7
1954	1.1	7.2	9.1	6.5	5.1	2.1	4.0
1955	1.9	6.7	7.5	10.0	6.6	0.1	0.9
1956	3.3	5.1	6.3	9.4	4.4	0.6	1.9
1957	2.1	4.8	7.6	8.4	4.4	0.5	3.2
1958	4.9	6.3	8.8	7.2	2.2	4.1	6.6
1959	1.8	8.7	10.2	7.3	6.0	2.7	4.2
1960	2.2	8.0	10.2	12.7	6.8	1.3	3.4
1961	2.1	8.5	9.8	8.7	5.5	3.0	4.3
1962	3.9	8.9	10.2	8.8	4.4	4.5	5.8
1963	3.9	9.2	10.7	8.5	4.1	5.0	6.6
1964	3.2	9.0	10.4	10.5	6.0	3.0	4.4
1965	3.9	7.6	10.2	8.7	4.4	3.2	5.9
1966	3.6	6.4	10.3	7.4	3.4	3.0	6.8
1967	2.7	6.5	11.2	5.7	3.1	3.4	8.1
1968	3.0	7.8	12.5	8.3	5.1	2.7	7.4
1969	3.9	5.4	10.2	11.3	5.9	−0.5	4.3
1970	4.9	7.5	10.0	13.1	5.1	2.4	4.9
1971	6.0	12.4	13.5	11.0	3.4	9.0	10.1
1972	6.2	14.0	16.6	10.7	3.9	10.1	12.7
1973	7.9	10.8	17.1	13.6	5.8	5.0	11.3
1974	11.9	9.8	14.6	13.0	1.8	8.0	12.8
1975	12.2	13.6	13.9	12.3	−1.1	14.7	15.0
1976	10.0	11.3	13.3	14.9	5.0	6.3	8.4
1977	9.8	11.3	12.6	11.7	2.0	9.3	10.6
1978	7.3	14.7	13.2	11.8	3.2	11.5	10.0
1979	9.2	12.5	12.9	12.9	3.4	9.0	9.5

Note: for definitions of series used and list of sources, see note at beginning of Appendix.

TABLE 4.A2. *Inflation in the United States and in Europe*

	United States				Europe			Ratio of European to United States price indices (col. 6 ÷ col. 1)
	Index: 1975 = 100	Percentage changes from previous year	Index: 1975 = 100	Percentage changes from previous year	Exchange rate *vis-à-vis* dollar (index: 1950 = 100)	Inflation in dollar terms (col. 3 × col. 5)	Percentage changes from previous year	
1950	44.7	−1.3	33.9	−0.6	100	33.9	−0.6	0.76
1951	48.3	8.1	37.7	11.1	100	37.7	11.1	0.78
1952	49.3	2.1	39.5	4.7	100	39.5	4.7	0.80
1953	49.7	0.8	39.2	−0.7	100	39.2	−0.7	0.79
1954	49.9	0.4	39.6	1.1	100	39.6	1.1	0.79
1955	49.8	−0.2	40.4	1.9	100	40.4	1.9	0.81
1956	50.5	1.4	41.7	3.3	100	41.7	3.3	0.83
1957	52.3	3.6	42.6	2.1	99	42.2	1.1	0.81
1958	53.7	2.7	44.7	4.9	96	42.9	1.8	0.80
1959	54.2	0.9	45.4	1.8	93	42.3	−1.4	0.78
1960	55.0	1.5	46.5	2.2	93	43.2	2.2	0.79
1961	55.6	1.1	47.4	2.1	94	44.8	3.6	0.81
1962	56.2	1.1	49.3	3.9	95	46.8	4.5	0.83
1963	56.9	1.2	51.2	3.9	95	48.6	3.9	0.85
1964	57.6	1.2	52.8	3.2	95	50.2	3.3	0.87
1965	58.6	1.7	54.9	3.9	95	52.1	3.8	0.89
1966	60.4	3.1	56.9	3.6	95	54.0	3.6	0.89
1967	62.0	2.6	58.4	2.7	95	55.3	2.5	0.89
1968	64.6	4.2	60.2	3.0	92	55.6	0.5	0.86
1969	68.1	5.4	62.5	3.9	92	57.7	3.7	0.85
1970	72.1	5.9	65.6	4.9	93	61.2	6.2	0.85
1971	75.2	4.3	69.5	6.0	93	64.6	5.6	0.86
1950–71[a]		2.5		3.5		−0.3	3.1	

Note: for definitions of series used and list of sources, see note at beginning of Appendix.
[a] Average annual percentage changes

European totals are obtained by adding the figures for the following nine countries, with the 1975 GDP weights in brackets: France (0.24), Germany (0.29), Italy (0.12), United Kingdom (0.16), Belgium (0.04), Denmark (0.02), Netherlands (0.06), Norway (0.02), and Sweden (0.05).

TABLE 4.A3. *Inflation in nine European countries*
(percentage changes from previous year)

	France	Germany	Italy	United Kingdom	Belgium	Denmark	Netherlands	Norway	Sweden
1950	8.0	−6.3	−1.0	2.7	−1.0	6.0	8.6	5.3	0.7
1951	17.6	7.8	12.5	9.9	9.5	10.2	12.2	15.9	16.2
1952	12.0	2.1	1.8	6.3	0.9	3.8	..	9.0	7.7
1953	−2.1	−1.9	1.5	1.6	−0.2	1.0	..	1.7	1.4
1954	0.6	0.2	2.9	1.6	1.3	..	4.1	4.5	0.8
1955	0.9	1.7	2.3	3.5	−0.7	5.6	1.8	1.1	3.2
1956	4.2	2.5	3.3	4.3	2.9	5.9	1.8	3.7	4.4
1957	−0.6	2.2	1.3	3.2	3.2	2.6	6.6	2.8	4.5
1958	15.3	2.2	2.9	2.8	1.2	0.9	1.7	4.7	4.3
1959	5.8	0.9	−0.5	0.6	1.2	1.7	0.9	2.4	0.9
1960	4.0	1.6	2.3	1.1	0.4	1.1	2.5	0.2	4.1
1961	2.5	2.1	2.0	2.7	1.0	3.6	−0.7	2.3	2.2
1962	5.1	3.1	4.7	4.0	1.4	7.4	2.3	5.7	4.7
1963	5.3	3.0	7.5	2.0	2.2	5.9	3.3	2.4	2.9
1964	3.0	1.8	5.9	3.2	4.0	3.3	5.8	5.7	3.4
1965	2.7	3.8	4.3	4.6	4.1	5.2	5.9	4.4	5.2
1966	2.7	3.5	2.4	3.9	4.3	7.1	5.7	3.2	6.4
1967	2.8	1.6	3.7	2.7	2.9	8.2	3.4	4.4	4.3
1968	4.5	1.7	1.5	4.8	2.6	8.0	3.9	3.4	2.0
1969	6.2	1.8	2.6	5.4	3.9	3.6	7.3	3.1	2.6
1970	5.8	3.3	4.8	6.3	3.9	6.5	3.8	10.8	7.1
1971	5.5	5.3	5.0	9.4	4.3	5.8	7.4	6.1	7.5
1972	6.2	5.6	5.7	7.3	5.4	6.6	7.9	7.3	6.0
1973	7.4	6.9	10.8	9.1	6.9	9.4	8.0	7.3	6.7
1974	13.7	7.0	19.1	16.0	12.7	15.2	9.6	9.4	9.9
1975	11.7	5.9	17.0	24.2	12.7	9.6	10.5	11.7	9.8
1976	9.6	4.3	16.8	16.5	9.2	9.0	8.8	9.1	10.3
1977	9.4	3.6	17.0	15.9	7.1	11.1	6.4	9.2	11.4
1978	9.1	2.8	12.1	8.3	4.5	10.1	4.1	8.1	9.9
1979	10.7	4.1	14.7	13.4	4.4	9.6	4.2	4.8	7.3

Note: for definition of series used and list of sources, see note at beginning of Appendix.

TABLE 4.A4. *Growth of broadly defined money supply
in nine European countries*
(percentage changes from previous year)

	France	Germany	Italy	United Kingdom	Belgium	Denmark	Netherlands	Norway	Sweden
1951	17.3	..	..	..	..	−0.3	1.3	3.9	10.4
1952	15.8	..	19.3	..	6.8	1.7	8.9	8.9	8.2
1953	12.6	20.8	25.8	3.3	4.5	6.2	8.1	6.1	7.0
1954	13.0	20.1	12.8	4.1	3.1	4.0	7.6	5.2	8.0
1955	13.4	16.9	12.0	0.5	3.9	2.4	9.3	5.2	4.8
1956	11.6	13.0	12.1	−0.7	4.0	4.4	4.1	5.5	5.3
1957	10.5	15.4	10.6	2.4	1.4	5.7	0.9	5.1	8.1
1958	8.2	17.2	12.1	3.4	3.5	9.3	8.8	3.8	7.7
1959	9.9	16.0	15.0	4.6	6.0	12.0	12.6	4.3	9.6
1960	15.2	13.5	14.7	4.2	4.7	8.1	11.1	6.1	7.7
1961	17.0	12.1	15.4	2.8	7.2	7.4	9.6	6.1	4.7
1962	18.0	12.0	17.1	0.3	8.7	9.3	8.9	6.2	7.6
1963	16.2	11.6	15.4	3.3	9.0	10.8	10.7	6.9	8.7
1964	11.8	12.3	10.9	7.0	8.8	11.2	11.1	7.3	7.8
1965	10.4	12.8	12.5	6.5	8.0	9.9	10.8	9.0	6.9
1966	10.7	12.1	15.2	5.5	8.7	11.4	9.3	9.2	7.7
1967	11.9	12.9	14.3	7.2	7.9	11.1	.0.4	9.2	10.5
1968	12.3	15.3	13.1	8.9	8.5	11.2	13.8	11.0	11.8
1969	8.0	13.6	12.0	5.1	7.4	11.6	13.4	11.2	8.5
1970	10.1	11.4	13.5	6.3	6.9	7.6	12.4	12.9	5.8
1971	16.9	13.3	15.8	11.4	10.8	6.9	13.5	14.1	8.2
1972	18.7	15.3	17.3	21.0	14.9	11.2	14.4	12.9	11.4
1973	16.5	13.3	20.9	27.7	15.1	13.5	15.3	13.0	13.2
1974	16.3	10.4	19.2	19.4	11.2	10.8	16.1	12.2	12.0
1975	16.7	11.6	20.4	9.9	12.1	18.1	14.4	13.3	11.5
1976	13.9	11.1	22.5	9.4	13.8	18.4	15.3	12.7	8.3
1977	13.5	9.5	21.7	10.6	10.3	10.4	14.8	14.0	6.5
1978	13.3	10.2	22.7	12.3	7.9	7.8	12.0	14.6	13.0
1979	13.1	8.6	21.1	13.5	6.8	8.4	11.5	12.9	17.9

Note: for definition of series used and list of sources, see note at beginning of Appendix.

THE EUROPEAN ECONOMY

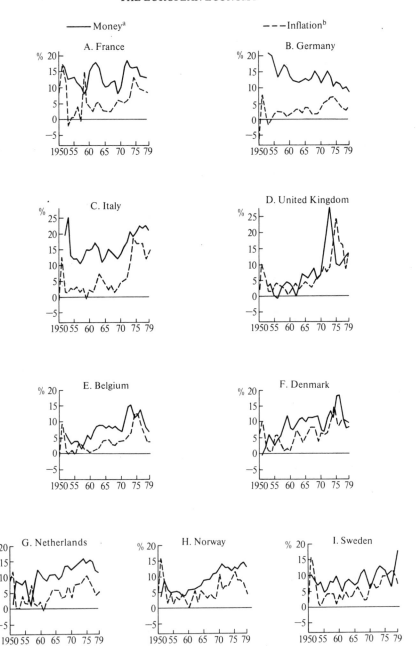

FIG. 4.A1. *Monetary growth and inflation in nine European countries* (percentage changes from previous year)
a Broadly defined money supply
b Consumer prices
Source: IMF, *International Financial Statistics* (1980 Yearbook).

Bibliography

The revival of monetarism in the 1960s and 1970s owes much to the pioneering work of Milton Friedman. The limitations of monetary policy are stressed in M. Friedman, 'The Role of Monetary Policy', *American Economic Review*, March 1968. Two recent review articles are: D.D. Purvis, 'Monetarism: A Review', *Canadian Journal of Economics*, February 1980, and D. Laidler, 'Monetarism: An Interpretation and an Assessment', *Economic Journal*, March 1981.

A good source for the monetary approach to the balance of payments, which emphasizes the difference between fixed and floating exchange rates is H.G. Johnson, 'The Monetary Approach to Balance-of-Payments Theory', in M.B. Connolly and A.K. Swoboda (eds.), *International Trade and Money*, London 1973. The effects of devaluations and the difference between traded and non-traded goods is set out in R. Dornbusch, 'Devaluation, Money and Nontraded Goods', *American Economic Review*, December 1973. Another useful source which includes many of the themes treated in this chapter is A.K. Swoboda, 'Monetary Policy under Fixed Exchange Rates: Effectiveness, the Speed of Adjustment and Proper Use', in H.G. Johnson and A.R. Nobay (eds.), *Issues in Monetary Economics*, Oxford 1974.

Two valuable summaries of inflation, with many references, are: D. Laidler and M. Parkin, 'Inflation: A Survey', *Economic Journal*, December 1975, and D. Laidler and A.R. Nobay, 'Some Current Issues Concerning the International Aspects of Inflation', in E. Claasen and P. Salin (eds.), *Stabilization Policy in Interdependent Economies*, Amsterdam 1972.

Many of the empirical sources quoted in the chapter are to be found in M. Parkin and G. Zis (eds.), *Inflation in the World Economy*, Manchester 1976. Other sources for the major European economies which stress the importance of money in the inflationary process are A. Fourcans, 'Inflation and Output Growth: The French Experience, 1960–1975', and M.J.M. Neumann, 'The Impulse-Theoretic Explanation of Changing Inflation and Output Growth: Evidence for Germany', both in K. Brunner and A.H. Meltzer (eds.), *The Problem of Inflation*, Carnegie-Rochester Conference Series on Public Policy, Vol. 8, 1978; M. Fratianni, 'Money, Wages and Prices in Italy', *Banca Nazionale del Lavoro Quarterly Review*, December 1980; and A.P. Budd, S. Holly, J.A. Longbottom, and D.B. Smith, 'Does Monetarism fit the UK Facts?', in B. Griffiths and G. Wood (eds.), *Monetarism in the UK*, London 1982.

5

Competitiveness and the Current Account

JOHN LLEWELLYN AND STEPHEN POTTER*

Introduction

There are various reasons for examining the behaviour, and determinants, of the current account of the balance of payments. There may be concern about the ability to finance a deficit, or about the cost of doing so. The current account may have implications for the exchange rate, and hence inflation, or for interest rates and the general conduct of monetary policy. A country may have an aim in respect of the desired transfer of resources to or from abroad, which, taking one year with another, the current account will need to match. More importantly, the evolution of the current account, over a run of several years, may represent a constraint on policy, preventing achievement of desired levels of activity.

In the post-war environment, in which most countries grew, by their earlier standards, at a high and steady rate, international trade was able to play a constructive role, both in supplying an important and growing component of aggregate demand, and in permitting firms to specialize and produce in far larger quantities than would be demanded in the home market alone, enabling important economies of scale to be realized. But the external balance did, on occasion, also represent a constraint. While imports of raw materials, in volume, have generally grown roughly in proportion with real GDP in major European economies, imports of finished manufactures have, on average, and reflecting increased specialization and openness, grown about twice as fast as GDP.[1] With income elasticities of this order, relative cyclical positions among countries have been a major short-term influence on current accounts. Thus, a typical European country whose domestic demand increased, relative to trend, 2 percentage points faster than that in its trading partners, could well find that its GDP increased only 1 per cent faster than theirs while its current account deteriorated by 1 per cent of GDP — normally thought of as quite a large swing.

Cycle-induced current account deficits could usually be dealt with by a modest amount of deflation, or could even be corrected without any action on the deficit country's part if demand abroad picked up, increasing world trade and thereby the deficit country's exports. But in some countries balance of payments deficits on current account were inclined to be more persistent, or more recurrent, than could be accounted for by explanations couched purely in cyclical terms. The United Kingdom was perhaps the most severe of such cases, showing a persistent tendency towards current account deficit whenever

---

* Department of Economics and Statistics, OECD. The views expressed are those of the authors and do not necessarily reflect those of the OECD.
[1] For a summary of the probable reasons for this, see T. Barker, 'International Trade and Economic Growth: An Alternative to the Neoclassical Approach', *Cambridge Journal of Economics*, March 1977.

demand turned up, even if GDP growth was moderate relative to that experienced by its trading partners.

In such countries the balance of payments may have exerted a restraint not only during stages of relative cyclical upswing, but also on the trend rate of growth of output. It is at least arguable that, had the rate of growth of exports been higher, and the rate of growth of imports lower, a faster growth of real demand could have been maintained. This would depend, of course, on whether higher levels of supply could be forthcoming. If not, then the economy was essentially supply-constrained, and the persistence of current account deficits was a *reflection* of this fact, rather than a cause in its own right of slow growth. Such issues remain uncertain. It is impossible to replay history under a different set of rules or assumptions, and so it is in turn impossible to reach definitive conclusions.

Considerations such as these suggest that countries' fundamental, or trend, current account positions may be determined by the same sort of forces as underlie their growth rates of productivity — which economic research has not explained very successfully. Nevertheless, there is one factor, apart from demand, with a well-attested influence on trade flows: changes in relative competitiveness, as measured by the development of a country's costs or prices compared with a suitably weighted average of those in partner countries. There is extensive econometric literature pointing to significant price elasticities of demand for both imports and exports, particularly of manufactures, with time lags of up to three years.[2] In addition to changes, the relative *levels* at which different countries emerged from the immediate post-war period probably had a substantial bearing on subsequent history.

The discussion of the period from the late 1940s is divided into three parts. The first, which covers the period of dollar shortage and post-war reconstruction, is taken as ending in 1958, with the reintroduction of dollar convertibility. The second covers the 'golden' age which lasted until 1973, when a period of rapid growth and generally fixed exchange rates came to an end with a commodity price boom of exceptional magnitude, a quadrupling of crude oil prices, and the generalized floating of major currencies. The third and last period is taken as being from then to the end of 1979 (Table 5.1).

The main concern is with the four largest economies, starting with Germany, probably the economy which, judged from a macroeconomic point of view, performed the most satisfactorily; from time to time it was necessary to correct its over-strong external position. Italy and France also performed well, although each on occasion saw the emergence of significant current account deficits; adjustment proved possible on each occasion, however, without, in the case of France at least, any perceptible check to macroeconomic performance. Indeed, there may even have been, for much of the period up to 1973 at least, a tendency towards higher French growth in each post-adjustment epoch. Last in the consideration of the major European economies comes the United Kingdom, which, while performing reasonably well relative to earlier periods in its history, continually disappointed in its failure to match the achievement of its continental

---

[2] For a survey see R.M. Stern, J. Francis, and B. Schumacher, *Price Elasticities in International Trade*, Trade Policy Research Centre, London 1976.

TABLE 5.1. *Longer-run output and trade trends in OECD Europe*
(average annual percentage changes)

	1950–79	1950–59	1959–73	1973–79
GDP	4.3	4.6	4.9	2.4
Exports[a]	7.2	7.0	8.4	5.0
Imports[a]	7.3	6.6	9.0	4.3
Export performance[b]	1.0	1.1	1.0	0.9
Import performance[c]	1.7	1.4	1.8	1.8

[a] Of goods and services at constant prices
[b] Ratio of export growth to total OECD export growth of goods and services
[c] Ratio of import growth to growth of GDP
Sources: OECD, *National Accounts of OECD Countries, 1950–1968 and 1950–1979.*

neighbours. An attempt to adjust the underlying current account situation came late, with the sterling devaluation of 1967, and proved more difficult to sustain than might have been expected on the basis of the theoretical writing of the time. And devaluation did not lead to any demonstrable secular improvement in performance, either absolutely or relative to other countries. In addition to the four largest economies, some attention is also paid to key balance of payments episodes in a number of the smaller economies, including particularly Spain, Belgium, the Netherlands, Sweden, and Switzerland.

The discussion usually proceeds from a brief description of the current balance experience to a tentative assessment of the competitive performance of the various countries. This assessment uses the available evidence on movements of relative costs and prices on the one hand, and two main indicators of performance in manufacturing trade on the other — the share of countries in world[3] exports of manufactured products, and the share of manufactured imports in countries' GDP. Although both these indicators are at current prices rather than in volume terms, and although the second one exhibits an upward trend in all the countries of Europe, they can provide some prima-facie indication of the extent to which measured changes in competitiveness affected the relevant trade flows. No discussion is attempted, on the other hand, of overall balance of payments experiences, such as the reasons for particular swings in capital accounts or in official reserves. References to these are given in Chapter 11 on Monetary Policy and in the country chapters of Part III of this book.

I. From Post-war Reconstruction to Convertibility

In the late 1940s, as European economies embarked on post-war reconstruction, their dominant balance of payments concern was the dollar shortage. In 1947 Europe was close to financial bankruptcy, with an overall deficit which, in the absence of foreign aid, would have virtually wiped out its total gold and dollar holdings. Europe's exports of goods and services were at less than 60 per cent of

---

[3] In fact, in the exports of the twelve major exporting countries: France, Germany, Italy, the United Kingdom, Belgium-Luxembourg, Netherlands, Sweden, Switzerland, Canada, the United States, and Japan.

their 1938 level, and would have covered only 60 per cent of a single year's imports – compared with approximate balance before the war. The resulting deficit of $7 billion, a truly enormous amount at the time (5 per cent of Europe's GDP), was financed largely by grants and loans from the United States, which was running the counterpart surplus. Indeed, American aid played a crucial role in the period 1947–50, sufficing to pay for one-quarter of Europe's total imports of goods and services, or almost two-thirds of its merchandise imports from the dollar area. The importance of Marshall Aid in financing essential import needs, and accelerating investment and reconstruction, can scarcely be over-stated.

Hand in hand with reconstruction efforts went a major liberalization of trade, first within Europe and later with countries outside. At the outset, prospects for freeing trade did not appear auspicious. In addition to their huge combined deficit, the European economies were afflicted by controls and shortages, and on the external trade side restrictions and bilateralism were general. Yet liberalization proceeded rapidly. By the end of 1949, approximately half of intra-European trade had been freed from quantitative restrictions and by 1956 some 90 per cent was free. Liberalization of imports from North America had inevitably to wait somewhat longer; it got going in earnest in 1954 and was about two-thirds complete by 1958. Several reasons can be put forward for this quick progress. First, some lessons had been learnt from the 1930s – it was now widely realized that the task of restoring production and financial stability would not only facilitate, but be facilitated by, the freeing of trade. Second, domestic demand management policies were apparently proving successful: 'In a climate of full employment and high and growing prosperity, efforts to cut tariffs and expand trade encountered no strong resistance.'[4] Third, the United States was strongly in favour of liberalization – indeed, it made Marshall Aid conditional on a removal of the bilateral trade barriers existing within Europe.[5]

Trade grew rapidly. The volume of intra-European visible trade, which in 1947 was little more than half that before the war, exceeded the pre-war level by 1950 and doubled it by 1957. This was in sharp contrast to the interwar experience, when intra-European trade at its peak in 1929 was still 6 per cent below its 1913 level. Apart from liberalization, the major reason for the expansion was rapidly rising European production (output grew by 6 per cent per annum between 1947 and 1957, as against 3½ per cent between 1920 and 1929). Exports to countries outside Europe were further boosted temporarily by the Korean War boom of 1950–1 and, for a somewhat longer period, by the 1949 devaluations against the dollar which increased Europe's competitiveness. Imports from outside Europe followed a somewhat different path. Despite the needs of reconstruction and increasing raw material requirements for industry, balance of payments difficulties initially dictated the limitation of imports to levels significantly below those recorded before the war. From 1953 onwards, as the strengthening external position led to more liberal trade and payments

[4] G. Ohlin, 'Trade in a Non-*Laissez-Faire* World', in P. A. Samuelson (ed.), *International Economic Relations*, London 1969, p. 158.
[5] A. Maddison, *Economic Growth in the West*, London 1964, p. 167.

policies, imports grew more rapidly, broadly in parallel with exports; the pre-war level was exceeded in 1954.

In considering the evolution of Europe's external balance on goods and services over this period, it is important to distinguish volume and price changes. Overall, the terms of trade were less favourable than they had been before the war: primary product prices were higher relative to those of manufactured goods, reflecting generally stronger world economic activity. In the immediate aftermath of the war, however, this factor was overlaid by the overvaluation of European currencies: the terms of trade were actually slightly higher in 1947 than in 1938. But, given the general increase in trade prices over this period – a virtual doubling – and the gap between imports and exports, the effect of price changes was greatly to worsen the balance (Table 5.2). Then, between 1947 and 1951, Europe's terms of trade worsened by a quarter, as a result partly of the

TABLE 5.2. *Europe's balance on goods and services, 1938-1955*
(\$ billion)

| | 1938 | 1947 | 1951 | 1955 | Changes | | |
					1938 to 1947	1947 to 1951	1951 to 1955
Exports[a]	9.4	11.1	20.6	25.9	1.7	9.5	5.3
volume change[b]					−3.9	11.3	6.4
price change					5.6	−1.8	−1.1
Imports[a]	9.9	18.3	21.9	24.5	8.4	3.6	2.6
volume change[b]					−0.2	−0.2	6.8
price change					8.6	3.8	−4.2
Balance	−0.4	−7.2	−1.3	1.4	−6.8	5.9	−2.7
volume change[b]					−3.7	11.5	−0.4
price change					−3.0	−5.6	3.1

[a] Goods and services
[b] Volume changes are calculated at the prices ruling in the first year of each period
Source: R. Triffin, *Europe and the Money Muddle*, New Haven 1957.

widespread devaluations of 1949 and then of the Korean commodity price boom. But given that, over this period, export volumes doubled while import volumes were little changed, the deficit on goods and services was almost eliminated. Subsequently, as commodity prices declined rapidly again, the terms of trade returned to about 90 per cent of their pre-war level. With import and export volumes now rising in parallel, a small current account surplus emerged (\$1½ billion on average between 1950 and 1958).

Within this total there were, of course, pronounced inter-country divergences (Table 5.3). At one end of the spectrum was Germany, whose current account was in persistent and growing surplus throughout the 1950s. With capital outflows relatively small, substantial reserves were accumulated, and by the late 1950s there was talk of the need for revaluation of the DM. At the other end was France, whose position was fragile in view of a relatively high rate of inflation and the burden of two colonial wars. After some temporary surpluses in

TABLE 5.3. *Current balances, 1950–1958*
(annual averages, $ million)

	1950–58	1950–54	1955–58
France[a]	11	219	−250
Germany	795	558	1,091
Italy	3	−79	107
United Kingdom	365	316	427
Spain	..	..	−86
BLEU	155	68	265
Netherlands	144	207	66
Sweden	7	53	−49
Switzerland	126	155	90
Other European countries	−176	−112	−178
OECD Europe[b]	1,430	1,385	1,483

[a] With non-Franc Area countries
[b] Excluding Finland
Source: OECD, *Balance of Payments Statistics, 1950–1961.*

mid-decade, supported by restriction of imports, sizeable deficits re-emerged in 1956–8 and the franc was twice devalued (by as much as 30 per cent). The Italian and British positions were intermediate. Italy began by running deficits and was in substantial surplus only in 1958, but capital inflows were ample, so that by the end of the period the country's reserves were the third largest in Europe. The current account was thus not a constraint on economic policy. The United Kingdom, on the other hand, was generally in surplus, but this was achieved in part by import controls and the imposition of restrictive economic policy packages in 1951–2 and again in 1956–7. The payments position tended to be regarded as insufficiently solid for a country which was attempting to support a reserve currency role and which, almost alone in Europe, was a substantial net exporter of private long-term capital. Official reserve holdings remained small in relation to sterling liabilities, and there were several runs on the currency. Among the smaller countries, Belgium, the Netherlands, and Switzerland all recorded persistent and sizeable surpluses, equivalent on average to some 2 per cent of GDP. In the Dutch and Swiss case the surplus diminished through time as the German one grew, but Belgium moved into even larger surplus through the decade.

It seems that in the early post-war years individual countries' current account positions were determined more by the availability of financing, the degree of import restriction, and their ability to generate an exportable surplus than by competitiveness as measured by costs or prices relative to those of competitor countries. Over time, however, as production and trading returned to normal in the 1950s, competitive conditions probably played an increasing role in determining current balance developments. Although the relatively comprehensive measures of competitiveness available for the 1960s and 1970s cannot be produced for this period, Table 5.4 gathers together some partial indicators. The first two columns show how, on a very broad measure of cost competitiveness

TABLE 5.4. *Measures of competitiveness and export performance*

	Relative competitiveness		Absolute competitiveness		Export performance	
	GDP deflator relative to United States[a] (indices : 1938 = 100)		Cost of representative basket of goods and services[ab] (indices: United States = 100)		Share in 'world' exports of manufactures[c] (percentages)	
	1950	1958	1950	1955	1950–51	1958–59
France	97	112	77	97	9.8	7.8
Germany	52	55	75	72	8.2	18.4
Italy	82	87	73	76	3.9	4.1
United Kingdom	62	74	72	79	23.8	17.7
Belgium	115	113	82	101	7.0	5.9
Netherlands	66	74	62	67	3.2	4.0
Sweden	72	89	..	..	2.9	3.0
Switzerland	94	91	..	..	3.7	3.3
Total	74[d]	82[d]	74[d]	81[d]	62.5	65.1

[a] In dollars
[b] Obtained by averaging the figures shown in the original source for a basket with United States and own country consumption weights
[c] Share in the exports of manufactures of the twelve major exporting countries
[d] Using 1955 trade weights

Sources: R. Triffin, *Europe and the Money Muddle*, New Haven 1957, and OECD, *National Accounts of OECD Countries, 1950–1979*, for first two columns; M. Gilbert and Associates, *Comparative National Product and Price Levels*, OEEC, Paris 1958, for third and fourth columns; NIESR, *Economic Review*, and UN, *Monthly Bulletin of Statistics* (various issues), for last two columns.

(the GDP deflator), costs in Europe (measured in dollars) had developed *vis-à-vis* those in the United States since before the war. On this basis, two countries – France and Belgium – stand out as having relatively high post-war costs in both 1950 and 1958, while Germany's are shown throughout the decade as being only half as high relative to those in the United States as they had been in 1938. Most of the other countries appear to have gained a distinct advantage in cost terms *vis-à-vis* the United States by 1950 (partly reflecting the 1949 devaluations), but by 1958 the competitive position of the European countries had worsened, on average by around a tenth. The next two columns provide estimates of absolute price levels in Europe relative to the United States. In these terms, Europe emerges with generally lower costs. The development suggested over time (from 1950 to 1955) is consistent with the movement of the first indicator. Overall the European level is seen to rise by approaching 10 per cent relative to the United States, with French costs increasing particularly rapidly and those of Germany perhaps declining slightly.

There would seem to be some relation between these various competitive indicators and the movement of individual countries' shares in world exports of manufactures. Germany's high absolute level of competitiveness and its gain in relative terms through the period *vis-à-vis* its European trading partners is shown by its very sharp rise in market penetration abroad to a level, by 1958, already above that of the United Kingdom. The country was clearly launched on a path of high export-led growth, made possible by an increasingly undervalued exchange rate.[6] Conversely, France, Belgium, and Switzerland, whose competitiveness was poor at the outset and/or deteriorated sharply through the period, are seen as losing export shares.

The very sharp United Kingdom loss, however, is not so readily explicable purely in terms of the competitiveness indicators. Although Britain's performance on costs and prices seems to have been below average, it was no worse than that of, for example, France, yet the loss in market share was considerably more pronounced. To some extent this may have reflected an unfavourable geographical composition of exports, with the slow-growing Sterling Area markets holding a much larger share than the faster-growing European market. But a more fundamental reason may have been an inadequate supply response of the economy. Investment and productivity growth were both relatively low, and non-price competitiveness was almost certainly declining.

Germany and the United Kingdom thus provide two polar examples. The former was the fastest-growing economy in Europe in this period (on average 8 per cent per annum between 1950 and 1958), with the highest investment ratio (excepting Finland and Norway) (Table 1.4), and an external position going from strength to strength. Britain was the slowest-growing country, other than Ireland (2½ per cent per annum), with the lowest investment ratio and with an external position which was increasingly perceived as a constraint on improving upon the modest growth being recorded.

Belgium and the Netherlands show a somewhat similar pattern, albeit on a smaller scale. Both ran current surpluses through the period, although one was losing market shares while the other was gaining. In the Belgian case low initial competitiveness was clearly a factor, but, as in the United Kingdom, an insufficient supply response through the 1950s may well have played an important role. Growth was very slow in the period as a result of restrictive anti-inflationary policies. In the Dutch case, on the other hand, growth was relatively high and investment shares in GDP were above the European average. And though inflation was more rapid in the Netherlands (3½ per cent there versus 2¼ per cent for Belgium per year on average for consumer prices), profitability in the tradeable sector of the Dutch economy may well have risen faster than in Belgium (where low capacity utilization was adversely affecting profits) due to the successful incomes policies of the time.

The absence of very marked divergences in current account positions and the limited role which capital flows were still playing at the time meant that most of these trends in competitiveness, trade performance, or in the current balance were not seen as particularly worrying. The French 1957–8 situation was a partial exception, as was the United Kingdom's increasing vulnerability to speculation on sterling, but such events were seen at the time as temporary crises rather than as the appearance of fundamental problems. Yet with the benefit of hindsight, the beginnings can be discerned of many of the trends which were later to become more marked and troublesome.

[6] See Ch. 16 below.

II. From Convertibility to the First Oil Crisis

The years from 1959 to 1973 were a period of unparalleled performance,[7] with Europe's output rising at virtually 5 per cent per annum. Not only was growth faster than in the 1950s, but it was also smoother, with GDP falling only once in one country (Germany in 1967) as against the more frequent declines of the previous decade (let alone the synchronized recession of 1975). There was also an acceleration in the growth of world trade to some 8½ per cent per year, with European exports growing at about the same rate and European imports somewhat faster. This reflected Europe's steady terms of trade improvement (by about 5½ per cent for the period as a whole), primary commodity prices remaining relatively weak *vis-à-vis* those of manufactured goods. The achievement of full non-resident convertibility at the end of 1958 almost certainly facilitated this unprecedented increase in world trade; the trade-creating effects of the EEC (and EFTA), particularly in the early 1960s, were a further major factor, as was rapid domestic income growth, which made for an increasing variety of wants not so easily satisfied within the confines of individual countries. But the rapid internationalization of the world economy brought with it a number of dangers, which became increasingly apparent. With rising trade shares in output countries were more open to the international transmission of inflation, more affected by foreign cyclical disturbances, and thereby more vulnerable to synchronized slowdowns and expansions. Rising capital mobility made the control of domestic monetary conditions, and the defence of parities, much more difficult. In a world in which growth, competitiveness, and inflation performance were inevitably different across countries, the pegged exchange rate system of Bretton Woods, in which changes of parity had tended to become major political events, could ultimately not survive.

Current balances

Over this fifteen-year period, Europe was generally in current surplus (Table 5.5). The current account dipped into small deficit in the early 1960s, but thereafter moved steadily into surplus, ending the period at some $5 billion, or ½ per cent of Europe's GDP, about the same relative size as in 1959-61. The $30 billion cumulative surplus was equal to less than half Europe's total reserve accumulation in this period. Reserves rose relatively rapidly in the early 1960s, due partly to large United States direct investment in the EEC, remained stationary in the mid-1960s when all the four major countries became sizeable long-term capital exporters, but were then multiplied by as much as two and a half in the early 1970s as the United States balance of payments went into massive overall deficit.

Within Europe, Germany and Italy emerged clearly as 'surplus countries', together accounting for the whole of the area's current surplus. Germany was in deficit only on two occasions in these years (1962 and 1965), and the strength of its external position created frequent upward pressure on the currency. Indeed, the DM was revalued in 1961 (by 5 per cent *vis-à-vis* the dollar), and in effective terms by 11½ per cent in 1969 and some 6 per cent at the time of the

---

[7] Although the period covered in this section notionally dates from 1958, 1959 is taken as a starting-point to avoid any distortions arising from the low level of demand pressure prevailing in 1958 through most of Europe.

TABLE 5.5. *Current balances, 1959–1973*
(annual averages, $ million)

	1959–73	1959–64	1965–69	1970–73
France	−193[a]	−171[a]	−405	45
Germany	1,062	480	1,189	1,775
Italy	995	270	2,178	604
United Kingdom	110	−84	−15	558
Spain	31	90	−428	516
BLEU	401	60	317	1,018
Netherlands	260	184	−30	736
Sweden	62	30	−136	358
Switzerland	64	−176	273	164
Other European Countries	−855	−423	−895	−1,460
OECD Europe	1,937	260	2,048	4,314

[a] 1960–73 and 1960–64

Sources: OECD, *Balance of Payments of OECD Countries, 1960–1977*; OECD, *Economic Outlook*, July 1981.

Smithsonian realignment. Italy's experience was different, and the lira never found itself a candidate for revaluation. If anything, the early 1960s saw the opposite danger as the current account weakened, a near-crisis developed in 1963, and a very restrictive policy package had to be imposed. In the years 1965–9, however, the current account returned to very substantial surplus, equivalent to 3 per cent of GDP, but this was largely offset by capital exports (most of which were illegal). Current surpluses of the order of 3 per cent of GDP were also recorded by some of the smaller countries which had already shown a tendency towards persistent surplus in the 1950s. Switzerland was in particularly large surplus in 1968–9, the Netherlands in 1972–3, and Belgium throughout the early 1970s.

Three countries which were much closer to current account balance through this period: France, the United Kingdom, and Spain each devalued their currency. France had already done so, in 1957 and in 1958, and did so again in 1969 (by 11 per cent *vis-à-vis* the dollar); Britain and Spain both devalued by just over 14 per cent in 1967. Despite the various devaluations, France was actually in deficit in most years of the 1960s, although it was only in 1968–9 that this deficit was at all large. The United Kingdom's position seemed even more precarious than in the 1950s, with surpluses alternating with deficits between 1959 and 1968. Thereafter, however, relatively large surpluses were recorded until 1971–2.

Competitiveness

As in the 1950s, these current account developments could be attributed to a mixture of competitiveness factors and differential growth rates. And as in the 1950s, two countries continued to stand out with relatively good and poor performances respectively – Germany and the United Kingdom – even if the gap was somewhat less marked than it had been (Table 5.6 and Fig. 5.1). The

TABLE 5.6. *Competitiveness and trade performance*

| | Manufacturing | | Changes in: | | |
	relative unit labour costs[a]	relative export average values[a]	Export shares[c]	Import shares[d]	Trade balance in manu- factures[e] (cif-fob)
	percentage changes, 1963–4 to 1971–72[b]		in percentage points, 1959–60 to 1972–73		
France	−20.2	−2.8	0.2	5.6	−4.0
Germany	21.7	5.4	2.4	3.6	−0.5
Italy	5.0	−4.0	2.6	3.7	1.7
United Kingdom	−4.4	2.3	−7.1	6.1	−4.3
Spain	..	..	(0.9)[f]	2.9[f]	0.2[f]
BLEU	−0.1	−5.8	0.7	12.5	−0.3
Netherlands	7.7	−9.0	1.1	2.2	1.4
Sweden	−2.0	7.9	0.3	2.3	3.6
Switzerland	−6.2	16.5	−0.2	5.2	−4.4

[a] In common currency

[b] The period chosen begins in 1963–64 because of unavailability of data before then, and ends in 1971–72, prior to the generalized floating of 1973 which is unlikely to have affected trade performance in that year

[c] Share in 'world' exports of manufactures

[d] Share of imports of manufactures (SITC 5 to 8, less 68, cif) in GDP at current prices

[e] Share of trade balance in manufactures (SITC 5 to 8, less 68, cif-fob) in GDP at current prices

[f] 1961–62 to 1972–73

Sources: OECD, 'The International Competitiveness of Selected OECD Countries', *OECD Economic Outlook – Occasional Studies*, July 1978, updated by the OECD Secretariat; OECD, *Statistics of Foreign Trade, Series B* (various issues); OECD, *National Accounts of OECD Countries, 1950–1979*; NIESR, *Economic Review*, and UN, *Monthly Bulletin of Statistics* (various issues).

French and Italian performances were more mixed. Although Italy was in large surplus through most of the period, this was at times due to low domestic demand pressures. France, on the other hand, was in small deficit, but was able to grow very rapidly, at a rate second only to that of Spain.

Germany's export-led growth of the 1950s had made some appreciation of the exchange rate inevitable. Though only very small, the 1961 revaluation appears to have checked the country's export performance.[8] After uninterrupted growth in market shares every year between 1950 and 1961, Germany's share stabilized in 1962–3. Between then and 1969 the growth of nominal incomes in manufacturing, taken in conjunction with the growth of productivity and the DM's constant parity, resulted in virtually no change in competitive position, whether measured by relative costs or prices (Fig. 5.2).[9] In the period exports grew at roughly the rate of world trade in manufactures, while import penetration

[8] E. Spitäller, 'The 1961 Revaluations and Exports of Manufactures', *IMF Staff Papers*, March 1970.

[9] The only major exception was the fall in costs during the upswing from the 1967 recession which led to a pronounced profit boom in the economy's tradeable sector and precipitated the 1969 'wage explosion'.

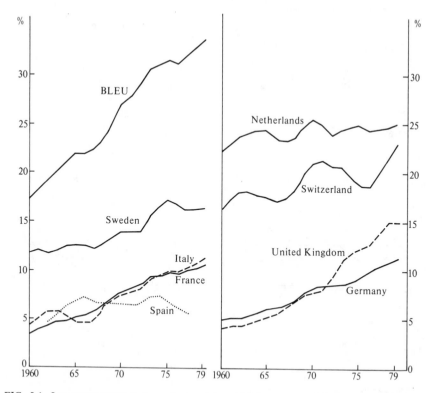

FIG. 5.1. *Import penetration* (manufactured imports[a] in per cent of GDP at current prices; three-year moving averages)
[a] SITC 5 to 8, less 68.
Sources: OECD, *Statistics of Foreign Trade, Series B* (various issues), and *National Accounts of OECD Countries, 1950–1979.*

rose steadily but more slowly than in the other major European countries. The 1969 revaluation, prompted by a combination of a large current account surplus and speculative capital inflows, reduced German cost competitiveness but was not at first reflected in a deterioration on the price front. Profits suffered, but export shares were maintained. As it became clear, however, that the cost position was unlikely to improve, a view reinforced by further appreciation under the float and subsequent Smithsonian realignment in 1971, export prices were raised. The effects, however, were to be felt only in the years following the first oil crisis.

Looking at the period as a whole, it would appear that although revaluations had temporary effects, their impact on Germany's longer-run external performance was small. Between 1959 and 1972, the DM's effective exchange rate probably rose by some 25 per cent, yet Germany's trade surplus in manufactures (on a cif-fob basis) declined only from 8½ to 8 per cent of GDP, its exports of manufactures rose above those of the United States, and its share of imported manufactures in GDP remained lower than those of both France (which had devalued in the period) and the United Kingdom (which had not participated in

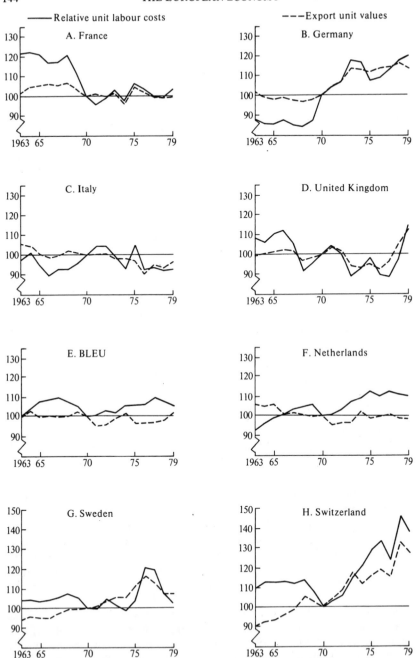

FIG. 5.2. *Relative unit labour costs and export unit values in manufacturing* (indices in $ terms: 1970 = 100)

Source: OECD, 'The International Competitiveness of Selected OECD Countries', *OECD Economic Outlook – Occasional Studies*, July 1978, updated by the OECD Secretariat.

the EEC trade creation movement).[10] To some extent the effects of revaluation were to be seen in the next period. One important reason for this performance is that the change in relative price competitiveness in this period was far smaller than the cumulated revaluation of the DM. A second reason for the apparently weak link between exchange rate changes and trade performances may well have been the characteristics of Germany's exports. These were (and are) heavily weighted in favour of machinery (SITC 7 represented nearly 50 per cent of manufactured exports in the early 1960s and some 55 per cent in the early 1970s), often sold in fairly monopolistic markets in the absence of close substitutes. Presumably for this reason, German export prices are among the least sensitive to the movement of competitors' export prices,[11] and, according to numerous econometric estimates, the price elasticities facing German exports are typically low (often below unity).[12]

The opposite was probably true for Italy. Italy's exports were (and are) much more heavily concentrated in semi-manufactures and consumer goods (some 50 per cent of the total) for which substitutability on world markets is likely to be much greater. Nevertheless, it does not appear that the country's success in increasing its market share abroad, and in containing the rise in imports, from the mid-1960s onwards was due to an improved competitive performance on the price or cost front. Although competitiveness, whether measured by relative unit labour costs or relative prices, fluctuated sharply on occasions, it showed little trend movement. Italy's current account surpluses are no doubt largely attributable to the low demand pressures that prevailed, in particular in the years 1964 to 1968. In this period while domestic demand was growing by 4 per cent per annum (a sharp deceleration from the previous five years' 7¼ per cent), foreign demand grew by 12½ per cent and import penetration actually declined. Rapid inflation in the early 1970s, largely consequent upon the 'Hot Autumn' of 1969, began, however, to affect the economy's performance, with the import share rising by 3½ percentage points between 1969 and 1974, export shares falling somewhat, and export profitability markedly eroded until the depreciation of 1973.

A noticeable element of the performance of France's foreign sector was its smooth behaviour, which paralleled domestic trends. Relative export prices remained virtually unchanged, and export shares were remarkably stable; and the import share rose very smoothly. That relative agricultural prices, important in French trade, should have shown little movement is perhaps unsurprising, given that a major instrument of the Common Agricultural Policy has been the stabilization of farm prices. But manufactured export prices, too, changed little in relation to those of France's main competitors. From 1963 to the second quarter of 1968, relative export prices fluctuated in a narrow band only about

---

[10] A study by M.C. Deppler ('Some Evidence of the Effects of Exchange Rate Changes on Trade', *IMF Staff Papers*, November 1974) also showed very little effect from DM revaluation in 1969.

[11] See, for instance, OECD, *Economic Outlook*, July 1973, p.86, or R. Dornbusch and P. Krugman, 'Flexible Exchange Rates in the Short Run', *Brookings Papers on Economic Activity*, No. 3, 1976, p. 567.

[12] See, for instance, M.C. Deppler and D.M. Ripley, 'The World Trade Model: Merchandise Trade', *IMF Staff Papers*, March 1978, p. 180.

5 percentage points wide, with no discernible trend; relative unit labour costs over that period, however, fell fairly steadily by about 8 per cent overall. The wage explosion following the May 1968 *événements* increased manufacturing unit labour costs by some 5 per cent, but after about a year the franc was devalued, more than restoring cost and price competitiveness. Thereafter, to the Smithsonian Agreements and beyond, export price competitiveness was essentially unchanged, while relative unit labour costs fell gently. Overall, this behaviour was characteristic of a manufacturing sector which, initially small in relation to Germany, France's largest trading partner, took prices essentially as given; with the authorities prepared at intervals to devalue the franc, relative costs moved so as to yield producers a profit sufficient to sustain high investment and thereby a high rate of growth.

The willingness to use devaluation as a tool of economic policy was probably the most interesting feature of the French experience. On the two occasions when large current account deficits could have constrained growth (in 1957-8 and in 1968-9), devaluations which went beyond the restoration of lost competitiveness freed policy-makers and spurred the economy. Nor was it considered essential to run large current account surpluses after these episodes. On the contrary, the small deficit recorded over the period as a whole suggests that the country grew as fast as was consistent with its overall trade performance. The United Kingdom's experience was an almost total contrast. The unwillingness to devalue until it was unavoidable meant that expansion was continually reined in by balance of payments considerations without the 'stop' phases of the 'stop-go' cycle generating either a lasting improvement in competitiveness or large current account surpluses.

Britain started the period with what was almost certainly an unfavourable relative cost position (Table 18.2). Despite several incomes policies, which temporarily restrained the growth of nominal incomes each time but arguably had little overall effect, competitiveness worsened, particularly after 1965. The current account, in deficit by 1 per cent of GDP in 1960 and by ¾ per cent in 1967, and never more than in slight surplus, was insufficient to support Britain's residual capital-exporting and reserve-currency role, leading ultimately to a large depreciation in late 1967. This, in conjunction with a tight fiscal policy, improved relative cost and price competitiveness for a period, and the current account went into substantial surplus for three years, reaching nearly 2 per cent of GDP by 1971. By that time, however, almost all of the cost competitiveness gained by the devaluation had been lost, and in 1972 the surplus was again only a modest ¼ per cent of GDP.

The most noteworthy performance among the smaller European countries — and indeed including the larger European economies as well — was that of Spain, another country which grew as fast as the balance of payments position would permit, and which devalued twice (in 1959 and 1967). Two major factors on the external front allowed Spain to expand as rapidly as it did (7 per cent on average between 1959 and 1973) — an improving performance on manufacturing trade and a sharp rise in invisible receipts. Spain's share in world exports of manufactures may have grown from close to zero at the beginning of the period to over 1 per cent in 1973. Although manufactured imports also grew rapidly in the early 1960s, in the wake of the liberalization programme of 1959, continued heavy protection and the 1967 devaluation helped stabilize their share in output from the mid-1960s onwards. Paucity of data makes an assessment of trade competitiveness difficult, but it seems that rapid export growth was mainly due to substantial additions to supply resulting from large-scale investment, particularly in new industries such as steel, chemicals, and motor cars. The combination of new manufacturing capacity with real wages which were low by the standards of the major European countries must have created a substantial cost advantage. Low real wages were probably also important in stimulating tourism. Spain's share in the total tourist receipts of the Southern European countries (Greece, Italy, Portugal, Turkey, Yugoslavia, and Spain itself) rose from 30 per cent in 1960-1 to 40 per cent in 1972-3, or in absolute terms from $350 million to $2¾ billion per year.

The fortunes of the other smaller and more mature European economies were (and still are) determined mainly by their larger trading partners. The smaller countries tend to be price-takers in product markets as well as broadly following wage developments in the major countries. Of the four countries considered in this chapter, only in Sweden can the current account be identified as having represented a fairly immediate constraint upon a more rapid expansion of demand. In Belgium, the Netherlands, and Switzerland, on the other hand, this was far from being the case. Trade performance was average for this group of countries. Switzerland seems to have lost market shares abroad, and saw its surplus on manufactured trade shrink from some 4 per cent of GDP in 1959-60 to virtual balance in 1973, but a rising surplus on invisible account more than offset this trade deterioration. The Benelux countries and to a lesser extent Sweden gained market shares, and the Netherlands and Sweden also managed to maintain a modest rise in imports. In Belgium, on the other hand, the share of imports in GDP increased from 16½ to 29 per cent, but this does not seem to have reflected any marked loss in cost or price competitiveness on the domestic market. In this period Belgium used its comparative locational advantage as a country at the heart of industrial Europe, integrated in the EEC, and with good communications, to develop a very large processing industry whose raison d'être was international trade. Hence between 1964 and 1974 the share of intra-industry in total trade increased in Belgium by more than in any other EEC country, reaching 79 per cent in 1974 (a figure second only to that of France).[13]

It is arguable that in these years supply forces probably played a smaller role than they did in the 1950s, a period which had seen more rapid structural change and the restoration of traditional trade channels. While both the German and Italian performances were perhaps not strongly influenced by changes in price and cost competitiveness, in other countries these forces seem to have been more important. In particular, the four major devaluations of the period (France in 1958[14] and 1969 and the United Kingdom and Spain in 1967) did apparently lead to improvements in both trade performance and current account

---

[13] B. Lassudrie-Duchêne and J.-L. Mucchielli, 'Les échanges intra-branche et la hiérarchisation des avantages comparés dans le commerce international', Revue économique, May 1979.

[14] Though France's devaluations of 1957 and 1958 took place in the earlier period, their effects only really came through between 1959 and 1962.

TABLE 5.7. *Comparative indicators of devaluation performance*
(percentages)

		Per caput GDP growth[a]	Per caput 'real wages'[ab]	Consumer price inflation[a]	Terms of trade[c]	Export shares[d]	Import shares[d]	Trade balance in manufactures (cif-fob)
					Changes in:			
France	1954–58 to 1958–62	0.6	0.3	−0.5	−1.8	1.1	1.0	0.6
France	1965–69 to 1969–73	0.2	1.0	2.2	2.2	1.9	−1.0	0.3
UK	1963–67 to 1967–71	−0.1	0.6	2.8	−0.2	1.5	–	−0.2
Spain	1963–67 to 1967–71	–	−2.5	−3.0	−1.9	(0.2)	−2.9	2.0

[a] Difference between average annual percentage changes in post- and pre-devaluation periods
[b] Compensation of employees deflated by implicit private consumption deflator
[c] Difference between terms of trade for goods and services in devaluation year and four years later
[d] Difference between percentage point changes in post- and pre-devaluation periods
[e] Difference between average annual shares in GDP in post- and pre-devaluation periods
Sources: OECD, *National Accounts of OECD Countries, 1950–1979*, OECD, *Statistics of Foreign Trade, Series B* (various issues), OECD, *Manpower Statistics, 1950–1962*; OECD, *Labour Force Statistics* (various issues); IMF, *International Financial Statistics* (1980 Yearbook); NIESR, *Economic Review*, and UN, *Monthly Bulletin of Statistics* (various issues).

positions. Yet these four episodes differed from each other. Table 5.7 tries to bring together an array of very summary indicators showing how the three countries performed in the four years before and after the parity changes. The figures try to allow for trend developments by (usually) presenting 'changes of changes'.[15] Although the data provide only a very partial picture, they suggest that the devaluations by France (in 1958) and by Spain were particularly successful. In neither case did real wages actually fall (indeed their growth accelerated in France), but their change was kept below that of per capita incomes, thereby allowing the necessary rise in profits. This was not, however, achieved in the United Kingdom. Also, inflation actually decelerated in France in the early 1960s and in Spain in the late 1960s, despite the devaluations and in contrast to the sharp acceleration in the United Kingdom. Finally, the terms of trade deteriorated in France and Spain, but remained unchanged in Britain. The second French devaluation was in many ways an intermediate case, with growth accelerating but by less than in 1959–62, inflation and the terms of trade rising

[15] Thus, for instance, the 1.5 per cent figure shown for the United Kingdom in the 'Exports share' column does not mean that Britain gained market shares but rather that its loss between 1967 and 1971 (−1.5 percentage points) was smaller than its loss between 1963 and 1967 (−3.0 percentage points). Similarly, the −2.5 per cent figure shown for Spanish 'Real wages' does not mean that real wages declined, but that their growth decelerated from an average annual rate of 7.7 per cent between 1963 and 1967 to one of 5.2 per cent in the subsequent four years.

rather than falling, but both export and import performance improving. More importantly, perhaps, France and Spain seem to have made better longer-term use of the breathing-space allowed by devaluation in so far as price competitiveness was preserved in both countries and non-price competitiveness may have improved.

Different policy attitudes were probably important in explaining these different reactions to devaluation. Both France in 1959 and Spain in 1968 made room for the tradeable sector by imposing severely restrictive fiscal policies around the time of devaluation. But subsequent years saw some relaxation which allowed investment to expand. In the United Kingdom, on the other hand, fiscal policies became progressively more restrictive. By 1969, the 'full employment' budget balance was in large surplus, equivalent to some 2½ per cent of output.[16] Arguably, this both stifled investment and contributed to the resentment that led to the 1969 wage explosion. Finally, non-economic factors may also have played a role: in Spain the break with a highly *dirigiste* and controlled economic system may have encouraged entrepreneurial initiative, while in France the return to political stability and entry into the EEC may have improved expectations. No such sharp change in trend, on the other hand, took place in the United Kingdom.

Despite the various differences, an overall judgement on these four episodes remains positive, and this would seem to be corroborated by a number of much more detailed studies.[17] The conclusion that devaluations were instrumental in allowing both a better trade performance and faster (or equally fast) growth for a number of years is important. Although the initial price advantages were to some extent eroded, the summary evidence presented in Table 5.7 suggests that in the conditions of the time this erosion was far from rapid, competitive gains being maintained for at least four years if not longer. This was to become one of the key issues of the period beginning in the early 1970s, when inflation was more rapid and floating exchange rates became generalized.

III. From the First Oil Crisis to the Second

The decade and a half of rapid OECD expansion culminated, in 1973, in the fastest growth recorded since 1964 (6.2 per cent), a commodity price explosion, and a quadrupling of the price of internationally traded oil. From March of that year, major countries' exchange rates were no longer pegged (indeed some currencies, in particular the pound and the Swiss franc, had been floating since 1972 and much greater exchange rate variability had set in in 1970-1). Not only did 1973 usher in a period of slower growth, but the events of that time led also to a number of other new developments, including:

---

[16] R.W.R. Price, 'Budgetary Policy', in F.T. Blackaby (ed.), *British Economic Policy, 1960-74*, NIESR, Cambridge 1978, p. 187.

[17] For France see, for instance, J. Mistral, 'Vingt ans de redéploiement du commerce extérieur', *Economie et statistique*, October 1975; for the United Kingdom, NIESR, 'The Effects of the Devaluation of 1967 on the Current Balance of Payments', *Economic Journal*, March 1972, or J.R. Artus, 'The 1967 Devaluation of the Pound Sterling', *IMF Staff Papers*, November 1975; for both countries as well as for Germany and the Netherlands, Deppler, 'Some Evidence'.

(i) A more rapid growth, in real terms of European exports (5 per cent on average, for goods and services) than of imports (4¼ per cent), reflecting the terms of trade shift to OPEC;

(ii) A high rate of inflation, as the commodity — but more importantly the oil–price increases became built into 'domestically generated' inflation,[18] the average rise of the GDP deflator amounting to nearly 12 per cent;

(iii) A substantial deficit on current account ($11 billion on average between 1974 and 1979), which, though slowly eroded in the years to 1978, re-emerged with the second oil price rise in 1979.

Within this overall picture there was considerably more divergence in the experience, policy, and performance of individual countries than in the earlier periods. In retrospect, at least, this is perhaps not surprising. The 1973–4 quadrupling of oil prices not only imparted a sharp inflationary impulse, but also had a number of other effects. It changed the pattern of relative costs, and hence of relative prices. It resulted in a change in the structure of final demand as OECD consumers and investors reacted to changed relative prices, and as OPEC oil producers, with tastes and needs different from OECD consumers, began spending newly acquired income. As the product composition of output began to change, and the various inputs of production began to be combined in different proportions, some economies were in a better position than others to respond to these unprecedentedly large shocks. This had important implications for the current account of the balance of payments, for exchange rates, and for overall macroeconomic performance.

Current balances and nominal exchange rates

Two of the traditional surplus countries of the 1950s and 1960s (Germany and Switzerland) remained in substantial surplus in this period too (Table 5.8). Germany's performance in 1974 was particularly notable. Monetary policy had been tightened markedly that year; and, due in important part to fiscal drag, the swing in the constant employment budget in 1973 had been of the order of 1½ per cent of GNP.[19] As a result, import volumes grew only very modestly, in contrast to the buoyant growth of exports. Hence, despite the terms of trade deterioration, the German current account surplus actually rose in 1974 (from $4½ to $10 billion). This was in sharp contrast to the experience of all the other European economies. It seems that this demand management policy stood the German economy in good stead to make the adjustments required by the changes in the structure of demand that followed the increase in oil prices.

First, and perhaps most importantly, the rate of 'domestically generated' inflation, which had averaged around 6.6 per cent over the previous four years, accelerated only fractionally, to 6.9 per cent, in 1974. This contrasts, for example, with the experience of Europe as a whole, where the implicit GDP deflator, after averaging 7.3 per cent growth between 1969 and 1973, accelerated to 11.8 per cent growth in 1974. This relatively favourable initial inflation

[18] Proxied by the implicit GDP deflator.
[19] Authors' estimates.

TABLE 5.8. *Current balances and effective exchange rates, 1973-1979*

	Current balances (annual averages, $ million)	Effective exchange rates (percentage changes over whole period)
France	−1,699	−5.7
Germany	4,375	35.8
Italy	382	−39.2
United Kingdom	−2,691	−21.6
Spain	−1,787	−22.9
BLEU	−710	11.8
Netherlands	629	20.0
Sweden	−1,542	−3.0
Switzerland	2,757	76.4
Other European countries	−10,705	..
OECD Europe	−10,991	..

Sources: OECD, *Economic Outlook*, July 1981; IMF, *International Financial Statistics* (1980 Yearbook).

response led, in conjunction with large current account surplus, to a virtuous circle over successive years. The effective exchange rate of the DM began to appreciate early in 1973. This meant that import prices in domestic currency were rising less quickly than in the average of other countries. German inflation in turn began to decelerate, the rate falling sharply, to only 3.3 per cent in 1976; by contrast for Europe as a whole the 1976 rate of 10.1 per cent was only slightly down on the 1974 figure. And the virtuous circle continued; by 1979 the exchange rate had, in effective terms, appreciated by 36 per cent in six years. Nor did the current balance appear to suffer much from this experience. It remained in large surplus through the years 1975-8 and went into deficit only in 1979, largely as a consequence, it seemed, of the second rise in oil prices.

Switzerland's performance was in some ways even more remarkable than Germany's. In Switzerland, too, policies were restrictive at the outset; and little relaxation took place through the period. The exchange rate appreciated very sharply — by as much as 76 per cent in effective terms between 1973 and 1979 — with predictable effects on inflation. Consumer prices rose by only 4 per cent per annum, the GDP deflator by 3.7 per cent, which was *less* than the 3.9 per cent recorded in the years 1950-73. Here, as in Germany, the revaluation seemed to have little effect on the current account, which remained in substantial surplus throughout the period. Indeed, the Swiss current surplus represented as much as 4 per cent of GDP (as against Germany's figure of not quite 1 per cent), probably the highest figure recorded by a European country for such a prolonged period, and this at a time when the rest of OECD Europe was in deficit to the tune of 0.7 per cent of GDP.

The other countries which revalued in effective terms through this period, although to a much lesser extent, were Belgium and the Netherlands, whose currencies were at least partly pegged to the DM. Inflation was relatively low in both countries, and well below the European average, but Belgium's erstwhile large surplus gave way to a large and growing deficit, while the Netherlands, although in surplus on average, also saw a gradual deterioration, despite the advantage of near self-sufficiency in energy.

At the other end of the spectrum were what came to be known as the 'weaker' countries of Europe. Among them, France and Sweden, though in substantial current deficit, experienced little depreciation. Both were countries that, for a time at least, tried to contain the rise in unemployment and to maintain relatively rapid growth. Both recorded inflation rates (of the order of 9½ to 10½ per cent per annum) that were stable and close to the European average. British, Italian, and Spanish inflation rates, on the other hand, were much higher, ranging from 15½ per cent per annum in the United Kingdom to 18 per cent in Spain. The dispersion in exchange rate developments was also much larger. Italy's exchange rate declined sharply in 1974 (when the pound, although depreciating, was boosted by inflows of OPEC funds, while the peseta seems to have been helped by official intervention). Given the wage indexation mechanism, inflation in Italy accelerated; and, in contrast to Germany's virtuous circle, the country entered into a spiral in which domestic money incomes rose to offset higher import prices, the exchange rate depreciated further, and so on. Spanish developments after 1974 were similar, but the return to surplus on current account in 1978-9 helped to boost the value of the currency (something that did not occur in Italy, where the authorities accepted a depreciation that offset continuing inflation differentials). The pound's movement was more erratic, with, in particular, a very sharp depreciation in 1976. This was reversed, however, in subsequent years, despite a continuing inflation differential between the United Kingdom and the rest of the world. Following the adoption of stabilization measures at the turn of 1976, exchange markets apparently began to be influenced by the prospect of the country becoming self-sufficient in oil by the early 1980s, and the pound's effective rate first stabilized and then rose, particularly in 1979.

The three countries also experienced very different current balance developments. Italy was in small surplus on average, while the United Kingdom and Spain were in large deficit. But both Italy and Spain, whose 1974 deterioration had been closely comparable to that of the United Kingdom, improved their positions sharply during the period. Between 1974 and 1979 the Italian current account swung from deficit into surplus by some $13 billion and the Spanish one by $4½ billion, equivalent to 6 and 3½ per cent of average GDP of the period respectively. The United Kingdom, in contrast, and despite output growth of only 1¼ per cent per annum, was in deficit in five years out of six, with little evidence of a trend improvement, even though its trade deficit in fuels (on a cif-fob basis) was reduced by as much as $6 billion.

Competitiveness and 'real' exchange rates

It is difficult to assess the experience of these years. For one thing, the period is too recent to permit a fully balanced and detached look. For another, it is too brief to allow an appraisal of the advantages and disadvantages of the floating exchange rate regime. Flexible exchange rates certainly appear to have added a new dimension of difficulty to economic management, and some European governments have at times laid a substantial part of the blame for worsened macroeconomic performance at their door. But how far the system has been an independent source of difficulty in a world of highly mobile capital, rapid and internationally divergent inflation rates, and supply-side shocks – whether, indeed, any other system could have worked in the circumstances – remains controversial. On the surface, at least, the new arrangements displayed disquieting characteristics. Exchange rate fluctuations were numerous and sharp, with the amplitude of day-to-day, month-to-month, and even year-to-year movements probably going well beyond what proponents of floating had expected at the outset. The stabilizing speculation predicted by the textbooks was frequently conspicuous by its absence. This was true both within Europe, despite attempts at stabilization (e.g. the creation of the European 'snake' arrangements and later the EMS), and between European currencies and the dollar or yen.

Turning to the particular concern of this chapter, current account positions sometimes seemed to react disappointingly slowly, if at all, to exchange rate changes even when these were large and went consistently in one direction. The most notable examples were those of Germany and Switzerland (but also Japan) – three countries whose large nominal revaluations seemed for a time to call forth larger rather than smaller surpluses, and not just because of short-run 'J-curve' effects. But among the 'deficit' countries, too, it was felt that both Britain and Italy were hardly helped by the steep depreciation of the pound and the lira.

Scepticism about the effectiveness of exchange rate changes arose not so much because of what in the 1950s and 1960s had been called 'elasticity pessimism' (the belief that price elasticities in international trade were frequently too low to generate desired shifts in current account positions), but rather because it was thought difficult to bring about and sustain desired changes in competitiveness or 'real' exchange rates. This view was held by adherents of widely contrasting intellectual positions. Thus unsophisticated monetarists tended to argue that exchange rate changes were essentially neutral because they 'merely reflected' inflation differentials (in turn related to relative rates of monetary growth); while those with a simplistic cost–push view of inflation held that virtuous or vicious circles in revaluing and devaluing countries respectively were bound quickly to wipe out any competitive advantage or disadvantage and hence reinforce inflation in some countries and price stability in others. Although these beliefs did not square well with econometric evidence that 'pass through' effects (the extent to which exchange rate changes led to changes in domestic prices or costs) were relatively small over time-spans of up to four or five years following depreciation or appreciation,[20] it was argued that in the climate of inflationary expectations prevailing in the later 1970s such evidence, often obtained from the behaviour of the 1960s, was irrelevant or even misleading.

But the 'stylized fact' that both schools of thought were seeking to explain –

---

[20] For a general survey see M.E. Kreinin, 'The Effect of Exchange Rate Changes on the Prices and Volume of Foreign Trade', *IMF Staff Papers*, July 1977; for more specific country evidence, P. Artus *et al.*, 'Les enseignements de METRIC sur l'analyse du court terme', *Economie et statistique*, June 1978 (for France), or NIESR, *Economic Review*, February 1978 (for the United Kingdom); for an opposite view on Italy see C. Chiesa *et al.*, *Un modello di analisi e previsione del settore bilancia dei pagamenti correnti*, Banca d'Italia, Rome 1978.

the constancy of 'real' exchange rates – was not a good approximation to real-world behaviour, and the implied conclusions for the balance of payments adjustment process were unjustifiably negative. The figures presented in Table 5.9 suggest that the period did witness changes in 'real' exchange rates, as proxied

TABLE 5.9. *'Real' exchange rates and trade performance*

	'Real' exchange rate			Changes in:		
	Nominal effective exchange rate	$(1)^a$	$(2)^b$	Export shares[c]	Import shares[c]	Trade balance in manufactures[c] (cif-fob)
	average annual percentage changes, 1970–79			in percentage points, 1974–1979		
France	..	0.8	0.5	0.9	1.7	0.9
Germany	5.5	3.3	2.0	−1.4	2.8	−1.7
Italy	−6.5	−1.8	−1.5	1.6	2.4	4.3
United Kingdom	−4.0[d]	0.5	0.8[d]	0.3	4.4	−1.2
Spain	−2.7	..	..	(0.6)	−1.8	1.4
BLEU	1.7	−0.3	−0.1	−0.8	3.5	−3.9
Netherlands	2.7	0.6	0.6	−0.3	1.7	−1.6
Sweden	0.1	−1.4	−	−0.3	2.4	0.2
Switzerland	8.4	3.2	3.3	0.2	2.0	2.7

[a] Relative unit labour costs in manufacturing in common currency adjusted for cyclical movements in productivity
[b] Average of relative normalized unit labour costs, relative wholesale prices, and relative export unit values in manufacturing in common currency
[c] See notes to Table 5.6
[d] For the period 1970–78 the figures are −5,4, −1.1, and −0.3 per cent respectively
Sources: IMF, *International Financial Statistics* (1980 Yearbook); NIESR, *Economic Review*, and UN, *Monthly Bulletin of Statistics* (various issues); OECD, *Statistics of Foreign Trade, Series B* (various issues); OECD, *National Accounts of OECD Countries, 1950–1979*.

by two rough indicators – one of costs and one of both costs and prices in manufacturing. The figures shown for exchange rates stretch back to 1970 on the plausible assumption that because of lags in the adjustment process the trade performances of the various European countries between 1973 and 1979 were likely to have been influenced by earlier currency movements, but even if the observations had been restricted to the six years from 1973, the figures would have looked very similar. It will be seen that, if only roughly, there is some evidence that, as suggested for a somewhat larger sample of countries, 'A 3 to 5 per cent change in the nominal effective exchange rate has been associated with a change in the real rate of 1 per cent',[21] particularly if, for the United Kingdom, the last year (1979), when the value of the pound was being strongly influenced by factors other than the competitiveness of the British economy, is ignored.

[21] N. Thygesen, 'Exchange-Rate Experiences and Policies of Small Countries: Some European Examples of the 1970s', *Princeton Essays in International Finance*, No. 136, 1979, p. 3.

Equally significant, the 'real' exchange rate changes that took place can be seen to have had effects on the (manufactured) export and import performance of the various countries. In contrast to the experience of the 1960s, Germany and the Benelux countries lost market shares even though Germany, at least, was particularly well placed to gain shares in the new and rapidly expanding OPEC market, given its comparative advantage in the 'traditional' metal-intensive machinery and equipment demanded in the area. Italy, the United Kingdom, and Spain, on the other hand, all gained market shares. The Italian performance was remarkable, in that the gains were larger than those of any other country (including Japan). The British performance was equally remarkable in that the country had regularly lost market shares from 1950 to 1974, and, in peace time at least, probably since the nineteenth century. Similarly, import penetration fell below trend in France and Spain, but rose relatively rapidly in Germany.

There are, however, apparent exceptions to this picture. Switzerland saw a fairly sharp real appreciation but no deterioration in export performance and no acceleration in import penetration, both contrary to the experience of the 1960s. Hence, the Swiss current account surplus, rather than declining, actually rose, but this may have been largely due to exceptionally low demand pressures at home rather than to a particularly low responsiveness of trade flows to price changes. Over the six years, Swiss domestic demand *fell* by 1 per cent while foreign demand grew by 31 per cent: the country substituted export for domestic demand growth. In Britain, while export performance was improving, import performance was deteriorating very rapidly. The share of imported manufactures in GDP rose from 9 per cent in 1972 to nearly 16 per cent in 1979, or by more than the whole of the rise in the preceding twenty-two years. EEC trade-creation effects were one factor at work, but non-price influences seemed also to be important.

More generally, the current balance developments noted above seem to have been strongly influenced by a combination of longer-run output trends and shorter-term policy responses that often masked the impacts of the depreciations or appreciations. Thus, in this period, 'a marked reduction in the long-run rates of growth in the three surplus countries, the Federal Republic of Germany, Japan, and Switzerland, was accompanied by a fall in domestic investment relative to saving',[22] while, at least initially, France, Italy, the United Kingdom, and Spain hoped to be able to maintain growth rates close to earlier pre-oil-price-increase levels. More importantly, the policy response to exchange rate changes may not always have been symmetrical. While devaluing countries did ultimately follow the disabsorption policies required to achieve the necessary resource shift into the foreign sector, surplus countries arguably did not fully offset the deflationary impacts stemming from revaluation. This was clearly the case for Switzerland, where output fell over the period, but may well have also been the case for Germany, at least until the stimulatory measures of mid-1978. Indeed, as Germany (and Japan) embarked upon reflation, their manufacturing trade surpluses either declined or rose less rapidly in 1979 and 1980 (and their current balances swung into large deficit).

[22] J.R. Artus and J.H. Young, 'Fixed and Flexible Exchange Rates: A Renewal of the Debate', *IMF Staff Papers*, December 1979, p. 661.

In summary, therefore, if current accounts failed to respond as hoped for over much of the period, this could probably be attributed more to the demand management policies that were followed than to the vagaries of the exchange rate regime. 'Flexible rates did not work better because, in part, demand management policies were not usually directed toward adjustment of current account imbalances. Cutting the inflation rate, even at the cost of sluggish domestic aggregate demand, was the major policy target in the surplus countries.'[23] As a result, the deficit countries were probably forced into an even more restrictive stance than the one they would have chosen in order to make their devaluations effective. Whether in these circumstances the floating system itself can be said to have imparted a deflationary bias to Europe as a whole (contrary to what would have been expected at the outset) is debatable. In so far as curbing inflation was almost certainly the primary target of most governments, at least by the end of the period, such a bias might actually have been welcome, although making external adjustment *per se* more difficult than it would otherwise have been.

Conclusions

In drawing together the main findings of this brief survey of the last thirty years, perhaps the first point to emerge is the remarkable rapidity with which Europe broke free from the extreme financial constraints it faced in the immediate aftermath of the war. Few could have expected that, even with significant American aid, European countries would so quickly be capable of combining fast growth, an ambitious programme of trade liberalization, and balance in their combined current account. Evidently Europe as a whole enjoyed something of a virtuous circle of trade and growth in the early post-war period. Within the overall picture, some countries performed consistently better than others. The question whether this was evidence of a process of export-led growth or of growth-led exports can hardly be settled here. Suffice it to say that the relative competitive positions of different countries and the pattern of their relative growth rates were mutually consistent; moreover, from the late 1940s to the late 1960s most countries maintained high levels of activity, and exchange rate changes were few. One conclusion which might be drawn is that the realignment of European currencies in 1949 was particularly well judged. But it is also hard to avoid the impression that, to a degree, relative growth rates adapted to relative competitive positions.

After fifteen years of strong European growth, strains began to develop. Partly these were due to greatly increased capital mobility and to the rapid growth of international banking and multinational corporations, but longer-run underlying forces were also at work. By the mid-1960s, the United Kingdom's growth performance was widely perceived as being constrained by inadequate competitiveness, while Germany tended to have a strong external balance even at full employment. France had not yet lost all the competitiveness gains achieved by devaluations in the late 1950s, although after the wage explosion of 1968 further depreciation seemed inevitable. Between late 1967 and 1969 the

---

[23] Ibid., p. 662.

three largest countries each changed their exchange rates, with Germany on balance appreciating by over 20 per cent relative to France and Britain. The wage explosion in Italy then reduced that country's competitive edge. This combination of changes moved current account positions in the desired directions, and was nearly sufficient to carry these countries through to the floating period, only small effective changes being made at the Smithsonian realignment.

It is difficult to draw clear-cut conclusions regarding the period starting in 1973. At first glance the simultaneous occurrence of widespread current account deficits and markedly slower growth would suggest that growth was being constrained by balance of payments considerations. But a much more complete analysis would be required, paying attention *inter alia* to the role of rapid inflation, big inflation differentials, currency floating, and higher oil prices. Public statements issued during the period suggest that virtually all countries saw inflation as the main reason underlying their pursuit of restrictive demand policies; but for some, notably a number of smaller countries, external considerations were probably a powerful reinforcing factor. In the circumstances, 'external considerations' were liable to mean the need the attract capital inflows and/or the avoidance of unwanted exchange depreciation as much as the desirability of reducing current deficits.

A full assessment of how well the floating exchange rate regime has served European countries is beyond the scope of this chapter. For present purposes it may be noted that while it had undoubtedly become more difficult to make a real exchange rate change 'stick' in a world of considerable real wage rigidity, real changes nevertheless did occur. Moreover, those that were sustained were generally speaking in the direction required for better payments balance and had significant effects on trade flows. As Europe entered the 1980s, there were, however, signs of disillusionment with floating exchange rates. It was felt that 'overshooting' had been too frequent, exchange rate changes often going significantly beyond what would have been warranted by underlying differences in competitiveness and in inflation differentials (e.g. Switzerland's appreciation in 1977–8 or the pound's slide into devaluation in 1976 and subsequent revaluation in 1979, let alone 1980). One major reaction against this took the form of the creation of the EMS in early 1979, a system that attempted, with a reasonable degree of success, to restore some exchange rate stability within Continental Europe, if not *vis-à-vis* the pound, which remained outside the system, or, of course, the dollar.

There were also signs that another trend might be emerging at the turn of the decade. Faced with increasing difficulties at home, a number of countries, both in Europe and elsewhere, were in danger of shifting to a more protectionist stance. The movement towards greater interference with trade was only partial and circumscribed. In Europe, in particular, it was very largely directed at imports from non-West-European countries. Within the EEC, if anything, trade liberalization progressed further. With the effectiveness of demand management policies in coping with unemployment and inflation being increasingly questioned, creeping protectionism was an indication that policy-making had not satisfactorily resolved the problems of securing domestic objectives in an interdependent trading world.

Bibliography

Two accounts of post-war payments problems, from different perspectives, are D. MacDougall, *The World Dollar Problem*, London 1957 (and the same author's 'The Dollar Problem: A Reappraisal', *Princeton Essays in International Finance*, No. 35, 1960), and R. Triffin, *Europe and the Money Muddle*, New Haven 1957. In addition to those sources, the statistical picture of that period presented here is derived from M. Gilbert and Associates, *Comparative National Products and Price Levels*, OEEC, Paris 1958, and A. Maizels, *Industrial Growth and World Trade*, NIESR, Cambridge 1963.

The measurement of international competitiveness is discussed in OECD, 'The International Competitiveness of Selected OECD Countries', *OECD Economic Outlook – Occasional Studies*, July 1978, and C.A. Enoch, 'Measures of Competitiveness in International Trade', *Bank of England Quarterly Bulletin*, June 1978.

A classic source for trade elasticities is H.A. Houthakker and S.P. Magee, 'Income and Price Elasticities in World Trade', *Review of Economics and Statistics*, May 1969. For a discussion of conceptual problems, see E.E. Leamer and R.M. Stern, *Quantitative International Economics*, Boston 1970. For examples of the use of elasticities in the context of a world trade model, see L. Samuelson, 'A New Model of World Trade', *OECD Economic Outlook – Occasional Studies*, December 1973, and J.R. Artus and R.R. Rhomberg, 'A Multilateral Exchange Rate Model', *IMF Staff Papers*, November 1973. Other examples of analyses of the effect of relative price changes on trade flows are H.B. Junz and R.R. Rhomberg, 'Prices and Export Performance of Industrial Countries, 1953–1963', *IMF Staff Papers*, July 1965, and M.E. Kreinin, 'The Effect of Exchange Rate Changes on the Prices and Volume of Foreign Trade', *IMF Staff Papers*, July 1977; an analysis of cyclical effects can be found in F.G. Adams and H.B. Junz, 'The Effect of the Business Cycle on Trade Flows of Industrial Countries', *Journal of Finance*, May 1971.

It is beyond the scope of the present bibliography to survey the vast literature on different approaches to balance of payments theory. An example is H.G. Johnson, 'Elasticity, Absorption, Keynesian Multiplier, Keynesian Policy, and Monetary Approaches to Devaluation Theory: A Simple Geometric Exposition', *American Economic Review*, June 1976. For a discussion of the significance of the current account, see J. Salop and E. Spitäller, 'Why Does the Current Account Matter?', *IMF Staff Papers*, March 1980.

6

The Labour Market and Unemployment

FRANCO BERNABÈ*

Introduction

This chapter deals mainly with the labour market response to changing economic and institutional conditions in post-war Europe. It is divided into two sections. The first concentrates on the supply response of labour through the period. It stresses, in particular, the difference between the experience of the 1950s and 1960s and that of the 1970s. While in the former period the rapid increase of labour demand was met by a corresponding increase of supply, despite adverse demographic conditions, in the latter period supply kept growing despite adverse economic conditions which were expected to discourage people from entering the labour market. This section pays particular attention to international migration, because of its importance in modifying domestic labour force trends both in sending and in receiving countries. The second section analyses the political and institutional consequences of full employment and their feedbacks on to labour market behaviour. It concentrates, in particular, on the institutional changes which seem to have affected labour supply and unemployment in the 1970s and on the increasing segmentation of European labour markets in this period. The chapter concludes with a short assessment of the consequences of almost a decade of growing unemployment in Europe and a tentative evaluation of future labour market prospects.

The chapter is not intended to be a survey of all relevant aspects of the post-war European experience. Rather, it concentrates on what seems to be the main feature of this experience – the long cyclical wave in the relative bargaining power of labour. In the 1950s and early 1960s strong demand dried up the open and hidden labour reserves which existed in the European countries after the war. The prolonged conditions of full employment which labour markets enjoyed in the 1960s strengthened the bargaining power of workers and allowed them to increase their relative income share and improve the institutional conditions regulating the labour market. Partly as a consequence of higher wages and of a large degree of job security, demand for labour slowed down and the bargaining power of workers decreased again from the mid-1970s onwards. It is readily admitted that there were numerous other reasons for the slower growth of labour demand in the 1970s, some of which are totally unrelated to the labour market. There are none the less grounds for believing that changes in the functioning of labour markets caused by the prolonged period of full employment were at the origin of some of the difficulties Europe encountered in that decade.

Full employment is the really distinctive feature of the post-war experience. By historical standards the achievement of full employment in the 1960s was completely unprecedented. For the first time not only were urban workers fully

*Economic Studies Department, FIAT.

employed but underemployment in agriculture and other low productivity sectors had also fallen to very low levels. For the economy as a whole, the major consequences of full employment were the end of a long period of only moderate wage growth and a large redistribution of income from capital to labour. These aspects have been widely analysed and will not be given extensive treatment in this chapter. Instead, the focus will be on the accompanying social and institutional consequences which have so far attracted less attention.

The political environment was relatively favourable to social reforms because in most European countries the attainment of full employment in the mid-1960s coincided (not by accident) with the coming to power of social-democratic governments or of coalitions including left-wing parties. At first these reforms involved a gradual extension of the welfare state.[1] The major changes specifically affecting labour market behaviour came, however, somewhat later and were mostly directed at improving the income and job security of workers. It should be noted that although these measures were extended during the 1974–5 recession the institutional framework was set mostly at the end of the 1960s and the beginning of the 1970s. The reforms of this period had two major consequences for the functioning of labour markets – they increased the attractiveness of entering the market and they made the access to prime jobs more difficult as the demand for labour became more selective.

Increasing job and income security mark a radical departure from the experience of market economies since the industrial revolution. To appreciate the importance of the change it is necessary to put it into a broader historical perspective. In a pre-capitalist society work was only one aspect (and perhaps not the most important one) of a complex system of social and personal relations. The labour market simply did not exist. In most cases the mobility of workers was restricted, as was the possibility of changing occupation. But, as the apprentice could not leave his master, the master could not lay off his apprentice. Along with this form of job security went various forms of income security – subsidies for the poor, assistance of the guilds to their members, and others.[2] All this disappeared with the progress of the industrial revolution when the development of manufacturing and factory work required, among other things, an elastic supply of labour. It has, indeed, been argued convincingly that the creation of a free labour market was one of the most important innovations introduced by capitalism and was decisive for its take-off.[3]

The return to a greater degree of job and income security has in the 1970s raised fears that a new form of economic feudalism may be appearing.[4] The shifting emphasis of employment policies from a macroeconomic approach, aimed at keeping aggregate demand at a level which allows full employment, to a microeconomic approach, aimed at preserving each job, could have negative implications for growth. The decreasing mobility of the labour force caused by higher job security may hamper the process of structural adaptation and therefore slow down productivity growth. It can also slow down employment growth

[1] See Ch. 7.   [2] A. Dal Pane, *Storia del lavoro in Italia*, Milan 1958, p. 288.
[3] K. Polany, *The Great Transformation*, New York 1949. The first to stress this point of view was, of course, Marx.
[4] See, for instance, OCDE, 'Mesures d'ajustement positives en matière de politique de main d'oeuvre et d'emploi', *mimeo*, Paris 1979, p. 55.

because firms may be less willing to hire if they know that it could be hard to lay off redundant employees. The fears of a secular stagnation as a consequence of a large degree of job security may however have been exaggerated. A study of the effects of employment protection laws shows that their major impact was on the selection and training policies of firms.[5]

It should also be noted that the higher degree of job security was a consequence not only of the greater bargaining power of workers but also of the changing needs of the productive system. As production grows more complex and more automated, the need for an abundant supply of undifferèntiated and unskilled labour such as that characteristic of the nineteenth and early twentieth centuries decreases, while increasing specialization stimulates employers to provide job security in order to promote training in skills as specific to the firm as possible.[6] The most important consequence of this process is that the instantaneous clearing mechanism of the labour market, postulated by neo-classical theory, is made even more unrealistic, and rationing becomes a much more common adjustment mechanism.[7]

There is much controversy over the appropriate policies for achieving full employment in these changed circumstances. But there is, perhaps, a more fundamental question that should be raised first. Can full employment under these new conditions still be considered a primary policy objective or should governments concentrate on other aims? The destruction of feudal institutions which deprived people of alternative sources of income compelled them to exchange work for income in order to survive. In such a context, Keynesian policies were designed mainly to assure to everybody an income by providing jobs. But in Europe's industrialized countries of the late 1970s, where almost half of national income was redistributed in various forms by the state, work and income appeared increasingly separated, and, paradoxically, the latter was often easier to provide than the former. It could, therefore be argued that the full employment objective need no longer be seen as a question of basic social justice. Its attainment may still be considered desirable, but more for socio-philosophical reasons than because it reduces deprivation and poverty. If this is true, government action could be redirected towards designing policies for the best use of leisure time rather than trying to tackle a problem which has defied solutions over at least a decade.

I. Characteristics of Labour Supply

The supply of labour is determined by four major factors: the size of the population, its demographic structure, the attachment of each age and sex group to the labour market, and the number of hours of work that the labour force is willing to supply. More recently a fifth factor, work effort, has received increasing attention, despite obvious measurement difficulties. Each of these can

---

[5] W.W. Daniel and E. Stilgoe, *The Impact of Employment Protection Laws*, Policy Studies Institute, London 1978.

[6] W.Y. Oi, 'Labor as a Quasi-Fixed Factor', *Journal of Political Economy*, December 1962.

[7] E. Malinvaud, *The Theory of Unemployment Reconsidered*, Oxford 1977.

be modified by overall economic conditions. The size and structure of the population, which depend upon exogenous demographic factors, can be altered by migration stemming from differential growth rates of demand for labour. Participation rates, which are determined by institutional factors, by specific social conditions, and by changes in the relative costs of work and leisure, can and are modified by cyclical fluctuations in the economy. Working hours are governed by custom and by contracts as well as by the level of economic activity. Even work effort, which depends primarily on job satisfaction, attachment to the firm, and custom, can respond to labour market pressures.

The distinction between economic and non-economic factors influencing labour supply which is usually introduced for analysing the short-run behaviour of labour markets is less relevant in a longer term perspective. Very often apparently exogenous institutional and social changes are themselves the consequences of earlier changes in labour markets or of particular features of the growth process. The length of compulsory education and the age limits for retirement depend on, among other things, the level of per capita income, and even birth rates follow to some extent the level of economic activity, as is indicated by their fall in the 1930s and 1970s and their strong recovery in the first half of the 1960s. Most factors affecting labour supply may therefore, to some degree, be considered endogenous with respect to the overall growth process, though the direction in which they operate may be indeterminate a priori and the lags at time rather long. This section will concentrate on the endogeneity of labour supply with respect to the post-war growth process. Its aim is to show that growth created favourable supply conditions in the labour market that allowed the growth process to become self-sustained.

For the purposes of this section the post-war period has been divided into three distinct phases. The first, from the beginning of the reconstruction process to the mid-1950s, was characterized in many countries by an excess supply of core labour force in the non-agricultural sectors and by the limited contribution of both demographic factors and intersectoral migration to urban labour supply. The only external supply source, limited to a few countries, was refugee migration. The second period, up to the mid-1960s, was characterized by massive intersectoral and international migration of the core labour force. The third period, from the late 1960s to the late 1970s, was characterized by the stagnation of total employment and by two distinct phases of supply developments — a first phase in which the growth of the labour force decelerated in line with demand and a second one in which it accelerated again despite rising unemployment (Table 6.1).

This subdivision is in some ways arbitrary because, although these phenomena have been common to a large part of Europe, their temporal and geographic dimensions have differed between various parts of the continent. It has, however, the advantage of corresponding to the three main phases of growth — reconstruction, super-growth in the late 1950s and 1960s, and semi-stagnation in the 1970s. It therefore allows a better appreciation of the link between labour supply and economic development.

In the 1950s and the first half of the 1960s, Europe's rapid growth process stimulated a large increase in labour demand mostly in manufacturing and construction. But the male labour force, particularly in prime age brackets, was in

TABLE 6.1. *Demand and supply for labour in the EEC*
(average annual percentage changes)

	1950–55	1955–65	1965–73	1973–79
Population of working age	0.6	0.6	0.4	0.6
Labour force	0.8	0.4	0.2	0.6
Total employment	1.0	0.6	0.1	0.1
of which: Agricultural employment	..	−3.5	−4.4	−2.9
Independent non-agricultural employment	..	−0.2	−0.4	−
Dependent non-agricultural employment	..	1.7	0.9	0.5

Sources: EEC, *Population and Employment, 1977*; OECD, *Manpower Statistics, 1950–1962*, and *Labour Force Statistics* (various issues); author's estimates.

short supply in urban labour markets, partly for demographic reasons and partly because of falling participation rates and earlier retirement that led to more than seven million people withdrawing from the labour force in fifteen years. Table 6.2 shows that from the mid-1950s to the late 1960s in the EEC countries the natural growth of urban labour supply contributed hardly at all to the increase in dependent employment in industry and services. The labour force necessary to match demand and supply had therefore to come from countries and regions where it was abundant.

In the 1970s the pattern of labour supply changed substantially, with the natural growth of the urban labour force increasingly contributing to the satisfaction of labour demand. Probably the most important reason for this change was the increasing participation rate of women in virtually all European countries. This was stimulated in part by the awareness that a job could be one way

TABLE 6.2. *Contribution of different supply sources to dependent non-agricultural employment growth in the EEC*
(percentages)

	1955–60	1960–65	1965–70	1970–75	1975–78
Growth in dependent non-agricultural employment[a]	1.7	1.7	0.8	0.4	0.5
Contribution of:[b]					
Urban labour force	0.20	0.08	−0.16	0.19	0.72
Unemployed	0.57	−0.04	−0.07	−0.48	−0.51
Immigrant labour force	0.33	0.52	0.29	0.20	0.04
Migration from agriculture	0.64	1.02	0.72	0.41	0.27
Self-employed and family workers outside agriculture	−0.04	0.12	0.02	0.08	−0.02

[a] Average annual percentage changes
[b] In percentage points

Sources: author's estimates based on data in EEC, *Population and Employment, 1977*; OECD, *Manpower Statistics, 1950–62*, and *Labour Force Statistics* (various issues).

to achieve emancipation from a subordinate role within the family, but also in part by the growing demand for labour in the service sector and in public administration. Another factor contributing to the changing structure of supply was a more rapid growth of the domestic working age population, mainly in the younger age groups. In the presence of a continuing, although moderate, migration from agriculture, and given much lower growth rates of output, this led to a very large increase in urban unemployment.

Reconstruction, 1945–55

A number of political factors had an impact on the European labour market during this period, and also later. Particularly important was refugee migration from Eastern to Western Europe, notably the flow of East Germans, which lasted from the end of the war to the raising of the Berlin wall in 1961. It has been estimated that in that period twelve million people coming from territories taken over by the Soviet Union and Poland and from the GDR entered the Federal Republic. According to Kindleberger, this may have increased the German labour force by almost seven million people.[8] Less important from the point of view of the number of people involved, but certainly not less important from a social and political standpoint, was the migration of Poles during and after the war. The UNECE estimated that in France, the United Kingdom, and Belgium alone there were at the beginning of the 1950s half a million Poles.[9]

In the period up to the second half of the 1950s, the role of domestic demographic growth was marginal (Table 6.3). It was only in Italy and Scandinavia

TABLE 6.3. *Labour force and employment growth in the EEC, 1950–1955*
(average annual percentage changes)

	France	Germany	Italy	United Kingdom	EEC
Population of working age	–	1.4	1.0	0.1	0.6
of which: From 15 to 24 years	−1.0	2.2	–	0.3	..
From 25 to 54 years	0.2	0.6	1.1	−0.2	..
From 55 to 64 years	3.9	3.0	1.8	1.1	..
Labour force	0.1	1.8	0.5	0.8	0.8
Total employment	0.1	2.7	0.4	0.9	1.0

Sources: author's estimates based on data in EEC, *Population and Employment, 1977*, and A. Maddison, 'Long Run Dynamics of Productivity Growth', *Banca Nazionale del Lavoro Quarterly Review*, March 1979.

(the latter not shown in the table) that demographic growth made some contribution to labour supply (the German figure being heavily influenced by immigration). Particularly marked all over Europe was the stagnation, and in some countries the decline, of the 15 to 24 age group, partly offset by a considerable increase in the older population. Unfortunately, few figures on labour market trends are available for the first half of the 1950s and the ones presented

[8] C.P. Kindleberger. *Europe's Postwar Growth*, Cambridge, Mass. 1967.
[9] UNECE, *Labour Supply and Migration in Europe*, New York 1979.

in Table 6.3 should be used with some caution. As they stand, they suggest, first, that the rapid employment growth recorded by Europe in these years was largely due to Germany, and, second, that labour supply appears to have been particularly responsive to demand conditions. In Germany and the United Kingdom a strong growth in employment led to an increase in participation rates, while in Italy a rate of employment growth only half as rapid as that of population resulted in a sharp drop in participation rates. As for hours worked, these rose marginally in the period, at least outside Scandinavia.

In the light of the above, it would seem worth stressing that the European labour market in the early post-war years provided conditions which were relatively favourable to stable non-inflationary growth. The countries in which the process of post-war reconstruction was generating a strong demand for labour benefited from having an abundant prime labour force, which, in the case of Germany, was even highly skilled. In the other countries, demand was not particularly high, but as supply was in some cases shrinking there was no need, with the exception of Italy, to aim at a particularly rapid growth of output to ensure full employment.

The acceleration of labour demand growth and international migration, 1955–65

The following decade saw a sharp acceleration in labour demand growth in almost every country accompanied by a marked shortening of the length of the working week. Employment between 1954 and 1965 (i.e. the period of maximum growth) rose by more than 1½ per cent per annum in industry and 2 per cent per annum in services, with unemployment falling to very low levels by the mid-1960s. The acceleration in labour demand was matched by more favourable conditions on the supply side than in the 1950s. Demographic growth picked up in those countries in which it had stagnated in the early 1950s and was particularly rapid in the 15 to 24 age group. The ranking of growth rates per country was however virtually reversed compared to the early 1950s (Table 6.4). The country with the largest increase in prime age population was France,[10] while in Germany,

TABLE 6.4. *Labour force and employment growth in the EEC, 1955–1965*
(average annual percentage changes)

	France	Germany	Italy	United Kingdom	EEC
Population of working age	0.9	0.6	0.6	0.4	0.6
Labour force	0.4	0.5	−0.1	0.5	0.4
Total employment	0.4	0.9	0.3	0.5	0.6
of which: Agricultural employment	−3.7	−4.0	−3.5	−2.3	−3.5
Independent non-agricultural employment	−1.0	−0.4	0.6	−0.4	−0.2
Dependent non-agricultural employment	2.0	2.1	2.6	0.7	1.7

Sources: EEC, *Population and Employment, 1977*; OECD, *Labour Force Statistics* (various issues).

[10] The French figure is to some extent influenced by a special factor — the end of the Algerian war at the beginning of the 1960s which forced the return of one million colonists as well as the demobilization of more than 600,000 soldiers.

despite heavy immigration and some increase in the total prime age population, there was a fall in the 15 to 24 age bracket (−0.4 per cent per annum between 1955 and 1965). Overall participation rates, however, started to decline, despite the appearance in a number of countries of rising activity rates for prime age women.

The spontaneous growth of the labour force would, however, have failed to cover the urban labour market requirements without intersectoral and international migration. The rate of migration from agriculture almost doubled between the second half of the 1950s and the first half of the 1960s. An important contribution also came, from the early 1960s onwards, from the decline in the number of the self-employed outside agriculture. But the most impressive phenomenon in that period was international migration, which deserves closer examination not only for the importance it had in modifying demographic and labour market conditions in the various countries, but also for its impact on their socio-political conditions.

In quantitative terms, migration was a phenomenon of vast proportions in post-war Europe, even if probably on the whole less important than the emigration from Europe that had marked the end of the last century and the beginning of this.[11] By the mid-1970s, when the process had come to an end, the alien population in European receiving countries, apart from the United Kingdom, had reached some 11 million people, or 7 per cent of the population (Table 6.5). The figure was probably similar for the United Kingdom if children

TABLE 6.5. *Alien population in major European receiving countries, 1975*

	Number (000s)	Per cent of population
France	4,196	7.9
Germany	4,090	6.6
Belgium	835	8.5
Luxembourg	84	23.5
Netherlands	351	2.6
Sweden	410	5.0
Switzerland	1,013	16.0
Total	10,978	7.1
United Kingdom[a]	3,045	5.5

[a] Foreign-born population, 1971
Source: UNECE, *Labour Supply and Migration in Europe*, New York 1979.

of alien parents born in the country and given British nationality were included. But immigration into the United Kingdom was in some ways different, in so far as over 50 per cent of the immigrants had come from outside Europe (for the continental countries the proportion of non-Europeans in the immigrant

[11] Twenty million people before 1914, according to G. Maselli, 'World Population Movements', *mimeo*, 2nd European Population Conference, Council of Europe, 1970; 18 million between 1901 and 1915 according to D. Kirk, *Europe's Population in the Interwar Years*, Princeton 1946.

population in the early 1970s ranged from 5 per cent in Sweden and Switzerland to 38 per cent in France), and were, therefore, more permanently established in the country. The bulk of the migratory movements took place between the end of the 1950s and the beginning of the 1970s, especially between 1957, year of the first important migration peak, and 1973, year of the last peak.

It may be interesting to note that post-war migration in Continental Europe differed from that of the beginning of this century in so far as it was closely correlated with cyclical trends in receiving countries. The marked slackening of the flow between 1966 and 1968, a period of decelerating growth in almost all European countries, and again in the later 1970s, is clear evidence of this. This cyclical tendency also accounts for the temporary nature of much immigration. Another important feature was the growing distance of sources of supply as the nearer ones ran out. In France, for example, while Italian immigration was dominant in the 1950s and Spanish in the first half of the 1960s, subsequent immigrants came above all from Portugal and Morocco. In Germany, the same phenomenon occurred, but in a shorter space of time, with Italians remaining the main component of immigration till the middle of the 1960s, but then being replaced by Yugoslavs, Greeks, and finally by Turks.

A second differentiating aspect of post-war emigration was its concentration on the labour force. Around 1970 active aliens represented 7 per cent of the total active population in the major receiving countries, while they formed only 5 per cent of the total population. The greater impact on the labour force than on the population as a whole was due both to the demographic structure of the immigrant population and to its relatively higher participation rates.[12] Immigrants in most receiving countries were above all men, and mostly young (Table 6.6). Interestingly, these young people had also decidedly higher participation rates than their local contemporaries. For the 15 to 24 age group, for instance, the rates were about 20 per cent higher.[13]

There thus emerges an important element which has probably not received sufficient attention, namely the fact that immigration led to a qualitative improvement in the labour force in receiving countries. These were able to increase their growth potential not only through more rapid labour force growth but also via a higher growth of productivity. In addition to this economic effect it can

[12] From a demographic standpoint the immigrants differed from the local population both because of their lower sex ratio (ratio of females per 100 males) and because of the concentration of the population in the 15 to 34 age bracket. Around 1970, according to the UNECE (*Labour Supply and Migration*), the sex ratio varied from a minimum in Germany of 60 for immigrants versus 113 for the indigenous population to a maximum in Sweden of 96 for aliens as opposed to 100 for the native population. At the same time, the 15 to 34 age group included 51 per cent of the immigrant population versus 27 per cent of the local population. More normal values were found in France (33 per cent versus 28 per cent).

[13] These data refer to the censuses of the early 1970s. If the corresponding censuses of the 1960s are considered it may be observed that this situation was the result of a process that went on throughout the decade, and that in many countries led to a different behaviour of participation rates between the indigenous population and the immigrants. In Germany, for example, the male participation rate for the local population between 1960 and 1970 fell by 5 percentage points, going from 82.8 to 77.8; that of aliens rose by 4.5 percentage points, from 89.9 to 94.4. The same pattern is also found in Austria, the Netherlands, and Switzerland.

TABLE 6.6. *Contribution of international migration to growth of total labour force by age and sex, 1960–1970*
(percentages)

	Total labour force growth	Migration		Other components[a]
		men	women	
Germany[b]				
Total	1.9	4.3	1.4	−3.8
From 15 to 24 years	−15.3	3.0	2.1	−20.4
From 25 to 34 years	17.3	8.4	1.9	7.0
From 35 to 54 years	8.7	3.9	0.9	3.9
From 55 to 59 years	−14.0	0.3	−	−14.3
Switzerland				
Total	13.4	6.9	3.7	2.8
From 15 to 24 years	9.7	8.7	7.3	−6.3
From 25 to 34 years	24.2	14.1	5.2	4.9
From 35 to 54 years	11.3	2.7	1.2	7.4
From 55 to 59 years	4.3	0.6	0.5	3.2
Italy[b]				
Total	0.7	−2.6	−0.7	4.0
From 15 to 24 years	−9.0	−1.8	−1.0	−6.2
From 25 to 34 years	−1.2	−5.2	−1.0	5.0
From 35 to 54 years	7.4	−1.8	−0.4	9.6
From 55 to 59 years	3.4	−1.5	−0.4	5.3
Portugal				
Total	0.6	−17.1	−3.7	21.4
From 15 to 24 years	5.2	−20.7	−5.0	30.9
From 25 to 34 years	−13.0	−25.6	−5.7	18.3
From 35 to 54 years	4.4	−10.8	−1.9	17.1
From 55 to 59 years	11.7	−5.6	−1.3	18.6

[a] Natural increase plus changes in participation rates
[b] 1961–71
Source: UNECE, *Labour Supply and Migration in Europe*, New York 1979.

also be argued that migration increased social stability in receiving countries, since migrants frequently filled those jobs that increasing prosperity was rendering incompatible with the aspirations of the local population.[14] Moreover, non-unionized foreign labour probably diminished the degree of industrial conflict. On the other hand, for the sending countries, emigration provided a safety-valve for too rapid demographic growth and for difficulties in creating urban jobs.[15]

[14] For a more general discussion of these aspects, see M. Piore, *Birds of Passage: Migrant Labor and Industrial Societies*, Cambridge 1979.
[15] The advantages and disadvantages of migration for the sending and receiving countries have been the most widely discussed issue in the literature on migration. Traditionally, migration has been considered advantageous for both sending and receiving countries (Kindleberger, *Europe's Postwar Growth*). In the 1960s, however, it became increasingly

While international migration has attracted a good deal of attention because of its socio-political implications, internal migration – which in quantitative terms had been even more important – has not been so carefully examined, partly because of the lack of reliable data. The extensive empirical work done by the UNECE points, however, to a great similarity between the two flows. Migrants from the country to towns tended to be young, mostly concentrated in the 15 to 34 age bracket, and male. Only at ages over 45 years did women tend to outnumber men. It is likely, however, that over time the age composition of internal migrants altered with a progressive increase in the proportion of older people.

In view of what has been said above it seems fairly evident that intersectoral and international migrations were endogenous with respect to the growth process. Only in the late 1960s, however, did it become clear that the growing demand for labour was in some sense creating its own supply. Kindleberger and Kaldor first perceived and analysed the problem. Their works rejected the prevailing supply-oriented approach to the analysis of migration – mostly based on the experience of the period before World War I – in favour of a demand-oriented approach, much more appropriate for interpreting what was occurring in Europe. Both the Kindlberger and Kaldor models are discussed elsewhere in this book in the context of Europe's growth performance.[16] As far as labour market developments go, the models, which use a modified version of the Marx–Lewis dual-economy approach, stress the importance of wage differentials between sectors and profit growth in manufacturing in creating an excess demand for labour in the more developed regions or countries.

More recent data than those available at the time of the Kindleberger and Kaldor studies would also confirm the heuristic validity of dual-economy models. Hill's reconstruction of the manufacturing sector's gross profit series from 1955 shows that the share of gross profits in value added underwent negligible swings in the 1950s for all the countries examined.[17] Between 1960 and 1964, by contrast, the share of profits fell rapidly as wage differentials declined, surplus labour supply was exhausted, and full employment achieved (except for Denmark and the United Kingdom, where the phenomenon occurred later and which were in any case only marginally involved in the rapid growth process of other European countries). For the rest of the 1960s, profits were stabilized at lower levels, with cyclical swings. This pattern followed fairly closely that of labour demand which, as already said, reached a peak in the mid-1960s.

Changing characteristics of labour supply, 1965-79

The third period, from the mid-1960s to the late 1970s, was marked by a major change in the employment situation. After the rapid growth of the previous

---

clear that the greatest benefits were accruing to the receiving countries, and most of the literature accepts this point of view (for a review, see R. Reyneri, *La catena migratoria*, Bologna 1979). More recently it has been argued that in the long run migration is disadvantageous for both sending and receiving countries (M. Livi Bacci, 'L'emigrazione italiana verso l'Europa', *Rassegna economica*, No. 1, 1973).

[16] See Ch. 1 above.

[17] T.P. Hill, *Profits and Rates of Return*, OECD, Paris 1979.

TABLE 6.7. *Labour force and employment growth in the EEC, 1965-1973*
(average annual percentage changes)

	France	Germany	Italy	United Kingdom	EEC
Population of working age	0.9	0.4	0.3	–	0.4
Labour force	1.0	−0.1	−0.3	0.1	0.2
Total employment	0.9	−0.1	−0.4	−0.1	0.1
of which: Agricultural employment	−3.7	−4.7	−5.2	−3.5	−4.4
Independent non-agricultural employment	−1.0	−0.8	−0.6	2.6	−0.4
Dependent non-agricultural employment	2.1	0.5	1.5	−0.1	0.9

Sources: EEC, *Population and Employment, 1977*; OECD, *Labour Force Statistics*
(various issues).

decade, total civilian employment stagnated between the mid-1960s and the
early 1970s and declined from 1973 onwards, despite a very rapid decline in
hours worked. Only dependent employment kept growing, although at progressively slower rates. Despite the relative homogeneity of employment trends
throughout the period, the pattern of supply changed considerably around
1973. While before that period labour force growth had decreased in line with
employment (Table 6.7), between 1973 and 1979 labour force growth picked
up again in the EEC at rates higher than those experienced in the previous
twenty years (Table 6.8). This pattern was seen in all countries. Even in Germany, the only country experiencing a substantial fall in the labour force mostly
due to return migration, the decline was only half that recorded by employment.

The impact of this change on unemployment was dramatic. While moderate
labour force growth till 1973 had kept unemployment at relatively low rates
despite a declining growth of labour demand, the subsequent reversal of this
trend, for both demographic and socio-economic reasons, brought unemployment, at the end of the 1970s, to levels unprecedented by post-war standards.
On the demographic side, the available data show a marked increase from the
beginning of the 1970s in the 25 to 54 age group and a marked decrease in the
numbers of the older generations. More important than demographic factors in
determining the growth of total labour supply in this period was, however, the
turn-around in participation rate trends and their changed response to aggregate
demand conditions and cyclical fluctuations.

Cyclical influences on participation rates may reflect a change in the real
determinants of labour supply, or may be due to the changing propensity of
people to register as unemployed or to declare themselves unemployed in the
sample surveys. The direction of the latter effect is not obvious a priori. Normally, participation rates decline in periods of high unemployment, since
marginal workers tend to leave the labour market because of difficulties in
finding a job. However, unemployment affecting the principal income earners
may compel previously non-active family members to seek employment. As
both these effects appear over the cycle, the first, which is referred to as the

TABLE 6.8. *Labour force and employment growth in the EEC, 1973-1979*
(average annual percentage changes)

	France	Germany	Italy	United Kingdom	EEC
Population of working age	0.7	0.3	0.8	0.3	0.6
Labour force	0.8	−0.3	1.2	0.5	0.6
Total employment	0.3	−0.8	1.0	0.1	0.1
of which: Agricultural employment	−3.6	−3.7	−2.4	−2.0	−2.9
Independent non-agricultural employment	−0.2	−1.3	1.2	−0.5	−
Dependent non-agricultural employment	0.8	−0.4	1.9	0.2	0.5

Source: OECD, *Labour Force Statistics, 1968-1979.*

'discouraged worker' effect, will prevail over the latter, which is referred to as the 'additional worker' effect, when the number of people dropping from the labour market outweighs the number of people entering it.

In the 1960s, a number of tests done by the OECD and by independent scholars had shown strong evidence of pro-cyclical variations in participation rates for a number of European countries (Germany, Italy, the United Kingdom, and Belgium) and a prevalence of the 'discouraged worker' effect.[18] The only country in which the 'discouraged worker' effect did not seem to have been at work was France. In the 1970s, the situation seems to have been reversed. An OECD simulation of expected labour supply growth for the years 1973-6, using the coefficients estimated over the period 1960-73, showed a strong systematic underprediction of participation rates in Italy, the United Kingdom, and Sweden, some underprediction for France, and a systematic overprediction for Germany.[19]

The traditional 'additional worker' effect could explain part of this reaction of labour supply to the more difficult labour market conditions of this period. Another hypothesis is that measures to prevent the fall of employment during the recession and more generous unemployment benefits encouraged a large number of people, mainly in the secondary labour market, to remain in the labour force or even to re-enter it. Where policies to maintain the level of employment take the form of direct job creation, either in the private or in the public sector, it is likely that demand for labour will discriminate less against

[18] For a general review of the literature see J. Mincer, 'Labor Force and Unemployment', in R.A. Gordon and M.S. Gordon (eds.), *Prosperity and Unemployment*, New York 1966. Tests on different European countries are reported in OECD, 'Labour Market Developments', *mimeo*, Paris 1973; for Italy, G. La Malfa and S. Vinci, 'Il saggio di partecipazione della forza lavoro in Italia', *L'Industria*, October–December 1970; for the United Kingdom, B.A. Corry and J.A. Roberts, 'Activity Rates and Unemployment: The Experience of the United Kingdom: 1951-66', *Applied Economics*, March 1970.

[19] OECD, *A Medium-Term Strategy for Employment and Manpower Policies* (Annex II), Paris 1978, p. 124.

certain socio-demographic groups. The measures taken to improve unemployment insurance may, on the other hand, have played a less important role. They consisted of more generous allowances but they did not change the eligibility conditions. This may have helped to keep people in the market, but is unlikely, as is sometimes suggested, to have drawn people wanting to benefit from unemployment insurance into the labour market.

A full explanation for the turnaround in participation rates must, however, throw light on the reasons for the sharp increase in the activity rates of married women (Table 6.9) who, in most countries, more than offset the falling participation rates of non-married women. This turnaround marked a major change

TABLE 6.9. *Changes in participation rates*[a]
(percentages)

| | Total participation rate | | | Participation rate of women aged 25 to 54 | | |
	1960	1970	1975	1960	1970	1975
France	69.9	67.8	67.9	39.7	46.8	52.9
Germany	70.3	69.5	66.6	44.5	47.6	50.3
Italy	64.1	56.0	55.7	25.7	30.2	33.1
United Kingdom	71.7	72.4	73.4	..	53.9	56.9
Belgium	62.2	63.0	64.0	29.7	36.1	38.4
Denmark	71.2	74.9	76.8	37.0	56.1	69.2
Netherlands	59.5	59.0	57.1	17.1	19.4	28.5
Norway	64.3	64.1	69.7	21.5	31.8	..
Sweden	74.3	74.3	78.5	36.9	64.2	74.3

[a] Labour force in per cent of 15 to 64 age group
Source: OECD, *Demographic Trends, 1950–1990*, Paris 1979.

in labour market behaviour and appeared to be more of a secular nature than cyclically determined. From the supply side at least four factors contributed to it: the innovations in housekeeping technology that allowed a dramatic increase in the productivity of housework; the diffusion of oral contraceptives that decreased fertility rates and therefore the amount of time spent raising children; the improvement of external child-care facilities which allowed mothers to remain active; finally the women's liberation movement which encouraged outside activity in order to obtain emancipation from the subordinate role within the family. On the demand side, the increasing demand for labour in the service sector and in public administration made working arrangements more flexible than those prevailing in industry, and allowed an increase of part-time work, while discrimination against women became more difficult as a consequence of equal opportunity legislation introduced in many countries.

The case of Germany, atypical of the trends described above, deserves some discussion. The main reason for Germany having a lower labour force in the later 1970s than could have been expected on the basis of earlier evidence was the reversal of the flow of migrant workers. Germany therefore appears to be the only European country that throughout the period had a highly responsive supply of labour — increasing when demand was high and decreasing when it started to fall. It is difficult to assess how large a contribution this has made to the German economic success story, but it can safely be said that the elasticity of labour supply provided that country with a degree of freedom in policy-making that other countries have not enjoyed.

II. The Consequences of Full Employment

Unemployment rates fell in the 1950s as the growth process gathered strength, and reached an all-time minimum in the mid-1960s (Fig. 6.1). According to EEC

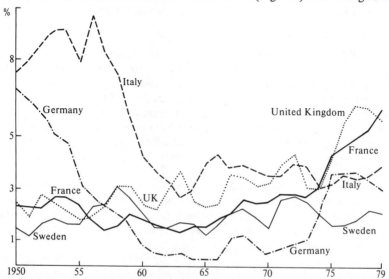

FIG. 6.1. *Unemployment rates*[a] (in per cent of the labour force)
[a] Adjusted to international concepts
Sources: C. Sorrentino, 'Methodological and Conceptual Problems in Measuring Un-
employment in OECD Countries', *mimeo*, OECD, Paris 1976; updated by J.
Moy, 'Recent Labor Market Trends in Nine Industrial Nations', *Monthly Labor
Review*, May 1979, and OECD, *Economic Outlook*, July 1981.

estimates, for the Common Market as a whole the unemployment rate came down to 1.9 per cent of the labour force in the years 1964–6. The trend, how-ever, was reversed in the second half of the decade, with unemployment rising, if only slightly, at each cyclical peak until 1973. After that date increases were much more rapid, and for Europe as a whole unemployment reached a post-war peak in the late 1970s (5½ per cent in the EEC). It was said at the beginning of this chapter that increasing unemployment in the 1970s was partly a conse-quence of the situation of full employment in the 1960s. Full employment gave a greater bargaining power to workers which was mostly used for improving job and income security. The latter, in turn, contributed to increasing the seg-mentation of labour markets and thus to unemployment.

It could, of course, be argued that there was no causal relation between full employment and institutional changes. After all, greater job and income security were implemented in the early 1970s after the wage explosions of the late 1960s and in a period in which labour market conditions, as measured by the normal indicators, were already deteriorating. In other words, institutional changes may have simply reflected the greater concern of governments with growing unemployment.

It must be borne in mind, however, that measured unemployment rates at the time were not a very helpful guide for understanding what was happening in the labour markets. The wage explosions, with all their institutional consequences, can only be explained by considering full employment not as an instantaneous event measured by a definite rate of unemployment but as a characteristic of labour markets which lasted almost a decade.

The European wage explosions

Seen in this light, it would seem certain that Europe was approaching full employment conditions in the first half of the 1960s. This is consistent with a number of other facts that have already been examined, in particular the massive increase of international and intersectoral migration in these years. If one argues along Phillips-curve lines, however, the wage explosions at the end of the 1960s came, in a sense, 'too late'. In France and in the United Kingdom unemployment had been rising since the mid-1960s, and in other countries the unemployment rates of 1968-9 were not lower than the ones that had seemed consistent in the past with fairly moderate rises in wages.

The chronicle of events is well known and will be only briefly reviewed. The first signal came from France, where, between May and June 1968, a three-week general strike brought to a halt two-thirds of the labour force (there are however no precise figures on the number of hours of strike for that year) and caused an increase in real wages of 7½ per cent. In Germany and Italy the French events were repeated in 1969, although with different intensity in the two countries. In Italy 4 million industrial workers went on strike and obtained a 16 per cent increase in real wages, while in Germany strikes involved one million workers and real wages increased by 8½ per cent. The only major country where the phenomenon did not happen suddenly was the United Kingdom. However, the number of days lost in strikes increased from 2.7 million in 1967 to 4.6 in 1968, to 6.8 in 1969, and reached 11 million in 1970, a level which had not been recorded since the General Strike of 1926. In the United Kingdom the increase in real wages was, however, much more moderate than in the three other countries. A common feature of all these explosions was the fact that they arose at rank and file level. It was only later that trade union organizations attempted to control them.

The events of these years gave rise to an abundant sociological and political literature, but unfortunately there was a lack of economic analysis. A symptom of this has been the abuse of dummy variables for that period in the estimates of wage equations in many European econometric models. There are at least three possible interpretations of the wage explosions. The first is based on a modified version of the Phillips curve which takes into account the possible inadequacy of the unemployment rate as a measure of the degree of tension on the labour market. The second overturns the logic of the Phillips curve by maintaining that full employment acts on the supply side in determining wage increases. The third argues simply that the Phillips curve was unable to detect the tensions on the labour market because of the incomes policies adopted in those years.

The inadequacy of the unemployment rate in indicating tensions on the demand side was particularly stressed by empirical research done in the United States. It was shown, in particular, that the cyclical variability of participation rates could lead to an underestimation of unemployment rates in low demand conditions. Similarly, relatively high unemployment rates due to the entry of marginal workers on to the labour market in periods of upswing could overshadow tensions on the demand side deriving from the insufficient substitutability between the various segments of the labour force.[20] This argument, together with the observation of the substantial changes occurring in the labour force as a result of demographic changes, prompted Perry in the United States to use a weighted unemployment rate to measure tensions on the demand side.[21] A more radical criticism of the use of the unemployment rate as an indicator of demand tensions came from the work on the functioning of the labour market begun especially by Holt at the end of the 1960s.[22] The main conclusion that can be drawn from Holt's work is that the unemployment rate is an extremely rough indicator of what is happening on the labour market, and should be handled with great care. Unemployment rates are in fact the result of a great number of flows in the labour market involving an extremely large number of people. Each of these flows is influenced by economic, social, and institutional conditions which change through time and alter the significance of any given unemployment rate.

Some of these objections to the adequacy of unemployment rates in indicating tensions on the demand side would appear to find no support in Europe, where the recording of unemployment has been of a relatively 'objective' nature until very recently.[23] With the exceptions only of Italy and Sweden, the numbers of the unemployed are recorded on the basis of unemployment registers; this tends to limit greatly the effect of discouraged workers on unemployment statistics. It is unlikely that discouraged or encouraged workers, leaving or looking for work, will register as unemployed, whereas they are recorded as unemployed in labour force surveys. This is even truer in the absence of a compulsory system of unemployment insurance, as was the case in France, for example, before 1967. The same would be true when the secondary labour force is excluded from benefits, as has been the case in the United Kingdom, where workers had to have at least twenty-six weeks of employment covered by the unemployment insurance system before they were eligible for compensation.[24]

---

[20] N.J. Simler and A. Tella, 'Labor Reserves and the Phillips Curve', *Review of Economics and Statistics*, February 1968.

[21] G.L. Perry, 'Changing Labor Markets and Inflation', and 'Determinants of Wage Inflation around the World', *Brookings Papers on Economic Activity*, No. 3, 1970, and No. 2, 1975; see also the literature quoted in A.M. Santomero and J.J. Seater, 'The Inflation–Unemployment Trade-Off: A Critique of the Literature', *Journal of Economic Literature*, June 1978.

[22] C. Holt, 'Job Search, Phillips Wage Relations and Union Influence', in E. Phelps (ed.), *Macroeconomic Foundations of Employment and Inflation Theory*, New York 1970.

[23] A careful and detailed survey has been made for the OECD by C. Sorrentino, 'Methodological and Conceptual Problems in Measuring Unemployment in OECD Countries', *mimeo*, Paris 1976.

[24] It is true, however, that in the United Kingdom most unemployed male workers could qualify for 'supplementary benefits' without any waiting period.

As for changes in the age–sex composition of the labour force between the beginning and the end of the 1960s, European countries did not seem to have experienced the dramatic shift that had taken place in North America. Nor can Holt's analysis be adapted uncritically to Europe in view of the differences in turnover rates between Europe and the United States. While in the United States there are large flows within the labour market and the average duration of unemployment is low, in those European countries for which figures are available, the opposite seems to be the case.

The only major objection to the use of unemployment rates as indicators of demand conditions in labour markets in Europe comes from the large inter-sectoral and international migration flows. It is likely that though full employment in urban labour markets had already been reached in the early 1960s, the existence of hidden reserves of labour had allowed a situation of high demand for labour to continue until the late 1960s, when European countries hit the full employment ceiling in a broader sense.

In this context, the second explanation of the wage explosions appears complementary to, and not in conflict with, the first one. Workers' pressure as well as excess demand for labour can generate wage increases. In an essay written in 1943, Kalecki, analysing the political implications of full employment, argued that maintaining full employment could bring about radical changes in socio-political conditions, not least because dismissals 'would cease to play their role as a disciplinary measure'.[25] The rank and file origin of the 1968–9 movements, the political content of workers' requests, and the lack of visible signs of excess demand for labour before the start of the movement may support the view that the events of the late 1960s were the consequence of a prolonged period of full employment, and that the marginal increases in unemployment at the end of the decade were insufficient to shift the balance of power in the labour market.

Some supporting evidence can also be mustered in defence of the third explanation. In the major European countries wages were increasing moderately in the mid-1960s, and there was a certain improvement in profitability. This subdued wage trend seems to have been largely due to the introduction of in-comes policies and/or to self-moderation in trade union wage claims.[26] In the United Kingdom, the Labour government established a statutory incomes policy as from July 1966. In Germany, the unions agreed to the programme of action established in the same year, when the social democrats entered the government. In France, the government successfully managed to introduce an incomes policy, if only in the public sector. In Italy there was no formalized incomes policy, but from indirect evidence it may be deducted that the moderate wage demands on the occasion of the 1966 contract renewals were dictated by the fear of a repetition of the events that had led to the 1964 deflation. This interpretation can be incorporated in a modified Phillips-curve framework, because the wage explosions may be seen as a catch-up on the increases that had been forgone in the preceding period of moderation.

[25] M. Kalecki, 'Political Aspects of Full Employment', in *Selected Essays on the Dynamics of the Capitalist Economy*, Cambridge 1971, p. 140.

[26] L. Ulman and R.J. Flanagan, *Wage Restraint – A Study of Incomes Policy in Western Europe*, University of California Press 1971. This thesis is also accepted by P. McCracken *et al.*, *Towards Full Employment and Price Stability*, OECD, Paris 1977.

These three interpretations are therefore only apparently in conflict. The first and the last maintain that excess demand in the labour market was not visible due to the inadequacy of one of the two variables entering the Phillips curve. The second holds that it was the increased bargaining power of workers, caused by the prolonged maintenance of conditions of full employment, that determined the wage increases. All three, however, are in agreement that the wage explosions largely originated because of the full employment conditions which Europe had been enjoying through most of the decade.

Job security and labour market segmentation

The change in income distribution was not the only, and perhaps not even the most important consequence of full employment. Much more important for the functioning of the labour market were the drastic limitations on the possibility of dismissal introduced by collective agreements or laws in the period immediately after 1968-9. France and Germany made the first moves in this direction. In 1969 in France an agreement was reached to regulate lay-offs made necessary by changing economic conditions, and to define a series of procedures and checks on the occasion of redundancies. The importance of this agreement was little more than formal, but it provided a basis for subsequent measures in which conditions became stricter. Thus, the 13 July 1973 law on individual redundancies laid down that dismissals were only possible in cases of 'real and serious reasons', in the absence of which the employer had to reinstate the dismissed worker or compensate him for damages. But an even more important law passed in January 1975 stipulated that lay-offs on economic grounds were subject to administrative authorization. This offered the Ministry of Labour's *inspecteur du travail* a certain freedom of action, including the possibility of refusing to approve redundancies.

In Germany, too, a law on redundancy was passed in 1969. This laid down that every redundancy had to be socially justified, otherwise the dismissal was considered void and the worker had to be reinstated (unless the court decided that it was impossible for the working relationship to continue and allowed the firm to pay the dismissed worker compensation). In 1972 the legislation concerning redundancies was amplified in the Works Constitution Act. This law not only reinforced the employer's obligations in the case of dismissal, but also imposed prior consultation with the Factory Council which could refuse approval and take the matter to court. In the United Kingdom, the 1971 Industrial Relations Act defined justified causes of dismissal and forbade dismissal on grounds of trade union activity, while the 1975 Employment Protection Act established principles on redundancy procedure. In the United Kingdom, however, the change in labour legislation was much less striking than in the other countries considered here. As for the smaller countries, similar measures were adopted in the early 1970s in Sweden and in 1977 in Ireland.

The country which seems to have undergone the most radical change was Italy. The passing of the 1970 Workers' Statute severely limited the employers' autonomy in the field of redundancies, ensuring for the unfairly dismissed worker the right to keep his job. Paradoxically, however, no administrative control of collective redundancies was introduced to parallel those which covered individual redundancies. It would seem that this derived from a choice intended to provide more scope for trade union negotiation and initiative in the field. In fact in Italy, but also partly in France, there was intense trade union activity throughout the 1970s both to cover legislative gaps with *ex-ante* agreements and to define ways of avoiding dismissals in the case of single firms. In the other two major countries, on the other hand, collective contracts seem mainly to have been concerned with defining ways of handling redundancies and ensuring income security.

One element which is worth underlining was the continuity between the job security measures taken between the end of the 1960s and the beginning of the 1970s, and the strengthening of such measures at the time of the 1974–5 crisis. There was also a clear connection between these policies and the provision of funds financing short-time work and helping firms in difficulty with the explicit aim of safeguarding jobs.

Inevitably, these various measures generated a greater rigidity in the use of the labour force and a tendency to overmanning. An indication of this can be found in the already mentioned systematic underestimation of employment that appeared in most employment equations for the period after 1973. The OECD estimated that, with the exception of Germany where the phenomenon seemed confined to 1975, in the other major European countries, employment was in the mid-1970s more than 1 per cent higher than could have been expected on the basis of past relationships between output and employment. For the United Kingdom the underestimation of employment for the years 1974–6 was of the order of 3 per cent of the labour force.[27] These estimates are confirmed by Gennard's evaluations, according to which there would have been about a million more unemployed in 1975 in the United Kingdom, in the absence of the selective financial assistance to firms and employers designed to avoid redundancies. Gennard also estimated that without the subsidization of short-time working in Germany there would have been another 250,000 unemployed in that country, while for the same reason in France there would have been at least another 100,000 unemployed.[28] It is true, however, that all these estimates concentrated on the recession period, when it is likely that other elements also contributed to keeping employment levels above what might have been expected.

A structural excess of employment is not necessarily, however, the most important problem raised by increasing job security. The analyses carried out by Doeringer and Piore in the United States show that the existence of an internal labour market whose members enjoy job security and career possibilities has as a counterpart a secondary labour market characterized by considerable employment instability and by 'dead-end jobs'.[29]

There are, indeed, indications that the contractual and legislative job security mechanisms of the 1970s brought about a segmentation of the market in several European countries, heavily affecting some parts of the secondary labour force, in particular youth. Of course, segmentation was not only caused by job security – ethnic, racial, and other social and institutional factors may also have been at

[27] OECD, *A Medium-Term Strategy*.
[28] J. Gennard, *Job Security and Industrial Relations*, OECD, Paris 1979.
[29] P.B. Doeringer and M.J. Piore, *Internal Labor Markets and Manpower Analysis*, Boston 1971.

work. The country in which most attention has been paid to this phenomenon is Italy, because segmentation there was more widespread and probably had deeper roots and more complex causes than elsewhere in Europe. The phenomenon originally attracted attention because Italy's overall labour force participation rate seemed abnormally low compared to that of other countries at a similar stage of development. This gave rise to a series of micro-investigations which pointed to the existence of a considerable amount of activity escaping official surveys. The investigations revealed that the labour market was split into two segments. In the main segment were found mostly prime age men, fully covered by the existing laws and regulations on job and income security, job safety, pension rights, etc. The members of the other segment were largely the young, women, and older men on piece-work and with little or no institutional protection. An interesting feature of the Italian secondary labour market, which seemed to differentiate it from other such markets, the American one for example, was that to some extent at least 'secondary' jobs appeared to be desired by both employers and employees. Just as there were firms which preferred to recruit workers on the secondary labour market so as not to be forced to observe official work regulations, there were also numerous people already enjoying protection on other grounds (being pensioners or even workers in other sectors or firms) who merely wanted to supplement their first source of income.

In France, the segmentation of the labour market in the 1970s had different characteristics to that of Italy. Particularly interesting in this respect was (and still is) the phenomenon of the so-called *intérimaires* workers. These were workers who were taken on for a temporary period to meet heavy workloads or for particular requirements. These workers shared all the characteristics of secondary workers, having neither guarantees of continuity nor prospects of promotion, yet in some ways they might have had a guaranteed income if they were on the pay-roll of agencies dealing in *travail intérimaire*. It is interesting to observe how the secondary labour market was entirely official and even encouraged. A major reason why such forms of work have developed, and not only in France, was that firms preferred not to expand capacity for fear of being caught in a recession and unable to shed excess manpower.[30]

The causes of youth unemployment

A further aspect of labour market segmentation common to most European countries in the later 1970s which can have far-reaching implications for growth and social stability was the increasingly difficult employment situation of the young. This problem attracted a great deal of attention after the 1974-5 recession, when in many European countries youth unemployment rates reached double-digit figures. There is evidence, however, that the employment opportunities for youth began deteriorating earlier than that (Table 6.10). In countries for which figures are available, unemployment rates doubled between the mid-1960s and 1973. It is interesting to observe that during the same period there was little evidence of other segments of the labour force having been affected by worsening employment opportunities. Unemployment rates for prime age males showed an upward trend only after the 1974-5 recession, and prime age women registered a faily stable growth of employment from the mid-1960s.

[30] M.J. Piore, 'Dualism in the Labor Market', *Revue économique*, January 1978.

TABLE 6.10. *Youth unemployment rates*[a]
(percentages)

	1960	1973	1979
France	4.2[b]	6.3	13.3
Germany	0.7[c]	1.0	3.8
Italy	3.1	11.9	24.6
United Kingdom	..	2.8	11.9
Spain	..	4.6	22.8
Finland	..	4.5	11.7
Sweden	..	5.3	5.0

[a] Unemployed aged 15 to 24 in per cent of labour force aged 15 to 24; figures are not
  strictly comparable between countries
[b] 1962
[c] 1958
Source: OECD, *Economic Outlook*, July 1980.

The reasons for this differential behaviour of youth unemployment are complex, not least because the labour market for youth seems to work in a different way from that of the rest of the work-force. Particularly in the early stages of work experience, trading on the labour market implies not only an exchange of labour services but also of information. Suppliers of labour demand information and on-the-job training; firms, in turn, do not just buy a technologically determined work service with a measurable productivity, but also information on the potential of young workers. Moreover, as firms sell the possibility of getting trained on the job, they buy general human capital services which they need in the process of adaptation to the changing economic environment.

The major reasons behind the increasing employment difficulties faced by the young would seem to have been: declining turnover rates in prime jobs; a lower propensity of firms to hire induced by the transformation of labour into a quasi-fixed factor of production; very rapid supply growth; increasing disequilibrium between wages and productivity, and the relation between insufficient information on the youth labour market and growing uncertainty among employers.

The first two factors were clearly a consequence of greater job security. The effect of declining turnover rates on youth employment prospects is quite straightforward. Most vacancies are available through normal turnover and since the internalization of labour markets tends to decrease turnover it also decreases available vacancies. The lower propensity to employ is related to the higher risk a firm takes when it hires a young worker with no career record to allow proper screening and who will be difficult to dismiss if he proves to be unsuitable for the job.

The excessively rapid supply growth was emphasized in particular by the OECD, which argued that, with the exception of Finland and Sweden, those countries which had seen a relatively large increase in their female and young labour force were also the ones with the largest youth unemployment problems.[31]

[31] OECD, *Youth Unemployment*, Paris 1979.

The reason why rapid supply growth did not affect women may be found in the qualitative differences in the nature of the jobs available to the two groups. Most women seem to re-enter the labour force at a fairly late stage and look for jobs that do not require extensive on-the-job training by the firm. Because of this, entering and leaving employment is relatively easy. Youths, by contrast, compete much more directly for jobs held by primary workers who may have considerable experience, frequently as a result of costly on-the-job training by the firm. This ensures a certain occupational stability and may provide a career once a job has been obtained, but can increase the difficulty of finding and holding one in the first place. The existence of two separate labour markets for these segments of the labour force means that the outlook for one segment may deteriorate without affecting opportunities open to the other.

Turning to the disequilibrium between wages and productivity, it has been argued that increases in minimum wages in a number of European countries did not allow the productivity differentials of younger and of more mature workers to be reflected in corresponding wage differentials. This does not imply, *per se*, that there were no employment opportunities for young workers, but simply that they were pushed towards jobs that had little or no skill content and in which the productivity differentials among different groups of workers were minimal. The increasing formal education of European youth may have worsened the situation, since it led to unjustified expectations concerning job status and earnings.

The last interpretation looks more closely at certain specific features of youth labour markets, and argues that to minimize training costs, employers rank potential workers on the basis of their existing skills or their proxies (such as age, formal education, work experience, and so on). External conditions will then determine how far down the queue workers will be hired.[32] If aggregate demand is low or the outlook is uncertain, employers will take only workers who need little or no experience. Although a quantitative assessment of employers' expectations is difficult, it is likely that such a mechanism was at work through the 1970s, when accelerating inflation reduced the confidence in the basic upward momentum of the European economies and induced employers to slow down training in parallel with the reduction of investment.

The effects of unemployment insurance

To conclude this section on the effects of the changing institutional environment on the labour market, a few comments will be made on the relation between unemployment benefits and the level of unemployment – an issue which became particularly important in the second half of the 1970s when many governments substantially improved the existing unemployment insurance systems.

There is widespread feeling that for a number of reasons more generous unemployment benefits increase the level of 'full employment unemployment'. A worker benefiting from unemployment compensation may well search longer for a new job than he would have done without such compensation. By itself this may not influence the aggregate unemployment rate if the worker finding a better job reduces his lifetime unemployment probabality. However, this does

---

[32] L.C. Thurow, *Generating Inequality*, New York 1975.

not always seem to be the case. The time spent searching increases only to a limited extent the chances of finding a better job, and, therefore, the longer-run unemployment probability of a worker may be little affected. If this is the case, there will be a longer period spent unemployed over the lifetime, and the ultimate effect will be higher unemployment rates and an inefficient use of resources. Moreover, the private benefits of the system in terms of lifetime working conditions will be much lower than the social costs.

There are, however, other ways in which unemployment compensation affects unemployment rates. In some cases the decreasing cost of leisure relative to work (corresponding to the difference between pay and unemployment benefits) may stimulate a different allocation of a person's time between work and non-work activities. In this case an individual may remain formally in the labour force even if he does not really look for a job. A more important effect could stem from an increase in the labour force induced by improved benefits. Secondary age-sex groups who would not have joined the labour market under normal conditions, may look for employment opportunities even of a highly unstable character, just to be eligible for unemployment benefits. Should these various effects be at work, the policy consequences could be to impart an inflationary bias to the economy if governments try to reduce aggregate unemployment by increasing aggregate demand.

The impact on unemployment depends also upon the particular institutional arrangements which regulate unemployment insurance in various countries. The loss of earnings offset by unemployment compensation tends to vary between countries and, within countries, among persons with different work experience, family circumstances, and earnings level. The duration of unemployment also affects the income 'replacement rate' (e.g. benefits can be reduced or suppressed after six to twelve months). Taxation, social security contributions, and income support schemes other than unemployment compensation make the determination of the 'income replacement' ratio complex. Table 6.11 presents estimates of this ratio in four countries in 1974. Differences in coverage can be wide among the unemployed, but the table helps to show that the 'cost' of unemployment could be low, particularly in the short-term. Yet people may prefer to work rather than live on social security, since in the value system of Western societies social and individual self-esteem depends greatly on the productive role performed by an individual. Furthermore, it is only through work that people have an opportunity of advancing to higher income levels.

A number of econometric studies have attempted to quantify the impact on unemployment rates of unemployment benefits. Unfortunately, they are limited to few countries and largely use the same methodology. In the United States, a country for which different estimates exist, the dispersion of results seems to be fairly wide. While Feldstein found that unemployment benefits were adding almost 1.2 percentage points to unemployment rates in the early 1970s, other authors provided much lower figures, going from only 0.2 to 0.6 percentage points.[33]

[33] M. Feldstein, 'Lowering the Permanent Rate of Unemployment', *mimeo*, Washington 1973; S.T. Marston, 'The Impact of Unemployment Insurance on Job Search', *Brookings Papers on Economic Activity*, No. 1, 1975; H.G. Grubel and D.R. Maki, 'The Effects of Unemployment Benefits on U.S. Unemployment Rates', *Weltwirtschaftliches Archiv*, May 1976.

TABLE 6.11. *Unemployment compensation: rates of replacement*
of a worker's average earnings, 1974
(percentages)

	Unemployment benefits (in per cent of former gross wage)	Disposable income (in per cent of former disposable income)
France		
Single	50	58
Married[a]	55	64
Germany		
Single	42	63
Married[a]	50	68
United Kingdom		
Single	27	39
Married[a]	46	61
Sweden		
Single	41	67
Married[a]	41	60

[a] Couple with two dependent children, wife not working.
Source: OECD, *Unemployment Compensation and Related Employment Policy Measures*, Paris 1979.

For Great Britain it has been estimated that unemployment rates in the late 1960s were 0.6 per cent higher because of benefits.[34] But these results were questioned by Sawyer, who has shown that the number of extra beneficiaries of Earnings Related Supplements (ERS) was actually below the alleged increase in unemployment.[35] The results of a careful inquiry by a Working Party of the Department of Employment suggested that, taking into consideration the coverage ratio and the effective average increase of benefits, there was evidence of only a very small effect on the unemployment rate of the Redundancy Pay Act of 1965 and of ERS in 1966.[36] A survey done by the Office of Population Census revealed that only 11 per cent of those actually receiving Redundancy Payments (the latter being a small fraction of all the unemployed) remained longer on the market to look for a better job. The impact of ERS was similarly small, since only 33 per cent of men receiving unemployment benefits in 1967 were in receipt of ERS, and the average benefit received was only 5 per cent higher in 1967 than in 1965. The conclusion of the Working Party was, therefore, that ERS and the Redundancy Pay Act may have increased the trend unemployment rate by no more than 0.3 per cent – less than one-fifth of the increase in the unemployment rate between 1966 and 1973.

Summing up, it seems fair to say that unemployment benefits were not a major cause of increased unemployment in the 1970s, although they may

[34] D. Maki and Z.A. Spindler, 'The Effect of Unemployment Compensation on the Rate of Unemployment in Great Britain', *Oxford Economic Papers*, November 1975.

[35] M.C. Sawyer, 'The Effect of Unemployment Compensation on the Rate of Unemployment in Great Britain: A Comment', *Oxford Economic Papers*, March 1979.

[36] Department of Employment, *Final Report of the Working Party on the Changed Relationship between Unemployment and Vacancies*, London 1976.

have had an impact. In particular, rising unemployment benefits are unlikely to have had much effect on youth unemployment, because in most cases the young were not eligible for assistance as a result of insufficient contributions to the insurance schemes. The increasing unemployment associated with greater income security has posed at most the problem of redefining the unemployment rate consistent with full employment, a problem which seems hardly relevent at the beginning of the 1980s after almost a decade of growing Keynesian unemployment.

Conclusions

The present chapter has briefly described some of the salient trends in labour demand and supply over the three decades from post-war reconstruction to the end of the 1970s. A theme which has run through the text has been that the gradual achievement of full employment in Western Europe, itself largely a consequence of very rapid output growth, was, in some ways, carrying the seeds of its own destruction. At a highly aggregate level, the strengthening of labour's bargaining power which full employment implied, led, on the one hand, to a gradual decline in the share of profits in national income and, on the other, to an acceleration in the rate of wage inflation, particularly dramatic at the time of the wage explosions of the late 1960s. Both these had macroeconomic consequences on private investment and on the stance of demand management policies which must have contributed to the deceleration of the growth of labour demand which, begun in the mid-1960s, became progressively more pronounced in the 1970s.

At the level of the labour market itself, the successes which countries had in diminishing fluctuations in aggregate unemployment first and in reducing its size later, seem to have prompted increasingly ambitious demands for institutional reform. While initially policies were designed to minimize macroeconomic cyclical disturbances, as time went by 'the scope of "fine tuning" was, *de facto*, extended to encompass individuals' income fluctuations'.[37] In other words, legislation was passed which increasingly insured members of the work-force against both dismissals and/or sudden poverty, while at the same time the emphasis of policies was being shifted (as was said in the Swedish context) from concern with 'the average unemployment rate (to) the employment opportunities for various groups of people . . . housewives, the handicapped, the elderly, etc.'.[38]

The result was a gradual decline in the very high degree of flexibility of Europe's early post-war labour markets. In the full employment conditions of the mid-1960s, dismissals began to lose their disciplinary function, as both aggregate demand management and special labour market measures were trying to guarantee employment to as many members of the labour force as possible. In the unemployment conditions of the mid-1970s, dismissals could not fulfil

---

[37] A. Boltho, 'Course and Causes of Collective Consumption Trends in the West', in R.C.O. Matthews and G.B. Stafford (eds.), *The Grants Economy and Collective Consumption*, London 1982, p. 149.

[38] A. Lindbeck, *Swedish Economic Policy*, London 1975, p. 237.

this function because legislation had by then severely limited the freedom of enterprises to fire members of the established work-force, just as demand for labour was decelerating and female labour supply accelerating. As a result, hiring policies became much more selective, mobility declined, labour market segmentation increased, and the burden of rising unemployment was largely borne by the young.

At the turn of the 1970s it could be argued that the European labour market was both more rigid and in some ways more 'dual' than that of twenty or thirty years earlier, despite the much higher level of education of the work-force and the virtual disappearance of an underemployed agricultural population. The new dualism reflected a difference between a protected 'permanent' labour force employed in large-scale firms, in public administration, and in public sector enterprises, and a precarious labour force, often old or young (or female) deprived of many of the rights and benefits associated with the status of full-time workers.

In this respect, Europe would seem to be different from both the United States and Japan, which have been able to maintain, or indeed acquire, a much greater degree of flexibility in recent times. The United States labour market is well known for its relatively high degree of geographical, professional, and employment mobility — (multi-directional) regional migration is more frequent, upward/downward movements in the social scale are less constrained by rigid social structures, and flows into and out of employment, unemployment, and inactivity are much greater. It is also a market in which institutional restrictions, the power of trade unions, and government intervention are much less present than in Europe, for complex historical reasons. But even Japan, a country which has often been termed 'feudal' and in which characteristics such as 'life employment' would suggest very little scope for labour market flexibility, has in fact registered a much higher degree of mobility (particularly since the oil crisis) than is commonly appreciated — largely because of the presence of numerous low-wage smaller firms which act as shock-absorbers for the surplus labour of the large-scale enterprise sector in times of difficulty. These differences, between Europe on the one hand, and the United States and Japan on the other, may not be unconnected with the remarkable employment growth recorded by the latter two countries in the 1973-9 period, despite the difficult macroeconomic climate, in contrast to the virtual stagnation of employment in Europe.

Yet Europe's situation need not be permanent. Indeed, it is quite possible that the 'feudal' characteristics which the labour market was increasingly acquiring from the mid-1960s onwards have already been eroded in some instances. Thus, trade-union bargaining power seems to have weakened in the late 1970s. While, after the first oil shock, labour was able to shift the burden of changing terms of trade over to other factors of production, this was less the case after the second oil shock. OECD calculations show, for example, that real wages did not only rise more slowly than productivity in 1978-9, but also more slowly, in some cases at least, than the 'room' allowed by productivity and terms of trade changes.[39] Similarly, some of the institutions that had improved workers' conditions in the 1960s and 1970s, notably income and job security, came under pressure for reform. Ostensibly, the intention was to eliminate the alleged

[39] OECD, *Economic Outlook*, July 1980.

distortions that these institutions had introduced into the working of the market mechanism, but clearly the underlying aim was often that of trying to establish a different balance of power in the labour market.

Whether these various trends will continue throughout the 1980s will largely depend on the macroeconomic context in which European labour markets find themselves. This is not the place to embark upon a forecast, but some broad indications can be provided. On the demand side, few would predict a return to rapid employment growth. In an environment constrained by rising real oil prices, continuing inflationary pressures, and likely balance of payments deficits, the scope for autonomous consumption and investment growth or stimulative policies would seem to be severely limited. And the pressures to restrain government spending will, in addition, cut down on virtually the only source which provided new jobs between 1973 and 1979 – the public sector.

Yet at the same time as employment opportunities may rarify, demographic forces will be leading to a continuing growth of the population of working age. Both OECD and EEC projections suggest that this could be around ½ per cent per annum throughout the 1980s and closer to 1 per cent in the first half of the decade.[40] Much will depend on whether this growing population will be discouraged from joining the labour market by adverse demand conditions, or will tend to increase its participation rate irrespective of employment trends, as was the case in the later 1970s. Looking at some of the factors that may affect activity rates suggests at best only moderate falls. School attendance rates are levelling off in most countries. Hence a further large decline in participation rates in the 15 to 24 age group appears unlikely. The availability of prime age women for labour market activity will keep increasing because of the continuing decline of birth rates and a more uncertain outlook for household incomes. It is only in the 55 to 64 age group that labour market participation may decrease because of more liberal policies towards retirement.

This impressionistic review of some of the forces that may be at work suggests that the 1980s could well witness further rises in unemployment. On the basis of trends since the mid-1970s, this is likely to lead to a further decline in the bargaining power of workers, and could conclude the long cycle which began with the high growth rates of employment in the 1950s and peaked around the late 1960s or early 1970s. This would then confirm what was tentatively argued in Section II above, namely that the Phillips curve is a complex long-term phenomenon, rather than simply a short-run relation between wage rates and unemployment.

Whether Europe will be able to live with very high open unemployment for a prolonged period of time is, of course, an open question. Much will depend on attitudes and on policy reactions to such attitudes. In particular, it can be argued that governments could try to tackle one issue – the very sharp distinction between gainful activity on the one hand and enforced idleness on the other – which, even more than the income differentials between the employed and the unemployed, is probably the greatest socio-political problem which prolonged unemployment might create. In so far as this led to a better spread of a (reduced) total amount of work over the population and over each individual's life cycle,

[40] See, for instance, OECD, *Demographic Trends*, Paris 1979.

it might be considered (returning to the comments made at the beginning of this chapter) as a 'feudal' or 'neo-feudal' objective, but one which, unlike job or income security, need not clash with the working of the labour market mechanism.

Bibliography

For a general review of European contributions to labour market economics in various countries, see J. Corina, *Labour Market Economics: A Short Survey of Recent Theory*, London 1972 (for the United Kingdom); L. Frey, 'Stato e prospettive delle ricerche sul mercato del lavoro in Italia di fronte ai problemi di disoccupazione-sottoccupazione', *Quaderni di economia del lavoro*, No. 1, 1975 (for Italy); and B. Mériaux, 'Point de vue sur les recherches françaises en économie du travail', *Revue économique*, January 1978 (for France).

Discussions of European labour market problems in historical perspective can be found in W. Galenson, 'The Labour Force and Labour Problems in Europe, 1920–1970', in C.M. Cipolla (ed.), *The Fontana Economic History of Europe*, Vol. 5, Glasgow 1976; UNECE, *Labour Supply and Migration in Europe*, New York 1979; C.P. Kindleberger, *Europe's Postwar Growth: The Role of Labor Supply*, Cambridge, Mass. 1967. The major changes in European and North American labour markets over the last fifteen years are discussed in OECD, *A Medium-Term Strategy for Employment and Manpower Policies*, Paris 1978. Longer-run demographic trends are analysed in W.R. Lee (ed.), *European Demography and Economic Growth*, London 1979, and in UNECE, *Post-war Demographic Trends in Europe and the Outlook Until the Year 2000*, New York 1975.

Most of the European literature on labour force participation is built on the conceptual framework provided by W.G. Bowen and T.A. Finegan, *The Economics of Labor Force Participation*, Princeton 1965, and J. Mincer, 'Labor Force Participation of Married Women', in NBER, *Aspects of Labor Economics*, NBER, Princeton 1962. Participation rates in some European countries are analysed by J.K. Bowers, 'British Activity Rates: A Survey of Research', *Scottish Journal of Political Economy*, February 1975, and G. La Malfa and S. Vinci, 'Il saggio di partecipazione della forza lavoro in Italia', *L'Industria*, October–December 1970.

On migration, a classic work is that of Kindleberger (*Europe's Postwar Growth*). Immigration in the main European countries is examined by E.G. Drettakis, 'Données sur les migrations et sur la croissance démographique en Allemagne Fédérale, 1950–72', *Cahiers de l'INED*, 1974; G. Tapinos, 'L'immigration étrangère en France, 1946–73', *Cahiers de l'INED*, 1975; W.R. Böhning, *The Migration of Workers in the United Kingdom and the European Community*, London 1972; and K.B. Mayer, 'Foreign Workers in Switzerland and Austria', *European Demographic Information Bulletin*, No. 3, 1971. On the causes and consequences of restrictions to migration introduced in most European countries after 1973, see OECD, *Migration, Growth and Development*, Paris 1979.

The original framework for the analysis of segmentation in the labour market was provided by J.T. Dunlop, 'The Task of Contemporary Wage Theory', in G.W. Taylor and F.C. Pierson (eds.), *New Concepts in Wage Determination*, New York 1957, and C. Kerr, 'The Balkanization of Labor Markets', in E.W. Bakke *et al.*, *Labour Mobility and Economic Opportunity*, New York 1954. The most important recent contribution in this area of research is by P.B. Doeringer and M.J. Piore, *Internal Labor Markets and Manpower Analysis*, Boston 1971. For European countries see M.J. Piore, 'Dualism in the Labor Market, *Revue économique*, January 1978 and M. Paci, *Mercato del lavoro e classi sociali in Italia*, Bologna 1973.

On the analysis of the institutional framework regulating job and income security see J. Gennard, *Job Security and Industrial Relations*, OECD, Paris 1979; and OECD, *Unemployment Compensation and Related Employment Policy Measures*, Paris 1979; while on the effect of transfer payments on labour supply it may be interesting to consult H.W. Watts and A. Rees (eds.), *The New Jersey Income Maintenance Experiment*, New York 1977.

7

Income Distribution and the Welfare State

Introduction

An outstanding and almost universal feature of Western European countries in the post-war era has been the growth of social welfare expenditure, and the accompanying increases in taxation. It can be argued that the creation and consolidation of the 'Welfare State' must, at least in the 1950s and 1960s, have reflected general political and social pressures in its favour. But the aims of the welfare state, whilst broadly egalitarian, were diverse, and seldom precisely stated. This is one reason why achievements in this area are hard to assess. Major problems also arise, however, even if one looks more narrowly at the effects of welfare expenditure on income distribution. The quantification of trends in distribution and of differences in inequality between countries is notoriously difficult; the role of value judgements is strong; and there are serious deficiencies in the available data. And, of course, welfare expenditures and taxation are not the only influences on income distribution. Other forces, demographic or economic, have to be allowed for if the impact of the welfare state is to be assessed.

In practice, it is not possible to provide a complete picture of the changes that have occurred over the period, nor to discuss, except in broad terms, the aims of economic policy in this area. This chapter concentrates on three major topics:

(i) The great expansion of the welfare state in the post-war period;
(ii) The much smaller changes in income distribution that have gone with it;
(iii) The impact of welfare spending on income distribution and poverty.

The first section discusses the growth of social welfare expenditure, particularly transfer payments under social security systems. Since, however, what matters for income distribution is not only expenditure changes but also the changes in taxation that go with them, much of the discussion is concentrated on the financing of rising welfare budgets and on the consequences for households of increasing income tax and social security contributions. The second section is concerned with earnings and income disparities between individuals and households. After analysing the position in the early 1970s, some information is provided on the changes which have taken place over the period; information which is, unfortunately, limited by scarcity of data. A theme running through this section is that, despite great expectations, the development of the welfare state does not appear to have been accompanied by a marked trend towards

* University of York.

greater equality. Indeed, the continued existence of poverty, a special and perhaps the most serious aspect of inequality, would seem to confirm this. Section III surveys the evidence on the impact of transfers on income distribution and poverty and thereby provides a link between the first two parts of the chapter. Finally, some of the reasons why social transfers and progressive taxation have been less efficient than was perhaps hoped for are very briefly discussed in the Conclusions.

I. The Growth of the Welfare State

By the end of the 1930s, in most Western European countries, the foundations of the welfare state had been laid in the sense that there was some state provision of, and/or involvement in, old-age pension arrangements as well as in health, unemployment, and industrial injury insurance. These provisions were, however, generally limited in coverage, and would often apply only to better-paid manual workers in manufacturing, mining, and construction industries. Thus, non-manual and lower-paid manual workers in these sectors, as well as workers in agriculture and services, were often excluded. By the end of the 1970s the population of Western Europe was, with only few exceptions, covered by universal old-age pension systems (usually arranged through public or quasi-public institutions), unemployment, sickness, and industrial injury insurance schemes, child benefit provisions, and, in most countries, disability pensions. The majority of these schemes are of an insurance type in which the benefits payable to an individual and his family are to a greater or lesser extent based on the contributions (number and value) made by that individual and his employer. In addition, the state is heavily involved in the health field through either public provision at low or zero cost at the time of use (as in the United Kingdom), or compulsory public insurance schemes with some nationalized element of health care provision (as in France). Finally, there are public assistance schemes which pay out means-tested benefits. In most countries, however, these form only a small part of total transfer payments.

The broad similarity between countries at the end of the 1970s stands in contrast to the much greater inter-country variety that prevailed in the late 1940s and early 1950s. Not only were welfare arrangements at the time much more developed in some countries than in others, but the nature of government involvement differed between two basic approaches. The first one, particularly prevalent in the original members of the EEC, sought to provide through the state an insurance scheme under which benefits were linked to contributions. State provision arose because private insurance was felt in some way to be deficient. The second approach, which could be found in the United Kingdom and in Scandinavia, provided cash to those reckoned to be in need. It is likely that no system ever fitted exactly into either the social insurance or the social assistance mould (for example, insurance-based schemes have usually involved an element of redistribution as compared with actuarially based schemes), and through time they have clearly converged. Countries began with a system which was close to one of the approaches and grafted on elements of the other. This is most apparent for old-age pension arrangements. At present, the flat-rate component is often unrelated to social security contributions and represents the social assistance approach (and indeed may be means-tested). The earnings-related component, which is linked to contributions, represents the social insurance approach.[1]

Expenditure

The impact of developments in the welfare state on public expenditure is illustrated by the figures in Tables 7.1 and 7.2. Table 7.1 shows the growth of transfers and subsidies to households from the mid-1950s to the mid-1970s.

TABLE 7.1. *Share of transfers and subsidies to households in output* (in per cent of GDP at current prices)

	1955–57	1967–69	1974–76
France	13.2	16.8	19.9
Germany	12.0	12.0	15.4
Italy	(9.7)	15.3	19.4
United Kingdom	6.1	9.3	11.3
Austria	10.2	13.3	13.8
Belgium	9.4	13.6	18.1
Denmark	7.1	10.4	14.4
Finland	5.4	7.8	9.0
Ireland	6.5	7.9	12.9
Netherlands	8.1	17.2	25.3
Norway	6.6	11.4	16.0
Sweden	7.4	11.2	17.1
Switzerland	5.2	7.8	12.1
Average	8.2	11.8	15.7

Source: OECD, *Public Expenditure Trends*, Paris 1978.

Though these payments cover more than just social security disbursements, they are restricted to payments made directly to households, and exclude, for example, agricultural and industrial subsidies. In drawing conclusions from this table, particularly of an inter-country type, the different methods of financing health care should be borne in mind. In a country, such as France, where the patient pays for some treatment at the time of use, and then receives virtually full reimbursement from the state health insurance scheme, these reimbursements are included as transfer payments. By contrast, in countries such as the United Kingdom, where health care is provided free of charge at the time of use, public expenditure is recorded as expenditure on goods and services rather than as transfer payments. If, for instance, the United Kingdom or Sweden had followed similar institutional arrangements to those of the other countries, their GDP shares of transfers and subsidies to households would, in the mid-1970s, have been boosted by some 4½ and 5 percentage points respectively. But despite these differences, the general sharp rise in the ratio of transfer payments to GDP is clear. The unweighted average of this ratio nearly doubled between the

---

[1] It could alternatively be argued that 'need' is the overriding principle in the provision of pensions, where the 'needs' of an individual in retirement depend upon his previous living standards.

THE EUROPEAN ECONOMY

mid-1950s and the mid-1970s, rising from 8.2 to 15.7 per cent. Although countries which initially had a relatively high ratio (France, Germany, and Austria) increased their ratio relatively slowly, there are no cases where the ratio declined during this period. In many countries it doubled, and in the Netherlands it even tripled.

Focusing more narrowly on income maintenance expenditure (essentially public assistance and social security, excluding health), a rapid growth in this form of public expenditure during the 1960s is indicated by the figures given in Table 7.2. On average, expenditure on income maintenance rose from the

TABLE 7.2. *Share of public expenditure on income maintenance and health in output*
(in per cent of GDP at current prices)

	Income maintenance		Health	
	c. 1962	*c.* 1972	*c.* 1962	*c.* 1972
France	11.8	12.4	3.1	5.3
Germany	11.9	12.4	2.5	5.2
Italy	7.5	10.4	2.9	5.2
United Kingdom	4.4	7.7	3.2	4.6
Austria	14.1	15.3	2.9	3.7
Belgium	11.7	14.1	3.1	4.2
Denmark	6.5	9.9	3.7	6.5
Finland	6.7	9.9	2.5	5.5
Ireland	5.3	6.4	2.8	5.4
Netherlands	8.6	19.1	2.8	5.1
Norway	5.1	9.8	2.5	5.3
Sweden	6.0	9.3	3.6	6.7
Average	8.3	11.4	3.0	5.2

Source: OECD, *Public Expenditure Trends*, Paris 1978.

equivalent of 8.3 per cent of GDP to 11.4 per cent in a decade. The expenditure by the public sector on health care also increased substantially between the early 1960s and the mid-1970s, from an average of 3 to over 5 per cent of GDP.

Why has this expansion of the welfare state taken place? At one level a complete set of explanations is virtually impossible. One could point to the emergence and growth of trade unions and political parties of the left, who were early advocates of the welfare state; to reactions to the interwar depression and mass unemployment; to general beliefs in the benefits and advantages of state action, etc.[2] This line of argument is not of direct relevance to the main themes of this chapter.[3] But it may be interesting to look at some of the more proximate causes of the change in expenditure.

---

[2] For empirical support for the view that governments with strong left-of-centre representation tend to expand the public sector faster than other types of government, see D.R. Cameron, 'The Expansion of the Public Economy: A Comparative Analysis', *American Political Science Review*, December 1978.

[3] See Ch. 13 for a discussion of the general rise in public expenditure.

It would appear that the introduction of new programmes was not a major reason for this change. Virtually all the schemes presently in existence were already in place in the late 1930s. The only major exception is child benefits, but these were introduced in the early post-war years and existed in all countries by 1950. They cannot, therefore, account for the increase in expenditure from then onwards; it is true that a few countries in the 1960s and 1970s phased out tax allowances for children and replaced them with child benefits,[4] but the effect of this on total expenditure was relatively small.

A much more important cause of the growth of welfare expenditures arises from the broadening of existing social security programmes. Groups like non-manual workers or the self-employed, originally excluded from state schemes, had generally been incorporated into the social security system by the end of the 1960s. In many cases, the major part of this extension of coverage was undertaken in the immediate post-war period. In the United Kingdom, for instance, the national insurance scheme replaced previous arrangements, and extended coverage from manual workers to most of the population in 1947.[5]

A second major expansionary force on expenditure has been demographic change, in particular the increase in the numbers of the old. In the case of pensions, this effect was reinforced by the encouragement given to retirement by the existence of pension schemes. Some indication of the importance of these two factors is given in Appendix Table 7.A1, which shows the proportion of the population aged sixty-five or more in c. 1960 and c. 1970, and activity rates for that age group. Not only is there a clear increase in the proportion of the older population but also a substantial decline in its labour force participation.

A third factor which has played a role, if only in the area of pensions, is the apparently increasing generosity with which the older population has been viewed by society. Thus, individuals who are of pensionable age, but have not made sufficient contributions to the social security scheme during their working lives to qualify for an insurance pension, are often granted a pension. For example, in Belgium, a *revenu garanti* extended to 5 per cent of the population aged sixty-five or more provides a minimum retirement benefit. In France, those with low incomes who do not qualify for a contributory pension are eligible for a pension under special schemes.[6] More generally, it would seem that the scale of old-age benefits has increased more rapidly than GDP per capita, suggesting that increased weight has been placed on the welfare of the aged.

The OECD has made some tentative calculations which try to quantify the importance of these three effects.[7] Relative to GDP, expenditure on old-age pensions rose by 36 per cent in the EEC countries between 1962 and 1972. Demographic changes meant that the over-65 age group increased by nearly 13 per cent (relative to the total population) during this period. Extensions in

---

[4] The change was made in Denmark and Norway in the early 1960s, in Germany in 1975 (when child benefits were extended to the first child), and over a number of years in the late 1970s in the United Kingdom (this also included extension to the first child).

[5] Married women were allowed, until 1978, to opt out of most contributions and benefits if they wished to.

[6] The *Allocation aux vieux travailleurs salariés* (AVTS) and a supplementary allowance paid by the *Fonds national de solidarité* (FNS).

[7] OECD, *Public Expenditure on Income Maintenance Programmes*, Paris 1976, p. 39.

coverage and an increased 'take-up' ratio were responsible for an increase of over 10 per cent in the number of people receiving pensions. Hence, the increase in the value of pensions relative to GDP per capita accounted for the remaining 10 per cent.[8] Similar calculations for other items of income maintenance expenditures (child benefits, sickness and unemployment insurance) show much less pronounced increases both in total expenditure and in the relative generosity of per capita benefits.

If a general conclusion is at all warranted after this brief survey of some selected features of the growth of the welfare state in post-war Europe, it would probably be that the pronounced rise in expenditures was most obviously associated with an expansion of the coverage of most welfare arrangements — public education (which is not a direct concern of this chapter), health schemes, pension systems, and other forms of social insurance. As put by the OECD:

As a very broad generalisation . . . it could be suggested that society, over the last decade, has more or less succeeded in fulfilling what might be called its "democratic" objective — the extension of coverage to as large a share of the relevant population as possible. Only slow progress, however, has been made towards fulfilling its more "egalitarian" aims involving selective help to the economically vulnerable and socially disadvantaged. Indeed insofar as the effort to achieve generalised coverage has restricted the increase of benefits, these two objectives may even have been in conflict.[9]

Taxation

Social welfare expenditure, with other forms of public expenditure, has to be financed. This subsection reviews some of the trends and inter-country variations in this area. The main focus is on the reliance which different countries place on different forms of taxation, since this allows some assessment of the impact of taxation on the distribution of income.

The distributional effects of taxes vary quite substantially. Thus, income taxes on households are usually progressive, but the extension of income tax to larger segments of the population can have regressive effects because it often involves a lowering of tax thresholds. Other regressive effects may arise from the existence of non-universal tax allowances (e.g. on house purchases), which may increase faster than income and imply that richer members of society gain more from them than poorer members.

The distributive effects of taxes on goods and services depend upon who ultimately pays these taxes. It has usually been assumed in work on the incidence of indirect taxation that the consumer bears the bulk of such taxes in the form of higher prices. If this is true, the distributive impact then depends upon the nature of these taxes (for example, the extent to which higher rates apply to 'luxury' goods and lower rates to 'necessities') and on the extent to which the propensity to consume declines with income. When, as is usually the case, the rich spend a lower proportion of their income than the poor, indirect taxes effectively fall more heavily (relative to income) on the poor than the rich.

---

[8] The precise figures were: total change in GDP share: 36.1 per cent, of which 12.9 was due to demographic changes, 10.2 due to changes in coverage, and 9.4 due to increases in pensions relative to GDP per capita.

[9] OECD, *Public Expenditure Trends*, Paris 1978, p. 30.

Social security contributions could be viewed as payments into an insurance fund from which the insured draws when aged, unemployed, sick, etc. But the compulsory nature of these contributions, and the general lack of actuarial balance between contributions and benefits, leads to the treatment of social security contributions as a tax. In this light, one can look at the distributive impact of social security contributions separately from the impact of the benefits. The available evidence suggests that employers' social security contributions are ultimately paid from real wages, although it is not possible to say whether this arises from higher prices or lower money wages.[10] When employers' social security contributions lead to higher prices the contribution will effectively be paid by consumers. The distributive consequences will then be similar to those of indirect taxes.

However, if social security contributions lead to lower money wages, then the distributive effects depend upon the contributions scale. These scales are typically regressive, and place proportionately higher taxes on lower earners than on high earners. This arises from the imposition of a proportionate rate of deduction up to an earnings ceiling only. The existence in some cases of separate rates and ceilings applying to different parts of the social security system (health care, unemployment insurance, old-age pensions, etc.), does not alter the general regressivity. The same regressivity, of course, applies also to social security contributions paid by employees.

Bearing these considerations in mind, Table 7.3 presents data on changes in

TABLE 7.3. *Changes in shares of taxation in output, 1955-57 to 1974-6* (percentage point changes in shares of GDP at current prices)

	Personal income taxes	Social security contributions	Indirect taxes	Other	Total
France	2.0	5.5	−2.3	1.1	6.3
Germany	4.7	6.0	−2.2	−1.6	6.9
Italy	2.8	6.3	−2.3	0.1	6.9
United Kingdom	6.6	3.5	−0.1	−2.6	7.4
Austria	2.8	3.1	3.1	−0.6	8.4
Belgium	6.5	5.7	1.0	1.6	14.8
Denmark	15.3	−0.7	5.3	−1.9	18.0
Finland	6.7	3.5	−0.7	−2.5	7.0
Ireland	5.5	3.5	1.3	−0.2	10.1
Netherlands	4.4	12.6	0.9	−0.7	17.2
Norway	3.9	10.0	5.0	−1.9	17.0
Sweden	8.8	7.7	6.2	−1.9	20.8
Switzerland	5.3	4.1	−0.3	1.2	10.3
Average	5.8	5.4	1.1	−0.8	11.6

Sources: OECD, *Expenditure Trends in OECD Countries, 1960-1980*, Paris 1972; OECD, *Public Expenditure Trends*, Paris 1978; OECD, *Revenue Statistics of OECD Member Countries, 1965-1979*.

[10] J.A. Brittain, *The Payroll Tax for Social Security*, Brookings Institution, Washington 1972.

the main forms of taxation as a percentage of GDP for the same time-periods as those shown in Table 7.1. On average, from the mid-1950s to the mid-1970s, taxation rose relative to GDP by nearly 12 percentage points (a figure higher than the change shown in Table 7.1 since, of course, taxation had to finance more than just increases in transfers to households).[11] Virtually the whole increase came from direct taxes and social security contributions, with the weight of corporate taxes falling slightly. Evidence from a somewhat shorter time-period (from the mid-1960s only) suggests that most of the rise in social security contributions came from increases in employers' rather than employees' contributions.

A somewhat more detailed picture of the structure of taxation existing in the late 1970s is provided by Table 7.4. The two features common to most countries are the generally limited yield of taxes on corporate income and on property on the one hand, and the high weight of income taxes and social security contributions on the other. But the dispersion amongst countries is substantial. Personal income tax accounts, on average, for 13.2 per cent of GDP, but this average hides the considerable difference between France (5.2 per cent) and Italy (6.2 per cent) at the lower end, and Sweden (22.2 per cent) and Denmark (22.1 per cent) at the higher. The Nordic countries with high income-tax yields make, however, little use of employee social security contributions. Hence, if one looks at direct 'visible' taxation (income tax plus employees' social security contributions) the variation diminishes, with the French and Italian figures rising to 9 and 8 per cent respectively, while Sweden and Denmark remain at around 22 per cent. Whilst there is some tendency for countries with low reliance on direct taxation to make greater use of indirect taxation (e.g. France and Italy, but also Austria and Ireland), countries with high direct taxation (such as the Netherlands and Sweden) raise only slightly less through indirect taxation than the low reliance countries.

The next step is to look more closely at the structure of 'visible taxes', i.e. income tax and employees' social security contributions. The structure of income tax varies from country to country in a bewildering fashion (apart from being bewildering within a country), with differences in the concept of income for tax purposes, in the definition of the tax unit (for example a husband and working wife may be counted as one tax unit or two tax units depending, in some instances, on legal provisions and in others on the couple's choice), and in deductions and allowances against tax, etc. The only way forward at the moment appears to be to estimate the tax position of a number of clearly defined households. This is the course of action followed by the OECD Committee on Fiscal Affairs, which takes an 'average production worker' (hereafter APW) in each country, and calculates the tax position of such an APW when single, married with two children, etc. The discussion which follows draws heavily on the results of these investigations.[12]

---

[11] In particular, non-defence government consumption, which includes some elements of welfare state expenditure, rose over the same period by 6 percentage points of GDP on average for the sample of countries here considered.

[12] See in particular: OECD, *The Tax/Benefit Position of Selected Income Groups in OECD Member Countries, 1972–76*, Paris 1978.

TABLE 7.4. *Shares of major forms of taxation in output, 1976–1978*
(in per cent of GDP at current prices)

	Income tax		Social security contributions		'Visible' taxation[a]	Taxes on goods and services	Total[b]
	Total	Personal	Total	By employees			
France	7.3	5.2	16.4	3.8	8.9	12.4	39.6
Germany	13.4	11.4	12.8	5.7	17.1	9.6	37.5
Italy	8.6	6.2	14.1	2.0	8.2	9.0	32.8
United Kingdom	14.7	12.5	6.5	2.4	14.9	9.2	35.3
Austria	10.4	9.0	11.6	5.1	14.1	13.2	39.8
Belgium	17.0	14.3	13.2	3.7	18.0	11.5	42.9
Denmark	23.6	22.1	0.6	0.3	22.5	15.8	42.5
Finland	19.8	18.1	4.1	—	18.1	13.6	38.5
Ireland	11.1	9.5	4.7	1.8	11.3	16.3	34.7
Netherlands	15.3	12.3	17.3	7.4	19.6	11.8	46.1
Norway	19.3	17.1	8.4	—	17.1	18.0	46.8
Sweden	23.9	22.2	13.3	—	22.2	12.7	52.7
Switzerland	13.7	11.5	9.3	(4.4)	(15.9)	6.2	31.5
Average	15.2	13.2	10.2	2.8	16.0	12.3	40.1

[a] Sum of personal income taxes and employee social security contributions
[b] Total includes payroll, property, and other miscellaneous taxes
Source: OECD, Revenue Statistics of OECD Member Countries, 1965–1979.

TABLE 7.5. *Tax rates for a married couple with two children, 1976*
(in per cent of earnings)

	Marginal tax rate[a]	Earnings of average production worker				Twice earnings of average production worker			
		Average tax rate			Value of child allowance in cash	Average tax rate			Value of child allowances in cash
		Total	Income tax	Social security contributions		Total	Income tax	Social security contributions	
France	16	10.0	0.3	9.7	9.7	12.5	5.3	7.2	3.5
Germany	34	27.0	11.2	15.8	5.6	28.7	17.9	10.8	2.8
Italy	23	13.3	5.5	7.8	9.7	19.8	12.0	7.8	4.8
United Kingdom	41	25.4	19.6	5.8	2.3	31.6	27.6	4.0	1.0
Austria	28	13.3	0.8	12.5	8.9	20.8	12.5	8.3	4.5
Belgium	37	21.9	11.9	10.7	13.0	32.4	22.6	9.8	6.5
Denmark	55	32.5	29.0	3.5	3.7	47.0	43.1	3.9	1.4
Finland	49	29.2	25.6	3.6	5.2	41.2	37.5	3.7	2.1
Ireland	39	19.6	15.1	4.5	2.1	30.5	28.2	2.3	1.1
Netherlands	42	31.8	11.4	20.4	6.5	35.2	23.1	12.1	3.2
Norway	42	26.9	19.7	7.2	4.4	40.3	32.6	7.7	2.2
Sweden	63	35.0	35.0	–	6.8	53.0	53.0	–	3.4
Switzerland	27	17.1	6.9	10.2	3.6	25.5	15.4	10.1	1.9
Average	38	23.3	14.8	8.6	6.3	32.2	25.4	6.7	3.0

[a] The marginal tax rate is calculated as the proportion of income accruing to the government when the earnings of the specified household increase by 10 per cent

Source: OECD, *The Tax/Benefit Position of Selected Income Groups in OECD Member Countries, 1972–76*, Paris 1978.

Table 7.5 summarizes the tax system in a number of European countries in terms of the marginal and average tax rates levied on a household of husband, wife, and two children with earnings of an APW and with twice those earnings.[13] The first column of the table records the marginal tax rate, while the second one shows the average tax rate. The latter is then divided into an average income tax rate and an average social security contributions rate. The fifth column indicates the value of child allowances relative to APW earnings. Some of this information is reproduced in the table's last four columns for a household on an income double APW earnings. The calculations which underlie the table only incorporate basic tax allowances, credits, and deductions. Thus any offset against income tax arising from, for example, expenditure on health and housing, is not included.

The degree of progressivity revealed in the table is a combination of the progressivity of the income tax system and the regressivity or proportionality of the social security contributions. Taking income tax first, the average rate shown in the table ranges from 10 per cent (France) to over 30 per cent (Denmark, the Netherlands and Sweden), but the range of marginal tax rates is much greater, going from 16 per cent (France) to 63 per cent (Sweden). A comparison of the first two columns, and of the second and sixth columns, indicates that the direct tax system, at least over the range here considered, is intended to be progressive in all the countries shown. But there are considerable differences in the degree of progressivity over this range. Thus, for example, in Germany the proportion of income deducted for tax purposes when earnings rise from 0 to 1 is 27 per cent. The deduction on the slice of income from 1 to 2 is 30 per cent. In France the corresponding figures are 10 and 15 per cent. These are the two countries where the tax rates in the two ranges are most similar, indicating a low degree of progressivity. At the other end of the spectrum are the four Scandinavian countries, where the figures range from 29 and 33 per cent for Finland to 35 and 71 per cent for Sweden.

Moving on to social security contributions, it should first be pointed out that, unlike for tax rates, no allowance is made for family size. Thus, while the average income tax rate declines as the size of household increases (for example, from an average of 29 per cent for a one-person household with earnings of the APW to 23 per cent for a four-person household), there is no such change for social security contributions, which remain at some 8½ per cent of income whether the APW is single or married with two children. As for the progressivity of these contributions, a comparison of the fourth and eighth columns indicates that only Denmark and Norway have a (very mildly) progressive (i.e. rising average) social security contributions scheme. Three countries (Finland, Italy, and Switzerland) have a proportional contributions schedule, whilst Sweden does not have any employee contributions. The remaining seven countries have a regressive, and in some cases quite sharply regressive, contributions system. This arises largely because the earnings ceiling, up to which contributions are proportional, falls close to the earnings of the APW.

Finally, the value of child allowances has a progressive effect. Thus, the last column of the table shows that, relative to income, these allowances are halved

---

[13] In this range of earnings, different household sizes do not alter the results shown significantly.

as earnings double (reflecting their constant cash value), or even more than halved in cases in which the cash transfer is either (negatively) income related or subject to taxation.

What conclusions can be drawn from the evidence so far? Bearing in mind the earlier discussion on the incidence of various forms of taxation, a distinction should perhaps be made between the effects of visible forms of taxation (personal income tax and employees' social security contributions) which affect directly the post-tax income distribution figures to be presented below, and other taxes (taxes on goods and services and employers' social security contributions), whose impact on income distribution is indirect. In so far as the latter tend to be passed on to prices, much will depend on how higher prices affect different groups. Some limited information on the incidence of indirect taxes is shown in Table 7.6. It will be seen that in France, the ratio of VAT to

TABLE 7.6. *Incidence of indirect taxation*
(tax in per cent of consumption or disposable income per income class)

	France[a]	Italy[b]	United Kingdom[c] 1977	
	1970 VAT	1971 VAT	Total indirect taxes	VAT
Income classes				
1	10.7	5.9	22.1	2.5
2	11.3	7.0	23.9	3.0
3	11.1	7.5	22.8	3.3
4	11.4	8.0	21.3	3.4
5	11.6	8.9	19.3	3.2

Note: the figures are based on the average of data given for a larger number of size classes in the various sources (6 for France, 18 for Italy, and 10 for the United Kingdom).
[a] VAT in per cent of consumption; income classes based on total household income
[b] VAT in per cent of expenditure; income classes based on total household expenditure
[c] Taxes in per cent of disposable income; income classes based on total household income
Sources: INSEE, 'Données statistiques sur les familles', *Collections de l'INSEE*, série M, No. 48, 1975; C. Fiaccavento, 'L'imposta sul valore aggiunto come strumento di perequazione tributaria', *Rivista di politica economica*, October 1973; CSO, 'The Effects of Taxes and Benefits on Household Income', *Economic Trends*, January 1979.

consumption expenditure is practically constant for different income classes. A declining propensity to consume would imply that VAT was regressive with respect to income. In Italy, VAT appears progressive with respect to expenditure, and given the extent of that progressivity, is probably progressive in terms of income as well. For the United Kingdom, total indirect taxes are slightly regressive, whereas the evidence for VAT is less clear-cut. As they stand, these findings do not suggest that indirect taxes are very strongly regressive, and, in so far as they have decreased in importance in most countries (see Table 7.3), their overall regressive impact may also have declined somewhat over time.[14]

[14] A conclusion supported by earlier United Nations findings for Western Europe: 'It appears that indirect taxation has in most countries a somewhat regressive effect when compared with original income (income before taxes and transfer payments) but perhaps more nearly proportional when related to disposable incomes for the majority of households.' UNECE, *Incomes in Post-war Europe*, Geneva 1967, Ch. 6, p. 41.

This very tentative conclusion need not be true, however, for Scandinavia, where the share of indirect taxation in GDP has risen rapidly over the period, nor does it take into account the effect of changing indirect taxation structures.

Employers' social security contributions have, as was mentioned earlier, risen quite rapidly in importance through the period. If this has been mainly reflected in prices, the effect could have been regressive, not only because of the, admittedly only mild, apparent regressive incidence of indirect taxation, but also because the effects on prices would have been less discriminating than those of changes in indirect rates which are often levied more heavily on 'luxuries' than on 'necessities'. In so far as employers' social security contributions were in fact passed back in the form of lower wages, then their impact will probably have been more regressive, as suggested by the earlier discussion on employee social security contributions.

On the income tax side, the evidence collected in Table 7.5 shows that, on balance, rising income tax rates have more than offset constant or declining social security contribution rates, so that, overall, there is a rising average tax rate as one moves from the earnings of the APW to twice those earnings. But this provides only a first indication of the effective progressivity of the direct tax system as a whole. One reason for hesitation is the obvious one that only part of the range of income has been investigated (although over 90 per cent of wage-earners earn less than twice the earnings of the APW). Other reasons have already been mentioned (e.g. the existence of non-universal tax allowances or of tax evasion). A further reason for caution is that no allowance has, as yet, been made for the differing levels of income at which tax may become payable. This is an important feature of a tax system, as it not only throws some further light on progressivity, but also leads into the problem of people in poverty being taxed and of overlap between the tax and social security systems. Table 7.7 summarizes the available information. It shows the level of earnings relative to those of the APW at which income tax becomes payable for the single individual, the married man, and the married man with wife and two children (social security contributions are generally payable immediately on earnings).[15]

It is clear that income tax becomes payable at a level of earnings substantially below the earnings of the APW, and in some countries (including Germany, the United Kingdom, and Sweden) does so for a single individual around one-fifth of the earnings of the APW. Given the available information, it was not possible to calculate this tax threshold for all countries, but from other figures provided by the OECD[16] it can be said that, with the exception of France, a single man with earnings equal to half those of the APW would be paying income tax in all the European countries. This inevitably implies that segments of the population close to, or at, poverty levels, are subject to income tax. Some confirmation of this is provided in an earlier paper by the present author.[17] Estimates of poverty lines for a number of OECD countries show that for a single-person household these were beginning at levels equivalent to between 33 and 40 per cent of APW

[15] The only exception to this is the United Kingdom where contributions, in the later 1970s, were not payable on earnings below 20 per cent of those of the APW.

[16] OECD, *The Tax/Benefit Position*.

[17] M.C. Sawyer, 'Poverty in Some Developed Countries', *mimeo*, Paris 1975.

earnings, and for a married man with wife and two children between 66 and 80 per cent of APW earnings.

TABLE 7.7. *Income tax thresholds, 1976*

	Tax thresholds in per cent of earnings of an average production worker		
	Single man	Married man	Married man with two children
Germany	20.5	35.6	35.6
United Kingdom	20.9	30.8	44.9
Netherlands	32.3	40.4	46.8
Norway (i) Local tax	8.2	12.1	17.1
(ii) National tax	50.2	72.4	72.4
Sweden	20.3	62.6	62.6

Source: calculated from OECD, *The Tax/Benefit Positions of Selected Income Groups in OECD Member Countries, 1972–76*, Paris 1978.

The large increases in personal income taxation of a progressive nature which Europe has witnessed in the post-war period may, therefore, not have had as pronounced effects as hoped on income distribution in view, first, of the concomitant increase in social security contributions, and, second, because of the lowering of tax thresholds to (relatively) poor segments of the population. Clearly, the strength of these effects varies across countries (and is further complicated by the possible incidence of price-raising taxes on various income groups). Little more can be said on changes through time given the limited availability of data. But a very rough conclusion on how countries stood in the late 1970s can be hazarded. Taking as indicators the importance of direct income tax and employees' social security contributions in GDP, as well as the rates of average and marginal income tax on households earning twice the earnings of an APW, it would seem that progressivity rises with latitude. The most tax-progressive countries, in line with what would have been expected, are the Scandinavian ones, with Sweden and Denmark at the top of the list, followed by Finland and Norway. Next comes a group which includes the United Kingdom, Ireland, the Benelux countries, and Germany. Finally are to be found Switzerland, Austria, Italy, and France. The reasons for these differences are as numerous as those which were invoked earlier when trying to account for the rise in the welfare state — political pressures, differently held beliefs about the role of state action, etc., but also, and very importantly, stages of social and economic development.

The structures of taxation, like those of welfare expenditures, have probably come closer in Europe over the period, and though substantial differences remain, some generalizations are possible. Thus, all thirteen countries have experienced a rapidly rising ratio of taxation to levels which were often thought previously to be intolerable. In the mid- to late-1970s a typical European country levied taxes equivalent to 40 per cent of GDP, of which over one-third came from personal income taxation, and a quarter from social security contributions. The latter have increasingly been levied on the employer rather than the employee. In a typical country, the social security contribution rate for an employee was around 10 per cent of earnings up to a ceiling equivalent to the earnings of the APW. In addition, income tax was paid on earnings less than half those of the APW, a level which in many countries would be regarded as below the poverty line.

II. Income Distribution

This section examines the inequality of incomes between households (including a look at the extent of poverty) and the inequality of earnings between individuals. The first part reports on incomes and earnings distribution in the 1970s, while the second part traces the changes in inequality in the post-war period.

Any discussion of equality or inequality is fraught with numerous methodological difficulties, the more so if it covers inter-country comparisons. Three major sets of problems will be briefly raised in what follows:

(i) The difficulties involved in obtaining consistent and comparable data across countries and across time;
(ii) The problems raised by the presentation of these data in a convenient form;
(iii) The inadequacy of the available data as indicators of inequality.

The problems of measurement arise in defining income, the income unit (individuals or households), and in determining the coverage in terms of the population for the distribution. These difficulties are always present but cause particular problems in an international context since each country adopts its own solution to them. Pre-tax income is defined as the sum of wages and salaries, entrepreneurial income, property income, and current transfers. Post-tax income covers the same items but deducts direct income taxes and social security contributions. These income concepts should refer to households defined either as a single person or as a group of people sharing housing accommodation and food provision.

The figures reported below, particularly in Tables 7.9 and 7.10, have on the whole been drawn from sources which follow these criteria relatively closely. But this, of course, is not sufficient to ensure full comparability. A major obstacle comes from the knowledge that some incomes are under-reported in the available data and that the extent of under-reporting varies between countries (and probably at different points in time). Entrepreneurial and property incomes are categories particularly prone to under-reporting — indeed, according to some international evidence, this under-reporting can go as far as 50 per cent or more. Since these income categories are disproportionately received by high income groups, the under-reporting will lead to a bias towards equality in the figures.[18]

The extent of inter-country distortion this introduces is difficult to gauge. A broad indication may perhaps be obtained from the share of employee

[18] For a fuller discussion of these various problems, see A.B. Atkinson, *The Economics of Inequality*, Oxford 1975, and M. Sawyer, 'Income Distribution in OECD Countries', *OECD Economic Outlook — Occasional Studies*, July 1976, pp. 12–13.

compensation in national income, since it is known that the under-reporting of wage and salary income is very limited. Such figures suggest that, among the countries for which data are shown in Tables 7.9 and 7.10, the degree of artificial bias towards equality should, *ceteris paribus*, be least in the United Kingdom, Norway, and Sweden, and highest in France, Italy, and Spain.

A second problem arises in connection with the presentation of the available data. In presenting income distribution figures, use is made of decile shares. In this approach, households are ranked in terms of their income, and the shares of successive tenths of the population reported. No such information is available for the distribution of earnings in the sources used. Hence quantile ratios will be shown, e.g. the decile ratio or ratio of the earnings of the worker one-tenth from the top to those of the worker one-tenth from the bottom of the earnings distribution. There is a temptation to go a stage further, and try to reduce the income distribution to one figure – a single measure of inequality. There are two pitfalls here. The first is that a lot of potentially interesting information is not presented and is therefore lost to the reader. The second is that the impression is created that, by use of a single number, income distributions, whether between countries or over time, can be compared in terms of the degree of inequality. As Atkinson and others have argued, any measure of inequality incorporates value judgements on the nature of inequality, and these judgements may not be found acceptable if they are spelt out.[19]

Hence the temptation to use a summary indicator will, on the whole, be resisted. Only very sparing recourse will be made to one, widely used, measure of inequality, the 'Gini coefficient'.[20] This measure, like all others, incorporates its own value judgements. But a number of the sources quoted below use it as the sole indicator of the distribution of income and hence it will be reported.

Finally, even assuming that reasonably comparable figures have been assembled and presented in a reasonably convenient form, this will still be inadequate for an understanding of inequality in economic welfare amongst individuals. Data for the size-distribution of income amongst households still fall short for at least

[19] A.B. Atkinson, 'On the Measurement of Inequality', *Journal of Economic Theory*, September 1970.

[20] This coefficient can be defined in terms of the diagram. In drawing this diagram, for a hypothetical distribution, income units have been ranked by their income. The horizontal axis refers to the cumulative proportion of income units (starting with those with least income), and the vertical axis to the cumulative proportion of income accruing to income units. The Gini coefficient is defined as the ratio of the shaded area ABC to the area ADC, and the value of the coefficient varies between 0 (complete equality) and 1 (complete inequality).

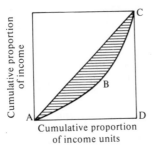

two reasons as indicators of the distribution of economic welfare. First, income is usually measured as money income (sometimes with the addition of the value of employer-provided 'fringe benefits'). Even when post-tax income is used, this does not coincide with real income. In particular, the benefits of public expenditure (especially those like health care and education which in the main accrue directly to individuals), are omitted from income. There may also be differences in prices faced by differing groups. This can arise from regional variations in prices, the different incidence of indirect taxation, and, in an international context, from different relative prices, so that, for example, the goods purchased mainly by the rich are cheaper in one country than in another.

Second, households differ in the number of their members, and an income which provides affluence for a one-person household may spell poverty for a large household. Though some allowance for this can be made by looking at the per capita distribution of household income, this may well be insufficient given that the age composition of the household should also be taken into account.

Inequality in the 1970s

In view of these various problems, this section begins by looking at what are probably the least contentious data available in an international context — figures on *individual earnings* which bypass at least such problems as household definition, under-reporting, or household size. This is not to say that statistical difficulties do not arise, but they are probably less formidable than for size distribution data. A study by Saunders and Marsden provides comparable statistics on the distribution of earnings for six European countries in the early 1970s.[21] The work focuses on the distribution of pre-tax hourly earnings (for manual workers) and monthly earnings (for non-manual workers) in 'industry',[22] with the statistics covering all full-time workers. The findings are summarized in Table 7.8 in terms of ratios of the top decile to the bottom decile and ratios of the top quartile to the bottom quartile. These can only be summary measures and do not capture, for example, the extent of inequality within the top or bottom ten per cent. These figures indicate that, in general, earnings are more unequally distributed in France, Great Britain, and Italy (with Great Britain often seen as the most unequal), than in Germany, Belgium, and the Netherlands. In the latter country, however, inequality amongst female workers is particularly high.[23]

The data for Great Britain are drawn from a different source from that used for the other five countries,[24] and though they have been adjusted to bring them in line with the other countries' figures, differences may still remain which

[21] C. Saunders and D. Marsden, *A Six-Country Comparison of the Distribution of Industrial Earnings in the 1970s*, HMSO, London 1979.

[22] The sectors covered were mining, manufacturing, public utilities, and construction.

[23] This has only a small effect on the overall distribution since female workers are a relatively small proportion of the Dutch labour force.

[24] The British figures are based on Department of Employment, *New Earnings Survey, 1972*, HMSO, London 1973, while those for the other countries are derived from a survey conducted by the EEC statistical office.

TABLE 7.8. *Distribution of pre-tax earnings in industry, 1972*
(full-time workers)

	France	Germany	Great Britain	Italy	Belgium	Netherlands
	Ratio of top to bottom decile					
Female manual	1.65	1.64	1.97	1.74	1.65	2.29
Male manual	1.97	1.59	2.14	1.88	1.72	1.68
Female non-manual	2.40	2.08	2.48	2.40	2.15	2.92
Male non-manual	3.14	2.13	3.02	2.99	2.54	2.50
All workers	2.68	2.34	3.18	2.57	2.28	2.29
	Ratios of top to bottom quartile					
Female manual	1.29	1.29	1.40	1.33	1.28	1.55
Male manual	1.42	1.26	1.50	1.40	1.30	1.26
Female non-manual	1.56	1.46	1.50	1.54	1.49	1.72
Male non-manual	1.74	1.47	1.67	1.74	1.57	1.56
All workers	1.65	1.46	1.79	1.61	1.47	1.43

Note: earnings of manual workers relate to hourly pay; earnings of non-manual workers and all workers relate to monthly (for Great Britain weekly) pay.

Source: C. Saunders and D. Marsden, *A Six-Country Comparison of the Distribution of Industrial Earnings in the 1970s*, Royal Commission on the Distribution of Income and Wealth, Background Paper No. 8, HMSO, London 1979.

could lead to some overestimation of British inequality. It is unlikely, however, that if such remaining biases could be adjusted for, this would remove the differences in inequality between Great Britain and the three less unequal countries.

Turning from individual earnings to *household incomes*, Tables 7.9 and 7.10 provide some information for a number of European countries on both pre- and

TABLE 7.9. *Distribution of pre-tax income*
(percentages)

	Decile shares									
	1	2	3	4	5	6	7	8	9	10
France (1970)	1.5	2.8	4.2	5.7	7.1	8.7	10.4	12.6	16.0	31.0
Germany (1973)	2.5	3.4	4.5	5.6	6.8	8.3	9.9	12.2	15.7	31.1
United Kingdom (1977/78)	2.5	3.6	4.6	5.9	7.3	9.1	11.0	13.4	16.3	26.2
Ireland (1973)	4.1		11.1		16.5		23.8		16.4	28.1
Netherlands (1967)	2.3	3.6	4.9	6.0	7.3	8.5	9.9	11.7	14.7	31.1
Norway (1970)	1.7	3.2	4.9	6.7	8.2	9.8	11.3	13.3	16.4	24.5
Sweden (1972)	2.0	4.0	5.3	6.1	7.9	9.5	11.2	13.1	16.1	24.4

Sources: CSO, 'The Distribution of Income in the United Kingdom, 1977/78', *Economic Trends*, February 1980; M. Sawyer, 'Income Distribution in OECD Countries', *OECD Economic Outlook — Occasional Studies*. July 1976; T. Stark, *The Distribution of Income in Eight Countries*, HMSO, London 1977.

post-tax distribution. There are numerous reasons for not drawing strong conclusions from these figures, for whilst they are as comparable as possible,

TABLE 7.10. *Distribution of post-tax income*
(percentages)

	Decile shares									
	1	2	3	4	5	6	7	8	9	10
France (1970)	1.4	2.9	4.2	5.6	7.4	8.9	9.7	13.0	16.5	30.4
Germany (1973)	2.8	3.7	4.6	5.7	6.8	8.2	9.8	12.1	15.8	30.3
Italy (1967)	2.3	3.9	5.1	6.2	7.3	8.6	10.3	12.4	15.8	28.1
United Kingdom (1977/78)	3.0	4.4	5.2	6.2	7.7	9.3	11.3	13.4	16.2	23.3
Spain (1973–4)	2.1	3.9	5.3	6.5	7.8	9.1	10.6	12.5	15.6	26.7
Finland (1971)	2.5	4.1	5.5	6.8	8.2	9.7	11.2	13.0	15.0	23.5
Netherlands (1967)	2.6	3.9	5.2	6.4	7.6	8.8	10.3	12.4	15.2	27.1
Norway (1970)	2.3	4.0	5.6	7.3	8.6	10.2	11.7	13.0	15.1	22.2
Sweden (1972)	2.2	4.4	5.9	7.2	8.5	10.0	11.5	13.3	15.7	21.3
Average	2.4	3.9	5.2	6.5	7.8	9.2	10.7	12.8	15.6	25.9

Sources: Banca d'Italia, *Bollettino*, April–September 1978; Central Statistical Office of
Finland, *Finnish Survey on Relative Income Differences*, Helsinki 1976; CSO,
'The Distribution of Income in the United Kingdom, 1977/78', *Economic
Trends*, February 1980; M. Sawyer, 'Income Distribution in OECD Countries',
OECD Economic Outlook — Occasional Studies, July 1976.

difficulties remain. Many of the reasons for these were mentioned in the introduction to this section. Others could arise from the possibility that countries
were in different phases of the trade cycle in the years shown, since the level
of activity may influence income distribution. Finally, it should be remembered
that the translation of any conclusions from these tables to conclusions on the
inequality of real income would need to incorporate information on the provision and distribution of the benefits of public expenditure, and on the differences in prices facing different groups.

A look at Tables 7.8 and 7.9 both of which present data on pre-tax incomes,
would show that the implied ranking of countries in terms of inequality are, in
a number of respects, rather different. But, it is worth remembering that the
distribution of earnings is only a part, often the middle part, of the distribution
of income. In particular, the upper part of the distribution is heavily influenced
by self-employment and property income, whereas the lower part of the distribution is strongly affected by transfer payments. Further, the distribution of
earnings is the distribution across individuals, whereas the distribution of income is the distribution across households.

The two most interesting findings suggested by Tables 7.9 and 7.10 relate to
inter-country differences on the one hand, and to the differences between the
pre- and the post-tax distributions on the other. For those countries for which
direct comparisons are possible, it would appear that direct taxes play an equalizing role everywhere, but one which varies considerably between countries. On
the basis of six measures of inequality, the reduction in inequality generated by
the tax system is largest in Norway, Sweden, and the United Kingdom, followed
by the Netherlands, Germany, and France (where there is virtually no change).[25]

[25] The measures of inequality used were the Atkinson measure (with values of 0.5 and
1.5 for the 'inequality aversion' index used), the Gini coefficient, the Theil measure, Kuz-

Turning to differences between countries, these tend to be particularly marked at the two extremities of the income distribution. In the post-tax distribution, the share of the lowest decile varies from 1½ per cent (France) through to 3 per cent (United Kingdom), so that relative income varies by a factor of two. The share of the highest decile varies from around 30 per cent (France and Germany) to around 25 per cent (Norway and Sweden). On average, the bottom decile receives 2½ per cent of total income and the second decile 4 per cent, with the top decile receiving 26 per cent.

It is possible to make a tentative ranking of countries in terms of the inequality of post-tax income distribution. Using the average position given by applying six measures of inequality (described in n. 25), one obtains the following ranking (with the least unequal first): Sweden, Norway, United Kingdom, Finland, Netherlands, Spain, Italy, Germany, and France. Of course, the positions vary depending on the measures used (although there is a large amount of agreement between them). This ranking, however, can only be tentative, for besides problems of measuring inequality there are problems arising from the unreliability of the data. This, as was mentioned earlier, may arise from a variety of causes, but the under-reporting of certain types of income is clearly one of the most important. If anything, allowance for this factor would probably reinforce the conclusion that the Scandinavian countries and the United Kingdom are relatively equal in terms of income distribution, while France is unequal. But correction for under-reporting could well alter the positions of Germany on the one hand (for which in fact under-reporting in the data base shown is zero), and for Italy and Spain on the other (for which under-reporting is likely to be very sizeable).

Tables 7.9 and 7.10 are, however, unable to throw light, except indirectly, on one particularly important aspect of the distribution of income – namely the extent of *poverty*. There are two important dimensions to the concept of poverty, which can be labelled 'absolute' and 'relative'. The absolute dimension reflects that aspect of poverty which arises from the lack of the necessities of life, particularly a lack of sufficient food for adequate nutrition, lack of shelter, and of clothing. The relative dimension focuses on a low command over resources *relative* to the rest of the community. The two dimensions are more closely linked than these bold statements might indicate. It is likely, for example, that the popular concept of poverty at any time (in a particular country) will be thought of in terms of an inability to purchase a certain level of goods and services. Yet these notions of poverty may change over time in response to changes in real income.

Three approaches to the concept of poverty can be distinguished. First, an absolute standard of poverty, which defines poverty in terms of the inability of a household to achieve a certain living standard fixed in real terms. Second, a relative standard of poverty, which defines the poor as those with income less than x per cent of the average (with households distinguished by size). Third, an approach which regards the poor as those at the bottom of the income

---

nets' index, and the variance of logarithms. For a definition of these measures, see Sawyer, 'Income Distribution'. The proportionate reduction in the measures of inequality varied for, e.g. Norway, from 30 per cent (variance of logarithms) to 13 per cent (Kuznets' index).

distribution, i.e. the lowest y per cent of the size-distribution. This last approach leads to a poverty problem which can never be eliminated, though the position of the poor may improve or worsen.[26]

Clearly if poverty is defined in terms of the inability to achieve a certain standard of living, with that standard fixed, then the extent of absolute poverty will generally decline over time (provided that the relative position of the poor does not continually worsen). In contrast, changes in relative poverty require changes in the distribution of income, particularly at the lower end. An indication of the sharp difference which arises from taking an absolute approach to poverty rather than a relative one is provided by estimates for the United Kingdom.[27] These show that, between the early 1950s and the early 1970s, poverty defined in absolute terms declined very sharply — the proportion of individuals in poverty fell from 4.8 to 0.2 per cent of the population if one uses as a (fixed) benchmark the 1953–4 National Assistance Scales, and from 21.0 to 2.3 per cent if one uses the 1971 Supplementary Benefits scales. A relative concept of poverty based on current (moving) National Assistance or Supplementary Benefits scales, leads to a much smaller decline (from 4.8 to 3.0 per cent of the population).

During the 1950s and into the 1960s, it was often assumed that poverty had diminished, and that, with continued economic growth, it would be eliminated in the foreseeable future. The 'rediscovery' of poverty in the early 1960s may reflect, in part, an essentially relative view of poverty, but with a lag before the notions of poverty adjust to rising real incomes. The fact that poverty is still discussed as a problem in the developed countries also indicates the relative nature of poverty. A quick reading of earlier writings on poverty (e.g. the work by Rowntree at the beginning of the century),[28] detailing the goods and services the lack of which was taken as defining poverty, gives an indication of the much higher living standards of those now considered poor.

The measurement of poverty is made particularly difficult by the requirement of defining a poverty line, especially when one wishes to make international comparisons. Table 7.11 reports the available evidence. It is clear that no comparisons can be made of the degree of poverty in various countries using the national definitions, since the poverty lines used differ in severity and there are also differences in concepts of income and income unit. The comparability of the so-called 'standardized' figures is also open to some doubt. Some of these figures were obtained by the OECD on the basis of a set of uniform (but inevitably

---

[26] Examples of these three approaches can be found in: (a) B.F. Rowntree, *Poverty — A Study of Town Life*, London 1901, who constructed a poverty line for the city of York based on the cost of a diet providing minimum requirements of protein and calories, some allowance for clothing, and rent. The poverty line widely used in the United States, which originates from M. Orshansky, 'Counting the Poor: Another Look at the Poverty Profile', *Social Security Bulletin*, No. 28, 1965, is based on a multiple of the cost of a minimum cost diet; (b) present-day British investigations which have often based their poverty line on the scale rates used for Supplementary Benefits/National Assistance; (c) T. Goedhart, V. Halberstadt, A. Kapteyn, and B. van Praag, 'The Poverty Line: Concept and Measurement', *Journal of Human Resources*, Fall 1977.

[27] G. Fieghan, P. Lansley, and A. Smith, *Poverty and Progress in Britain*, Cambridge 1977.

[28] Rowntree, *Poverty*.

TABLE 7.11. *Estimates of poverty, early 1970s*
(per cent of population below relative poverty line)

	National definition	'Standardized definitions'[a]	
		ILO	OECD
France	15–20	..	16
Germany	..	..	3
United Kingdom	13	10[b]	7½
Belgium	14	6	..
Ireland	24	..	..
Norway	..	7½	5
Sweden	..	..	3½

[a] For definitions, see original sources
[b] Great Britain

Sources: W. Beckerman, *Poverty and the Impact of Income Maintenance Programmes in Four Developed Countries*, ILO, Geneva 1979; OECD, *Public Expenditure on Income Maintenance Programmes*, Paris 1976.

arbitrary) assumptions and using the not always very reliable income distribution data discussed above. The data basis is better for the figures produced at the ILO, but the assumptions remain arbitrary and are not identical to those used by the OECD. Hence the purpose of the table is not so much that of providing precise international comparisons of the extent of poverty in Europe, but to indicate that poverty, however defined, remains, and is seen to be, a continuing problem.

Thus, whilst the material conditions of the poor have undoubtedly improved in the post-war period, relative poverty and deprivation remain considerable issues. But the causes of poverty have probably changed. Although this is difficult to document, a study for the United Kingdom concluded that the two factors which were associated with poverty in earlier years ranked some way down the list in the early 1970s.[29] Whilst the risk of poverty for households with an unemployed head was high, such households did not account for a particularly large proportion of the poor in 1971. Secondly, although the risk of poverty for households with large numbers of children (five or more) was also high, the numerical importance of poverty had become less significant. Risk and numerical importance had remained high only for retired and single-parent households.

Changes in inequality

The changes in the distribution of income which have occurred since 1945 are difficult to document. In many countries, it is only recently that income distribution data have been collected on a regular basis. Indeed, many of the statistics used in Tables 7.9 and 7.10 come from special 'one-off' surveys, so that data for previous years do not exist. Even where information is available for a number of years, improvements made in definitions and methods of collection introduce elements of incomparability. In addition, the reliability of the figures may be affected by changes through time in the degree of under-reporting and in

[29] Fieghan, *et al.*, *Poverty and Progress*, p. 57.

TABLE 7.12. *Changes in the distribution of pre-tax earnings in industry*

		Ratios to median of:		
	upper decile	upper quartile	lower quartile	lower decile
France: all workers				
1964	202	138	71	50
1968	210	140	72	53
1972	204	..	..	54
all male workers				
1964	208	138	73	52
1968	217	142	75	55
1970	213	140	75	58
1972	212	..	..	55
Germany: all manual workers				
1966	144.7	118.4	82.9	66.1
1972	140.3	118.9	82.6	66.1
all male manual workers				
1957	134.9	116.8	85.3	73.3
1966	135.7	121.7	82.6	70.6
1972	135.8	116.9	86.7	75.7
United Kingdom: all male workers				
1968	161.4	126.7	80.1	65.7
1978	157.9	125.1	80.6	66.8
all male manual workers				
1886	143.1	121.7	82.8	68.6
1938	139.9	118.5	82.1	67.7
1960	145.2	121.7	82.6	70.6
1968	147.8	122.3	81.0	67.3
1973	146.1	121.2	82.4	69.5
Ireland: all adult male workers				
1960	147.5	122.4	78.4	61.0
1968	151.4	126.2	77.7	62.1

Sources: CSO, *British Labour Statistics* (various issues); T. Stark, *The Distribution of Income in Eight Countries*, HMSO, London 1977.

the extent of tax evasion (when the data are partly based on tax records), by the development of incomes in kind and fringe benefits, and by the growth of the 'black economy' to levels frequently reported as in the range of 7 to 15 per cent of GDP. Finally, the use of different sources introduces at times an element of incomparability between the earnings and income data for the 1970s presented in Tables 7.8 to 7.10 and those in Table 7.12.

Bearing these caveats in mind, a summary of changes in the distribution of earnings for four countries is shown in Table 7.12. The first visual impression given by the figures is one of stability in the earnings distribution in the four countries concerned. Though the sample here shown is limited, earlier evidence for a much larger number of countries confirms that the structure of pre-tax earnings has indeed remained remarkably stable in post-war Europe,[30] and, in

[30] UNECE, *Incomes in Europe*; see also OECD, *Wages and Labour Mobility*, Paris 1965.

the United Kingdom, for as long as a century.[31] It is difficult to know whether this stability is due to economic or other factors. The UNECE has, for instance, argued that 'The pay structure may even appear to have become an exogenous variable, determined independently by history and social institutions, rather than the result of the play or market forces.'[32]

It would seem that government intervention in the process of earnings formation (e.g. incomes policies) has not generated substantial changes in the distribution of earnings. The introduction of minimum wage legislation may have had some initial impact on the distribution of earnings, but no further effects seem to have taken place, at least in the three countries in which minimum wage legislation has been implemented in recent years (France, Italy, and the Netherlands), since such minimum wages appear to have moved in line with the general level of wages, and thus have tended to leave the distribution of earnings unchanged. Thus, in the Netherlands the minimum wage was pitched at a relatively high level initially, but has since stayed around two-thirds of the average wage. In France, the minimum wage has generally, in the post-war period, increased at a slower rate than average earnings. There was a dramatic exception with a rise of 35 per cent in 1968. However, the proportionate increases in the minimum wage and average earnings were exactly the same over the twenty-one year period up to 1975. In Italy there has been a complex of minimum wages for different sectors of the economy, but in manufacturing the minimum wage has moved roughly with average wages.

One area where changes in social opinion and legislation appear to have had an effect is the earnings differentials between men and women. Table 7.13 provides some figures on male–female differentials in much of the non-agricultural sector (varying from manufacturing industries only through to all non-agricultural industries). The figures are not strictly comparable across countries, for they refer to somewhat different sectors and vary in other small ways, but they do refer to hourly earnings of manual workers throughout. The general pattern is one of stability in the male–female differential during the 1950s (with Germany and the Netherlands as exceptions), a narrowing of the differential in about half the countries during the 1960s, and a general narrowing in the 1970s. Over the twenty-five year period ending in 1979 the differential remained virtually unchanged in only France and Switzerland. Elsewhere, it narrowed, though at the end of the period male earnings still exceeded female earnings in all countries by, on average, some 30 per cent.

Information on changes in income distribution is less easily forthcoming. Some of the available data are presented in Table 7.14. These suggest some movement towards equality in that the top decile has tended to lose some share of total income, whilst the bottom deciles have tended to gain. In France, a loss of 7 per cent by the top decile is matched by gains in the bottom three deciles. However, this comparison may indicate a greater shift towards equality than actually took place, since the statistics omit means-tested pensions, which go

---

[31] There may, however, have been some exceptions to this general rule in e.g. Italy and Sweden, where evidence for the 1960s and early 1970s shows that wage differentials have narrowed quite sharply − see Ch. 12 below.

[32] UNECE, *Incomes in Europe*, Ch. 5, p. 33.

TABLE 7.13. *Changes in male–female earning[a] differentials,*
non-agricultural sector[b]
(indices: female earnings = 100)

	1954	1960	1970	1979
France	115	118	115	114
Germany	165	152	144	138
United Kingdom	163	165	166	142
Belgium	172[c]	171[c]	150	144
Denmark	153	149	138	118
Finland[d]	148	150	142	133
Ireland[d]	177	173	177	150
Netherlands[d]	172	163	139	123[e]
Norway[d]	147	146	133	124
Sweden[d]	144	145	121	112
Switzerland	150	155	159	150
Average	155	153	144	132

[a] Hourly earnings or rates for manual workers
[b] Unless otherwise stated
[c] Estimated from differentials in weekly earnings
[d] Manufacturing only
[e] 1978
Source: calculated from ILO, *Yearbook of Labour Statistics* (various issues).

predominantly to the poor, but include earnings-related insurance pensions. The former were gradually replaced in the post-war period by the latter. In Germany, there appears to have been little change since 1950 in absolute shares, although the income share of the bottom decile moved up from 2.1 per cent in 1950 to 2.8 per cent in 1974, a relative gain of one-third. For Italy, the figures cover only the decade since 1967, and suggest a fairly marked shift, with the top decile losing 2.5 per cent and the bottom decile gaining 0.7 per cent (a relative gain of nearly one-half). In fact the changes may have been even more pronounced than this, since the underlying statistics have been gradually improved through the decade to include more items of income. The extensions are likely to have caused measured inequality to increase, as the extra income included has tended to be income derived from various types of capital. For the United Kingdom, both the top decile and the bottom half lost ground between 1949 and 1959, while the sixth to ninth deciles gained. The top decile continued to lose ground after 1959 but the bottom quintile improved its position. The largest change in absolute share terms has been the fall from 6.4 per cent in 1949 to 3.9 per cent in 1977/8 in the share of the top 1 per cent. The data for the Netherlands also indicate a shift from the top decile to the bottom deciles between 1954 and 1967.

The general picture which emerges is thus of losses in the share of income by the top decile, with the bottom deciles being the main gainers in this process. But the changes which have occurred can hardly be described as dramatic, although the relative gains by the bottom decile are of the order of a quarter to a half.

But are the changes what they appear? Quite apart from the already mentioned

TABLE 7.14. *Changes in the distribution of post-tax income*
(percentages)

	Decile shares									
	1	2	3	4	5	6	7	8	9	10
France[a]										
1956	——— 3.0 ———			3.9	6.9	8.2	10.3	12.8	18.8	36.2
1962	0.9	1.1	3.0	4.5	6.9	7.5	10.8	12.0	17.3	36.1
1965	1.1	2.5	3.4	5.5	6.6	8.4	9.7	12.3	16.5	34.0
1970	1.1	2.7	4.3	5.7	6.9	8.2	11.1	12.5	18.3	29.3
Germany										
1950	2.1	3.4	4.7	6.0	7.3	8.7	10.3	12.5	15.8	29.3
1960	2.5	3.5	4.7	6.0	7.3	8.8	10.5	12.6	15.8	28.1
1970	2.5	3.4	4.6	5.8	7.1	8.5	10.2	12.3	16.3	29.3
1974	2.8	3.8	4.7	5.7	6.9	8.3	10.0	12.2	15.8	29.8
Italy										
1967	1.6	3.2	4.8	6.2	7.6	8.8	9.9	12.0	15.5	30.5
1972	1.8	3.6	4.9	6.1	7.2	8.5	10.0	12.0	15.6	30.2
1977	2.3	3.9	5.1	6.2	7.3	8.6	10.3	12.4	15.8	28.1
United Kingdom										
1949	——————— 26.5 ———————					9.5	10.5	11.9	14.5	27.1
1959	6.0		5.2	6.6	7.2	9.9	11.2	12.9	15.7	25.2
1967	7.1		4.9	7.1	7.7	9.7	11.0	13.0	15.2	24.3
1973	3.2	4.2	5.4	6.4	7.8	9.5	11.2	13.2	15.5	23.6
1976/77	3.0	4.5	5.1	6.6	7.7	9.3	11.3	13.4	16.0	23.1
Netherlands										
1954	1.7	3.3	4.8	6.1	7.5	9.3	10.3	12.0	15.1	29.9
1959	2.3	3.2	4.8	6.4	7.8	9.2	10.5	12.2	15.0	28.8
1967	2.6	3.9	5.2	6.4	7.6	8.8	10.3	12.4	15.2	27.7

[a] Pre-tax income (excluding family allowances and minimum pensions)
Sources: Banca d'Italia, *Bollettino*, April–September 1978; Deutsches Institut für Wirt-
schaftsvorschung, *Wochenbericht*, No. 31, 1975; M. Sawyer, 'Income Distribution
in OECD Countries', *OECD Economic Outlook – Occasional Studies*, July 1976.

statistical and other problems, any assessment of these changes must consider
demographic and other structural factors which may have led to changes in the
overall distribution of income. Three particular changes will be briefly discussed
below – demographic changes, changes in average household size, and changes in
the socio-economic distribution of the labour force. Other factors can, of course,
also play a role (e.g. increased female participation rates or migration from poor
to rich regions), but given the paucity of empirical estimates as to their effects,
they will not be treated.

Probably the most important demographic change in post-war Europe has
been the gradual ageing of the population, for which some evidence is presented
in Appendix Table 7.A1. It is well known that the old tend to have a lower than
average income. Thus, roughly half the households in the bottom two deciles
were headed by persons aged sixty-five or over in six OECD countries in the late
1960s or early 1970s.[33] Hence an increase in the proportion of elderly people
tends to swell the numbers in the lower income groups, and, *ceteris paribus*, to

[33] Sawyer, 'Income Distribution', p. 20.

increase measured inequality. The effect of this ageing of the population has been estimated for the United Kingdom via a shift–share analysis.[34] This basically assumes that the total distribution is composed of a number of sub-distributions corresponding to subgroups in the population, and that demographic changes lead to changes in the weights of the sub-distributions in the total. Thus a counterfactual distribution for the end of the period is constructed with the weights of each subgrouping taken from the beginning of the period. From 1951 to 1971, the effects of changes in the proportion of the population which is elderly and in the female–male ratio within the elderly population are estimated to have caused a 2.6 per cent relative increase in the share of the top percentile, and a 1.0 per cent relative decrease in the share of the bottom quintile.[35] The effect of an ageing population on the Gini coefficient was to increase it by 1.6 per cent. While similar evidence for other countries has not been found, it is plausible to assume that the changing age structure has also increased measured inequality elsewhere, even if the effect is likely to have been only small.

A similar effect may have arisen from another general trend over the post-war period, namely the fall in the size of households (which is partially but not entirely related to the ageing of the population). Here again, some average figures for a number of OECD countries show, for example, that nearly 90 per cent of households in the bottom decile and 80 per cent of the next decile consisted of one or two members.[36] This change too is therefore likely to have increased measured inequality. This is confirmed by one estimate for the United Kingdom which showed that a hypothetical Gini coefficient based on the 1961 household composition was 3.5 per cent lower than the actual coefficient.[37]

The impact of more general socio-economic changes is less easy to predict. Thus, the effect of, for instance, the decline of a particular sector, such as agriculture, on the distribution of income, will depend both upon the extent of inequality and on the average income of the sector relative to the rest of the economy. Some of the available evidence is summarized in Table 7.15. In France there is a general tendency for the Gini coefficient to decline for each sector, but the decline in the overall coefficient is somewhat more pronounced than that of the average of the Gini coefficients for all sectors, suggesting that some of the movement towards greater measured inequality arose from structural change. The opposite is true for Germany between 1950 and 1973. Overall distribution changed little, but this appears to have been composed of two separate trends. Inequality within socio-economic groups declined, but shifts between the socio-economic groups as well as other factors led to increases in inequality. Yet another example is provided by the Netherlands, where structural changes seem to have played only a small role. Thus, the decline in inequality for the period 1954 to 1967 arises mainly from a sharp decline in inequality amongst pensioners and the non-employed and from small changes in the other two groups.

[34] R. Dinwiddy and D. Reed, *The Effects of Certain Social and Demographic Changes on Income Distribution*, HMSO, London 1977.

[35] Thus, whereas in the actual distribution for 1971/2 the lowest quintile accounts for 4.47 per cent of total income, in the counterfactual distribution (based on the 1951 age structure) the share is 4.52 per cent.

[36] Sawyer, 'Income Distribution', p. 20.

[37] M. Semple, 'The Effects of Changes in Household Composition on the Distribution of Income', *Economic Trends*, December 1975.

TABLE 7.15. *Changes in the distribution of income by
socio-economic group*
(Gini coefficients for France and Germany; Theil coefficients[a] for
the Netherlands)

	1962	1970
France		
Self-employed in agriculture	0.57	0.53
Agricultural workers	0.37	0.31
Independent professions	0.47	0.47
Top-level management	0.36	0.28
Middle management	0.32	0.27
Other non-manual workers	0.32	0.31
Manual workers	0.29	0.28
Economically inactive	0.52	0.47
Total	0.51	0.44
	1950	1973
Germany		
Self-employed	0.38	0.26
Salaried workers	0.34	0.33
Manual workers	0.31	0.28
Economically inactive	0.41	0.33
Total	0.38	0.38
	1954	1967
Netherlands		
Self-employed	0.40	0.37
Wage and salary earners	0.22	0.19
Economically inactive	0.35	0.19
Total	0.32	0.26

[a] The Theil coefficient is a measure of inequality defined as: $\sum_{i=1}^{N} s_i \log Ns_i$

where s_i is the income share of unit i and N is the number of units. As with the Gini
coefficient, a decline in its value denotes a reduction in inequality.
Source: M. Sawyer, 'Income Distribution in OECD Countries', *OECD Economic Outlook —
Occasional Studies*, July 1976.

Finally, a detailed study for the United Kingdom concludes that the sum of
a large number of both demographic and other changes has had only a very small
effect on the distribution of income.[38] A counterfactual distribution based on
1951 social and demographic characteristics, in terms of marriage rates, population structure, proportion of the elderly, women's economic activity, and
education in the 15 to 24 age group, resulted in a Gini coefficient for 1971/2
only marginally below the actual one. The impact of the changes has been to
lower the share of each of the five lowest deciles and of the top decile.

In summary, this subsection has shown that in the post-war period, and
despite a surprisingly stable pre-tax earnings structure, the distribution of
(usually) post-tax income has none the less changed towards greater equality

[38] Dinwiddy and Reed, *The Effects of Social Changes.*

in those European countries for which reasonably reliable data are available. Fairly pronounced changes have taken place in Italy, the United Kingdom, and the Netherlands; more modest ones in France and Germany. This conclusion is strengthened if allowance is made for the likely effects of two important demographic and social changes – the ageing of the population and the decline in household size – both of which are likely to have increased measured inequality. On the other hand, it is possible that some of the move towards greater equality resulted from other socio-economic changes such as rising female participation rates, the decline in the number of the self-employed and the agricultural population, and more general regional changes. The available evidence on the importance of these two factors is too scanty to allow many generalizations, but probably the effects of such changes on measured equality were more pronounced in countries such as France, Italy, or Spain, which had relatively large primary and/or unincorporated sectors at the outset, than in countries such as Germany or the United Kingdom, in which the overall effects of such socio-economic transformations on income distribution seem to have been relatively small.[39]

III. Transfers and Distribution

This section briefly discusses some of the links between the trends in welfare expenditure, taxation, and income distribution which have been looked at so far. These various developments impinge on each other in a number of ways. *Inter alia*:

    (i) Changes in welfare payments will alter the pre-tax distribution of income;

    (ii) Changes in taxation will alter the post-tax distribution;

    (iii) Changes in other benefits provided by the state (education, housing, etc.) will have further indirect effects on distribution;

    (iv) These various forces can all have (positive or negative) feedback effects on the pre-tax structure of earnings.

The discussion concentrates on the impact of income transfers, largely because their distributive effects are most firmly based. But before turning to these, brief mention must be made of the effects of taxes and non-transfer benefits. The effects of taxation have already been discussed in Sections I and II. It was shown, first, that the structure of direct taxation in Europe is progressive, though less so than income tax alone would suggest, both because of the strongly regressive nature of employee social security contributions and because the changes in taxation over the period may not have gone in the direction of much greater progressivity. The first statement was corroborated by some of the evidence presented in Section II – in particular, the move towards income equalization shown by post-tax relative to pre-tax size distribution data. The second statement is hardly open to empirical verification at present, in view of data insufficiency, but the lack of a pronounced shift towards equality through the period, according to the few post-tax figures available, may suggest that the progressivity of tax policies has not changed very greatly.

[39] See Ch. 14 for some evidence on the narrowing of regional income differentials.

Turning to the benefits provided by the state, other than direct transfers to households, the allocation of such benefits is very difficult, if not impossible (e.g. law and order or defence). Many studies on the distributive effects of public expenditure allocate benefits across income groups by assuming that each individual receives the same per caput benefits.[40] This is, however, an arbitrary assumption. Restricting the discussion to welfare benefits (e.g. education, health care provided directly rather than financed via social security transfers, housing provision), a plausible a priori argument is that such benefits, even if they accrue to a larger extent to high than to low income groups, are unlikely to be distributed in the same proportion as income. In other words, while the top decile in the income distribution may receive 26 per cent of total income, and therefore nearly eleven times more than the bottom decile, this same decile is unlikely to be able to consume eleven times more health care than the poorest decile. But beyond this generalization, which would clearly point to some favourable effects of public expenditure on distribution, little can be said. Indeed, as far as education goes, the OECD has concluded that the large increases in public expenditure in this area until the early 1970s had only small effects on measured inequality and little if any impact on social mobility.[41]

Somewhat clearer conclusions emerge, however, from a look at the impact of income transfers on income distribution and poverty. The assessment of such an impact usually relies on a comparison of a pre- and post-transfer situation made on the assumption that, if all transfers were removed, nothing else would change. This is likely to result in an overstatement of the effects of income transfers. For example, it implicitly assumes that there would be no increase in private provision in the absence of public provision. It also ignores any effects on labour force participation induced by income transfers – e.g. the encouragement to retire provided by the existence of public old-age pension schemes. Table 7.16 summarizes some of the evidence on the possible impact of transfers on household income distribution (more detail is provided in Appendix Table 7.A2). It shows the change in the share of quintiles between pre- and post-transfer income due to transfers and the extent to which each quintile relies on transfers as part of its income. It should be noted that the type of income which is used to rank households, and thereby determine the quintiles, varies between countries, and this is an added reason for the figures not being fully comparable. The most noticeable feature is that transfers represent a very considerable part of the income of the bottom quintile — everywhere over 60 per cent. Transfers also allow a significant change in the income share of this bottom quintile, while they

---

[40] For some estimates of the distributive effects of public expenditure, see: articles entitled 'The Effects of Taxes and Benefits on Household Income' (for the United Kingdom), published annually in CSO, *Economic Trends*; K. Bjerke and S. Brodersen, 'Studies of Income Redistribution in Denmark for 1963 and 1971', *Review of Income and Wealth*, June 1978; A. Foulon and G. Hatchuel, 'The Redistribution of Public Funds in France in 1965 and 1970', *Review of Income and Wealth*, September 1979; T. Franzen, K. Lövgren, and L. Rosenberg, 'Redistributional Effects of Taxes and Public Expenditure in Sweden', *Swedish Journal of Economics*, No. 1, 1975; R. Suominen, 'Empirical Results Concerning Vertical and Horizontal Redistribution in Finland', *Review of Income and Wealth*, March 1979.

[41] OECD, *Public Expenditure on Education*, Paris 1976, p. 38.

TABLE 7.16. *Impact of transfers on the distribution of income*
(percentages)

	Quintile shares				
	1	2	3	4	5
France (1970)[a][b]					
Change in income share	2.0	1.7	0.6	−0.8	−3.5
Transfers in per cent of income	64.2	30.1	17.2	9.7	6.5
Germany (1969)[a]					
Change in income share	3.5	2.3	−0.3	−1.3	−4.3
Transfers in per cent of income	63.2	32.1	16.1	12.3	8.3
United Kingdom (1973)[a]					
Change in income share	3.5	1.4	−0.6	−1.4	−3.1
Transfers in per cent of income	71.7	18.7	6.2	4.1	2.0
Spain (1973–74)[c]					
Change in income share	6.6	0.9	−0.5	−1.7	−5.1
Transfers in per cent of income	89.3	20.3	9.3	5.8	3.3
Norway (1970)[a]					
Change in income share	2.8	1.8	−0.3	−1.4	−3.0
Transfers in per cent of income	60.2	23.4	7.0	4.1	2.3
Sweden (1972)[c]					
Change in income share	9.3	5.6	−0.1	−3.1	−11.6
Transfers in per cent of income	108.4	55.5	20.5	13.8	8.1

Note: for more detail, see Appendix Table 7.A2.
[a] Households ranked by post-transfer income
[b] Transfers consist only of pensions
[c] Households ranked by pre-transfer income
Source: M. Sawyer, 'Income Distribution in OECD Countries', *OECD Economic Outlook –
Occasional Studies*, July 1976.

depress the income shares of the two top quintiles. This notwithstanding, as can
be seen in Appendix Table 7.A2, in some countries a significant proportion of
transfers (reaching 20 per cent in France and Germany) accrues to the upper
quintiles. This is perhaps not as surprising as it may seem since most transfers
are in fact not means-tested and include universal benefits like child allowances.
Another factor is that these distributions are for households, and hence no
account is taken of household size.

A study undertaken by Beckerman for the ILO[42] investigates the comparative
power of income transfers in reducing poverty in four countries, of which three
(Great Britain, Belgium, and Norway) are European. The main results are summarized in Table 7.17. These compare the extent of poverty when only pre-
transfer income is considered with the extent when transfers are included as
part of income. This type of comparison provides an upper limit to the poverty-
decreasing power of income transfers. In the absence of transfers, for example,
it is clear that some private provision of pensions and continued work by the
elderly would have lead to poverty at a lower level than that reported in the
table.

[42] W. Beckerman, *Poverty and the Impact of Income Maintenance Programmes in Four
Developed Countries*, ILO, Geneva 1979.

TABLE 7.17. *Impact of transfers on poverty, around 1973*
(percentages)

	Great Britain	Belgium	Norway
Incidence of poverty[a]			
Pre-transfer	22.2	20.5	24.9
Post-transfer	9.9	6.1	7.7
Poverty gap[b]			
Pre-transfer	3.2	4.8	5.0
Post-transfer	0.4	0.7	0.5

[a] Percentage of population below relative poverty line; the poverty lines have been standardized across countries

[b] The poverty gap for a particular household is the difference between the poverty line for that size of household and the household's actual income; the total poverty gap here shown is the sum of the poverty gaps of individual households and indicates the percentage of GDP required to eradicate poverty

Source: W. Beckerman, *Poverty and the Impact of Income Maintenance Programmes in Four Developed Countries*, ILO, Geneva 1979.

Though the figures, despite the use of a 'standardized poverty line', are not, for a variety of reasons, strictly comparable across countries, it can none the less be seen that transfers achieve a significant reduction in the incidence of poverty in all the three countries — an average of one-third. The decline in poverty measured by the figures on the poverty gap is even larger — the post-transfer gap is less than 15 per cent of the pre-transfer gap for each of the three countries, and no larger, on average, than ½ per cent of GDP.

In conclusion, therefore, it would appear that government intervention in the form of income transfers, at least for the countries for which data are available, has apparently made an appreciable difference to the income position of the lowest deciles and of the poor. And this impression could be strengthened by the brief and admittedly only vague considerations put forward at the beginning of this section on the effects of non-pecuniary benefits provided by the state on the one hand, and of progressive taxation on the other.

Conclusions

This chapter has briefly surveyed some developments of welfare states and income distribution in post-war Europe. The discussion has often had to rely on a very imperfect and incomplete data base; the reliability and comparability of many of the figures which have been used is limited; and the country coverage has often been insufficient. Hence many of the generalizations and conclusions which have been put forward are inevitably tentative and partial.

Bearing these caveats in mind, one of the themes which the chapter has tried to develop has been the general convergence of European countries in the post-war period in some broad areas. Thus, whilst there are innumerable minor differences between the social security systems in use in the late 1970s in Europe, there is also an impressive similarity. The general pattern includes old-age pension schemes, with a pension payable to everyone at age sixty-five at the latest, and composed of two elements – a flat-rate part and an earnings-related part. Unemployment, sickness, and industrial injury insurance provide the vast majority of the work-force, after a short waiting period, with transfer payments, related to previous earnings, for up to a year. Flat-rate child benefits are payable to families with children, though the impact of these benefits on household income varies considerably. Whilst the foundations of these schemes were often in place before the war, they have generally been extended and consolidated in the years since.

The changes in the distribution of income which have occurred have generally been of an equalizing nature, and have often involved shifts in income from the top decile to the bottom two or three deciles. Some of these changes may have arisen from structural changes in the economy, but government intervention seems also to have played a role. Thus, transfer payments form a substantial part of the income of the bottom two deciles, and their growth may have caused some of the changes in the distribution of income through time. As for direct taxation, it also seems to have had an equalizing impact in all those countries for which figures are available. And both these findings are confirmed by the evidence on the income equalization achieved by taxes and transfers at the regional level contained in Chapter 14. Further reasons for the belief in the importance of government action stem from the evidence of a surprising stability in the distribution of pre-tax earnings, which does not correspond with the changes observed in the overall distribution.

But this recital of achievements does not mean that all problems have disappeared nor that all objectives have been reached. The persistence of poverty shows that benefit levels may still be insufficient. There may also be a general feeling that achievements have fallen short of objectives in view of the massive changes that have taken place in taxation and expenditure and the relatively small changes that have occurred in income distribution. To some extent this may be unfair, since it is very difficult to pinpoint the objectives of governments in the income distribution arena. The description of the objectives of a single government at a moment of time would be difficult enough. But the objectives themselves and the urgency attached to the objectives change over time for any particular government, and often shift with a change in government.

It may also be unfair since not all the changes in taxes and expenditure were introduced with specific income distribution aims in mind. While it may often be thought that the intention of social security and social assistance is to change the distribution of income and alleviate poverty, usually there are many pressures at work which lead to the introduction of such programmes, only some of which are connected with egalitarian aims. Thus, one reason for promoting income transfers may arise because of 'market failure' arguments, i.e. the contention that the private market mechanism is not capable of providing the desired result. This argument then leads to the provision of social insurance in place of private insurance.

Neither such provision of social insurance nor an increase in direct taxation need have favourable effects on income distribution. The former is often earnings-related and not means-tested and thus can perpetuate income disparities from active into inactive life; the latter can be regressive when it takes the form of social security contributions or when it extends the tax thresholds downwards. This in turn can have pronounced effects on poverty, as shown by the reported existence of so-called 'poverty traps' — the possibility, because of lack of sufficient integration of the social security and tax systems, for people on low incomes to pay effective marginal tax rates in excess of 100 per cent.[43] And poverty can, of course, also persist because of an incomplete 'take-up' of welfare benefits on the part of those who are theoretically entitled to them. Finally, increasing taxes and benefits can have feedback effects on earnings (e.g. widening the pre-tax differentials), or on the target groups (e.g. increasing the number of relatively low-income pensioners), which could, at the end of the day, lead to no change or even a deterioration in the measured post-tax distribution.[44]

In view of these and other reasons for expecting only a muted impact from increased government intervention in the welfare area, the results achieved in post-war Europe, while perhaps smaller than those which had been hoped for by the advocates of the welfare state, are none the less significant. On the basis of the available evidence, most governments have achieved a measurable and substantial impact on the position of less fortunate members of society. In the light of this conclusion, the changes in the climate of opinion which have taken place in the late 1970s in a number of European countries are viewed with disquiet. Threatened reductions in the level of social assistance and of unemployment compensation, or declines in the progressivity of direct taxation, could be expected to lead to perceptible changes in income distribution at a time when, if the generally pessimistic macroeconomic forecasts made for the 1980s materialize, the need for income transfers on welfare grounds would tend to increase.

Appendix: Supplementary Statistical Material

The two tables in this Appendix provide some further statistical information on demographic and labour market trends for the old-age population (which are discussed in Section I), and on the impact of transfers on income distribution (which is surveyed in Section III).

Bibliography

The evolution of public expenditure from the mid-1950s to the mid-1970s is discussed in OECD, *Public Expenditure Trends*, Paris 1978, which also provides some information on the evolution of taxation. A more detailed picture of the taxation side is given in the annual editions of OECD, *Revenue Statistics of OECD Member Countries*, Paris. Public expenditure on social welfare programmes is analysed for the period from the early 1960s to the mid-1970s in the following three publications by the OECD: *Public Expenditure on Education*, Paris 1976; *Public Expenditure on Income Maintenance Programmes*, Paris 1976; and *Public Expenditure on Health*, Paris 1977.

---

[43] The 'tax' rate here refers not only to extra tax and social security contributions, which become payable as income rises, but also to the concurrent loss of benefits.

[44] For a fuller discussion of various feedbacks, see OECD, *Public Expenditure on Income Maintenance*, Ch. 6.

TABLE 7.A1. *Statistics on the over-65 age group*
(percentages)

	Proportion of population over 65		Participation rate of the over-65 age group					
	1951	1978	year	male	female	year	male	female
France	11.4	13.8	1954	36.1	13.3	1975	10.6	5.0
Germany	10.2[a]	15.4	1950	26.8	9.7	1978	8.4	3.4
Italy	8.2	11.8	1951	43.7	7.1	1978	13.4	3.7
United Kingdom	10.7	14.6	1951	31.4	5.3	1971	19.3	6.3
Austria	10.4	15.1[b]	1951	31.3	13.4	1971	8.0	3.2
Belgium	11.0	14.0[b]	1947	24.7	5.4	1970	6.8	2.2
Denmark	9.0	14.2	1955	33.2	8.4	1978	20.9	5.6
Finland	7.1	10.8[b]	1950	56.7	20.6	1976	10.8	3.1
Ireland	10.7	10.9[c]	1951	58.4	17.0	1975	29.0	7.2
Netherlands	7.7	9.8[c]	1947	35.5	6.3	1977	6.3	1.4
Norway	9.6	14.1[c]	1950	42.1	8.6	1970	25.7	5.6
Sweden	10.3	15.3[b]	1960	27.3	4.7	1975	11.0	3.5
Switzerland	9.6	13.4	1950	50.7	11.9	1970	31.7	9.7
Average	9.7	13.3		38.3	10.1		15.5	4.6

[a] 1956
[b] 1976
[c] 1977

Sources: ILO, *Yearbook of Labour Statistics* (various issues); OECD, *Manpower Statistics, 1950-1960*; UN, *Demographic Yearbook, 1978*.

A description of the social security system is provided by P.R. Kaim-Candle, *Comparative Social Policy and Social Security*, London 1973 (for Austria, Denmark, Germany, Ireland, the Netherlands, and the United Kingdom) and T. Wilson (ed.), *Pensions, Inflation and Growth*, London 1974 (for old-age retirement pension schemes in Belgium, France, Germany, Italy, the Netherlands and Sweden).

In tabular form, information on these systems is given in EEC, *Comparative Tables of the Social Security System*, Brussels, and the US Department of Health, Education and Welfare, *Social Security Programmes throughout the World*, Washington (both of which are updated at intervals). A. Maynard, *Health Care in the European Community*, London 1975, discusses the evolution and situation in the early 1970s of the health care system in the EEC.

A general discussion on the economics of inequality of income, earnings, and wealth; of poverty, and policies to alleviate poverty is provided by A.B. Atkinson, *The Economics of Inequality*, Oxford 1975. A more detailed discussion of the distribution of income than given in this chapter is contained in M. Sawyer, 'Income Distribution in OECD Countries', *OECD Economic Outlook–Occasional Studies*, July 1976.

T. Stark, *The Distribution of Income in Eight Countries*, HMSO, London 1977, provides a comprehensive coverage of the information on the distribution of income and earnings in France, Germany, Ireland, Sweden, and the United Kingdom (the other three countries of the eight mentioned in the title are non-European). A number of publications by the Centre d'étude des revenus et des

TABLE 7.A2. *Impact of transfers on the distribution of income*
(percentages)

	Quintile shares				
	1	2	3	4	5
A. *Households ranked by*					
pre-transfer income					
Spain (1973–4)					
Share in pre-transfer income	1.0	10.3	16.8	24.4	47.4
Share in transfers	50.9	17.2	11.5	10.0	10.5
Share in post-transfer income	7.6	11.2	16.3	22.7	42.3
Sweden (1972)					
Share in pre-transfer income	0.1	7.2	18.3	27.0	47.2
Share in transfers	37.3	26.1	13.8	12.2	10.7
Share in post-transfer income	9.4	12.8	18.2	23.9	35.6
B. *Households ranked by*					
post-transfer income					
France (1970)[a]					
Share in pre-transfer income	2.8	8.5	15.2	23.4	50.2
Share in transfers	17.8	20.9	19.5	17.7	24.3
Share in post-transfer income	34.8	10.2	15.8	22.6	46.7
Germany (1969)					
Share in pre-transfer income	2.9	10.3	18.0	24.9	43.9
Share in transfers	23.7	23.5	16.7	17.0	19.1
Share in post-transfer income	6.4	12.6	17.7	23.6	39.6
United Kingdom (1973)					
Share in pre-transfer income	1.8	10.6	18.7	25.5	43.5
Share in transfers	42.4	24.9	12.6	10.9	9.3
Share in post-transfer income	5.3	12.0	18.1	24.1	40.4
Norway (1970)					
Share in pre-transfer income	2.1	9.8	18.3	26.0	43.8
Share in transfers	33.2	30.6	14.5	11.2	10.5
Share in post-transfer income	4.9	11.6	18.0	24.6	40.8

[a] Transfers consist only of pensions
Source: M. Sawyer, 'Income Distribution in OECD Countries', *OECD Economic Outlook –
Occasional Studies*, July 1976.

coûts (CERC) (especially *Dispersion et disparités de salaires à l'étranger*, Paris 1976) illustrate various aspects of the distribution of income and earnings in France, with some international comparisons. V. George and R. Lawson (eds.), *Poverty and Inequality in Common Market Countries*, London 1980, examines, on a country by country basis, the evidence on trends in inequality and poverty. W. Beckerman, *Poverty and the Impact of Income Maintenance Programmes in Four Developed Countries*, ILO, Geneva 1979, seeks to apply a common approach to the estimation of poverty, and three of the four countries included in the study (Great Britain, Belgium, and Norway) are European.

8

The Economic Impact of the EEC

MICHAEL DAVENPORT*

Introduction

This chapter deals with the economic impact of the EEC. But it should be recognized that the establishment of the EEC is a step in the search for an ideal in which economics has never been the dominant motive. The ideal of a United States of Europe can perhaps be traced back through Napoleon and Charlemagne to Julius Caesar. The modern concept, however, is to be found *inter alia* among the non-Communist resistance movements in occupied Europe in the early 1940s.[1] The Council of Europe was established by ten Western European countries in the summer of 1949, but this was an inadequate instrument to satisfy the ambitions of federalists such as Jean Monnet and his Action Committee for the United States of Europe. Monnet proposed the establishment of a European Coal and Steel Community (ECSC) in 1950, an idea taken up enthusiastically by Robert Schuman, French Foreign Minister at the time, Konrad Adenauer, the German Chancellor, and Alcide De Gasperi, the Italian Prime Minister. But Monnet stressed from the outset that the ECSC or any other economic institutions on the European scale were primarily instruments to further political integration. Political integration *per se* found expression in the proposals for a European Defence Force in 1950, but these proposals were effectively buried by the French assembly in 1954.

In 1955, the Benelux countries sought to maintain the momentum towards European integration with the Messina Conference. This directly led to the signing of the Treaty of Rome in 1957, which established the institutions of the European Economic Community. The Treaty also laid down the competences of the different institutions, the Council of Ministers, the Commission, the Assembly, the Court.

The major achievements of the Community were, in the early days, the establishment of a customs union or common market and the development of the Common Agricultural Policy (CAP). Customs duties between member states were eliminated over a ten-year transitional period. The first part of this chapter examines the economic gains to the original six members which were expected to derive from the customs union, and, to some extent, the gains of the United Kingdom, Denmark, and Ireland, who joined the customs union definitively, that is after a five-year transitional period, in 1978.

While the establishment of the common market paid some respect to liberal

---

*Wharton Econometric Forecasting Associates, Philadelphia.
[1] W. Lipgens, 'European Federalism in the Political Thought of Resistance Movements during World War II', *Central European History*, March 1968.

trading principles, the CAP was founded on a belief that protectionism was essential in the agricultural sector. The CAP has often been described as the French quid pro quo for the free market in manufactured goods which was foreseen as benefiting most of all the German economy. That is perhaps an over-simplification, and the Germans have never been notable for their reforming zeal as regards the CAP. The economic impact of the CAP is examined in the second part of this chapter.

The third major goal was from the beginning that of Economic and Monetary Union. The EMU, like its avian homonym, never took off. The history of plans — from Barre, through Werner and Marjolin to MacDougall — is witness to the failure to develop the necessary unified institutions such as a European central bank or effective European policy instruments. On the other hand, some progress was achieved in the later 1970s in the areas of the co-ordination of demand management policies, the development of centralized loan instruments, particularly for member states in balance of payments difficulties, and most notably in the establishment of a zone of relatively fixed exchange rates, the European Monetary System (EMS). The economic impact of these developments is discussed in the third section of the chapter. That section also incorporates some brief discussion of the major so-called structural policies of the Community, industrial, regional, commercial (i.e. tariff) policy, and so on. Important though these policies may have been to certain firms or even industries, they have been of little macroeconomic significance, with the possible exceptions of steel and textiles. This is not to disparage the importance of the micro-project approach, which characterizes the regional, social, and agricultural guidance funds, and only slightly less so the industrial and transport policies, or the case-method approach of competition policy. But this chapter sets out to get some feel for the macroeconomic impact of the first twenty-two years of the Community, and this, together with space constraints, justifies the short shrift given to these activities and those in the fields of energy, education, and so forth which are getting under way at the beginning of the 1980s.

I. The Community as a Customs Union

The theoretical literature on the economic gains associated with the formation of a customs union makes an important distinction between 'static' gains (or gains deriving from 'trade creation' net of losses due to 'trade diversion') and 'dynamic' gains linked to the favourable impact of larger markets and greater competition. It also distinguishes between the static effects of customs unions on consumption and on production and is, on the whole, rather agnostic as to whether customs unions will or will not increase overall economic welfare. The empirical literature is more limited in scope and almost entirely confined to estimates of trade creation and trade diversion. There seems to have been no quantitative work following the analytical division between production and consumption effects and very little on dynamic effects — admittedly, these are inherently difficult to quantify. This section presents a brief overview of the main results that have been reached in trying to determine whether the creation of the Common Market has had beneficial effects on member countries.

Trade creation and trade diversion

The literature on static trade creation and trade diversion effects is extensive, and a survey of some of the major studies is attempted in the Appendix to this chapter. A summary impression of the main results can be obtained from Table 8.1, which presents various estimates of trade creation and trade diversion due to the Common Market for the six original EEC member countries combined at the turn of the 1960s. Though the studies cited in the table usually obtained a

TABLE 8.1. *Estimates of trade creation and trade diversion in the EEC*[a]

	Date	Coverage	Trade creation ($ billion)	Trade diversion ($ billion)
Truman	1968	manufactures	9.2	1.0
Balassa	1970	manufactures	11.4	0.1
Balassa	1970	all goods	11.3	0.3
Verdoorn and Schwartz	1969	manufactures	11.1	1.1
Aitken	1967	all goods	9.2	0.6[b]
Kreinin	1969–70	manufactures	7.3	2.4
Resnick and Truman	1968	manufactures and raw materials	1.8	3.0

[a] Original six member countries only
[b] Diversion from EFTA countries only
Sources: see Appendix.

number of alternative results, the ones shown tend to be the authors' preferred estimates or those which appear to be based on the most defensible assumptions. The methodologies used to obtain the figures differ quite substantially, yet a cursory look at the table suggests that the divergence in estimates is relatively limited, with the majority clustered in a range going from $7½ to $11½ billion for trade creation and from $½ to $1 billion for trade diversion. Indeed, standardization to a common year would have brought the various estimates marginally closer. A major exception is provided by the Resnick and Truman study — apparently the only one in the whole literature on the subject which obtains an excess of trade diversion over trade creation — but the approach used by these two authors probably underestimates the positive effects of the elimination of tariffs on trade flows, for reasons which are discussed in the Appendix.

If the amount of trade creation is taken as, say, $10 billion in 1970 and trade diversion as $1 billion, the net gain would represent some 10 per cent of the combined imports of goods of the EEC at the time, or nearly 2 per cent of Community GDP — a non-negligible gain from the creation of a free trade area. What this could have meant in terms of static welfare gains, that is the greater satisfaction of consumer wants through access to lower cost and more diverse sources of supply, has received scant qualitative attention. On the basis of the so-called 'welfare triangles', Balassa tentatively suggests that an $11.4 billion increase in trade in manufactures is associated with a welfare gain of only $0.7 billion or 0.15 per cent of GNP.[2] These conjectures are however fraught with conceptual

[2] B. Balassa, 'Trade Creation and Trade Diversion in the European Common Market: An Appraisal of the Evidence', in B. Balassa (ed.), *European Economic Integration*, Amsterdam 1975.

as well as statistical problems. The net stimulation to trade following the form-ation of the Common Market was expected to have, and almost certainly had, a greater overall impact on real incomes through increased opportunities for economies of scale, increased competition, and the expansion of investment activity, the 'dynamic' effects, than it had through the static gains and losses of trade creation and diversion.

Dynamic effects

By 'dynamic effects' are usually meant all the direct and indirect influences of the formation of a customs union on the rate of economic growth in the member countries. Because of the many and complex channels through which such in-fluences may operate, the concept has remained vague and ill-defined, and to a large extent a cover-all phrase for all the effects excluded from the static gains and losses associated with trade creation and diversion. In general, though, three principal 'dynamic effects' have been identified and emphasized in the literature:

(i) The opportunities presented by the elimination of tariffs for the exploitation of a larger market and thus economies of scale;
(ii) The gains in productivity and cost reductions associated with the in-centives of greater competition – the often-cited 'cold shower of competition' argument;
(iii) The spur to investment presumably to a large extent associated with economies of scale or greater competition, and thus the acceleration of economic growth.

Certainly the dynamic effects played a considerable part in the early economic justifications offered for the formation of the Common Market. They also played a prominent role in the debate in the United Kingdom both before the enlargement and subsequently in the referendum campaign.[3] Nevertheless, the arguments are difficult to subject to rigorous theoretical analysis and certainly do not easily lend themselves to quantitative appraisal.

There are a number of weaknesses, for instance, behind the economies of scale effect. If the ability to exploit economies of scale is limited by the sizes of tariff-free markets, one would expect production costs to be higher and living standards lower in small countries. This was certainly not the general pattern in Europe before the EEC and EFTA were established.[4] Nevertheless, whether the welfare gains are 'dynamic' or 'static', the formation in Europe of two customs unions with free trade in manufactured goods between them and the opportu-nities for scale-economies must have furthered rationalization and concentration in, for example, the motor-car industry. To what extent the market would have been unified and the scale economies exploited without the elimination of customs duties is speculative. Certainly Japan and Spain were able to remain competitive in this market despite the tariff barriers. The economies of scale

[3] For Example, J. Williamson ('Trade and Economic Growth', in J. Pinder (ed.), *The Economics of Europe*, London 1971) estimated that, by 1978, the static welfare gains for the United Kingdom would amount to some £19 million, while benefits from economies of scale would add another £210 million, or 4 per cent of GDP.

[4] M.B. Krauss, 'Introduction', in M.B. Krauss (ed.), *The Economics of Integration*, London 1973, p. 14.

gains can only be assessed industry by industry in the context of the interplay of trade creation and diversion, changing industrial structures due to new technologies, relative factor costs, and so on. But they cannot be dismissed out of hand.

The 'cold shower of competition' argument is equally difficult to pin down. It presupposes that producers do not follow the cost-minimizing rules postulated in neo-classical theory, but that their effort to minimize costs, or reduce 'X-inefficiency', will be greater the more they are exposed to competition, in this case from foreign suppliers following the abolition of tariffs. The argument is plausible − as are the various 'satisficing' theories of firm behaviour to which it is obviously related − but it is clearly not easily subject to verification.

The third major dynamic effect is that of the spur given to investment by the formation of a customs union. This is closely related to the foregoing arguments, since the exploitation of economies of scale of the galvanizing impact of foreign competition are often realized through investment in new plant and equipment. New investment merely designed to take advantage of the increased market size is presumably offset by reduced investment in sectors where foreign producers can now dominate the home market. Here, again, verification is bound to be difficult, but an attempt to estimate the increased growth due to higher investment following the formation of the EEC and EFTA was made by Krause.[5] He took the increase in the average ratio of business investment to GDP between the periods 1955–7 and 1960–4, and using Denison's methodology imputed to the increased investment an average annual increment to the GDP growth rate. The methodology, however, is suspect − the incremental capital–output ratio was for several countries higher in the latter period for cyclical reasons, while the translation from investment ratios, through capital–output ratios, into GDP growth rates raises numerous methodological problems. For what the results are worth, they show that the growth effect of the formation of the EEC ranged from 0.18 per cent per annum in Germany to 0.22 per cent in Italy.

Much more impressionistic evidence as to whether the 'investment effect' was at all important is presented in Table 8.2, which shows GDP and machinery and equipment investment growth rates in the original EEC countries over selected periods. The years 1954–8 predate the establishment of the customs union, while the periods 1958–63 and 1963–8 are years of transition, since the last tariffs on intra-Community trade in industrial products were not eliminated until 1968. Obviously, the comparisons of growth rates over these three quinquennia are fraught with problems. They are not, for example, adjusted to eliminate business cycle effects (which are particularly important in the case of Italy). Also, the growth rates in the earlier period may to some extent have been pushed up by investment in anticipation of the formation of the Community. Still, it is probably reasonable to conclude that the increase in the growth rates of investment and GDP in the period 1958–63 in Italy and Belgium were to some extent due to the stimulatory impact of tariff reductions. No clear impact is, however, apparent in France, Germany, and the Netherlands.

The Italian example is particularly interesting since Italy joined the EEC at a lower stage of development than the other five countries − its per caput income

[5] L.B. Krause, *European Integration and the United States*, Brookings Institution, Washington 1968.

TABLE 8.2. *Growth of GDP and investment in machinery and equipment*
(average annual percentage changes)

	GDP			Investment		
	1953–58	1958–63	1963–68	1953–58	1958–63	1963–68
France	4.7	5.6	5.1	10.0	(8.2)	7.5
Germany	7.2	5.7	4.2	10.0	(6.1)	2.8
Italy	5.0	6.6	5.1	5.3	14.0	−0.8
Belgium	2.7	4.6	4.3	. .	8.7	4.8
Netherlands	4.0	4.9	5.6	9.1	9.3	7.5

Source: OECD, *National Accounts of OECD Countries* (various issues).

in 1958 was only 60 per cent of the Community average at the time and agriculture still represented some 18 per cent of output and 35 per cent of total employment, against figures elsewhere in the range 7 to 11 and 8 to 24 per cent respectively. Yet, according to Johnson, a country will only wish to enter a customs union, or an existing union will only want to accept a new member, if the new and the old members are at a similar stage of development. The new member must believe its industrial production will gain from being within the union, and the existing members must believe their own industrial competitiveness able to withstand competition from the new member.[6] This raises the possibility that not all countries need necessarily benefit from dynamic effects and that, for instance, the industrially more competitive partners may, in the longer run, gain at the expense of weaker members, particularly if exchange rate changes are either not possible or ineffective. The apparent success which Italy had in the early days of the EEC in weathering the competition of its more advanced neighbours suggests, however, that the country benefited from dynamic effects on scale economies, competition, and investment. Over the period, the capital goods industries, in particular chemicals and iron and steel, and the durable consumer goods industries developed very rapidly, and in Italian exports there was a marked decline in the share of agricultural products.

Among the newer member countries, Ireland was also relatively less developed when it joined the Community in 1973, but it was in a particularly advantageous position to gain from the CAP. In 1974, the guarantees section of the CAP subsidized Irish agriculture to twice the extent of the pre-accession 1972/3 Irish budget. Apart from large transfers aiding both the balance of payments and public revenues, farm incomes benefited greatly, and this no doubt to some extent encouraged investment in agriculture and related industries.

But the possibility that the dynamic effects of a customs union may not be positive has been raised in connection with United Kingdom membership. In 1970, the government described the advantages of membership as:

The creation of an enlarged and integrated European market would provide in effect a much larger and a much faster growing "home market" for British industry. It would provide the stimuli of much greater opportunities – and

[6] H.G. Johnson, 'An Economic Theory of Protectionism, Tariff Bargaining, and the Formation of Customs Unions', *Journal of Political Economy*, June 1965.

competition – than exist at present or would otherwise exist in future. There would be substantial advantages for British industry from membership of this new enlarged Common Market, stemming primarily from the opportunities for greater economies of scale, increased specialisation, a sharper competitive climate and faster growth. These may be described as the "dynamic" effects of membership on British industry and trade.[7]

And in the concluding section:

This would open up to our industrial producers substantial opportunities for increasing export sales, while at the same time exposing them more fully to the competition of European industries . . . The acceleration in the rate of growth of industrial exports could then outpace any increase in the rate of growth of imports, with corresponding benefits to the balance of payments. Moreover, with such a response, the growth of industrial productivity would be accelerated as a result of increased competition and the advantages derived from specialisation and larger scale production.[8]

These quotations have prompted a study which set out to measure *ex post* some of the benefits and costs of United Kingdom membership.[9] The main argument advanced was that the welfare benefits of trade creation would not be realized if the trade accounts of a member country in a weak competitive position deteriorated and forced the authorities to contractionary policies reducing real national income. Using alternative values for demand and relative cost elasticities of imports and exports to adjust the deviations over the years 1973 to 1977 from the extrapolated 1958-72 trend, the authors of the study estimated the amount by which British manufactured trade had been affected by membership. Depending on the elasticities used, the average export effect varied from + £0.4 billion to − £0.6 billion and the average import effect from + £0.1 billion to − £2.4 billion (all at 1970 prices) – a very wide range. The authors' preferred estimate – of a net import effect of £1.1 billion ($1.9 billion) – led them to conclude, following simulations made on the Cambridge Economic Policy Group econometric model, that, in view of a balance of payments constraint, the authorities had to constrain the level of real national income by an average 6 per cent per annum below what it would otherwise have been, and nearly double this figure in 1977. If the transfer costs of the Community budget, which they estimated to be of the order of £1 billion ($1¾ billion) in 1977, were added, the total cumulated cost to real national income by 1977-8 was of the order of 15 per cent.

Though the exact calculations may be disputed, the conclusion that the United Kingdom suffered a 'dynamic loss' is a serious charge. It implies that Britain was unable to withstand the 'cold shower' of European competition, and it presumably means that the promised dynamic gains of economies of scale, greater efficiency, and induced investment were not realized on a substantial scale. The conclusion hinges, however, on the idea that over the period examined

---

[7] *White Paper on Britain and the European Communities* (Cmnd. 4289), HMSO, London 1970, p. 26.

[8] Ibid., p. 37.

[9] M. Fetherston, B. Moore, and J. Rhodes, 'EEC Membership and UK Trade in Manufactures', *Cambridge Journal of Economics*, December 1979.

it was the balance of payments deficit which called for demand-restraining policies, and inflation played no role.

The argument that the balance of payments impact was negative has, in any case, not gone unchallenged. A subsequent study argued that British exports of manufactures benefited significantly from EEC membership, so that despite the increase in imports, there was a net gain to the balance of payments.[10] By comparing actual United Kingdom exports of manufactures to the EEC to what these exports would have been had the United Kingdom's share in EEC imports moved with the United Kingdom's share in the rest of the world, the author estimated that, by 1977, the total cumulative export 'gain' was of the order of £1 billion. The tariff cuts associated with joining the EEC were estimated to have increased British imports by some £0.7 billion, leaving a small net improvement of about £0.3 billion ($½ billion) in 1977, compared with the Cambridge estimated loss for that year of over £3 billion or $5 billion (both at current prices).[11]

The methodologies used in the two studies are, of course, different, but even if one were to adopt the more optimistic analysis of the balance of payments effects, it would be difficult to argue that the small gains in the trade account could offset the substantial and increasing budgetary costs of membership. Nor do there seem to have been any studies which have claimed that the United Kingdom reaped significant dynamic gains. This is not, of course, to say that Britain's relative industrial decline might not have been faster without the net gains in exports of manufactures which are consistent with the calculations in both papers.

Foreign direct investment

Creation of the Common Market might also have stimulated an inflow of non-EEC direct investment into the area. The so-called 'tariff discrimination hypothesis' states that the erection of a common external tariff higher than the average earlier rates of duty will reduce the levels of trade in goods with the rest of the world but increase the inflow of foreign investment aimed at avoiding the higher tariff barriers. Mundell demonstrated the thesis theoretically by relaxing the usual assumption of trade models that factors of production are internationally immobile.[12] The conditions for the hypothesis to work seem to have been satisfied, as shown by Table 8.3, which provides information on the 1962 EEC external tariffs and on the previous national tariff of the dominant supplier of each product.

The empirical studies testing the hypothesis as it pertains to United States investment in the EEC have produced conflicting evidence. The major difficulty lies in developing a robust econometric model to explain direct foreign investment, since merely looking at gross or trend-adjusted flows before and after

[10] A.D. Morgan, 'The Balance of Payments and British Membership of the European Community', in W. Wallace (ed.), *Britain in Europe*, RIIA, London, 1980.

[11] For the sake of completeness, a third set of unpublished estimates prepared by the British Treasury should also be mentioned. According to *The Economist* (5 January 1980), the study's conclusion is that 'the best central estimate may be to regard the net balance unchanged'.

[12] R.A. Mundell, 'International Trade and Factor Mobility', *American Economic Review*, June 1957.

union leaves too many alternative explanations available. A review of the literature over a decade, from the late 1960s to the late 1970s, shows that some
authors found no evidence of increased United States investment due to the
formation of the Common Market,[13] whereas others claim to have found such
evidence.[14]

TABLE 8.3. *Comparison between 1962 EEC[a] external tariff and previous
national tariff of dominant supplier country*
(number of commodities)

	Higher	Equal	Lower
Chemicals	10	–	2
Textiles	3	1	3
Other manufactures			
Classified by material	14	3	2
Machinery and transport	11	–	–
Other	8	1	3
Total	46	5	10

[a] Original six member countries only
Source: L. B. Krause, 'European Economic Integration and the United States', *American
Economic Review*, May 1963.

Such direct foreign investment from outside the EEC as was stimulated by
the external tariff has probably been distributed unevenly among the member
states. Belgium seems to have been particularly attractive to foreign investors in
the 1960s, with the United States the predominant source. Between 1959 and
1969 the United States accounted for 64 per cent of foreign direct investment
projects in Belgium, and the latter, in turn, represented half of all net manufacturing investment in the Community.[15] Belgium seems to have gained from
its skilled labour force, favourable geographic situation, good infrastructure,
attractive tax and credit incentives, and the *laissez-faire* attitude of the public
authorities. Less foreign investment went to Belgium in the later 1970s, but
multinational enterprises still accounted for 20 to 25 per cent of industrial
employment. In the 1970s it was Ireland which attracted a good deal of foreign
investment. A wide range of fiscal and credit inducements clearly played a role,
but 'jumping' the external tariff may also have been an important factor.

In summary, there would seem to be some evidence of substantial dynamic

[13] A. Scaperlanda, 'The E.E.C. and U.S. Foreign Investment: Some Empirical Evidence',
Economic Journal, March 1967; R. d'Arge, 'Note on Customs Unions and Direct Foreign
Investment', *Economic Journal*, June 1969; and A. Scaperlanda and L.J. Mauer, 'The Determinants of U.S. Direct Investment in the E.E.C.', *American Economic Review*, September
1969.

[14] K.F. Wallis, 'The E.E.C. and United States Foreign Investment: Some Empirical Evidence Re-examined', *Economic Journal*, September 1968; A. Schmitz, 'The Impact of
Trade Blocs on Foreign Direct Investment', *Economic Journal*, September 1970; and A.
Schmitz and J. Bieri, 'EEC Tariffs and U.S. Direct Investment', *European Economic Review*, No. 3, 1972.

[15] See Ch. 20 below.

gains from the customs union, but these have probably been short-lived adjustments to the extension of free trade to a larger market. They may also have been concentrated in countries which for a number of reasons, including an important policy emphasis, were attractive to direct foreign investments, such as Belgium and Ireland, or offered major opportunities for a technological catch-up, such as Italy. The static gains are easier to identify, but in absolute terms seem to have been fairly insignificant relative, say, to year-to-year fluctuations in growth rates.

II. The Community as an Agricultural Regime

Before attempting to assess the economic impact of the Common Agricultural Policy, it is useful to recall its objectives and briefly review the basic mechanisms that it has used to pursue them. Article 39 of the Treaty of Rome set out the five objectives of the CAP as:

> (i) To increase agricultural productivity (the productivity of labour being especially mentioned);
> (ii) To ensure a fair standard of living for the agricultural community;
> (iii) To stabilize markets;
> (iv) To assure the availability of supplies;
> (v) To ensure that supplies reach consumers at reasonable prices.

Furthermore, these objectives were meant to be pursued within the more general aim of the Community to develop an integrated market. This section will not make a balance sheet for each of these objectives, which in very general terms would show that there have been dramatic rises in agricultural labour productivity, that farmers are on average no longer relatively poor, that products reach the market, and that although prices are high relative to world prices, food takes up a small and shrinking share of income. It will instead briefly outline the mechanisms of the CAP and then consider the impact of agricultural policies within member states, between member states, and on the rest of the world.

The structure of the Common Agricultural Policy

At the start it is worth recalling that setting up the CAP was the result of hard bargaining between the original member states. While they agreed that some agricultural policy was necessary, they each had different domestic policies.[16] It was thus a much more delicate political affair than merely reducing tariffs to create the common market for industrial goods. The basic agreement was to follow three principles: (a) free internal trade; (b) preference for member countries, and (c) common financial responsibilities. Given that preference for the agricultural sector was accepted, the policy was not illiberal — in fact rather the opposite, as it frequently replaced quantitative controls by market-dependent mechanisms. The main policy instrument was to be the setting of common prices, not necessarily because that was considered to be the most efficient way, but because it was the method which minimized the direct budgetary cost of

---

[16] For a detailed account of the development of the CAP between 1958 and 1970, see J. Marsh and C. Ritson, *Agricultural Policy and the Common Market*, RIIA, London 1971.

the system. This was of importance both because unseen transfers were (and still are) politically more acceptable than seen ones (the more so when the transfers are between states rather than between sectors within a given nation), and because of the limited size of the EEC budget. Price has therefore always been the crucial variable, and even at the start of the system the compromise on the common price level was at the top of the existing range of national prices. It will be seen that, as the CAP developed, this tendency persisted.

The CAP has two basic parts: a market policy which guarantees prices, and a structural policy which is meant to make funds available for improving agricultural efficiency. Despite the continuing lip-service being paid to enlarging the share of structural policy from the 'Mansholt Plan' of 1968[17] onwards, this aspect has been mostly covered by the member states acting individually. In 1979, out of a total budgetary expenditure of over $14 billion on agriculture, only $450 million was spent on structural policy. The main mechanism of the market policy is a price-support system, or in the jargon of the Community, the guarantee section of the European Agricultural Guidance and Guarantee Fund (EAGGF). The support arrangements are not the same for all agricultural commodities,[18] but they include at least some of the following basic features:

(i) Prescribed prices for products. The exact system differs from product to product, but, as an illustration, the system for cereals links three prices: a *target* price in the wholesale market set to enable farmers to plan production and give an economic indication to all market users; a *threshold* price for imports, calculated such that threshold price plus transport costs equals the target price; and an *intervention* price at which national intervention agencies are obliged to purchase produce meeting quality requirements;

(ii) Variable import levies to bridge the gap between the lowest price at the EEC community frontier and the threshold price;

(iii) Export subsidies granted to enable Community-produced excess supplies to be sold on lower-priced world markets while maintaining the internal price;

(iv) Subsidies for domestic markets.

The direct financing for these general support arrangements is borne in common by all the member states through the EEC budget. This cost has grown very considerably in the 1970s, from around $1.8 billion in 1968 to $3.5 billion in 1974, and was over $14 billion in 1979, or about 3½ per cent of total expenditure on food. Table 8.4 shows this budgetary expenditure in 1979 for the largest part of the system, the guarantee section of the EAGGF. The table does not include expenditure by the guidance section, which only accounted for some $410 million in 1979, but does include spending on monetary compensation amounts (MCAs), which accounted for about $1 billion.

The reason for these payments stems from the existence of so-called 'green'

---

[17] 'Memorandum on the Reform of Agriculture in the EEC', submitted to the EEC Council of Ministers, 1968.

[18] For details of workings of each market organization, see EEC, *The Common Agricultural Policy*, Brussels 1978.

TABLE 8.4. *CAP expenditure by sector*,[a] *1979*

	$ million	Per cent of total
Cereal and rice	2,213	15.7
Milk products	6,055	42.9
Sugar	1,376	9.7
Fruit and vegetables	571	4.0
Beef, veal, pigmeat, poultry, and eggs	1,150	8.1
Oils and fats	812	5.7
Wine and tobacco	420	3.0
Other	478	3.4
Monetary compensation amounts	1,055	7.5
Total	14,131	100.0
of which: Refunds	6,438	45.6
Intervention	6,639	47.0

[a] Expenditure by Guarantee section of the European Agricultural Guidance and Guarantee Fund (EAGGF)
Source: EEC, *The Agricultural Situation in the Community*, Brussels 1980.

currencies, which introduce a further complication into the system.[19] Although there is a common market in that the whole of the EEC can be regarded by any producer or trader of agricultural products as an extension of his own domestic market, there is no common market for consumers. Casual empiricism shows that food prices differ between member states, and it is not only food prices that vary but also guaranteed prices of basic agricultural products. Common prices are set at the annual price-fixing in units of account, but these are converted into national currency using representative (or 'green') exchange rates. As these rates have been set by decision of the Council of Ministers the relationship between them has not necessarily been the same as the relationship between market exchange rates. In fact, as 'green' rates have only been changed infrequently and have been set primarily to determine national price levels, there have been persistent differences between the two sets of exchange relationships. Germany's 'green' currency has been undervalued between 1969 and 1979, and the United Kingdom's has been overvalued most of the time between accession and 1979. This resulted in the so-called common price for guaranteed products being higher in Germany than in Britain when valued using market exchange rates. Without a system of border taxes and subsidies, all United Kingdom produce would have been sold to German intervention stores to collect the guaranteed price in DM which could have been exchanged on the market for more pounds than could have been obtained by selling the produce in Britain. Furthermore, no German produce would ever have been exported to the United Kingdom, as the DM equivalent of the price there would have been less than the intervention price in Germany. These taxes and subsidies, the MCA system, do not balance out and have normally resulted in a substantial cost which is borne by the Community budget.

[19] For a full account of this system, see T. Josling and S. Harris, 'Europe's Green Money', *The Three Banks Review*, March 1976.

Transfers within member countries

Within each country the total size of the transfer from the non-agricultural to the agricultural sector depends (a) upon the size of the agricultural sector, and (b) upon how high prices are set above the level which they would otherwise have reached. While the first of these variables can be measured relatively easily, there is no clear measure of the second, which, it should be remembered, over time will have an effect on the first. For want of anything better, the measure often used is the world price level. Some idea of how EEC price levels have stood in relation to world market prices for certain key products is provided in Table 8.5. The figures show a high degree of variability, but on average Community prices have been well above world prices over the period surveyed. In the late 1970s, for a large number of products, they were nearly twice as high, and for some commodities (e.g. butter and skimmed milk powder) a staggering four or five times higher.

TABLE 8.5. *CAP – ratio of selected EEC prices to world market prices*[a]

	1968/69	1970/71	1972/73	1974/75	1976/77	1978/79
Soft wheat	195	189	153	107	204	193
Rice	138	210	115	81	166	157
Barley	197	146	137	107	147	225
Maize	178	141	143	106	163	201
White sugar	355	203	127	41	176	276
Beef	169	140	112	162	192	199
Pigmeat	134	134	147	109	125	155
Butter	504	481	249	316	401	403
Skimmed milk powder	365	218	145	139	571	458
Total[b]	(229)	(195)	(149)	(139)	(208)	(229)

[a] The world market prices used are not necessarily those at which the EEC could import more than marginal quantities of the products in question
[b] Roughly obtained by applying the average of production, total domestic use, and final private consumption weights to the price differentials
Source: EEC, *Yearbook of Agricultural Statistics* (various issues).

However, as mentioned above, world prices are not a wholly satisfactory benchmark, partly because they have been in themselves highly influenced by EEC prices. For a number of products the EEC is a major world supplier and consumer, and hence its own prices have had a marked effect on world prices. This raises, of course, major problems for calculating the transfer to the agricultural sector as a function of the difference between the two price levels. The world price could not be expected to remain unchanged if the EEC were to abandon its price support policy. Though admitting to the existence of this problem, a 1980 study has made some estimates of the total transfers between consumers and producers in each member state on the simplifying assumption that, in the absence of the CAP, world prices would not have been very different from what they were.[20] The estimates are subject to two further methodological difficulties which relate to the values of the demand and supply elasticities

[20] C.N. Morris, 'The Common Agricultural Policy', *Fiscal Studies*, March 1980.

(which in some cases are either not known or seem to be highly variable) and to the problem of aggregation over products which are substitutes. Given some fairly arbitrary assumptions to overcome these difficulties, the author arrived at the estimates shown in Table 8.6.

TABLE 8.6. *CAP — estimates of consumer losses and producer gains,*[a] *1978*
($ million)

	Consumer loss	Producer gain
France	6,081	6,993
Germany	8,828	7,747
Italy	6,553	4,333
United Kingdom	3,431	2,204
BLEU	1,392	1,306
Denmark	559	1,369
Ireland	336	783
Netherlands	1,713	2,694

[a] Due to within-country transfers resulting from the CAP
Source: C.N. Morris, 'The Common Agricultural Policy', *Fiscal Studies*, March 1980.

Even allowing for measurement problems, the magnitudes shown are substantial and raise distributional issues as well as the question of whether the transfers are having the desired effect — in particular whether the expressed aim of the CAP of ensuring a fair standard of living to the agricultural community has been achieved or whether relatively rich farmers became richer and whether this was at the expense of the relatively poor. The second question can be answered fairly easily. As the basic mechanism of the CAP support system is to hold food prices above the level at which they would otherwise have been, the cost is borne by consumers. Since Engel's law, which states that the proportion of income spent on food decreases as income rises, is well substantiated, the cost of the CAP must in the first instance fall more heavily on the relatively poor, though of course governments can correct this effect. An estimate for the United Kingdom shows, for instance, that in 1965 a two-adult family with no children in the lowest income bracket would have borne costs equivalent to 5.75 per cent of after-tax income (the estimate for pensioners was even higher), whereas the cost borne by the same type of household in the highest income group would have been of only 0.14 per cent.[21]

The other question, of whether the already rich farmers were made richer by the CAP, cannot be considered from the distributional point of view alone. Though there is evidence suggesting that richer farming regions obtained a disproportionate amount of the CAP's budget, it may be that the rich are more efficient, and a perfectly legitimate aim of the system is to encourage the efficient.[22] The evidence on the distributional question is scarce, not least because farmers on the whole have traditionally been rather inefficient at filling in

[21] T.E. Josling and D. Hamway, 'Income Transfer Effects of the Common Agricultural Policy', in B. Davey, T.E. Josling, and A. McFarquhar (eds.), *Agriculture and the State*, Trade Policy Research Centre, London 1976.
[22] Whether it has done so is, virtually impossible to document.

income tax forms. Overall, farm income, measured in terms of gross value added at factor cost, increased in real terms at an average annual rate of 3.3 per cent between 1970 and 1978, compared with the rate of 3.0 per cent for the rest of the economy.

Transfers between member countries

The CAP, however, cannot be considered only in the light of its effects within countries. Both because of the very large trade flows between them, and because the whole system is financed through the Community budget, in which the contribution key is very different from the expenditure key, the consumers in one member state may make transfers to the producers in others, and large flows of funds are generated between countries, not least because of the MCAs. Taking into account the different national price levels and the MCA system, the magnitude of the inter-country transfers then depends for each product upon:

(i) The amount of trade between member states that is subject to preferential pricing arrangements. There is a transfer to exporters to enable them to export products to other EEC markets at the same conditions as they could obtain on their own markets, and the importing countries bear the cost;

(ii) The flows through the EEC budget because of the common financing of the system.

In what follows the first amounts are called trade effects and the second budgetary effects.

As the pattern of agricultural expenditure is related to the output of the subsidized producers in each country and is therefore independent of the pattern of member state contributions,[23] some countries who make large contributions to the budget receive relatively little, and vice versa. The overall budget problem is relatively well documented, and there have been a large number of estimates of its magnitude, especially in conjunction with various British demands to pay a 'fair share'.[24] Estimating the net budgetary flows attributable to the CAP from these overall figures needs some assumptions, but the scope for error is relatively small, as agricultural expenditure has been the dominant item (nearly three-quarters) of total expenditure. The major problem is how to treat the MCAs, i.e. whether to attribute MCA payments on imports as expenditure in the exporting or importing country. The Commission's studies have presented both sets of figures. However, although the data on net budgetary transfers give the correct direction of the flows, the magnitudes involved are in themselves misleading until the trade effects are also considered. A number of estimates of these effects

---

[23] At the margin, the contribution key is determined by relative amounts in the total VAT potential; this gave the following percentages in the late 1970s: France 24.7, Germany 32.8, Italy 10.9, United Kingdom 17.4, Belgium 4.5, Denmark 2.6, Ireland 0.8, Luxembourg 0.2, Netherlands 6.1. For a complete description of the budgetary financing system, see D. Strasser, *Les finances de l'Europe*, Paris 1975.

[24] In conjunction with the 1975 'renegotiation', see M. Emerson and T.R. Scott, 'The Financial Mechanism in the Budget of the European Community', *Common Market Law Review*, May 1977, and for the late 1970s position, EEC, 'Net Cash Transfers in 1978 between Member States Resulting from the Community Budget', Press Release, 6 April 1979.

have been made.[25] The studies are not strictly comparable because of different periods covered, different concepts of costs and benefits, and different valuation methods.

The two studies which will be used to illustrate the magnitudes involved are by the Cambridge Economic Policy Group and by Rollo and Warwick.[26] The latter authors abstract from the problem of using a direct measure of world prices and use instead current rates of levies and 'restitutions' (i.e. export subsidies), as a measure of the difference between EEC and world price levels. This method avoids the problem of the price effects of CAP itself on world price and supply levels and hence facilitates the calculation of the trade costs and benefits consistent with the amounts shown in EEC budgets. It implies that the member states would have had the same price level in the absence of the CAP as they had with it, and that support would have been given in the same way. The study therefore measures the balance of payments effect of the common system rather than the effects of the price level itself. It is however quite doubtful whether some of the countries which receive large net benefits from the common system, especially Denmark and Ireland, would have been prepared to maintain prices at EEC levels if all the financing had had to come from within.

The Cambridge study, on the other hand, uses an estimate of world prices to assess the net trade receipts and payments on internal trade on the assumption that trade would have taken place at these world prices in the absence of the CAP. For some products, like beef and grains, for which there is a substantial volume of trade, it considers that importers would have had no difficulty in obtaining any desired supplies at current market prices; for other products, like sugar, butter, and cheese, it assumes that importers would have had to obtain supplies at a price considerably higher than the world one. It also makes an estimate of the prices that exporters might have got on the world market. For all products this was lower than what could have been obtained by selling within the EEC, and substantially lower for some products.

The results of the two studies are presented in Table 8.7. Though the figures are not strictly comparable because of differences in coverage, reference periods, and approach, the divergence in the estimates is not very pronounced. In absolute terms, the United Kingdom, Italy, and Germany (in that order) were the largest contributors to the CAP, while the Netherlands, Denmark, France, and Ireland reaped the greatest benefits. On a per caput basis the net gains of the latter three smaller countries were, of course, much more pronounced.

The CAP and world agricultural trade

The EEC is a very substantial trader in agricultural products. It is the world's

[25] Josling and Hamway, 'Income Transfer Effects'; E.A. Altwood, 'The Consequences of Participation in the Common Agricultural Policy to the Irish Economy', in M. Whitby (ed.), *The Net Cost and Benefit of EEC Membership*, Centre of European Agricultural Studies, Wye 1979; and P. Blancus, 'The Common Agricultural Policy and the Balance of Payments of the EEC Member Countries', *Banca Nazionale del Lavoro Quarterly Review*, December 1978.

[26] *Cambridge Economic Policy Review*, April 1979, and J.M.C. Rollo and K.S. Warwick, 'The CAP and Resource Flows among EEC Member States', *Government Economic Service Working Paper*, No. 27, 1979.

TABLE 8.7. *CAP – estimates of net gains/losses to member countries*[a]
($ million)

	Rollo and Warwick 'central' estimate 1978	Cambridge Economic Policy Group estimate 'composite' year[b]
France	1,100	1,350
Germany	−950	−950
Italy	−1,600	−1,150
United Kingdom	−1,500	−1,700
BLEU	−50	100
Denmark	1,200	1,000
Ireland	950	750
Netherlands	1,400	1,100

[a] Due to inter-country transfers resulting from the CAP
[b] Obtained by adding estimated 'trade costs' and 70 per cent of 'net budget costs' as given in the original source
Sources: J.M.C. Rollo and K.S. Warwick, 'The CAP and Resource Flows among EEC Member States', *Government Economic Service Working Paper*, No. 27, 1979; *Cambridge Economic Policy Review*, April 1979.

largest single importer on either a net or gross basis and is also well up in the ranking of exporters. In 1979, for example, its gross food exports amounted to some $22 billion compared with a figure of $35 billion for the United States. The CAP has, however, been generally inward-looking and it can justly be accused of being protectionist and of adding to instability on the world markets.[27]

The protectionist nature of the CAP has come under international examination on several occasions. In 1958, a GATT committee critically looked at the agricultural articles of the Treaty of Rome. In 1960–2, before the mechanisms of the system had been fully worked out, the 'Dillon Round' also attempted to weaken the CAP, and indeed some EEC agricultural duties (e.g. on cotton, soya beans, and protein meals) were eliminated. But the EEC achieved what it really wanted, i.e. an international acceptance of the whole concept of a common agricultural support system. This was a major concession, mainly on the part of the United States, which had most to lose. But America at the time wished to encourage European integration; moreover its bargaining position was weakened by its own illiberal attitudes to agricultural trade, which included claiming unlimited rights to restrict trade by quotas and duties.[28] Though the CAP came under much greater attacks during the 'Kennedy' and 'Tokyo' rounds of trade negotiations, its protectionist nature escaped largely unchanged.

As well as being protectionist and thereby limiting world agricultural trade, the mechanisms of the CAP have added to the instability of world markets[29]

[27] T.K. Warley, 'Western Trade in Agricultural Products', in A. Shonfield (ed.), *International Economic Relations of the Western World, 1959–1971*, RIIA, London 1976.

[28] V. Sorenson, 'Contradictions in US Trade Policy', in E.F. Ferguson (ed.), *United States Trade Policy and Agricultural Exports*, Iowa State University Centre for Agriculture and Rural Development 1973.

[29] T.E. Josling, 'Agricultural Protectionism and Stabilization Policies. An Analysis of Current Neo-Mercantilist Practice', paper presented to the Symposium on International Trade and Agriculture, Tucson, Arizona 1979.

since the EEC has purchased agricultural products abroad only when domestic supplies were short and has sold on world markets at a subsidized price. It is this latter policy instrument which has caused the major problems – on an increasing scale, as the level of EEC surpluses rose in line with prices. It could be argued that the effects of a variable import levy are the same as those of a variable export subsidy in that it does not matter to other suppliers how demand for their products is decreased. In practice, however, the export subsidy has tended to be more disruptive than the import levy for a number of reasons. Traditional suppliers to a given market were badly affected by the sudden influx of some subsidized produce, and even if they were not put out of business they found it hard to re-establish themselves in the market. There has also been (and still is) a much greater political acceptance, both internally and externally, that high cost countries protect their producers by restricting imports, than that they should continue this support to such a degree that their producers eventually become exporters. In this case the formerly largely hidden subsidy becomes clearly evident and is resented, both by the foreign producers and the domestic taxpayers who see that they are subsidizing foreign consumers.

While the overall judgement on the customs union which was ventured above was clearly favourable, a similar overall judgement on the CAP must be negative. The system has almost certainly kept European food prices somewhat above the levels they would otherwise have reached; it has required significant financial transfers between member countries which from an international equity point of view would seem largely inappropriate; it has, similarly, led to substantial internal redistribution from consumers to producers which may well have conflicted with the distributional aims which governments were pursuing; finally, it has generated vast surpluses of some commodities whose subsidized exports have at times destabilized world markets and (much more than the CAP's protectionism, shared after all by most major agricultural areas) created a good deal of international ill feeling. It is true that against this must be set the fact that the EEC is, broadly, agriculturally self-sufficient – no mean achievement in a world in which food, just like energy, can be used as a weapon. But self-sufficiency could probably have been reached in a less expensive and economically more rational way.

III. The Community as a Policy-Maker

A glance at the *General Report on the Activities of the European Communities for 1979* indicates that in that year the EEC undertook a project with the aim of drawing up a consolidated balance sheet of ground water resources with a view to better use thereof, completed an initial screening of 30,000 human blood samples for lead content, and decided that certain stockbrokers were 'natural persons' to whom, therefore, freedom of establishment did not appear to be of practical interest. The Community, at the initiative of the Commission, has endeavoured to implement policies in an enormous range of fields. To an important extent these policies are seen to be necessary to protect competition in the customs union. Anything from bathing-water to tractors' rear-view mirrors may be harmonized to prevent member states obtaining an advantage for their own suppliers by making 'safety' or other rules designed to prevent imports of certain goods. But over and above the monitoring of the customs union, and the agricultural, external, and economic policies which are discussed separately, the EEC also has or is attempting to define an employment and social policy, an industrial policy, an energy policy, a regional policy, an environmental and consumer protection policy, a fisheries policy, a transport policy, all of which have been developed with much time-consuming negotiation. Many of these areas can be subsumed under the vague heading of structural policy. This section begins with a discussion of structural policy, inevitably selective, goes on to survey EEC policy *vis-à-vis* the outside world, and ends by looking at the EEC as a centre for macroeconomic policy, and, in particular, as a monetary union. If, at the end, any broad theme has emerged, it is one of small, hesitant steps towards integration and eventually unity of policy.

'Structural policy'

The words 'structural policy' are used as a portmanteau for a large range of different activities at the EEC level. Some of these are of potential macroeconomic importance, in particular industrial policy, energy policy, and regional policy. Only the first of these has already had a significant impact particularly as regards the steel sector, and will be discussed in this section. Energy policy up to the late 1970s was still very much at the debating stage, and the Commission's efforts to push the member states along this road had not got very far. Regional policy at the EEC level has suffered from the major drawback that 'additionality' has been difficult to ensure. In other words, the regional grants and loans provided by the EEC institutions on proposal by the member states did not always represent additional finance for regional development, but were offset by less finance from national administrations. But even if it were assumed that all the expenditure under the regional fund had represented additional resources, the total in 1979 still only amounted to 5 per cent of Community budgetary expenditure, or 0.04 per cent of the EEC's GDP. Clearly, no matter how wisely utilized, the macroeconomic impact of such expenditure was bound to be insignificant. Social fund expenditure has been even more limited, though its operation in industrial retraining, assistance to migrant workers and handicapped persons, and so forth has shown an imaginative approach often absent at the national level.

Regional policy stemmed largely from fears that regional disparities in productivity or living standards were a political obstacle to further integration. It has also been argued that economic integration, by encouraging industrial concentration in certain areas, with superior infrastructure, lower transport costs, and the availability of skilled labour would itself aggravate these disparities. There is little information on regional output per head with which to assess the argument that integration has increased the differentials between regions. Regional income data are more readily available, but are, of course, affected by interregional transfer payments. As they stand, they show perhaps some reduction in relative disparities between the early 1960s and the late 1970s.[30] But the regional fund can only have played a very unimportant part in these relative changes. In terms of EEC redistributive mechanisms, agricultural expenditure

---

[30] See Ch. 14 below.

has been many times more significant, but it has been based on criteria essentially unrelated to income levels.

The importance of a common industrial policy was in the early years stressed by the French and Belgians, whose economic policies were fundamentally *dirigiste* and in favour of medium-term planning, and opposed by the Germans who were economically more liberal (regardless of the party or coalition in power). The typically Community compromise was for a mixture of limited financial powers (outside the separate funds for the coal and steel industries), and substantial EEC legislation originally designed to remove legal obstacles and to encourage concentration within European industries, believed necessary to counter competition from United States firms. The steel industry (which falls under the somewhat different ECSC regime) provides an example of the sort of intervention which can arguably be best practiced at the EEC level. The European steel industry was the first important sector to experience the problems of overcapacity, fierce competition from Japan and newly industrialized countries, regional concentration, and a high-age-group labour force, problems which have since become manifest in other sectors, such as shipbuilding and textiles. By the late 1970s the industry had not yet recovered from the 1974–5 recession. Between December 1974 and June 1978 some 12 per cent of the EEC's steel workers were made redundant, while output fell by 20 per cent.

Since the ECSC was established, with particular interventionist powers, the EEC has spent a lot of money on plant modernization (close to $½ billion in 1978), loans to establish alternative industrial plants, and social aids for supplementary unemployment benefits, retraining, and relocation costs. More radically, the 1977 'Davignon Plan', which was accepted by the European steel industry, restricted imports from the most serious competitors outside the EEC, imposed ceilings on productive capacity and compulsory minimum prices for particularly sensitive products, tried to outlaw national aids to the steel industry which gave rise to unfair competition, and provided aid for modernization and rationalization of companies and for industrial reconversion and diversification in the major steel-making areas. The 'Davignon Plan' represented a radical intervention by the EEC into the affairs of one industry. It was agreed upon by both the member countries and the major private steel firms in the Community as an acceptable way of cushioning the social problems of a declining industry, while gradually modernizing it and rendering it competitive with the low-cost producers outside the EEC.

External policies

It is interesting to speculate on the impact which the development of the EEC has had on the balance between free trade and protectionism in the outside world. It is sometimes argued that because the Commission has been responsible for the Community's commercial policy *vis-à-vis* the rest of the world, it has served to limit concessions to the demands of special interest groups in individual countries for further protectionist devices. At the very least, the national governments may have been able to use the Commission as a scapegoat in this respect. On the other hand, in sensitive areas, it is likely that the EEC has, at times, come closest to the most restrictive position. But probably the most important contribution the EEC has made to greater freedom of trade is that its existence as a customs union has made possible such wide-reaching and substantial negotiations as the 'Kennedy' and 'Tokyo' rounds. Without the EEC there would have been no interlocutor of sufficient weight for the United States to justify such time-consuming negotiations and the attendant domestic problems of a distrustful and often openly protectionist Congress. To the extent that the United States or any other country could have taken liberal initiatives, these would have tended to be through sets of bilateral agreements specific to particular products and hence very much more limited in scope.

While the 'Kennedy Round' was initiated by the United States, the 'Tokyo Round' followed a Community initiative. Though the outcome of the negotiations was not dramatic (apart from the adoption of some 'codes of conduct' in international trade, EEC tariffs on industrial goods were cut from 9.8 to 7.5 per cent), it was considered important to maintain the momentum of trade liberalization, particularly in a period of world recession. The one area which gained least from the 'Tokyo Round' was the developing world, which failed to obtain the concessions it was seeking on such key products as steel, fertilizers, or leather goods. Indeed, in the field of textiles, the 'Multi Fibre Agreement' reimposed bilateral quotas for individual developing countries. But arguably the EEC's greatest contribution to the Third World resides in the two Lomé Conventions of 1975 and 1979 (themselves inheritors of the older Yaoundé Convention of 1963).

The second Lomé Convention was signed by fifty-eight developing countries. These countries, known collectively as the ACP (African, Caribbean, and Pacific) states, include all of Africa south of the Sahara, except for Zimbabwe, South Africa, Angola, and Mozambique, and most former English and French colonies in the Caribbean and in the Pacific. The overall conception of the conventions and the many years of negotiation which preceded them were remarkably free of ideological arguments. The ACP countries, despite their political differences, displayed a high degree of cohesion, and this certainly contributed to improving the terms of the conventions from their point of view. There have been three main aspects to the agreements: (a) non-reciprocal trade co-operation; (b) a guaranteed export earnings scheme, and (c) provisions for aid.

The principal idea behind trade co-operation has been that of a common market extending to all the EEC and ACP countries. An important aspect of these provisions has been that of non-reciprocity. This has been often demanded by developing countries in the past, but rarely achieved and certainly never on the same scale. Whereas almost the total of ACP exports to the EEC have been freed of import quotas or duties, the ACP states have not been required to offer more than the existing preferences, or if none, then 'most favoured nation' status, and to refrain from discrimination between EEC countries in return. Over 90 per cent of ACP exports to the EEC were admitted duty-free in 1977. The only major goods still subject to import duties were those which competed with EEC agricultural products (in particular beef and sugar). Beef was given further preferential treatment in the 1979 convention. For sugar, particularly crucial to the West Indian economies, it was agreed that the ACP countries would receive a guaranteed price for annual quotas (of some 1.4 million tonnes a year) defined country by country. In practice, since 1976, the first operating year, the negotiated price has followed the price guaranteed to sugar-beet farmers in the EEC and considerably exceeded the world price. In 1978–9, for instance, the average world price was $16.15 per tonne, while the guaranteed price was $36.78 per tonne.

The 'Stabex' mechanism of guaranteed export earnings has been claimed as a model for future aid schemes for developing countries. It was the first scheme to assure a minimum revenue for raw material producers, whose export earnings were especially subject to vagaries in production or fluctuations in world market prices. Under 'Stabex', shortfalls in export earnings have, under certain conditions biased in favour of the poorest countries, been compensated for by interest-free loans by the European Development Fund (EDF). The commodities covered have included most ACP agricultural exports. By mid-1979, the fifth year of operation, $365 million had been transferred under the scheme, including $216 million in the form of grants. The $365 million only represented 2½ per cent of the value of EEC imports from the ACP countries in 1978, but for some of the poorer ACP countries the importance of 'Stabex' was considerable.

Financial aid (channelled through the EDF) during the five years of the first convention came to $4.3 billion, of which the bulk (some $2.7 billion) was earmarked for outright grants. The 1979 convention planned for an average annual aid flow of $1¼ billion over five years. These figures compare with a sum of more than $19 billion of net official development assistance from the Western developed countries (members of the Development Assistance Committee of the OECD) to the developing countries in 1978, and a total of more than $6 billion of official bilateral aid from individual EEC countries in the same year. Though the EDF flows may thus seem relatively unimportant, they are concentrated on fifty-eight, generally small, countries. Total net bilateral development aid to all the ACP countries was about $5 billion in 1978. Thus if there is no reduction in bilateral aid — and the EEC member countries have committed themselves to not partly offsetting their payments through the Lomé Convention by cutting their direct aid — the convention could increase the total flow of aid to the ACP area by as much as a quarter.

Two features of the conventions appear to have been of great value to the ACP countries. First, aid has been provided on a contractual basis with the contract including the maintenance and extension of free access to markets on a multilateral basis. This has been an important advance on the bilateral trading privileges which have tended to characterize bilateral aid. Second, the conventions have provided for a measure of security. The ACP countries have been enabled to plan ahead in agriculture and industrial development with some confidence that development aid would be available over a five-year period and with certain export earnings guarantees. This is not to deny that the conventions have been of economic and of course political value to the EEC as well. Some 40 per cent of EEC exports to the outside world were in the late 1970s going to the developing countries. Increased aid has thus had a quick return in the form of additional EEC exports given that the imports of the ACP countries have been heavily weighted towards the Community.

Macroeconomic policies

Until the mid-1970s, macroeconomic policy co-ordination did not really figure in the armoury of EEC policies. The Commission was not hesitant to proffer advice on short-term economic policy to the member states through its quarterly reports on the economic situation. This advice, however, was not particularly EEC-oriented. It tended to pick some point on the 'expand to reduce unemployment − contract to reduce inflation' locus depending on the relative severity of the problems in the countries concerned − without looking at the issues from a Community viewpoint, perhaps because there was no very apparent EEC business cycle till the early 1970s. The advice quite often took the form of a tough monetary stance to cut inflation with an expansionary fiscal policy to reduce unemployment. To the extent that there was policy co-ordination it was at the sharing-of-information level.

The greater synchronization of cyclical fluctuations since the first oil crisis prompted a search for greater co-ordination not only at the OECD, but also at the EEC level. This found its first expression in the 'concerted action' programme prepared by the Commission and national authorities and adopted at the Bremen 1978 European Council meeting. This programme, in some cases, defined precisely the contribution of each country to fiscal expansion. Germany, the Netherlands, and Luxembourg were, for instance, to take stimulatory measures so as to boost demand initially by about 1 per cent of GDP. The contribution of the other member states was expressed in various terms, for some more precisely than others, but in all cases referred to instruments of fiscal policy including the central government budget as a whole. What was striking about the programme was that no references were made to monetary policy. This was partly because the Commission had not up to that point ever made a quantitative recommendation about a member country's monetary policy, and on the eve of the establishment of the EMS this did not seem an appropriate innovation, and partly because detailed discussions about monetary policies tended to be conducted behind the very closed doors of the committee of governors of central banks at the BIS. Though a monetary dimension was subsequently introduced in EEC discussions, monetary policy co-ordination tended to be confined to technical matters of central bank co-operation, largely in exchange rate intervention.

Yet the ideal of a monetary union is as old as that of the EEC itself. Through most of the 1960s the Community had been relatively complacent about monetary integration, which seemed to be taking place of its own accord. During that period the idea gained ground that, with the increasing integration in trade and especially with the fixing of common agricultural support prices in units of account, exchange rate adjustments had become nearly impossible and the EEC had *de facto* become a monetary union. As the 1960s drew to a close (and international currency crises became more frequent) the flow of reports and proposals for closer economic and monetary co-operation started. Thus, the Hague summit of December 1969 set up a committee to prepare a plan to establish economic and monetary union by stages. That plan (the 'Werner Plan')[31] stated that: 'The group considers that economic and monetary union is an objective realizeable in the course of the current decade,' and monetary union was taken to imply the irreversible fixing of parity rates. Overall, the plan was a compromise

---

[31] EEC, 'Report of the Council and the Commission on the Realization of Stages of Economic and Monetary Union in the Community', *Bulletin of the EEC Commission*, Supplement No. 11, 1970.

between a 'monetary' school of thought which considered linking exchange rates and monetary policies as a necessary and sufficient condition for integration, and an 'economic' school of thought which considered (as Chancellor Erhard is quoted as having said) that 'the use of monetary schemes to promote economic integration is like putting the bridle on the tail of the horse'. In any case, the upheavals of 1971 and the breakdown of the Bretton Woods system made it impossible to implement the first steps of the plan, let alone its final goals. The idea that the Community was a viable currency area persisted, however, and a number of proposals were put forward in following years.[32]

The year 1972 also saw the establishment of an exchange rate mechanism — the 'snake'. This did not for any length of time encompass all member states and could not be compared in comprehensiveness to the Bretton Woods system, but, despite many gloomy predictions, it not only survived the turbulent years to 1979 but it can also be seen as one of the major ingredients in the setting-up of the EMS.

The EMS should be seen as as much of a political as an economic achievement. Extensive political and technical discussions accompanied its birth and led to the adoption of measures designed to strengthen the economies of the less prosperous member states. The latter was the quid pro quo for Italy and Ireland to join the system. These countries' argument was mainly based on the 'economist' side of the 'economist' versus 'monetarist' controversy. It was maintained that monetary integration could not take place without economic integration, and that as well as strengthening co-operation and co-ordination, it would be necessary to give special aid to the less prosperous countries which would have extra adjustment costs in keeping up with the discipline of the richer and stronger currency member states. The argument was further supported by the proposition from the 'MacDougall Report' that in an integrated Europe there would have to be much larger interregional transfers.[33] The measures consisted of loans of up to $1.4 billion available each year over a five-year period and subsidized by up to $300 million per year.

The economic impact of these transfers is unlikely to be large, and that of the EMS itself is extremely difficult to assess. At the time of writing the system was in a transitional phase, and its eventual impact will depend upon as yet unanswered questions about the existing mechanisms, the reserve asset and settlement instrument of the system, the ECU, and the development and characteristics of the new institution (the European Monetary Fund, or EMF). The EMS will have a significant economic impact if the Fund is set up in such a way that it can grow over time into a European Central Bank with discretionary powers over liquidity creation through control over the supply of its liability, the ECU.

[32] For a comprehensive review of monetary integration in the EEC before 1972, see A.I. Bloomfield, 'The Historical Setting', in L.B. Krause and W.S. Salant (eds.), *European Monetary Unification and Its Meaning for the United States*, Brookings Institution, Washington 1973. For post-1972 developments, a chronology of the 'snake' is given as an annex to N. Thygesen, 'The Emerging European Monetary System: Precursors, First Steps and Policy Options', in R. Triffin (ed.), 'The Emerging European Monetary System', *Bulletin de la Banque Nationale de Belgique*, April 1979.
[33] EEC, *Report of the Study Group on the Role of Public Finance in European Integration* (MacDougall Report), Brussels 1977.

The exchange rate mechanism adopted in 1979 was neither a fully fixed nor a fully floating system.[34] Each participant declared a central rate and was obliged to intervene to hold its currency within 2¼ per cent margins (6 per cent for Italy) around this rate; but central rates could be, and have already been, changed. The important provision was that central rates had to be adjusted by 'mutual agreement and by a common procedure'.[35] Depending upon how these words will be interpreted, this could represent a significant shift away from the position that determining one's own exchange rate is an essential pillar of a national economic sovereignty. A further important question will be how the system as a whole will behave *vis-à-vis* the rest of the world. Originally, the 'snake' was in a 'tunnel', i.e., there was a declared rate against the dollar, but this arrangement only lasted until March 1973. Subsequently, the choice lay predominantly with the dominant economy, Germany. This solution would not seem to be open to the EMS, which contains more than one large economy. Again, the Brussels resolution admits the problem but does not provide a specific answer. The second set of questions concerns the role of the ECU as the EMS's reserve asset. Under the transitional arrangements, each central bank transferred 20 per cent of its gold and dollar reserves to a fund in return for a quantity of ECU. This mechanism, which through gold price changes resulted in just over one year in a spectacular growth in the quantity of ECU from 26 to 46 billion (or from some \$36 to \$64 billion), is hardly appropriate for a system whose declared intention is to create a zone of monetary stability. The quantity of ECU reserves available to the system will also depend on the credit facilities, which were expanded to a potential total of nearly \$30 billion. The stated intention is that in the next phase these credit arrangements will be consolidated into the system, although it is neither clear what is meant by that term nor what role credit can or should play within a regional grouping which seems to have more than adequate liquidity and which is composed of participants able to get all the financing they may need from the international markets.

The answers to these questions about the nature of the exchange rate mechanism, the reserve asset, and the credit facilities will in part determine whether the system survives in its original form or not. Failure in any of the fields is more likely to lead to adapting the arrangements than to abandoning the whole attempt,[36] and so a more important question than survival is success. The latter must be judged in terms set by the system itself — monetary stability, implying both internal price stability and external exchange rate stability. This brings one back to the old 'monetarist' versus 'economist' debate. Can the EMS alone lead to stabilization and create economic and monetary union? The answer is almost

[34] For a comprehensive account of the mechanisms of the EMS, see Deutsche Bundesbank, 'The European Monetary System: Structure and Operation', *Monthly Report*, March 1979; and EEC, *European Economy*, July 1979.

[35] 'Resolution of the European Council of 5 December 1978 on the Establishment of the European Monetary System and Related Matters', in EEC Monetary Committee. *The Compendium of Monetary Texts*, Brussels 1979, Article 3.2.

[36] See C. McMahon, 'The Long-run Implications of the European Monetary System', in P.H. Trezise (ed.), *The European Monetary System: Its Promise and Prospects*, Brookings Institution, Washington 1979, in which he concludes that 'if the EMS did not exist, it — or something similar — would have to be invented' (p. 92).

certainly no. A well designed monetary system would greatly contribute to achieving these goals, just as the lack of order during the 1970s contributed to the growing divergences in the EEC in terms of growth, unemployment, and inflation rates. It is, however, also essential that other measures be taken and that political will be engaged. Supporters of the EMS would say that the system both provides the first elements of the necessary monetary dimension and clearly demonstrates the existence of political will.

Conclusions

The previous discussion has shown that in most areas it is difficult to say whether the economic effect of the EEC has been positive or negative, let alone to assess quantitatively its impacts. A major difficulty in trying to answer such a question is the benchmark against which to make any measurements. The economies of the member states have changed fundamentally since the formation of the EEC, but so have those of non-member states. And though the EEC is essentially an economic community, its political dimension must also be taken into account in any assessment. The initial intention was that gradual step-by-step integration in specified areas would have spill-over effects and lead to political integration. In the late 1970s, with direct elections to the European Parliament, increased co-operation in foreign policy, and the setting-up of the EMS, there have been renewed signs that this approach could work. Previously it had seemed as if the strategy had been dealt a death blow in 1965 by de Gaulle's blocking of the evolution of the Community to the phase prescribed in the treaty, when certain decisions might be taken by less than unanimous vote, and by his dashing of the hope that the Commission might be able to strengthen its independence *vis-à-vis* the national governments. Certainly there have been achievements, but they remain far short of the dreams of a unified Europe.

Returning to the specifically economic areas, the corner-stone of the EEC is the customs union. The EEC speeded up the process of reducing tariffs between its member states, a process which would probably have in time happened to much the same extent in any case. The direct impact of the customs union on trade flows does not appear to have been very large — probably less than 1 per cent of GDP. The beneficial effects of the customs union also arise, however, in unquantifiable ways such as increased consumer choice and indirect stimuli to growth, at least in some countries. *Vis-à-vis* the rest of the world the EEC may appear more protectionist. Yet it is not clear whether the overall degree of protectionism has been greater or less as a result of negotiating as a Community rather than as individual nations. On the positive side is the fact that a smaller number of parties may facilitate agreements, and that one negotiator representing a block with slightly different interests may be able to offer more permutations for compromises than if each different interest was seeking only its own goal. On the negative side is the powerful argument that the compromises adopted as the EEC solution before negotiations began with other parties may have been closer to the most restrictive position than to the mid-position. This is closely tied to the problem of veto and unanimous voting used in Community matters, which has often resulted in common policies representing the lowest common denominator.

Agriculture has always been treated as a special case, and the EEC's record in that sector is certainly protectionist. It is also, as was suggested in Section II, disruptive to world trade. The EEC's high price policy has made it more than self-sufficient in a number of agricultural products, leading to surpluses which have often been sold off on the world market with subsidies. This has been even more disruptive than the policy of taxing imports with a system of variable levies on the difference between the world and the EEC price. Internally, the CAP's impact is difficult to assess with any accuracy, again mainly because the individual national policies in the absence of the CAP cannot be known. Most studies looking at the effects of the CAP have assumed that world prices would prevail in the EEC if the CAP did not exist, but, especially for products for which the EEC represents a substantial share of the world market, the validity of this assumption is dubious. It is, however, almost certain that the common financing of the CAP has resulted in a higher degree of transfers to the agricultural sector of some countries, especially Denmark and Ireland, than would have been available from the national exchequers.

Agriculture was responsible for the two most pressing problems the EEC faced in the late 1970s. The high price policy leading to structural surpluses and disruption of the world market had pushed the EEC budget to its financing limit, and had caused unjustifiable financial flows between member states. Whereas it may have made sense in terms of the wider goals to have made substantial transfers to Ireland, the same cannot be said for Denmark, which had the highest per capita income in the EEC. This problem came to a head again in 1979, with United Kingdom demands for substantial reductions in its own contributions, and crisis was only averted by a temporary solution which involved adapting the so-called 'financial mechanism' which had been created in 1975 in answer to exactly the same problem. The major reason for the difficulties was that nearly three-quarters of total expenditure went to the agricultural sector. This situation had been allowed to persist because the EEC's 'own resources' (customs duties, agricultural levies, and up to 1 per cent of national VAT revenues) had grown sufficiently rapidly to allow the financing of these expenditure flows. But the prospect of the CAP taking an ever-increasing share of the budget, and of a budgetary ceiling being reached, may provide the necessary spur to reform that was lacking previously.

So far the so-called 'neo-functional' approach to integration has failed to live up to expectations. The underlying idea, associated particularly with the thinking of Monnet, was that of taking small steps in specified areas, selected by a politically motivated bureaucracy as symbolic, but sufficiently technical and uncontroversial that the decisions would be left to experts. Integration was to be achieved almost behind the backs of the governments who had been unwilling to take the underlying political decision. The process was meant to gather momentum and spread from the initially chosen areas. Events have worked out differently. Instead of spill-overs from the original areas and growing momentum, some institutions like Euratom never got off the ground, and other areas like agriculture gave rise to reticence about, rather than enthusiasm for, further efforts. The bureaucracy might have lacked ingenuity and motivation, but, above all, the governments were not taken in by the strategy.

In many ways, it seems as if the EEC in the late 1970s was running out of steam. International organizations, it is sometimes said, are always designed to prevent the last war, and to some extent the cold war made the EEC redundant from the start. Europe has been held together not by the Treaty of Rome but by geopolitical circumstances. If it had not found itself between two opposed superpowers, developments might have been very different. As it was, the underlying political aims as opposed to the explicit economic goals could largely be attained without surrendering sovereignty through integration. In foreign policy and defence, as well as in the economic sphere, co-ordination was perhaps achieved more through the tutelage of the United States than through the efforts of the EEC member states.

Appendix: A Survey of the Literature on Trade Creation and Trade Diversion

The theoretical literature on customs unions and economic integration more generally has been closely associated with the formation of the Common Market. The first important works were by Viner and Meade.[37] Viner first developed the concepts of trade creation and trade diversion, and made the fundamental point that there can be no general presumption as to whether the formation of a union increases overall economic welfare. Trade creation takes place when there is a shift from higher-cost domestic sources to sources in the partner country of the union which have become relatively cheaper since tariffs have been abolished. Trade diversion takes place to the extent that trade is switched from lower-cost foreign sources to domestic or partner country producers due to the erection of the common external tariff.

Later, Meade and Lipsey introduced the distinction between the effects of the formation of a customs union on consumption as distinct from production. Lipsey argued that when 'consumption effects are allowed for, the simple conclusions that trade creation is good and trade diversion bad are no longer valid'.[38] While trade diversion implies a switch to higher-cost but tariff-free sources of supply, it eliminates the divergence between domestic and international (customs union) prices caused by tariffs. Therefore consumers who were previously purchasing a more-than-optimal quantity of domestic goods can usefully reallocate their expenditures between commodities. Whether the loss in welfare due to the shift to a higher-cost source of supply is greater or less than the gain due to the removal of the tariff constraint on consumer equilibrium is, in principle, an empirical question, but not one to which a straightforward empirical test can be applied.

Quantitative research on the impact of the European Common Market *qua* customs union has been almost entirely confined to the estimation of the Vinerian trade creation and trade diversion effects. The following text surveys a selection of this research, concentrating on relatively recent works that appear methodologically sound.[39] The studies chosen can be grouped under four broad headings:

    (i) Single-country demand for imports approaches;
    (ii) Gravitational models;

[37] J. Viner, *The Customs Union Issue*, New York 1950; J.E. Meade, *Problems of Economic Union*, London 1953, and *The Theory of Customs Unions*, Amsterdam 1955.

[38] R.G. Lipsey, 'The Theory of Customs Union: Trade Diversion and Welfare', *Economica*, February 1957.

[39] A complete survey of the literature can be found in D.G. Mayes, 'The Effects of Economic Integration on Trade', *Journal of Common Market Studies*, September 1978.

(iii) Control-country approaches;
(iv) Multi-country models.

Examples of studies that have adopted the *single-country demand for imports approach* are those by Truman and Balassa.[40] The approach is based on the assumption that had it not been for the formation of a customs union, the imports of the member countries would have increased over time according to some rule, for example that of constant shares of domestic and foreign supplies in total absorption (Truman), or constant income elasticities of import demand (Balassa), and that the difference between the actual level of imports and that implied by the rule can be attributed to the formation of the customs union.

The approach has a number of drawbacks. First, the chosen rule is all-important. The validity of the results depends on how accurate is the representation of the hypothetical path of imports over time in the absence of the customs union (the counterfactual). Second, the choice of the base period over which the elasticities or shares are estimated is critical, and in particular there is the danger of cyclical distortions. Third, a number of variables are implicitly or explicitly assumed to be unchanged by the establishment of the customs union. In the foregoing case of an elasticity with respect to GDP rule it is assumed that GDP is independent. If, in fact, the formation of the customs union accelerates economic growth, the application of the rule will underestimate the extent of trade creation.[41] Finally, in the specific case of the EEC, both before and after the abolition of all tariffs among the original six countries, trade liberalization on a broader scale was taking place within the framework of the 'Kennedy Round' and later on between the EEC and EFTA.

Truman's methodology is richer than that of most earlier studies in that it allows for double trade creation where both non-member countries and member countries gain shares at the expense of domestic production in the importing member country. This is most likely to happen when the new common external tariff is lower than the tariff previously protecting the importing country. Also, Truman distinguishes internal and external trade erosion, which occurs when the share of domestic suppliers rises after the customs union is formed and either the share of member or non-member countries or both fall. External trade erosion may occur when the common external tariff is higher than the previous national tariff. It is difficult, however, to understand how the formation of a customs union alone could lead to internal trade erosion.

To counter the argument that the assumption of share constancy will lead to overestimates of trade creation and underestimates of erosion because during the 1960s trade shares were growing under the impact of multinational tariff reductions, Truman, in a second set of comparisons, took the shares for 1968 as predicted by regressions of shares against a cyclical variable and a time trend estimated over the period 1953–60. The results indicated less trade creation ($2.5 billion rather than $9.2 billion), less internal trade creation and external diversion ($0.5 billion rather than $1.0 billion), and more trade erosion. It seems likely that the inclusion of a linear time trend, which assumes that the multinational tariff reductions induced the same average annual rate of growth in trade between 1961 and 1968 as they did between 1953 and 1960, will seriously

[40] E.M. Truman, 'The Effects of European Economic Integration', and Balassa, 'Trade Creation and Diversion', both in Balassa (ed.), *European Economic Integration*.
[41] It is true that this is going somewhat beyond Viner's definition of trade creation. But the various methodologies on the whole cannot distinguish between trade creation in the pure Vinerian sense and that consequent upon an increased growth rate in the union.

overestimate the level of trade in the counterfactual, and thus underestimate the effects of the customs union. But the wide divergence in estimates indicates the problems in quantifying the pattern of trade as it would have been if duties had not been abolished.

A similar 'residual-imputation' methodology was adopted by Balassa, only rather than use a shares-in-consumption rule, he preferred an elasticity rule. Like Truman, Balassa ignores the effects of changes in relative prices (or assumes that they are all brought about by the integration process), and such dynamic changes as might affect income or consumption. Following a criticism of an earlier study,[42] he is careful in selecting the periods over which he takes percentage changes in imports and GNP to calculate the elasticities. The periods chosen are 1953-9 and 1959-70, with the following elasticities for all EEC imports taken together.

	1953–59	1959–70
total	1.8	2.0
intra	2.4	2.7
extra	1.6	1.6

Thus, at the global level there is indication of internal trade creation but not of trade diversion. Values of trade creation and diversion are calculated for each sector by taking differences between the actual and the hypothetical (constant elasticity) trade flows.

The difficulty of ignoring other factors affecting the elasticities is well exemplified by considering Balassa's analysis of the food category. The GNP import elasticities of food imports do not show evidence of trade creation. However, if GNP is replaced by total food consumption or industrial production there is evidence of trade creation, because 'the income elasticity of demand for food fell during the period under consideration and the rate of growth of industrial production declined while that of GNP increased slightly'.[43] All the results are interpreted in terms of particular *ad hoc* factors, which throws doubt on the usefulness of the basic methodology.

A second group of studies of trade creation and diversion in the European Common Market by Verdoorn and Schwartz, and by Aitken, is based on the so-called *gravitational models*, first developed in the regional science field and only later applied to international trade problems.[44] The basic idea is that the size of a trade flow between any pair of regions or countries is a positive function of demand in the importing country and supply in the exporting country, and a negative function of tariff and non-tariff barriers including transport costs. The most straightforward empirical application of the gravitational model for the assessment of the trade impact of the formation of a customs union is through cross-section estimation of bilateral trade functions with dummy variables or average tariff time series to measure the customs union effect.

Verdoorn and Schwartz estimate a number of such functions, among which the most satisfactory yields the estimates for trade creation and diversion shown in Table 8.1. But perhaps the most interesting conclusion of their work is that

---

[42] W. Sellekaerts, 'How Meaningful are Empirical Studies on Trade Creation and Trade Diversion', *Weltwirtschaftliches Archiv*, No. 4, 1973.

[43] Balassa, 'Trade Creation and Diversion', p. 83.

[44] P.J. Verdoorn and A.N.R. Schwarz, 'Two Alternative Estimates of the Effects of EEC and EFTA on the Pattern of Trade', *European Economic Review*, No. 3, 1972; N.D. Aitken, 'The Effect of the EEC and EFTA on European Trade: A Temporal Cross-Section Analysis', *American Economic Review*, December 1973.

the relative price variables, which compare alternative sources of supply after taxes and tariffs, only capture a minor part of the extra trade flows which follow the establishment of a customs union – the greater part seems due to the dummy or average tariff variables. This is explained by the fact that prior to the union some of the duties, even though possibly fairly low in percentage terms where there was considerable competition, effectively prohibited trade for the commodity in question. When those tariffs were eliminated, trade in that commodity could expand rapidly, but this rate of expansion would not be caught in the coefficients on the price relatives. In addition to the impact of the abolition of effectively prohibitive tariff barriers are what Verdoorn and Schwarz call the 'promotional effects' (e.g. increased flow of information to markets, development of repair and distribution networks, reduced risk of the re-establishment of tariff or non-tariff barriers), all of which are best captured by dummy variables.

In another application of the gravitational model, Aitken uses cross-section regression analysis to estimate the customs union impact, but he estimates successive equations for each year, with dummy variables to represent tariff cuts, deriving a measure of the customs union effects over time. The original seven EFTA members and the original five EEC trading countries (Belgium and Luxembourg being aggregated in the trade statistics) are included in the study. Two alternative estimates for trade creation in the EEC for 1967, of $11.1 billion and $9.2 billion, are obtained. In the case of EFTA they are of $2.4 billion and $1.3 billion. The lower projection estimates are marginally to be preferred in that their equations take more explicit account of trade diversion between the two communities. Trade diversion was estimated at the relatively small levels of $0.6 billion and $0.2 billion for the EEC and EFTA respectively. Thus, despite the apparent advantages in capturing the effects of increased integration, the gravitational models have not yielded much higher estimates of trade creation than the residual-imputation approach discussed earlier.

The first major study using a *control-country approach* was that of Williamson and Bottrill.[45] Their basic hypothesis is that the share performance of a given supplier in markets where there are no preferential tariff changes gives a good indication of that supplier's hypothetical performance in markets being affected by integration. In their case they use the rest of the world as the 'control country'. Thus the difference between the 'control-country' and the 'residual-imputation' approaches is that rather than invoke some rule of constant elasticities or shares or other measure to reconstruct the counterfactual, the control-country approach adopts the assumption that the performance of countries outside the union, when appropriately evaluated, permits the estimation of the hypothetical trade flows as they would have developed in the absence of the union.

Kreinin takes the control-country approach further and more heroically than Williamson and Bottrill both in terms of country and product-disaggregation.[46] His principal method is to compare percentage changes in the United States and EEC import–consumption ratios in different manufacturing industries. It is initially assumed that the EEC external import–consumption ratios would have moved by the same amount as the United States total import–consumption ratios without the customs union. This gives a measure of trade diversion. It is

[45] J. Williamson and A. Bottrill, 'The Impact of Customs Unions on Trade in Manufactures', *Oxford Economic Papers*, November 1971.

[46] M.E. Kreinin, 'Effects of the EEC on Imports of Manufactures', *Economic Journal*, September 1972.

further assumed that the ratios of external to total EEC imports would have remained unchanged at their 1959–60 values. The change in the EEC ratio of total imports to consumption minus the change in the American ratio, 'blown up' by the EEC base year total-to-external-imports ratio, gives an estimate of trade creation. In fact between 1959–60 and 1969–70 the United States import-consumption ratio for all manufactures rose by 2.1 per cent, while the EEC external import–consumption ratio rose by only 1.3 per cent, implying trade diversion of some $1.1 billion. The EEC total import ratio rose by 7.5 per cent, which implies trade creation of $8.5 billion.

The methodology might appear excessively simplistic, in particular in that it assumes away differential price and income movements. Kreinin tries crudely to adjust for the effects of these on import–consumption ratios. First, using an independent estimate of the income elasticity of import demand, he raises the United States import–consumption ratio to reflect the country's lower income growth over the period. Second, he adjusts for the loss of United States competitiveness in certain industries by reducing imports in those industries by a percentage equal to the decline in the United States share in third markets.[47] After these adjustments, the estimate for trade creation in 1969–70 falls to $7.3 billion and that for diversion rises to $2.4 billion.

Finally, among the studies discussed here, Resnick and Truman adopt a *multi-country model approach*.[48] They propose a model for the imports of ten EEC and EFTA countries (excluding Portugal and Finland, and combining Belgium and Luxembourg) which takes the form of a decision tree. Total non-food imports of each country are assumed to be a function of relative domestic and import prices, real income, and a pressure of demand variable. Total imports are then allocated to suppliers on the basis of relative prices in a hierarchical way. First, the shares in total imports from the other nine European countries and those from the rest of the world are separately related to relative import prices. The first group is then divided into the shares from the EEC and the shares from EFTA. Finally, in each customs union the shares coming from each country are related to all relative prices in that union. Thus there is one total import equation to be estimated for each of the ten countries, one Europe and one non-Europe share equation, one EEC and one EFTA share equation, four EEC member and five EFTA member share equations. In some cases difficulties in obtaining good ordinary least squares estimates led to the combining of some of the supplying countries' shares.

Once estimated, this set of import-allocation equations permits the simulation of any number of different customs union arrangements, provided the arrangement can be translated into a relative price change. For example, the impact of the 'Dillon Round' of multilateral tariff cuts can be isolated from that of the formation of the EEC customs union, provided that some view is taken as to what the 'Dillon Round' would have meant for the tariffs of the six if the first EEC tariff reductions had not intervened. In fact, it was assumed that the tariffs of the six would have been reduced by 10 per cent, the average cut for other participants in the 'Dillon Round'. The trade creation and diversion effects

[47] This is justified on the grounds that 'in quantitative terms U.S. manufacturing imports happen to be roughly equal to U.S. manufacturing exports to markets outside the EEC' (ibid., p.911). If this is merely a question of coincidence, the logic of adjusting in this way is difficult to see.

[48] S.A. Resnick and E.M. Truman, 'An Empirical Examination of Bilateral Trade in Western Europe', in Balassa (ed.), *European Economic Integration*.

following the formation of the two customs unions can be calculated from the price elasticities.

After abstracting the effects of the 'Dillon Round', the EEC is calculated to have generated only $1.9 billion of trade creation and $3.0 billion of trade diversion in 1968 at current prices. These are apparently the only results in the literature which show trade diversion in excess of trade creation. Resnick and Truman suggest some biases which may have arisen because of the use of particular time-series. In addition, the only regression coefficients which can pick up the effects of membership of the same trading bloc are those attached to relative prices, and Verdoorn and Schwarz showed that these will only pick up a minor part of the effects of tariff cuts. The effects of the elimination of prohibitive or nearly prohibitive duties will be all but missed.

Bibliography

There seems to be a lack of historical surveys of the EEC. An introduction to the economics side is D. Swann, *The Economics of the Common Market*, London 1978 (4th edn.). Some general books which provide historical background are: J. Pinder (ed.), *The Economics of Europe*, London 1971; A. Cairncross *et al.*, *Economic Policy for the European Community*, London 1974; L. Tsoukalis, *The Politics and Economics of European Monetary Integration*, London 1977; B. Burrows, G. Denton, and G. Edwards, *Federal Solutions for European Issues*, London 1978; H. Wallace, W. Wallace, and C. Webb, *Policy-Making in the European Community*, New York 1977; P. Coffey (ed.), *Economic Policies of the Common Market*, London 1979; A.M. El-Agraa (ed.), *The Economics of the European Community*, Oxford 1980.

On the customs union issue, the two most complete surveys are B. Balassa (ed.), *European Economic Integration*, Amsterdam 1975, and D.G. Mayes, 'The Effects of Economic Integration on Trade', *Journal of Common Market Studies*, September 1978. An earlier account can be found in E. Dalbosco and F. Pierelli, 'Evoluzione della struttura del commercio estero dei paesi membri della CEE', in Banca d'Italia, *Contributi alla ricerca economica*, No. 3, 1973.

The Common Agricultural Policy is surveyed in: J. Marsh and C. Ritson, *Agricultural Policy and the Common Market*, RIIA, London 1971; Commission of the European Communities, *The Common Agricultural Policy*, Brussels 1978; C.N. Morris, 'The Common Agricultural Policy', *Fiscal Studies*, March 1980; R. Fennell, *The Common Agricultural Policy of the European Community*, London 1979. A continuing useful source is the *European Review of Agricultural Economics*.

General issues about economic and monetary union are raised in M. Fratianni and T. Peeters (eds.), *One Money for Europe*, London 1978. More specific references to EMS can be found in P.H. Trezise (ed.), *The European Monetary System: Its Promise and Prospects*, Brookings Institution, Washington 1979, while the original system is explained in EEC, *European Economy*, July 1979. The implications of economic union for financial transfers are investigated in EEC, *Report of the Study Group on the Role of Public Finance in European Integration* (MacDougall Report), Brussels 1977. Regional policy is analysed in T. Buck, 'Regional Policy and European Integration', *Journal of Common Market Studies*, December 1975. For discussion of the operation of the Lomé Convention and relations with the Third World in general, see the Commission's own journal, *The Courier* (various issues), as well as P. Coffey, *The External Relations of the EEC*, London 1976.

Other aspects of EEC economic policy not treated in the chapter are covered in, *inter alia*, M. Shanks, *European Social Policy, Today and Tomorrow*, Oxford 1977; N.J.D. Lucas, *Energy and the European Community*, London 1977; A.P. Jacquemin and H.W. de Jong, *European Industrial Organisation*, London 1977; L. Tsoukalis, *The European Community and its Mediterranean Enlargement*, London 1981. Finally, some more general essays on EEC problems can be found in W. Hallstein, *Die europäische Gemeinschaft*, Düsseldorf 1974, and in R. Triffin, R. Aron, R. Barre, and R. Enalentio, *L'Europe de la crise*, Brussels 1976.

9

Eastern and Western Europe

NITA WATTS*

Introduction

As a prelude to a comparison of macroeconomic developments in Eastern and Western Europe, it is a commonplace to say that one is comparing the experience or achievements of very different economic systems. In the West are predominantly *managed market economies*; managed mainly through fiscal, monetary, and exchange rate policies affecting aggregate demand. Selective and direct interventions to support income and employment in particular regions or sectors, to control wage inflation, to influence foreign trade flows, etc., have also been resorted to, but there have been considerable variations from country to country in the degree to which such more discriminating interference with the market system has occurred. Thus, the West German economy was probably a good deal less 'managed' than the French one through most of the post-war period; the Italian one became progressively more controlled as time went by; while the Spanish one, highly *dirigiste* in the 1950s, was gradually liberalized in the next two decades. Similarly, the share of total government expenditure in GDP varied in the late 1970s from figures above 50 per cent in the Benelux, Norway, and Sweden to figures often below 30 per cent in the less developed Mediterranean countries. Yet, whatever the degree of government influence, the public ownership sector of the economy, whether measured in terms of its share in employment or in expenditure, or in its contribution to national income, was everywhere the smaller part of the whole.

All the Eastern European countries, on the other hand, have been in principle, and to a large extent in practice, *centrally planned economies* throughout most of the period here considered. The means of production are predominantly in public ownership, market forces play a very minor role, and governments transmit instructions through a hierarchy of administrative bodies out to the individual enterprise, farm, shop, etc., to secure a level and pattern of output, investment, consumption, and foreign trade conforming with the centrally determined national plan. Such a description is, of course, an over simplification, and, as in the West, there has been a good deal of inter-country diversity − with the Hungarian 'New Economic Mechanism', introduced in 1968, as the system furthest removed from the stereotype of a 'Soviet-type' centrally planned economy.[1] The picture of predominantly public ownership of the means of production also requires some qualification. The organization of industry into state enterprises and co-operatives was practically completed by 1950 in most Eastern European countries (and much earlier in the Soviet Union). But Eastern Germany (the GDR) was an exception, with private and mixed private-and-

*St. Hilda's College, University of Oxford.

[1] This system, as it operated in the late 1960s and early 1970s, was intended to transform Hungary into a socialist managed-market economy.

state-owned enterprises until the latter were nationalized in 1972, at which time they employed some 12½ per cent of the industrial labour force and contributed about the same share of global industrial output.

Agriculture has remained an area within which private sector output is significant in every Eastern European country, and also in the Soviet Union. Collectivization had, by the early 1960s, reduced private farms to no more than 10 per cent of the cultivatable area in all countries except Poland, where, throughout the period, small peasant farming accounted for about 80 per cent of both the agricultural area and gross farm output. However, in all the other countries the private sector, represented mainly by the household plots of members of collective farms, has remained an important contributor to total agricultural production. In Hungary, for example, the household plots in the co-operative farms provided about 20 per cent of the gross value of agricultural output in the mid-1970s and other 'auxiliary farms of the population' a further 13 per cent, though together accounting for only about 15 per cent of the agricultural area. But everywhere private sector output incorporates significant inputs of fodder grown on collective or state land.

A second important difference between Western and Eastern Europe lies in the level of economic development. An indication of this is provided by Table 9.1, which shows tentative UNECE estimates for per caput GDP in 1965 – a mid-point in the period under observation. It is clear that none of the Eastern European countries was at all comparable with the more mature economies of the West such as the high-welfare Scandinavian and Benelux countries or even the United Kingdom. But such differences were less pronounced with some of the central and southern countries in the 'Western' group, where per caput GDP appears closer (and in some cases very close) to levels in Eastern Europe.

TABLE 9.1. *GDP per caput, 1965*[a]
(dollars)

Sweden	2,170	East Germany	1,440
United Kingdom	1,930	Czechoslovakia	1,430
BLEU	1,890	Soviet Union	1,050
Switzerland	1,860	Hungary	1,020
West Germany	1,850	Poland	990
Denmark	1,820	Bulgaria	880
Netherlands	1,800	Romania	700
Norway	1,670		
France	1,620		
Finland	1,590		
Austria	1,460		
Ireland	1,240		
Italy	1,190		
Spain	940		
Greece	760		
Portugal	730		
Total	1,560	Total	1,060

[a] Estimates based on 'physical indicators'
Source: UNECE, *Economic Survey of Europe in 1969*, Pt. I, New York 1970.

Bearing in mind differences in both institutions and levels of economic development, this chapter attempts to compare broad macroeconomic trends in Eastern Europe during the post-war period with those in some Western countries which started at more or less similar stages of development. On the Eastern European side attention will be concentrated on six countries of the area, excluding Albania (for lack of data) and also the Soviet Union, whose vast size, almost comprehensive endowment of natural resources, and small dependence on external trade make significant comparison with any Western European country rather difficult. On the Western side, the countries chosen, partly in the light of the evidence presented in Table 9.1, will be Greece and Portugal — among the area's least mature economies and most similar to Bulgaria and Romania; West Germany and Austria, which come closest to the two most developed Eastern European countries; and Italy and Spain as intermediate cases, with Spain, at least, sharing some of the economic characteristics of Poland.

TABLE 9.2. *Share of agriculture in total employment*[a]
(percentages)

	1950	1979		1950	1979
West Germany	24	6	East Germany	22[c]	10
Austria	34[b]	11	Czechoslovakia	39	13
Italy	46	15	Hungary	50	19
Spain	(46)	20	Poland[d]	56	23
Greece	(53)[b]	31	Bulgaria	70[c]	24
Portugal	(60)	31	Romania	74[b]	31
Total	(39)	14	Total	52	21

[a] Differences in methods of calculating employment in agriculture, in particular, make international comparisons hazardous

[b] 1951

[c] 1952

[d] If male employment only is considered (less likely to be distorted by differing statistical conventions), Poland becomes more comparable with Italy or Spain than with Greece or Portugal.

Sources: OECD, *Manpower Statistics, 1950–1962*; OECD, *Labour Force Statistics* (various issues); UNECE, *Economic Survey of Europe in 1969*, Pt. I, New York 1970, and *Economic Survey of Europe in 1980*, New York 1981.

Such a selection is clearly arbitrary, but is at least partly supported by the further evidence presented in Table 9.2. It should be stressed that in this area (and in others) differences in statistical conventions make precise international comparisons impossible. Hence the comparative evidence presented throughout this chapter must be treated with caution.

I. The Growth Experience

In looking at economic growth in Eastern and Western Europe, this section begins with a brief account of the actual growth performances. This is followed by some consideration of the stability or otherwise of growth rates recorded over the period and by a discussion of some of the major factors which propelled growth.

TABLE 9.3. *Growth of output*
(average annual percentage changes)

A. GDP 1950–52 to 1967–69			
West Germany	6.2	East Germany	5.7
Austria	5.0	Czechoslovakia	5.2
Italy	5.4	Hungary	4.8
Spain	6.1	Poland	6.1
Greece	6.0	Bulgaria	6.9
Portugal	5.1	Romania	7.2
Total	5.9	Total	6.0
B. GDP 1967–69 to 1979		**B. NMP 1967–69 to 1979**	
West Germany	3.6	East Germany	4.9
Austria	4.4	Czechoslovakia	5.1
Italy	3.5	Hungary	5.4
Spain	4.5	Poland	6.3
Greece	5.6	Bulgaria	7.3
Portugal	5.0	Romania	9.3
Total	3.8	Total	6.3

Note: Eastern European data on a GDP basis were estimated by the UNECE by reweighting official sectoral NMP data to an approximate '1963 factor cost' price basis, by adding capital depreciation, and making an allowance for 'non-productive' services, based on employment data for that sector and an assumed 1 per cent annual increase in labour productivity.

Sources: UNECE, *Economic Survey of Europe in 1971*, Pt. I, New York 1972, for part A; OECD, *National Accounts of OECD Countries, 1950–1979*, and UNECE, *Economic Survey of Europe* (various issues), for Part B.

The pace of economic growth

It is probably safe to say that in Eastern Europe, as in Western Europe, post-war rates of economic growth were everywhere higher and fluctuations generally less than during the interwar years, though changes in national boundaries and/or inadequate statistics make precise comparisons virtually impossible in some cases. In most of the Eastern countries recovery from the impact of the 1914–18 war and the immediate post-war troubles was hardly completed before the mid-1920s. Thereafter, Bulgaria appears to have been relatively little affected by the 'Great Depression', and national income is estimated to have increased by about 4 per cent a year, but elsewhere growth rates were relatively low (between 1¼ and 3½ per cent per annum)[2] and similar to those recorded by Western Europe (Table 1.1). Despite differences of coverage and methodology these rates are

[2] Data assembled by B.R. Mitchell (*European Historical Statistics, 1750–1970*, London 1975) and N. Spulber (*The State and Economic Development in Eastern Europe*, New York 1966) show the following annual average growth rates for Eastern Europe: Czechoslovakia (GDP, 1924–37) 3.1 per cent; Hungary (NNP, 1925–37) 3.4 per cent; Poland (NMP, 1929–38) 1.6 per cent; Bulgaria (NNP, 1924–37) 4.3 per cent; Romania (NMP, 1926–38) 1.2 per cent. No data are available for East Germany, but a rough guess would be that the country grew at rates not very dissimilar to those of what is now West Germany, i.e. at some 3 per cent per annum between 1922 and 1937.

sufficiently below those shown in Table 9.3 for one to say with some confidence that growth accelerated in the period after World War II in all the countries of both East and West.

Turning to the post-war experience, inter-area comparisons are impaired by well-known differences in national accounting methodology. Part A of Table 9.3 shows, however, UNECE estimates of Eastern European growth in the 1950s and 1960s on a 'service inclusive' GDP basis. These suggest that growth in the two decades was very similar in Eastern Europe and in the sample of Western countries here chosen (some 6 per cent a year in both cases), though inclusion of the Soviet Union would boost the Eastern block's rate to 7 per cent per annum, while the inclusion of other Western European countries would bring the growth of OECD Europe down to not quite 5 per cent per annum. The two most industrialized Eastern European countries – the GDR and Czechoslovakia – appear to have experienced growth rates somewhat faster than those of Austria and Italy, though slower than that of West Germany; but allowing for the margins of error in the calculations, the differences may well not be very significant. Of the two 'intermediate' Eastern European countries, Hungary's growth rate appears to have been rather below those of the most rapidly expanding Western economies, and Poland's was about the same.

Bulgaria and Romania seem to have grown a good deal faster than less developed Western Europe. But in Romania and Bulgaria the 'monetization' of the economy could well have imparted a somewhat greater upward bias to the growth statistics than in the less developed Western economies, partly because of the collectivization of agriculture. Moreover, the disappearance of much small-scale trading and artisan activity probably resulted in reductions in some outputs never recorded in the statistics, so that some of the replacement production from larger-scale socialist enterprises appeared as a net addition.

Comparable data for the 1970s are not available, except for Hungary, where GDP growth accelerated to a 6.1 per cent annual rate during 1970–5 but fell thereafter. It is known, however, that in all the Eastern European countries employment in 'non-productive' services increased faster than total employment in the decade. A *very* rough adjustment[3] to the official data on the growth of NMP (which excludes the output of 'non-productive' services) shown in Part B of Table 9.3 would suggest that the growth of GDP in the first half of the 1970s was probably not very different in Bulgaria from the rate for the 1950s and 1960s shown in Part A of the table; it probably accelerated somewhat in Czechoslovakia and the GDR, and certainly there were accelerations in Poland and Romania. Though economic growth slowed down everywhere in the later 1970s, for reasons discussed below, the slowdown does not appear to have been as marked as that recorded in the West, so that, both for the 1970s as a whole, and for the 1974–9 crisis years, Eastern Europe grew faster than Western Europe.

The same would probably be true for the whole of the post-war period. While output in West Germany, Austria, Italy, and Spain (as well as Portugal) rose by some 5 per cent per annum between the early 1950s and the late 1970s and in OECD Europe as a whole by 4¼ per cent, the four more industrialized countries of the East appear to have achieved growth rates between about 5½

[3] On the lines described in the Note to Table 9.3.

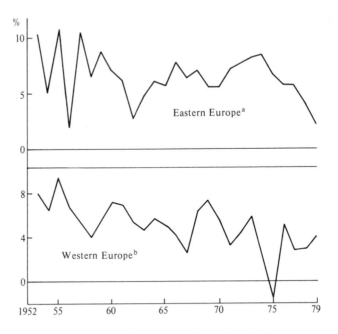

FIG. 9.1. *Cyclical fluctuations* (annual percentage changes in output)
[a] NMP, excluding Soviet Union
[b] GDP, sum of West Germany, Austria, Italy, Spain, Greece, and Portugal
Sources: UNECE, *Economic Survey of Europe* (various issues); OECD, *National Accounts of OECD Countries, 1950-1979*.

and 6½ per cent per annum. Greece recorded a similar rate of increase but Bulgaria and Romania probably expanded at annual rates of 7 to 7½ per cent.

Cyclical fluctuations

It could be expected that, despite higher growth rates, Eastern Europe would have exhibited greater cyclical stability than Western Europe, thanks to central planning. This is only partly borne out by Fig. 9.1, which shows that the amplitude of fluctuations in activity may have been roughly similar in the two 'comparable' groups of countries. Eastern Europe recorded pronounced swings from the early 1950s to the early 1960s, but smoother trends thereafter, at least until the late 1970s, while the six countries of Western Europe experienced several mild cycles in the first two decades and a pronounced recession in the mid-1970s.

These very aggregate findings are confirmed by Table 9.4, which presents a very simple proxy for the amplitude of fluctuations – the standard deviation of annual percentage changes in GDP and NMP. The figures, of course, are not strictly comparable. Thus, the use of NMP data probably imparts an upward bias to the East European indicators, since the output of 'non-productive' services is excluded. On the basis of Western evidence at least, this output could be expected to fluctuate much less than that of agriculture or industry. Allowing for this, the prima-facie impression is that there is no obvious tendency for growth rates to have been more stable in one area or the other. East Germany

TABLE 9.4. *Variability of output growth, 1953–1979*

	Average annual percentage change in GDP	Standard deviation		Average annual percentage change in NMP	Standard deviation
West Germany	4.8	2.9	East Germany	5.3	1.8
Austria	5.1	2.5	Czechoslovakia	5.4	2.7
Italy	4.7	2.4	Hungary	5.3	5.5
Spain[a]	5.3	3.0	Poland	6.6	3.1
Greece	6.1	3.1	Bulgaria	7.5	4.1
Portugal	5.2	3.0	Romania	8.7	5.3
Total	4.9	2.1	Total	6.4	2.1

[a] 1954–79

Sources: OECD, *National Accounts of OECD Countries*, 1950–1979; UNECE, *Economic Survey of Europe* (various issues).

certainly appears to have performed relatively well (indeed as well as the most stable Western economies, such as France or Norway), and so did Poland up to the mid-1970s or Hungary from the late 1950s onwards (the country's very high standard deviation reflects extreme instability in the 1950s — and not only the events of 1956). Among the less developed countries, however, Greece and Portugal appear to have experienced less variation than Bulgaria and Romania. It may be interesting to note that despite generally somewhat more pronounced individual country fluctuations in Eastern Europe, the amplitude of the area's overall 'cycle' seems to have been no larger than that of the Western European six. This would suggest that simultaneous fluctuations in activity were less marked in the East than in the West (which is more open to international demand and price transmissions).

Though cyclical fluctuations were experienced in both areas — and were, on the whole, relatively mild in both, particularly in comparison with the pre-war years — their causes were, of course, very different. The reasons for business cycles in Western Europe in the post-war period are well known and reflect mainly the interactions between government demand management policies and the two major 'exogenous' components of demand (exports and private investment). The upswings of the mid-1950s and the late 1960s were largely investment-led; the downswings of the period, on the other hand, reflected slowdowns in North America, particularly in earlier years, and, increasingly, the influence on economic policies of balance of payments difficulties and/or inflationary pressures. This was particularly true of 1975 (the only year in the three decades with negative growth). Governments, faced by unprecedented balance of payments deficits and price rises, deliberately swung into a very restrictive policy stance that accentuated a recession initiated by the shift of the terms of trade in favour of OPEC and an autonomous deceleration in consumer demand.

The story of variations in growth rates in Eastern Europe is very different, and one in which inadequate levels of foreign or domestic demand play no part. One major source of fluctuations was the agricultural sector. During the 1950s official attitudes to and measures affecting the private farms alternated between pressures intended to induce movement into the collectives, which discouraged production, and relaxation of such pressures, which tended to halt the process of collectivization but encouraged output. By the early 1960s collectivization was a *fait accompli* everywhere, except in Poland; but still agriculture as a sector had in most countries been starved for many years of both direct investment — in buildings, machinery, transport, and storage facilities — and also of inputs of fertilizers, pesticides, etc. The result was a level of technique which kept output very heavily dependent on weather conditions.

While the countries of the 'less-developed fringe' of Western Europe suffered rather similar — though less extreme — fluctuations in overall growth rates as a result of varying climatic conditions and consequent fluctuations in farm output, the 'developed' Western countries were far less susceptible than Eastern Europe. This does not only reflect the smaller shares of farm output in their economies but also the more advanced technical level of their agriculture and related facilities (grain-drying, storage, transport, etc.).

A second reason for fluctuations in Eastern Europe is to be found in changes in government policy objectives as well as in mistakes and inadequacies in planning and policies. As pointed out by a number of observers,[4] such factors led to the appearance of actual investment cycles in a number of East European countries which, in the earlier part of the period, were also partly synchronized across the area.[5] The process started usually with over-ambitious central investment plans and/or excessive eagerness of ministries and enterprises to invest; this led to too many starts on new projects, lengthening completion periods, intensified shortages of materials, balance-of-payments strains and/or pressures on living standards; cut-backs in investment authorizations followed, with a decline in construction output and probably decline or slower growth in other sectors as inputs were constrained by the need to right the balance of payments.

In the early 1950s the intense drive for industrialization adopted in every country as its Communist Party came to power reflected both the ambitions of national party leaders and also Soviet pressures, which were intensified as East–West relations worsened. National plan targets set for the first half of the 1950s, which were originally often over-optimistic as a result of an encouraging earlier recovery of output, were generally revised upwards under Soviet pressure and with an increased concentration on investment in heavy industry.[6] Resources were everywhere poured into large slow-maturing projects, shortages of fuels and materials intensified, and living standards generally stagnated or fell. With all the Eastern European countries concentrating on similar patterns of development, all faced similar shortages which could not be relieved by importing from Western

[4] J. Goldmann, 'Fluctuations and Trend in the Rate of Economic Growth in Some Socialist Countries', *Economics of Planning*, No. 2, 1964; K.A. Soós, 'Causes of Investment Fluctuations in the Hungarian Economy', *Eastern European Economics*, No. 2, 1975–6; J.G. Zielinski, *Economic Reforms in East European Industry — Poland*, London 1973.

[5] UNECE, *Economic Bulletin for Europe*, Vol. 18, No. 1, 1966; A. Bajt, 'Investment Cycles in European Socialist Economies: A Review Article', *Journal of Economic Literature*, March 1971.

[6] In Hungary, to take one example, an already ambitious investment plan for the five years 1950–4 was increased by 70 per cent in May 1951, and the allocation to heavy industry alone was doubled.

.countries, trade being inhibited both by political factors and by the lack of readily available and saleable Eastern exports. By 1952 or 1953, with bad harvests also depressing living standards, the strains became intolerable and pressures for investment and growth were relaxed, only to intensify again in the later 1950s.

Fluctuations in output in these years were very pronounced (as can be seen in Fig. 9.1). Hungary provides an extreme example – NMP rose by some 17 to 18 per cent in 1950 and 1951, but growth then decelerated to little more than 3 per cent a year over the next four years, to be followed by an absolute and considerable fall in output in 1956 as a result of the uprising and a fairly rapid recovery thereafter. No other country suffered such extreme fluctuations, but for the Eastern European countries taken together the strains induced by the intensity of the early investment drive brought about a reaction from an NMP growth rate of some 8 per cent annually during 1950–2 to about 5½ per cent a year from 1952 to 1954. Thereafter, the rate rose again to about 7½ per cent from 1954 to 1960. These fluctuations of course understate the sum of the swings in individual countries, since turning-points did not exactly coincide.[7]

The next period of 'recession' was 1960–3, when the growth rate fell to 4½ per cent on average, recovering to an annual rate of about 6½ per cent over the later 1960s. Some poor harvests, the effects on construction activity of one particularly bad winter, and the cutting of trade links with China all played some part in this slackening. But, again, a significant factor was a recoil from an over-intense investment drive. A rather satisfactory period of expansion after 1954, based partly on the coming into operation of capacities started in earlier years, led governments once again to adopt plans for intensified investment efforts and very rapid growth. Investment ratios generally rose in the later 1950s, too many new starts again produced mounting stocks of unfinished projects, and the increase of processing capacities – particularly in the heavy industries – again tended to outrun their 'feeder' industries.

Czechoslovakia and East Germany were the two countries which experienced the most marked slowdown in growth in the early 1960s. In the former country, the level of NMP was no higher in 1964 than in 1961, having actually fallen in 1963, and in the GDR the annual rate of growth fell to little more than 2½ per cent between 1960 and 1963 from about 8 per cent in the preceding three years. In both countries, labour shortage was becoming a constraint on growth by the end of the 1950s, and in both countries the authorities saw a need for changes in the pattern of expansion, both on this account and to relieve endemic balance of payments difficulties. Half-hearted 'reforms' resulting mainly in loss of central control, and a general economic and political malaise, revealed only later, complicated the picture in Czechoslovakia, while in the GDR preparations for the introduction of the 'New Economic System' announced in 1963 may have contributed to the slowdown.

The following decade was to witness rather steady growth in the area as a whole up to 1974, to be followed by a striking deceleration in the later 1970s. The only major 'cyclical' episode of the early 1970s was the acceleration of growth in Poland – largely made possible by substantial borrowing from Western

[7] UNECE, *Economic Survey of Europe in 1971*, Pt. 1, New York 1972.

sources to finance coinciding consumption and investment 'booms' — which was followed by a major crisis at the end of the decade.

Looking at the 'cyclical' experience of the two groups of countries over the three decades, there are both similarities and differences. The similarities are in the amplitude of fluctuations and in the presence of one common driving force behind these fluctuations, namely investment. The differences lie largely in the changing role of government policies. In the 1950s and 1960s, Eastern policies were to some extent engineering cycles — if unwillingly — while Western policies were trying to stabilize levels of activity, and with some measure of success (according to Chapter 10 below). In the later 1960s and in most of the 1970s, the amplitude of fluctuations in Eastern Europe diminished, while Western policies, faced with mounting difficulties, played an increasingly pro-cyclical role. At the very end of the decade, finally, inflation in the West and balance of payments problems in the East (to name only the two major difficulties) were forcing both sets of governments into increasingly restrictive policies.

Factors in growth

The similarities between the two areas are probably more pronounced when looking at the factors that propelled economic growth. Though pre-war data are scanty and unreliable, it seems almost certain that the acceleration of growth in the post-war period was accompanied by an acceleration of both labour and capital inputs in East and West alike. While it is almost impossible to assess the extent of this acceleration between the two periods, some comparisons of developments in the two areas are possible for the years after 1950.

Turning to labour first, the growth of the population of working age seems to have been roughly similar in Eastern Europe and in the sample of Western countries here considered (0.6 to 0.7 per cent per annum over the three decades). But labour inputs grew more rapidly in the centrally planned economies (around 1 per cent per annum, including employment in 'non-productive' services) than in the market economies (just over ½ per cent per annum) (Table 9.5). Participation rates fell in the West through most of the period (not only after 1973), while they rose in the East, particularly for women.

Within these broad aggregates, there were, however, substantial inter-country differences. In Western Europe, the growth of the active population was relatively uniform in five of the six countries here considered, with only Austria's stagnating. But the falls in participation rates varied — they were most pronounced in Italy and, to a lesser extent, in Western Germany and Austria, while relatively modest in the developing countries. Almost the opposite was the pattern in Eastern Europe, where participation rates fell quite sharply in Bulgaria and Romania (as a consequence not only of improving educational and pension provisions but also of migration from countryside to towns and relatively rapid natural population growth), while they rose elsewhere.

The most pronounced rise in activity rates was in the GDR, where the working-age population fell sharply in the 1950s as a result of wartime losses and emigration to the West (which of course allowed the Federal Republic's labour force to grow relatively rapidly).[8] In the mid-1960s the GDR had the highest

---

[8] Emigration from East Germany during the twenty years 1949–69 has been estimated

TABLE 9.5. *Growth of employment and labour productivity*
(average annual percentage changes)

A. 1950–52 to 1967–69

	Employment	Productivity[a]		Employment	Productivity[a]
West Germany	1.2	5.0	East Germany	0.4	5.3
Austria	0.1	5.0	Czechoslovakia	1.2	4.0
Italy	0.4	5.0	Hungary	1.0	3.8
Spain	0.8	5.3	Poland	1.8	4.2
Greece	0.9	5.0	Bulgaria	0.5	6.4
Portugal	0.2	4.9	Romania	0.9	6.2
Total	0.8	5.0	Total	1.1	4.9

B. 1967–69 to 1979

	Employment	Productivity[a]		Employment	Employment in the 'productive' sphere	Productivity[b]
West Germany	−0.2	3.8	East Germany	0.5	0.2	4.7
Austria	−0.1	4.5	Czechoslovakia	1.1	0.9	4.2
Italy	0.5	3.0	Hungary	0.6	0.3	5.1
Spain	−0.3	4.8	Poland	1.1	0.8	5.4
Greece	0.4	5.2	Bulgaria	0.6	0.1	7.2
Portugal	0.4	4.6	Romania	0.4	0.1	9.2
Total	0.1	3.8	Total	0.8	0.5	5.7

[a] GDP per employed
[b] NMP per employed

Sources: UNECE, *Economic Survey of Europe in 1971*, Pt. I, New York 1972, for Part A;
OECD, *National Accounts of OECD Countries, 1950–1979, and Labour Force Statistics, 1968–1979*, and UNECE, *Economic Survey of Europe* (various issues), for Part B.

overall activity rate in Europe, and although the rate for men later fell somewhat, women's participation continued to increase until by the mid-1970s there was an insignificant difference between the male and female activity rates (measured in relation to working-age groups). The mid-1970s picture in Czechoslovakia and Hungary, also countries with relatively slowly growing working-age populations, was similar to that of the GDR. At the other extreme, Poland had throughout an abundant labour supply. The 1½ per cent annual increase of the working-age population was the highest in Eastern Europe, and in Western Europe it was matched only by the Netherlands and Switzerland – both, and especially the latter, countries of large-scale immigration. The female participation rate rose in Poland also, thus contributing to the fastest growth of employment in any European country, excluding the Soviet Union.

A further contribution to overall economic growth came from the possibility of transferring workers out of agricultural into industrial (or service) employment

---

at some 2.9 million or 16 per cent of the population: G. Leptin and M. Melzer, *Economic Reforms in East European Industry – East Germany*, Oxford 1978.

without significant loss of farm output. While this happened everywhere in Europe during the period, the extent of the shift differed from country to country. Table 9.2 above suggests that, except in Eastern Germany, the transfers that took place were proportionately more important in Eastern Europe than in the West. Simple OECD estimates of the contribution of such intersectoral shifts to the growth of output put this at roughly 15 per cent for West Germany, 25 per cent for Austria, and 35 per cent for Italy over the years 1955–68.[9] A very rough guess would be that for Eastern Europe as a whole this contribution could come close to the Italian figure.

The contribution of elastic labour supplies to growth in the West probably exceeded the simple mechanical effects of shifts from low to high productivity sectors. In Kindleberger's well known dual-economy model, the presence of abundant labour depresses urban wages, boosts profits, encourages investments, and perpetuates growth,[10] an argument that is developed in Chapter 1 above. Such a mechanism was clearly not at work in Eastern Europe. Yet, arguably, elastic supplies of labour for the non-farm sectors may have boosted investment just as much, if not more, in the centrally planned economies, if only because planners knew that they could count on available labour reserves and could therefore embark on ambitious growth strategies.[11]

Turning to capital inputs, precise comparisons are virtually impossible, given significant differences in national accounting conventions. This is particularly true for capital stock data, which are difficult to calculate at best and which, even when available in the West, are not always comparable across countries. A better indicator of the investment effort should in principle be provided by shares of investment in GDP, but a comparison of such ratios between East and West is made difficult by differences in national price structures. Not only was turnover tax concentrated almost entirely on consumers' goods in the Eastern economies, but there were also at times heavy subsidies paid to some capital goods industries. The Polish Statistical Office attempted to calculate the distribution of net material national income in the mid-1950s at something like factor cost, and produced an estimated 28 per cent share for net accumulation (compared with 20 per cent at official market prices),[12] and this could be consistent with a similar or even slightly higher ratio of total gross investment to service-inclusive GDP. Western attempts to calculate such ratios have produced fairly wide ranges of figures. Zauberman's estimate of total gross investment (including stock accumulation) to service-inclusive GDP in the late 1950s suggests ratios of the order of 35 per cent for Poland and Czechoslovakia and of 25 per cent for East Germany.[13] A UNECE estimate on the same basis put the ratio in the late 1960s at some 35 per cent for the area as a whole, compared with about 25 per cent in industrial Western Europe.[14]

---

[9] OECD, *The Growth of Output, 1960–1980*, Paris 1970.

[10] C.P. Kindleberger, *Europe's Postwar Growth*, Cambridge, Mass. 1967.

[11] It is true, however, as was seen above, that in the early years of the period such strategies often turned out to be over-ambitious.

[12] UNECE, *Economic Survey of Europe in 1958*, Geneva 1959.

[13] A. Zauberman, *Industrial Progress in Poland, Czechoslovakia and East Germany, 1937–1962*, RIIA, London 1964.

[14] UNECE, *Survey in 1971*, Pt. 1.

Even allowing for a relatively high share of stockbuilding in output, which is characteristic of the Eastern European economies, these various figures suggest that the fixed investment effort in the 1950s and 1960s was greater in the centrally planned than in the market economies here examined, where the (current price) fixed investment shares ranged from a low of 15 per cent in Greece and Portugal in the 1950s to a 26 per cent peak in Austria in the 1960s, with an average figure of about 22 per cent for the two decades as a whole. There are also less direct indications of intense savings and investment efforts in Eastern Europe in the period. There was an extreme squeeze on personal consumption in Hungary in the early 1950s, and in other countries also standards stagnated for some years or actually fell. In every individual country gross fixed investment ratios rose from the 1950s to the 1960s, and over these two decades the annual growth of fixed investment in the region as a whole has been estimated at some 9½ to 10 per cent, compared with some 6 to 6½ per cent for personal and collective consumption[15] (the figures for the six Western countries here examined are 8½ and 5½ per cent respectively).

An important feature of the Eastern European investment drives was, however, their 'unbalanced' nature. In most countries of the area the expansion of the capital stock was very rapid in the industrial sector, but slow in construction, transport, and all other services. Of course, this reflects in part the long neglect of housing construction, but in other more 'productive' sectors growth of total output depended upon rising employment and rising labour productivity without any great increase in capital per worker. This implied an increasingly intensive use of certain types of equipment (e.g. the railways), and the smaller scale or virtual absence of other developments (e.g. road building and improvement or motor transportation) which were important in the West.

The differences in overall investment performance probably became more pronounced in the 1970s. In Western Europe investment ratios fell virtually everywhere in the later part of the decade, as a consequence of the recession, with the (current price) figure down to 21 per cent in the years 1974–9, whereas in the East investment ratios may, if anything, have risen further. A few available comparable figures in fact suggest such a conclusion. An official Polish estimate yields a ratio of 41 per cent in 1974, a year in which the import surplus was equivalent to 18 per cent of gross domestic investment; and an official Hungarian calculation for the same year shows a ratio of 36½ per cent, with an import surplus equivalent to 13 per cent of gross domestic investment.[16] On the other hand, for the one centrally planned economy, Hungary, covered by a recent study which has revalued national income data for a number of countries on the basis of, as nearly as possible, identical concepts and 'international dollar' prices, an average for 1970 and 1973 gives a ratio of gross capital formation (including net external investment or disinvestment) to GDP of about 27 per cent, compared with 25 per cent in Italy, but as much as 36 per cent in West

---

[15] Ibid.

[16] T.P. Alton, 'Comparative Structure and Growth of Economic Activity in Eastern Europe', in Joint Economic Committee, Congress of the United States, *East European Economies Post-Helsinki*, Washington 1977.

Germany.[17] In national prices the ratio was higher for Hungary and either un-changed or lower for the Western countries.

While in aggregate higher rates of investment were associated in the East with higher growth rates of output than in the West, it is more difficult to find evidence of a close relationship between the two variables for individual countries in either area. This is particularly true of the 1950s in Eastern Europe, where the country with the lowest investment ratio (East Germany) grew fastest, and that with the highest (Hungary) grew most slowly; and in the 1970s in Western Europe, where the fall in demand pressures distorted the relationship between growth and investment. However, in Western Europe in the 1950s (a period of relatively rapid and smooth growth) and in Eastern Europe in the 1960s, the link between investment and growth appears closer.

The evidence so far suggests that both capital and labour inputs grew more rapidly in the Eastern than in the Western European countries over the last three decades. Though overall growth was also more rapid, it is arguable that factor productivity growth was not,[18] particularly before the oil crisis depressed the performance of the market economies (Table 9.5). In other words, growth was more 'extensive' in Eastern Europe and more 'intensive' in Western Europe, and the role of technological progress less in evidence in the former than in the latter area. This may seem readily understandable for 'disembodied' technological progress, since the pursuit of 'X-efficiency' is usually lacking in a centrally planned economy, but could come as a surprise for 'embodied' technological progress, in view of the very considerable research effort made in every Eastern European country. There is ample evidence that this research effort has not produced commensurate advances in general industrial application, and this has probably been due to lack of incentives and bureaucratic impediments. It is true that an insatiable demand by industrial ministries and enterprises for investment resources is a feature of these economies, but this demand has tended to reflect ambitions to expand on the basis of existing techniques and products, not eagerness to innovate; and studies of the effects of the import of technology have revealed long delays before it was put to even limited effective use, and very slow, or non-existent, diffusion.

Whatever the absolute growth rates of capital and labour productivity may have been, both East and West probably recorded in the 1970s a slowdown, more pronounced on the labour side in the West (Table 9.5) and on the capital side in the East where the incremental capital–output ratio (on an NMP basis) rose from 4½ to 8 between the first and the second halves of the decade.[19] The Western deceleration in the growth of output per man seems to have been primarily due to the overall deceleration in growth rates of output. The slackening growth of capital productivity in the East may also have been affected by slower growth, but other longer-run factors were at work, e.g. the progressive

[17] I.B. Kravis et al., *International Comparisons of Real Product and Purchasing Power*, Baltimore 1978.

[18] This is confirmed by an earlier growth-accounting estimate by B. Balassa and T.J. Bertrand, 'Growth Performance of Eastern European Economies and Comparable Western European Countries', *American Economic Review*, May 1970.

[19] The acceleration shown in Table 9.5 for East Europe's labour productivity growth is entirely due to the change from a GDP to a NMP basis.

exhaustion of easily mobilized labour reserves and possibly the changing economic objectives in many countries – an enhanced priority for agriculture; a
genuinely increased concern with consumers' welfare, producing somewhat
greater emphasis on development of light industries and on housing construction; more interest in trade with Western countries. All such attempts to change
the pattern of growth could well have tended – temporarily at least – to lower
capital productivity, particularly within planning and management systems
which themselves made it difficult to achieve well-co-ordinated structural
change. At the same time the observed slowing growth of capital productivity
and of labour supplies, together with increasing stress on improving living
standards, everywhere resulted in growing official emphasis on boosting factor
productivity and less on increasing labour and capital inputs; and this, in turn,
has underlined the need for more efficient methods of economic planning
and management.

This leads to a consideration of the role of economic policies in the growth
process. Chapter 1 above has argued that this had been very important in Western
Europe. United States policies at the beginning of the period, in contrast to
experience after World War I, had greatly facilitated the European reconstruction
effort and imparted a momentum to growth that generated optimistic expectations. These expectations were then sustained in later years by the belief that
governments committed to full employment and growth would make efficient
use of demand management policies to these ends. The first factor, of external
support, was clearly lacking in Eastern Europe. Rather than granting aid, the
Soviet Union extracted reparations from the 'ex-enemy' Eastern European
countries in the early post-war years, and also tended to exploit Eastern Europe
generally through its foreign trade pricing. Only in the second half of the 1950s
did this picture change; reparations deliveries had come to an end and the mixed
companies had been dissolved, and, although it can be said that over the long
period every Eastern European country has been obliged to 'pull itself up by its
own bootstraps', some Soviet credits have been available to help tide these
countries over particularly difficult times, and Soviet pricing in foreign trade had
by the 1960s ceased to be exploiting. At times, indeed, it has since tended to be
more favourable to some of the USSR's Eastern trade partners than trade on a
strict 'world-price' basis would have been.[20]

Government management of the economy has, of course, taken completely
different forms in Eastern Europe from those in the West. Whether the central
planning system has raised Eastern growth rates above what they would otherwise have been is difficult to assert with complete confidence, in that the alternatives to central planning that might have been are unknown. What one can say
is that throughout most of the post-war period fast growth and, particularly,
rapid expansion of heavy industry was the major aim of economic policy. The
central planning system effectively squeezed high rates of saving and investment
out of relatively poor societies, assured full employment and massive redeployment of labour from agriculture to industry (and even an excessive mobilization

---

[20] In principle, intra-CMEA trade has until recently been conducted at the world prices
of a particular year or average of years, these changing at fairly long intervals. For the
change in the second half of the 1970s, see below.

of labour in some countries), and generally proved effective in concentrating resources on the limited range of top priority objectives of the earlier years. The
system had its inefficiencies, to some extent linked with the intense drives for
maximum output at all times and for rapid growth. There was some obvious
waste of resources in various forms – some investment projects abandoned un-
completed, or having to be reconstructed or scrapped, excessive use of materials
to produce goods to meet output targets fixed in terms of gross value or of
weight, etc. There was also less obvious waste in the form of too diversified
patterns of production with loss of scale, irrational patterns of foreign trade,
tying-up of resources in too slowly completed investment projects, and excessive stock accumulation. In addition, there was a general tendency not to
match detailed output patterns at all closely to the preferences of the users and
consumers of those outputs. These inefficiencies undoubtedly held per caput
output at any time below the level it would have reached in a 'model' centrally
planned economy. Some of them were probably more significant for the more
highly industrialized and/or more trade dependent economies than for the
Soviet Union, Bulgaria, or Romania; and they also tended to become more
important, as brakes on economic growth, as labour 'reserves' diminished or
were exhausted and the objective of increasing living standards reached a
higher priority.

However, it may be doubted whether these inefficiencies have very significantly slowed the long-term rates of growth of these economies, even if they
were becoming more significant by the 1970s. In other words, an overall judgement on the planning experience remains positive. The planners wanted growth
and achieved it. Western policy-makers probably wanted growth as well, even if
aims were not as clearly spelt out, but had fewer means at their disposal to obtain it. In the event, they were also successful, helped, as in the East, by permissive supply conditions. But their success stemmed more from a fortunate
combination of events than from conscious design, as the events of the later
1970s were to show.

II. Unemployment, Inflation, and External Relations

Traditionally, the main concerns of Western governments' demand management
policies have been seen as unemployment, the rate of price inflation, and the
state of the balance of payments. The first has hardly been a 'problem' in
Eastern Europe, and although planners in those countries have certainly been
concerned to limit price inflation and to achieve satisfactory balances of payments, the constraints under which they have operated have been very different
from those affecting their Western opposite numbers.

Unemployment

Though post-war levels of unemployment in the West were much lower than
those of the pre-war years – and were much lower in the late 1960s than in the
early 1950s as structural unemployment was absorbed – cyclical (or demand-
deficient) unemployment was none the less recorded at times, and particularly
so since 1973. But though fluctuations in activity have also occurred in post-
war Eastern Europe, there has been no officially recognized unemployment in

any of these economies throughout nearly the whole period. Some unrecorded, usually very short-term, 'frictional' unemployment has undoubtedly existed, but 'cyclical' unemployment has generally been kept within the farm or factory gate. Workers once taken on by an enterprise could not easily be dismissed, except for gross misconduct (political or other), and the normal climate of intense pressure for output and relative disregard of costs made enterprise directors generally willing to absorb available labour, even when it could not be fully employed.

There have been reports at times of shortages of opportunities for non-farm employment in particular regions or in some small towns, but while attempts were everywhere made — continuously or spasmodically — to limit the rate of migration to the large urban centres, the migrants who reached these centres were generally readily absorbed into employment. It is true that one Western estimate of Soviet unemployment (on comparable 'Western' definitions) obtained a figure of 1.3 per cent of the labour force in 1962-3.[21] But even if such a figure were applicable to Eastern Europe, it would still compare relatively favourably with most of the Western figures of the time (e.g. ½ per cent for West Germany, 4 per cent for Italy, 2¼ per cent for Spain, 2¾ per cent for Austria), let alone with the much higher rates experienced in the years 1974-9 (3 to 5½ per cent on average in the countries here examined).

Indeed it could be argued that in Eastern Europe (and particularly in those countries with abundant labour supply) employment was 'fuller', and the leisure available — particularly to married women and the elderly — less, than should have been necessary to achieve the levels of output actually registered, at least in the earliest years. Intense pressure to expand output in the priority producer-goods sectors meant that everywhere in the 1950s, and in most countries into the 1960s, enterprises could exceed their plan targets for employment and/or wage bill if they also produced more than their planned levels of output. With priority for material inputs given to the producer-goods sectors, it was in these sectors that output and employment targets were most likely to be exceeded, and plans for consumer-goods production were frequently underfulfilled because of shortage of material inputs. Thus, above-plan numbers of wage-earners and below-plan consumer-goods production tended to result in slow — and slower than planned — growth of per caput real wages; and this tended to drive more married women and old people to seek work in order to achieve an adequate family income, thus giving another turn to a spiral of too intense employment and depressed labour productivity and real per caput wages.

Some idea of this state of 'over' full employment is provided by Table 9.6. which shows ILO estimates of male, female, and elderly participation rates in the two areas in 1970. It will be seen that for the last two categories of workers, activity rates were usually higher in the Eastern countries than in their Western counterparts, and often by very large percentages. While the high participation rates of women and the old in Poland, Bulgaria, and Romania may have been largely due to the persistence in these countries of sizeable agricultural populations, the female participation rates of Czechoslovakia and East Germany

[21] P.J.D. Wiles, 'A Note on Soviet Unemployment on U.S. Definitions', *Soviet Studies*, April 1972.

TABLE 9.6. *Participation rates, 1970*
(percentages)

	Male[a]	Female[a]	Older workers[b]		Male[a]	Female[a]	Older workers[b]
West Germany	92.3	48.2	9.7	East Germany	96.1	69.8	15.1
Austria	88.5	50.9	5.5	Czechoslovakia	84.0	65.7	9.2
Italy	84.9	30.6	8.4	Hungary	85.5	59.0	9.0
Spain	92.2	21.5	12.1	Poland	88.5	71.2	41.8
Greece	92.5	42.1	19.4	Bulgaria	90.6	67.3	24.5
Portugal	101.2	29.8	26.0	Romania	96.7	74.8	39.2
Total	90.2	36.5	10.9	Total	90.5	69.3	24.9

[a] Total labour force in per cent of population aged 15 to 64
[b] Labour force aged 65 and more in per cent of population aged 65 and more
Source: ILO, *Labour Force Estimates and Projections, 1950–2000*, Geneva 1977.

are particularly striking. Indeed, the 70 per cent figure recorded by East Germany was above that of all Western European countries at the time (only Sweden and Denmark reached rates of just over 70 per cent in the very last years of the 1970s).

Inflation

While the fact of virtually full employment as a normal state in Eastern Europe is undisputed, there is more dispute about the claim that these economies also avoided inflation — at least after the raging inflations of the immediate post-war years were brought to an end, as they were everywhere by the early 1950s.[22]

In the consumer-goods markets, price stability after the early 1950s was impressive, at least as measured by official price indices. Over the twenty years to 1975, the consumer price index fell in the GDR and rose by less than ½ per cent annually in several other countries (the most rapid rise recorded was an average annual increase of about 1½ per cent in Poland). In the next quinquennium the rates of increase gradually accelerated, though exceeding 2 per cent only in Hungary and Poland (where they reached 6 to 7 per cent). This record is to be set against annual increases up to 1975 ranging from a low of 3¼ per cent in West Germany to a peak of 8 per cent in Spain, not to mention the double digit rates of most West European countries in the later 1970s.

But the official price indices are widely mistrusted, both in the Eastern European countries and by most Western observers. It is argued that in some countries they incorporate only 'official' prices and not those charged in the free markets (important for foodstuffs), and that they do not reflect the replacement of low-priced goods (no longer available though still in the official price lists) by higher priced variants which do not represent genuine improvements in quality. It is also true that the effective price to the consumer of particularly scarce goods may be increased by conditional sales, black market transactions, bribery, and the time spent in queues (or money spent on hiring 'queuers').

---

[22] What follows is a brief summary of part of the author's paper 'Inflation in the USSR and Eastern Europe', in S.F. Frowen (ed.), *Controlling Industrial Economies*, London (forthcoming).

Whether the incidence of such extra charges has increased over time is perhaps doubtful; on the other hand, the incentive for concealed price rises — when enterprises claim higher prices for spurious improvements in the quality of their products — may well have increased. A higher price could always be to the advantage of an enterprise with an output or sales target fixed in gross value terms; in the 1970s, an increasing emphasis on profit among enterprises' success indicators probably added to the incentive to raise prices where this was possible.

An estimate by the President of the Hungarian Price Office of the incidence of concealed price increases 'in conditions of market tension' in Hungary put it at an extra 2 per cent a year to be added to the official consumer price index.[23] A number of attempts by Western observers to check official data on either price trends or changes in consumers' real incomes have led to similar conclusions — that the understatement of the annual rate of price increase in these countries by the official indices is probably no more than about 1 to 2 per cent a year.

If so, there still was, by Western European standards, an impressive degree of consumer price stability up to the mid-1970s, with the average annual increase held to some 3 per cent or less in most countries, though somewhat greater in Poland. If one asks how this was achieved, the short answer is through control of wage bills and of personal incomes of farm families (via control of farm gate prices) on the one hand, and through the planning of an equivalent volume of supplies of consumer goods on the other. This system was, of course, not watertight. 'Wage-bill drift' has not been unknown, and sudden changes in priorities (e.g. in favour of defence), a worsening of the terms of trade, or, above all, a bad harvest could cause problems for the fulfilment of supply plans.

But temporary increases in tension in the consumer-goods market did not result in any automatic diversion of resources from investment or exports; shortages caused irritation but were not automatically relieved by means which could hamper the achievement of other objectives. Moreover, increases in wage costs per unit of output were not automatically transmitted to domestic market prices, at least in the short run — the possibility always remained of 'recouping' the rise in unit costs in subsequent years. The danger of a cost–price spiral was (and still is) minimal in these countries as compared with those of Western Europe.[24] Finally, consumer credit could be tightly controlled and advance payments for particularly scarce goods could be used both to encourage and to immobilize consumers' savings.

While there is little dispute about the achievement of relatively slow rates of price inflation in Eastern Europe, there is less agreement among both Eastern and Western observers about the degree of suppressed inflation in the consumer-goods market. Certainly, people have been obliged to accept patterns of consumption different from what they would have chosen if, with their existing money incomes, unlimited supplies of all goods and services had been available at the actually ruling prices. In the early years, virtually everything available was absorbed by the consumer; increasingly since the late 1950s shortages of some goods and services have been accompanied by a tendency for stocks of others to

[23] B. Ciskós-Nagy, 'Profit in Socialist Economy', *Economie appliquée*, No. 4, 1972.
[24] Not all the foregoing argument is applicable to Hungary under the 'New Economic Mechanism'.

build up – unsaleable until prices were cut or production patterns changed. Personal savings deposits have risen everywhere, and at times the increases have certainly reflected shortages of goods to buy rather than 'voluntary' savings; but there is little doubt that living standards were high enough by the mid-1970s for people to choose to hold large money balances, in the hope of eventually finding the goods they wanted rather than immediately taking what they could get.

External relations

In Western economies foreign trade has tended to play a dual role in economic growth. On the one hand, the opening to international exchange has led to welfare-enhancing resource reallocation and, more importantly, has stimulated competition and probably investment. On the other hand, countries have become more vulnerable to cyclical fluctuations both at home and abroad as well as to changes in competitiveness, since these have translated themselves into balance of payments problems and/or exchange rate changes. The seen need to maintain a given parity, or a particular surplus on current account, has often become a constraint on economic policy-making.

A very summary judgement on Eastern Europe would be that the planning system has diminished both the advantages and disadvantages potentially resulting from rising trade dependence, and that it is questionable whether the actual development of foreign trade has been particularly helpful to Eastern Europe's economic growth. In the immediate post-war years political pressure from the Soviet Union, later reinforced by Western trade policies including 'strategic controls', forced the Eastern European countries to concentrate on trade with the USSR and with each other. This concentration reached a peak in ·1953 when intra-CMEA exchanges accounted for 65 per cent of the area's total trade. Thereafter this share decreased only slowly until the 1970s when, partly as a consequence of relative price changes, it declined to 52 per cent in 1979 – national percentages ranging from 74 per cent in Bulgaria to 35 per cent in Romania.

But trade dependence nevertheless increased. From 1955 to 1970, the trade of Eastern Europe (including the Soviet Union) grew in volume by 8½ per cent a year – a rate very similar to that of Western Europe as a whole but somewhat less than the 11½ per cent recorded by the group of Western countries here selected. Import elasticities for the same period (ratio of trade growth to growth of output) were estimated at about 1.2 for Eastern Europe and 1.8 for Western Europe as a whole, with export elasticities identical at 1.7. Over the subsequent years, up to 1978, the import elasticity for the former area rose slightly and the export elasticity appears to have fallen to about 1.2.[25]

But although the growth of trade dependence after 1955, as measured by import or export elasticities, was fairly similar in Eastern and Western Europe, the degree of trade dependence was probably less in the Eastern European countries than in their most comparable Western neighbours. A tentative UNECE estimate of deviations between calculated and actual ratios of trade to GDP (the calculated ratios being a function of per caput income levels and population size) suggested

[25] UNECE, *Survey in 1971*, Pt. 1, and *Economic Bulletin for Europe* (various issues).

that the three more industrialized Eastern European countries (East Germany, Czechoslovakia, and Hungary) were much less trade-dependent than virtually all Western industrialized countries in the 1950s and 1960s. On the other hand, Spain, Greece, and Portugal's calculated trade ratios were well above their actual values, in contrast to Bulgaria and Romania which, in fact appeared, 'too' trade dependent.[26] More recent comparable figures are not available except for Hungary, for which, on Western definitions, the export ratio stood at some 25 to 30 per cent in the mid-1970s, a figure close to that of the larger Western European countries, but well below that of the smaller ones.

Increasing trade dependence in Eastern Europe was not accompanied by increasing liberalization of trade. While virtually free and multilateral trade and payments were progressively established as the norm in post-war Western Europe, the trade of the Eastern European countries continued to be conducted on the basis essentially of national central planning and bilateral balancing. Medium-term (usually five-year) trade agreements between pairs of CMEA countries were the framework within which 'operational' annual trade agreements and some long-term contracts were negotiated; payments were normally intended to balance, subject only to small short-term credits. There has even been a strong tendency for exchanges of 'hard' goods (those generally in short supply within the area or readily saleable in Western markets) and of 'soft' goods to be separately balanced in each exchange.[27]

Nor did CMEA achieve very much success in planned sector-by-sector integration. Efforts up to the end of the 1960s took two main forms – joint investment in new capacities in areas of common interest, and specialization agreements intended to ensure that potential economies of scale were realized in lines of production where they could be significant. In fact, effective specialization agreements seem to have been rather few, though by 1977 they were said to cover about 20 per cent of total intra-CMEA trade and about 34 per cent of intra-trade in machinery.[28] The preference system was always one of 'nationally administered' preference, not formalized in a common external tariff, and the 'world prices' at which intra-CMEA trade was in principle conducted clearly did not reflect relative costs, or relative scarcities, within the area. Any proposed specialization agreement was thus quite likely to encounter opposition either from a country protesting that it was being asked to expand capacity for too low a reward in relation to cost or from potential customers for the product who would have preferred to remain free to buy – with more choice of quality – from the Western world or to expand or install their own capacity. In these circumstances, while trade did alleviate shortages to some extent, it clearly did not play its role of a resource allocator to the same extent as in the West.

On the other hand, bilateral balancing meant that balance of payments problems could in theory be avoided. In practice, they appeared in the form of shortages which could not be filled with imports, for lack of suitable export supplies. In the West the emergence of deficits usually led to restrictive policies and to a deceleration of growth; incipient or actual deficits in the East had

[26] UNECE, *Economic Bulletin for Europe*, Vol. 21, No. 1, 1970.
[27] Z. Juhar, 'Commodity Trade in Consumer Goods', in T. Kiss (ed.), *The Market of Socialist Economic Integration*, Budapest 1973.
[28] UNECE, *Economic Bulletin for Europe*, Vol. 30, No. 1.

often similar effects, mainly because of the appearance of unavoidable bottle-necks. But in the 1970s, some Eastern balance of payments deficits came into the open, in the form of larger trade gaps and mounting levels of indebtedness to Western countries.

However, while the disadvantages of the CMEA countries' trading principles and practices may be obvious, it may still be asked whether losses through allo-cative inefficiencies were not balanced — at least in relation to the objective of rapid economic growth — by the advantages of their chosen system. The con-centration on intra-trade lessened their vulnerability to demand fluctuations in the Western world, national planning made it possible to concentrate foreign exchange resources on the satisfaction of priority needs, and the negotiation of trade agreements and long-term contracts with CMEA partners gave some degree of certainty to both flows of imports and export possibilities. The balance of advantages and disadvantages probably varied from one country to another, with the most naturally trade-dependent countries tending to lose most from allo-cative inefficiency and the Soviet Union to lose very little.

III. Reactions to the Post-1973 World

The impact which the oil crisis had on the West is well known. Combined with an earlier commodity price boom and with restrictive policies originating in growing anxieties about domestically generated cost-pressures, it led to a sharp acceleration of inflation, to the first real post-war recession, and to record levels of unemployment. More seriously, it appeared to destroy the momentum of Western growth. Despite ample margins of spare capacity, Western Europe was unable to return to earlier rates of expansion in the later 1970s, nor did in-flation decelerate much as the recession developed — even before the second oil price rise at the end of the decade.

Eastern Europe did not remain unaffected by these developments, but thanks to its planning system the impact was more diffused. While in the West, the oil price rise had, at one and the same time, an inflationary effect (via cost-push pressures on oil users), and a deflationary effect (via a reduction in aggre-gate demand consequent upon a purchasing power shift from high to low ab-sorbing countries), neither of these effects was directly significant in the East.[29] But the Eastern European countries were affected by the inflation-cum-recession in the industrialized West, and there was a lagged change in terms of trade within the CMEA area as a consequence of the OPEC decision. It was lagged because the CMEA countries decided to move from a system using average 1965-9 world prices in their intra-trade to a system using five-year moving averages of world prices in 1975. The immediate effect was estimated as improvements in the Soviet Union's terms of trade with individual Eastern European countries ranging from some 2½ per cent *vis-à-vis* Poland and Romania to some 12 to 20 per cent *vis-à-vis* Hungary, Czechoslovakia, and Eastern Germany.[30]

---

[29] For a comprehensive discussion of how the oil crisis impinged on Eastern Europe see R. Portes, 'Effects of the World Economic Crisis on the East European Economies', *The World Economy*, June 1980.

[30] M.R. Kohn and N.R. Lang, 'The Intra-CMEA Foreign Trade System: Mayor Price Changes, Little Reform', in Congress of the United States, *East European Economies*.

TABLE 9.7. *Indicators of performance, 1973–1979*

	1972–1976	1973–1979		
	Change in terms of trade[a] (percentages)	Slowdown in growth[b]	Reduction in absorption[c]	Change in indebtedness[d] ($ billion)
		(average annual percentage changes)		
East Germany	−13.7	−0.5	−0.7[e]	4.5
Czechoslovakia	−11.3	−0.4	−0.9	2.0
Hungary	−12.7	−0.3	2.2	5.0
Poland	− 2.5	−1.7	−0.2[e]	14.5
Bulgaria	− 7.3	−1.4	−1.7	2.0
Romania	..	−2.4	..	3.9
Total	− 8.8[f]	−1.2	−0.4[g]	31.9

	1972–76	1973–1979		
	Change in terms of trade[h] (percentages)	Slowdown in growth[j]	Reduction in absorption[c]	Current balance[k] ($ billion)
		(average annual percentage changes)		
West Germany	−7.1	−2.1	0.3	26.2
Austria	−2.6	−1.9	−0.1	− 8.6
Italy	−19.9	−2.7	−1.1	2.3
Spain	−10.8	−4.5	−0.3	−10.7
Greece	−9.1	−4.1	−0.8	− 6.9
Portugal	−18.5	−4.2	−0.8	− 5.3
Total	−10.8	−2.6	−0.2	− 3.0

[a] Goods only
[b] Difference between actual and planned NMP growth
[c] Difference between total domestic demand and NMP/GDP growth
[d] Between end-1974 and end-1979
[e] 1973–78
[f] NMP weights; excluding Romania
[g] Excluding Romania
[h] Goods and services
[j] Difference between actual and average 1960–1973 GDP growth
[k] Cumulative current balance, 1974 to 1979
Sources: R. Portes, 'Effects of the World Economic Crisis on the East European
Economies', *The World Economy*, June 1980; OECD, *National Accounts of
OECD Countries, 1950–1979*, and *Economic Outlook*, July 1981; UNECE,
Economic Bulletin for Europe, Vol. 32, 1980.

The indirect effects of the Western recession were felt mainly through increased competition in, and more difficult access to, Western markets, and,
again, through a worsening in the terms of trade. Some estimates of the overall
change in the terms of trade are presented in Table 9.7. These almost certainly
underestimate the longer-run deterioration suffered by the GDR, Czechoslovakia,
and Hungary since, in 1976, some further increases of energy prices in intra-
CMEA trade were still to come. Allowing for this, it could be argued that the
two groups of countries shown in the table may have fared relatively similarly
in aggregate, with the richer countries doing best in the West and the poorer
ones in the East.

It is not easy to distinguish the impact of the terms of trade changes and of
increased Western competition and protectionism from the effects of other
forces also at work in the later 1970s and indigenous to the Eastern economies −

input constraints, inefficiencies, policy changes, or errors. But relative to the West, the impact on employment was non-existent and on inflation was small. While the rate of unemployment rose from 3 per cent in 1973 to 5½ per cent in 1979 both in Western Europe as a whole and in the present sample, full employment was maintained in the centrally planned economies. Most Eastern European governments also continued to operate their economies with stable, or only very slowly rising, consumer prices until the end of the decade. In Bulgaria annual rates of increase were below 1 per cent until 1978, when a 1½ per cent rise was followed by a 4½ per cent increase in 1979. In Czechoslovakia a rise of 4 per cent in 1979 followed annual increases ranging from less than one per cent to 1½ per cent in earlier years. East Germany reported almost complete price stability throughout the decade; in Romania increases of less than 1 per cent a year were followed by rises of 1½ to 2 per cent in 1978 and 1979. These very modest accelerations of consumer price increases at the end of the decade seem everywhere to have reflected decisions to limit or reduce the mounting subsidy bill bridging the gap between producers' and consumers' prices, itself reflecting *inter alia* increasing energy prices.

Hungary and Poland were, however, the exceptions to this general picture of continuing relative price stability. The initial Hungarian reaction to external inflation was to preserve domestic stability by subsidizing some imports and tightening control both of home-market prices and of wage increases. But to preserve an equitable income distribution it then proved necessary to introduce special taxes to skim off profits of enterprises realizing particularly high prices for their exports (often incorporating subsidized imported inputs). There was a tremendous proliferation of enterprise-specific special taxes and subsidies, which soon made rational calculation of the likely future profitability of any contemplated investment virtually impossible for the enterprise, and so led to a marked extension of *de facto* control of investment, once again, by the industrial ministries. Progress in bringing the 'New Economic Mechanism' into full operation was halted, and to some extent reversed. Despite subsidies rising to the equivalent of 14 per cent of the total value of retail trade turnover by 1979, the annual rate of increase of the consumer price index averaged nearly 4½ per cent between 1975 and 1978 and rose to 9 per cent in 1979 – this increase reflecting the government's announced decision to undertake a drastic realignment of domestic prices to reflect the international price structure, to sweep away within a short time the accretion of special taxes and subsidies, and to resume progress towards a 'market economy'.

In Poland the average annual rate of increase of consumers' prices between 1974 and 1979, at 5¼ per cent, exceeded those in all other countries of the region (and even that of West Germany). The reasons were many: deliberate increases in farm prices intended to improve incentives; the half-hearted reforms of the economic system which gave enterprise directors, with profit as a 'success-indicator', incentives to raise prices where possible; wage increases, conceded at least in part in recognition of popular discontent, producing excess demand pressure as domestic inefficiencies (including poor levels of farm output) and balance of payments problems limited supplies to the consumers' market. Even so, subsidies to consumer prices mounted, to account for some 40 per cent of total budgetary expenditure by the end of the decade, and the recorded price increase did not prevent accentuating shop shortages, black-market dealings, and other symptoms of suppressed inflation.

Though price inflation accelerated, it was generally mild in comparison with rates in the West. But the deceleration of economic growth in Eastern Europe was pronounced. Growth rates declined everywhere. Some decline might have been expected, in the light of shrinking labour supplies, and had been foreseen in the Five Year Plans for the second half of the 1970s, but the planned rates of expansion were not in fact achieved – the shortfalls ranging from ¼ per cent per year for Hungary to over 2 per cent for Romania for the years 1973-9 (covering the recession years in the West; see Table 9.7). For the Western countries, the table shows the difference between longer-run (1960–73) trend growth rates and actual output growth in the post-1973 years. The figures almost certainly over-estimate the slowdown from the 'potential' rate in these countries, since some deceleration from the rates of the 1960s could have been expected in the 1970s already before the oil crisis; but they still suggest that the effects of the crisis were significantly greater in the West than in the East.

The shortfall in the centrally planned economies' growth rates was not en-tirely due to worsened terms of trade or balance of payments difficulties. The adverse effects of these two factors were reduced by the relative ease with which the Eastern countries found themselves able to raise credits in the West to finance part of their import bills. This meant that the reduction in absorption that was necessary to pay for the terms of trade shift was delayed – something that occurred in Western Europe as well. Indeed, Table 9.7 shows that, on the Western side, only West Germany and Italy were able to restore current account balance over the period – West Germany thanks to a sharp recession already in 1974, Italy via a protracted squeeze on domestic absorption. But elsewhere in both areas, though domestic demand grew more slowly than total output (except in Hungary), net indebtedness also rose (or net asset positions fell), particularly in Poland and Spain.

By the end of the decade most of the Eastern European economies, but also the less developed Western ones, were still facing balance of payments problems which could constrain their growth in the future. Over the years 1973-9, how-ever, the centrally planned economies undoubtedly performed more favourably. The system partly sterilized and partly delayed the effects of world changes in the terms of trade and Western recession; and the West's willingness to lend further lengthened the lags between terms of trade and absorption changes. There was thus relatively moderate recession, no rise in unemployment, and no open runaway inflation, and though the growth of living standards slowed down, this decleration was less marked and probably less unevenly spread than in the West.

Conclusions

The preceding brief look at Eastern and Western European economic perform-ance in the post-war period suggests that both experiences were 'success stories'. By the standards of the pre-war years or earlier, growth was very rapid in both sets of countries, full employment was ensured or nearly ensured through most of the period, and fluctuations in activity were usually mild. Given the relatively limited economic contacts between East and West, particularly at the outset, this growth process must have been largely endogenous to each area and its main propelling forces need not have been the same.

In fact, a number of factors were similar. Thus, labour supply was abundant during most of the period in all the countries here considered (except Austria and East Germany), transfers of labour from agriculture to industry boosted productivity growth in both sectors, and saving and investment ratios rose to unprecedented heights everywhere. The West benefited at the outset from Marshall Aid, and throughout the period from imported American technology, but may have suffered from the transmission of cyclical fluctuations via the foreign trade multiplier, with attendant balance of payments crises and restrictive policies. Eastern Europe imported little technology and was insignificantly helped by aid or credit flows from the USSR or any other source; but the more developed countries enjoyed relatively favourable terms of trade within the CMEA in the 1960s and early 1970s, and the near-absence of transmission of intra-area fluctuations in activity may have helped all countries by facilitating the planning process.

The crucial role in the growth experience seems, however, to belong to the government. In the West, this was indirect, as argued in Chapter 1 above. The belief in the government's power to control and stimulate the economy strongly contributed to raising business expectations and therefore investment, with success breeding further success. The process was, however, temporary. When the mid-1970s crisis broke out, governments were seen not to be as all-powerful as had perhaps been assumed. The momentum was broken, confidence declined, and countries, with varying degrees of commitment, returned to more *laissez-faire* policies. In the East, the role of planning was much more direct, since it was the central plan which mobilized the available labour and capital resources in a conscious and determined effort to raise growth rates. Planning was the real 'engine of growth', and despite early errors, a successful one both in the relatively calm 1960s and in the more troubled 1970s, when East European governments were able to dampen the unfavourable effects of terms of trade changes and Western recession. But the weaknesses of the planning and management systems became more apparent in the East as exhaustion of 'reserves' made efficiency increasingly important; and the fashionable late 1970s accusation in the West against 'too much government' was increasingly paralleled in the East by one of 'too much planning'.

In Western Europe the most pressing question must be whether the 1980s will see a return to anything like full employment as understood, and experienced for much of the time, in the post-war years up to 1973. The answer may well depend first on whether, and how quickly, government policies in the major countries intended to control inflation and to change expectations about future inflation, work. If they do appear to be effective in the reasonably near future, the second question will be whether national demand management policies become effectively expansionist and without involving 'beggar-my-neighbour' measures. The third question will then be whether labour market conditions, government policies, and the future 'rules of the game' of international trade and payments can once again permit general expansion, not crippled – in one country or in all – by excessive, or excessively varied, resumption of cost inflation and/or balance of payments problems. If present policies, placing major emphasis on countering inflation, do not work, the question becomes simpler to ask and impossible to answer — when and how will policy priorities, and policies, change?

Western growth in the 1980s is thus likely to be determined mainly by the growth of overall demand. The Eastern European prospect is very different. Not only is there full employment, but in the more industrialized countries, at least, easily mobilized reserves of labour (married women, pensioners, surplus farm workers) have virtually ceased to exist. Similarly, much of the 'inherited' capital stock in infrastructure (particularly in transport) has been used too intensively in the past and needs urgent improvement and replacement. At the same time, commitments to, or popular pressures for, raising living standards, on the one hand, and persistent difficulties in raising farm output, complicate balance of payments problems (intensified in several cases by debt-service commitments to the West) and/or constrain investment efforts. Barring an unlikely technological 'leap forward', these supply prospects imply a slowdown which is, indeed, incorporated in the planned growth rates of the 1981–5 Five Year Plans — noticeably less ambitious than any past plans in all the countries for which targets have yet been published. And while there is no reason to suppose that the inefficiencies of the planning and management systems, which have been reiterated for so long by both Eastern and Western commentators, are getting worse, they may be becoming a more important constraint now that growth increasingly depends on raising factor productivity.

Bibliography

Comparative studies of Eastern and Western European economies are few, but developments in both regions are regularly reviewed in the UNECE's *Economic Survey of Europe* (annual), *Economic Bulletin for Europe* (varying number of issues each year), and occasional additional studies. Specifically comparative East/West studies by the UNECE include: *Some Factors in Economic Growth in Europe during the 1950s* (*Survey* for 1961, Part II); *Structural Trends and Prospects in the European Economy* (*Survey* for 1969, Part I); *The European Economy from the 1950s to the 1970s* (*Survey* for 1971, Part I); *Labour Supply and Migration in Europe* (*Survey* for 1977, Part II); and *Structure and Change in European Industry*, 1977.

In addition to the UNECE *Surveys* and *Bulletins*, works covering a number of Eastern European countries (not always with explicit comparisons) include: Joint Economic Committee, Congress of the United States, *Economic Developments in Countries of Eastern Europe*, Washington 1970; H.-H. Höhmann, M.C. Kaser, and K.C. Thalheim (eds.), *The New Economic Systems of Eastern Europe*, London 1975; D. Granick, *Enterprise Guidance in Eastern Europe*, Princeton 1975; Z.M. Fallenbuchl (ed.), *Economic Developments in the Soviet Union and Eastern Europe*, New York 1975; Joint Economic Committee, Congress of the United States, *East European Economies Post-Helsinki*, Washington 1977; F.D. Holzmann, *International Trade Under Communism*, London 1976.

On individual countries interesting surveys can be found for *Bulgaria* in R. Feiwel, *Growth and Reforms in the Centrally Planned Economies — The Lessons of the Bulgarian Experience*, New York 1977; for *Czechoslovakia* in J. Goldmann and K. Kouba, *Economic Growth in Czechoslovakia*, New York 1969;

and H. Gordon-Skilling, *Czechoslovakia's Interrupted Revolution*, London 1976; for the *GDR* in G. Leptin and M. Melzer, *Economic Reform in East European Industry – East Germany*, Oxford 1978; for *Hungary* in M. Timár, *Reflections on the Economic Development of Hungary 1967–1973*, Budapest 1975, and P. Hare, H. Radice, and N. Swain (eds.), *Hungary, A Decade of Economic Reform*, London 1981; for *Poland* in J.G. Zielinski, *Economic Reforms in East European Industry – Poland*, London 1973; and for *Romania* in I. Spigler, *Economic Reforms in East European Industry – Romania*, Oxford 1973.

PART II

ECONOMIC POLICIES

10

Demand Management

JOHN BISPHAM AND ANDREA BOLTHO*

Introduction

Demand management policies may be defined as those concerned with regulating the total amount of expenditure in the economy by acting, via changes in fiscal and monetary instruments, on the major components of aggregate demand. The need for regulation arises from the presumption that a modern mixed economy, if left uncontrolled or subject merely to some simple fiscal or monetary 'rule', would exhibit unwelcome or excessive fluctuations in the level of employment, while if controlled in much greater detail would probably show less efficiency and open or hidden tensions on the price front. Demand management would presumably not be necessary in a perfectly competitive self-stabilizing market system or in a perfectly planned centralized economy, but it was felt to be clearly required in Western Europe in the period under review.

At the outset, and throughout the 1950s, its function was first to achieve a high level of utilization of resources, and then to assure the maintenance of this level in as stable a way as possible. No doubt views differed across Europe on the appropriate role of government intervention, but it would seem generally accepted that in that decade reductions in unemployment levels were seen as a prime target for policy in a large number of countries. The aims of demand management policies were relatively clear and so were its achievements – unemployment fell rapidly to levels which bore no comparison to those of the interwar period and were even below those which the early inspirers of demand management (e.g. Beveridge in the United Kingdom or Myrdal in Sweden) had hoped for.

The successes of the 1950s – which were not, of course, due solely to demand management – probably led policy-makers into increasingly ambitious views of what could be achieved – views which became progressively more apparent in the course of the 1960s. Low unemployment remained a priority, but it was coupled with a number of other aims which governments increasingly felt were within their reach – not just high employment but also rapid growth, not only the avoidance of pre-war-type recessions but the evening-out of more minor fluctuations. It is in this decade that the term 'fine tuning' gained general acceptance, without the pejorative overtones which it acquired in the 1970s. Yet precisely at the time at which ambitions were growing, the nature of the problems facing Europe was changing – intermittent balance of payments difficulties and a more generalized acceleration of inflation imposed (usually temporary)

* Bank for International Settlements, Basle and Magdalen College, University of Oxford respectively. The views expressed are those of the authors and do not necessarily reflect those of the BIS. The authors would like to acknowledge the helpful comments received on an earlier draft from W.A. Allen and W.H.B. Brittain formerly of the BIS and from Chris Allsopp, who, of course, bear no responsibility for any errors of fact or logic which remain.

redirections of the aims of demand management away from the 'real' preoccupations of employment or stabilization to the more 'financial' ones of the price
level and the level of foreign reserves.

This redirection became much more pronounced in the 1970s when the context in which demand management policies had to operate changed sharply. The
most fundamental difficulty was the rapid acceleration in domestic inflation.
But policy had also to cope with a commodity price boom, two major oil price
hikes, and the accompanying disequilibrium in world payments, and with the
new environment of floating exchange rates. The reaction to this period has
often been described as a retreat from traditional demand management towards
the use of simpler (more or less fixed) policy 'rules'. While no doubt the academic
world moved in this direction, experience up to the late 1970s suggests that
there was little real change in the way governments used their instruments. What
gradually changed were the goals of policy-makers. The decade was marked not
so much by a retreat from demand management as by a retreat from the short-
term full employment goal towards policies aimed at controlling inflation.

These changing views must be borne in mind when looking at the record of demand management policies over the period. Far too often successes or failures have
been assessed rather narrowly in terms of just stabilization or employment levels.
This is perhaps appropriate for the 1950s and 1960s, which are surveyed in the
first two sections of this chapter. Section I outlines the various attitudes to demand
management which prevailed in European countries throughout the period.
Section II reviews policies and assesses their success. It looks, in particular, at the
frequently formulated criticism that demand management policies, even in this
era of high growth and low unemployment, were, in practice, destabilizing.

Assessments of this kind are no longer appropriate for the 1970s, when demand management policies were used, and often quite actively, but with different
aims in mind. This more troubled decade forms the background for the Section
III survey of the 'retreat from full employment'. Finally, the Conclusions take
a somewhat longer-term view by arguing that demand management policies,
whatever their short-run effects on their primary targets — be these unemployment or inflation, the balance of payments or the trade cycle — can also be
assessed in a longer-run perspective as one of the important influences shaping
expectations and behaviour over the whole period. Much greater government
intervention in the economy than hitherto may well have added to the longer-run
expansionary forces at work in the 1950s and 1960s, just as it may well have
worsened the pessimistic atmosphere and climate which prevailed in the 1970s.

While both the chapter's narrative and the assessment in principle cover the
twin instruments of demand management — fiscal and monetary policies — in
practice the emphasis is more on the former in view of the presence in this
book of a chapter specifically devoted to monetary policy.[1]

I. The 1950s and 1960s — Instruments and Policies

The Keynesian 'revolution'

The implementation of demand management policies in the 1950s and 1960s
was marked by three major breaks with the past:

[1] Ch. 11 below.

(i) The increased importance of government revenues and expenditures which conferred a greater potential role to automatic stabilizers;

(ii) The acceptance by most governments that budget deficits could be tolerated, at least in the short run, which transformed the increased degree of potential stabilization into actual stabilization;

(iii) The additional willingness, by some governments at least, to supplement the counter-cyclical workings of automatic instruments with discretionary measures as well.

Reliable data on pre-war public sector revenues and expenditures are not always available, but on the basis of the, admittedly imperfect, evidence assembled in Table 10.1, which covers only selected public transactions, there would seem to have been a very sharp increase in the weight of taxation between the pre-depression years and the early 1950s (the 1930s were omitted from the table because recession and rearmament distort some of the figures). Piecemeal evidence on the expenditure side also suggests a similarly sharp break between the

TABLE 10.1. *Selected indicators of pre- and post-war government transactions* (in per cent of GNP at current prices)

	Central government revenues		General government non-defence consumption expenditure	
	1928–29	1950–51	1929	1950
France	13.8[a]	20.4		
Germany	8.1[b]	16.6	11.8	10.8
Italy	12.3[c]	15.2[c]	4.6	8.6
United Kingdom	16.7	31.3	7.1	9.8
Spain	12.8	7.7		
Austria	9.5	17.3		
Belgium	16.3[d]	18.4		
Denmark	6.0[c]	9.5[c]		
Finland	15.5	21.8		
Ireland	12.5[e]	18.9		
Netherlands	7.8	24.2		
Norway	8.3[c]	15.8[c]	6.7	6.6
Sweden	7.5[c]	13.2[c]	7.6[f]	12.9[f]
Switzerland	4.0[c]	7.5		
Average	10.8	17.0		

Note: figures, particularly for the first two columns, are not strictly comparable for a variety of reasons and are shown only as an indication of broad trends.

[a] 1925–34

[b] NNP rather than GNP

[c] Revenues for financial years, GNP for calendar years

[d] 1927

[e] 1929

[f] Including defence expenditure

Sources: B.R. Mitchell, *European Historical Statistics, 1750–1970*, London 1975; A. Boltho, 'Course and Causes of Collective Consumption Trends in the West', in R.C.O. Matthews and G.B. Stafford (eds.), *The Grants Economy and Collective Consumption*, London 1982.

late 1920s and the post-war period, at least for some countries. Through the 1950s and 1960s, as is well known, this trend continued. All the European economies experienced rising public expenditures as a proportion of total output, together with the higher rates of taxation needed to pay for them. In addition, all strengthened and/or widened the scope of their public social security systems, including unemployment compensation, while existing tax systems were made more progressive.[2] Though these developments were usually motivated by longer-term social aims, they provided, as a very important by-product, a considerable degree of automatic counter-cyclical stabilization to the budgetary systems.

This, of course, would not have been sufficient *per se* to prevent the occurrence of a serious cumulative downturn had governments not been willing to face the consequences of slowdowns or recessions in the form of larger budget deficits. In this respect too the post-war period stands in marked contrast to earlier years, in great part, probably, thanks to Keynesian prescriptions. As is well known, at the core of Keynesian economics lies the notion that the balance of the government budget can be used to influence the level of total spending in the economy. Thus, if spending by the private sector is insufficient to ensure full employment, the government can step in with corrective 'overspending' of its own – a budget deficit. This simple but revolutionary notion flew in the face of the conventional wisdom of the 1930s, which held that governments, like any prudent private individual, should always balance their accounts. Hence, when the economy was subjected to a deflationary shock, budgetary policy tended at times to reinforce the deflation rather than correct it.

This was not a universal reaction, of course. It was true for the United Kingdom and also for France and Germany in the very early 1930s, when orthodoxy prevailed and governments tried to cut back expenditures to counteract falling tax revenues, thus compounding the original shortfall. But it was already less true, at that same time, of Italy, where the state came to the rescue of large industrial sectors threatened by bankruptcy, and became progressively less true through the decade as the governments of various countries (e.g. Germany but also France, and, of course, 'New Deal' America) intervened to sustain demand.[3]

However, these various attempts at counteracting cyclical developments remained limited, and were, essentially, of an *ad hoc* nature. It required Keynesian economics to provide a theoretical underpinning for such policies, and the experience of World War II to show that the possibility of full employment had not vanished. The combination of these two factors strongly contributed to the changed climate of the 1950s and 1960s. Temporary deficits were now accepted with a much more relaxed attitude than hitherto, and the counter-cyclical working of automatic stabilizers was understood and indeed welcomed in a number of countries.

Keynesian economics had, of course, further implications for the conduct of economic policies. As mentioned earlier, the Keynesian 'revolution' did not

---

[2] See Ch. 7 above and Ch. 13 below.

[3] See, for instance, R. Boyer and J. Mistral, *Accumulation, inflation, crises*, Paris 1978, Ch. 8; P. Ciocca and G. Toniolo (eds.), *L'economia italiana nel periodo fascista*, Bologna 1976; or W. A. Lewis, *Economic Survey, 1919–1939*, London 1949.

consist solely in a recommendation to tolerate budget deficits in cyclical down-turns, and, possibly, surpluses during booms. It also envisaged more active inter-vention, since experience had shown that while automatic effects could serve to check any disastrous slide in activity, they were not sufficient to prevent sig-nificant cycles from occurring. To avoid this, discretionary action was also required in the form of both fiscal and monetary measures (e.g. reductions in taxation, increases in expenditure, cuts in interest rates, removal or easing of credit controls, etc.). This latter message was probably received with less enthu-siasm in some European countries at the start of the period — particularly those that had suffered from too much government intervention in the 1930s. But it gained ground progressively, and by the late 1960s had become part and parcel of the 'consensus' view of economic policy-making, having received explicit approval by the OECD in the form of a well-known report by an international group of experts.[4]

While in principle, therefore, demand management had become one of the main economic instruments in the hands of all European policy-makers in the 1950s and 1960s, its actual use differed between countries for a variety of reasons. Some of these were ideological — the *commitment* to demand manage-ment varied across Europe in part at least because of political preferences, with social-democratic countries generally more in favour of active counter-cyclical policies than Christian-democratic ones. Other reasons were more economic — the *need* for counter-cyclical policies differed depending, for instance, on the openness of the country and on the stability/instability of its private sector. Others, finally, were institutional — the *ability* to engage in fine tuning could be severely constrained by the availability and effectiveness of the necessary instruments.

The commitment to demand management

Looking at the degree of active commitment to demand management first, one can begin with a broad-brush classification of the European economies. It would seem fairly clear that those most committed to intervention were the United Kingdom, Norway, Sweden, and, possibly, Austria, while those apparently least committed were Germany, Switzerland, and, in the 1950s perhaps, the Nether-lands. There was also a third, intermediate group comprising France, Italy, and Belgium (with the possible inclusion of Spain and Finland). Over time, however, there was also some tendency for movement between groups — for example, the Netherlands clearly moved away from their non-interventionist stance in the 1960s, and Germany behaved similarly. In addition, there was perhaps changing emphasis as the two decades unfolded. The 1950s were still dominated in many cases by post-war reconstruction problems, while the 1960s saw a fairly general movement (at various levels of commitment) towards more intervention.

To some extent these different attitudes to demand management were really different attitudes to policy goals, which were in turn a function of subjective values. While countries no doubt varied in the extent to which they wished to engage in fine tuning, the more relevant distinction was really between those that gave priority to employment and those that did not. The latter tended to

[4] W. Heller *et al.*, *Fiscal Policy for a Balanced Economy*, OECD, Paris 1968.

be not so much less interventionist as more conservative in their fiscal and, especially, monetary policies. Past experiences clearly played a role in this. Thus Germany was especially concerned to avoid inflation, partly because of the two hyperinflationary episodes within living memory. Countries which had only experienced unemployment as their main interwar problem saw the situation in a different light and were more prepared to compromise earlier principles of 'sound finance'. An illustration of these various attitudes to policy is provided by the notions of what constituted a 'balanced' or neutral budget in some European countries: For once the simple rule was abandoned that the budget should always balance, the question arose of how to assess any particular imbalance given the well-known two-way causation between the economy and the budget due to automatic stabilizers.

Among the more fiscally conservative countries, the Netherlands in the early 1960s evolved the notion of the 'Structural Budget Deficit'.[5] This held that tax rates and expenditure plans should be set so that at full employment the public sector balance would be equal (with the opposite sign) to the sum of the full employment private sector suplus and a balance of payments surplus on current account of the order of 2 per cent of GNP. The hypothetical full employment level of private investment was calculated so as to be compatible with the medium-term growth of the economy, while the target external surplus was to be the 'real' counterpart of aid flows to developing countries and other 'structural' capital outflows. Another way of looking at the Dutch rule is to say that government borrowing was to be restricted to what could be financed in the capital market without recourse to money creation. That is, only 'genuine' *ex-ante* savings were to be tapped. It is interesting to note that there was a monetary counterpart to this early fiscal rule. Already in the 1950s Dutch monetary policy had stressed the need for a relatively steady and not fully accommodating stance embodied in a target for the 'liquidity ratio' (or ratio between nominal income and a relatively broad monetary aggregate).[6] Yet this early combination of a money supply policy and of a fiscal rule was accompanied by an elaborate system of incomes policies and, increasingly in the 1960s, by more detailed fiscal policy changes taken in the framework of so-called Dutch planning.[7]

A little later a rather similar guideline concept, the 'Cyclically Neutral Budget', was put forward in Germany by the semi-independent Council of Economic Experts.[8] A base year, 1966, was chosen, in which the economy was thought to be at full employment. So long as any actual budget incorporated the same proportion between government expenditures and potential GNP and the same ratio of tax revenues to actual GNP as in the base year, it was defined as neutral.

At the other end of the spectrum, the United Kingdom apparently felt little need for some such theoretical justification for deficit financing. In fact, it probably came as close as any country in Europe to adopting the position that

---

[5] See, for instance, D.A. Dixon, 'Techniques of Fiscal Analysis in the Netherlands', *IMF Staff Papers*, November 1972.

[6] See Ch. 11 below.

[7] OECD, *Techniques of Economic Forecasting*, Paris 1965, Ch. IV.

[8] See, for instance, T.F. Dernburg, 'Fiscal Analysis in the Federal Republic of Germany: The Cyclically Neutral Budget', *IMF Staff Papers*, November 1975.

the real thrust of the budget should be such as to achieve the required pressure of demand at a (fairly early) specified time, with the implication for the budget balance being simply accepted as the inevitable and harmless accompaniment. The same might be said of Sweden. Before 1960, however, there was here a strong feeling that, although the budget should be varied according to the state of the cycle, it should nevertheless on average be in surplus.[9]

Degrees of commitment were also influenced by beliefs about the inherent stability/instability of the private sector. The interventionists tended to fear that the economy, left to itself, would be unacceptably erratic, while others took comfort from theories stressing the self-correcting forces at work. In addition, however, the interventionists probably hoped for wider benefits from a secularly high level of activity and employment. On the one hand, by encouraging both investment and labour mobility, it was hoped that the long-run efficiency of the economy could be substantially improved. On the other, and in complete contrast to the 'demand pressure' view of inflation, it was sometimes hoped (particularly in the 1960s) that by offering a high level of employment, organized labour could be brought into more harmonious co-operation with the two other 'social partners', business and government. In this way, low nominal wage rises might be traded for high employment and, possibly, larger real wage gains than otherwise. Austria was perhaps the outstanding case of success in this respect, a success which continued, at least relatively, through the more turbulent 1970s. But Norway and Sweden can also be cited for a large part of the period. The outstanding contrary case was, of course, that of the United Kingdom, where even fairly explicit attempts at some form of 'social contract' were a failure. Conversely, it is possible to point to counter-examples among the less interventionist countries. Germany and Switzerland enjoyed a high degree of non-inflationary consensus between the social partners, as well as high and growing levels of output and productivity, without any overriding commitment to full employment policies.

The need for demand management

On a rather more objective level, there is also the question of how much need there was in fact for discretionary action to even out the cycle. This probably varied across countries depending on a number of factors. One of these, which has already been mentioned, was the almost universal growth in the relative size of the public sector, which automatically increased the degree of built-in stability in fiscal systems. This was due in particular to the rise in unemployment compensation payments on the expenditure side and income-elastic tax receipts on the revenue side. It is not easy to document precisely either of these phenomena, but according to OECD figures the (cyclically adjusted) value of unemployment benefits in the EEC area rose from 0.4 to 0.7 per cent of GDP between the early 1960s and the early 1970s,[10] while evidence presented by Hansen suggests that tax elasticities with respect to GDP were above unity in the 1955–65 period in all the six European countries he surveyed (the four largest economies, Belgium, and Sweden) and, in his judgement, particularly high

[9] Heller, *Fiscal Policy*, p. 58.
[10] OECD, *Public Expenditure on Income Maintenance Programmes*, Paris 1976.

in the latter two countries and in France.[11] This rising weight of automatic stabilizers had important consequences which went beyond the borders of each country. Single economies were cushioned against cumulative declines in activity, not only by their own fiscal systems, but by those of their trading partners as well.

Greater overall stability in the world economy clearly lessened the need for stabilization policies at home. Rapid growth in world trade had similar consequences, since buoyant export demand supplemented strong domestic investment growth in progressively reducing unemployment, particularly in the 1950s. This implied that active fiscal or monetary intervention to stimulate activity was often unnecessary, particularly in countries which had begun the period with either elastic labour supplies and/or favourable exchange rates (e.g. Germany, Italy, Spain, the Netherlands). Demand management was required, particularly in the 1960s, to cope with balance of payments problems given that the automatic return to equilibrium which would have been assured by the monetary consequences of persistent surpluses or deficits was felt by all governments concerned to be far too protracted and, therefore, unacceptable. But the need for demand management obviously differed depending on the nature of the balance of payments problem. In Germany (and to a lesser extent in the Netherlands until the early 1960s), continuous surpluses stimulated inflationary pressures and monetary policy was used to reduce them. But as monetary policy was tightened, with the current account already in surplus, there were disruptive inflows of short-term capital which threatened either to push up the exchange rate, or to undermine the domestic stance of monetary policy itself. In France (in 1957-8 and again in 1963 and 1968-9), in Italy (in 1963 and in 1969-70), and in the United Kingdom (throughout the period until 1967), the problem was of an opposite kind. The emergence of balance of payments deficits required restrictive policy moves; the subsequent rises in unemployment called for a return to stimulation.

With the exception of Italy, all the countries just mentioned used the exchange rate weapon, but initial reluctance to revalue or devalue meant that demand management policies were necessary. The balance of payments swings that called them forth, were, however, often a function of domestic forces rather than of sudden cyclical changes in foreign demand. This is evident if one looks at the development of the two most volatile major demand components (apart from stockbuilding), which are also the ones least amenable to government control — gross fixed investment and exports (of goods and services). Though export instability was often an important element in such cyclical developments as occurred (e.g. in the 1958 recession and, to some extent, in the 1972-3 boom), it would not seem to have been severe. This is difficult to document precisely, but using a very simple proxy for instability (the standard deviation of annual percentage volumes changes), it appears that exports were a more stable component of demand than gross fixed investment in most of the European countries over the period (Table 10.2). This is even true for some of the small and very open economies of the Benelux or Scandinavia, in which fluctuations seem clearly to have been moderate relative to the absolute growth of exports. The

---

[11] B. Hansen, *Fiscal Policy in Seven Countries, 1955-1965*, OECD, Paris 1969.

TABLE 10.2. *Variability of exports and investment, 1955-1973*

	Gross fixed capital formation		Exports of goods and services	
	average annual percentage change	standard deviation	average annual percentage change	standard deviation
France	7.4	2.0	9.0	6.0
Germany	5.1	4.8	8.9	3.8
Italy	5.2	6.0	12.1	5.1
United Kingdom	4.8	4.2	4.5	3.5
Spain	8.7	6.4	14.6	14.1
Austria	6.9	5.1	9.9	7.4
Belgium	4.9	5.7	8.3	3.9
Denmark	7.5	6.4	6.6	2.3
Finland	5.3	5.9	7.3	5.4
Ireland	6.2	8.9	6.9	5.1
Netherlands	5.5	6.8	8.9	3.6
Norway	4.5	7.2	6.7	3.3
Sweden	4.7	3.0	7.5	3.4
Switzerland	6.0	6.5	7.0	3.1
OECD Europe	5.9	2.2	8.0	2.5

Source: OECD, *National Accounts of OECD Countries, 1950-1979* and *1953-1969*.

only exceptions are France, Spain, Austria, and Sweden, and of these the case of Spain is partly explained if it is borne in mind that as late as in the early 1970s, over half of the country's exports consisted of agricultural commodities and tourist receipts, both of which are a good deal more volatile than manufactured exports.

The lack of great cyclical variability in exports was probably due to both demand and supply factors. On the demand side, as already mentioned, world trade grew relatively steadily. On the supply side, exports often played an automatic stabilizing role, being increased in periods of domestic slowdown and curtailed in booms. This would seem to have been the case in all the major countries. At a simple level, clear episodes of counter-cyclical export performance can be found in Germany during the 1967 recession and in Italy between 1964 and 1969, when weak demand pressures at home were an important factor behind rapid export growth and the achievement of a current balance surplus equivalent to nearly 3 per cent of GDP. More formally, relative demand pressure variables were found to be statistically significant for France, Germany, and Italy (as well as Belgium)[12] in two OECD world trade models, while for the United Kingdom there is a body of evidence suggesting some counter-cyclical export behaviour as well.[13] In some of the smaller countries, in addition to the possible workings of this mechanism, the composition of exports may also have played a role. Thus in Sweden, for instance, the presence of both primary products and manufactures

[12] F.G. Adams, H. Eguchi, and F. Meyer-zu-Schlochtern, *An Econometric Analysis of International Trade*, Paris 1969; L. Samuelson, 'A New Model of World Trade', *OECD Economic Outlook – Occasional Studies*, December 1973.
[13] Surveyed in A.P. Thirlwall, *Balance of Payments Theory*, London 1980, Ch. 9.

in total exports, the demand cycles for which tended to offset each other, helped overall stability.

The presence of fairly pronounced instability for total investment spending suggests, on the other hand, that policy might have been needed to control this component of demand. This conclusion is reinforced by the observation that the only two countries which experienced very smooth investment growth — France and Sweden — were also those that most actively intervened in this area. In France, the environment provided by indicative planning,[14] as well as considerable fiscal aid to private investment and management of public investment,[15] were all factors which probably played a role. In Sweden, the main form of government intervention was a cyclical investment tax mechanism (or Investment Fund System) which allowed firms to deduct from taxes in boom periods funds which they undertook to use for investment purposes during slowdowns. According to the available evidence, this system was able to modify the timing of investment decisions in a counter-cyclical way.[16]

In summary, therefore, owing to the presence of domestic and foreign automatic stabilizers, and in a climate of relatively rapid growth, it would seem that the need for an active stabilization policy was perhaps not as pressing as had been expected at the beginning of the period, when memories of the 1920s and 1930s were still vivid. Private and public consumption behaviour was relatively steady, and so was foreign demand. Unemployment was rapidly declining in many countries, and in a number it did not represent a major constraint because of the existence of a large number of immigrant workers. At a time of recession, members of this section of the labour force moved back to their countries of origin (Southern Europe, Northern Africa, but also Finland or Ireland). Thus the unemployment consequences of recession, at least as measured in, say, Germany or Switzerland, were less than in other cases, and downturns did not lead to as much political pressure for counter-cyclical action as they might otherwise have done.[17] The major source of 'exogenous' cyclical instability came from the investment side, and it is really only in this area that government intervention would seem to have been required.

While the discussion so far may suggest that demand management policies in fact had only a minor stabilizing role to play (apart from their use in responding to undesirable balance of payments or inflation developments), this partial assessment ignores, of course, the fact that the apparent *ex-post* self-stabilizing capacity of the European economies in this period was not fortuitous. Indeed, in many ways it could be argued that it was the *ex-ante* knowledge of the presence of an armoury of counter-cyclical weapons which stabilized the economy and lessened the *ex-post* need for active intervention. The concluding section will return to this theme.

[14] A point made, for instance, by J.-J. Carré, P. Dubois, and E. Malinvaud, *French Economic Growth*, Oxford 1976.

[15] See Ch. 15 below, and OECD, *Economic Survey of France, 1975*.

[16] A. Lindbeck, *Swedish Economic Policy*, London 1975, Ch. 6.

[17] The extreme example was probably Switzerland, where even during the major recession of 1975, when output fell by 7½ per cent, the unemployment rate rose to only 0.3 per cent of the labour force.

The ability to manage demand

In addition to differing value judgements and different objective needs for active stabilization policy, European countries have differed in their technical ability to engage in active demand management. In particular, the availability and effectiveness of the necessary instruments has varied considerably between countries. Thus in France, for instance, the traditional centralization of all ad-ministrative decisions (whatever its other drawbacks) allowed a close and con-tinuous supervision of both public and private economic activity. In Germany, on the other hand, after the war, the government decision-making process was deliberately decentralized by the occupying powers, making the co-ordination of fiscal policy in the interests of national stabilization very difficult. This may have been one factor behind the relatively slow attainment of full employment during the 1950s. The authorities apparently systematically overestimated the German contribution to the occupation costs and underestimated fiscal drag,[18] so that large budget surpluses appeared. But with no major centralization of the budgetary process, any offsetting action would have been difficult to engineer, even if it had been desired. In Switzerland, too, given the high degree of devo-lution of fiscal powers to the cantons and communes, it was basically only monetary policy which could be used as a national economic policy tool.

However, in Germany, as the disadvantages of too great a reliance on mone-tary instruments became apparent in the 1967 recession, some changes were made. New legislation, the 'Stabilization Law', was passed which, in addition to certain administrative changes facilitating easier use of discretionary fiscal policy, affirmed four major aims of policy (growth, low unemployment, stable prices, and external balance), where previously there had, *de facto*, been only one – steady prices. In the event, Germany's apparent move into the ranks of the 'demand managers' coincided with the general acceleration of inflation in the late 1960s. Hence, reluctance to support the level of employment at the ex-pense of any inflationary risk remained an important feature of German policy.

Even where more centralized fiscal systems existed, there were still problems in some cases in using them for demand management purposes. For example if, as in Italy, there were long and uncertain delays in the collection of taxes, timely stabilization measures were difficult to implement. Indeed, they could very easily turn out to be pro-cyclical, and were indeed so in some years of the period, according to Hansen.[19] Alternatively, if tax receipts were not lagged, pro-cyclical behaviour could still arise if government agencies exhibited what Myrdal called a 'natural budget reaction',[20] and immediately increased their expenditure in response to rising revenue – something which has been known to happen in some countries. There were also, on occasion, problems connected with the control of public expenditure regardless of revenue considerations. In particular, spending at the local authority level sometimes led a life of its own – for example in the United Kingdom and in the Netherlands. And even at the central govern-ment level large capital spending projects could have an uncertain timing profile – for example as a result of the vagaries of the weather and terrain in the cases

---

[18] Heller, *Fiscal Policy*, p. 45.
[19] Hansen, *Fiscal Policy*, p. 316.
[20] Ibid., p. 306.

of major construction projects, or just because of bureaucratic inefficiencies, as was the case in Italy.

On the tax side, too, the administrative practice of scheduling budgets only once a year could obviously be a constraint on timely intervention. This was certainly felt to be the case in the United Kingdom, where in the early 1960s the government attempted to ease this constraint with the introduction of the 'regulator'. This was a statutory provision to permit the government to vary certain indirect tax rates, within specified limits, at any time of the year without prior parliamentary approval.

On the monetary policy side, the limitations on timely action were clearly less severe, and the power of discretionary changes much greater. But problems could arise because of lack of co-ordination (or even of agreement) between governments and central banks in those cases in which the latter were either formally, or *de facto*, relatively independent from political pressures (e.g. Germany, Italy, or Switzerland). Also, monetary policy was seen to suffer from a number of limitations which diminished the efficacy of demand management policies in those countries which mainly relied on it. In particular, its impact tended to be asymmetrical – being more effective in reining in booms than in stimulating an upswing. Also its effects tended to be heavily concentrated on rather narrow sectors like house-building or business investment – both elements of expenditure that governments usually wished to encourage, rather than re-duce, in the interests of welfare and longer-term growth. Finally, the efficacy of monetary policy during the period was increasingly eroded by the international mobility of financial capital, which led at times to massive and disruptive shifts of funds across the exchanges in response to interest-rate variations.

Nevertheless, monetary policy was used in Europe throughout the period, and particularly in the 1960s, partly to back up fiscal policy, and partly to re-place it when it was felt that fiscal policy formulation or implementation were subject to considerable lags arising from political, institutional, or administrative constraints. In Germany, up to the mid-1960s, it was virtually the only instru-ment used to control export-led booms – though with undesired effects on foreign capital flows. Italy too was forced to place heavy reliance on monetary policy because of inadequacies in fiscal instruments. Elsewhere, it was usually the case that a certain amount of monetary ease or restraint marched in step with fiscal counter-cyclical policies.

Finally, the degree of openness of the economy could also affect the technical ability to influence the pressure of demand. Partly this was a question of the constraint imposed by the balance of payments. The greater the share of imports in domestic spending, the more any demand management stimulus affected the external balance, and the less did it affect the demand for domestic output. Partly it was a function of the internationalization of the domestic capital market. The greater this was, the smaller was the effectiveness of monetary policy (under fixed exchange rates) in controlling activity. The former con-straint was particularly strong for the small and very open economies; the latter for those larger economies whose currencies were used for international trade (the United Kingdom, but by the end of the period also Germany) or which had developed important international financial markets at home (again the United Kingdom and Germany, but also Switzerland).

II. The 1950s and 1960s – Results and Achievements

Was policy destabilizing?

Any assessment of the effectiveness of demand management policies over the two decades from the early 1950s to the early 1970s faces a number of difficulties. For one thing, it is not always easy to know what particular aim the authorities of any country were pursuing. While a high and stable level of employment was clearly desired everywhere, demand management also affected other important variables such as the balance of payments and, possibly, price stability. Though these should more aptly be regarded as constraints, for many countries they came to be viewed as desirable objectives in themselves, between which trade-offs were believed to exist.

Second, even if one knew precisely what the aims of policies had been, deviations between actual and desired outcomes could not necessarily be ascribed to policy errors, but could have been due to a variety of other causes. In particular, later data revision (a frequent occurrence), errors in forecasts or errors in the assessment of the transmission mechanism (e.g. size of multipliers, length of time-lags), could all have impaired the effectiveness of what would otherwise have been appropriate action. Though the technology of short-term forecasting became increasingly sophisticated over the post-war period, there is little evidence that forecasting accuracy improved *pari passu*.

Third, any formal forecast had to be based, at least implicitly, on a theory of how the economy actually worked – something which was, and still is, by no means settled. It also required projections, for example, of the growth of export markets or international commodity prices, which might have depended in part on policy changes yet to be made in other countries. Not surprisingly, it was quite natural for GDP forecasts a year ahead to be out by 1 or 2 percentage points. This might not seem a large error until it is recalled that this is the same order of magnitude as the effects of the policy changes normally considered.

And finally, even if such difficulties could be surmounted, any assessment could still be ambiguous because, for instance, the unfavourable outcome of a particular policy move could have been due to the 'hijacking' of demand management away from a stabilization objective to help deal with other policy problems, or to the deliberate taking of risks with short-term stabilization in the interests of longer-term growth, just as much as to simple policy errors.

Diversions of policies from pure stabilization objectives were indeed frequent, particularly at times of foreign exchange crises. In France, for example, in 1957–8, the Algerian situation required large increases in public expenditure at the same time as an international recession was developing. The ensuing current account deficit led to a run on the franc, which forced a restrictive package on the economy (the Rueff Plan) and was accompanied by devaluation. A minor version of the same story was replayed – without devaluation – in 1963. And in 1968, following the large wage increases granted as a result of the May *événements*, the franc again came under pressure and both monetary and fiscal policy became more restrictive. Even so the franc was devalued in 1969. Clearly, the first of these examples of French policy changes in response to external pressures contains elements of earlier policy errors as well as simply the need to direct policy away from stabilization.

The same was true of the policy changes implemented when the Italian lira came under severe pressure in 1963. Monetary tightening came first and budgetary correction followed in 1964, by which time the economy was already in recession. The restrictive move was necessary as a compensation for previous excesses, but it was both overdone, since the economy was already turning down at the end of 1963 of its own accord, and delayed, at least as far as the fiscal component was concerned.

The United Kingdom is perhaps a purer example of the diversion of policy to deal with external problems which were themselves not always the simple consequence of earlier policy mistakes. There is a sense in which the country's margin for manœuvre was much less than for other European countries – though it is also true that governments set themselves relatively ambitious goals for full employment. The United Kingdom emerged from the war with a current external account weakened by the loss of earlier investment income flows (foreign assets had been sold off to help pay for war-related imports) and with a weak reserve position. To this was added further weakening of the current account because of a relatively poor industrial (and therefore trade) performance, and yet a continuing international reserve role for sterling was maintained. This meant that any emerging deficits on current account were quickly magnified by external financial flows – the familiar 'sterling crises'. On several occasions demand management 'stops' had to be hurriedly introduced in the interests of maintaining the exchange rate. Paradoxically, it was the very reserve role of sterling which made governments feel that devaluation, or floating, was not an option. Nevertheless, the pound was devalued twice – in 1949 and again, after a long and costly struggle, in 1967.

The deliberate taking of risks with short-term stability in the hope of longer-term gains was, perhaps, less of a general phenomenon. But examples can be found. In the French case, for instance, risks were taken, but not so much with the stability of growth and employment as with the balance of payments and inflation. Influenced by the stagnation of the pre-war period, the French authorities were anxious to see a high pressure of demand maintained even in the face of deteriorations on the external and inflationary fronts. In contrast, say, to the British or Italian cases, there was thus a greater willingness to devalue in the face of balance of payments pressures.

The United Kingdom experience shows two much clearer examples of deliberate risk-taking in the short run: two 'dashes for growth', both undertaken by Conservative administrations in 1962-3 and 1972-3. Even by the early 1960s, the relatively low British growth rate had become a matter of concern. Starting from a degree of recession in 1961, therefore, it was hoped that an upturn of sufficient strength and duration could be engineered so that investment spending would rise to such a degree that the upturn would become self-reinforcing. An initial sustained boost to demand would bring forth – eventually – the desired boost to supply and competitiveness, via the productivity-raising effects of higher investment. As is well known, the experiment ran into balance of payments problems well before any of the self-reinforcing benefits appeared. The same was true of the 1972-3 episode, even though that began with a higher degree of slack in the economy and an explicit commitment to 'let the exchange rate go' if necessary rather than resort again to a 'stop'. It is true that this second attempt had the bad luck to run into the first commodity and oil price explosion. Even so, in both instances, there was probably an element of simple policy error — especially in the overestimation of the balance of payments 'leeway' which was available, and of the true degree of spare capacity.

While these various episodes may suggest that the role of outright policy errors was not major, a number of examples exist which show that straightforward policy mistakes — often connected explicitly or implicitly with erroneous forecasts — had been a fairly general cause of inappropriate policy stances. Sometimes destabilization was linked to electoral considerations (e.g. Germany in 1965, the United Kingdom on several occasions). At other times, as was seen above, policies were too bold or too timid (e.g. France in 1957-8, Italy in 1964-8). And with hindsight, of course, policy mistakes can easily be catalogued in all countries. The over-expansionary stance of German fiscal policy in 1965 and the serious under-prediction of the severity of the 1967 recession are cases in point. In Belgium, too, a contractionary policy stance in 1957 contributed to the recession of the following year, while the opposite error was probably made in 1963-4. Even in Sweden, for example, one can point to the bad timing of the release of Investment Reserve funds in 1958, the under-forecast strength of the 1963-4 upswing, and the consequent inflationary stance of policy in 1964 and 1965. And finally, of course, mention must be made of the excessive and simultaneous fiscal stimulus cum monetary expansion engineered by most OECD countries in the years 1971-2 (on which more in the next section), which led to the 1972-3 inflation and ushered in the much more troubled years which followed the first oil shock.

It is perhaps not surprising in these circumstances that a relatively large number of observers have concluded not only that policy performance had in many cases been well below its theoretical potential but also that it had often been destabilizing rather than stabilizing. This view became progressively more fashionable throughout the 1970s, but had already received support in the 1960s. The United Kingdom provides the best-known example of these arguments. A number of authors have criticized British fine tuning policies, starting from Dow's early assessment of the 1952-60 record,[21] and the quantitative evidence assembled by Hansen (see Table 10.5 below) gave grist to the mill. Similar disparaging assessments were made elsewhere as well. For Germany, for instance, the OECD argued that the counter-cyclical record over the years 1960-72 had only been modest,[22] while a study by several German authors reached an even more pessimistic conclusion.[23] In the Netherlands it was argued that discretionary policy had been destabilizing, at least in the early 1970s,[24] and the

[21] J.C.R. Dow, *The Management of the British Economy, 1945-60*, NIESR, Cambridge 1964; see also, *inter alia*, R.W.R. Price, 'Budgetary Policy', in F.T. Blackaby (ed.), *British Economic Policy, 1960-74*, NIESR, Cambridge 1978.

[22] OECD, *Economic Survey of Germany, 1973*.

[23] 'The public sector has chiefly aggravated and not alleviated the fluctuations of the level of utilization around the target size of full employment': D. Biehl, G. Hagemann, K.-H. Jüttemeier, and H. Legler, 'On the Cyclical Effect of Budgetary Policy from 1960 to 1970 in the Federal Republic of Germany', *German Economic Review*, No. 4, 1973, p. 290.

[24] W.H. Buiter and R.F. Owen, 'How Successful has Stabilisation Policy been in the Netherlands? A Neo-Keynesian Perspective', *De Economist*, No. 1, 1979.

same may have been the case for Finland from the mid-1960s to the mid-1970s.[25] Though more favourable assessments can also be found, a selective reading of the literature could leave one with the impression that demand management over this period had at best been rather ineffectual, and at worst actually counter-productive.

A tentative assessment

This chapter cannot possibly try to answer the question of whether demand management was really ineffective over the period. To do so properly would require estimates of 'policy-free' underlying cycles, or, alternatively, detailed calculations of the demand effects of budgetary and other policy changes actually implemented. Either would require empirical knowledge of the structure of at least half a dozen economies – in fact detailed econometric models. In the absence of such an ideal means of analysis, one is forced to rely on more *ad hoc* methods of empirical assessment. Two in particular will be chosen – a qualitative review of the period, mainly in tabular and graphical form, and a summary of a few standardized if simplified comparative studies.

TABLE 10.3. *Pre- and post-war growth, inflation, and unemployment*

	GDP		Consumer prices		Unemployment[a]	
	1925–38	1955–73	1925–38	1955–73	1925–38	1955–73
	average annual percentage changes				annual averages	
France	–	5.4	–	4.9	2.6[b]	1.9
Germany	4.1	5.1	–1.0	2.9	7.4	1.2
Italy	1.6	5.4	–	3.9	4.4[b]	5.9
United Kingdom	1.7	3.0	–1.0	4.3	10.1	2.9
Spain	1.1[c]	6.1	..	7.1	..	2.5
Belgium	2.3[d]	4.3	–	3.1	5.9	2.5
Netherlands	1.3	4.7	..	4.3	6.3	1.1
Sweden	3.1	3.9	–0.5	4.4	4.5	2.1

[a] In per cent of the labour force; figures not strictly comparable across countries
[b] Selected years only
[c] 1925–35
[d] 1924–38

Sources: Columns 1 and 2: B. R. Mitchell, *European Historical Statistics, 1750–1970*, London 1975; OECD, *National Accounts of OECD Countries, 1950–1979*. Columns 3 and 4: W. Heller *et al., Fiscal Policy for a Balanced Economy*, OECD, Paris 1968; IMF, *International Financial Statistics* (1980 Yearbook). Columns 5 and 6: A. Maddison, 'Western Economic Performance in the 1970s: A Perspective and Assessment', *Banca Nazionale del Lavoro Quarterly Review*, September 1980; ILO, *Bulletin of Labour Statistics* (various issues); C. Sorrentino, 'Methodological and Conceptual Problems in Measuring Unemployment in OECD Countries', *mimeo*, OECD, Paris 1976; OECD, *Labour Force Statistics* (various issues); OECD, *Economic Outlook*, July 1981; EEC, *European Economy*, November 1980.

A factual summary of the period is provided by Table 10.3, which shows the pre- and post-war experience of a number of European economies in terms of growth, inflation, and unemployment, and Table 10.4, which presents the

[25] OECD, *Economic Survey of Finland, 1977.*

TABLE 10.4. *The cyclical and unemployment record, 1955–1973*
(annual averages)

	Gap between actual and potential output[a]	Unemployment in per cent of the labour force[b]	
		1955–73	1964–73
France	0.5	1.9	2.2
Germany	1.3	1.2	0.8
Italy	2.1	(5.9)	5.5
United Kingdom	1.5	2.9	3.1
Spain	1.3	(2.5)	2.8
Austria	1.5	(2.2)	1.7
Belgium	1.5	(2.5)	2.3
Denmark	1.8	(1.7)	(1.1)
Finland	2.0	2.1[c]	2.3
Ireland	1.8	(4.9)	(4.9)
Netherlands	1.4	(1.1)	1.3
Norway	0.7	(2.2)	1.7
Sweden	1.1	2.1	2.1
Switzerland	1.2	(—)	(–)
Average	1.4	(2.4)	(2.3)

[a] Sum of both positive and negative deviations of actual from potential output in per cent of potential GDP
[b] Figures in brackets not strictly comparable across countries
[c] 1958–73

Sources: OECD, 'The Measurement of Domestic Cyclical Fluctuations', *OECD Economic Outlook-Occasional Studies*, July 1973; ILO, *Bulletin of Labour Statistics* (various issues); C. Sorrentino, 'Methodological and Conceptual Problems in Measuring Unemployment in OECD Countries', *mimeo*, OECD, Paris 1976; OECD, *Labour Force Statistics* (various issues); OECD, *Economic Outlook*, July 1981; EEC, *European Economy*, November 1980.

stabilization and unemployment record of Europe in the years 1955–73. In addition, a more detailed graphical presentation is available in Fig. 10.A1 in the Appendix to this chapter, which sets out for each of eight countries the actual output cycle and policy responses in the context both of the related unemployment cycle as well as of inflation and the balance of payments. As shown in Table 10.3, and as described in greater detail in other chapters, the real economic performance of European countries between 1955 and 1973 was vastly superior to that between the wars. Output and living standards grew at unprecedented rates to unprecedented levels, and unemployment was on average very low. Although there were fluctuations, they were more in the nature of 'growth cycles' (i.e. variations in the rate of growth, rather than in the level of activity), and no country experienced recession on anything like the scale of the 1930s. On the other hand, especially from the mid-1960s onwards, inflation became an increasingly severe and general problem – in North America and Japan as well as in Western Europe.

Looking at Table 10.4, which presents the comparative post-war performance, the countries that would appear, at this very aggregate level, to have been most successful in controlling cyclical fluctuations, are clearly France, Sweden, and

Norway. The latter two are examples of countries that actively used demand management policies. France, in which the growth of all major demand components was exceptionally steady, may have paid less lip-service to the idea of fine tuning, but did, none the less, use both fiscal and monetary policies to control the economy on a short-term basis. At the other end of the spectrum are Italy – a country with inadequate policy instruments – and the two other Scandinavian countries (Denmark and Finland), whose relatively large gaps between actual and potential output may have stemmed from the influence of destabilizing tax systems and external shocks (at least in Finland, where fairly pronounced demand effects from export changes were usually reinforced by changes in the same direction in the terms of trade). Looking at unemployment, a comparative assessment is made difficult by conceptual differences in the underlying data. But broadly, concentrating on the more recent (1964–73) period for which the statistical basis is somewhat more reliable, Germany and Switzerland stand out as having had very low or virtually non-existent unemployment levels, though in both cases, of course, this was helped by the already mentioned presence of foreign workers. The primacy given to the full employment goal is evident in several of the Scandinavian countries and in the Netherlands (though the latters' figures may well underestimate the actual unemployment levels). And the diagrams show that whatever fluctuations there may have been in unemployment, these were, on the whole, very moderate.

These various results do not, of course, suffice to show that policies were successful, since achievements may have been due to other factors (as demonstrated, for instance, by the example of Switzerland, which enjoyed both relatively stable growth and virtually no unemployment, despite the near-absence of a conscious counter-cyclical policy on the fiscal side, and very limited powers of control on the monetary side). For a more direct assessment of policy effectiveness, one can turn to the estimates of the demand impact of fiscal policy made by Hansen and the OECD. These attempt to measure the proportion of the underlying cycle which budgetary policy prevented from occurring. The available evidence is presented in Table 10.5. The period covered stops at 1971 rather than 1973 because in the inflationary 1972–3 years the simple estimates of the real demand effects used here could be very misleading – for example, positive demand impacts such as those recorded in Italy or the United Kingdom (see Fig. 10.A1), while leading to a narrowing of the gap between actual and potential output, were also contributing to accelerating inflation.

The results in the first column, which have often been quoted in the literature, are particularly striking in that they show, at least for the United Kingdom, that policy was actually destabilizing, thus confirming the findings reported earlier. But as seen from the second column (which has been computed using Hansen's basic data), this result is entirely due to the inclusion of public enterprises in the estimates. While it can be argued that one arm of the government should be aware of the actions of other parts of the public sector machine, the inclusion of public enterprise investment decisions in estimates of the short-run effectiveness of counter-cyclical policies is open to some doubt. Countries differ, of course, in the extent to which they can influence the nationalized industries' sector, but, broadly, in the sample here covered, that influence was exercised primarily for medium-term purposes (with the possible exception of

TABLE 10.5. *Effects of fiscal policy on GNP*
(stabilization of GNP growth around trend or potential)

	Percentage stabilization achieved by general government				
	Including public enterprises (around trend) 1955–65	Excluding public enterprises			
		(around trend)		(around potential)	
		1955–65	1955–65	1966–71	1955–71
France[a]	12[b]	2[b]	53	39	50
Germany	..	35	52	8	27
Italy[a]	31	42	35	17	26
United Kingdom	−11	7	18	20	18
Spain[a]	..	..	..	31[c]	40[d]
Belgium	31	29	32	..	..
Netherlands	..	..	..	11	23[e]
Sweden	31	33	45	29	40

[a] Measured on non-agricultural GNP
[b] 1958–65
[c] 1966–70
[d] 1963–79
[e] 1962–71

Sources: A. Boltho, 'British Fiscal Policy, 1955–71 – Stabilizing or Destabilizing?', *Oxford Bulletin of Economics and Statistics*, November 1981; OECD, 'The Measurement of Domestic Cyclical Fluctuations' and 'Budget Indicators', *OECD Economic Outlook – Occasional Studies*, July 1973 and July 1978; OECD, *Economic Survey of Spain, 1972*.

France). The next three columns present the Hansen and subsequent OECD estimates, not only excluding public enterprises, but also relating effects to potential output (in line with an approach developed by Snyder),[26] rather than to a trend growth rate – probably a more appropriate indicator of the thrust of policy. The overall findings look plausible. France and Sweden (as well as Spain) top the list in terms of their stabilization efforts, while the United Kingdom comes last. Though in that country policies do not seem to have been positively destabilizing, results have clearly fallen short of the (rather ambitious) aims.

An interesting finding which arises from a comparison of the third and fourth columns of the table is that the successes of fiscal policies seem to have declined through the period. This suggests two major conclusions. On the one hand, the potential for successful stabilization was probably greater in the earlier period when inflationary pressures were not severe and balance of payments difficulties (particularly in the inconvertible world of the 1950s) did not yet constrain governments to the same extent as later. On the other hand, it is possible that the greater ambitiousness of policy in terms of fine tuning to achieve several objectives at once, which was nurtured by earlier successes, itself led to later difficulties. In other words, policy intervention may have been subject to diminishing returns. As put by Lindbeck in the Swedish context in the early

[26] W.W. Snyder, 'Measuring Economic Stabilization: 1955–65', *American Economic Review*, December 1970.

1970s: 'We might even start to wonder if the attempt to do "fine tuning" in stabilisation policy – to remove the small fluctuations that remain in unemployment – is worth while, in view of the inconveniences that are created for the economy by the stream of policy measures by the authorities,' and 'The complexity of targets in recent years has partly paralysed stabilisation policy.'[27]

No similar comparative and quantified evidence is available on the monetary policy side, for reasons explained in the following chapter. But the tentative conclusions reached by the OECD at the end of a cross-country study of monetary policy over this period suggest that monetary policy had had considerable effects in all the six major economies of the area which were surveyed, particularly in the United States and Japan, but also in Germany.[28] Indeed, and despite the evidence that effects of policy changes continued to build up over time, the OECD argued that: 'The most that can be safely concluded is that the potential contribution of monetary policy to demand management over a six to twelve month horizon has been so considerable as to make it unlikely that the disadvantages of longer-term instability could outweigh it.'[29]

A summary impression that arises from what has so far been presented in this subsection is that both fiscal and monetary policy did contribute to the stabilization of output growth and, especially, to the continuation of high employment levels throughout the period, even if this contribution may have declined through time and have fallen somewhat short, in some cases at least, of what might have been hoped for. It is true that some evidence exists to the contrary, evidence at times based on a more careful year-to-year study of the impact of policy changes on the economy than the much more broad-brush indicators used here. But looking at Europe as a whole *vis-à-vis* the pre-war period, and at the differential performance of many European countries in the post-war period, an admittedly impressionistic conclusion would still be that demand management policies were of clear assistance in achieving the rather impressive successes that were recorded in the unemployment and stabilization fields.

III. The 1970s – The Retreat from Full Employment

The single most important factor shaping the posture of demand management policies in the 1970s, in particular since the oil crisis of 1973, was clearly the acceleration in inflation. Broadly, just as the reduction of unemployment had been the major aim of policies in the 1950s, the curbing of inflationary pressures became that of the 1970s. In addition to inflation, however, a number of other factors influenced policies, in particular the increasing internationalization of the world economy (which weakened the power of individual government intervention), and the various exogenous shocks to which the world was subject through this period. After a brief survey of these changed circumstances, this section turns to a discussion of policy attitudes, looking in particular at the hypothesis that the period marks a general retreat from demand management, before surveying results and achievements.

[27] Lindbeck, *Swedish Policy*, pp. 235, 239.
[28] OECD, *The Role of Monetary Policy in Demand Management*, Paris 1975.
[29] Ibid., p. 134.

Changed circumstances

Inflation had been accelerating through the late 1960s, and this had led to attempts to quell it by orthodox deflationary measures. It was these measures that precipitated the 1971 slowdown. They were, however, insufficient to curb inflationary pressures. In the choice between rising prices or rising unemployment, countries, often facing electoral deadlines, preferred the former, and from the end of 1971 there was a general switch to reflationary policies.[30] With hindsight, there is little doubt that, taking the industrial world as a whole, this stimulus was overdone, since it powerfully contributed to accelerating domestic and world inflation.[31]

Over and above this obvious error of forecasting came the so-called 'oil shocks' of 1973 and 1979. The first one was preceded by an abrupt rise in commodity prices which was by far the most spectacular since the speculative commodity boom at the time of the Korean War. *The Economist's* index of world commodity spot prices (excluding oil) rose by more than 120 per cent between 1971 and the early part of 1974. A major part of this rise was no doubt due to exceptional disturbances on the supply side, particularly as far as food was concerned. World grain production fell by 3 per cent in 1972 following poor harvests in the Soviet Union and the Far East. There were also supply difficulties with industrial materials, but for both commodity types (and especially the second) the price rise would not have been so severe had the boom in demand not been so strong.

The huge oil price rise which followed posed a number of serious and novel problems.[32] It exacerbated the already very strong inflationary pressures and plunged most oil importing countries into massive trade deficits. The diversion of income from consumers in the industrial countries, who had a high propensity to spend, to governments and individuals in OPEC countries who had, on balance, low spending propensities, caused an upward shift in the world's saving propensity. Interestingly, domestic saving propensities rose at the same time, probably reflecting the acceleration in inflation,[33] thus compounding the contractionary impact. For Europe as a whole, therefore, the oil price rise was at one and the same time inflationary, deflationary, and a drain on the balance of payments. The dilemma for demand management could hardly have been more acute.

[30] This whole episode is covered in greater detail in P. McCracken *et al.*, *Towards Full Employment and Price Stability*, OECD, Paris 1977, Ch. 1.

[31] Although, as the Appendix diagrams show, this upswing did not take the pressure of demand to exceptional *levels* in Europe (or indeed elsewhere), as measured either by the gap between actual and potential output or by the level of unemployment, the speed of the upswing was temporarily very fast indeed. In the first half of 1973 output in the OECD area as a whole was rising at nearly 9 per cent per annum. In the United Kingdom the rate was an astonishing (if distorted) 15 per cent (and it was 13 per cent in Japan). In France, Germany, and Italy (as well as the United States), the rates ranged from 5 to 7 per cent.

[32] This episode is covered in more detail and at a rather more technical level in C.J. Allsopp, 'The International Demand Management Problem', in D. Morris (ed.), *The Economic System in the UK*, Oxford 1979 (2nd edn.).

[33] For some evidence on how inflation affected saving behaviour in the four major countries see EEC, *European Economy*, March 1980.

And the dilemma repeated itself at the end of the decade, at the time of the second sharp oil price increase, with an added twist. Though, quantitatively, the 1979–80 oil shock was of a similar magnitude to the 1973–4 one (and policy-makers were better prepared to face it thanks to the earlier experience), on the latter occasion a new danger emerged. In 1973–4, at least after the initial embargo period, the physical supply of oil was not a problem, only its price and the related financial difficulties. By late 1979, in contrast, there was doubt about whether increasing supplies were going to be available in the future. There appeared to be much less willingness on the part of major producers to go on increasing output from existing reserves whatever the price.

At the same time, other, longer-run, forces were also working in the direction of weakening the traditional powers of fiscal and monetary instruments. Foremost among these was the increase in the degree of interdependence between all the Western industrialized countries and in particular the European ones. This took a number of forms. At the most obvious level, the proportion of output exported had risen sharply since the mid-1950s and, by the late 1970s, was roughly as high as one-half in the Benelux and in many other cases a quarter or more (Table 10.6). These proportions were considerably higher for private sector

TABLE 10.6. *Share of exports[a] in output*
(in per cent of GDP at current prices)

	1954–56	1976–78
France	13.2	21.0
Germany	16.2	25.8
Italy	10.7	26.0
United Kingdom	23.0	29.7
Spain	4.8	14.5
Belgium	37.3	55.1
Netherlands	48.0	50.1
Sweden	22.7	27.7
OECD Europe	18.7	27.5

[a] Goods and services
Source: OECD, *National Accounts of OECD Countries, 1950-1979.*

output, and, of course, for manufacturing. National control over the pressure of demand had thus gradually diminished at the same time as national policy goals had become more ambitious.

This partial loss of autonomy on the 'real' side was reinforced by the effects of the liberalization of international capital flows on domestic monetary policies. In theory, neither of these two factors ought to have presented very serious problems after the move to generalized floating in 1974. Any sudden changes in foreign demand or foreign capital flows should merely have influenced the exchange rate, with no more ultimate net effect on competitiveness than was required for a satisfactory balance on current account. In practice, the floating system did not live up to these optimistic expectations.[34] Capital flows turned

---

[34] J.R. Artus and J.H. Young, 'Fixed and Flexible Exchange Rates: A Renewal of the Debate', *IMF Staff Papers*, December 1979.

out to be extremely volatile, while domestic costs did not prove to be sufficiently flexible. And in those countries whose currencies depreciated, the resulting rises in import prices often only exacerbated domestic inflation, leading, in turn, to further pressures on the exchange rate.

Thus both trade and financial interdependence reduced the scope for independent fiscal and monetary action in individual countries even with floating exchange rates. The effects of increased financial interdependence were probably more visible than those in the field of trade and were especially highlighted at times of exchange market crisis. Trade interdependence was not so obvious, but was at least equally important in that it tended to reduce the apparent effectiveness of policy by increasing the import leakage. Conversely, the demand management actions of other countries had a greater effect on any individual economy. It was perhaps the failure to perceive this that was in part behind the excessive degree of stimulus simultaneously administered by most countries and the resulting synchronized upswing in 1972-3.

But there was a further and probably more important sense in which demand management policies were constrained by increasing internationalization – the actions of any individual government were much more conditioned than hitherto by the actions of other governments. While in the 1950s and 1960s, despite fixed exchange rates, it was usually assumed (and with good reason, as was seen above) that the rest of the world would, by and large, continue to grow at its trend rate, in the 1970s, despite floating exchange rates, countries found themselves in a situation of 'oligopolistic interdependence'. Expansionary action in one country, not followed elsewhere, would lead to large balance of payments deficits, depreciation, and inflation. Restrictive action, on the other hand, could well lead to interest rate escalation in other countries. It may not be too far-fetched to suggest that, in these circumstances, the best strategy often appeared a very negative one with no initiatives of any kind.[35]

Changed policies

The inflationary situation of 1972-3 had already prompted some policy tightening in most European countries even before the oil shock occurred. The policy reaction to the inflation and balance of payments problems which this shock created varied depending on country. At one extreme, Germany fully accepted the deflationary impact of the oil price rise and followed a strictly non-accommodating monetary policy throughout 1974. Money supply growth actually decelerated[36] and inflation fell sharply through the year. Italy and the United Kingdom, on the other hand, felt that some offsetting action had to be taken so as to prevent the negative demand effects of the oil price rise and of a gathering world recession from plunging the economy into an unwanted slump, and a similar line was taken in some of the smaller economies, in particular Sweden. France followed an intermediate policy, with an immediate tightening giving way to some reflation by the end of 1975.

---

[35] There may be an analogy here with the behaviour of firms in oligopolistic markets often represented as facing a kinked demand curve.

[36] The stock of central bank money, which became the Bundesbank's target aggregate, rose by 6 per cent in 1974 as against 10½ per cent in 1973.

The diversity of policy responses – in the world economy and within Europe – reflected differing views about the role of demand management policies in curbing inflation. At one extreme, Germany and Switzerland gave very high priority to inflation control and were prepared to discount the risks of world recession. For these countries, deflationary demand management policies were the appropriate response to rising prices however caused. In other countries there was more scepticism about the efficacy of demand management in bringing down inflation – in part because experience in 1970-1 had been unfavourable. There was also a greater tendency to regard the problems caused by oil as special and to give greater weight to the risk of major world recession. Characteristically, in those countries where it was felt that recession would have only a limited effect on inflation or that the effect would be perverse, greater reliance was put on incomes policies or other non-conventional responses to the problem.

On balance, however, the combination of earlier moves of retrenchment, of the deflationary effect of the oil price rise itself (equivalent to some 2 per cent of GDP), and of the already mentioned upward shift in household saving propensities, led Europe into the deepest recession since the war. Though output still grew in 1974, it fell by 1 per cent in 1975 – the first peace-time decline in forty years. Between 1975 and 1978 policy turned in a somewhat more expansionary direction, though in a number of countries episodes of relaxation alternated with renewed tightening, as pressures developed on (now largely floating) exchange rates, or inflation rates reaccelerated. The tightness was particularly pronounced in those countries which had previously tried to follow relatively expansionary policies (e.g. France, Italy, and the United Kingdom), and which found their position untenable as their external payments balance deteriorated. In France, after a 'dash for growth' in 1975-6, it came in the form of the 'Barre Plan' which imposed much stricter budgetary and monetary norms on the economy. In Italy and in the United Kingdom it was prompted by runs on the currency in 1976. In both these countries, restrictions took the form of sharp rises in interest rates,[37] quantitative credit restrictions, and fiscal packages. In all these countries restraint prevailed from then on until the end of the decade, despite some cuts in direct taxation in Britain preceding the 1979 general election.

During this period economic growth recovered, but only to levels well below those prevailing in the pre-oil-crisis years, inflation decelerated, but only slowly, and the balance of payments returned to surplus, but only in 1978 (Table 10.7). While policy-makers in the 'weaker' countries, constrained by exchange rate pressures and still high rates of inflation, had little option but to continue their tight policies, the mounting costs these policies implied in terms of rising unemployment prompted them to support what came to be known as 'locomotive' strategies for world expansion – i.e. the adoption of expansionary measures in the 'stronger' countries (principally Germany and Japan, but to some extent also the United States), in the interests of a generalized recovery in the world economy.

This pressure from the weaker countries started as soon as it became apparent that the recovery in 1976 was going to peter out into slow growth with continuing

---

[37] Bank rate rose from 6 to 15 per cent between end-1975 and end-1976 in Italy and from 9 to 14¼ per cent during 1976 in the United Kingdom.

TABLE 10.7. *OECD Europe – major macroeconomic indicators*

	GDP	Inflation[a]	Unemployment[b] per cent of	Current balance $ billion
	percentage changes		labour force	
1973	5.8	8.4	2.9	2.1
1974	5.2	12.7	2.9	−20.2
1975	−0.9	12.6	4.1	−10.0
1976	4.7	10.5	4.7	−19.5
1977	2.3	11.0	5.1	−14.5
1978	3.0	8.5	5.4	16.2
1979	3.3	10.1	5.6	−18.0

[a] Consumer prices
[b] Average of eleven countries (representing some 80 per cent of the European labour force) for which comparable figures are available
Sources: OECD, *National Accounts of OECD Countries, 1950-1979*, and *Economic Outlook*, July 1981; IMF, *International Financial Statistics* (1980 Yearbook).

high levels of unemployment. Initially it led to little in the way of action apart from over-optimistic targets and projections at, for example, the London summit meeting of 1977. Eventually, however, the advice was heeded, and both Germany and Japan stimulated their economies through reflationary packages announced at the Bonn summit in 1978. This did impart a significant stimulus to activity, and output growth which had fallen to a rate of less than 2 per cent during 1977 accelerated again to some 4 per cent through 1978 and into 1979. This synchronized 'mini-boom' had some impact on commodity prices – *The Economist's* (dollar) index rose by nearly 50 per cent in the two years to the end of 1979 – but in real terms this had little effect on Europe, compared to the earlier price explosion, not only because of the smaller overall rise, but also because of continuing domestic inflation and dollar depreciation. Oil prices however, rose as sharply as during the 1973-4 crisis. Though the main trigger for this was, as on the previous occasion, political turmoil in the Middle East, the relative firmness of demand in Europe (and in Japan) probably facilitated the leap-frogging of prices engaged in by OPEC countries in the course of 1979.

Taking stock at the end of the decade of what had happened to policy throughout this difficult period, three major trends appear to have been important, if at different times and to different extents depending on country:

(i) There was during most of the period a genuine hesitation on the part of policy-makers as to the correct attitude to take;
(ii) There was also a gradual movement through the period towards a less accommodating monetary stance;
(iii) There was, by the very end of the period, a realization that prolonged tightening was probably inevitable.

That there were hesitations, false starts, abrupt changes, etc., in policy over this period is clear. All the four major countries changed their stance on several occasions; all four followed policies of reflation and deflation (using most of the instruments at their disposal in pursuing their changing targets). Ironically, perhaps, by the end of the period, the two countries which until then had given the greatest priority to full employment (France and the United Kingdom), had become most restrictive, while the country which had until then favoured price stability and a strong balance of payments was the most expansionary. These various changes reflected, of course, the real problems which faced policy-makers. In this new world of stagflation it was difficult to know what targets to pursue, since the traditional trade-off no longer seemed to apply. Nor was economic theory of great help – the doctrinal quarrels between monetarists and Keynesians, combined with the arrival on the scene of the 'new' classical macroeconomics (which was hardly 'new', since it had been already tried, with disastrous consequences, in the very early 1930s), added to the confusion. In addition, some of the instruments which had traditionally worked in the past (e.g. changes in interest rates, investment incentives, or exchange rate movements) seemed to have lost a good deal of their effectiveness.

Within this confused picture, one trend which did become fairly firmly established was the move towards the adoption of targets for monetary aggregates.[38] Combined with a somewhat greater cautiousness in any fiscal reflationary move, this prompted the thought that demand management policies were indeed on the retreat and that Europe (as well as North America) was moving towards the more monetarist prescriptions of steady money-supply growth and more or less fixed fiscal rules. There is no doubt some truth in this argument, and the best example is provided by the switch in this direction by two erstwhile very interventionist countries – France and the United Kingdom. The 'Barre Plan' marked a fairly radical departure from earlier detailed interference with the economy. The Thatcher government of 1979 rejected Keynesian demand management in an even more pronounced way. Nevertheless detailed and continuous fiscal measures were still being taken in a number of specific areas (be these selective aids in the form of regional, industrial, or labour market subsidies, or general moves to restraint, in the form of tax changes or controls on civil servants' wages). And, on the monetary side, it was often interest rates rather than money supply itself which were being controlled – not a very great departure from earlier Keynesian prescriptions.

What was different, however, was that these measures, which in some sense were not that different from fine tuning, were increasingly being taken to deal with inflation rather than to move demand and employment in any particular direction. As the dust of the 1970s was settling, policy-makers in the majority of the European countries were, perhaps reluctantly, coming to the conclusion that traditional reflationary measures had, for the time being at least, to be shelved. Some considered them ineffective anyway, even though the experience of the Bonn package and of the United States in that period were clear proof to the contrary. Rather, the view was that if taken individually such measures were likely to exacerbate inflation to unacceptable levels via exchange rate depreciation, while if taken collectively they would interact with an increasingly restricted supply of oil and lead to rising oil prices. No doubt this orthodox policy was helped by the muted social and political reaction to rising unemployment. Just as in earlier years countries of immigration had been able to pursue deflationary policies with relative ease because of the outflow of foreign workers,

---

[38] Discussed in greater detail in Ch. 11 below.

on this occasion most countries found that they could 'afford' rising unemployment since this was, at least until the end of the 1970s, being concentrated among the less vocal members of the secondary labour force – women and the young.

Changed outcomes

Given that policy, on the whole, hesitated between curbing inflation and stimulating output through much of the period, it is difficult to assess its successes or failures. As shown by Table 10.7, it could be argued that, in fact, for Europe as a whole, it was unsuccessful on both fronts, since unemployment clearly rose sharply to record post-war levels, while inflation, though coming down until 1978, did so only very slowly and not enough to curb inflationary expectations (as seen by the sudden reacceleration in 1979). Of course, within Europe, countries differed (Table 10.8), and some, like Germany, Austria, the Netherlands, and Switzerland were able not only to curb price pressures (thanks also to revaluations of their currencies), but also to keep the rise in unemployment to modest, or even trivial proportions. Elsewhere, successes were much less marked and in some instances the deterioration on both fronts was particularly severe, notably in most of the larger economies of the area.

TABLE 10.8. *Changes in inflation, unemployment and 'discomfort index',* [a] *1973–1979*
(changes in percentage points)

	Inflation[b]	Unemployment[c]	'Discomfort index'[a]
France	3.3	3.3	6.6
Germany	−2.8	2.3	−0.5
Italy	3.9	1.3	5.2
United Kingdom	4.3	2.7	7.0
Spain	4.2	6.0	10.2
Austria	−4.0	1.0	−3.0
Belgium	−2.5	5.6	3.1
Denmark	0.2	4.6	4.8
Finland	−3.5	3.7	0.2
Ireland	2.1	2.3	4.4
Netherlands	−3.8	1.9	−1.9
Norway	−2.5	0.5	−2.0
Sweden	0.6	−0.4	0.2
Switzerland	−5.1	0.3	−4.8
OECD Europe	1.7	2.8	4.5

[a] Changes in the 'discomfort index' (which was used in P. McCracken *et al., Towards Full Employment and Price Stability*, OECD, Paris 1977) are obtained by adding deteriorations (or improvements) in performance, with purely arbitrary *equal* weights given to unemployment and inflation. Results could clearly differ sharply if other weights or economic indicators were used. Cyclical situations also varied across countries in the two years here chosen, thus somewhat impairing cross-country comparisons
[b] Consumer prices
[c] In per cent of the labour force

Sources: IMF, *International Financial Statistics* (1980 Yearbook); OECD, *Economic Outlook*, July 1981; EEC, *European Economy*, November 1980; ILO, *Bulletin of Labour Statistics* (various issues).

To what extent were these various outcomes induced by policy? It is difficult to be sure about the impact of monetary policy. The experience with the new policy trend of announcing aggregate targets is too short and no robust empirical evidence could be found to assess it, apart from the rather general assertions that in some countries at least, the announcement of targets had favourable expectational effects on wage bargaining not dissimilar to those of an incomes policy. On the fiscal side, it could be argued prima facie that the very large budget deficits that prevailed through the period were an indication of a relatively relaxed stance and should have, other things being equal, helped the level of employment. This argument, however, fails to take into account the monetary consequences of such deficits. Indeed, the 1970s saw a concerted attack on the whole idea of an expansionary fiscal policy in an environment in which money supply growth was being constrained. Far from supporting activity, it was argued, prolonged deficit financing was contributing to the continuation of relatively depressed demand conditions and slow growth, since these deficits could only lead to higher interest rates and therefore lower private spending. The public sector was 'crowding out' the private one.

At the theoretical level it can be accepted that higher interest rates could have some partially offsetting effects on private investment — though even this has to be balanced against any 'accelerator' effect of net government demand. What is more difficult to accept is the existence of some additional 'financial' or 'portfolio' crowding-out mechanisms capable of swamping entirely any changes in net public sector demand, and more.[39]

A priori doubts about the significance of this mechanism are supported by available simulations of econometric models which suggest, at least for France, Germany, and the United Kingdom, that the multipliers from bond financed (and hence interest-rate-raising) changes in government expenditure were not only positive in the short run, but remained positive five to six years after the initial expenditure decision.[40] There is, perhaps, some evidence of crowding-out in Italy (though again this is unlikely to have been total), not, however, because of interest rate effects, but because of credit rationing.[41] And the importance of crowding-out in this period would seem to be further diminished by the data

[39] This whole subject is tackled comprehensively in B.M. Friedman, 'Crowding Out or Crowding In? Economic Consequences of Financing Government Deficits', *Brookings Papers on Economic Activity*, No. 3, 1978.

[40] In the United Kingdom, a simulation carried out on three major econometric models suggests that the average reduction in the value of the multiplier for a bond-financed rather than a money-financed increase in government expenditure was of, at most, 0.1 after one year, 0.2 after four years, and 0.5 after six years (with all the multipliers remaining positive): J.S.E. Laury, G.R. Lewis, and P.A. Ormerod, 'Properties of Macroeconomic Models of the UK Economy: A Comparative Study', *NIESR Review*, February 1978. In France, a similar exercise on two models suggests values very close to the British ones — 0.1, 0.3, and 0.7 respectively: P. Artus and P.-A. Muet, 'Une étude comparative des propriétés de six modèles américains et cinq modèles français', *Revue économique*, January 1980. For Germany, a simulation made on the University of Hamburg 'Sysifo' model also suggests very limited 'crowding-out' effects: U. Westphal, 'Empirische Aspekte des Crowding Out', in W. Erlicher (ed.), *Geldpolitik, Zins und Staatsverschuldung*, Berlin 1981.

[41] A. Verde, 'Ancora sul crowding-out: un tentativo di stima per l'Italia 1974–1977', *Banco di Roma Economia Italiana*, No. 2, 1979.

TABLE 10.9. *Budget balances*[a] *and 'real' interest rates*[b]
(annual averages; percentages)

	1969–73	1976–79	Change between two periods
France			
Budget balance	0.9	−1.0	−1.9
'Real' interest rate	1.9	−0.1	−2.0
Germany			
Budget balance	0.4	−3.0	−3.4
'Real' interest rate	1.2	2.4	1.2
Italy			
Budget balance	−6.9	−9.0	−2.1
'Real' interest rate	−1.2	−2.1	−0.9
United Kingdom			
Budget balance	−0.4	−4.0	−3.6
'Real' interest rate	0.3	−	−0.3
Spain			
Budget balance	0.4	−1.2	−1.6
'Real' interest rate	1.0	−4.2	−5.2
Belgium			
Budget balance	−2.2	−6.1	−3.9
'Real' interest rate	0.7	3.0	2.3
Netherlands			
Budget balance	−0.1	−2.3	−2.2
'Real' interest rate	0.1	0.7	0.5
Sweden			
Budget balance	4.5	0.8	−3.7
'Real' interest rate	2.3	−0.7	−3.0

[a] General government net lending in per cent of GDP at current prices
[b] Long-term government bond-yields less percentage change in implicit gross fixed investment deflator
Sources: OECD, *National Accounts of OECD Countries, 1962-1979,* and *Economic Survey of Spain, 1981*; IMF, *International Financial Statistics* (1980 Yearbook): EEC, *European Economy,* November 1980; Banco de España, *Boletín estadístico,* December 1980.

shown in Table 10.9 which give some indication of what actually happened to budget deficits and to (a simple proxy for) 'real' interest rates in the years immediately preceding the oil crisis and in the years 1976-9.[42] It will be seen that while deficits did rise everywhere quite sharply, 'real' interest rates in no way paralleled that movement. They did rise in Germany and Belgium, but they remained roughly unchanged, or actually fell, in several other countries — a prima-facie indication that simple crowding-out could hardly have taken place.[43]

But if fiscal policy was not impotent because of crowding-out, the question

---

[42] The years 1974-5 have been left out because of recession-induced distortions. Their inclusion would, if anything, reinforce the argument.

[43] It is, however, true that high nominal interest rates may have inhibited investment spending, since in the short run they may have unfavourable effects on firms' cash-flows, while in the longer run they could exert strong pressure on profitability should inflation decelerate.

could be asked as to why relatively large budget deficits did not have more pronounced effects on output growth. Two major reasons can be advanced for this.
The first stems from the effects of inflation on the budget deficit. As has been
argued by Artis:

There is an argument that, in inflationary conditions, any measure of fiscal
policy which . . . is based on the cash flow of government expenditures and
revenues is an upward-biased indicator of fiscal stance and will give a misleadingly
expansionary impression of policy. This argument is based on the observation
that the rising price level implies a fall in the real value of outstanding national
debt, an act of confiscation which should be regarded as a special form of tax
(an inflation tax), but one which is not reflected in the cash flow definition of
tax revenues. Compounding the bias, from this point of view, is the fact that the
increased debt costs associated with the inflation induced increase in interest
rates *will* be reflected in the cash flow definition of government expenditure.[44]

This argument is illustrated by Table 10.10, which shows EEC estimates for
the years 1975-9 which, if somewhat crudely, allow for inflation. It will be seen
that what are, ostensibly, record high deficits, turn out to be much smaller
deficits in an underlying 'real' sense. Indeed, in the United Kingdom's case, the
adjusted figure shows a surplus.[45]

The second reason why deficits were perhaps less expansionary than might
have been thought has to do with the well-known and already mentioned two-
way causation between the budget and the economy. Though deficits were
large, they usually reflected automatic stabilizer effects, given the very large
margins of spare capacity that had been built up since 1973. In a 'full' or 'high'
employment sense, budgets may well have been in balance or even in surplus.
This is difficult to document precisely, because of the conceptual problems involved in constructing a 'high employment' budget balance in these years, but
scattered evidence suggests that the effect was likely to be sizeable. Thus, for
Germany, OECD estimates of the 'cyclically adjusted' budget balance for the
years 1975-8 show that an actual deficit equivalent on average to 3.7 per cent of
GDP is reduced to 1.6 per cent.[46] Similar NIESR estimates for the United Kingdom made for the financial years 1976/7 to 1978/9 turn an apparent average
deficit equivalent to 5.6 per cent of GDP to a surplus of 0.3 per cent.[47] And for
Belgium, a 'full employment' estimate suggests that the deficit, rather than being
of the order of 5½ per cent of GDP, was close to 2 per cent only.[48] If one were
to extrapolate these findings to other countries (something which is not totally
implausible), and were then to add the inflation adjustments mentioned above,
Europe might well appear to have been in cyclically adjusted real budget surplus,
and possibly in substantial surplus, through most of the later 1970s.

[44] M.J. Artis, 'Fiscal Policy and Crowding Out', in M. Posner (ed.), *Demand Manage-
ment*, NIESR, London 1978, p. 168.
     [45] For a relatively similar result for the United Kingdom, see C.T. Taylor and A.R.
Threadgold, ' "Real" National Saving and its Sectoral Composition', *Bank of England
Discussion Paper*, No. 6, 1979.
     [46] OECD, *Economic Survey of Germany, 1979.*
     [47] See *NIESR Review*, various issues in the late 1970s.
     [48] W. van Rickeghem and P. Bekx, 'The Belgian Full Employment Budget Deficit in the
Seventies', *Tijdschrift voor Economie en Management*, No. 3, 1979.

TABLE 10.10. *Budget deficits and inflation, 1975-1979*
(annual averages; in per cent of GDP at current prices)

	General government net lending	Inflation adjustment[a]	General government net lending less inflation adjustment
France	−1.2	0.8	−0.4
Germany	−3.5	1.2	−2.3
Italy	−9.6	6.9	−2.7
United Kingdom	−4.2	6.5	2.3
Belgium	−5.7	3.5	−2.2
Netherlands	−2.1	1.8	−0.3

[a] The inflation adjustment attempts to measure the erosion by inflation of the real value of the outstanding stock of public sector debt.
Source: EEC, *European Economy*, November 1980.

This suggests, therefore, that fiscal policy was, on balance, restrictive in these years, whether by accident or design, and that this degree of restriction was superimposed on the deflationary effects of the oil price rises twice in the period. It may be no wonder in these circumstances that private sector reactions, in the form, for instance, of higher savings or lower investment propensities, also worked in the direction of lowering output growth. Confidence may have earlier been nurtured by a period of rapid growth, but confidence and expectations could easily turn in the opposite direction as soon as policy was seen to fail in its attempts at coping with stagflation, and almost certainly did so. Indeed, given popular attitudes to budget deficits, it may be that large nominal borrowing has itself had some adverse effects on confidence and on inflationary expectations. What is perhaps more surprising is the modesty of the success in fighting inflation, despite unprecedented policy tightness, rising unemployment, and also an appreciating exchange rate, at least for Europe as a whole. The answer to these questions clearly goes beyond the scope of this chapter, but the demand management experience between 1973 and 1979 clearly suggests that traditional instruments are very blunt indeed when used to curb what appear to be deep-seated inflationary pressures in the system. It was earlier remarked that monetary policy has asymmetrical effects — it can curb a boom but not engineer an expansion. Perhaps the overall workings of demand management policies are similarly asymmetrical — they can stimulate an economy but not bring down inflation, or, better still, they can act relatively quickly on quantities but only very slowly on prices. Perseverance with the orthodox medicine may perhaps succeed in bringing inflation down, but this could well be at the cost of unemployment levels closer to those of the 1930s than to those of the late 1970s.

Conclusions

At the end of this brief review of demand management one may now turn to a tentative assessment of the contribution of fiscal and monetary policies to the economic achievements, as well as failures, of post-war Europe. It may be appropriate to divide the period into two, as was done in the preceding narrative.

For the 1950s and 1960s, the demand management record can be approached on at least three different levels. On the first, one can of course point out that a major slump was decisively avoided. How much of this success can be credited to demand management policy as such can be disputed. In part it was no doubt due to the avoidance of deflationary errors in monetary and fiscal policy, rather than to positive intervention in more appropriate directions. And in any case by no means all European countries were deliberately indulging in demand supporting policies as such. Nevertheless, the growth of the automatic budgetary stabilizers and the spread of the Keynesian message no doubt created a more permissive climate of opinion towards at least temporary budget deficits, so that self-reinforcing confidence could grow in the ability of the system to avoid a recurrence of cumulative deflationary disaster. In addition, those countries, both inside and outside Europe, which did deliberately pursue full employment policies, gave indirect support to others by maintaining a high and rising demand for imports.

Hence, although other factors were no doubt important, such as the strong autonomous push in the release of pent-up wartime consumer demand and postwar reconstruction, it is probably not an overstatement to say that, even if only indirectly and passively in many cases, the Keynesian revolution (rather than active demand management *per se*) played a key role in avoiding for a quarter-century any major set-back. The fact that, in the event, no such major reverse had to be faced does not necessarily invalidate the notion that business confidence and private spending were supported by the belief that, if it had, the means were at hand to counteract it.[49]

While a verdict on the avoidance of major depression is thus clearly favourable, it is not so easy to come to a judgement about demand management in the fine tuning sense — that is, the counter-cyclical adjustment of output around its growing full employment potential. On the one hand it seems fairly clear from the historical narrative that stabilization policy achieved only a fraction (though possibly a large one) of its theoretical potential. On the other, not all European countries were actively pursuing fine tuning policies, while those which were were subject to the inevitable uncertainties involved in forecasting. In addition, it is difficult to judge how much of the cyclical instability can in some sense be 'excused' by the need to cope with balance of payments and price pressures. To the extent that these pressures were themselves the result of earlier inappropriate policy stances, clearly they cannot be counted as excuses. But even where they were not, the question also arises whether such pressures were in part the result of policy mistakes in other areas. For example, should balance of payments pressures have been dealt with more directly and promptly in the contrasting cases of Germany and the United Kingdom? The French willingness to use the exchange rate to maintain an appropriate level of competitiveness and, hence, stability of export growth, is perhaps a pointer. Even more difficult to decide is the extent to which inflation 'ought' to have been dealt with by more direct means. Incomes policy of course is not a technical matter like exchange

---

[49] This argument has also been put forward for the United States: see M.N. Baily, 'Stabilization Policy and Private Economic Behavior', *Brookings Papers on Economic Activity*, No. 1, 1978.

rate policy, but rather a delicate social and political instrument. Nevertheless, it remains true that more effective direct control of inflation would in several cases have meant greater freedom to pursue stabilization policies as such.

What then were the costs of the instability which did occur? Complete success in evening-out the cycle would probably have resulted, in most cases, in an average level of output only one or two percentage points higher than might have occurred under the automatic stabilizers alone. In addition, unemployment might on average have been perhaps a percentage point or so lower. Although this would no doubt have been an important fact for the several million Europeans themselves involved in cyclical bouts of joblessness, it would not have been a major gain by more general standards (this judgement might need modifying, however, to the extent that cyclical unemployment tends to be particularly and repeatedly concentrated on minority groups — especially ethnic minorities and the young).

There is also the criticism that fine tuning turned out to be inflationary. As the record shows, this was clearly true on occasions, when policy was mistakenly expansionary. But what is more difficult to believe is that these isolated bouts of excessive demand pressure played much more than a relatively minor role in the secular rise of the inflationary problem. That is, the idea of a virginity of stable prices which, once lost in a rash moment, can never be regained, seems rather unlikely.[50] Especially with the hindsight of the 1970s, when the degree of slack was allowed to rise to much higher levels than previously, it seems fairly clear that inflation has a strong momentum of its own. Nevertheless, while perhaps not the prime cause of the secular acceleration of price rises, over-expansionary fine tuning errors may have exacerbated the phenomenon to some degree.

Another criticism sometimes made is that the instability resulting from fine tuning errors was disruptive of private sector medium-term planning and that business investment spending was thereby held back. In the United Kingdom this was summed up in the 'stop-go' label applied to policy. This is essentially an argument about uncertainty — that is, that fine tuning errors increased the degree of uncertainty faced by firms when trying to project the likely level of demand for the products of new investment expenditures. It has, however, to be set alongside the major reduction in uncertainty thought by many to have occurred as the belief grew in the Keynesian ability to avoid major slumps, as opposed to mere growth recessions. This, indeed, is the third and final level of the assessment of policy in the 1950s and 1960s. And, as seems to be the case with all the interesting and important questions in economics, it is of course not possible to give a watertight answer. However, so long as the belief in the end of serious slumps was reasonably firmly held, one might well imagine that the high average pressure of demand should have been a bigger factor in stimulating private investment than growth recessions were in inhibiting it.

To sum up, it is difficult to avoid giving relatively low marks to demand management performance in the fine tuning sense. Discretionary actions were

[50] An opinion which is reinforced by Tobin's judgement on the United States record: 'I do think that it is disingenuous to give the impression, so prevalent today, that the whole inflationary experience could have been costlessly avoided by conservative demand management': J. Tobin, 'Stabilization Policy Ten Years After', *Brookings Papers on Economic Activity*, No. 1, 1980, pp. 43-4.

too often either ill-timed or constrained by the need to meet other, non-stabilization, policy goals. At the same time it seems that the automatic stabilizers were not sufficient on their own to prevent some cyclical behaviour in the economy, so that the attempt to do better was worth the try. And, with the possible exception of the United Kingdom, discretionary action probably did not on average lead to greater instability than might have occurred in any case. In most cases it was probably less. In other words, given also that the total elimination of the growth cycle would have resulted in only a relatively small increase in the average level of output, the partial failure of fine tuning was perhaps not too important anyway. On the other hand, the achievement and maintenance of a high average pressure of demand was almost certainly beneficial to capital investment and therefore to output in general.

How do these judgements look in the light of much poorer economic performance in the 1970s? Clearly the low marks given to fine tuning cannot be redeemed. The 1971 recession and especially the synchronized upswing of 1972-3 were destabilizing and were brought about by discretionary measures in many European countries – and elsewhere. But while part of the error in 1972-3 was no doubt due to the failure to see the world multiplier consequences of general reflation, the explosion in the prices of raw materials and oil probably owed more to exogenous shocks on the supply side. After that, the progressive redirection of demand management away from stabilization and towards reducing price pressures was less than wholly successful. It led to higher unemployment than policy-makers would have wished (or would even have expected to be politically acceptable), while at the same time making only a minor dent in inflation.

Do these judgements on the latter 1970s imply that even if demand management had been successful earlier on, it had outlived its usefulness and that a more radical, monetarist and non-interventionist stance was appropriate? On the European record, at least, the monetarists' criticism that forecasts, and therefore fine tuning policies, are liable to error clearly has more than a little substance. And, while their faith in the self-stabilizing properties of the economic system may be over-strong, it is not obviously outrageous. Rather paradoxically, however, an important reason for this endogenous stability is no doubt the thoroughly Keynesian one of the increasing scale of government involvement in the economy. For not only has this meant a significant measure of built-in stability in the fiscal system, but it has also, by definition, increased the proportion of total demand which is independent of the normal commercial criteria. It would also seem difficult to accept the monetarists' implicit assertion that the inflationary bias of the economy could be permanently eliminated relatively painlessly – that is, without more than a small and temporary rise in unemployment – by bringing down the rate of increase of the money supply.

Another view, however, and a much more pessimistic one, is that it is not fine tuning errors, but the avoidance of major depression over a long period which has been important – the distinction which has been drawn several times throughout this chapter. The high average pressure of demand may have at least permitted the underlying inflationary bias of the modern economy to become apparent – a bias which was effectively hidden by the severe economic conditions in the interwar period. High secular demand pressure effectively strengthens the degree of economic security enjoyed by most economic agents, a factor which has probably been strengthened still further by the development of social security systems. In this situation, organized labour has, in many countries, been increasingly willing to use its potential power to press for increasingly inflationary wage rises. And large corporations, especially, have found that they possessed the market power to pass on most of the resulting increase in costs into higher prices. Governments, who in many cases were in at the start of this process in their provision of high levels of aggregate demand, also found themselves in again at the end, faced with the choice between accommodating higher levels of costs and prices or risking recession.

Does all this imply that one should change one's mind about the net benefits of the (on average) full employment economy? Are the beneficial effects of capital investment and productive potential offset by the generation of inflation? To some extent at least the answer must be 'yes', in the sense that that is how it has actually worked out for many countries in the 1970s. With price shocks from outside as well, not even Germany and Switzerland have escaped some degree of inflation over the decade.

However, it is probably more fruitful to see the level of demand as the permissive factor in the rise of inflation rather than the prime causal mover. In the latter role one can more realistically cast the uncompetitive nature of many of the more important markets in the modern economy. The textbook model of perfect atomistic competition is a far cry from real world labour markets and from the markets for many manufactured goods. These are characterized, in Hicks's term, by their 'fix-price' (as opposed to 'flex price') nature, or, more graphically, by the presence of market power. And, while the provision of high aggregate levels of demand certainly facilitates the exercise of this market power, it is not the prime cause of its existence in the first instance. The implication of this is that to fight inflation solely by means of demand management policy might be very costly indeed in terms of its effect on the real economy. In other words, the notion that the answer to inflation is the permanent abandonment of a commitment to reasonably full employment is probably a sterile one. One would simply exchange one problem – inflation – for another – chronic unemployment.

To return to the extreme of prolonged depression is clearly a non-solution to the problem. Apart from the resulting unemployment and the accompanying loss of output in the short run, there would be longer-run costs too. In particular the longer-run supply potential of the economy would suffer: if sustained high demand was on balance good for capital investment, sustained low demand pressure would presumably be bad.

To sum up, it seems that demand management policy has become less and less capable of being used alone. Some policy on aggregate demand is clearly necessary for good economic performance – indeed it is inevitable given the present scale of government activity – but it is not sufficient. Demand management can apparently no longer provide a reasonably acceptable combination of both high employment and stable prices, nor, of course, can it deal with the energy problem. Without supporting policies in the inflation and energy areas it seems inevitable, as has already happened in the 1970s, that demand management will be diverted from its primary task of supporting the level of activity. It would be foolish to forget, however, that the European economy achieved unprecedented levels of general economic well-being during the 1950s and 1960s. And, while it can obviously not be claimed that this was all due to high average demand pressures, let alone to conscious policies in favour of such pressures, it is difficult to deny that they played an important role.

Appendix: Selected Cyclical Indicators for Eight Countries

The diagrams of Fig. 10.A1 provide for the years 1955–73 the actual output cycle and the policy response in the context both of the related unemployment cycle as well as of inflation and the balance of payments. The output cycle is proxied by the gap between actual and potential output, the latter having been obtained from OECD estimates made for the period 1955–73, thus avoiding the main effects of post-war recovery and the special situation of the mid-1970s. The fiscal policy indicators are for the most part taken from estimates given by Hansen for 1955–65 (which include multiplier effects), and, for more recent years, from OECD figures (which do not allow for multiplier effects). The latter have, however, become less important as import 'leakages' have generally tended to increase over the post-war period. In the few instances where no figures were available, the diagrams show changes in general government net lending as a percentage of GDP. Thus, in all three sources used, the fiscal indicator measures include both discretionary and automatic effects, and only the third does not employ some method of 'demand weighting' for changes in the different items of revenue and expenditure. For the four largest countries, the diagrams also give a qualitative indication (in the form of arrows) of the stance of monetary policy – qualitative because there are no agreed estimates of the precise demand effects of monetary policy changes.

The following sources have been used:

GDP gap: OECD, 'The Measurement of Domestic Cyclical Fluctuations', *OECD Economic Outlook – Occasional Studies*, July 1973 (for all countries).

Fiscal policy indicator: B. Hansen, *Fiscal Policy in Seven Countries, 1955–1965*, OECD, Paris 1969 (for France, Germany, Italy, the United Kingdom, Belgium, and Sweden for the years 1955–65); OECD, 'Budget Indicators', *OECD Economic Outlook – Occasional Studies*, July 1978 (for France, Germany, Italy, the United Kingdom, and Sweden for the years 1965–73; OECD, *Economic Survey of Spain, 1972* (for Spain for the years 1963–70); OECD, *National Accounts of OECD Countries, 1962–1979* (for Spain for the years 1970–3), and *1953–1969* (for the Netherlands for the years 1955–62); OECD, *Economic Survey of the Netherlands, 1976* (for the Netherlands for the years 1962–73); EEC, *European Economy*, November 1980 (for Belgium for the years 1965–73).

Monetary policy indicator: authors' estimates.

Unemployment rate: C. Sorrentino, 'Methodological and Conceptual Problems in Measuring Unemployment in OECD Countries', *mimeo*, OECD, Paris 1976 (for France, Germany, Italy, the United Kingdom, and Sweden for the years 1955–64); OECD, *Economic Outlook*, July 1981 (for all countries for the years 1965–73); OECD, *Labour Force Statistics* (various issues) (for Spain for the years 1956–64); ILO, *Bulletin of Labour Statistics* (various issues) (for Belgium and the Netherlands for the years 1955–7); EEC, *European Economy*, November 1980 (for Belgium and the Netherlands for the years 1958–64).

Consumer prices: IMF, *International Financial Statistics* (1980 Yearbook) (for all countries).

Current balance: OECD, *Balances of Payments of OECD Countries, 1960-1977* (for all countries for the years 1960-73); IMF, *International Financial Statistics* (1980 Yearbook) (for all countries, except France and Sweden, for the years 1955-9); OECD, *National Accounts of OECD Countries, 1950-1979* (for Sweden for the years 1955-9 and for all the GDP data).

Bibliography

The international demand management experience does not seem to have called forth a vast literature. Comparative studies are, in fact, rather rare, and even national surveys are not as widespread as might be expected. Since a bibliography on monetary policy is presented at the end of the following chapter, this brief list of references will be limited to either general works on demand management or more specific studies of fiscal policy.

Brief international surveys of policy experience over the post-war period can be found in A. Maddison, *Economic Growth in the West*, London 1964, and A. Shonfield, *Modern Capitalism*, Oxford 1965. The period up to the first oil crisis is analysed in P. McCracken *et al.*, *Towards Full Employment and Price Stability*, OECD, Paris 1977, and the period since that crisis in L. Izzo and L. Spaventa, 'Macroeconomic Policies in Western European Countries: 1973-1977', in H. Giersch (ed.), *Macroeconomic Policies for Growth and Stability*, Institut für Weltwirtschaft, Kiel, Tübingen 1980. In addition, year-by-year surveys can be found in the regular publications of the BIS, *Annual Report* (since the end of the war); the OECD, *Economic Outlook* (since 1967); and the EEC, *European Economy* (since 1978). An interesting article on demand management problems in general is A. Lindbeck, 'Stabilization Policies in Open Economies with Endogenous Politicians', *American Economic Review*, May 1976.

On the fiscal policy side, the best known comparative work is, of course, that by B. Hansen, *Fiscal Policy in Seven Countries, 1955-1965*, OECD, Paris 1969, and the follow-up study by the OECD, 'Budget Indicators', *OECD Economic Outlook – Occasional Studies*, July 1978.

On individual countries, the OECD again provides in its annual *Economic Surveys* continuous year-by-year coverage of the demand management experience of all the Western Countries. Other information can be found in, for instance, chapters in E.S. Kirschen *et al.*, *Economic Policy in our Time*, Amsterdam 1964 (which consider the four major countries, the Benelux, and Norway in the 1950s) and in E. Lundberg, *Instability and Economic Growth*, New Haven 1968 (which looks at early British, Dutch, and Swedish economic policy).

More specific national references are as follows: for *France*, Ch. 14 of J.-J. Carré, P. Dubois, and E. Malinvaud, *French Economic Growth*, Oxford 1976, gives a bird's-eye view of some economic policy problems of the period up to the late 1960s. For *Germany*, H. Giersch, *Growth, Cycles and Exchange Rates: The Experience of West Germany*, Stockholm 1970, and W. Kaspar, 'Stabilization Policies in a Dependent Economy: Some Lessons from the West German Experience of the 1960s', in E. Claasen and P. Salin (eds.), *Stabilization Policies in Interdependent Economies*, Amsterdam 1972, both look at the German balance of payments – exchange rate – monetary policy dilemma in the 1960s; for *Italy*, the Bank of Italy, *Annual Reports*, are fairly analytical; see also, L. Izzo, A. Pedone, L. Spaventa, and F. Volpi, *Il controllo dell'economia nel breve periodo*, Milan 1970. For the *United Kingdom*, two very comprehensive surveys

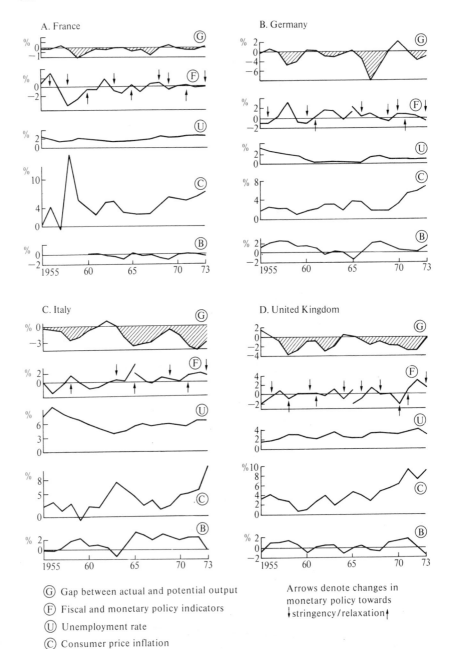

A. France   B. Germany   C. Italy   D. United Kingdom

Ⓖ Gap between actual and potential output

Ⓕ Fiscal and monetary policy indicators

Ⓤ Unemployment rate

Ⓒ Consumer price inflation

Ⓑ Current balance in per cent of current price GDP

Arrows denote changes in
monetary policy towards
↓stringency/relaxation↑

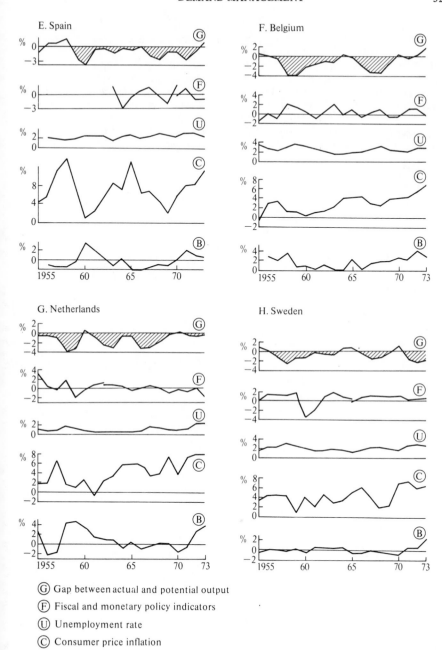

E. Spain

F. Belgium

G. Netherlands

H. Sweden

Ⓖ Gap between actual and potential output
Ⓕ Fiscal and monetary policy indicators
Ⓤ Unemployment rate
Ⓒ Consumer price inflation
Ⓑ Current balance in per cent of current price GDP

of the whole period are J.C.R. Dow, *The Management of the British Economy, 1945–60*, NIESR, Cambridge 1964, and F.T. Blackaby (ed.), *British Economic Policy, 1960–74*, NIESR, Cambridge 1978. For *Ireland*, K.A. Kennedy and B.R. Dowling, *Economic Growth in Ireland Since 1947*, Economic and Social Research Institute, Dublin 1975, discuss policies in Part IV. For the *Netherlands*, an early survey is J.G. Abert, *Economic Policy and Planning in the Netherlands, 1950–65*, New Haven 1969; later accounts are provided in a special number of *De Economist*, No. 1, 1979. For *Sweden*, regular surveys appear in the Konjunkturinstitutet, *The Swedish Economy*; a full account of the experience to the early 1970s is by A. Lindbeck, *Swedish Economic Policy*, London 1975.

11

Monetary Policy

NIELS THYGESEN*

Introduction

As a background to this survey of the role of monetary policy in the economies of Western Europe over the past twenty to thirty years it may be helpful to choose as an organizing principle for the analysis three main trends common to all countries:

(i) The changing international environment in which national monetary policies have had to be formulated and implemented;
(ii) The evolution of the views on how monetary actions influence macro-economic objectives;
(iii) The changing evaluation of the relative merits of market-oriented versus direct and selective methods of conducting monetary policy.

Discussion of these three themes — which interact in a chronological presentation — should bring out the way in which monetary policy has evolved from a largely accommodating posture in the 1950s through an increasingly ambitious, domestically oriented role in stabilization policy in the 1960s, to the longer-run largely external orientation of the 1970s. It should also indicate the extent to which this evolution has been reflected in a changing emphasis on the various instruments available. For some countries, other themes might have proved equally or more worthy of attention. It is necessary, however, to be highly selective if the reader is to retain any impressions at all from a survey of monetary policy in a number of countries.

Another problem is that of composing a proper country sample, sufficiently wide to cover the relevant range of monetary experience. To omit any of the four largest countries would not be defensible. But to survey only these four would throw insufficient light on the problems of monetary policy in smaller open economies, and thereby on the first two of the three issues outlined above. Three additional countries are therefore included — Denmark, the Netherlands, and Switzerland. The latter two are, despite their size, not only major trading nations, but also financial centres, and accordingly manage currencies that are frequently used and demanded internationally. Denmark is included as an extreme case of external orientation of monetary policy. Other smaller countries might have been included on equally valid grounds. The only defence for the particular choice is that it is sufficiently wide to allow illustration of the main trends in the monetary environment, in objectives, and in the instruments under significantly different institutional arrangements.

Apart from obvious differences in size and in external alignment, such institutional differences are important determinants of the design and effectiveness of

*University of Copenhagen.

monetary policy. It is impossible to do justice to the range of these differences in this chapter.[1] Some indication of their importance, however, is provided in Tables 11.1 and 11.2, which show certain financial variables on a comparable basis for the countries included in the present survey.

TABLE 11.1. *Ratio of money supply to nominal GNP*
(percentages)

	M 1[a]		M 3[a]	
	1958	1978	1958	1978
France	31.2	26.5	33.4	51.2
Germany	17.1	17.6	36.0	67.0
Italy	30.0	55.6	51.9	96.5
United Kingdom	20.5[b]	17.1	40.6	34.9
Denmark	22.0	23.4	49.1	44.7
Netherlands	28.2	21.2	44.7	58.8
Switzerland	52.9	48.2	98.5	125.9

[a] M1 and M3 stand for the narrow and broader definitions of the money supply respectively
[b] 1966
Sources: N. Kaldor, 'Memorandum', House of Commons, Treasury and Civil Service Committee, *Memoranda of Monetary Policy*, HMSO, London 1980; Danmarks Nationalbanks, *Beretning og Regnskab*, and *Economic Survey of Denmark* (various issues).

Table 11.1 reveals that there are significant differences with respect to the level of money holdings – in both a narrow and a broad definition – relative to income. The demand for money has been higher in Italy and Switzerland than in the remaining five countries; in the broad definition of money (M_3), which has been most commonly used in recent years as a monetary target and/or indicator, demand has been growing particularly fast in Germany, Italy, and Switzerland. Such structural differences must be kept in mind in cross-country comparisons, since they clearly suggest that parallel rates of monetary growth in different countries imply rather different policy stances. Perhaps surprisingly, there seems to be no clear relationship between the money–income ratio and the degree to which countries have relied on quantitative restrictions on the activities of the institutions whose liabilities are included in the definition of money. Thus one finds among the countries with a high and rapidly rising money–income ratio both Italy, which has used credit ceilings extensively, and Germany and Switzerland, which have not. The pattern of claims of all credit institutions on the private sector also reveals structural differences (Table 11.2), with British and Dutch institutions holding claims relative to income of only one-half to two-thirds of those found in the other five countries.

A third type of difference relates to the size of securities markets and, particularly in recent years, the financing of government deficits. The degree to which the latter have been financed either through bond sales to the non-bank sector, or via monetary financing through the central bank or the private banking

[1] The bibliography at the end provides references to works which discuss the institutional background more fully.

TABLE 11.2. *Credit institutions private sector assets*
(amounts outstanding in per cent of GNP)

	End–1965	End–1975		
		Total	Credit	Securities
France	45	80	72	8
Germany	60	75	73	2
Italy	59	82	75	7
United Kingdom	43	53	47	6
Denmark	102	92	90	2
Netherlands	30	47	45	2

Source: Secretariat of the EEC Monetary Committee.

system, has been an important determinant of monetary developments — usually more significant than the combined use of other instruments of monetary policy. But here the differences over time within each country have been at least as important as those between countries. In most of the seven countries in the present survey (and in other European countries as well) there has been a movement from initially sizeable government deficits in the early post-war period, through more balanced, but fluctuating government financial positions, back to unprecedentedly large deficits during the protracted recession of the 1970s.

The present chapter is organized along the following lines: Section I surveys the three main themes outlined above with a minimum of country detail. Sections II to IV discuss country experience and cover roughly the period prior to 1960, 1960–72, and the years from 1973 onwards respectively. A short concluding section summarizes the main trends and presents a tentative assessment.

I. The Changing Environment

International financial integration

The change in the degree of openness of national financial markets in Western Europe since the 1950s is striking. Two major factors have been at work in this area — the late-1958 move to convertibility and the subsequent and more gradual expansion of Eurocurrency markets from the early 1960s onwards. Throughout the 1960s most European countries had been able to conduct their monetary policies in relative isolation from each other — though balance of payments considerations did at times influence their stance, policies were not unduly affected by large and destabilizing movements across the exchanges. This era came to an end with the essential step taken by fourteen countries[2] on 29 December 1958 to restore convertibility to their currencies with respect to all payments and normal credits arising from current transactions. Although most European countries stopped well short of liberating capital movements other than short-term commercial credits, the integrating effects of that move were sufficiently strong to change qualitatively the degree of interdependence of national monetary policies.

[2] The six EEC countries, the four Scandinavian countries, the United Kingdom, Austria, Ireland, and Portugal.

The movement towards more closely integrated financial markets was not, however, a steady one. Most empirical studies find support for the view that integration proceeded smoothly up to the mid-1960s.[3] Such a trend can be illustrated by the gradually closer conformity to interest-rate parity observed over this period for the forward rate of the dollar *vis-à-vis* most European currencies. But after about 1965 this trend is no longer traceable. Initially it was checked by increasingly severe controls on private capital movements — barriers to inflows in strong-currency countries and to outflows in weak ones. A subsequent check was provided by the transition to floating exchange rates in the years 1971-3 — a period in which anticipations of changes in currency relationships were swamping the effects of interest rate differentials on capital movements. Indeed, the instability this created in financial markets strengthened support for the 1973 move to floating which, in theory at least, could have checked financial integration even further and restored a large degree of independence to national monetary policies.

As experience with floating exchange rates accumulated, this optimistic view of the virtues of floating was modified. It became evident that international interdependence had changed its outward expression, but remained present as a strong constraint on the ability to pursue nationally determined monetary objectives. There was no evidence that external flows had become less important in the course of the 1970s; if anything they had become relatively larger in the second half of the decade (Table 11.3). This clearly illustrated the heavily managed nature of the exchange rate system. The European countries were not prepared to accept the volatility of exchange rates which would have resulted from a hands-off policy; and some of them at times created such stringency by their domestic monetary actions as to generate strong upward pressure on their currency and/or large inflows. Many of these external effects were welcome and even well designed; yet their sheer size underlined the continuing and growing need to design domestic monetary policy with external considerations in mind.

The second aspect of international financial integration mentioned above was the evolution of the Eurocurrency markets. These have come to serve a number of purposes: they supplement national money markets as an outlet for short-term funds from banks and large non-financial corporations, they provide facilities for hedging, and they supplement the lending operations of banks working in their own currency domain. Indeed, rapid growth of the Eurocurrency markets has at times been speeded up by restrictive national monetary measures tending to create excess demand for credit and money in European countries and in the United States. As markets operating to clear national financial imbalances the Eurocurrency markets have to an important extent become the common reference point in the design of national monetary policies. From the later 1960s onwards, official publications as well as econometric studies of the interrelationships between the national money and credit markets have increasingly taken Eurocurrency rates as the reference point from which changes in relative interest rates are measured, as against the earlier bilateral comparisons with rates in the United States.

---

[3] V. Argy and Z. Hodjera, 'Financial Integration and Interest Rate Linkages in the Industrial Countries, 1958–1971', *IMF Staff Papers*, March 1973.

TABLE 11.3. *External and domestic contributions to changes in monetary base, 1970–1979*
(in per cent of initial monetary base)

	1970	1971	1972	1973	1974	1975	1976	1977	1978	1979
France										
Monetary base	4.4	10.6	31.6	7.5	13.2	−21.7	7.5	8.8	12.3	6.6
Foreign assets	8.6	18.6	7.7	−5.5	−1.1	37.4	−6.0	15.6	17.2	49.7
Domestic assets	−4.2	−8.1	23.9	13.0	14.3	−59.1	13.4	−6.8	−4.9	−43.1
Germany										
Monetary base	21.5	15.0	26.3	7.4	−1.1	2.9	10.2	7.9	13.1	5.2
Foreign assets	42.8	14.6	19.6	15.2	−8.6	2.9	2.0	1.3	13.4	−0.1
Domestic assets	−21.3	0.4	6.7	−7.8	7.5	—	8.3	6.6	−0.3	5.3
Italy										
Monetary base	12.4	17.0	14.0	17.1	13.2	44.3	12.8	17.4	25.8	13.1
Foreign assets	2.6	5.1	−3.9	1.0	3.9	−6.1	31.3	20.5	20.2	19.8
Domestic assets	9.8	11.9	17.9	16.1	9.3	50.4	−18.5	−3.1	5.6	−6.7
United Kingdom										
Monetary base	11.6	−5.1	21.2	31.5	4.1	11.4	19.9	5.3	9.9	9.8
Foreign assets	6.8	52.0	−26.0	−0.4	−1.7	−7.6	−6.4	32.2	−5.2	28.9
Domestic assets	4.8	57.1	47.2	31.9	5.8	18.9	26.3	−26.9	15.1	−19.1
Denmark										
Monetary base	−9.8	2.0	5.1	2.3	6.1	38.9	4.5	−16.7	7.8	13.6
Foreign assets	3.3	19.3	10.1	30.2	−35.5	1.2	−0.6	50.4	60.9	1.9
Domestic assets	−13.1	−17.3	−5.0	−27.9	41.6	37.7	5.1	−67.1	−53.1	11.7
Netherlands										
Monetary base	5.5	4.9	9.1	4.8	7.9	13.5	6.2	9.0	7.9	7.9
Foreign assets	25.7	5.5	28.5	27.0	−2.8	11.3	−2.5	2.4	14.1	9.9
Domestic assets	−20.2	−0.6	−19.4	−22.2	10.7	2.2	8.7	6.6	−6.2	−2.0
Switzerland										
Monetary base	12.6	18.5	7.9	5.1	3.0	2.0	7.5	3.5	17.2	−8.0
Foreign assets	15.0	19.0	7.4	1.8	−0.5	9.9	17.2	−3.4	18.2	−11.0
Domestic assets	−2.4	−0.5	0.5	3.3	3.5	−7.9	−9.7	6.9	−1.0	3.0

Note: the foreign assets data include valuation adjustments on international reserves; the figures are significantly influenced in the 1970s by changes in exchange rates for the dollar and in the valuation of monetary gold. Foreign assets also include net government borrowing which is usually fully sterilized, i.e. offset by opposite changes in domestic assets.

Sources: B.G. Hickmann and S. Schleicher, 'The Interdependence of National Economies and the Synchronization of Economic Fluctuations: Evidence from the Link Project', *Weltwirtschaftliches Archiv*, No. 4, 1978; IMF, *International Financial Statistics* (various issues).

The rapid growth of Eurocurrency lending, particularly in the 1970s, led to an intensive debate on the desirability of extending national controls to this largely unregulated market. While action was limited to improvements in the statistical base for monitoring the markets and particularly the risk aspects of Eurocurrency lending, the impression persisted in several European countries that the growth of the Eurocurrency market was in itself a major contributing factor to the erosion of domestic monetary autonomy. It is important to retain a sense of proportion in this debate. If one looks at estimates of non-bank deposits in Eurocurrency markets relative to comparable figures for money holdings, Eurocurrency deposits constituted less than 3 per cent of the total world money stock at the end of 1978 (Table 11.4). For three European countries,

TABLE 11.4. *Monetary aggregates and non-bank deposits in the Eurocurrency market, end-1978*

	Broad money supply	Eurocurrency deposits	
	billion dollars	billion dollars	per cent of money supply
World total	4,200	115	2.7
Eight reporting European countries			
France	261	2.9	1.1
Germany	470	4.4	0.9
Italy	243	2.1	0.9
United Kingdom	115	11.1	9.7
BLEU	54	5.1	9.5
Netherlands	85	3.2	3.8
Sweden	35	0.7	2.0
Switzerland	122	10.0	8.2
Total	1,385	39.3	2.9
Canada	94	9.5	10.1
Japan	918	3.2	0.3
United States	963	26.5	2.8
Rest of the world	840	36.0	4.3

Source: H. Mayer, 'Credit and Liquidity Creation in the International Banking Sector', *BIS Economic Papers*, No. 1, 1979.

the United Kingdom, Belgium-Luxembourg, and Switzerland, foreign currency deposits with domestic banks plus other Eurodeposits approached 10 per cent, while most other reporting European countries showed a ratio as low as 2 per cent. These figures do not suggest that the loss of control over monetary aggregates had assumed alarming proportions in Europe. This conclusion is reinforced when it is kept in mind that a substantial part of the Eurocurrency deposits – residents' foreign currency deposits in their national banking system – were typically already included in the domestic money stock figures; this important component was accordingly watched closely by the respective national authorities and should not be regarded as a complement to national money.

Changing views of the transmission mechanism

Paralleling the changes in the international environment, and in the degree of international financial integration, were changes in the design and aims of policies, which partly reflected changing economic conditions but partly also new analytical and empirical insights. Though the task of any precise dating of changes in strategies is complicated by the stress which central banks put on a high degree of continuity in their formulation, interpretation, and implementation of policies, it may still be possible to argue, if at the risk of oversimplification, that the three decades under review can be divided into the following three broad phases (crudely summarized in Table 11.5):

(i) Up to the beginning of the 1960s an extended period of monetary accommodation with no ambition of controlling short-run economic fluctuations;

(ii) Between the early 1960s and 1972–3 a period of relative optimism that the proper role of monetary policy had become sufficiently well understood to permit short-run activism ('fine-tuning');

(iii) The remainder of the 1970s, when the emphasis shifted from short-run stabilization towards longer-run control of the inflation rate; the catch-phrase became 'target-constrained' monetary policies, with the constraints being perceived as desirable particularly because of their stabilizing impact on exchange rate and inflationary expectations.

The first of these phases comprised the period of post-war reconstruction and trade liberalization. It would not be correct to classify the entire period as one of passive accommodation by the monetary authorities, since there were important exceptions, such as counter-cyclical efforts in the United Kingdom in 1957–8, and monetary restraint-cum-reform in France in 1958–9. But a modest and mainly supportive role was certainly assigned to monetary policy up to the early 1960s in most countries.

Intellectually, the most detailed and authoritative statement from this phase is the report of the so-called Radcliffe Committee which appeared in 1959.[4] It argued, along Keynesian lines, that the transmission mechanism through which monetary policy affects real demand and employment was subtle and complex, incapable of being summarized in a single indicator such as the money supply. A rather broader concept, 'the state of liquidity', reflecting borrowers' views of their scope for raising additional credit, was seen as the centre-piece, but this concept lacked an empirical counterpart. Interest rates were seen as the main short-run, or operating, targets for the monetary authorities. Changes in the structure of interest rates would impinge both directly and indirectly on spending decisions: directly as a cost element, and indirectly because financial institutions would tend to modify their lending policies and thereby credit availability – 'the state of liquidity' – in the economy. Possibly the main lasting contribution of the Radcliffe Report was to supply a reasonably clear analysis of the interaction of interest rate movements and credit availability or rationing.

[4] *Committee on the Working of the Monetary System, Report* (Racliffe Report), Cmnd. 827, HMSO, London 1959.

TABLE 11.5. *Main features of monetary policy, 1950–1979*

	Ultimate objectives	External conditions	Theoretical foundation	Primary method	General characterization
1950s	Promote private fixed investment and economic growth	Fixed rates, low capital mobility	Keynesian	Low and stable interest rates	'Accommodating'
End 1950s– c.1972–73	Influence real demand; internal and external equilibrium	Fixed, but adjustable rates; higher capital mobility	Refined Keynesian (portfolio models); monetary approach to balance of payments	Variations in interest rates and in credit rationing	'Activist'
After 1973	Control of inflation	Flexible rates; high capital mobility	Monetarism; monetary models of exchange rates	Target path for M via monetary base, interest rates, or credit rationing	'Target-constrained'

The main impression left by this assessment of the role of monetary policy was that the transmission mechanism was, if not weak and unreliable, then at least insufficiently quantifiable for short-run stabilization purposes. It is characteristic that the Radcliffe Committee proposed the temporary imposition of credit ceilings, if it was thought necessary to assure a rapid and strong impact, as the best way to prevent a further deterioration on external account.

While the Radcliffe Report, based as it was on a careful study of the working of United Kingdom financial institutions, addressed itself directly only to British monetary management, there is no doubt that it was broadly representative of monetary thought on the Continent also around 1960. Relative to the United Kingdom, financial markets were less fully developed, and interest rates more rigid, but the view of the transmission mechanism was not much different. It was a view that implied a supportive and accommodating, rather than an activist, role for the monetary authorities in stabilization policy, leaving the major role in demand management to fiscal policy.

During the 1960s monetary policy nevertheless came to be used increasingly as a tool of demand management. In part, this may be explained by the constraints on domestic fiscal action. In part it was a reaction, as the decade unfolded, to increasing international integration. At home, the time-lags involved in changing tax rates or expenditure policies were longer than those required to change interest rates, reserve requirements, or other monetary instruments.[5] In addition, the political onus of putting up taxes and/or cutting expenditures — and these were increasingly the direction of action required as labour markets tightened and inflation accelerated during the 1960s — became heavier. Some evidence of 'electoral cycles', i.e. of occasionally pro-cyclical fiscal actions, may be found in Germany in 1965, in France in 1968-9, and, more pervasively, in a number of European countries at the time of the 1972 'superboom', which was largely synchronous in all the major industrial countries.

While these practical and political difficulties encountered in designing an effective fiscal stabilization policy seem to supply the major explanation for the more active use of monetary policy, the role of changing analytical views on its effects were also important. Central bankers were being told with increasing confidence by their own staff, by international organizations, and by academic economists that the elusive parameters in the complex transmission process were after all beginning to emerge, and that their values were generally conducive to the adoption of more activist policies. The second half of the 1960s and the first years of the 1970s were, after all, the years of intensive efforts at macroeconomic model-building on a large scale. Although the efforts and the confidence they generated never quite reached the level in Europe which could be observed in the United States, Canada, or Japan — with the central banks in these three countries in a very prominent role — there was in important respects a similar trend.

But greater reliance on monetary policy for domestic fine tuning purposes was gradually undermined by external developments. Increasingly, large capital flows acted as a buffer, offsetting the impact of internal monetary actions. Accelerations of domestic relative to foreign money creation tended to cause

[5] W.W. Heller et al., *Fiscal Policy for a Balanced Economy*, OECD, Paris 1968; B. Hansen, *Fiscal Policy in Seven Countries, 1955-1965*, OECD, Paris 1969.

outflows matching a growing share of the initial expansionary action. Similarly, increases in the discount rate or in reserve requirements were often largely offset through capital inflows. An important example of shrinking policy autonomy as a result of increasing financial integration was that of Germany; by 1970 capital mobility had increased to such an extent, notably because international financial transactions had become routine to even modest-sized non-financial German firms, that domestically motivated monetary actions had lost most of their effect.

Faced with a shrinkage of policy autonomy, not only in small open economies, but also in the larger European countries − indeed, in all countries except the United States, which remained protected by its reserve currency role − the attention of policy-makers became focused on the predictability of the external rather than the domestic effects of policy. Here again, the major reason for the change in the aims of policy activism arose for practical reasons, but analytical advances may also have played a part. The basic notion that monetary policy could, in a system of fixed exchange rates, be assigned the task of managing the level of international reserves, leaving to fiscal policy the task of managing domestic demand, had already been formulated in the early 1960s by Mundell and Fleming.[6] The notion that it was possible to achieve a roughly predictable impact on private capital movements, through variations in domestic interest rates and/or the degree of credit rationing relative to conditions prevailing in other countries, responded well to the needs of the monetary authorities in Europe in the late 1960s. The impact proved less easily predictable once it had been recognized that the properly specified relationships were between relative monetary conditions and desired *stocks* of assets and liabilities, but nevertheless early models based on this portfolio view of capital movements appeared to account rather well for observed flows up to around 1969.[7]

But at the end of the 1960s, not to speak of the turbulent 1970-1 phase, capital flows ceased to be stably related to domestic monetary actions. Fine tuning of the external objective looked as elusive as pursuit of any precise impact on real demand components, for which it had been substituted in a number of European economies. It was in this climate of growing disillusionment among policy-makers with the efficiency of monetary policy as a tool of short-run external and domestic stabilization that the main theses of monetarism gained ground. It is important, if one is to get a proper perspective on the extent to which the monetarist challenge was absorbed into the central-bank practice in the 1970s, to recall briefly what exactly that challenge was.

Leaving aside the monetarist view of fiscal policy actions as a weak and temporary influence on real demand (and the inflation rate), there were three main points: (a) the time-lags with which changes in monetary instruments have an impact on spending decisions are both long and variable; (b) the monetary authorities cannot use their control over nominal quantities to peg a real quantity such as the real interest rate, the rate of unemployment, or real income; (c) it is advisable to select, in each country according to its institutional circumstances,

---

[6] R.A. Mundell, 'The Appropriate Use of Monetary and Fiscal Policy for Internal and External Stability', *IMF Staff Papers*, March 1962; J.M. Fleming, 'Domestic Financial Policies under Fixed and Floating Exchange Rates', *IMF Staff Papers*, November 1962.

[7] W.H. Branson and R.D. Hill, Jr., 'Capital Movements in the OECD Area', *OECD Economic Outlook − Occasional Studies*, December 1971.

some concept of the money supply as the prime target and to stick to a low and steady rate of expansion for this aggregate.

The first point challenges the confidence inspired by the apparent stability of Keynesian macroeconomic models in the 1960-72 period. These models would be consistent with the view that the time-lags are long, though they would point out that the short-run effects of monetary measures are significant, thus making their contribution to demand stabilization desirable. But the real point is that the gradual build-up over a long period, say two to three years, of the effects of monetary policy puts the monetary authorities in a dilemma. If some monetary measure is designed with a view to its effects within a one-year horizon, it is unlikely that the additional effects will fit well into the desired macroeconomic pattern for years 2 and 3; they may have to be at least in part neutralized by measures in the opposite direction. The consequence of the extended time pattern of the responses to monetary actions is to impose a notable instability upon the monetary actions themselves. And such fluctuations may be so upsetting to financial markets and thereby to the prospects of achieving a desired impact on real demand that they are not worth having.[8]

The second point was the central message of Friedman,[9] who argued that, by gearing monetary policy to the maintenance or lowering of an already modest level of unemployment, United States and other policy-makers of the late 1960s were causing steadily *accelerating* inflation — and not just a once-and-for-all upward shift in the inflation rate as advocates of ambitious Keynesian policies had claimed. Accelerating inflation was a price that central banks, whether they have a specific mandate from central banking legislation to devote attention particularly to the internal and external stability of the currency — as do, say, the German or Dutch banks — or not, were eventually bound to consider too high.

The third and most specific monetarist prescription — the low and steady norm for a chosen measure of the money supply — flatly contradicts the Radcliffean view of the money stock as an inadequate or outright useless policy target. The monetarist view is that nominal interest rates, so dominant in the 1950s and most of the 1960s as intermediate targets in policy, had become highly unreliable guideposts in a period of rapid and variable inflation; and to aim for some particular target for the 'real' interest rate, i.e. the nominal rate minus the expected inflation rate, was not feasible in view of the inobservability of the latter. The best alternative was to aim for a steady or gradually lower rate of expansion of the money supply, converging on the growth rate of productive potential of the economy. Such a policy would not only prevent overambitious activist policies, but could also be assumed to have a maximum stabilizing influence on exchange rate and inflationary expectations.

A later group of theorists — the neo-classical or neo-Austrian school — which stresses that policy achieves its effects largely through its influence on expectations, has tightened the monetarist prescription by advocating not gradualism, but the announcement of a rapid move towards a permanently low growth rate for the money supply. If such a policy looks credible over a medium-term

[8] The counter-argument is, of course, that a policy of sticking rigidly to a steady growth of a monetary aggregate would be likely to lead to pronounced volatility in short-term interest rates.

[9] M. Friedman, 'The Role of Monetary Policy', *American Economic Review*, March 1968.

horizon, price expectations should adjust quickly without requiring a sustained period of deflation and unemployment. This school also argues that activist monetary policies are ineffectual as long as they derive from a stable strategy of the monetary authorities, i.e. a strategy which can be predicted by the private sector of the economy. 'Only surprises matter,' as Friedman has argued.[10]

The views of the neo-Austrian school, with its emphasis on the role of expectations, represent the ultimate challenge to monetary policy-makers. These views have, not surprisingly, generally been rejected by both central bankers and by the majority of monetarists, who advocate gradualism. But the more general monetarist message is one that has largely been absorbed during the 1970s, initially by most central banks, and from the middle of the decade also by governments in Europe. The environment had worsened dramatically by then: the level of unemployment at which attempts to lower it through expansionary demand management policies lead to accelerating inflation appeared to have moved up as a result of structural changes in the labour market. The European economies were subjected to far larger external shocks than before, particularly the quadrupling of oil prices in 1973-4. Most important of all, national financial markets and, since widespread floating was introduced in 1973, exchange markets had become highly sensitive to any information pertaining to the inflationary outlook, including policy changes. Any such change by the monetary authorities, leaving open the interpretation that priorities had shifted in favour of expansion, could be seen in these circumstances to endanger both the internal and external stability of the currency through anticipations of higher inflation. The latter would also tend to push up nominal interest rates, nullifying or even reversing the effects of the initial easing of policy.

On the other hand, the breakthrough of monetarist prescriptions occurred at a time when their intellectual justification was gradually becoming less obvious than during the late 1960s, when monetarism, as summarized in the three propositions listed above, found its clearest formulation. First, the demand for money was becoming less stable, undermining the use of monetary aggregates as targets. Second, the degree of financial innovation accelerated in the sense that any one measure of the money supply was overtaken by some other closely related measure more frequently than before. Such a speeding-up of the process of financial innovation was prompted both by increasing financial integration across borders, which eroded the significance of traditional national monetary aggregates, and by methods of quantitative credit regulation which prompted attempts at evasion of normal financial channels — the so-called process of disintermediation. And, third, the major external shock — that of the oil price explosion — was not a demand, but rather a supply shock. Monetarist prescriptions are not necessarily relevant in such a situation. It is arguable that a once-and-for-all increase in the money stock to accommodate the impact of higher oil prices in 1974, with policy reverting subsequently to a relatively low and stable monetary growth rate, might have been preferable to the more rigidly monetarist course followed, notably in Germany.[11] The alternative policy might

[10] M. Friedman, 'Nobel Lecture: Inflation and Unemployment', *Journal of Political Economy*, June 1977, p. 456.

[11] F. Modigliani, 'The Monetarist Controversy or, Should We Forsake Stabilization Policies?', *American Economic Review*, March 1977.

have maintained a significantly higher level of employment at a small cost of additional inflation.

Market-oriented versus administrative approaches

A third, and very interesting observable trend in post-war monetary history in Europe has been the changing view on market-oriented versus administrative approaches to monetary policy. Most European countries — Germany is the main exception — have at some time or other experimented with quantitative regulation of bank credit. The motives have varied, but have typically included a desire to achieve faster and more predictable effects than by indirect methods; very often it has also been implicitly assumed that quantitative controls obviated the need for sharp increases in interest rates.

There is little clear evidence in favour of these two apparently reasonable propositions. Large-scale econometric models constructed to analyse the impact of policy in various countries show no superiority of quantitative credit regulation over market-oriented methods. It is interesting to note that the clearest evidence of strong macroeconomic effects of monetary policy were found in, on the one hand, the United States, and on the other Japan — two countries which could be said to represent extremes in monetary techniques.[12] The European countries span an almost equally wide range of arrangements and philosophies, with Germany towards the United States' end of the spectrum and France, Italy, and Spain towards the Japanese end, with no evidence to suggest that monetary policy is made more effective through reliance on credit ceilings.

The other argument usually advanced in favour of reliance on ceilings, namely that they obviate the need for sharp increases in interest rates, has to be qualified. When lending institutions find themselves constrained by a ceiling from meeting demands for loans at prevailing interest rates, they will try to raise the latter towards a market-clearing level. In other words, rationing will tend to be replaced by higher lending rates. To the extent that this succeeds, the authorities will typically be concerned with the distributional consequences. By appropriating the cartel-like revenue which observance of the ceilings in a phase of excess demand for credit makes possible, the lenders gain at the expense of the borrowers. This can be prevented by imposing ceilings on lending rates as a supplement to those on credits; there has indeed been a tendency for the two kinds of intervention to feed upon each other, which suggests that ceilings on lending may be regarded as a substitute for higher interest rates only when bolstered by further administrative intervention in the determination of the lending rates themselves.

During the 1960s and the early 1970s there was a movement away from direct public intervention into credit flows and/or interest rates. The most dramatic single step was taken in the United Kingdom in 1971, when the authorities abandoned credit ceilings on the main banks in a move towards creating more competition in the financial sector. Similar, though more gradual, reforms were made in France and Germany by withdrawing public approval from interest rate agreements among the banks. France also abandoned in 1970 her policy of ceilings on bank lending (*encadrement du crédit*).

[12] OECD, *The Role of Monetary Policy in Demand Management*, Paris 1975, Part IV.

It is clear that these and similar steps in other European countries over the same period were taken because the authorities were becoming increasingly worried about the longer-term costs in terms of loss of efficiency in the financial sector through more active competition. No country had succeeded in developing a design of direct control of lending combining effective control of aggregate credit flows with the changes in market shares and in specialization which are typically associated with a competitive banking sector. But there was also a concern in countries that had practised ceilings on lending for extended periods of time that these methods were gradually losing their impact as financial institutions and their customers found ways around the restrictions. Competition was not inactive, but it took forms that appeared detrimental to the institutions affected by the regulations.

While the movement in the early 1970s as a result of these misgivings about the longer-run effects of quantitative regulations was clearly towards greater reliance on market-related instruments of monetary policy, the perspective at the end of the 1970s was different. Several countries — France, Italy, and the United Kingdom among them — had reintroduced more direct methods of controlling the monetary aggregates. With increasingly difficult tasks assigned to monetary policy in a world of high inflation and large public sector deficits, the authorities had not found it possible to dispense with a differentiated range of instruments, including some that hinged more directly on bank lending decisions than squeezes on bank reserves and high money-market rates. The 'corset' system which operated in the United Kingdom between 1973 and 1980, and the progressive reserve requirement on transgressions of a loan ceiling in France, were examples of a partial return to direct methods of control, given the penal nature of the deposit requirements. And in some countries, where a non-monetary financing of public sector deficits had a high priority, control over interest rates offered by banks to holders of large deposits seemed a useful instrument for directly affecting the capacity of the government to sell its debt instruments to the non-bank public; Denmark provided a clear example of this type of motivation for reverting to direct intervention in interest rate formation.

In addition to these trends towards more frequent administrative measures, selective policy measures also became more frequent as the 1970s unfolded. Never absent in previous periods, particularly in the form of export credit schemes at preferential rates, they spread to domestic sectors threatened by unemployment and/or rapid restructuring: shipbuilding and steel were the most prominent examples. No systematic surveys of such special financing arrangements exist, but an impression of their importance may be gathered from, e.g., an OECD survey of 'positive' adjustment policies.[13]

It would, however, be an exaggeration to say that the more interventionist approach gradually adopted amounted to a total reversal of the earlier trend towards greater reliance on the market mechanism. It remained a highly significant fact that the political constraints on movements in the level of interest rates had weakened visibly during the decade. The period of high and variable inflation in the 1970s had effectively destroyed earlier notions of what could be regarded as a normal, or desirable, level of interest rates — or the more elaborate

[13] OECD, *The Case for Positive Adjustment Policies*, Paris 1979.

notions of, say, the Radcliffe Committee as to a 'low-', 'middle-', and 'high-gear' interest rate.[14] The significant development was not only that private agents had ceased to attach any precise meaning to such terms; the central banks had gained acceptance from politicians and from the public for the view that historically observed ranges of interest rates could not be used as a guide for what was tolerable. This was important both in paving the way to adoption of monetary targets as described above, but also in relieving the authorities of the burden of intervening in financial markets to keep nominal rates from reflecting fully rising inflation. Institutional changes (e.g. introducing variable interest rates rather than rates fixed for the maturity of the loan over a wider spectrum of contracts) helped to make this trend possible by sharing the apparent burden of higher rates more widely among debtors and thereby removing the sense of gross un-fairness caused by rapid changes in borrowing conditions for only new long-term debtors, notably private house-buyers. The political taboo which surrounded rapid movements or transgressions of sensitive target levels of interest rates had weakened so much as to arguably constitute the most important single factor in the evolution from the more rigid financial markets of the 1950s to the more market-oriented methods of conducting monetary policy of the 1970s.

II. The Early Post-war Phase — Support for Investment and Growth

According to all three of the proposed organizing principles, the early post-war phase has clear distinguishing features. The degree of openness was limited, at least prior to the introduction of convertibility at the end of 1958. Domestic policy objectives tended to dominate, at least after the external constraint was eased by Marshall Aid and the setting up of the EPU in 1950. But external ob-jectives — mainly a sustainable current account position — were never absent in some of the smaller economies, and tended to demand increasing attention to-wards the end of the 1950s in the large ones as well. Ambitions to regulate demand were largely absent, as witnessed by the formulation and implementa-tion of policy in the form of fairly low and stable interest rates. Towards the end of the decade some misgivings were voiced about the possibility of avoiding more significant changes in interest rates — the Radcliffe Committee advocated changes in their level and structure, a change in 'gearing', to use their terminology.

The clearest illustrations of the generally supportive and accommodating role assigned to monetary policy in this phase of rapid growth are those of Germany and Italy. Germany experienced exceptionally rapid growth with an annual in-flation rate of only 2 per cent on average between 1950 and 1960. The initial worry of an external deficit which dominated at the time of the launching of the EPU evaporated in the following year; from 1951 Germany became a surplus country *vis-à-vis* its EPU partners. In retrospect, monetary policy was remark-ably expansionary, with the growth rate of the money stock running perma-nently 3 to 4 percentage points above the growth rate of nominal incomes, and 5 percentage points above that of real output.

Towards the end of the 1950s a conflict between internal and external stability became apparent. Indeed, revaluation was first seriously discussed

[14] 'Radcliffe Report', para. 495.

around 1957[15] as a means of resolving what was to become the recurrent dilemma in German economic policy – the reconciliation of a cooling-off of domestic demand and better equilibrium on the current account. But initially orthodoxy prevailed and the conflict continued to be resolved in favour of domestic considerations up to and including a major tightening of policy in 1959.

Italy is another example of a country which was able to design its monetary policy so as to play a strongly supportive role during the phase of rapid growth which lasted for more than a decade and a half after the war. Resources were far from fully utilized. Though measured unemployment fell strongly as emigration abroad or to the north reduced surplus labour in the south, it remained well above levels registered elsewhere in Europe. The balance of payments was in a healthy condition throughout most of the period prior to 1962-3, and inflation was very moderate. It is therefore not surprising that monetary policy was accommodating or even expansionary, as was the case in 1958, which was a year of moderate recession in Europe.

Switzerland is a third example of an accommodating stance, though here it has never been possible to overlook the external influences and objectives. Already in the 1950s the growth of reserve money was largely externally generated. A small trade deficit was more than offset by net service earnings, the resulting current account surplus leaving – after some long-term capital exports – additions to Switzerland's international reserves sufficient to match the trend increase in the demand for currency and bank reserves. In no other European country – though possibly in some 'dependent' economy in the Sterling or Franc Areas where money creation was linked by law or custom to changes in holdings of international reserves – was the domination of external sources so complete or so smooth. In these circumstances, the one classical monetary instrument available to the Swiss authorities – changes in refinancing terms at the central bank – was not of much relevance, since banks were sufficiently well endowed with owned reserves to have very little need of indebting themselves to the central bank. In practice, the discount rate remained fixed at 1½ per cent up to 1957, and was only rarely changed in the following years.

This remarkably passive monetary stance did not give rise to any serious imbalances until the end of the 1950s, when an export-led boom got under way. When this produced severe bottle-necks in the labour market the Swiss authorities responded by encouraging immigration to supplement the country's own slow-growing labour force, instead of curtailing demand by deflation and/or revaluation. But although this policy worked well in a macroeconomic sense, some weaknesses in the Swiss monetary armour became visible. Apart from the largely ineffectual refinancing terms, the authorities had to rely either on making special arrangements for conducting open market sales – they had no permanent portfolio from which to sell – or on *ad hoc* gentlemen's agreements for which there was a long tradition. But this was hardly adequate when, for the first time, in 1960 during the international crisis surrounding the independence of Zaire, the Swiss franc had visibly become a refuge currency. So for Switzerland as for Germany, though for somewhat different reasons, it is appropriate to date the intensified external orientation in 1960.

[15] O. Emminger, 'The D-Mark in the Conflict Between Internal and External Equilibrium, 1948-75', *Princeton Essays in International Finance*, No. 122, 1977.

The predominance of domestic objectives in the 1950s is also evident in France. Under the Fourth Republic the monetary authorities were confronted with two major tasks — to contribute to a slowdown of the inflation rate, which tended to run well ahead of those in neighbouring countries, and to assist in the allocation of resources in accordance with the priorities set by the longer-term plans. It would not be misleading to describe monetary policy in the 1950s as largely an adjunct to the Plan — a description which has connotations of selective credit policies.

Even if the authorities had intended to pursue more activist policies it is doubtful whether the instruments available could have delivered the goods. The main instrument was changes in refinancing terms, but the discount and other lending rates varied less than in most comparable countries. Rediscount ceilings were applied to each bank, but they did not apply to categories of lending favoured for selective reasons, i.e. medium-term credits (and the banks retained ample scope for borrowing). To assist banks in their role of transforming short-term deposits into the needed long-term credits — a transformation which the deposit banks undertook on a rather narrow capital base — the Banque de France had also established other liberal criteria for borrowing. Without changes in the register of instruments or a very active discount rate policy, the French authorities had little scope for policies that were other than accommodating. New instruments (in the form of ceilings on bank lending and minimum ratios of Treasury bills and medium-term discountable paper to deposits) were developed in 1959–60, but policies continued to be largely accommodating well beyond the start of the Fifth Republic and up to the first phase of major restriction in 1963.

As regards the United Kingdom it is arguable that monetary policy was already developing in this early phase towards an increasingly external orientation. In their review of the use of monetary measures between 1951 and the end of 1958, the authors of the Radcliffe Report made frequent reference to external factors.[16] Spurred by the large 1949 devaluation of sterling, British exports rose rapidly, but the external position nevertheless remained precarious because of occasional domestic overheating and a relatively high degree of (primarily non-resident) capital instability. The very large volume of outstanding short-term Treasury debt also complicated the task of getting a firmer hold on domestic credit expansion. Sharp increases in interest rates were, however, engineered in late 1954 and again in the summer of 1957. On both occasions domestic indicators of demand pressure combined with an emerging current deficit (aggravated by adverse 'leads and lags' in external payments) and the government found it necessary to confirm its intention of sticking to the existing sterling parity of $2.80. In 1957 the restrictive measures also included a ceiling on bank lending to the private sector; when this ceiling was removed in mid-1958, advances accelerated strongly, a factor which apparently contributed to the boom which developed during 1959. The 'more conventional instruments (of monetary policy) have failed to keep the system in smooth balance', as the Radcliffe Committee noted.[17]

[16] 'Radcliffe Report', pp. 136–48.
[17] Ibid., para. 472.

Monetary policy in the Netherlands has attracted international attention since the interwar period, when the methods and strategy of the Nederlandsche Bank were first set forth in a clear and original way. It is no exaggeration to say that most of the elements in the monetary approach to the balance of payments which has become fashionable since the late 1960s were present in 'Dutch monetarism'.[18] The latter takes as a starting-point the notion of monetary equilibrium which prevails when the demand for a well-defined category of financial assets matches the supply of such assets at a low inflation rate. The designated category of financial assets includes, in addition to currency and demand deposits, secondary liquid assets, i.e. Treasury bills and notes and other easily encashable claims on the authorities. The empirical nature of the definition is underlined by the fact that it has been widened gradually to take account of new institutional developments which have imparted liquidity to a larger group of assets.[19] This empirical approach to the choice of an aggregate monetary objective conforms well to the prescriptions of Friedman and other early monetarists in selecting the most relevant concept of money stock.

To decide upon a proper definition of the aggregate is, however, only the first step. A second and equally important step is to interpret properly what constitutes an equilibrium level for the ratio of the aggregate to GDP — the liquidity ratio. The Dutch authorities aimed to reduce the ratio from the level of 0.5 prevailing in the early post-war period. In particular, during periods of strain in the current account, they refrained from sterilizing fully the external drain; conversely, they did not allow the external generation of liquidity in the late 1950s and early 1960s to become fully reflected in the ratio. This asymmetry of reactions, which was restated by Dutch officials in the late 1970s as a desirable course in the EMS, was based on the conviction that merely aiming to keep the growth of liquid assets in step with the growth of nominal income — i.e. a stable liquidity ratio — would in the long run imply an excessively accommodating policy. The Dutch authorities have several times stressed that their preferred way of expressing the monetary objective was not intended to convey accommodation. They have seen it as very similar to a money supply rule, though with some allowance for deviations from a steady path in order not to fully sterilize money creation through the external account, and not to permit too sharp increases in interest rates as a result of complete bond financing of public sector deficits. Thus the policy has in essence not been different from a pragmatic management of a monetary aggregate target; what was remarkable about it was rather that it evolved before monetarism had reached the public debate.

[18] H.G. Johnson, *Inflation and the Monetarist Controversy*, F. De Vries Lectures, Amsterdam 1972; the clearest statement of Dutch 'monetarism' can be found in Nederlandsche Bank, *Annual Report*, 1963, pp. 70–6.

[19] In particular, savings deposits were to some extent reclassified in the late 1960s; savings deposits are included fully in liquid assets if they have a high turnover rate, but only partially or not at all if they turn over slowly. In practice, only a minor part (10 to 15 per cent) of savings deposits are found to be liquid. Recent empirical work (M.M.G. Fase, 'The Demand for Financial Assets: Time Series Evidence for the Netherlands: 1963 II – 1975 IV', *European Economic Review*, October 1979), has suggested that the degree of substitution between 'money' and ordinary time deposits is low so that the latter could be left out of the definition.

The strong performance of the Dutch economy over the better part of the first two decades after the war reflected a mixture of cautious demand management policies and an undervaluation of the guilder between the 1949 devaluation of 30 per cent and the 1963 wage explosion. Monetary policy contributed strongly to this long period of non-inflationary growth. The excess liquidity left by the war was reduced drastically by a conversion in 1945, and the authorities subsequently aimed at keeping money creation at most in step with the growth of money income.

The tasks of monetary policy became, however, more difficult towards the end of the 1950s. The authorities were trying to curtail a domestic credit expansion and at the same time encourage capital exports to offset a persistent external surplus. Ceilings on bank lending were introduced with a view to keeping domestic money creation consistent with a liquidity ratio of at most 0.4. Combined with a rather restrictive fiscal policy and a 5 per cent revaluation in 1961, approximate internal and external balance was apparently maintained for a while until the wage explosion of 1963.

Denmark is another example of a small open economy for which the option of neglecting external objectives in the 1950s was not open – even less so than for the Netherlands. The task of defending the country's international reserves was dominant prior to 1957-8, when net reserves never rose far above zero and the scope for international borrowing was limited to the short-term facilities of the EPU. A remarkably explicit formulation of a monetary rule was incorporated in a written agreement between the government and the central bank in 1951, namely to allow any external deficit to be fully reflected in a contraction of the monetary base while requiring any external surplus to be sterilized by government bond sales. The agreement was closely akin in spirit to 'Dutch monetarism', though without the explicit theoretical basis developed by the Nederlandsche Bank. Observed monetary trends show that the agreement was never rigidly adhered to and that it was allowed gradually to fade into oblivion. But the rule nevertheless supplied a framework for evaluating the proper size of the government deficit and the division of its financing between money creation and bond sales – a framework only resurrected in the late 1970s.

III. From the Early 1960s to the Early 1970s – The High Tide of Policy Activism

As one moves into the 1960s the conflict between external and internal equilibrium becomes more pronounced in most European countries. With employment and capacity utilization generally at high levels and with a continuing strong underlying trend in real demand, often assured by rapid growth of public expenditures, there was no longer any need for largely accommodating monetary policies. Rather, the domestic situation required that policy be geared to assuring that the growth of demand be kept roughly in step with that of productive capacity. But there were occasions when an external constraint pushed policymakers into a restrictive stance earlier than warranted by domestic considerations. The focus was on the ability of the available monetary instruments to contribute to the prevention of domestic overheating and external current deficits, while the issue of whether demand could also be effectively stimulated through expansionary monetary action attracted rather less attention. There was a tendency to assume that the mere removal of the monetary brakes would be sufficient to put real demand back on its underlying rising trend — an assumption which proved erroneous, at least in some cases.

In France, the first major experience with activist policies was in 1963–5. In the light of accelerating inflation the authorities increased the minimum liquidity ratios of the banks and imposed ceilings on bank lending in the early months of 1963. All monetary aggregates decelerated significantly, i.e. by 5 to 10 percentage points relative to the high rates of growth in 1961–2. The effects of the policy appeared to be satisfactory; the annual rate of inflation decelerated from nearly 6 per cent early in 1963 to little more than 2 per cent from mid-1965 to mid-1967, and the current account swung back into a small surplus. These results were achieved without opening up any major gap between productive capacity and actual output. It would not be reasonable to attribute the major part of these effects to monetary policy, since fiscal policy and tighter supervision of prices and incomes also contributed. But the experience left the impression that monetary instruments were helpful in pursuing shorter-term stabilization goals — and that the main contribution came from credit rationing as banks complied with ceilings, rather than through interest rates; in fact nominal rates moved very little.

A second phase of activist policy occurred towards the end of the decade. The growth rate of the monetary aggregates jumped up sharply in 1968 to accommodate the increased borrowing needs of enterprises arising from the high wage settlements which ended the turbulent spring months. The liquidity situation facilitated major speculation on a realignment of the exchange rate. When it became clear in the autumn that no such decision was imminent, monetary policy was tightened in several ways: credit ceilings and exchange controls were reimposed, while interest rates were allowed to move up with unprecedented speed. But tight policies proved inadequate to contain inflation and the external deficit. A surprise devaluation in August 1969 — enlarged by a DM revaluation a month later — helped to bring the current account back to near balance in 1970; and there was a massive reflow of capital. Monetary policy, which had been further tightened in 1969, was gradually eased in the following year and the main instrument — the ceiling on bank lending — was removed.

Looking at the monetary indicators for the two periods of restraint, the second one looks more severe in terms of both interest rate increases and deceleration of bank lending. As regards interest rates, political sensitivity had receded and rates had become much freer to move after official controls on both lending and deposit rates had been eased during 1965–7. Since the discount rate was also used much more vigorously in the second phase, the upward shift of rates was at the same time much larger and more pervasive. Yet the impact on real demand was no stronger than in the earlier phase, and the inflation performance hardly improved, at least when measured in terms of consumer prices. Attainment of the ultimate domestic objectives through activist monetary (and fiscal) policies had become harder. On the other hand, the second phase of restraint (including devaluation) was very successful in reversing the deterioration in the current external account, and, particularly, in regenerating a capital inflow.

An equally clear illustration of the changing environment for monetary policy in the 1960s is supplied by Italy. Monetary restraint was applied vigorously in September 1963 in the face of simultaneous domestic and external indications of overheating. Bank reserves declined sharply well into 1964 following the limitation of foreign borrowing. The monetary aggregates decelerated and long-term interest rates rose significantly. But the phase of restraint was short; the policy was eased in the spring of 1964 as evidence of weakening demand became unambiguous. Despite this, the effects appear to have been both sizeable and durable. The current account was back in surplus by mid-1964 and continued to improve throughout 1965. The inflation performance improved steadily; both wholesale and consumer price indices decelerated gradually from a 6 to 8 per cent annual range down to 2 to 3 per cent per annum two years later. But this was achieved at the cost of an extended slowdown in the rate of growth of domestic demand which opened up a sizeable gap of unused resources and — more seriously in a long-run perspective — dampened private investment demand; industrial investment only surpassed the 1963 level in 1970.

It was a source of much dispute in Italy whether this remarkable change in the economic climate could be attributed largely to monetary restraint.[20] Business investment had begun to fall before restraint was applied and would probably have continued doing so for some time in view of the cost increases observed in 1962–63; the change in monetary policy reinforced the decline. But there seems to be general agreement that the application of the monetary brakes, reinforced by some modest increases in taxation and controls on hire purchases in the course of 1964, did have a lasting effect on the rate of inflation and on financial behaviour. This rather remarkable and drawn-out impact underlined the power and asymmetry of monetary policy — it seemed far easier to restrain than to encourage demand.

The intended ease and steadiness of policy found expression in stable growth rates for the monetary aggregates and for the chosen operational target in this period, the monetary base — but also, and more remarkably, in stable interest rates in the long-term bond market between mid-1966 and mid-1969; the Banca d'Italia publicly indicated its intention to peg rates in the face of a rapidly rising Treasury borrowing requirement. Surprisingly, this policy did not for a long time require large-scale purchases of government bonds by the bank, which would have undermined the steady creation of monetary base; rather, pegging led to a substantial upward shift in the demand for bonds from the private non-bank sector.

But, gradually, the level at which rates had been pegged was made unrealistic by the rise in foreign interest rates and in observed and expected inflation in Italy. The experiment in financial stabilization, in some ways reminiscent of policies in the 1950s, had to be interrupted by a second restrictive phase between mid-1969 and mid-1970, triggered off by accelerating inflation and a deteriorating current account, which began in the early part of 1969 but was substantially worsened by the 'Hot Autumn' events at the turn of the year. In response, the Treasury bill rate was allowed to rise for the first time in two decades and the

---

[20] See, notably, Bank of Italy, *Annual Report, 1964*, and F. Modigliani and G. La Malfa, 'Inflation, Balance of Payments Deficit and their Cure through Monetary Policy: The Italian Example', *Banca Nazionale del Lavoro Quarterly Review*, March 1967.

discount rate was put up, leading to an upward adjustment of bond rates of 2 percentage points. These measures quickly succeeded in reversing the worsening trend in capital outflows; in the course of 1970 the pre-1969 pattern with the current surplus partially offset by capital outflows was re-established. But there was no success comparable to that of 1963-4 in reducing domestic inflation. In this sense the Italian experience in the two phases of restraint is parallel to that of France — domestic objectives became less attainable. Activist policies had to be geared to external objectives, where, on the other hand, they proved effective.

The United Kingdom provides a similar illustration, though the external inspiration of monetary policy was clearer throughout the 1960s. During the early part of the decade policy continued along the same activist lines as in the 1950s. Swings in the external account necessitated several changes in policy stance, ranging from sharply restrictive in 1961 to expansionary in 1963. The traditional instruments of changes in the discount rate and in short-term market rates were actively used, as were changes in reserve requirements in the form of calls for 'Special Deposits'. But a growing public sector borrowing requirement (PSBR) from 1963 onwards imposed increasingly severe restraints on the feasible range of variation for interest rates. The Bank of England felt a conflict between its role in stabilizing and enlarging the market for government debt (requiring stable interest rates) and an activist policy. The conflict was (partly) solved by a more regular use of credit ceilings than envisaged by the Radcliffe Committee. A ceiling on lending in sterling by most deposit institutions was introduced in 1965 and retained for six years. Though it was gradually undermined by competition from non-regulated institutions, it remained the dominant instrument in this period.

By the time of the 1967 devaluation, policy had to some extent been redesigned within a macroeconomic framework suitable for an open economy with a fixed exchange rate. Major emphasis was put on a target in terms of Domestic Credit Expansion (DCE); in practice the major new element was that the PSBR was monitored more closely. By holding back on credit to both the private and the public sector, monetary policy contributed importantly to the dramatic improvement in the external position that followed the devaluation.

Turning now to surplus countries, Germany, after a small revaluation in 1961 prompted by speculative pressures, remained relatively close to both internal and external equilibrium until the mid-1960s. Monetary policy was fairly activist, being guided by small changes in the inflation rate and in indicators of pressure in the labour market. But cyclical movements were not fully avoided; there is evidence of overheating in 1964-5, and a short sharp recession developed in 1966-7. Contemporary analyses put most of the blame for these deviations from an otherwise successful performance relative to other European countries on failures of fiscal policy. Indeed, public expenditures appear to have moved procyclically in this phase, notably around the 1965 elections, and the experience led to the adoption in 1967 of the *Stabilitätsgesetz*, or 'Stabilization law'.[21]

The conflict between internal and external objectives arose once more in the course of 1968. The inflation rate had crept upwards in most European countries

[21] See Chs. 10 and 16.

and in the United States since the mid-1960s, whereas Germany came very close to complete price stability during the 1967 recession. Combined with very large current surpluses, this greatly reinforced expectations of a parity adjustment. Since no such decision could be agreed upon, capital inflows began to swell the German money supply in late 1968. Initially, they were sterilized by imposition of 100 per cent reserve requirements on the increase in bank external liabilities, and acceptance of non-resident deposits was made subject to licensing.

As a boom was clearly under way a further tightening of monetary policy appeared desirable. The Bundesbank saw the increase in foreign interest rates in early 1969 as providing the required scope for such a policy change, but movements in bank liquidity became increasingly dominated by capital flows. Furthermore, the observed decline in the main operating target, the ratio of bank liquidity to deposits, did not perceptibly change the readiness of the banks to increase credit to the private sector. It was only following a 9.3 per cent revaluation in October 1969 and a subsequent outflow of capital that the desired degree of monetary tightness was achieved — and then only briefly. In 1970 inflows became more massive than ever, as interest rates in Eurocurrency markets dropped. It appeared, even more clearly than ten years earlier, that these inflows were at times able to completely swamp or even reverse restrictive policy actions.

The German experience in the final stages of the fixed exchange rate system has been studied intensively, but interpretations differ. Initially, the analysis focused on Germany's ability to sterilize inflows, i.e. capital movements were regarded as an externally generated disturbance to which the Bundesbank reacted by putting up reserve requirements, lowering rediscount quotas, etc. Adopting this view, one author found that the Bundesbank had succeeded over the 1963–70 period in sterilizing 80 to 90 per cent of the net inflows of capital, leading to the conclusion that monetary autonomy had not been fully eroded.[22] But the German data also did not contradict a rather different hypothesis, namely that Germany's domestic monetary measures were the dominant cause of the volatile capital flows. Starting from this hypothesis, two studies concluded that net capital flows had offset on average as much as 80 per cent of the impact of the Bundesbank's domestic measures within one month.[23] This second view was close to the Bundesbank's own inferences from the 1970 experience and formed the conceptual basis for the German eagerness to abandon a fixed dollar exchange rate for the DM, when large inflows reappeared in the first two months of 1973.

More recent studies, emphasizing the tricky interdependence between domestic monetary actions and capital flows, have again somewhat reversed the relative importance of the two directions of causation by seeing the main link as the — on balance efficient — reactions of the Bundesbank to external disturbances during the fixed-rate period.[24] What is clear, however, is that the

[22] M. Willms, 'Controlling Money in an Open Economy: The German Case', *Federal Reserve Bank of St. Louis Review*, April 1971.

[23] M. Porter, 'Capital Flows as an Offset to Monetary Policy', *IMF Staff Papers*, July 1972; P. Kouri and M. Porter, 'International Capital Flows and Portfolio Equilibrium', *Journal of Political Economy*, May–June 1974.

[24] R.J. Herring and R.C. Marston, *National Monetary Policies and International Financial Markets*, Amsterdam 1977.

more successful the German authorities have been in sterilizing external flows, the more they have perpetuated the causes of such flows. The German experience of 1970 (and early 1973) marks a dramatic progression in the integration of German financial markets into the international system. When it turned out in 1972-3 that attempts at halting and reversing this evolution, by imposing on German firms borrowing abroad the requirement that 40 to 50 per cent of the proceeds be deposited into an unremunerated account in the Bundesbank (*Bardepot*), were ineffective, the conclusion was reached that monetary autonomy could only be restored by greater exchange rate flexibility around a level for the DM well above that established in December 1971.

While the internal–external conflict in the case of Germany was resolved primarily by revaluation from 1969 onwards, in the case of Switzerland such a course was resisted longer. The Swiss economy continued to grow very rapidly throughout the 1960s, and monetary policy was more accommodating than in Germany. One problem was that the Swiss monetary authorities lacked the necessary instruments for conducting a more activist policy. Swiss monetary history, up to 1969 at least, reads primarily as an account of how the Swiss National Bank struggled to get a firmer grip on lending through voluntary agreements with the banks. But in any case increasingly large and volatile capital flows made it very difficult to pursue domestically oriented objectives. The Swiss franc remained pegged to the dollar until early 1973, and the authorities continued to regard floating, even though temporarily following the German example in 1969 and 1971, as unfeasible.[25] Instead, the external–internal conflict was resolved by a mixture of four approaches: (a) allowing domestic demand to rise rather faster than elsewhere; (b) permitting some imported inflation through the pegged exchange rate; (c) revaluing by 14 per cent in two equal instalments in that year; and (d) gradually fortifying the defences against capital inflows (reserve requirements on non-resident deposits and/or prohibition of interest payments on such deposits).

In the Netherlands the wage explosion of 1963 brought to an end the period of a stable and relatively benign framework for monetary policy. What remained of undervaluation of the guilder after the 1961 revaluation was quickly eliminated by cost and price increases, and the current account swung into a small deficit for a number of years. The public sector deficit rose to a level which made it very difficult to pursue the previous course of a gently declining liquidity ratio. Monetary policy continued to be tight for most of the decade, with ceilings on bank lending as the main instrument. A short relaxation was allowed in 1967-8 when demand cooled off temporarily. It would not be wrong to describe the 1964-71 period as one of fine tuning, though around a level of activity that at least the Nederlandsche Bank considered as being unsustainably high. Gradually, the liquidity ratio was reduced – by 1971 to a historical minimum of little more

---

[25] Lademan, writing shortly before the Swiss franc started to float, expressly repudiates monetarism as being unfeasible under fixed exchange rates; and on the alternative of floating he states that 'There is very little support for the permanent adoption of a flexible exchange-rate policy, which is generally thought to be unrealistic and impracticable for the country'; J.R. Lademan, 'Monetary Policy in Switzerland', in K. Holbik (ed.), *Monetary Policy in Twelve Industrial Countries*, Federal Reserve Bank of Boston, Boston 1973, p. 459.

than one-third – despite large capital inflows. But inflation continued to accelerate and rose clearly above the rates experienced in neighbouring countries. Had it not been for the effects of the exploitation of the gas resources in the Dutch sector of the North Sea on the current account, the deterioration in competitiveness would no doubt have prompted strong restrictive measures.

In the case of Denmark there was prior to 1969 a surprisingly low degree of conformity to the general pattern for the smaller countries of heavier emphasis on external objectives within a framework of generally activist policies. Although the Danish current account was from 1961 – with only a brief interruption in 1963 – in continuing and mostly growing deficit, monetary policy must be described as primarily oriented towards domestic objectives and largely accommodating. Although the whole level of interest rates was allowed to shift in 1964-5 to what was then considered 'high', the smooth functioning of the bond market remained – as in Italy and, to a lower degree, the United Kingdom – a major objective. Through a mixture of rationing of private bond supplies and sizeable open market purchases the authorities largely stabilized long-term interest rates and even embarked on a lowering of rates in 1968-9. This largely accommodating policy broke down in the spring of 1969, when the money stock had risen to such an extent that capital outflows could not be contained. The ensuing loss of a major part of the country's international reserves imposed from then on a Mundellian external orientation of monetary policy. Such a policy, implemented through a mixture of high domestic interest rates and credit ceilings, from 1969-70 induced or forced private borrowers to satisfy a substantial part of their credit demand in international markets.

IV. The 1970s – Inflation Control and Monetary Targets

As discussed in Section I, the period between the end of the 1972-3 boom and 1979 is marked by significant changes in all three dimensions of monetary policy. The external environment was modified by the transition to greater exchange rate flexibility in a system that can best be described as managed floating; this restored some policy autonomy, though far less than was expected. Greater exchange rate flexibility removed the narrow constraint on the ability of individual countries to deviate from an international inflation average, but this did not enable policy-makers to pursue their respective domestic objectives (apart from the inflation rate) with greater activist determination than before. Rather, they found it necessary to rely increasingly on longer-run targets for the monetary aggregates and let any shorter-run activist ambitions be constrained – and be seen to be constrained – by these monetary targets (Table 11.6). Finally, the authorities in several countries became so anxious to keep the monetary aggregates close to their targeted path, than an unusually active discussion of monetary techniques suitable to this end arose towards the end of the 1970s. The present section aims to illustrate these general trends by describing the experiences of individual countries.[26]

[26] For an analysis of the foundation of, and the experience with, monetary targets, see particularly OECD, *Monetary Targets and Inflation Control*, Paris 1979, and the BIS, *Annual Reports*.

TABLE 11.6. *Monetary targets and monetary growth*
(percentage changes from previous year[a])

	1975	1976	1977	1978	1979
France (M2)[b]					
Target			12½	12	11
Outcome			13.9	12.3	14.4
Germany (CBM)					
Target	8[c]	8	8	8	6–9[d]
Outcome	10.0	9.2	9.0	11.5	6.3
Italy (Total DCE)[b]					
Target		17¾	16	19¼	18½
Outcome		19.8	17.8	21.2	18.5
United Kingdom (£M3)[e]					
Target		9–13	9–13	8–12	8–12[f]
Outcome		7.8	14.9	11.4	13.1
Spain (M3)[b]					
Target			21	17	17½
Outcome			18.7	19.5	18.0
Switzerland (M1)					
Target	6[c]	6	5	5	
Outcome	5.9	8.0	5.4	16.2	

[a] Unless otherwise stated
[b] End-year to end-year
[c] End-1974 to end-1975
[d] 1978 Q.4 to 1979 Q.4.
[e] Financial year to April of following year
[f] October 1978 to October 1979
Sources: OECD, *Monetary Targets and Inflation Control*, Paris 1979, and *Economic Survey of Spain* (various issues); EEC, *European Economy*, November 1980; Instituto nacional de estadística, *Boletin mensuel de estadística*, February 1981.

In the group of countries here considered the move towards monetary targets originated in Germany. Targets were set for the first time for the year 1974, but not communicated outside the Bundesbank. Since the restrictiveness of monetary policy during that year came as a surprise to the public and led to a sharp rise in unemployment, it was decided to announce publicly in December 1974 the current target for the growth rate of the chosen measure, the central bank money stock (CBM), for 1975.[27] A broadly similar procedure was followed thereafter.

The German evaluation of experience since 1975 is positive – even though the target was exceeded moderately in 1975-7 and in a major way in 1978. The targets are thought to have had an important impact on price expectations: if labour unions and employers recognize that the growth of nominal demand will be effectively dampened by the target – and experience in 1974 supplied a base for such a belief – so that a rate of wage increase in excess of what the target

[27] The CBM comprises currency plus required bank reserves, but excludes the volatile element of excess reserves. CBM is a proxy for a broad monetary aggregate, but with a larger weight for currency; this feature makes CBM more difficult to control, since currency reflects largely past or contemporaneous movements in income.

implies will lead to slower growth in output and employment *and* these consequences are regarded as undesirable, the conditions are met for a direct impact from the monetary target on prices and wages.

In fact, the announcement of the targets then becomes akin to the declaration of an indirect norm for prices or wages, i.e. a non-mandatory incomes policy. It is difficult to assess in any quantitative way the specific contribution of the monetary targets to the remarkable slowdown in German inflation between 1974 and 1978. The formulation and announcement of the target was part of an integrated and comprehensive 'concerted action' involving the government, the Bundesbank, and the labour market parties; there was no question of springing next year's monetary target on an unprepared public. Any investigation of the German efforts must therefore focus attention on the factors which made this approach to stabilization policy feasible, rather than on its monetary component in isolation.

The central bank money target probably helped, along with Germany's remaining exchange rate commitments *vis-à-vis* partners in the 'snake' and in the EMS, in stabilizing the important relationship to the dollar relative to the volatility during the first two years of floating in 1973-4. By choosing a target which focused on currency and excluded bank reserves Germany had, possibly inadvertently, contributed to the kind of non-sterilization policy which made the remains of a fixed exchange rate system in Europe feasible. Larger interventions by the Bundesbank to support other European currencies, or to stem a slide in the dollar, had relatively little effect on the target aggregate. Such interaction boosted excess bank reserves (which were outside the target), and other bank deposits which affected the target only in proportion to the reserve ratio applying to them. There was, of course, no escape ultimately from the conclusion that Germany had to, as long as it aimed for a lower inflation rate than most other countries, occasionally see its currency appreciate if it wished to avoid losing control of its monetary aggregates. But the particular brand of monetarism adopted in the second half of the 1970s in Germany seemed well designed to insulate German financial markets from a repetition of the violent disruptions experienced in the early part of the decade (Fig. 11.1).

Since the Swiss franc was set free to float in March 1973, the authorities pursued targets for the narrow money stock (M_1), though such targets were not publicly announced until early 1975. Subsequently, annual targets were announced for each of the next three years, but only met in 1975 and 1977. In 1976 there was a moderate transgression, but in 1978 observed M_1 growth rose to over 16 per cent, more than three times the targeted figure. Nevertheless, the Swiss authorities became the favourites of monetarist economists and, with help from a survey by Niehans, it is possible to see why.[28]

The major aim of Swiss monetary policy in the 1970s continued to be to assist in achieving a low and fairly stable inflation rate. But since most price indices were rising at some 10 per cent a year in 1973-4, a sharp recession was allowed to develop in 1975-6, made tolerable by the possibility of limiting

---

[28] J. Niehans, 'Monetary Policy with Overshooting Exchange Rates', *mimeo* (paper presented at the Trinity College Summer Seminar on Small Open Economies, Dublin, July 1979).

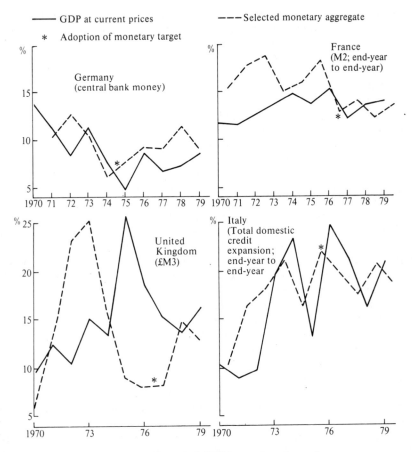

FIG. 11.1. *Monetary aggregates and nominal GDP* (percentage changes)
Sources: OECD, *National Accounts of OECD Countries, 1950-1979*; Banque de France,
           Bulletin trimestriel, December 1980; Deutsche Bundesbank, *Statistische Beihefte
           zu den Monatsberichten, Reihe 4* (various issues); Banca d'Italia, *Annual Reports*
           (various issues); *NIESR Review*, November 1980.

measured unemployment through return flows of foreign workers. This determined stance, underlined by the fairly low monetary target, led to a sharp rise
in the Swiss franc and to the closest approximation to price stability achieved
anywhere in Europe by 1977-8. Swiss policy was seen at that time as a successful application of traditional monetarism.

The pragmatic – or sophisticated – attitude of the authorities was revealed in
1978. As the dollar weakened again in the early months of the year, Swiss franc
assets were greatly in demand and the authorities were faced with the dilemma
of either allowing a severe loss of competitiveness or making a mockery of the
target for M_1 by intervening to sustain the dollar. The latter course was chosen
in recognition of the fact that the demand for Swiss francs had been severely
underestimated. The monetarist prescription of a stable (and low) growth rate

for the money stock rests on the assumption that the demand function for the chosen measure of money is stable. If that can be demonstrated to be patently incorrect, as was becoming evident in 1977–8, it is quite consistent with qualified monetarism to substitute an exchange rate target for a monetary one.

The foreign currency interventions, alarmingly large as they were, even proved to be self-correcting. Once the market had accepted that the Swiss authorities were willing and able to prevent the franc from rising further against the dollar, there was a shift back into the market for dollar assets. The Swiss money stock returned in 1979 approximately to where it would have been if it had continued along its 5 to 6 per cent annual growth path. Thus, the stabilization of the franc turned out to be a precondition for achieving longer-run stability in the growth rate of the monetary aggregate chosen as prime target.

Despite the violently unstable external environment and the increasing international role of the Swiss franc, Swiss monetary policy would appear to have worked better than in the calmer 1960s. A *modus vivendi* with the banks was arrived at, with domestic credit regulated by informal agreement. Additional powers were obtained on an *ad hoc* basis to control movements of non-resident funds. The Swiss experience suggests that it is possible to design an effective monetary policy without strong statutory powers, though admittedly other factors have rendered the task less unmanageable than it appeared elsewhere. The generally moderate behaviour of labour and of price-setters in industry, together with the scope for reducing labour supply through emigration, greatly eased the tasks confronting the Swiss monetary authorities.

Germany and Switzerland are without doubt the two countries which came closest to a monetarist approach. There is, in particular, in the pronouncements of the respective monetary authorities the notion, central to later versions of monetarism, that monetary targets are important in shaping price expectations and that they may offer a way of influencing the longer-term inflation rate more directly than through their impact on real demand. To the extent that trade unions and others who have a major influence on strategic prices in the economy pay attention to the monetary target, because they are concerned about the real impact of a conflict between their wage or price claims and 'what the market will bear', the monetary target does achieve a highly desirable direct transmission.

In the other countries where monetary targets were adopted in the mid-1970s their purpose appears, initially at least, to have been more modest. The targets for the broad monetary aggregates which were publicly announced in France and the United Kingdom in 1976 seemed above all to have provided a conveniently comprehensive framework for discussing both fiscal and monetary policies. At a time when public sector borrowing requirements were rising fast as a result of both automatic mechanisms and discretionary action, an overall framework was required to assess the proper balance between public and private contributions to liquidity creation. A target for a broad monetary aggregate supplied such a framework.

In France the monetary target was introduced as an integral part of the anti-inflationary package of 1976 — the Barre Plan — and compliance has generally been fairly close, though with some transgression in 1979. Since the Bank of France has tended to intervene substantially in the foreign exchange market, whether it was under any formal obligation or not, the external impact on money growth has at times been large and volatile. Despite the adoption of monetary targets French official opinion has not put the same emphasis on the anti-inflationary benefits of this approach as, say, German policy-makers. Up to 1978 close supervision of, and extended control over, prices were regarded as the main anti-inflationary weapons. With price controls substantially eased in 1978, the importance of the overall money stance as well as of a strong exchange rate came closer to the centre of the public debate. At the same time tools for better control of the aggregates were put into place, making for a sharp contrast with the 1950s and 1960s.

In the United Kingdom some emphasis was already given to broad monetary aggregates at the time of the 1967 devaluation. But this emphasis faded when a surplus in the current account emerged in 1969–71. As the surplus appeared to stabilize on a high plateau, while domestic demand proved to be weaker than expected, a major easing of monetary policy was undertaken. Under the heading of 'Competition and Credit Control' the ceilings on bank lending which had been in existence since 1965 and the agreements constraining movements in banks' interest rates were scrapped. As its title indicates, the reform had the double purpose of activating competition and of improving control. That the former purpose was achieved is obvious; in the course of the first two years the market share of the clearing banks in total credit to residents rose from 41 to well over 60 per cent. But competition also led to an explosive growth in the overdraft facilities available. Though no explicit targets for money or credit growth were set in 1971–2, it soon became clear that the rate of expansion of the monetary aggregates was unsustainably rapid. There were special and temporary reasons for a large part of this excess; but above all there was a larger pent-up demand for bank credit than had been foreseen.

In these circumstances there was inevitably a long time-lapse before control over the broad monetary aggregates, represented by sterling M_3, could be reasserted. The fact that it took the better part of three years to get M_3 under control, and that the main instrument used to this end proved to distort the information conveyed by M_3, did not strengthen the credibility of monetary targeting in the United Kingdom. The imposition, between late 1973 and mid-1980, of the so-called 'corset' — a supplementary and sharply progressive reserve requirement on increases in interest-bearing liabilities beyond a targeted rate of growth — was a recognition by the authorities that the more indirect channels of influence through bank liquidity and short-term interest rates were inadequate; in particular, control of the supply of reserve assets to the banks proved difficult.

Between late 1973 and late 1979 the growth of sterling M_3 became steadier and the average growth rate tended to be lower than that of nominal income — indeed, often lower than the rate of inflation, causing the real money stock to contract. While a stable and moderate growth rate for M_3 was an internal and informal objective from late 1973, it was only in July 1976 that the government publicly committed itself by announcing a 9 to 13 per cent target for the fiscal year 1976/7. A sharp fall of sterling had convinced the authorities that a publicly announced target could help to stabilize expectations in the exchange market and prevent a renewed vicious circle of depreciation and inflation. In

December 1976 in the government's 'Letter of Intent' to the IMF at the conclusion of a 'stand-by' agreement, the main emphasis was on an objective for
DCE for 1976/7 and the following two fiscal years. But as the external balance
improved, efforts were made also to comply with an M_3 target. These efforts
consisted primarily in permitting sterling to rise substantially, notably during
two phases in 1977 and again in 1979.

Given the history of the early 1970s it is perhaps not surprising that the
authorities initially saw the announcement of the monetary target in a less
ambitious perspective than the more monetarist one, typified by Germany and
Switzerland. But the emphasis clearly changed with the election of the Conservative government in May 1979, which made the announcement of a gradually
shrinking annual target the crucial element in its medium-term strategy.

The United Kingdom experience at the turn of the decade also illustrated
the dilemma of a country trying to lower its inflation rate by gradually reducing
the growth rate of its money stock in an environment of floating exchange rates.
The exchange markets were impressed much more rapidly and thoroughly by the
monetary target than domestic wage- and price-setters. The result was a massive
appreciation of sterling at a time when the domestic inflation rate remained well
above those in most other European countries as well as in the United States.
The rise of sterling helped to reduce British inflation, but implied a severe
deflationary impact from the loss of competitiveness. This problem did not arise
in most other European countries – with the exception of Switzerland in 1977–
8 – because they had – or were thought to have – more definite commitments
in their exchange-rate policies.

In Italy policy formulation in the 1970s has relied heavily on a very broad
monetary aggregate, namely total domestic credit (TDCE), comprising both
bank credit, loans by specialized credit institutions, and bonds issued by public
or private borrowers. The choice reflects the empirically founded belief that
close substitutability prevails in Italian financial markets between monetary and
non-monetary assets. To achieve stated targets, the authorities use a number of
levers: control of bond issues, ceilings on bank credit, minimum quotas for bank
holdings of bonds, and, at times, import deposit requirements. Compliance has
been highly mixed; on at least two occasions – late 1975 and early 1978 – observed TDCE ran far ahead of targets, in both cases due to heavier Treasury
financing needs than anticipated. The first transgression caused a plunge of the
lira in 1976, while the second left less of a mark. Despite the overshooting of
monetary targets, ultimate policy objectives were largely achieved; the current
account returned to surplus and the lira was fairly stable in 1978–80, though
only at the price of an increasingly external orientation of Italian interest
rate policies.

In the Netherlands, the worsening of the competitive position, already
notable towards the end of the 1960s, continued into the 1970s. For three to
four years from 1972 onwards the guilder appreciated in effective terms by
some 4 per cent annually, while the Dutch cost level rose almost in line with
the international average, implying a severe squeeze on profits. At the same
time, the high degree of financial integration made it difficult to avoid large
inflows in response to any major increase in Dutch interest rates relative to
international, particularly German, levels. In this situation, policy was pushed

into a more accommodating stance than the authorities would have liked; and their chosen indicator, the liquidity ratio, rose significantly up to 1977. As fiscal and incomes policies began to contribute to the reduction of imbalance, notably by bringing down Dutch inflation, monetary policy could once more be targeted on the gradual lowering of the liquidity ratio. Credit ceilings, which had been removed in 1972, were reimposed in 1977.

In Denmark the external orientation of policy has been pronounced in the 1970s. Following the foreign-exchange crisis of 1969 a mixture of ceilings on bank lending commitments and interest rates increasingly far above international levels induced private capital inflows which were in most years sufficient to finance a persistent large current account deficit. With official borrowing in international markets also rising strongly, the international reserves increased substantially. The assignment of policy to an external role was so efficient that it removed for much of the decade – up to the second increase in oil prices in 1979 – any pressure to rapidly reduce the current account deficit. The one short period in 1975-6 when this assignment was eased and monetary policy was allowed to assist in expanding demand quickly reminded the authorities of the pressing nature of the external constraint. After that the monetary aggregates rose more slowly than nominal income, though explicit monetary targets were not given much emphasis, the philosophy being that the exchange rate commitments *vis-à-vis* other European currencies made it both impracticable and unnecessary to have such targets.

There are some similarities with Dutch policies. Both countries lost competitiveness in international markets in the early 1970s by pegging to a low-inflation currency (DM), and both had to give a largely external orientation to their monetary policy. But differences emerged in the second half of the decade when the Netherlands had greater success in reducing inflation, while Denmark made a series of exchange rate adjustments which perpetuated the need for maintaining a very large interest rate differential over international levels. But in both countries the conflict persisted between on the one hand external constraints and on the other domestic pressures for more accommodating policies – and particularly lower interest rates – to ease the problem of a general profit squeeze.

Conclusions

Looking at the whole time-span covered by this chapter, it may now be appropriate to ask how effective monetary policies were in achieving whatever aims had been assigned to them. This is, however, a very difficult question to answer. For one thing, these aims were never clearly specified, and, more importantly, changed through time from internal accommodation through external equilibrium to control of inflation. For another, the circumstances surrounding monetary policies were also significantly modified through institutional reforms, internationalization of financial markets, and the move to floating. More importantly, perhaps, a proper assessment of monetary policy effects would require the existence of econometric models with well-specified monetary channels of transmission. Yet, with the possible exception of the United Kingdom's Treasury model at the very end of the 1970s, econometric model-building in Europe never reached the sophistication it did in North America, particularly as far as monetary interactions went. This already limits the extent to which the effects of monetary policies can be traced to the ultimate goal variables which the authorities would wish to influence. And this limitation would be even more glaring if one accepted the monetarist claim that changes in money supply have an all-pervasive effect on total expenditure. In such a case, as argued by Laidler, narrowing the channels of causation that such models investigate to a few expenditure functions ensures that only relatively weak links between money and economic activity will be discovered.[29] A final, and perhaps more important problem, is that of disentangling the relative contributions of fiscal and monetary influences on any particular monetary policy change. It is not by accident, therefore, that most longer-run assessments of monetary policy in Europe tend to shy away from quantitative estimates, often limit themselves to graphical evidence, and almost invariably reach only qualitative conclusions.[30]

Accepting such inevitable limitations, the evidence surveyed in this chapter suggests that, as far as the 1950s go, monetary policy was probably successful in achieving the rather limited aims which it had been set — accommodating a rapid growth process — and this success was repeated in the one instance (Denmark) in which this accommodating role was pursued in the 1960s. But elsewhere the story of the second decade is somewhat more mixed. It will be recalled that in the 1960s policy had become more ambitious just as the external environment was probably impairing some of its effectiveness. Very broadly, monetary instruments were assigned a domestic fine tuning role in the first half of the decade and an external one in the second half. It is in this period that the basic asymmetry of monetary policies became most apparent. Countries which used monetary instruments to rein in domestic demand were, on the whole, successful at least in the early 1960s (e.g. France and Italy), but monetary relaxation alone was unable to restore growth rates to former levels. Similarly, countries that in the second half of the 1960s tried to reduce their external deficits achieved a fair measure of success with the help of monetary measures (and, of course, devaluations, at least in France and the United Kingdom), but countries in surplus (notably Germany, but also Switzerland), were unable to restore external equilibrium by monetary measures alone.

The lesson of the 1960s should probably have been that monetary instruments were too blunt to fine tune an economy, particularly a very open one, but this lesson was not learnt or else was forgotten in the early 1970s when, in a generalized attempt to stimulate demand, control over monetary expansion was virtually lost. Countries were either unwilling, or unable, to sterilize the effects of large United States balance of payments deficits on their domestic monetary aggregates, and in some cases even added to such expansion by internal measures (most obviously in the case of the British 'Competition and Credit Control' reforms). The move to a more monetarist stance that followed was no doubt partly also a reaction to this apparently glaring failure of activism.

In the move towards target constrained policies in the later 1970s it is possible

---

[29] D. Laidler, 'Money and Money Income: An Essay on the "Transmission Mechanism"', *Journal of Monetary Economics*, April 1978.

[30] See, for instance, the various studies published by the OECD in its Monetary Studies Series listed in the bibliography.

to detect several rather different forces at work. At the practical level, the failure of policy in the early 1970s and the dramatic increases in the rate of inflation everywhere were bound to lead to policies of greater monetary restraint. Inflation itself, and the volatility of expectations, meant that the stance of policy could not be easily assessed in terms of interest rates and attention was directed to the control of nominal monetary aggregates. This move was strongly reinforced and supported by the intellectual tenets of monetarist theory as well as by the growing disillusion with policy activism in general. In this environment, explicit and publicized targets appeared to offer the chance of directly stabilizing expenditures. But another way of seeing the move to reliance on monetary targets is as a kind of substitute for the discipline implicit in the maintenance of fixed exchange rates under the Bretton Woods system. With the move to generalized floating, and with the marked increase in external shocks to which national economies were subjected in the 1970s, it was felt necessary, on pragmatic grounds, to establish some overall indicator or target against which the general thrust of policy could be assessed. Previously, balance of payments problems or exchange market pressure performed this role, and both monetary and fiscal policy were often modified in line with external objectives. Pressure on monetary targets in the 1970s could similarly be seen as calling for general economic policy action of a pervasive kind; including, of course, as a possibility, a change in, or relaxing of, the target — akin in some ways to devaluation in the 1960s.

Particularly on this latter interpretation monetary targets should be seen in a rather general light, and not simply as dependent upon monetarist theory. Moreover, if seen as a substitute for external targets, it is likely that monetary and exchange rate considerations would come into conflict from time to time, especially in the face of external shocks. It was seen that at the end of the 1970s both Germany and Switzerland were prepared to resolve the conflict in favour of the exchange rate objective when appreciation appeared likely to get out of hand. In both cases this pragmatic response was understandably aided by the clear commitment of the authorities to an anti-inflationary stance. In the United Kingdom a similar conflict (occurring in part because of the build-up in North Sea oil revenues) tended to resolve in favour of the domestic monetary target.

The experience of the later 1970s is too short to provide sufficient evidence for an assessment of the success of policies over this period. But, broadly, it would seem that targets that were seen to be observed did perform a useful function in Germany and Switzerland, even though, or perhaps because, there was a good deal of flexibility in the way in which policy was implemented. In Italy and the United Kingdom, however, it seems probable that the direct effect of the targets was rather small, and that their chief role was as an element in a generally anti-inflationary and deflationary policy stance.

A bird's-eye view of this varied experience of partial success alternating with temporary mistakes in a rapidly changing institutional and economic environment suggests a fundamental similarity between the early and the last phase. In both, the emphasis was on providing a stable longer-run framework. In the 1950s low and stable interest rates were designed to induce private capital formation and economic growth. In the 1970s low and stable money-supply growth rates were aimed at reducing long-run inflation. Both objectives require that some constraints are put on shorter-term stabilization aims. Accordingly other policies – expenditure, tax, structural, and incomes policies – have to be assigned the major, or even exclusive, role in pursuing these objectives. Practical monetarists would not disagree with the Keynesian view of twenty years ago that these other policies have a considerable comparative advantage in such a task.

Bibliography

No concise survey exists reviewing European monetary policy over the whole of the post-war period, and the literature on the 1950s is also very scanty. For the 1960s and early 1970s a general treatment can be found in EEC Monetary Committee, *Monetary Policy in the Countries of the European Economic Community*, Brussels 1972; D.R. Hodgman, *National Monetary Policies and International Monetary Cooperation*, Boston 1974; and OECD, *The Role of Monetary Policy in Demand Management*, Paris 1975. The later 1970s experience has seen a proliferation of writings. Among the more interesting surveys see R.J. Herring and R.C. Marston, *National Monetary Policies and International Financial Markets*, Amsterdam 1977; OECD, *Monetary Targets and Inflation Control*, Paris 1979; and BIS, *The Monetary Base Approach to Monetary Control*, Basle 1980. More technical material can be found in F. Masera *et al.*, *Econometric Research in European Central Banks*, Bank of Italy, Rome 1975; and J.M. Boughton, 'Demand for Money in Major OECD Countries', *OECD Economic Outlook – Occasional Studies*, January 1979 (which covers France, Germany, Italy, and the United Kingdom). On the Eurocurrency markets a relatively early article is W. McClam, 'Credit Substitution and the Eurocurrency Market', *Banca Nazionale del Lavoro Quarterly Review*, December 1972; and H. Mayer, 'Credit and Liquidity Creation in the International Banking Sector', *BIS Economic Papers*, No. 1, 1979.

On individual countries, papers covering the institutional background for the late 1950s can be found for all the countries here covered, except Denmark, in R.S. Sayers (ed.), *Banking in Western Europe*, Oxford 1962, while the 1970s are surveyed in Inter-Bank Research Organisation, *Banking Systems Abroad*, London 1978. The experience of the 1960s is reviewed in six country chapters (all the countries except Denmark) in K. Holbik (ed.), *Monetary Policy in Twelve Industrial Countries*, Federal Reserve Bank of Boston, Boston 1973, while a later account of the move to targets can be found for France, Germany, Italy, the United Kingdom, and Switzerland (as well as for other European countries not included in the present survey) in J.E. Wadsworth and F.L. de Juvigny (eds.), *New Approaches in Monetary Policy*, Alphen aan den Rijn 1979.

Other works on *France* are: J.-H. David, *La politique monétaire en France*, Paris 1974; OECD, *Monetary Policy in France*, Paris 1974; R. de la Genière, 'Les moyens de la politique monétaire vus de la Banque de France', *Revue banque*, May 1976; and M. Chazelas, J.-F. Dauvisis, and G. Maarek, 'L'experience française d'encadrement du crédit', *Cahiers économiques et monétaires*, No. 6, 1978. For *Germany*, O. Emminger, 'The D-Mark in the Conflict between Internal and External Equilibrium, 1948–75', *Princeton Essays in International Finance*, No. 122, 1977, covers the whole period up to the move to floating, with emphasis on the conflict between internal and external equilibrium, while the OECD, *Monetary Policy in Germany*, Paris 1973, reviews the 1960–72 experience.

For *Italy*, a similar survey (OECD, *Monetary Policy in Italy*, Paris 1973) covers the 1960s. For later evidence see T. Padoa-Schioppa, 'Selective Credit Policy: Italy's Recent Experience', *Banca Nazionale del Lavoro Quarterly Review*, December 1975; G. Vaciago, 'Monetary Policy in Italy: The Limited Role of Monetarism', *Banca Nazionale del Lavoro Quarterly Review*, December 1977; F. Cotula and S. Micossi, 'Some Considerations on the Choice of Intermediate Monetary Targets in the Italian Experience', *Cahiers économiques et monétaires*, No. 6, 1978; and A. Fazio, 'La politica monetaria in Italia dal 1947 al 1978', *Moneta e Credito*, September 1979. For the *United Kingdom*, institutional background is provided by Bank of England, *Monetary Policy in EEC Countries – UK Institutions and Instruments*, London 1974, while surveys of policies in the 1950s can be found in J.C.R. Dow, *The Management of the British Economy, 1945-60*, NIESR, Cambridge 1964; and for the 1960s and early 1970s in articles by Tew and Artis in F.T. Blackaby, *British Economic Policy, 1960-74*, NIESR, Cambridge 1978.

The *Danish* experience of the 1950s and 1960s is surveyed in N. Thygesen, *The Sources and the Impact of Monetary Changes: An Empirical Study of Danish Experiences, 1951-68*, Copenhagen 1971, and that of the 1970s in E. Hoffmeyer and L. Hansen, 'Danish Monetary Policy During the Last Decade', *Kredit und Kapital*, Heft 2, 1978. The *Dutch* 'monetarist' view is exposed most clearly in Nederlandsche Bank, *Annual Report, 1963*. A survey of the whole post-war period is provided by E. den Dunnen, 'Post-war Monetary Policy', *De Economist*, No. 1, 1979, and a more personal interpretation by J. Zijlstra, 'Monetary Theory and Monetary Policy: A Central Banker's View', ibid. A somewhat more theoretical exposition of *Swiss* monetary policies can be found in J. Niehans, 'Monetary Policy with Overshooting Exchange Rates', unpublished paper presented at Trinity Summer Seminar on Small Open Economies, Dublin, July 1979.

Among the countries not covered in this chapter, a survey of *Swedish* monetary policies to the early 1970s can be found in A. Lindbeck, *Swedish Economic Policy*, London 1975, while *Austria, Belgium*, and *Norway* are covered in the already cited work by K. Holbik (ed.).

12

Incomes Policy and Centralized Wage Formation

KARL-OLOF FAXÉN*

Introduction

Incomes policies have often been described as a third instrument of demand management policy arising from the need to control wages and prices if high employment is to be maintained. In general terms, they can be described as government efforts to co-ordinate wage and salary developments with monetary, fiscal, and exchange rate policies by means of direct pressures on collective bargaining. In this open-ended sense, some form or other of incomes policy has been in operation in nearly all European countries at least since the early 1960s, and in some cases much earlier. There are, however, major differences between countries in the reasons for the adoption of incomes policies, in the specific form they have taken, and in the institutions which have been used for their implementation. In some countries – all of them small – incomes policies have become a more or less permanent feature of the bargaining process. Others, such as the United Kingdom, are characterized by repeated attempts to apply incomes policies alternating with periods of reliance on monetary and fiscal policies alone. It is an important theme of the present chapter that this contrast between temporary and permanent incomes policies reflects quite fundamental differences in trade union organization and in the institutions of collective bargaining.

The general perception of the role of incomes policies has changed quite markedly over time. At a theoretical level, there was always a recognition that use of the demand management instruments to promote high employment and growth carried with it the serious risk of increasing cost–push pressures in the labour market. At a more practical level, the institution of wage and price controls in many countries in the period of post-war reconstruction was prompted by the limited short-run effectiveness of conventional demand management instruments in those disturbed conditions. These controls were mostly dismantled as growth got under way in the 1950s. In the early 1960s, incomes policies returned to the stage and became widely accepted as part of economic policy. This is illustrated by the publication of a report of a group of experts to the OEEC which expressly recommended their introduction.[1] At that time, the justification offered was that such policies could help in achieving a lower rate of inflation for any given level of unemployment, or, alternatively, could allow the maintenance of higher employment and output for a given rate of inflation. They were, thus, seen as improving the trade-off between inflation and un-

---

* Swedish Employers Confederation, Stockholm.
[1] W. Fellner, *et al.*, *The Problem of Rising Prices*, OECD, Paris 1964, particularly Ch. V. It should be noted that this recommendation was not unanimously endorsed.

employment, i.e. as shifting the 'Phillips curve' towards the origin – a highly desirable end which monetary and fiscal policies were unable to reach.

By the late 1970s, this optimistic view had changed. In a new report by a group of experts to the OECD, the suggested role of incomes policies had shrunk to, at best, a contributory element in a strategy to wind down inflationary expectations.[2] This change in attitude probably stemmed from a variety of causes – earlier negative experiences with incomes policies, the generally more disturbed economic conditions of the 1970s, the increased difficulties met in controlling inflation, and even changes in economic thinking. It was now felt that there was no longer a trade-off between unemployment and inflation. Instead, a reduction of inflation was increasingly seen as necessary in order to maintain employment and restore growth. Incomes policies, to the extent that they acted on expectations of future price and wage increases, could perhaps be an adjunct to a restrictive policy stance and help in reducing the unemployment costs associated with bringing down inflation. They were thus seen in much the same light as other possible influences on expectations, such as central bank declarations on future monetary growth. In the longer run, their role appeared clearly restricted. Indeed, in an important segment of public opinion, there was no room for incomes policies at all. Full employment could only be secured, after a period of transition, through a determined and restrictive monetary policy.

Whilst incomes policies have so far been considered in the context of strategies against inflation, it is clear that they may have a more general role in improving economic performance. The experience of smaller open economies under fixed exchange rates indicates the importance of analysing incomes policies in a sufficiently broad context. In such economies, it is well known that the inflation rate is strongly influenced by external factors,[3] and so are levels of activity. It would be unrealistic to suppose that incomes policies could have pronounced effects over the longer term either on inflation, or on levels of unemployment. They may, however, have a general impact on the trade-off between investment, growth, and a favourable balance of payments on the one hand, and immediate consumption on the other. Their effects may be on productivity or on the international competitiveness and dynamism of the economy.

As described so far, incomes policies are an aspect of macroeconomic policy, and their successes, or lack of them, should be assessed in terms of their efficiency in helping to achieve macroeconomic goals. Yet, particularly in looking at the experience of the smaller economies, it is necessary to go further than this and consider labour relations. It can be argued that in some European economies, the emergence of incomes policies was a response, not to macroeconomic difficulties, but to problems and conflicts in the labour market. Even when incomes policies are presented as acts of government policy against inflation, their true origin may often be a desire to create an institutional framework in which trade union and employer organizations can reach agreements reasonably predictably, and at a frequency of open conflict which is acceptable to society at large.

This view may be illustrated by the following quotation from a Finnish

---

[2] P. McCracken *et al., Towards Full Employment and Price Stability*, OECD, Paris 1977, particularly Ch. 8.

[3] See Chs. 3 and 4 above.

government official with a long experience of incomes policies in the country with the highest frequency of open conflicts and the lowest degree of political and social consensus among the smaller European countries considered in this chapter: 'By no means all income policy agreements made in Finland have been justified by considerations of employment and price stability. Some of them have simply been compromises made to keep the peace.'[4] On this interpretation, the achievements of incomes policies should be measured, not so much by their effects on inflation or growth, but by their effects in reducing social conflict, and in particular, in reducing the incidence of strikes.

Against this complex background, it is not surprising that the forms that incomes policies have taken have varied greatly between European countries. The term is usually reserved for situations in which the government actively and directly makes decisions about the content of collective agreements in the form of special legislation, or through a 'Pay Board' or similar kind of agency. Yet incomes policies can exist even outside such a formal framework. Thus the adoption of a centralized agreement between bargaining groups, taking into account macroeconomic considerations, but arrived at independently of government pressures, has been called an 'incomes policy'. The expression 'private incomes policy' for such cases serves to underline the independence of collective bargaining from government interference. In practice, there is a continuum of degrees of government influence over wage bargaining, and no exact and well defined dividing line between incomes policy and free collective bargaining can really be established.

Rather than focusing on different types of incomes policy, a much more important distinction needs to be made between centralized and more decentralized forms of collective bargaining. At one end of the scale are countries in which collective decisions are made at national level, through bargaining between central employers' and wage and salary earners' organizations or through tripartite government agencies. At the other end are countries in which the mechanisms of wage and salary formation are decentralized at branch, regional, or plant level, with varying degrees of government influence.

From an analytical point of view, what matters most is the contrast between a process of centralized wage formation on the one hand and a decentralized process on the other, subject at times to some form of incomes policy. The important question is not whether the government makes efforts to influence the outcome of collective agreements — this is done in almost all countries, if only because governments are such large employers themselves. The decisive distinction is instead whether or not there exist centralized organizations on the employer and trade-union sides or a permanent central government agency for co-ordination and supervision of collective agreements. If such institutions do not exist, the government has to work through a series of decentralized private agreements which make the achievement of any macroeconomic policy objective in the field of wage formation much more difficult. Indeed, in this latter case wage and salary changes may not be parameters for government action,

[4] K. Liinamaa, 'Problems of Relating the Outcome of Collective Bargaining to the Needs of National Economic and Employment Policies – Some Views', in OECD, *Collective Bargaining and Government Policies*, Paris 1979, pp. 133-4.

which they could be seen to be in situations where central institutions exist permanently.

This distinction between centralized and decentralized wage formation, which is very frequently, though not invariably, also a distinction between small and large countries, runs through the rest of this chapter. Differences in approach, in motivations, and in achievements can be traced back to it, and provide some of the themes that will be developed. In particular, it is not easy to draw lessons for the larger, more decentralized countries from the experience of so-called 'permanent' incomes policies in smaller countries with centralized institutions.

Some evidence on the relevance of this distinction is provided in Fig. 12.1, which has been derived from two charts developed by Blyth.[5] In the diagram,

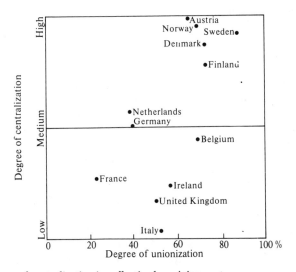

FIG. 12.1. *Degree of centralization in collective bargaining*
Source: derived from C.A. Blyth, 'The Interaction between Collective Bargaining and
            Government Policies in Selected Member Countries', in OECD, *Collective Bar-
            gaining and Government Policies*, Paris 1979.

the horizontal axis measures known degrees of unionization, while the vertical axis presents a more subjective assessment of the centralization of wage bargaining. This assessment is based on the effective centralization of employer and union federations, on the extent of power wielded by such bodies and on the influence of government and/or central tripartite institutions. Five countries (Austria, Denmark, Finland, Norway, and Sweden) are clearly close to the centralized wage-formation model and these will be considered in Section I below.

[5] C.A. Blyth, 'The Interaction between Collective Bargaining and Government Policies in Selected Member Countries', in OECD, *Collective Bargaining*. In the original diagrams which take into account only the centralization of wage bargaining and collective agreements, the Netherlands is placed between France and the United Kingdom; the present diagram, however, considers also the degree of government interference and hence puts the Netherlands in a somewhat higher position.

The Netherlands is also considered a centralized country because of its well-developed incomes policy before 1963 and the high frequency of direct government interference in other forms thereafter.

The second section looks briefly at the experience of the four major economies, which can be seen to be much less centralized. Only one of them (the United Kingdom) has regularly resorted to incomes policies. Section III provides some comparisions and contrasts between experiences in the two groups of countries, while the Conclusion summarizes the various arguments.

I. Centralized Wage Formation in Small Open Economies

This section considers the process of wage formation in countries in which collective bargaining is largely conducted at a central level. No general and detailed description is attempted. This can be found in the literature.[6] Rather, the text will select a few salient features of Europe's post-war experience with centralized wage formation. Prerequisites for such a process of collective bargaining to occur are the existence of strong national employer and trade-union federations which cover the great majority of enterprises and work-force in a country. Government intervention is not indispensable, but direct or indirect government influence in the negotiations is usually a feature of the process.

No European country fully satisfies all these conditions, but some, and in particular Austria, the Netherlands, and the four major Scandinavian countries come close to meeting at least several of them. Thus, for instance, five out of the six countries (the exception is the Netherlands) have a rate of unionization of the labour force of at least 60 per cent, and frequently of above 80 per cent for blue collar workers. On the employers' side, centralization is assured for Austria by mandatory membership in semi-official 'Chambers', while in Scandinavia the central employers' organizations (which cover directly 40 to 60 per cent of all employees in private business) have considerable statutory power over collective agreements and conditions of pay in member firms.

The high degree of centralization distinguishes these countries from other small open European economies such as Belgium, Switzerland, or Ireland. In Belgium, the degree of unionization is relatively high, but the unions are split into three organizations along both political and linguistic lines. In Switzerland, neither unions nor employer federations are strong at the national level. And in both countries wage bargaining is decentralized at branch or enterprise level, particularly in Switzerland, where neither centralized collective negotiations nor prices and incomes policies have ever existed. In Ireland, on the other hand, some moves towards more centralized bargaining took place in the 1970s, but in the absence of strong central employer and trade union organizations. The development of National Pay Agreements in this period was the consequence of the government's threat to legislate a prices and incomes policy. Thus, the

---

[6] See, for instance, the following surveys: UNECE, *Incomes in Post-War Europe*, Geneva 1967, Ch. 4; L. Ulman and R.J. Flanagan, *Wage Restraint*, University of California Press 1971; A. Romanis Braun, 'The Role of Incomes Policy in Industrialised Countries since World War II', *IMF Staff Papers*, March 1975; OECD, *Collective Bargaining and Government Policies in Ten OECD Countries*, Paris 1979; P. Schelde Andersen and P. Turner, 'Incomes Policy in Theory and Practice', *OECD Economic Outlook – Occasional Studies*, July 1980.

agreements were the result of free collective bargaining and did not constitute direct government involvement in wage formation, even if the government exercised considerable direct influence by means of co-ordinated tax measures.

The role of government

Differences among the six countries are more pronounced in the area of government intervention. In Austria, the absence of a strong, independent, and unified employers' organization in the early post-war period led to the establishment of a tripartite body by the government as part of the reconstruction effort. The arrangement remained in force in the next three decades, and government influence was strong. Since 1957 a 'Joint Wages and Prices Board' brought together government, unions, and employers to consider claims for, and disagreements on, wages. Despite the lack of legal status, and of power of sanctions,[7] the Board has not only survived under three different types of government, but, according to opinion polls, has also been widely supported by the population, and frequently viewed as having contributed to the success of the Austrian economy, notably in the 1970s. This could in part be due to the way in which such policies have been seen in Austria, i.e. as 'part of a general broader approach to participation in economic and social policymaking rather than as a series of measures specifically designed to restrict the rate of increase in prices and money wages in accordance with some quantifiable criteria or guidelines'.[8]

Between the early 1950s and 1963, the wage formation process in the Netherlands was channelled through several co-ordinating bodies which provided the most comprehensive centralized wage policy in Europe. Government intervention was important and considered highly successful. The collapse of that policy after 1963[9] (the formal end of the 'Guided Wage Policy' came in 1967) led to a more decentralized collective bargaining process, but government influence remained and became again increasingly important in the 1970s. Though the 1970 'Law on Wage Formation' had delegated the responsibility for wage determination to the two sides of industry, the latter were able to sign a central agreement only in one year – 1973. Direct government intervention was thus resorted to on six occasions in the decade.

In the four Scandinavian countries, the government's influence has been less institutionalized. Strong central employer federations were a tradition already in the 1940s. Union centralization can be seen as a response to the prior existence of such organizations. These were, of course, not formed for the purpose of conducting macro-oriented central wage policies. But the centralization of statutory power, established when such policies had not yet been heard of, proved useful when co-ordination of wage policy became important in the early post-war period. The later emergence of government influence may thus be interpreted as a consequence of the prior centralization of both employers' organizations and trade unions.

The degree of government influence is probably most pronounced in Finland, where intervention has, at times, been far-reaching and taken the form, for

[7] J. Mire, *Country Labor Profile: Austria*, US Department of Labor, 1979.

[8] H. Suppanz and D. Robinson, *Prices and Incomes Policy. The Austrian Experience*, OECD, Paris 1972, p. 46.

[9] See Ch. 20 below.

instance, of legislative action or of combined wage-fiscal policy 'package deals' imposed by presidential authority. An example was the Stabilization Agreement of March 1968, which followed the December 1967 devaluation. Exchange rate considerations also loomed large (at least implicitly) in the 'packages' of the late 1970s.

Sweden is probably at the other end of the scale, with a minimum of direct government influence. Denmark and Norway come somewhere in between. In Denmark, the government has intervened repeatedly by legislating on the basis of the last proposal made by the mediators. The 1973 general conflict was ended in that way, as were the 1975 and 1977 bargaining rounds. In 1979, however, the government legislated directly. In Norway, during the earlier part of the post-war period, a government institution, the *Rikslönnemnda* (or National Wage Council) was often used to arbitrate between the central bargaining partners. Since the mid-1960s the emphasis of government policy has been more on the preparatory stages, with much economic and statistical research carried out jointly under the auspices of the authorities, designed to publicize a realistic assessment of the scope for income increases. In spite of this, legislation has sometimes been used, for instance to stop wage drift in the late 1970s.

Another form of government intervention common to virtually all the six countries is what has often been called 'tax bribery'. With rapid inflation and progressive (nominal) income tax rates, fiscal drag made it more or less impossible to increase real wages without tax adjustments. This link between fiscal policy and wage determination became the basis for mutual pressures inside as well as outside consultative institutions and joint decision-making bodies in all the six countries. Politically, the tax adjustments were presented as measures to influence prices, wages, and the climate for negotiations. Use was made of reductions in indirect (including payroll) taxes (Denmark, Finland, Sweden) as well as in direct income taxes (Austria, Finland, Norway, Sweden). Probably the most comprehensive attempt in this area was made in the Netherlands in the form of a social contract in the early 1970s, in which the government offered tax concessions as well as a larger volume of public expenditure and employment guarantees in exchange for wage and price moderation.[10]

Wages and profits

Turning from this brief description of some features of the institutional background to wider issues, it could be argued that in the six small countries with centralized wage formation, the coverage of collective agreements is wide enough to make a discussion of the general distribution of income between labour and capital meaningful. Indeed, it could be expected at first sight that trade unions would be able to increase labour's share more successfully when bargaining is centralized than in partially unionized countries. This is, however, not borne out by the experience of the post-war period. Isolated episodes in which the functional distribution of income shifted in favour of one or the other factor can be found (often in fact, in favour of capital, as, for instance, in Finland in 1968–70 or in Sweden in 1972–4), but over the longer run it is unlikely that centralized wage formation made much difference.

[10] In Ireland, too, direct and indirect tax cuts were frequently used by the government in the second half of the 1970s to influence National Pay Agreements.

TABLE 12.1. *Gross profit share in manufacturing*[a]
(percentages)

	Actual shares			Trend changes[b]	
	1960–66	1967–73	1974–79	1960–73	1973–79
France	24	27	23	1.52	−3.54
Germany	36	34	30	−1.29	0.71
Italy	39	35	32	−2.10	0.35
United Kingdom	30	27	22	−1.32	0.17
Austria	44	42	33	−1.01	−2.40
Belgium	36	36	31	−0.17	−1.53
Denmark	28	26	23	−1.36	−2.29
Finland	38	37	35	−0.17	−0.88
Netherlands[c]	40	36	30	−1.53	−3.14
Norway	20	20	19	1.07	−8.83
Sweden	28	26	23	−1.61	−7.40

[a] Operating surplus in per cent of value added at current prices
[b] Percentage rate of change in shares obtained from regression estimates of exponential
trends
[c] Excluding petroleum and gas
Source: unpublished Swedish Employers Confederation estimates based on a variety of
national accounts sources.

Indicators of profitability are not easy to interpret, but according to the evidence presented for eleven countries in Table 12.1 there would seem to have been a general decline in the share of gross profits in manufacturing value added in Europe from at least the mid-1960s onwards, decline which became more pronounced after the oil crisis. This broad conclusion, based upon available national accounts data, is confirmed by studies of more relevant measures for a smaller number of countries. Thus, negative trends for the net rate of return on capital were found for Germany and the United Kingdom, Austria, and Sweden.[11]

Comparing the profit performance of the six centralized wage formation countries on the one hand, and that of the four major economies on the other, no significant differences emerge both in the period 1960–73 and in the more troubled years after 1973. Table 12.1 would seem to support the view that average profit levels in an economy are in the medium term determined at a macroeconomic level by factors other than centrally negotiated wage increases. Demand management and exchange rates are more important.

Centralized bargaining can have an influence in the short run, but even this is limited by the variability and importance of wage drift. Between the mid-1960s and the late 1970s the annual range of variation of wage drift was 10 percentage points in Finland, 6 in Norway, and 5 in Denmark, Sweden, and Austria (using the Nordic definition of wage drift). Moreover, wage drift accounted for 40 to 55 per cent of the total rise in wages for periods of several years in the

[11] See T.P. Hill, *Profits and Rates of Return*, OECD, Paris 1979; K. Aiginger and K. Bayer, 'Entwicklung des industriellen Cash-Flow 1980', *Monatsberichte*, WIFO, No. 10, 1980; and J. Ortengren, unpublished material for the Industrial Institute for Economic and Social Research, Stockholm.

four major Nordic countries during the 1960s and 1970s, and for 25 to 35 per cent in different manufacturing branches in Austria between 1966 and 1975. As observed by Schelde Andersen and Turner, 'One important feature of collective bargaining is that wage drift is usually much higher under centralized than decentralized systems'.[12] In part, this may stem from differences in definitions of wage drift. Probably a more important reason is to be found in the more uniform nature of the wage bargain settled upon at the national level, combined at times with elements of a 'solidaristic' wage policy (common to most of the countries) dictated by egalitarian income distribution considerations. This inevitably leads to compensating bargains being struck at the plant level. But such compensating bargains are influenced by the state of the labour market. Thus an analysis of wage drift in, for instance, Sweden, and its dependence upon profits and vacancy levels,[13] leads to the conclusion that a significant deviation of the outcome of wage bargaining at central level is compensated through wage drift after about three years. This dependence of wage drift on market forces suggests an important conclusion – conflicts can achieve little in the longer run.

General strikes or lock-outs have occurred in Finland, Denmark, or Sweden for periods of one or a few weeks, but were unable to shift income distribution between labour and capital in a visible way. Similarly, the dependence of wages on market forces limits what the government could try to achieve in preaching, or imposing, wage moderation. None of the social partners has been able, via centralized collective bargaining, to have more than a marginal and temporary effect on the macroeconomic distribution of income between wages and profits. The results cannot be more dramatic than the machinery, as well as economic forces, permit.

These limits which the central bargaining partners encounter in their influence upon the distribution of income between wages and profits were a main theme in the Swedish joint employer–trade-union report 'Wage Formation and the Economy'.[14] Following the earlier Norwegian 'Aukrust Report',[15] the authors defined a 'main course' for the development of wages and salaries, surrounded by a 'corridor'. The determination of the 'main course' belonged to economic analysis and could be made jointly by economic experts. The 'corridor', on the other hand, defined the scope for collective bargaining. If the upper wall of the 'corridor' was touched, investments would be depressed and productivity and growth would decelerate in a way that was against the interests of both parties. If, instead, the lower wall was touched, wage drift would increase and correct the imbalance. Thus, there was no point in seeking an agreement outside the 'corridor'.

[12] Schelde Andersen and Turner, 'Incomes Policy', p. 37.

[13] N.H. Schager, 'The Duration of Vacancies as a Measure of the State of Demand in the Labour Market. The Swedish Wage Drift Equation Reconsidered', in G. Eliasson, B. Holmlund, and F.P. Stafford (eds.), *Studies on Labour Market Behaviour: Sweden and the United States*, Industrial Institute for Economic and Social Research Conference Reports, Stockholm 1980; see also OECD, *Economic Survey of Sweden, 1981*, Annex III.

[14] First published in Swedish in 1968 and subsequently in English; see G. Edgren, K.-O. Faxén, and C.-E. Odhner, *Wage Formation and the Economy*, London 1973.

[15] *Innstilling II fra utredningsutvalget for inntektsoppgjørene i 1966, avgitt 20. oktober 1966* (Second Report by the Reporting Committee for the 1966 Income Settlement), Office of the Prime Minister, Oslo 1967.

The purpose of this analysis, subsequently dubbed the 'Scandinavian Model', was to define an interval for the bargainers, sufficiently narrow to make an open conflict economically uninteresting. The establishment of this framework, first in Norway and then in Sweden, was as much a description of principles already followed in central bargaining as a tool for the future. In fact, the actual determination of wage increases in Sweden since the introduction of central agreements in the mid-1950s had already been made following the 'main course' formula of the model. Since, with a fixed exchange rate, the 'main course' was determined by international prices and productivity in the competitive sector, the bargaining partners did not attempt to push inflation below the level that followed from international factors.

The nature of wage bargaining

The 'Scandinavian Model' also widened the frame of reference and the content of wage bargaining. The minimum profits necessary for the financing of investments required for increasing productivity defined the upper wall of the 'corridor'. Movements of the equity–debt ratio in the company sector created a link between wage policy and fiscal policy. Thus, the ground was laid for the 1970s joint consultation in the preparatory work on government medium-term projections in Sweden, and the joint incomes policy analysis in Finland. The fact that the state (especially the President) played a more active role in Finland made more far-reaching co-ordination between wage policy and fiscal and exchange rate policy feasible in that country. For instance, Finnish central agreements in the late 1970s contained clauses that were intended to limit the freedom of action for exchange rate policy. In the Netherlands, such links between centralized wage formation on the one hand, and fiscal and exchange rate policies on the other, had already been established by the Centraal Planbureau in the 1950s as a basis for Dutch incomes policies before 1963.

Thus, in central negotiations, general economic policy issues like exchange rates, taxes, investment, growth, and productivity are necessarily involved in addition to nominal wages and inflation. There is no longer a clear dividing line between the wage bargain and more general political and economic considerations. Trade unions are in a position to influence government decisions on economic policy in relevant areas such as public expenditure, taxation, or even labour market and industrial subsidies, or to exercise political pressure for higher employment and less unemployment.

Government incomes policies may emerge out of this process when institutional, historical, and political factors are appropriate. Under other circumstances, the central bargaining partners may be able to retain their independence from the government and yet establish a working relationship. A formal and visible government involvement in centralized collective bargaining is thus not essential. The centralization itself, whether brought about through private employer and trade-union interaction or through government policy, is the crucial factor.

A further factor that needs to be emphasized is the political nature of centralized collective bargaining. When bargaining is centralized, and the economic issue is general, a strike or a lock-out has to be general. A general open conflict is, on the other hand, an expensive and not very rational way to settle an issue.

Neither side can regain what is lost in income during the conflict (as they can in partially organized labour markets), and this is usually understood among members of both the union and the employers' side.

When strikes occur, they result from conflicts between groups of wage and salary earners. Centralization is seen as a method of dealing with such conflicts in a regular and predictable way and is often supported by employers as a policy to minimize strikes. This is particularly important when small groups in key positions are organized.[16] Centralization becomes a method to exercise pressure upon and 'contain' such groups. The amount of inter-union pressure necessary to reach a central agreement serves to emphasize its political nature.

In conclusion, therefore, it can be said that in spite of the fact that, in the longer run, centralized wage formation is unlikely to have much influence on factorial income distribution, it remains none the less an integral and indispensable feature of the six economies here surveyed. It has become an essential element of economic policy formation both because it avoids, at least most of the time, the dangers of an open and expensive conflict, and because it provides a means by which unions and employers can exert their influence on government policy.

II. Incomes Policies in Larger Countries

In the four larger European economies the degree of unionization is much smaller than in the six countries with centralized wage formation discussed above. It ranges from about 20 to 25 per cent in France, to about 50 to 55 per cent in the United Kingdom, while national employers' federations are weak. Collective bargaining is largely conducted at industry or even plant level. Economy-wide bargaining is limited to fringe benefits or indexing, as for the automatic escalator mechanism (*scala mobile*) in Italy. Partly as a result of these features, strikes are seen as a natural means for trade unions in particular plants or branches of industry to secure or maintain gains in living standards, and their costs are viewed as relatively small compared to possible gains. In such an environment, incomes policies are much less likely to be feasible, or at the least, their nature is fundamentally different. They are unlikely to be of a 'permanent' nature, as is more or less the case in the six countries discussed above. Rather, they tend to be introduced or experimented with only on a temporary basis as a response to particularly adverse macroeconomic conditions. The reasons for their acceptance by unions differ quite markedly from those in more centralized countries.

Experience with incomes policies

Of the major European economies, it is only the United Kingdom which has

---

[16] Cf. the statement made by H. Fjällström, the secretary responsible for wage negotiations in the Swedish LO (trade-union confederation), during the strike by the independent Harbour Workers' Union: 'LO-members demand increasingly that work is resumed in Swedish ports in order to protect their jobs. Groups that use their key positions to form independent unions act against the solidarity of the working class. Pay levels in the new agreement correspond to what other groups have obtained and should be accepted according to the LO solidaristics wage policy.' *Dagens Nyheter*, 3 June 1980.

both formally and frequently tried to use incomes policies as an instrument of economic management. In France (a country with a long history of price controls) and in Italy, government intervention in the process of wage formation has tended to be *ad hoc*. In France, for instance, the government influenced the Grenelle Agreements which followed the May 1968 *événements* and, in the late 1970s, issued recommendations to employers and unions to limit wage increases to the rate of consumer price inflation. In Italy there are no formalized institutions for government influence in wage formation, and 'Intervention by the public authorities in collective bargaining has normally taken place at the most dramatic stage of labour conflicts, and has involved an attempt to mediate or simply to attempt to bring about a resumption of negotiations.'[17] In Spain, where the highly controlled economic system of the 1950s and 1960s gave way to free trade unions only in the later 1970s, one experiment with a tripartite agreement was made in 1977 (the Moncloa Agreements), but lasted for only one year.

In Germany the situation is somewhat different. Though collective bargaining is decentralized, regional agreements, often in the metal industry, are 'pattern making', i.e. they cover large segments of the labour force (up to 25 per cent for the metal agreements), and influence the outcome in other branches. Though they do not determine an economy-wide framework as in the case of the Scandinavian central agreements, they have prompted an indirect form of government intervention in the form of the 'Concerted Action' programme. This was instituted in 1967 between the federal government, the unions, and employers' associations, as a forum for discussion of likely macroeconomic trends and desirable goals usually supplied by the independent Council of Economic Experts (*Sachverständigenrat*). The 'Concerted Action' formula made decisions in both economic policy and wage policy more transparent, without breaking the basic principle of non-interference in collective bargaining. Its suspension, on the initiative of the unions, in 1977, was related to the co-determination issue and not to dissatisfaction with the dialogue itself.

The United Kingdom, on the other hand, applied temporary incomes policies of various degrees of severity on numerous occasions (between 1948 and 1950, 1961 and 1963, 1966 and 1969, 1972 and 1974, and, most recently, 1975 and 1978). In the absence of a powerful central employers' federation, the establishment of these policies and of the institutions regulating them (e.g. the National Incomes Commission, the National Board for Prices and Incomes, the Pay Board), has been very much a government–trade-union affair. Among the instruments used by the government, apart from voluntary agreements or outright wage freezes, were some of the approaches followed in smaller countries (e.g. voluntary price restraints, price freezes, direct tax reductions), as well as, in the 1975-8 experiment, the threat of withholding public purchases from firms guilty of breaking wage guidelines.

The nature of incomes policies

The partial unionization of the work-force raises some important issues for the workings of incomes policies in countries such as the United Kingdom. When

[17] OECD, *Collective Bargaining in Ten Countries*, p. 37.

unionization is incomplete, unions can, in theory, achieve a significant wage differential in relation to unorganized groups doing the same kind of jobs. This can arise, for instance, if some product markets are oligopolistic and mobility is limited by, for instance, seniority. In such cases, economic theory provides for the possibility that trade unions share 'oligopolistic rent' with the owners of such firms. A similar effect upon the wage structure may emerge from unionization and collective bargaining in competitive industries, where the union is able to organize an entire branch and reach a branch agreement. Wages can be made higher than in non-union branches (for the same level of skill, education etc.), and firms can still remain competitive. In both cases, of course, one is considering either relatively closed economies or floating regimes, conditions which, broadly, are better approximated by the major European economies (and the United States) than by the smaller countries. Alternatively, the discussion can refer to non-tradeable products. Thus, from a theoretical point of view, one could expect that wages, in some instances but not always, will be higher in unionized industries than in non-unionized ones.

The empirical evidence on the existence of such union–non-union wage differentials is scanty and mainly based on United States research. It is also evidence which must be handled with caution for two main reasons. First, the results seem to depend to a significant extent on the statistical techniques used – in particular, the methods adopted in standardizing for education, skill, age, industry branch, region, and other similar factors. Second, there is a problem of causality. Is unionization or coverage by collective agreements independent of background factors (such as skill and experience but also product market characteristics – e.g. degree of oligopoly as measured by concentration ratios and relative profitability), or has unionization been more successful in some combinations of background factors than in others? In other words, unionization may have been easier where it was relatively easier to raise wages.

With these caveats in mind, some of the evidence can be reviewed. The union–non-union wage differential in the United States has been estimated by different authors to lie between less than 10 per cent and up to almost 50 per cent.[18] A review of the issue concluded that, for the mid-1970s, a reasonable estimate for production and non-supervisory workers might have been of 20 to 30 per cent.[19] Evidence for the United Kingdom summarized in an OECD report suggests a very similar result: 'Recent studies indicate that for male manual workers, other things being equal, the average hourly wage in an industry whose labour force (irrespective of the degree of unionization) is completely covered by a collective agreement is around 25 to 35 per cent greater than the average wage in a completely uncovered industry.'[20] Less detailed work on Germany also suggests that

[18] See, for instance, the following works which obtain estimates of 10, 30, and 50 per cent respectively: P. Schmidt and R. Strauss, 'The Effects of Unions on Earnings and Earnings on Unions: A Mixed Logit Approach', *International Economic Review*, February 1976; Lung-fei Lee, 'Unionism and Wage Rates: A Simultaneous Equations Model with Qualitative and Limited Dependent Variables', *International Economic Review*, June 1978; L.M. Kahn, 'Unionism and Relative Wages: Direct and Indirect Effects', *Industrial and Labor Relations Review*, July 1979.

[19] D.J.B. Mitchell, *Unions, Wages and Inflation*, Brookings Institution, Washington 1980, p. 214.

[20] OECD, *Collective Bargaining in Ten Countries*, pp. 135–6.

unions can raise wage levels for their members,[21] though the extension by government decree of collective agreements to unorganized workers must limit German union–non-union differentials.

A union–non-union wage differential of the order of 25 to 30 per cent cannot be taken entirely from profits, and must originate, in part at least, from other causes. The evidence on this issue is even scantier. Two United States studies suggest that higher wages in unionized industries correspond to differentials in value added per worker which are, in turn, due either to productivity differentials, as indicated by the second of the two studies, or to oligopolistic pricing in unionized industries.[22] In either case, unionization effects upon the distribution of real income between different groups of wage and salary earners are much larger than the possible effects upon the distribution between all wage and salary earners on the one hand and capital on the other.

If this is so, the issue of an incomes policy is very different in a country like the United Kingdom, or any of the larger European industrialized countries, from the situation in small countries with centralized wage formation. Two lines of action are open to government policy in such circumstances. One would be efforts to establish equal pay for equal work in organized oligopolistic and un-organized competitive industries. This would constitute an argument for a permanent interference in wage formation of a different nature from interference based on macroeconomic considerations. This, however, has not been the policy followed in the United Kingdom, let alone in the other large countries in which incomes policies have been much less prominent. The second approach would be the more traditional one of using incomes policies to prevent cost–push inflation stemming from union pressures in a particular situation and in a special sector of the economy such as in large oligopolistic corporations. It is, of course, this second approach which has been prominent in practice. The real problem for policy has been to prevent or reduce a temporary cost–push situation from disturbing the general demand management of the economy.

United Kingdom policies

The success of such attempts seems to have been mixed. According to a relatively large body of literature which has investigated the effects of incomes policies in the United Kingdom,[23] results were only marginal and temporary, with frequent evidence of rebounds in the rate of wage inflation after termination of the incomes policy. Similar exercises, carried out for the United States, obtain broadly similar results. Yet, while this can, prima facie, be seen as a strong criticism of incomes policies since they would seem to be unable to alter longer-run inflationary trends, this conclusion can be tempered by a number of considerations.

---

[21] M. Neumann, I. Böbel, and A. Haid, 'Marktmacht, Gewerkschaften und Lohnhöhe in der Industrie der Bundesrepublik Deutschland', *Kyklos*, No. 2, 1980.

[22] C. Brown and J. Medoff, 'Trade Unions in the Production Process', *Journal of Political Economy*, June 1978; and K.B. Clark, 'The Impact of Unionization on Productivity: A Case Study', *Industrial and Labor Relations Review*, July 1980.

[23] See, for instance: R.G. Lipsey and J.M. Parkin, 'Incomes Policy: A Reappraisal', *Economica*, May 1970; S.G.B. Henry, 'Incomes Policy and Aggregate Pay', in J.L. Fallick and R.F. Elliott (eds.), *Incomes Policies, Inflation and Relative Pay*, London 1981; Schelde Andersen and Turner, 'Incomes Policy'.

First, it could be argued that 'Incomes policies are tested by much more rigorous criteria than are other forms of policy such as fiscal or monetary policies',[24] thus, perhaps, weighing the dice against them. Second, most of the econometric tests conducted in this field have based their results on estimates of domestic wage inflation in periods with and without incomes policies, with deviations from a longer-run trend of domestic wages during and just after policy periods denoting the effectiveness of such intervention. The validity of such econometric tests may, however, be limited. Other types of wage formation models might be more relevant. For instance, it could be argued that in a reasonably open economy such as that of the United Kingdom, international trends could also affect wage claims. Thus, if allowance was made in the wage equations for the influence of the late 1960s European wage explosions, this could well alter some of the conclusions derived from these findings (i.e. upward deviations from a longer-run trend could be seen not only as 'catch-ups' but also as, in part at least, responses to events abroad).

Thirdly, even if the success of incomes policies in moderating inflation can at most be put at only 1 or 2 percentage points (as, for instance, in the United Kingdom in the period 1973-4, according to OECD estimates),[25] this is not insignificant if translated into the unemployment increase which would have been necessary for a similar reduction in inflation by traditional demand management means. Finally, these estimates may not convey the full story. It could be argued that government incomes policy initiatives were rooted in the fear that, because of special circumstances in the bargaining sphere (union rivalries, contests for power, exogenous shocks, etc.), accelerations in inflation were imminent. If this were the case, the regression results quoted above would indicate success, not failure. A case in point could be the United Kingdom's experience in the 1975-9 period, which has not yet been subject to econometric testing. Though it is true that the Labour government's incomes policy collapsed in late 1978 and wage inflation accelerated significantly until 1980, it is doubtful whether this acceleration can really be considered as a full compensation for what would have happened in the absence of the incomes policy. The 'counterfactual' is virtually impossible to construct, given the situation of the mid-1970s, but it should not be forgotten that, in 1975 for instance, earnings rose by over 25 per cent and were widely expected to accelerate further without government intervention.[26]

Yet incomes policies are perceived, at least in the United Kingdom, as unable permanently to affect the inflation–unemployment trade-off. Their acceptance by unions (at least over certain periods of time), and the continued support for them expressed by some sections of public opinion may need explanation.

---

[24] D. Robinson, *Incomes Policy and Capital Sharing in Europe*, London 1973, p. 13.

[25] Schelde Andersen and Turner, 'Incomes Policy', p. 48.

[26] Thus, EEC surveys of consumers' expectations of inflation show that there was a downward shift at the turn of 1975 which could be associated with Phase II of the 'Social Contract' policy of the time. It should be noted, however, that a similar downward movement in inflationary expectations took place in the first half of 1979, despite the collapse of incomes policies in late 1978; F. Papadia and V. Basano, 'EEC-DG11, Inflationary Expectations – Survey–Based Inflationary Expectations for the EEC Countries', *EEC Economic Papers*, No. 1, May 1981. A significant effect of incomes policies on price expectations was also found by R.A. Batchelor and T.D. Sheriff, 'Unemployment and Unanticipated Inflation in Postwar Britain', *Economica*, May 1980.

There are probably several reasons for their continued popularity. First, they can be viewed as instruments to reduce uncertainty. In indeterminate situations, as those which arise out of the oligopolistic character of bilateral bargaining, there is always the possibility of an irregular, unforseeable element of decision-making. In the absence of incomes policies, such disturbances could create inflationary shocks that monetary and fiscal policy could find difficult to cope with. The response to the uncertainty arising out of this indeterminacy is centralization. A government incomes policy is one method, in the absence of an alternative such as the establishment of a central employers' organization with power to conduct bargaining on behalf of its members.

On the union side, motivations for accepting incomes policies must be different from those in centralized and highly organized countries, since strikes are still an efficient weapon. One explanation could be that an incomes policy appears a less costly way to reach agreements that (according to *ex-post* regression studies) yield almost the same results as those of more aggressive forms of strategy, which would, in addition, involve substantial risks of open conflicts. Indeed, if the final outcome (in terms of the development of earnings, including wage drift) is likely to be the same as without the policy, acquiescence might offer some advantage to trade unions. It would increase predictability in collective bargaining, reduce the risk of open conflict, and thus make the same economic result possible at lower cost for the union and its members. Evidently, such advantages are temporary in nature and do not justify a permanent incomes policy. In the basic economic bargaining of partially organized labour markets, a 'show of power' is necessary at some intervals of time. An incomes policy period can, however, be used between such intervals to ensure the consolidation of earlier gains and the strengthening of new positions.

III. Parallels and Contrasts

The preceding two sections have briefly looked at the incomes policy experience of two sets of countries which, partly because of size but more importantly because of institutions, are very different from each other in the field of collective bargaining. This does not preclude, however, an attempt at comparing some selected features and achievements. Three aspects in particular will be looked at, in which these policies could, a priori, be thought of as having had noticeable effects:

     (i) The influence of centralized wage formation and incomes policies on macroeconomic performance;

     (ii) The behaviour of wage and salary differentials through time;

     (iii) The incidence of open conflicts in various countries.

Inflation and unemployment

At the macroeconomic level, incomes policies have been seen in the larger countries very much as anti-inflationary instruments. Hence they have been assessed in the literature in terms of their contribution to lowering wage pressures. Experience to date, at least in the United Kingdom, suggests that, on the surface, they have not been very successful in achieving this aim. A similarly narrow technique of assessment would not be thought reasonable or possible for the smaller countries. Not only would it be impossible to distinguish the differential impact on inflation of a system such as centralized wage formation because this system was permanently in operation (i.e. there are no 'policy off' periods), but more importantly, inflation in such small open economies is to a large extent determined by external forces. In fact, a priori, one would expect inflation rates to differ little between the two groups of countries here considered (at least under a system of fixed exchange rates), and, indeed, this is confirmed by the longer-run evidence.

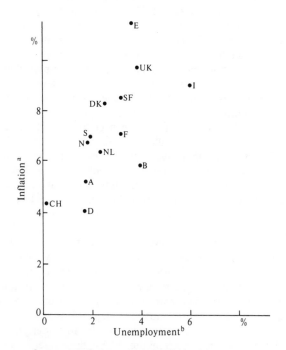

FIG. 12.2. *The unemployment–inflation trade-off, 1964–1979*
[a] Average annual percentage changes in consumer prices
[b] In per cent of the labour force
Sources: OECD, *Economic Outlook*, December 1980 and July 1981; EEC, *European Economy*, November 1980; ILO, *Bulletin of Labour Statistics*, (various issues); IMF, *International Financial Statistics* (1980 Yearbook).

As was argued in Section I, if centralized wage formation is to have an effect in a small open economy, this would work through higher rates of investment and growth or lower rates of unemployment rather than via a lower rate of inflation. But even in the growth area, it is unlikely that longer-run differences could be substantial, given that, first, factorial income distribution may not have been affected by the bargaining system in the countries with centralized wage formation, and, second, in view of the open nature of these economies which renders them very dependent on trends in the four major ones.

The relationship between unemployment and inflation may, however, be worth some analysis. If roughly internationally comparable unemployment data are used, it would seem that over the period 1964–79[27] there is little trace of a trade-off in Europe (Fig. 12.2). If anything, in such a longer-term analysis, the relationship appears to be the opposite to the one postulated by the Phillips curve. A European country could not gain lower unemployment by accepting more inflation – on the contrary, more inflation went along with higher unemployment. The six centralized wage formation countries did not fare better in this respect than other European countries. They are clustered in the middle of the diagram together with France and Belgium, with Austria closest to the German and Swiss observations, and Finland to the British and Italian ones. A shorter-run analysis is provided in Fig. 12.3, which splits the post-oil-shock years into two periods (1974–6 and 1977–9). In this instance there is some evidence for a Phillips curve trade-off (shown by the slopes of the country lines). In most countries, inflation was lower in the second sub-period and unemployment was higher. Among the six countries with centralized wage formation, Austria, the Netherlands, Norway, and Sweden were able to reduce their inflation with only limited increases in unemployment, as were Germany and Switzerland in the other group of European countries. The line for Finland, on the other hand, is almost parallel to those for France, Italy, the United Kingdom, or Belgium and indicates that the 'price' for a deceleration of inflation was a significant increase in unemployment. The experiences of Denmark and Spain were even more unfavourable. Thus it cannot be said that centralization of wage formation generally helped the six countries to overcome the inflationary effects of the first oil shock better than was the case elsewhere in Europe.

It should be remembered, however, that countries such as Germany and Switzerland and, to a lesser extent, France and Belgium, were in a more favourable starting-position in the 1970s – they could moderate the increase in domestic unemployment by repatriating immigrant labour. Among the smaller centralized wage formation countries, this was possible only to a more limited extent in Austria and the Netherlands. The suggestion that, after all, performance may have been somewhat better, at least in an underlying sense, in the smaller centralized countries, is strengthened by the evidence shown in Table 12.2, which presents OECD estimates for the 'room' for wage increases in the years 1972–9 in the light of the terms of trade and productivity changes (and assuming a constant profit share). It will be seen that, despite the lower scope for real wage rises in the six centralized wage formation countries, due to both sharper terms of trade deteriorations and lower productivity growth, their performance was somewhat better than that of the other countries. Though this may have been due to other causes, it could provide a prima-facie case for the usefulness of centralized collective bargaining mechanisms in circumstances in which the growth of real incomes must decelerate.

---

[27] The year 1964 has been chosen because it is the earliest one for which comparable unemployment data for a relatively large number of countries are available. The only unemployment data in Figs. 12.2 and 12.3 that are not comparable are those for Denmark and Switzerland.

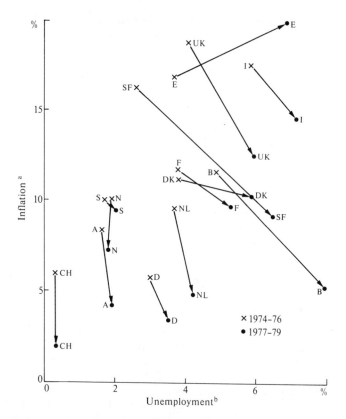

FIG. 12.3. *Changes in the unemployment-inflation trade-off, 1974–1979*
[a] Average annual percentage changes in consumer prices; 1973 to 1976 and 1976 to 1979
[b] In per cent of the labour force; 1974–76 and 1977–79
Sources: OECD, *Economic Outlook*, July 1981: EEC, *European Economy*, November 1980; ILO, *Bulletin of Labour Statistics*, No. 2, 1980; IMF, *International Financial Statistics* (1980 Yearbook).

Wage and salary differentials

A second area in which incomes policies are often perceived as having had pronounced effects is in compressing wage differentials. This can arise either because incomes policies in larger countries impinge mainly on the unionized sector and, therefore, lead to an erosion of the union–non-union differential discussed in Section II above, or because, in both large and small countries, flat rate elements in wage policies or 'solidaristic' wage efforts by unions inevitably imply lower percentage wage and salary increases for higher paid workers and employees.

There is, unfortunately, little evidence on these issues, particularly on the first one. The long-run stability in earnings differentials is reasonably well documented (and is discussed in Chapter 7 above). Looking only at shorter-run trends, mainly over the 1970s, and taking the large countries first, French statistics exhibit some narrowing of differentials after 1968 which, however, only compensates for the increase in dispersion that had been experienced since 1950.

TABLE 12.2. *'Warranted '*[a] *and actual real wage increases, 1972–1979*
(average annual percentage changes)

	'Warranted'[a] real wage	Actual real wage	Real wage gap
France	2.9	3.6	0.6
Germany	3.2	2.7	−0.5
Italy	1.8	2.6	0.8
United Kingdom	1.5	1.7	0.1
Spain	4.3	4.0	−0.3
Austria[b]	2.9	3.5	0.6
Belgium	2.5	4.3	1.7
Denmark	0.9	1.1	0.1
Finland	2.6	1.5	−1.1
Netherlands	2.3	2.6	0.3
Norway	2.2	1.8	−0.5
Sweden	0.5	−0.2	−0.7
Switzerland	1.3	2.0	0.7
Total	2.5	2.7	0.1

[a] Productivity growth less income effects of terms of trade changes
[b] 1972–78
Source: unpublished OECD estimates.

The stability of the German pay structure is even more pronounced. The skill differentials among male manual workers in industry (excluding construction) fluctuated within a range of only 1 to 2 per cent between 1966 and 1979.[28] Salary differentials were similarly stable.

More striking are the results for the United Kingdom and Italy. In the United Kingdom, where one could have expected some compression of differentials because of incomes policies, the consensus opinion is that there is very little evidence to support such an assumption. Though it is true that skill differentials were compressed in some branches during the 1970s, the timing was such as to suggest that forces other than incomes policies had been at work.[29] On the contrary, low-paid workers covered by Council Agreements suffered a relative loss when incomes policies in the 1960s were enforced more effectively upon them, and they were unable to recoup their position in the 1970s.[30] In Italy, on the other hand, and despite the absence of incomes policies, there was a dramatic compression of skill differentials, mainly following the 1969 'Hot Autumn' crisis in industrial relations. As an example, between 1964 and 1977 the

[28] C. Saunders and D. Marsden, *A Six-Country Comparison of the Distribution of Industrial Earnings in the 1970s*, Royal Commission on the Distribution of Income and Wealth, Background Paper No. 8, HMSO, London 1979; D. Marsden, 'A Study of Changes in the Wage Structure of Manual Workers since 1966', *mimeo*, EEC, Brussels 1980, p. 4.32.

[29] A.J.H. Dean, 'Incomes Policies and Differentials', *NIESR Review*, August 1978; C. Saunders, 'Changes in Relative Pay in the 1970s', in F.T. Blackaby (ed.), *The Future of Pay Bargaining*, NIESR, London 1980; K. Mayhew, 'Incomes Policy and the Private Sector', in Fallick and Elliott (eds.), *Incomes Policies*.

[30] R. Steele, 'Incomes Policies and Low Pay', in Fallick and Elliott (eds.), *Incomes Policies*.

percentage difference in average hourly earnings between the highly skilled and the unskilled in manufacturing was halved.[31] The major reasons for these developments were egalitarian forms of shop-floor bargaining on the one hand, and nationally agreed flat cost-of-living allowances on the other.

The trends among the smaller countries for which data are available (Austria, Denmark, Finland, and Sweden) are equally diverse. Austria exhibits much the same stability as Germany in the long run. Dispersion increased between 1953 and 1964, but decreased between 1964 and 1970 and remained stable in the 1970s, with structural changes in the labour force rather than trade-union bargaining explaining the major part of these movements.[32] Denmark, on the other hand, witnessed a significant decrease in differentials between the early 1960s and the late 1970s.[33] For workers, the compression can be seen as a consequence of collective agreements policies. For qualified salaried employees who are unorganized in Denmark and for whom private employers set salaries unilaterally, the dramatic compression that took place[34] may have been largely due to the use of flat rate cost-of-living allowances, following the example set by the public sector. Moreover, public sector workers who had gained relative to the private sector in the 1960s lost heavily in the 1970s, probably as a result of a stricter application of centrally agreed wage and salary norms in the latter decade. In Finland, both wage and salary dispersions were stable in the first half of the 1970s and slightly reduced during the second half.

Sweden, finally, recorded a drastic reduction in differentials in the 1970s. The coefficient of variation for both hourly earnings in manufacturing and monthly salaries for routine staff fell by about one-quarter in the decade. It is, however, an open question to what extent these developments can be attributed to wage and salary policies at the central level. Thus, it is remarkable that the reduction in differentials was equally pronounced for wages and salaries, even though flat rate increases were much more common for workers than for employees, and so were special contractual increases for the low-paid.[35] The compression of salaries for routine office staff must be seen as a result of plant-level bargaining rather than of rules and provisions in central collective agreements.

Clearly, these findings are too disparate and divergent for any definite conclusions. Wage and salary dispersions are affected by numerous factors such as conditions in labour markets, use of flat rate or percentage cost-of-living-allowances, social norms, and attitudes at the plant level, for it to be possible to

[31] Marsden, 'A Study of Changes', p. 4.18.

[32] J. Christl, 'Entwicklungstendenzen in der österreichischen Lohn- und Gehaltspyramid zwischen 1953 und 1979, *Empirica*, No. 2, 1980.

[33] Det Økonomiske Råds Formandskap, *Dansk økonomi maj 1981* (The Chairman of the Economic Council, The Danish Economy in May 1981), Copenhagen 1981, Table 2, p. 116.

[34] The differential in life salary between a university-educated engineer and a skilled metal-worker fell, for instance, from 115 per cent in 1970 to 55 per cent ten years later.

[35] L. Jonsson, 'Lönespridning: Arbetare, tjänstemän 1972–1980' (Wage and Salary Dispersions; 1972–1980), *mimeo*, Swedish Employers Confederation (SAF), Stockholm 1981; I. Ohlsson 'Den solidariska lönepolitikens resultat' (Results from the Solidaristic Wage Policy), in Swedish Confederation of Trade Unions (LO), *Lönepolitik och solidaritet* (Wage Policy and Solidarity), Stockholm 1980.

decide, one way or another, on the egalitarian effects of incomes policies on the basis of the available evidence.

The frequency of open conflict

Turning to strike frequency, it could be expected from what was said earlier that the evidence might be more conclusive. In a partially organized labour market open conflicts (strikes and lock-outs) are virtually inevitable. Trade unions in oligopolistic industries must sometimes strike as part of a mixed strategy to ensure a high wage-level for their members relative to the rest of the labour market. The cost of strikes is usually small compared to the potential gains (with a ratio of perhaps one to ten). The same is true for employer organizations for whom it can be economically advantageous to resist union claims and to answer, if necessary, by lock-outs if there is an element of profit above normal yields of capital that can be obtained permanently.

In a small economy with centralized bargaining, on the other hand, the general conflict does not have the same meaning for the wage formation process as a limited conflict in a partially unionized society. There is no non-union sector vis-à-vis which a differential can be established or maintained. Average profit levels in the economy are determined at a macroeconomic level by factors other than negotiated wage increases, at least in the medium term. The temporary gains that can be made through an aggressive policy from the employer or the union side are short-lived and small compared to the costs of a conflict. There is no ten to one relationship in centralized bargaining as there can be in plant bargaining in oligopolistic industries. There may even be a ten to one relationship in the opposite direction. This means that professional bargainers in a stable bargaining relationship try to avoid a general conflict. It is not part of a rational mixed strategy to take a non-negligible risk of that nature.

One could, therefore, expect that centralization would lead to significantly lower strike frequencies than in partially unionized countries. This seems, indeed, to be confirmed by the statistical evidence. Table 12.3 shows that, in both the 1960s and 1970s, the average strike frequency in the six smaller countries was less than half as great as it was in the other European countries. Thus the conclusion could be drawn that a centralized bargaining system usually provides a more peaceful way to arrive at results which are broadly similar to those achieved by other methods of bargaining (e.g. at plant, branch, or regional level). This could be true for Finland, for instance, where, as already mentioned in the Introduction to this chapter, it is felt that without wage centralization strike frequencies would be even higher.

But, as is so often the case, the opposite causal interpretation is also possible, at least for the other five countries. Centralized wage formation may be feasible only when strike frequencies are low for other reasons. In other words, it could be argued that a social consensus is a prerequisite for a peaceful centralized system just as much as that centralization is a factor which further strengthens the social consensus.

Conclusions

This chapter has briefly surveyed some selected issues in the area of incomes

TABLE 12.3. *Industrial disputes*
(working days lost directly through industrial disputes per 1,000 employees,
annual averages)

	1961–79	1961–70	1971–79
France	253	280	223
Germany	32	15	50
Italy	1,285	1,237	1,338
United Kingdom	385	191	580
Austria	30	48	10
Belgium	187	133	246
Denmark	227	177	283
Finland	410	178	668
Netherlands	26	14	40
Norway	62	77	46
Sweden	33[a]	21	47[a]
Switzerland	2	1	2
Average of six centralized wage formation countries[b]	131	86	182
Average of other countries	357	309	407

[a] 89 for 1961–80 and 157 for 1971–80, thus including the effects of the 1980 general strike and lock-out.
[b] Austria, Denmark, Finland, the Netherlands, Norway, and Sweden.
Source: unpublished Swedish Employers Confederation estimates based on ILO, OECD, and EEC data.

policies and centralized wage formation. One of the major themes that has been developed is that the traditional way in which incomes policies are seen in, for instance, the United Kingdom or the United States, as a government-determined anti-inflation package relying on a temporary consensus of the union movement is, at best, a very limited view which can often be misleading. It most nearly applies to relatively large and only partly unionized countries in which incomes policy episodes have been initiated by governments. But even in such countries, union participation in these policies has not necessarily reflected mere acquiescence for the sake of a national priority, but possibly a more positive acceptance dictated by the feeling that a temporary lull between bouts of aggressive bargaining may, in fact, be welcome.

In smaller countries, with virtual full unionization of the work-force and a strong national employers' federation, this two-way causation for incomes policies is even more obvious. Indeed, in some countries the prior existence of a central employers' organization may have led, first, to centralization of the union movement, and only later to government intervention in the collective bargaining process. Moreover, the evidence that such collective agreements are unable to control wage drift and have, therefore, only a short-run influence on wage formation, rather than weakening the resolve to continue the process, probably strengthens it.

The alternative (aggressive bargaining) is always risky and can end in expensive strikes or lock-outs, given that institutional and political conditions make it difficult for the central bargaining partners to use partial conflicts as an effective means of influencing the outcome of the central bargaining process. This increases the interest of both parties to the negotiations in obtaining an agreement some-where in the neighbourhood of the market equilibrium. It is also a factor in the willingness of the central bargaining partners to listen to government information and accept a government decision after the bargaining process has created a range for the possible outcome. It becomes more advantageous to accept a point inside that range than risk a general conflict. Centralized wage bargaining by its own internal dynamics may arrive at a situation when government assistance is needed for reaching an agreement. Thus, in small countries with a centralized bargaining system, there are more reasons for the existence or establishment of an incomes policy than just the government's desire to use wage developments as a parameter of action.

A second theme that has run through this chapter, is that incomes policies can have only limited effects on both macroeconomic variables and on income distribution. A distinction must again be made between large countries, in which unionization is only partial and in which union–non-union wage differ-entials are important, and small countries with full unionization and centralized wage formation. In the former, collective bargaining can significantly affect the distribution of income between unionized and non-unionized workers, but not very much the functional distribution between labour and capital. In the latter, the opposite could be the case, though in fact there is little evidence suggesting the existence of a systematic difference between changes in the distribution of income into profits and wages in these countries compared to other European economies. A similar conclusion may hold for the inflation–unemployment trade-off. The only empirically documented result from incomes policies is a reduction in strike frequency.

These conclusions have important consequences for policy. They suggest, first, that incomes policies should perhaps not be seen as a third demand manage-ment instrument. The long-run similarity in macroeconomic developments (inflation, profits, investment, productivity, growth rates), with or without an incomes policy, in different countries and periods of time in post-war Europe is much more obvious than possible differences. And second, it would appear that though they may have had favourable effects on conflict in small open economies, these cannot necessarily be easily repeated in decentralized countries by changes in the wage bargaining machinery towards a more centralized model. Their success may stem from more than just institutional differences between, say, Sweden and the United Kingdom, and reflect deeper-seated social charac-teristics of the six smaller open economies here considered.

Bibliography

The text has already mentioned the existence of a number of surveys of incomes policies in Europe. One of the first was carried out by the UNECE (*Incomes in Post-war Europe*, Geneva 1967). This covered the period from the early 1950s to the mid-1960s and, in addition to the six smaller centralized wage formation countries, also looked at British and French experience. The book by L. Ulman and R.J. Flanagan, *Wage Restraint – A Study of Incomes Policies in Western Europe*, University of California Press 1971, looks at the experience of the four larger countries, Denmark, the Netherlands, and Sweden to the end of the 1960s.

A more recent survey can be found in OECD, *Collective Bargaining and Government Policies in Ten OECD Countries*, Paris 1979, which again covers the four larger economies, Austria, and Sweden. All these sources provide a good deal of institutional background. More succinct reviews are presented by A. Romanis Braun, 'The Role of Incomes Policy in Industrialized Countries since World War II', *IMF Staff Papers*, March 1975, and P. Schelde Andersen and P. Turner, 'Incomes Policy in Theory and Practice', *OECD Economic Outlook – Occasional Studies*, July 1980. More limited surveys, covering four countries (Germany, the United Kingdom, the Netherlands, and Sweden) can be found in W. Galeson (ed.), *Incomes Policy: What Can We Learn from Europe?*, Ithaca 1973, and OECD, *Socially Responsible Wage Policies and Inflation*, Paris 1975.

Some of the conceptual issues raised by incomes policies are looked at in the already quoted Schelde Andersen and Turner paper, in OECD, *Collective Bargaining and Government Policies*, Paris 1979, and in D. Robinson, *Incomes Policy and Capital Sharing in Europe*, London 1973. More technical material can be found, *inter alia*, in M. Parkin and M.T. Sumner, *Incomes Policy and Inflation*, Manchester 1972, and, for the United Kingdom, in the various references quoted in n. 23 above.

On individual countries, the United Kingdom is covered in a number of works, e.g. D.C. Smith, 'Incomes Policy', in R.E. Caves (ed.), *Britain's Economic Prospects*, Brookings Institution, Washington 1968 (for the 1950s and early 1960s); F.T. Blackaby, 'Incomes Policy', in F.T. Blackaby (ed.), *British Economic Policy, 1960–74*, NIESR, Cambridge 1978 (for experience up to the mid-1970s), and by several articles in F.T. Blackaby (ed.), *The Future of Pay Bargaining*, NIESR, London 1980, and in J.L. Fallick and R.F. Elliott (eds.), *Incomes Policies, Inflation and Relative Pay*, London 1981. The Austrian experience is examined by H. Suppanz and D. Robinson, *Prices and Incomes Policy. The Austrian Experience*, OECD, Paris 1972, and E. Spitäller, 'Incomes Policy in Austria', *IMF Staff Papers*, March 1973; the early Dutch one in two papers by J. Pen, 'The Strange Adventures of Dutch Wage Policy', *British Journal of Industrial Relations*, October 1963, and 'Income Policy in the Netherlands', *Scottish Journal of Political Economy*, November 1964; a later and more technical article is by W. Driehuis, 'Inflation, Wage Bargaining, Wage Policy and Production Structure: Theory and Empirical Results for the Netherlands', *De Economist*, No. 4, 1975.

There is a vast literature on the Scandinavian experience. Early surveys of Danish, Norwegian, and Swedish policies can be found in E. Hoffmeyer, 'Incomes Policy in Denmark: Recent Developments', H. Skånland, 'Incomes Policy: Norwegian Experience', and K.-O. Faxén, 'Incomes Policy in Sweden: Problems and Developments', all in *British Journal of Industrial Relations*, November 1964. A more recent and comparative Scandinavian account is in N. Elvander, 'Collective Bargaining and Incomes Policy in the Nordic Countries: A Comparative Analysis', *British Journal of Industrial Relations*, November 1974. On other countries, see also OECD, *Wage Policies and Collective Bargaining Developments in Finland, Ireland, and Norway*, Paris 1979.

13

Public Expenditure

ANTONIO PEDONE*

Introduction

It is well known that public expenditure grew more rapidly than GDP in the post-war period in virtually all European countries. The economic reasons for, and the economic consequences of, this rapid growth are, however, less well known, and remain a subject of vivid controversy, fostered by the lack of adequate comparable data and by the inadequacy of many analytical schemes. Moreover, any interpretation of Europe's post-war experience in the area of public expenditure would require an examination not only of demographic, technological, and economic trends, but would also have to cover a wide range of political and social issues. The aims of this chapter are more limited.[1] It attempts a comparative analysis of some common patterns and of some basic differences in a few selected European countries. This analysis is merely intended to provide background material and to clarify some of the issues which surround the relationship between the economy and the public budget. It should not be taken as a sufficient basis for assessing the effects of the public expenditure policies which were followed in various countries at various times.

The limited scope of the following pages should not come as a surprise. After all, even if the post-war period has seen an impressive development of both normative and positive theories of public expenditure, the persistence of controversial methodological issues and the limited availability of comparable data still prevent the attainment of universally accepted results in the area. Most traditional theories of public expenditure have emphasized its allocative aspects, examining mainly the determinants and the effects of the provision of public goods (and occasionally of 'merit' goods). But the expansion of the government sector during the post-war period in Europe seems to have been mainly caused by expenditures incurred for redistributive or growth purposes. Unless redistribution and growth are treated as public or merit goods, the explanations provided by traditional theories of public expenditure are of no great help.

The chapter's first section briefly discusses two main obstacles to a satisfactory empirical analysis of public expenditure — the problems posed by the changing forms of government intervention and the inadequacies of available statistics. Section II describes the main features of public expenditure growth and financing in the four largest EEC countries (France, Germany, Italy, and the United Kingdom). No unique model of interpretation is used for all countries over the whole period, and only a few suggestions are made on the main structural causes and on the likely effects of public expenditure growth. The

---

* University of Rome.
[1] Indeed, a more appropriate title for it would be 'Some Notes on Public Expenditure'.

third section derives some policy implications with reference in particular to the planning and control of public expenditure and to the later 1970s' attempts to increase the flexibility of public budgeting.

I. Methodological Problems

Two main sets of problems limit any analysis of public expenditure growth in post-war Europe:

(i) Changes in the relationship between public expenditure and other forms of government intervention in the economy;

(ii) The inadequacy of the present statistical base, which does not classify public expenditure following logically consistent definitions.

International public expenditure comparisons in Europe are made difficult not only by the different sizes of the various countries' public sectors, but also by the wide diversity in the forms of public intervention in the economy. Despite the great importance of, for instance, regulations or direct interventions, both normative and positive analyses of the public sector have largely tended to ignore forms of government intervention other than expenditure and taxation.

On the normative side, public expenditure theory has focused mainly on the 'pure public goods' case and has found it difficult to accommodate the other cases of market failure. In such other cases – which cover a great variety of situations, from monopoly power to the unemployment of productive resources – forms of government intervention other than public expenditure may be appropriate. Unfortunately, no satisfactory definitive results have been reached as to when and how far expenditure should be preferred, especially when administrative aspects and costs are taken into account.[2]

On the positive side, the neglect of other forms of government intervention would be of slight consequence if the relationship between them and public expenditure remained broadly unchanged. This relationship, however, has not always been stable. In particular, one of the most important legacies of World War II was not so much a shift in the allocation of public expenditure, as an increased acceptance and use of numerous forms of direct and indirect government intervention. Thus, the dismantling of many controls and regulations in the immediate post-war years may have played some role in boosting the growth of public expenditure in that period. Similarly, in the later 1970s, the increased use of forms of government intervention that are public expenditure substitutes (e.g. 'tax expenditures' and non-budgetary practices) may have kept public spending from growing more rapidly than it did.

Given the existence of numerous forms of potential and actual government intervention, it becomes difficult to specify and to test precise relationships between them and public expenditure growth, in view of the substitutabilities

---

[2] Some of the theoretical and accounting problems which arise when defining 'public sector operations' in circumstances in which direct intervention is extended are analysed in A. Breton, *The Regulation of Private Economic Activity*, Montreal 1976. For a recent discussion and description of new forms of regulation, see the papers of M.L. Weidenbaum, M.J. Ulmer, and D.R. Fusfeld on 'The New Regulation: Pro and Con', *Journal of Post-Keynesian Economics*, Spring 1980.

and complementarities that may occur. Very often, increased direct intervention implies additional expenditure (if only to pay for the staffing and operating of the agencies in charge of the regulations, as in the case, for example, of environmental protection), but additional expenditure may also follow from a reduction in government intervention. Thus a lowering of protectionist barriers may involve a rise in transfers to some productive sectors, while a reduction in rent controls could lead to increased public expenditure in the construction industry.

These changing relationships between public outlays and other forms of government intervention, although difficult to assess and to measure, have clearly been important in Europe over the period. In the following analysis it may, therefore, help to bear in mind that public expenditure is neither a precise measure nor a good indicator of overall government intervention in the economy. Yet many discussions of, and proposals for, institutional changes aimed at a better control and co-ordination of government activities for economic policy purposes are concerned with overall intervention. In any case, if the extent of government intervention other than public expenditure is large and variable, it may be of limited significance to look for the determinants and the effects of public expenditure in isolation.

Even if one could neglect other forms of government intervention in the economy, it is highly doubtful that any single and convincing explanation of the post-war growth of public expenditure, or any definite appraisal of its economic effects, could be reached. This is partly for theoretical reasons. Any hypothesis made to explain the growth of overall public expenditure in relation to GDP on the basis of economic factors should take into account the distinctive properties of the many individual items that enter into it. But any explanation founded on economic theory – whether it came from the demand side (e.g. low price elasticity and high income elasticity of demand for public services) or from the supply side (e.g. productivity lag in the public sector and elasticity of tax revenues) – would seem ill-suited to account for the behaviour of every public expenditure component at every stage of a country's economic development.[3] Equally importantly, however, the nature, content, and coverage of the available data and the varying definitions of the public sector adopted in different countries severely restrict any comparative analysis of the many pressures for, and constraints on, the expansion of public expenditure.

This lack of consistent data over the post-war period also limits the economic analysis of expenditure determinants at a disaggregated functional level, where it is sometimes possible to identify a homogeneous output produced by the public sector.[4] Notwithstanding the efforts made to assemble comparable information

---

[3] If one left the world of simple and consistent economic theory and allowed for the many conceivable social and political factors one would probably end up by identifying 'Some 33 indicators of change which together appear likely to embrace the characteristics of the complex multidetermined phenomenon "the growth of goverment"'; A.T. Peacock and J. Wiseman, 'Approaches to the Analysis of Government Expenditure Growth', *Public Finance Quarterly*, January 1979, p. 19.

[4] Public outlays on a specific function cannot be considered as a good proxy for public output, not only because of changes in relative prices, but also because of the varying efficiency of the administrative process of public provision in the various European countries.

on public expenditure by functions,[5] very often it is only the proximate factors affecting the growth of expenditure that can be identified. The analysis of these factors can contribute to a better short-run forecast of public expenditure growth, particularly in view of the increased importance of contractual and open-ended programmes, but it can only seldom be taken as an explanation of why a given coverage or a given level of benefit rates was chosen or changed.

If at a disaggregated level the lack of consistent data impairs any analysis of the causes and effects of changes in the level and structure of public output,[6] at an aggregate level no comparable data are available on total expenditure including public expenditure on financial assets. It is to be noted that in most European countries many discussions on, and suggestions of, institutional changes have frequently been made with the purpose of curtailing 'excessive' *total* public expenditure or preventing it from 'running out of control' (even when it was recognized that the adequacy of total public expenditure could not be easily assessed). In these discussions reference was usually made to the total amount of resources flowing through the budget of the public sector, however defined. This financial approach to public expenditure analysis may be criticized on many grounds, but it remains true that the lack of consistent data at this level frustrates a complete evaluation of public expenditure policies in post-war Europe.

The only consistent data for international comparisons that are available come from national accounts statistics (see the Appendix). Such statistics are well suited for an analysis of public expenditure policy from the point of view of short-term demand management, but they are inadequate for an analysis of trends either from the point of view of functional categories (because of the limited degree of disaggregation) or from the point of view of aggregates (because of the exclusion of public expenditure on financial assets). If the two main issues of public expenditure analysis and policy are the determinants and the effects of spending by functions and of total expenditure, then the available consistent data can offer only a partial and incomplete empirical basis to any enquiry.

II. Trends in Public Expenditure Growth and Financing

Aggregate expenditure

The nature of the available comparable data accounts for the emphasis in the economic literature either on the growth of public sector claims on resources (as measured by government purchases of goods and services), or on the growth of public expenditure including transfer payments but excluding expenditure on financial assets. A trend analysis of these aspects, though not fully supported

[5] Particularly by the OECD; see OECD, *Public Expenditure Trends*, Paris 1978, and the special reports on *Public Expenditure on Education*, Paris 1976, *Public Expenditure on Income Maintenance Programmes*, Paris 1976, and *Public Expenditure on Health*, Paris 1978.

[6] At all levels, public expenditure analysis happens to be a field where 'The economist is not unfamiliar with wild goose chases after causal explanations of "phenomena" which turn out to be nothing more than mistakes which were made in the statistical office.' J.R. Hicks, *Causality in Economics*, Oxford 1979, p. 12.

by a sound theoretical basis and by adequate comparable data, may none the less give some insights and raise some interesting questions.

To begin with, at an aggregate level the similarities of public expenditure trends in the four main EEC economies seem very impressive. Inter-country differences appear to have declined through time, and were, by the end of the period, far less important than differences between these countries and other European countries (or the United States and Japan). In the mid-1970s the share in GDP of total public expenditure[7] for the four major EEC countries was in the range of 42 to 44 per cent and very close to the (unweighted) average for OECD Europe (43 per cent). Among other European countries, Sweden and Spain were at opposite extremes, the former with a share above 50 per cent (also recorded in the Netherlands), the latter with a share of only some 25 per cent (Table 13.1).

TABLE 13.1. *Public expenditure trends*

	Public expenditure in per cent of GDP[a]			Elasticity of public expenditure with respect to GDP[a]		
	1955–57	1967–69	1974–76	1960–76	1967–76	1972–76
France	33.5	39.4	41.6	1.09	1.06	1.25
Germany	30.2	33.1	44.0	1.23	1.26	1.62
Italy	28.1	35.5	43.1	1.19	1.21	1.19
United Kingdom	32.3	38.5	44.5	1.21	1.20	1.27
Spain	(17.0)	(21.4)	25.3	1.27	1.18	1.19
Sweden	(28.5)	41.3	51.7	1.38	1.32	1.35
OECD Europe[b]	27.4	35.0	42.9	1.24	1.24	1.37

[a] At current prices
[b] Unweighted average for 14 countries
Source: OECD, *Public Expenditure Trends*, Paris 1978.

The convergence reached among the four major countries was the result of a time profile showing an inverse relation between the size of public expenditure in the 1950s and its subsequent growth. France, which had the highest public expenditure share in GDP in Europe in the mid-1950s, also recorded the lowest elasticity of public expenditure with respect to GDP in the period 1960–76, while Italy's share, low at the outset, grew relatively fast.

This convergence is even more striking in the case of (general government) current expenditure. While in the 1950s the GDP share ranged from 30 per cent in France and in the United Kingdom to 24 per cent in Italy, in the years 1969–76 it was 36 per cent in France, Germany, and the United Kingdom, and 37 per

---

[7] All the data used come from the OECD's National Accounts publications and refer to the general government. As should be clear from the preceding discussion, this choice of coverage and content does not reflect any theoretical standpoint, but was imposed by the lack of comparable data on expenditure by function and on the government's financial transactions. The use of expenditure–GDP ratios seemed preferable to the use of arbitrary price deflators, although it is well known that such ratios are sensitive to cyclical movements. On the widely different results obtained by using nominal and real measures of public expenditure, see M. Beck, 'Public Sector Growth: A Real Perspective', *Public Finance*, No. 3, 1979.

cent in Italy. Relative stability was also maintained in the later 1970s — between 1977 and 1979 current expenditure represented 40 to 41 per cent of GDP in all countries. The coefficient of variation which was of the order of 0.10 in the 1950s had in the late 1970s declined to only 0.03.

This apparent convergence does not necessarily imply that differences in various identifiable economic and social determinants compensated each other, nor that one could expect approximately similar effects from growing public expenditure in each country. Other factors, such as the structure and financing of public spending, might have been more important than its overall level. Before examining these other aspects it may be appropriate to briefly comment on the role played by the increased ratio of total public expenditure to GDP. It has been argued that, although the size of budget deficits did not rise in the post-war period, at least until the mid-1970s, the increase in public spending financed out of taxation tended to raise output and employment.[8] Using a simple balanced budget multiplier model, it can be shown that, given zero deficit spending, national income is raised by the tax multiplier, the value of which increases with the tax ratio. Even allowing for the secondary effects of total public spending on the utilization of capacity in the private sector, the increased size of a balanced budget can play an expansionary role. But if it is true that sometimes and in some countries the pre-war technique of deficit spending was replaced after the war by the technique of increased public spending financed by taxation, and that this was practised on a much greater scale and with correspondingly greater effect on employment,[9] it can hardly be said that this happened in all countries during the whole of the post-war period.

The increases in the GDP shares of total public expenditure *and* total government revenue were not only large but also almost balanced between the mid-1950s and the late 1960s in the four major EEC countries (as well as in Spain and Sweden). Between the late 1960s and the mid-1970s, on the other hand, the public expenditure share rose much more rapidly than that of taxation, particularly in Germany, Italy, and the United Kingdom (Fig. 13.1). Preliminary data for the later 1970s suggest that changes in shares were relatively balanced, but expenditure was, of course, well in excess of revenues almost everywhere (Table 13.2).

A 'supply of funds–push' hypothesis to explain public expenditure growth may thus seem appropriate for the 1950s and the 1960s, but not for the 1970s, although in all the four EEC countries the income elasticity of tax revenue was not only above one, but also, with the possible exception of the United Kingdom, rising through time. This increasing income elasticity of tax revenue should, however, be compared with the income elasticity of public expenditure which, even though starting from a higher initial level, rose even more rapidly in the 1970s.

How much of the public expenditure growth in each country can be explained

---

[8] J. Steindl, 'Stagnation Theory and Stagnation Policy', *Cambridge Journal of Economics*, March 1979. A similar conclusion, using different hypotheses and a modified model, is also reached by R. Paladini, 'Spesa pubblica e sviluppo del reddito', *Rivista di diritto finanziario e scienza delle finanze*, December 1980.

[9] Steindl, 'Stagnation Theory'.

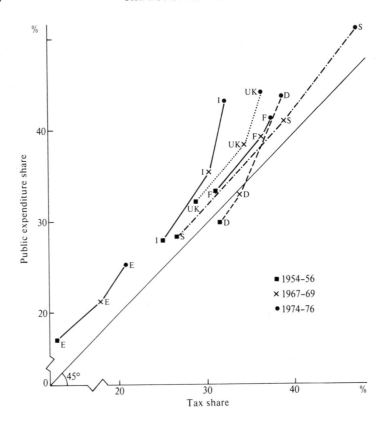

FIG. 13.1. *Shares of total public expenditure and total tax revenues in GDP at current prices* (percentages)
Source: OECD, *Public Expenditure Trends*, Paris 1978.

by the 'supply of funds–push' hypothesis depends on the degree of built-in flexibility of tax revenues and on the sub-periods chosen. It may be questionable whether any uniform periodization could fit equally well the experience of all countries considered. But, even if the precise initial and final years for each single country may not be the same, there seems to have been a noticeable break in the relationship between the economy and the budget in almost all countries some time in the late 1960s or early 1970s. While the availability of an expanding supply of revenue and the low and often falling cost of collecting taxes probably fuelled the growth of public expenditure in the 1960s, this conclusion would not seem to be applicable to the last decade.

In the 1970s, public expenditure rose exceptionally rapidly in Germany and Italy (as well as in Sweden) and outstripped the growth of tax revenues virtually everywhere. The ratio of current receipts to current disbursements, in particular, fell in the decade to levels well below those of the 1950s and 1960s (Table 13.3). This decline in public sector saving, or, as in Italy, the occurrence of dissaving, together with the problems of financing the government capital and financial transactions in an inflationary environment, led to a shift in the climate of

TABLE 13.2. *Changes in public expenditure and total taxation*
(percentage points of GDP at current prices)

	1955–57 to 1967–69		1967–69 to 1974–76		1974–76 to 1978–79[a]	
	PE[b]	TT[c]	PE[b]	TT[c]	PE[b]	TT[c]
France	5.9	5.3	2.2	1.0	3.0	2.3
Germany	2.9	2.2	10.9	4.7	0.8	1.5
Italy	7.4	5.3	7.6	1.6	4.6	4.7
United Kingdom	6.2	5.5	6.0	1.9	(−2.5)	(−1.5)
Spain	4.4	5.0	3.9	2.8	4.4[d]	2.7[d]
Sweden	12.8	12.6	10.4	8.2	11.0	6.2
OECD Europe[e]	7.6	6.3	7.9	5.1	(3.0)[d]	(1.9)[d]
Average annual change	0.6	0.5	1.1	0.7	(0.9)	(0.5)

[a] Not strictly comparable with previous columns
[b] Public expenditure
[c] Total taxation
[d] 1974–76 to 1977–78
[e] Unweighted average for 14 countries
Sources: OECD, *Public Expenditure Trends*, Paris 1978, and *Economic Outlook*, July 1981.

opinion in favour of public expenditure control and against public expenditure planning.

TABLE 13.3. *Ratio of general government current receipts*
to current disbursements

	1950–59	1960–69	1970–79
France	111.1	112.4	105.8
Germany	122.9	118.2	107.7
Italy	107.6[a]	98.5	86.6
United Kingdom	105.3	109.0	101.0
Spain	..	122.4[b]	111.5
Sweden	118.2	127.0	111.6

[a] 1951–59
[b] 1964–69
Source: OECD, *National Accounts of OECD Countries* (various issues).

The attempt to control spending by setting ceilings on budget deficits resulted in a decreasing expansionary effect of public expenditure. Since the deceleration in government revenue growth mirrored the slowdown in autonomous private investment, the attainment of a given target budget deficit figure required an increase in the total tax ratio (given that public outlays were still growing relatively rapidly). The increase in the tax burden had, in turn, a built-in stabilizing effect, by weakening the expansionary thrust of public expenditure growth. Unlike what happened in the 1950s and 1960s, the experience of the main European countries in the 1970s seemed to follow a new pattern and sequence – a slowdown would occur in the growth of investment, output, and tax revenues at a time at which public expenditure was still expanding rapidly; this would call forth the imposition of ceilings on the budget deficit (usually expressed as a percentage of GDP), and increases in the tax ratio; higher taxation would in turn impair the expansionary effects of public expenditure. Though attempts were made to encourage private investment by tax and expenditure policies, these proved insufficient. In most European countries the virtuous circle of auto-nomously induced GDP growth – tax dividend – public expenditure expansion – GDP growth seemed to have been broken and indeed replaced by an opposite cycle.

Expenditure components

The declining role of public expenditure in promoting economic growth has also been caused by changes in its structure and financing. Trends in these two areas do not seem to have been too dissimilar among the four major EEC countries, although two different subgroups (Germany and the United Kingdom on the one hand, France and Italy on the other) can be clearly discerned. Looking at major expenditure components, the GDP share of general government final consumption was in the 1950s much higher in the United Kingdom (some 17 per cent) than in the other three countries (12 to 14 per cent); since then, Germany's share has grown more rapidly, and in 1975-6 two countries (Britain and Germany) had an average ratio of 20 to 22 per cent, well above the 14 per cent of France and Italy (or even the 17 to 18 per cent of OECD Europe) (Table 13.4). To some extent such differences reflect different financial arrangements in the provision of some public services, which in the first two countries are directly provided by the public sector rather than being paid for initially by users who are then re-imbursed from public funds. The divergence, however, has been increasing through time (the coefficient of variation of the ratios of the four EEC countries rose from 0.13 at the beginning of the 1950s to 0.20 in the mid-1970s), and may arise from different government attitudes and from the increased cost and varying quality of many services publicly provided in the various countries.

TABLE 13.4. *Changes in major components of public expenditure,*
1955-57 to 1974-76
(percentage points of GDP at current prices)

	Government consumption		Transfers		Interest on public debt	Gross investment
	Total	Defence	Total	To households		
France	0.3	−2.1	6.9	6.7	−0.1	1.4
Germany	7.8	0.2	4.4	3.4	0.7	1.2
Italy	1.8	−0.5	10.6	9.7	2.0	0.4
United Kingdom	4.9	−2.4	6.8	5.2	0.4	1.3
Spain	0.7	..	8.2	6.8	−1.1	(—)
Sweden	9.2	−1.1	11.1	9.7	1.1	(1.0)
OECD Europe[a]	5.0	−0.8[b]	8.5	7.4	0.6	(1.1)

[a] Unweighted average for 14 countries
[b] Excluding Spain
Source: OECD, *Public Expenditure Trends*, Paris 1978.

Inter-country differences in the changing shares of total public expenditure in GDP may also arise because of the different input content of some of the main spending components. If the increase in the value of public consumption in the national accounts is made equal to the increases in nominal wages and salaries (in line with the usual assumption of zero productivity growth in the public sector), and if the relative size of the wages and salaries component is higher for government consumption than for public fixed investment or transfer payments, then even a constant volume of public services will imply an increasing public expenditure share in current price GDP. In addition, if the relationship between pay in the public and in the private sectors is erratic, sudden wage and salary increases for public employees may cause unpredictable financial pressures and inspire requests for expenditure cuts or the imposition of cash limits, particularly since the increase in public outlays appears unrelated to any current change in the level and quality of public services. This structural characteristic of general government consumption may be one reason why the attempts made to restrain public expenditure growth in the 1970s often focused on this particular component.

In virtually all the European countries, the single most important item responsible for the increase in the public expenditure–GDP ratio has been government transfers to households (the major exception to this general rule being Germany). In countries such as France and Italy the reasons for rapidly rising transfers may stem from a number of causes, e.g. attempts to compensate for more regressive tax systems, different social attitudes, different degrees of public expenditure consciousness, the competition among parties for political consensus, the higher political dividends of *ad personam* public expenditures, or even the convenience of administrative arrangements. All these factors have played a significant, even if unequal, role in the expansion of eligibility to benefits and in the increase in programme coverage, which have been the immediate cause of rising welfare public expenditure.[10]

Among the more general causes that have influenced the exceptionally rapid growth of transfer payments are the relative decline of traditional pure public goods (such as defence or justice) and the increasing demand for 'merit' goods (education, health, 'security'[11]) in most European countries. The case for direct public provision of merit goods is less clear than that of pure public goods. It can be argued that a more suitable approach to the provision of merit goods may often be that of leaving to individual preferences the choice of the way in which merit wants are to be satisfied. In view of the individualistic nature of most merit wants, a complex government administration may be a less efficient supplier than small flexible organizations.

Increased transfers to households, together with a rapidly growing amount of subsidies to producers and of interest payments on public debt (particularly in Italy and the United Kingdom), have led to a growing gap between public

---

[10] For further discussion see Ch. 7 above.

[11] For the definition of individual 'security' as a form of merit want, and on the causes of the increased supply of merit goods in general, see A. Boltho, 'Course and Causes of Collective Consumption Trends in the West', in R.C.O. Matthews and G.B. Stafford (eds.), *The Grants Economy and Collective Consumption*, London 1982.

expenditure growth and the growth of the public sector's claims on real resources. This in turn has meant that decisions about the final use of income
have increasingly moved away from the public to the private sector. Paradoxically, the most rapid expansion of public expenditure has been paralleled
by an enlarged role for individual decisions about resources use. Indeed, at
least in two countries (Italy and the United Kingdom) an increase in public
ownership has been accompanied by a concomitant expansion of the private
power to influence the ultimate destination of income from property.[12] These
trends underline the need to separate in any analysis the effects of transfer and
other non-exhaustive public expenditures on the decisions about the final uses
of income from the effects which other forms of public expenditure may have
as substitutes for private consumption. In other words, the public financing of
private expenditure should not be confused with the public provision of private
consumption.

Public expenditure financing

The speed of public expenditure growth has been influenced by the ease of
collecting tax revenues and by the forms of taxation mainly used in each country.
Differences among the four EEC countries in the ratio of total tax revenue to
GDP have been and still are quite large and persistent: the gap between the two
countries with the highest tax ratios (France and Germany) and the country
with the lowest tax ratio (Italy) was equal to some 6 percentage points of GDP
both in the mid-1950s and in the late 1970s (Table 7.4), while the coefficient
of variation on the yearly tax ratios of the four countries declined only slightly
between 1950 and 1976.

Large differences also persist in the tax structures of the four EEC countries
(Table 7.4), with the British and German shares of direct taxes in GDP almost
twice as large as those of France and Italy in the 1970s. Conversely, indirect
taxes and social security contributions accounted for nearly three-quarters of
French but less than 50 per cent of United Kingdom tax revenues. However,
changes in the shares of tax revenues in GDP have been a good deal more uniform over the twenty years to the end of the 1970s both at an aggregate and at
a category level (Table 7.3). In all four major EEC countries the share of government revenue in GDP rose by 6½ to 7½ percentage points, as against increases of
21 points in Sweden, 11 in Europe as a whole, and as little as 3 to 4 points in
Japan and the United States. Similar trends among the four EEC countries
appear also for major tax components. Social security contributions grew most
rapidly as a share of GDP (except in the United Kingdom), and direct taxes recorded a moderate increase, while the share of indirect taxation declined.[13]

Despite such similarities in changes through time, the initial differences in
tax structures remain broadly unchanged. These may reflect a variety of factors,
e.g. different attitudes to various forms of tax illusions, stronger preferences for

---

[12] That there is no one-to-one relationship between the amount of public ownership
and the amount of the economy's total real wealth which is in the unencumbered possession
of the state was pointed out in J.E. Meade, *Efficiency, Equality and the Ownership of
Property*, London 1964.

[13] For further details see Ch. 7 above.

levies more closely linked to individual benefits, attempts to increase household saving by making consumption relatively more expensive and compensating
for the adverse redistributive effects through a higher level of transfer expenditure, etc.

The influence of factors such as these is important in understanding not only
persistent inter-country differences in overall tax shares and tax structures but
also the various patterns of public expenditure growth, structure, and policy in
Europe. For example, if a lower overall tax ratio and a lower share of direct
taxes in financing public expenditure were to favourably affect household
savings, a budget deficit would probably have a smaller immediate effect on the
current account of the balance of payments and on private investment than a
similar deficit would have in a country with a higher tax level, a higher share of
direct taxes, and lower transfer expenditures. Considerations such as these may
throw some light on why for a long time only scarce attention was paid to the
problems of the financial control of public expenditure in, for instance, Italy.

Another example could be provided by a policy which rather than increasing
public transfers to productive sectors attempted to obtain similar results by reducing employees' social security contributions and then financed such a measure
by increasing indirect taxation. Several European countries in the 1970s proposed and used such a partial substitution of VAT for the payroll tax as an
effective way to reduce unit costs without directly affecting wage rates. In
countries (like France or Italy) where the payroll tax had become a substantial
source of revenue and its incidence on final prices was relatively high, it was
generally recognized that a reduction in social security contributions could lead
to some deceleration in inflation while leaving nominal wages unchanged. In
such cases, changes in the tax structure are in fact a substitute for some forms
of public expenditure. This example further underlies the variety of reasons
that may lie behind the different composition of public outlays across countries.

III. Public Expenditure Planning and Control

The deceleration in the growth of tax revenues and changes in its structure have
affected the role and popularity of public expenditure planning and control in
most European countries. Popular requests and parliamentary attempts to rein
in the expansion of public spending have, of course, been influenced by numerous other institutional, social, and political factors, but financial considerations have progressively become more important and have shaped various
countries' reactions and policies.

Planning in the 1950s and 1960s

In the 1950s, the growth of public expenditure gave rise, on the one hand, to
tax reforms designed to increase the elasticity of tax revenues, and, on the
other, to requests for strengthening the legal control over public expenditure and
to attempts to introduce some forms of managerial control.[14] What was primarily feared was wasteful, not excessive, public expenditure. The emphasis was

---

[14] A comparative survey from the point of view of parliamentary 'control' can be found
in D. Coombes *et al.*, *The Power of the Purse*, London 1976.

on the legal regularity of the public expenditure process, on preventing the mis-appropriation and misuse of public funds, and on securing efficiency in the activities of government departments. The efforts to implement these important traditional prerequisites of any public expenditure process, though not uniformly successful in all countries, had generally at least two important effects. The first, paradoxically perhaps, was to weaken the role of parliament in the 'control of the purse'. Although the legal and managerial forms of control that were intro-duced were intended to ensure that the budgetary choices of the legislature were loyally and efficiently carried out, they inevitably increased the role of those institutions which were in charge of legal control and auditing and of those sectors of the public administration which were entrusted with manage-ment functions. The second effect was to reinforce the traditional forms of accounts in which public outlays are described in terms of individual inputs or items of expenditure incurred by various organizational units. This, in turn, made it virtually impossible to know to what purposes public expenditure was being devoted.

Dissatisfaction with this situation was reinforced by another development of the period. The opportunities for choice in public spending were being reduced by the expanding size of prior expenditure commitments. The amount of 'un-controllable' rigid public expenditure was increasing because of changes in its composition towards a growing share of assistance and open-ended programmes. Preoccupation with future public expenditure commitments arising from legis-lation with long-term effects led to some limitations on parliamentary powers (as, for example, in France with the *Loi organique* of 1959). If public expendi-ture was to be still regarded and used as an effective 'instrument' of economic policy, it was felt necessary to have a detailed description of its allocation among the various areas of government activity and an overall view of its trends in relation to the expected growth of the economy.

During the 1960s some form of public expenditure planning was thus intro-duced in all the four major EEC countries. Though the specific forms this planning took varied (indeed in France and Italy it never achieved an independent status but was related to the already existing or tentative frameworks established for national economic planning), some common aims can be identified. The five major ones seem to have been:

(i) Public expenditure decisions were to be taken in the light of medium-term projections initially made on the assumption of unchanged policies (though plans could also be made on the basis of any proposed policy change);

(ii) Future public expenditure as a whole was to be evaluated in relation to 'prospective resources' (this was the main recommendation of the British Plowden Report of 1961,[15] and of the German reforms of 1964–7) or in the framework of the developments foreseen in the national eco-nomic plans;

(iii) The claims of public expenditure on these prospective real resources of

---

[15] HM Treasury, *The Control of Public Expenditure* (Plowden Report), Cmnd. 1432, London 1961.

the economy were to be expressed in volume terms obtained by con-
verting public expenditure to a constant price basis;

(iv) All public expenditure was to be considered together, and not only that
part of central government expenditure which required cash voted by
parliament; this implied that spending by local authorities and capital
expenditure by public enterprises were also to be brought into the
planning process;[16]

(v) Public expenditure projections were to be made by grouping similar
activities together, using a classification by functions or programmes no
longer linked to individual inputs but not yet based on output.

The declining role of public expenditure planning in the 1970s followed from
the difficulties met in fulfilling the five aims just listed, and from the increased
importance of financial control. Some of the difficulties met were mainly of a
socio-political kind. Thus, the fulfilment of aim (iv) depended on the financial
relations between various government levels and on the scope of public ownership prevailing in a country at the time, and not just on the details of budgetary
consolidation procedures or on the definition of capital expenditures.

Others were linked to lack of co-ordination. Thus, under (v) above, though
projections were made for functions and activities, no comparisons were carried
out for alternative programmes. Also, the emphasis remained on the macroeconomic implications of public expenditure. The various techniques designed
to improve the rationality of expenditure decisions at a microeconomic level
(like the French *Rationalité des choix budgétaires* system) were introduced
along a path largely unrelated to public expenditure decisions. But most of the
five points raised important technical and economic problems.

As regards points (i) and (ii), it has been observed that since the purpose of
the exercise was 'to provide a framework for taking decisions regarding public
expenditure over the medium term, the critical element has been seen as establishing what prospective resources are available and the "cost" of pre-empting
them for public sector use. Crucial to the former is the concept of the growth
of productive potential, or the path of "constant employment" output from
which variations in capacity utilisation have been abstracted.'[17] In fact, most
of the time it was the expected growth of GDP which was taken as the real constraint on public expenditure growth in the medium term. This, in turn, had two
important shortcomings which became apparent before long. The first one was
related to the consequences of traditional forecasting errors: over-optimistic
growth expectations could encourage 'excessive' government spending, while
forecasts that were too cautious could lead to a self-perpetuating restraint on
growth. The use of alternative or conditional growth paths, which would have
reduced the effects of forecasting errors, was rarely adopted because of the com-
plexities involved. Secondly, medium-term public expenditure projections
framed in a medium-term forecast of overall economic growth might have

[16] This recommendation was followed in the British Public Expenditure Survey Committee system (PESC) and in the system introduced at the local government level in Germany in 1967.

[17] R.W.R. Price, 'Public Expenditure', in F.T. Blackaby (ed.), *British Economic Policy,
1960-74*, NIESR, Cambridge 1978, p. 82.

conflicted with the short-term flexibility required for stabilization purposes. In theory, 'Fitting budgetary targets into regularly revised medium-term projections would provide the required flexibility to adjust the longer-run budget posture to unexpected events and changing public preferences with regard to longer-term economic and social priorities.'[18] In practice, however, counter-cyclical variations of public expenditure plans usually disrupted the medium-term expenditure projections and led to frequent reversals of policy. Of course, this was not a consequence of planning, but of a basic lack of agreement on some more general issues – the aims of a medium-term economic strategy, the definition of the budget target or rule, and the choice of the appropriate indicators of budgetary effects. These were, and still are, general obstacles not directly related to public expenditure planning, but paradoxically they contributed to its discredit as well as to the loss of favour of short-term demand management policies.

The problems posed by (iii) seem even less tractable. Public expenditure projections in real terms were intended to be a good indicator of the public sector's absorption of real resources, and, if corrected for the 'relative price effect' (the change in the prices of goods and services bought by the public sector relative to the average price of national output), also a good indicator of the volume of services supplied. But public expenditure analysis in volume terms raises at least three difficult problems. The first one relates to the correction for the relative price effect. This can be viewed as a measure of the slower growth of productivity in the public sector, but it 'may equally reflect, for example, a sharp rise in public service pay, of purchasing policies in the public sector . . . Thus in a very real sense the size of the relative price effect could be a direct measure of the scale of the lack of control of public expenditure.'[19] On the other hand, if public expenditure projections were not corrected for the relative price effect, this would be reflected in a smaller than intended volume of public services. The second problem arises independently of the relative price effect, and is related to the measurement of public expenditure at the constant prices of some base year. Whichever price deflator is used, a given amount of public expenditure in real terms will give rise to a variable amount of outlays depending on the rate of inflation. In times of rapid and unpredictable inflation, public expenditure set in real terms implies a loss of financial control. On the other hand, the introduction of cash limits or of other forms of control on nominal outlays nullifies any expenditure planning and makes the outcome of the public expenditure process completely unpredictable in terms of real public services to the citizens. The third problem relates to the need to match the public expenditure projections in real terms with corresponding and comparable tax revenue projections. This requires not only the choice of an appropriate price deflator for tax revenues but also the choice between alternative ways of public expenditure financing.

---

[18] P. McCracken *et al.*, *Towards Full Employment and Price Stability*, OECD, Paris 1977, p. 201.
[19] Expenditure Committee, *The Financing of Public Expenditure, Report*, Vol. I, HMSO, London 1975, p. vii.

Financial control in the 1970s

These various problems became increasingly important in the 1970s. The continuing growth of public expenditure without a corresponding increase in tax revenues and the efforts to finance massive government deficits in an inflationary environment shifted the emphasis of policy towards financial control and away from public expenditure planning. Particularly after 1973, the increased uncertainty about the economic environment, the more pronounced fluctuations in activity, and the pressing requests made on the public budget to sustain production and employment, severely limited the scope for the long-term planning of public expenditure. Although on average the overall share of public expenditure in GDP continued to increase in most European countries in the second half of the 1970s, year-to-year changes fluctuated more widely than before.

The increased variability reflected both the greater fluctuations in activity experienced by most European countries, and the varying policy responses to the slower economic growth imposed by the deterioration in the terms of trade. In addition, a lower and less regular growth of the economy made it more difficult to accommodate the effects on public expenditure of past decisions (especially in the fields of health and social security) without increased taxation or borrowing. Since increased taxation inevitably met with greater opposition most governments' financial balances went into large deficit. As a consequence, a larger share of current public expenditure in the later 1970s was devoted to the payment of interests on public debt.[20] This increase was probably one of the most important trends of the decade in the public expenditure field. It was a good deal more important than any increase in public subsidies to private industries or public corporations. Indeed, according to national accounts data, the latter remained relatively stable during the 1970s in the major European countries, despite the worsening of economic conditions. In this case, however, reference to national accounts statistics may be misleading, since effective subsidies to nationalized industries have been granted frequently through public acquisition of financial assets.

This increasing recourse to financial public expenditure in the second half of the decade (on which comparable international data are unfortunately not available) may in turn help to explain both the relatively stable share of public in total investment[21] and the greater attention paid to the financial role rather than to the real outcomes of public budgets. In sum, the economic turbulence of the 1970s seems to have mainly affected the attitude towards public expenditure rather than having induced any permanent shift in the overall level of spending or any substantial change in its composition (at least, as measured in the national accounts).

[20] As a share of total public expenditure, interest payments on public debt rose from 2.8 per cent in France in 1971-5 to 3.5 per cent in 1977-9; for Germany the figures for the same two periods were 3.2 and 4.2 per cent; for Italy 7.5 and 13.1 per cent, and for the United Kingdom 10.7 and 11.2 per cent.

[21] In the 1970s the share of government in total gross fixed investment rose slightly in Italy (from some 15 per cent in the first half of the decade to about 17 per cent in the second), declined slightly in France (from 14 to 13 per cent) and in Germany (from 16 to 15 per cent), and fell sharply in the United Kingdom (from about 25 to 16 per cent).

Conclusions

The preceding pages have very briefly reviewed a few selected aspects of public expenditure growth and control in post-war Europe. The review was selective because a comprehensive account faces the difficulties posed by frequent shifts in the boundary line between public expenditure and other forms of government intervention. These greatly impair both cross-country and through-time comparisons and analysis. More importantly, a full account was well beyond the scope of this chapter since the pervasiveness of the public expenditure phenomenon in post-war Europe is such that any interpretation would be equivalent to the economic and social history of the various countries.

The rapid growth of, and substantial convergence in, levels of public expenditure and taxation in Europe through the period under examination have often been underlined. Economic integration and demonstration effects meant that the forms of government intervention, the nature of public services provision, the characteristics of tax systems, etc., became increasingly similar across the area. No doubt, very significant differences still remained among the four major EEC countries at the end of the 1970s, but these were certainly much less pronounced than they had been thirty years earlier. Interestingly, perhaps, similarities were also to be seen in changes in the climate of public opinion which surrounded public expenditure. In the 1960s, the pressures were everywhere for growing outlays, but subject to rational choices and longer-term planning. In the 1970s these pressures had shifted to demands for much greater financial rigour and control.

Less well known perhaps was another common feature – a break in trend in the nature of the public expenditure growth process. While in the first two decades of the period public expenditure seems to have risen largely in parallel with mounting tax revenues (and falling defence commitments), in later years it appeared to have acquired a momentum of its own, irrespective of revenue growth. It is difficult to pin-point exactly the timing of this change, but it may well have preceded the slowdown in activity which followed the first oil shock. The latter, of course, added to the financing problems and hence to the pressures for restriction.

While in fact the growth of public expenditure in the later 1970s did not seem to have been curtailed very sharply by these pressures, the need to offset the unfavourable consequences of worsened terms of trade and slower economic growth have made a return to flexibility in budgetary policy a matter of great urgency. The experience of the last ten years has shown that attempts to plan public expenditure (and accept a loss of financial control) cannot be successful in an inflationary environment. It has also shown, however, that the opposite sort of policy (financial control without expenditure planning) is equally fruitless. If this conflict is not solved, it is probable that public expenditure will lose in importance (if not in size or growth) as a tool of public action in Europe in the coming years, to the benefit of other forms of government intervention.

Appendix: A Note on Differences in Public Expenditure Data

The availability and the use of consistent statistical information is essential to test the many alternative hypotheses about the determinants and the effects of public expenditure expansion. Data on public expenditure are made comparable and published by a number of international agencies. Detailed descriptions of the methodologies used and lengthy explanations of why and how the various international sources on government finance differ can be found in the manuals published by the same agencies and in the notes accompanying the individual country tables in each publication. The purpose of this Appendix is not to compare and evaluate the different methodologies used by the various sources but only to see whether large differences arise between the data which these sources publish.

To provide an idea of how large the discrepancies between the various sources may be, some of the available measures of public expenditure, expressed in per cent of GDP for 1975, are shown in Table 13.A1. The major sources used are,

TABLE 13.A1. *Public expenditure on various definitions, 1973*
(in per cent of GDP at current prices)

	Total expenditure			Current expenditure	
	OECD–UN[a]	IMF[b]	IMF[c]	OECD–UN[d]	IMF[e]
France	43.3	37.4	23.6	39.5	35.3
Germany	45.5	30.1	15.9	41.7	27.8
Italy	45.6	42.5	32.8	41.9	36.6
United Kingdom	46.3	40.2	38.5	41.4	37.7
Spain	25.4	21.2	12.2	22.5	18.5
Sweden	51.2	29.6	..	46.9	27.4

[a] General government current disbursements plus gross capital formation
[b] Total expenditure
[c] Government expenditure
[d] General government current disbursements
[e] Current expenditure
Sources: OECD, *National Accounts of OECD Countries, 1976*, and UN, *Yearbook of National Accounts Statistics, 1978* (for first and fourth columns); IMF, *Government Finance Statistics Yearbook, 1978* (for second and fifth columns); IMF, *International Financial Statistics*, December 1979 (for third column).

on the one hand, the National Accounts Statistics of the OECD and the UN, which differ between themselves only by very small amounts, and the IMF's data on government financial statistics. Taking total public spending first, the IMF data are below those of the OECD and the UN for all countries, but the percentage differences between the first two columns vary widely (with Sweden at one extreme and Italy at the other). These differences are largely due to the more restricted coverage of the IMF data, which cover only the central government, as defined by the UN standard national accounts, including, however, the national security fund and excluding monetary authority transactions and treasury deposit functions. The third column, which presents a different set of IMF data for government expenditure, shows figures lying below those of the previous two sources, again by varying amounts. In this instance it seems that the same coverage does not apply uniformly to the four EEC countries: government expenditure refers to the federal government in the case of Germany (with some non-cash transactions omitted), to Treasury operations in the cases of

France and Italy (where the figures refer only to the so-called *settore statale*), and to a larger definition of central government in the case of the United Kingdom (where expenditures comprise total current expenditures, gross domestic capital formation, and grants). The same unpredictable variability emerges from the data on current expenditure.

Despite these various problems and incompatibilities, most sources have often been used interchangeably. It is no wonder, in the circumstances, that many recent empirical studies in the field of public expenditure analysis (from tests of 'Wagner's law' to the assessment of the dynamic impact of government expenditure) obtain different results and reach different conclusions.

Bibliography

The literature on public expenditure is vast and the few lines that follow can only provide a very small selection. Some of the earlier comparative work on public expenditure changes is contained in S. Kuznets, *Modern Economic Growth*, New Haven 1966; F.L. Pryor, *Public Expenditure in Communist and Capitalist Nations*, London 1968; and R.A. Musgrave, *Fiscal Systems*, New Haven 1969. A more recent valuable source of data surveying the expenditure and financing of virtually all Western European countries is the OECD's *Public Expenditure Trends*, Paris 1978. On individual countries, longer-run historical surveys can be found in the classic work by A.T. Peacock and J. Wiseman, *The Growth of Public Expenditure in the United Kingdom*, London 1967, (revised edn.), and, for Germany, in H.C. Recktenwald, 'Umfang und Struktur der öffentlichen Ausgaben in säkularer Entwicklung', in F. Neumark (ed.), *Handbuch der Finanzwissenschaft*, Tübingen 1977.

Among the numerous discussions of methodological issues, E. Chester, 'Some Social and Economic Determinants of Non-Military Public Spending', *Public Finance*, No. 2, 1977, looks at problems of definition and measurement, while P.H. Heller, 'Diverging Trends in the Share of Nominal and Real Government Expenditure in GDP: Implications for Policy', *National Tax Journal*, March 1981, presents an appraisal of the problems raised by a real measure of public expenditure. For a critical survey of the literature on these various issues, see V.P. Gandhi, 'Trends in Public Consumption and Investment: A Review of Issues and Evidence', in H.C. Recktenwald (ed.), *Secular Trends for the Public Sector*, Paris 1978.

A. Breton, *The Regulation of Private Economic Activity*, Montreal 1976, is an important contribution to the discussion of the various forms of government intervention. The European experience of planning expenditure flows and the problems raised by inter-governmental relations in this process are reviewed in E. Gerelli and G. Pola (eds.), *La programmazione poliennale della spesa pubblica*, Bologna 1979, and in A. Robinson and B.C. Ysander, *Flexibility in Budget Policy*, Industrial Institute for Economic and Social Research, Stockholm 1981.

14

Regional Problems and Policy

WILLIAM NICOL AND DOUGLAS YUILL*

Introduction[1]

Regional problems arise when there is a marked and persistent economic inequality between different parts of a country. Such inequality normally shows itself in one or more of a number of standard problem indicators – high rates of unemployment, low activity rates, heavy emigration, and below-average income per head. Almost every country in Europe faces regional problems of some sort, although regional disparities vary considerably in intensity and also have a wide range of causes. Usually, however, they can be attributed to structural decline and, in particular, to the rundown of a region's traditional employment base – the agricultural sector or problem industries like coal-mining, textiles, heavy engineering, and shipbuilding.

In the face of such disparities most European countries have adopted a regional policy. Close to one-third of the population of the European Community live in areas designated as problem regions for policy purposes. Public expenditure on regional policy is high. Over $6 billion per year (or ¼ per cent of GDP) was spent in the late 1970s in the countries of the EEC on grants and 'soft' loans to firms alone, and there are, in addition, a wide range of other incentives in operation – including depreciation allowances, other tax concessions, and, in a few countries, employment subsidies. National governments are active in the provision of infrastructure and other investment in the problem regions, and in using controls (and disincentives) to affect the location of industry. Clearly both regional problems, and the policy response to those problems, are of considerable significance in the European economy.

From a wider perspective, differences between countries in Europe are as interesting, from a regional point of view, as the disparities within countries. At the European level, there is a marked tendency for regional difficulties to increase towards the periphery (see Fig. 14.1). Thus a description of regional differences tends to merge into an analysis of inter-country differences in growth, income, and employment – the subject-matter of other chapters of this book. This chapter concentrates on national regional policies.[2] Apart from their quantitative significance (noted earlier), there are two more fundamental reasons

* International Institute of Management, Wissenschaftszentrum, Berlin, and Centre for the Study of Public Policy, University of Strathclyde, Glasgow, respectively. The authors gratefully acknowledge the helpful comments of Kevin Allen on an earlier draft of this chapter. However, they alone are responsible for any errors of fact or judgement which remain.
[1] A number of international studies have been helpful in the preparation of this chapter. They are not acknowledged separately each time they have been used so as not to burden the text with too many footnotes, but are listed in the bibliography at the end of the chapter.
[2] For some information on EEC regional policy, see Ch. 8.

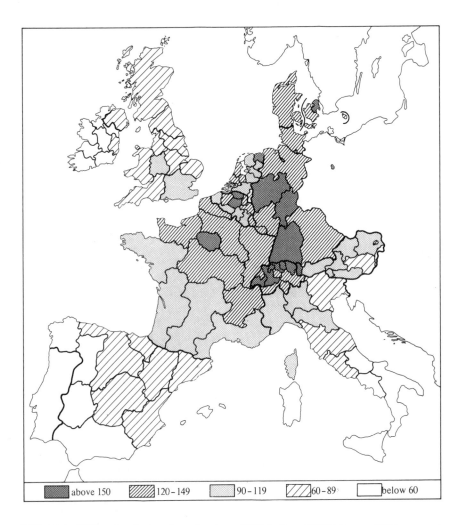

FIG. 14.1. *GDP per capita in selected regions, 1975* (indices: OECD Europe GDP per caput
= 100)
Note: Irish figures are based on total personal income
Sources: see Appendix.

for focusing on regional problems and policies within countries. The first is that
economic objectives for growth and income distribution are formulated, explicitly or implicitly, for the nation and not for some wider or narrower grouping.
The second is that countries are normally considered to have autonomy in the
sense of having control over their own monetary, fiscal, and exchange rate
policies. It is the absence of such autonomy at the regional level that, most
fundamentally, distinguishes a regional problem from a national one.

Clearly, however, even this distinction may be breaking down. European economies are becoming increasingly dependent on, and constrained by, their neighbours, and national autonomy may, in some respects, be more theoretical than real. Exchange rates may be linked to others, formally as in the case of Ireland when it was part of a common currency area with the United Kingdom, or less formally as under the EMS. Regional groupings may, moreover, have some autonomy, for example in fiscal policy, as is the case with the *Länder* in Germany. Moves towards European monetary union, should they occur, would have the effect of blurring further the distinction between national and regional economic problems, and, it is widely recognized, would carry with them a requirement for an increased scale of supra-national regional policy.[3] But for the purposes of a survey of developments from the early 1950s to the late 1970s, the regional problem can be viewed as essentially one pertaining to countries rather than to Europe as a whole.

This chapter is in three sections. In Section I information is presented on the size of regional disparities in European economies, together with an indication of how they have changed over time. Particular country examples are used to illustrate the main types of problem and their causes. Section II traces out the development of policy over the post-war period. Three phases are identified — the 1950s, a period of passive policy when regional problems had relatively low priority compared with other national objectives; the 1960s and early 1970s, a phase of active regional policy with considerable experimentation in the search for the most appropriate measures; and the period from the oil crisis to the late 1970s in which policy had matured, but in an economic environment which had become far more hostile. The third section then focuses on the effects of regional policy, while the Conclusions consider possible future developments in the light of the changing nature of the regional problem.

I. Regional Problems

This section concentrates on indicating the size of the regional problem in a number of European countries and on identifying its main causes. A first subsection provides some simple summary indicators of the extent of regional disparities and of their changes between the early 1960s and the late 1970s. This is then followed by a more detailed examination of the origins of such disparities. These are complex and vary from country to country. They fall, however, broadly into two types which are related to changes that have occurred in agriculture and industry respectively. A third type of problem, that of congested regions, really follows from the other two, but has become sufficiently important in some countries to merit special attention. For each type a somewhat simplified picture of the problem and its consequences is presented, followed by specific country examples. The examples are intended to be illustrative and do not represent a comprehensive treatment of regional economic issues in the country in question. In many countries there are, moreover, other aspects

---

[3] EEC, *Report of the Study Group on the Role of Public Finance in European Integration* (MacDougall Report), Brussels 1977.

TABLE 14.1. *Selected indicators of regional disparities, 1977*[a]

| | Number of regions | Per caput GDP[a] | | | Unemployment rates | | |
| | | Weighted coefficient of variation | Regional income level[b] | | Weighted standard deviation | Regional unemployment rate[c] | |
			Highest	Lowest		Lowest	Highest
France	11	0.23	145	75	0.93	3.4	6.9
Germany	11	0.15	172	83	0.81	2.5	6.5
Italy	11	0.27	134	64	4.41	2.6	16.8
United Kingdom	11	0.09	113	76	1.60	4.5	11.0
Spain[d]	11	0.22	128	59	3.08	2.0	11.9
Austria	9	0.17	127	61	0.96	0.7	4.8
Belgium	9	0.16	123	75	2.14	5.4	11.8
Finland[e]	10	0.20	133	79	2.61	3.4	11.5
Greece[f]	10	0.33	159	60	0.81	1.9	4.5
Ireland[g]	8	0.14	117	77	2.19	7.1	16.6
Netherlands	11	0.27	222	74	1.43	2.3	7.5
Norway	11	0.36	196	77	0.52	0.8	3.0
Portugal[h]	7	0.37	150	47	2.25	6.2	13.8
Sweden[j]	8	0.10	120	90	0.57	1.3	3.7
Switzerland	12	0.21	148	74	..	..	..
Average	10	0.22	146	71	1.74	..	..

[a] Unless otherwise stated
[b] National average = 100
[c] As per cent of labour force; figures not strictly comparable across countries
[d] GDP: 1975
[e] Household disposable income rather than GDP
[f] GDP: 1958; unemployment: 1971
[g] Personal income rather than GDP: 1973; unemployment: 1975
[h] GDP: 1970; unemployment: 1975
[j] Household disposable income rather than GDP
Sources: see Appendix.

of the regional problem which do not fit in the classification adopted.[4]

To provide an indication of the size of the regional problem in Europe, Table 14.1 assembles some of the available evidence, usually for the mid- or late 1970s. It is well known that no ideal statistical indicator exists which can summarize the diversity of experience. The best that can be done is to display a number of different indicators — in this instance, the spread of per caput incomes and un- employment rates between the most and least fortunate regions of a country, as well as two very simple summary measures of dispersion, the weighted coefficient

[4] Thus, for example, while regional problems in Belgium can be presented as the conse- quence of industrial decline in the Wallonian South, the basic North–South division of the country reflects, too, the linguistic and cultural split between the Flemish North and the French-speaking South. Again, in Northern Scandinavia the problem is not simply agri- cultural in nature but has the added dimensions of emigration and underpopulation, which create serious difficulties in relation to the minimum size of urban units required to provide basic services. And in the Zonenrandgebiet (Zonal Border Area) in Germany, economic problems have far less to do with agricultural or industrial decline than with the cutting off of many areas along the border from previous markets and economic hinterlands.

of variation and the weighted standard deviation.[5] The former is used for income disparities which are usually assessed in percentage terms. The latter is preferred for unemployment rates, where it is felt that a measure of absolute disparity provides perhaps a more comprehensive picture than one of proportionate dispersion. It is readily admitted that the figures shown hardly capture all the complexity of regional differences – in particular, they leave out two important facets (emigration and low participation rates), which, just as much as low income or high unemployment, may characterize poorer regions.

Another difficulty is that the available regional classifications are often far from ideal. If regions are too large, much variation may be concealed. On the other hand, too fine a classification, even if the data existed, may display variations which are not significant from a policy point of view in that they occur within an area which is generally regarded as a cultural or geographic entity. In practice, crude as the criteria are, the regional classifications generally adopted for statistical reporting purposes may not be too misleading, especially as many regional groupings do have a fairly strong historical, institutional, and cultural basis. Finally, the data shown are not always comparable across countries, in particular for unemployment, while the summary indicators of disparities can be sensitive to the number of regions used in their calculation. Hence the data in Table 14.1 have tended to use a roughly similar number of regions.[6]

With these caveats in mind, the comparative evidence presented in the table suggests, not surprisingly, that Europe's major regional problems are concentrated in the south. Italy, Spain, and Portugal (and Yugoslavia could, of course, be added to this list) suffer from both severe income and unemployment disparities. The difficulties in these countries (as will be shown in greater detail below) are largely linked to the existence of backward agricultural regions characterized by low productivity, heavy emigration, and low participation rates. In contrast, countries such as the United Kingdom and Belgium exhibit a different sort of problem – income levels are relatively equal across regions (indeed, in the United Kingdom, more equal than anywhere else), but unemployment rates differ quite sharply. The difficulties here arise most often from the rundown of basic industries which happen to be regionally concentrated, while wage levels remain relatively rigid (Ireland also falls into this category, but for different reasons discussed below). This kind of situation in the industrial problem areas has often been compared with the problems faced by countries when they become uncompetitive in international trade. At the national level the solution would be a devaluation of the currency: at the regional level a similar result could be achieved if there was sufficient wage flexibility between regions. This would, then, eliminate unemployment over time, at the expense, however, of lower living standards, at least in the initial period.

Several other countries in the table exhibit relatively severe income differentials, though not unemployment gaps. In some instances (France, Norway, Greece) these arise from the presence of one hypertrophied capital region which

---

[5] A much larger number of dispersion indicators for EEC countries can be found in, for instance, CEE, *Statistiques régionales, 1972*, and Eurostat, *Regional Statistics, 1970-77*.

[6] This has meant that in a few instances in which the available data were very detailed they were aggregated into somewhat larger groupings following rough geographical criteria.

monopolizes a country's activities. In a few other instances (Finland and again Norway) the disparities arise from the continuing presence of relatively poor agricultural areas located in the far north of the country. Finally, in a few countries such as Germany, Austria, or Sweden, regional problems clearly seem much less serious than elsewhere in Europe. On the whole, these various findings confirm that the regional problem tends to become more acute as one moves away from the 'centre' of Europe. The 'peripheral' nature of the problem is also confirmed by Fig. 14.1, which shows how incomes decline as one moves away from the centre of the Continent[7] – though, of course, such a diagram, which expresses regional incomes as a percentage of the per capita income of the European area of the OECD, combines indications of both regional and national problems.

Table 14.2 presents some evidence on changes in income and unemployment dispersal through time for those countries for which data were available for a sufficiently long time-span. Very broadly, it would appear that, with the exception of the Netherlands (for special reasons linked to the discovery of natural gas resources in one province), income disparities have probably decreased somewhat over the period, particularly in Italy and Spain. The gap between the highest and lowest income regions has narrowed virtually everywhere, the constancy in Germany not being, in a sense, very significant because of the very small weight of the rich Hamburg region. Interestingly, however, it would appear that success in closing income gaps was probably more pronounced in the 1960s than in the 1970s. To some extent this may have been due to migration. The large movements of population within countries and, indeed, across countries that characterized Europe, particularly between the mid-1950s and the mid-1960s,[8] have been a major equalizing factor from a regional point of view.[9] The later 1970s, however, have witnessed in a number of countries reverse migration flows (discussed below) so that the equalizing effects of migration may have become less important.

A similar improvement in the 1960s can be seen for unemployment, while the picture for the 1970s is more mixed. In percentage terms, disparities narrowed further, with the exceptions of Italy and, possibly, Spain, but in absolute terms there is a clear deterioration. This is sharp enough to suggest that, for the period as a whole, and with the exception of Austria, the situation may if anything have worsened slightly, in particular in Italy and Spain. To a large extent this arises, of course, from the general upward shift in national unemployment rates which has inevitably led to an increase in absolute dispersion.

Having given a broad indication of the intensity of the problem, the remainder of this section concentrates on identifying and describing three main types of problem regions – agricultural, industrial, and congested.

---

[7] Indeed, 70 per cent of the variance in regional per caput incomes in the EEC and Spain can be 'explained' by distance from the Düsseldorf–Cologne area; see D. Biehl, 'Determinants of Regional Disparities and the Role of Public Finance', *Public Finance*, No. 1, 1980.

[8] See Ch. 6.

[9] W. Molle, *Regional Disparity and Economic Development in the European Community*, London 1980.

TABLE 14.2. *Changes in selected indicators of regional disparity 1960–1977*[a]

	Indicator	Per caput GDP			Unemployment rates		
		1960	1970	1977	1960	1970	1977
France	(i)				..	0.57	0.93
	(ii)	0.23	0.26	0.23	..	0.48	0.19
	(iii)	1.9	2.1	1.9	..	5.2	2.0
Germany	(i)				0.59	0.21	0.81
	(ii)	0.16	0.15	0.15	0.59	0.36	0.20
	(iii)	2.1	2.1	2.1	7.0	5.0	2.6
Italy	(i)				1.04	2.63	4.41
	(ii)	0.35	0.28	0.27	0.26	0.61	0.69
	(iii)	3.0	2.2	2.1	2.3	5.4	6.5
United Kingdom[b]	(i)				1.04	1.21	1.60
	(ii)	0.11	0.11	0.09	0.70	0.46	0.26
	(iii)	1.8	1.5	1.5	8.6	4.3	2.4
Spain[c]	(i)				1.15	0.88	3.08
	(ii)	0.28	0.26	0.22	0.82	0.63	0.54
	(iii)	2.4	2.4	2.2	12.3	5.3	6.0
Austria[d]	(i)				2.43	1.43	0.96
	(ii)	0.28	0.22	0.17	0.66	0.59	0.53
	(iii)	2.8	2.4	2.1	12.3	8.9	6.9
Belgium	(i)				..	1.07	2.14
	(ii)	0.19	0.15	0.16	..	0.49	0.28
	(iii)	1.9	1.6	1.6	..	4.1	2.2
Netherlands	(i)				..	0.31	1.43
	(ii)	0.09	0.13	0.27	..	0.31	0.34
	(iii)	1.3	1.5	3.0	..	3.3	3.3
Average	(i)				..	1.04	1.92
	(ii)	0.21	0.20	0.20	..	0.49	0.38
	(iii)	2.2	2.0	2.1	..	5.2	4.0

Note: i = weighted standard deviation; ii = weighted coefficient of variation;
   iii = ratio of highest to lowest region.
[a] Unless otherwise stated
[b] Unemployment: 1965
[c] GDP: 1969 and 1975
[d] GDP: 1961 and 1971
Sources: see Appendix.

Agricultural problem regions

Since the emergence and persistence of regional problems can be traced to the processes of economic development – and within this, to shifts in technology and the pattern of demand – it is perhaps natural to begin a classification of regional problems by focusing on those strongly related to the decline of employment in agriculture. The move out of agriculture and towards industrial and tertiary activities is a process which all European countries have experienced or are still experiencing. While the speed and magnitude of adjustment has varied between countries, the decline of agricultural employment has everywhere been massive. Between the early 1950s and the late 1970s, the agricultural labour force in Western Europe declined by about 17 million. In the countries of North-West Europe agricultural employment fell from some 20 per cent to 6 per cent of the labour force. In the South, the decline was proportionately smaller due to the larger initial size of the agricultural sector (often exceeding 50 per cent of the labour force in the early post-war period), the higher rates of population growth, and the fact that there were relatively few alternative employment opportunities; but even so, the share of agricultural employment within the labour force in Southern Europe more than halved (from 45 to 18 per cent).

This major and secular decline in agricultural employment can be traced to two major processes. First, given rising real incomes and the nature of the income elasticity of demand for food products, the demand for these goods grew at a much lower rate than for other products. Secondly, technological change, in its widest sense, led to a sharp reduction in the need for agricultural labour, thereby exacerbating the effects of shifting demand. On the one hand, such factors as mechanization, land reform, and fertilizers allowed output levels to be increased with a smaller labour force, while, on the other, the development of the chemical and synthetics industries led to a substantial substitution of non-agricultural for agricultural products. The situation was, moreover, made worse by high rates of natural population increase and by the ability of other sectors to provide sufficient employment opportunities – at least in part a reflection of the general unattractiveness of agricultural problem regions to industry due to factors such as peripheral location, physical geography, lack of resources and human capital, and an underdeveloped infrastructure.

The extent to which agricultural decline has resulted in major interregional disparities has varied considerably within Europe. While the main focus of this section is, of course, on those countries where large areas can be classified as agricultural problem regions, in some countries the decline of agricultural employment, although substantial, has not created regional difficulties on a major scale. Indeed, in Denmark (where agriculture declined from 25 per cent of the labour force in 1950 to 8 per cent in 1978) recent trends show not only a convergence in the interregional unemployment picture and migration back to the rural and less populated areas, but also that previously lagging regions are now the ones with the highest rates of growth.

The Italian Mezzogiorno or South is the classic example of an agricultural problem region (Table 14.3). Nationally, agricultural employment declined by nearly 5 million in the 1951–78 period, from 44 per cent to 14 per cent of the labour force. By contrast, agriculture in the South employed over 40 per cent of the labour force in 1960 and still represented over 20 per cent of southern employment in 1978. Despite significant employment growth in other sectors, particularly tertiary and government jobs, the South has experienced a net loss of well over half a million jobs in the post-war period. As a consequence, the Mezzogiorno displays the typical symptoms of an agricultural problem region. Population in the South (20 million at the end of 1977) has grown by only 13 per cent since 1951, compared to over 22 per cent in the North, despite a high level of natural increase, because of substantial emigration (2.5 million net

TABLE 14.3. *Selected indicators of regional imbalance in Italy,
relative position of the South*[a]
(percentages)

	1951	1960	1970	1978
Population				
Share in total	37.2	36.9	35.2	35.3
Output				
Share in GDP	24.0	22.8	23.4	24.2
Share in manufacturing GDP	13.0	12.2	13.6	14.1
Share in industrial investment	13.0	15.2	26.3	22.0
Balance on goods and services				
in per cent of GDP	−15.0	−21.1	−20.9	−15.6
Ratio of per caput GDP	65	62	67	69
Labour force[b]				
Unemployment – national	6.6	4.0	3.1	7.2
Unemployment – regional	6.3	4.8	4.9	10.0
Participation rate – national	40.8	42.8	36.6	38.9
Participation rate – regional	35.1	37.6	32.1	34.8
Female participation rate – national	20.1	24.9	19.3	24.5
Female participation rate – regional	13.9	19.4	15.0	20.0
Share in industrial employment	..	24.3	22.6	21.5

[a] Abbruzzi, Molise, Campania, Puglia, Basilicata, Calabria, Sicily, and Sardinia.
[b] 1952 instead of 1951.
Sources: ISTAT, *Annuario di contabilità nazionale, Annuario di statistiche del lavoro*
(various issues), and *Bollettino mensile di statistica*, February 1980.

moving to the North and a further 1.6 million going abroad). Since the early
1970s, however, there has been a noticeable slowing down in this trend, the
1975 net loss to the North being 50,000 in comparison to 125,000 in 1971. In
part, this was due to significant return migration from the North following the
mid-1970s recession.

Despite the safety-valve of migration, unemployment rates in the South have
generally been well above the national average. In 1978, for example, the southern
rate was 10 per cent compared to 7 per cent in the North. Moreover, the unemployment gap is growing in absolute terms (and, unlike the position in most
other countries, also in percentage terms), with reduced emigration obviously
the major explanatory factor. Even these figures understate the extent of excess
labour supply; in spite of high emigration and underemployment, the participation rate in the South in 1978 was 34.8 per cent compared to 38.9 per cent
in the North – itself an extremely low rate by international standards.

While, after a period of worsening in the 1950s, progress has certainly been
made in the Mezzogiorno (with massive transfers of resources and changes in
industrial structure moving in the right direction), the area remains sluggish in
its adaptation and agriculture is still the largest single sector. The nature of expansion in other sectors, in particular with government and construction growing
faster than manufacturing and with much manufacturing development being
capital intensive, creates concern about the type of development taking place.
In terms of many of the key indicators, the North–South gap is growing while
the apparently improved position in terms of migration is at least partly due to
problems in the North rather than improvements in the South. These trends

suggest that the dualistic nature of Italy has not been fundamentally altered and that the South is still, indeed increasingly, a major regional problem area.

The decline in agricultural employment has also resulted in significant imbalances in Ireland. Nationally, agricultural employment fell between the early 1950s and the late 1970s, from 40 to 20 per cent of the labour force (more than 150,000 jobs). This quite major decline was, however, spread fairly evenly among the regions so that agriculture remains an important sector virtually everywhere. Only the East region had less than 5 per cent of its labour force in agriculture in 1975, while, elsewhere, agriculture represented from 25 to nearly 50 per cent of total employment. At the national level, expansion in other sectors was not quite sufficient to offset the decline in agricultural employment; manufacturing, despite relatively rapid growth (industrial production rose by some 6 per cent per annum from 1960 to 1979), generated only few additional jobs due to its small size, while the tertiary sector had the lowest growth of employment (less than one per cent) within the EEC. At the regional level, only in the East region was agricultural decline offset by expansion in other sectors. Elsewhere, employment either remained relatively stable or declined in absolute terms.

These trends have had major repercussions on Ireland's demographic position, where migration, both within Ireland and to other countries, has played a significant role. At the national level, Ireland's population began to grow in the 1960s for the first sustained period since the Great Famine (1846-7); previously, a high rate of natural increase had always been more than offset by emigration. At the regional level, migration has led to increasing demographic imbalances. The East region, covering 10 per cent of the area of Ireland but containing over a third of its population, is becoming increasingly dominant. In the 1960s, it was the only region to experience net immigration and a growing share of total population; while in the 1970s, as all regions began to experience increasing population, it was the region of highest growth – due primarily to a high rate of natural increase. The decline of agriculture, the inability of other sectors to provide a rapid growth of alternative employment opportunities, and a now-growing population have combined to increase the severity of the unemployment problem, both at the national and regional levels. Nationally, unemployment in Ireland grew from a low of just over 4 per cent in the early 1960s to some 8 per cent in the late 1970s, one of the highest national unemployment rates within the EEC. In addition, the regional distribution of unemployment was becoming increasingly unbalanced, with the gap between the regions of lowest and highest unemployment being much wider in the late 1970s than it was in the 1960s. Thus, while unemployment is a major national problem in Ireland, it also has a notable regional dimension.

A third example of major difficulties linked to the predominance of a backward agricultural sector can be found in Spain. Despite a relatively rapid growth of farm output (faster than that of virtually all other European countries in the 1960s and 1970s), increasing productivity has led to rapid declines in employment and resulted in large migratory flows from the countryside to the major cities of Madrid, Barcelona, and Valencia, as well as to France and Germany. Yet, despite these flows, measured unemployment problems, as in Italy, have worsened, partly as national unemployment rose sharply (from only 1½ per cent in 1955 to close to 10 per cent at the end of the 1970s), but partly also as people previously underemployed on the land left agriculture and swelled the ranks of the urban unemployed. In Andalucia and Extremadura, for instance, the two poorest regions, the unemployment rate stood at only 3¼ per cent in 1955, but had risen to over 11 per cent in 1977.

While Southern Italy, Spain, and Ireland represent acute examples of agricultural problem regions, comparatively less severe, but nevertheless nationally significant examples can be found elsewhere in Europe. In the Netherlands, for instance, rapid agricultural productivity growth caused the North to be the only Dutch region to suffer continuously from above-average unemployment in the post-war period. Fortunately, the rapid growth of the Dutch economy helped provide alternative employment opportunities (albeit elsewhere in the Netherlands and therefore resulting in net emigration), and thus kept the problem to 'manageable' proportions. Similarly, in Western France, the decline in agricultural employment and consequent emigration led to absolute falls in both population and employment until the mid-1960s. After 1968, however, the situation improved, with the region not only gaining population (through reduced emigration) but doing so faster than the national average. Again, the ability of expanding sectors to generate alternative employment opportunities and the fact that the west obtained a reasonable share of these kept the problem to a level well below that found in Southern Italy, Spain, or Ireland.

Industrial problem regions

To explain the origins of industrial problem regions, one has to go back a century or so to see that they were once very prosperous areas, being in the van of the industrialization process. The nature of this process, concentrated on mining, textiles, and heavy industry, led to a major growth of population in these areas and the attraction of many related industries, a consequence of the high degree of locational immobility of these basic activities and high transport costs. Over time, however, these areas lost their locational attractiveness and comparative advantage as a result of shifts in technology and demand and increasing international competition, leading to declining demand for labour and the emergence of regional problems.

In the coal industry, the major factors responsible for decline, despite rising world energy demand, were exhaustion of readily mined resources, increasing mechanization, the growth of production outside Europe, and, in particular, the shift in demand to other energy sources. The 1970s problems with oil and nuclear energy may, however, serve to reprieve in the 1980s many mining areas from the fate of earlier mining communities. With textiles, competition from low labour-cost countries and the effect of rising real incomes combined with a below-unit elasticity of demand for textile products have been the major factors associated with falling demand for labour. Within the rest of the manufacturing sector, the move from basic to process-oriented industry involved not only a greater degree of locational freedom but also the emergence of a new set of factors determining locational attractiveness (e.g. size and diversity of product and labour markets, communications, and business services) which generally resulted in areas outside the traditional industrial areas gaining the lion's share of these new industries.

The underlying nature of the problems facing industrial problem regions is generally discussed in terms of structural and 'regional' factors. While areas dominated by coal or textiles have an obvious structural problem (a concentration on industries declining nationally), other industrial regions have not only structural but also 'regional' features in that the region's industries, standardized for structure, perform poorly in relation to the national average. Amongst other things, this poor performance is associated with the changing determinants of locational attractiveness noted above.

These various forces, together with a lack of alternative employment opportunities, have created situations of excess labour supply in certain industrial regions. In turn, this has resulted in the traditional manifestations of regional problems — high unemployment, low activity rates, relative or absolute population decline, and high emigration. However, in contrast to the situation found in agricultural problem regions, interregional income disparities tend not to be substantial. This is the case, as was seen above, in the United Kingdom, where national wage negotiation procedures are a major explanatory factor. But this, in turn, means that low productivity — often a characteristic of the problem regions — causes them to be relatively expensive locations in terms of the 'efficiency' wage of labour. A further difference between industrial and agricultural problem regions is that the former have generally a greater regeneration potential, due primarily to the existence of a developed infrastructure and an industrial labour force. Indeed, many industrial problem regions have been able to attract considerable amounts of mobile investment.

The northern half of Great Britain (Scotland, Wales, and the Northern, North-West, and Yorkshire–Humberside regions of England) provides a good illustration of an industrial problem region, both in terms of the underlying causes of the difficulties as well as in the variety of problem types — related to the problems of coal, textiles, and traditional industry (Table 14.4). Not only has the national decline of employment in these sectors been substantial (coal losing 440,000 jobs, textiles 250,000, and shipbuilding 80,000 over the period 1959–73), but it has been highly concentrated in the northern half of the country, with 95 per cent of the job loss in shipbuilding, 90 per cent in coal, and 75 per cent in textiles, taking place in this area. Adding to these difficulties has been the relatively poor performance of the North in the expanding manufacturing and tertiary sectors. While national employment grew by 7 per cent in the 1950–70 period, growth in the northern regions ranged from 2 per cent to 5 per cent, leading to an increasing South–North gap in terms of employment. In the 1970s overall employment growth has, of course, been much lower (1.4 per cent only between 1970 and 1979), but northern employment has virtually stagnated (0.5 per cent in the same period).

This spatial imbalance shows itself clearly in terms of the traditional problem indicators, with trends in migration and unemployment being of particular interest. All five regions of the north have experienced net emigration (with the exception of Wales in the 1971–3 period), and the interregional migration pattern in the 1960s was one where a region generally lost population to regions to its south and gained population from those to its north. The 1970s saw a change in this picture — while the South as a whole still had a positive migration balance, the South-East region had a substantial net migration loss. Given a

TABLE 14.4. *Selected indicators of regional imbalance in Great Britain, relative position of the North[a]*
(percentages)

	1966	1970	1979
Population			
Share in total	42.2	41.7	41.2
Output			
Share in GDP	38.6	38.7	38.7
Share in manufacturing GDP	..	41.8	42.8
Share in industrial investment	..	57.5	50.9[b]
Balance on goods and services			
in per cent of GDP	(−0.1)[c]	..	..
Ratio of per caput GDP	91	92	94
Labour force			
Unemployment − national	1.4	3.4	5.7
Unemployment − regional	1.9	4.6	7.3
Participation rate − national	68.9	67.1	65.4
Participation rate − regional	68.9	67.1	64.9
Female participation rate − national	42.2	43.0	47.0
Female participation rate − regional	41.3	42.1	46.9

[a] Scotland, North, Yorkshire and Humberside, North West, and Wales
[b] 1978
[c] 1964
Sources: CSO, *Regional Statistics* (various issues); V.H. Woodward, *Regional Social Accounts for the United Kingdom*, NIESR, Cambridge 1970.

much reduced rate of natural population increase, migration is the major factor explaining interregional population trends. By 1975, all northern regions had a smaller share of total population than in 1961, while Scotland and the North and North-West regions (and, in the later 1970s, the South-East as well) have experienced absolute population decline. Matching the southern flow of population has been a northerly flow of mobile firms, particularly in the form of branch plants. Up to 1971, the northern regions as a whole received more than half of the moves, both indigenous to the United Kingdom and from abroad. Of particular note was the ability of Wales to gain indigenous moves and of Scotland as a recipient of foreign in-moves. Since the oil crisis, however, the share going to the northern regions has dropped off considerably, despite the fact that the total number of interregional moves has increased substantially.[10]

Despite these equilibrating tendencies, a clear South–North unemployment gap still persists. Since the 1950s, the northern regions have generally had unemployment rates well above the national average. While interregional disparities have been narrowing (at least in percentage terms), this is in no sense a reflection of any diminution in the problem, but rather stems from the increasing difficulties facing the once-prosperous south. Unemployment has more and more become a national rather than a specifically regional problem.

[10] It should be noted, however, that changes in data collection procedures may mean that the newer figures include more smaller moves than previously. This acts not only to increase the total number of moves but, since small firms generally move only relatively short distances, will also result in a smaller proportion of total moves going to the assisted areas given their peripherality.

Moving from the problems arising from industrial decline in general to those specifically related to one sector – coal – the Nord region of France, the southern part of Belgium (Wallonia) and the German Ruhr provide interesting examples of differing experiences. Though the decline of coal-mining has created problems elsewhere, too – most obviously in Britain – these may have been less severe, partly because mining employment fell less sharply in the United Kingdom and partly because the major coal-mining areas are less regionally concentrated than in the three other countries.

In France, employment in the coal industry declined by 69 per cent (some 250,000 jobs) over the 1947–71 period, with roughly two-thirds of this national decline being concentrated in the Nord region. The problems thereby arising were compounded by two other factors: first, the Nord had a high birth rate, even by French standards (15 per cent above the national average) and, secondly, there were major job losses in the other sectors important in the Nord (agriculture losing some 60,000 jobs and textiles 50,000 between 1954 and 1968). Despite this, the level of employment in the Nord remained relatively stable, due to high emigration as well as the rapid growth of the French economy. Between 1954 and 1962 the region had a net migration loss of over 20,000, which increased to nearly 50,000 in the 1962–8 period, it being second only to Lorraine in terms of net migration loss. At the same time the region experienced major growth (29 per cent) in the tertiary sector. As a result of these factors, the Nord's unemployment rate was, by the late 1970s, not much above the national average, despite further job losses in the mining sector as well as in textiles and agriculture.

The rundown of the coal industry was even sharper in Belgium, with total mining employment falling by 7 per cent per annum between 1953 and 1970, as against 4 per cent in France. The major area affected by this decline was the Wallonian South, particularly the Liège and Hainaut provinces, where employment in the coal industry declined by over 90 per cent during the 1953–73 period. Despite the rundown of the coal industry being facilitated by such factors as strong economic growth elsewhere in Belgium, early retirement policies, return migration of foreign workers, and the small size of the country (which helped promote geographical mobility), Liège and Hainaut still suffered considerably, their share of national unemployment increasing from 22 to 41 per cent over the 1960s. During the same period Liège had only 38 per cent of the national average rate of population growth and Hainaut 66 per cent, reflecting heavy migration losses. Thus, in comparison to the French Nord, Wallonia experienced a much more marked relative deterioration in its position, with its share of total population and labour force both falling. While the decline in coal played an important causal role here, an additional major force has been the increasing locational attractiveness of the Flemish North, leading to it receiving some 75 to 90 per cent of all foreign investment in the early 1970s.

Finally, the German Ruhr represents the interesting case where the decline of the coal industry led to a major short-term crisis, but, due to a rapid transformation and absorption process, many of the long-standing problems normally associated with the rundown of the mining sector were avoided. The German coal industry experienced annual average rates of decline sharper in relative terms than elsewhere in Europe. The major problems arose from the late 1950s onwards, and by 1973 the Ruhr had lost over 320,000 coal jobs. Absorption of the labour surplus was, however, relatively rapid, fostered by strong national growth as well as expansion in chemicals, the metal industry, and services within the *Land* of North Rhine–Westphalia where the Ruhr lies. In consequence, male unemployment rates generally remained below the national average, although there were serious pockets of unemployment in some mining communities. In addition, there was considerable migration out of the coalfields, but most of this was within the region. Thus, despite the major decline of coal, the strong national and regional climates of growth, and the ability to adapt to major sectoral change, allowed North Rhine–Westphalia to increase its share of total national employment from 24.5 per cent to over 26 per cent between 1950 and 1973, and to maintain a level of GDP per caput close to the national average.

Congested regions

During the 1950s and 1960s, but less so in the 1970s, the counterpart of regions displaying conditions of excess labour supply were regions experiencing excess demand for labour. These regions are generally called 'pressured' or 'congested' regions, these terms referring, from a regional policy perspective, to the difficulties posed by labour shortages and problems relating to the major externalities and bottle-necks created by the attractiveness of these areas to labour and capital.

In comparison to the areas of deficient labour demand, congested regions generally display the reverse characteristics in relation to population, migration, unemployment, activity rates, growth, and industrial structure and performance. The attractiveness of these areas to capital (and hence labour) stems from the considerable agglomeration economies they afford, causing them to gain major shares of modern industrial and tertiary developments. Although these external benefits are generally matched by a variety of external costs, these have not been such as to act as a natural limitation on the growth of these areas, primarily because they are often not incorporated into firms' decisions and because they can anyway generally be passed on. This traditional problem of market failure is aggravated by the 'satisficing' nature of firms' decision-making so that other locations — which could be superior from private as well as public perspectives — are often not examined, or are summarily dismissed. In consequence, a spatially suboptimal resource allocation is promoted since the optimal size of these areas for firms may be far in excess of the public optimum. Thus these areas enter the regional discussion and a number of countries have introduced regional 'disincentive' policies specifically geared to limit their rate of expansion.

The justification of measures to control the growth of congested regions has been both regional and national. At the regional level, the attractiveness of congested regions, which can be regarded as excessive from a public perspective, can play a causal role in the persistence of regional problems, since it hinders the equilibrating flow of capital which an efficiently operating market could stimulate. The resulting impact of these forces on labour migration is also seen as undesirable for both problem and congested regions. For the former, difficulties arise due to the selective nature of migration and the under-utilization and rundown of social overhead capital. For the latter, labour inflows can lead to congestion, urban sprawl, and pressure on the available infrastructure. In addition, migration into the pressured regions acts to reduce tightness in the labour market and thereby lessens the market pressures acting to push firms out of these regions. Taken together, therefore, migration can simultaneously reduce the attractiveness of the problem regions to mobile investments and weaken the market stimuli which foster relocation out of the pressured regions. At the national level, the wage increases generated by tight labour markets in the congested regions result in inflationary pressure which is often transmitted to areas of excess labour supply via the process of national wage negotiations. This macroeconomic or 'overheating' justification for specific disincentive policies has been an explicit feature of both British and Dutch regional policy.

Trends in the later 1970s show, however, that this picture of congested regions has become increasingly less appropriate (Table 14.5). Thus, in a number of countries (e.g. the United Kingdom, Austria, the Netherlands), these regions experienced net migration losses. In addition, the severity of the mid-1970s recession and the slowness to move out of it have caused particularly severe problems within the core of some of these regions (e.g. in London), so that some have acquired characteristics previously only associated with assisted areas. In other countries (e.g. France, Italy, Belgium), there was no longer-run decline in population until the late 1970s, but some stabilization with signs of increasing convergence in terms of output with the rest of the country. However, while the income gap between prosperous and poorer regions may have narrowed, the former type of region still appears to be increasing its more functional and qualitative dominance. Finally, in several Southern European countries (e.g. Spain or Greece), the process of congestion has continued in the 1970s and income differentials have, if anything, grown further.

The Paris region provides an excellent example of the domination of one region in a country's spatial structure. The growth of Paris became a major concern following Gravier's *Paris et le désert français* in 1947.[11] With just over 2 per cent of French territory, the Paris region has almost 20 and 23 per cent of total population and employment respectively, and both these shares have been increasing. The primacy of Paris in terms of population and employment is, however, overshadowed by measures of the region's qualitative or functional dominance. Close to 30 per cent of the country's output is produced in the area, and by the mid-1970s, Paris contained 40 per cent of all managers, 50 per cent of all engineers, and 66 per cent of all pure and applied researchers. Even more significant is the position of Paris as a control centre, having 78 per cent of all headquarter offices in 1975, in comparison to 75 per cent in the mid-1960s. These statistics reveal a major conflict within France, given, on the one hand, the interregional problems associated with such a spatial monopoly of high level functions and, on the other, the Gaullist desire to make Paris into a *ville internationale* and thus improve its competitive position with other major international centres.

The Randstad in the West Netherlands presents a different example of a dominant region, given its multipolar agglomeration structure. The Randstad has four major centres, Amsterdam and Utrecht on its northern wing and Rotterdam and The Hague in the south. While the domination of this area within the

---

[11] J. Gravier, *Paris et le désert français*, Paris 1947.

TABLE 14.5. *Changes in the predominance of selected congested regions* (percentages)

		Share in population			Share in GDP		
		1960	1970	1977	1960	1970	1977
France	Ile de France	18.1	18.9	18.8	26.8	28.5	27.3
Italy	Piedmont–Liguria Lombardy	25.4	27.2	27.2	37.2	37.2	36.0
United Kingdom	South-East	30.9	30.6	30.1	34.6	34.6	34.0
Spain	Madrid–Barcelona Valencia	22.6	27.3[a]	29.8[b]	32.3	35.3[a]	37.4[b]
Austria	Vienna[c]	23.0	21.7	21.1	33.8	29.3	26.8
Belgium	Brabant	21.5	22.5	22.6	27.5	26.8	26.2
Greece	Greater Athens	22.1	29.0	..	35.1[d]	..	39.5[e]
Ireland	East[c]	32.1	35.7	36.6[b]	..	41.8[f]	..
Netherlands	West	47.4	46.2	44.9	50.9	50.6	47.5

[a] 1969
[b] 1975
[c] 1961 and 1971
[d] 1958
[e] 1974
[f] 1973; share in total personal income
Sources: see Appendix

Netherlands is not so great as that of Paris in France, it has still led to the phrase 'The West and the Rest' being coined. Although the Randstad contained 33 per cent of total population in 1975, its share (and the share of the West as a whole – the provinces of North and South Holland and Utrecht) has been declining over time and at an increasing rate. Since the early 1950s, population growth rates in both the West and the Randstad have been below the national average, and, during the 1972–5 period, the Randstad's population fell by 2 per cent. A major factor explaining these relative and absolute declines has been the reversal in migration trends since 1960 from high gains to progressively larger losses.

The Randstad, like a number of other major agglomerations in Europe, is subject to 'disincentive' measures aimed at controlling its growth and attempting to stimulate relocation to the problem regions. However, the relative decline of the Randstad, coupled with the severe impact of the mid-1970s recession on it, appear to have led to a significant reduction in the desire to constrain the growth of the area. There is now a widespread feeling that the importance of agglomeration benefits and the role they can play in relation to improving efficiency and viability in low growth periods need to be reasserted and promoted.

Finally, the example of London and the South-East region can be used to illustrate a situation where, for London at least, the term 'congested' is no longer appropriate given the recent and major reversal in its fortunes. The South-East, with 12 per cent of the national territory, had 30 per cent (17 million) of the total population in 1978. Until 1971, its share of total population had been relatively stable, with population growing slowly, but between then and the late 1970s the region experienced an absolute decline of over 150,000 people, largely due to increased net emigration. The region was, however, still relatively prosperous, with, for example, unemployment rates well below and incomes per head above the national average, but since the mid-1970s the regional and national rates have been converging. The South-East unemployment rate was 60 per cent of the national rate in 1966 and 68 per cent in 1977-9, while relative per caput incomes declined marginally from 115 to 113 per cent of the national average. Like Paris, however, the region is still a dominant and dynamic centre as a location for high quality occupations and control functions, having approximately three-quarters of all headquarter offices and half of the research and development establishments.

Although the South-East as a whole still retains the mantle of a prosperous region, London is experiencing major problems related to substantial losses of population and employment. Population has not only been declining for some time, but has been doing so at an increasing rate, culminating in a loss of 5.5 per cent between 1971 and 1976. Over the 1961-76 period London lost over 1 million people. In terms of employment, too, London suffered a major reversal in its fortunes after 1960. A net gain of around 130,000 jobs in the 1950s turned to a net loss of 386,000 jobs in the 1960s. Over the 1961-76 period total employment in London fell by some 10 per cent, but for manufacturing the decline was 38 per cent, seven times the average for England and Wales as a whole. Perhaps the most striking feature of this trend has been that about three-quarters of the gross decline in manufacturing employment has been due to the death or contraction of firms, and that the problem is felt to be particularly severe in the small firm sector. While all major British cities are experiencing similar difficulties — so that this problem has been termed the 'inner area problem', given its particular severity in areas adjacent to city centres — the scale of the problem in London is such as to warrant the feeling that a 'London factor' (i.e. something specific to London) is at work.

II. The Development of Policy[12]

From the above review of the main types of problem regions, two major features stand out. First, the nature and intensity of the regional problem differ considerably between countries; secondly, there have been significant changes over the years. In this latter context, as was mentioned above, income differences across regions seem to have diminished in size over time. Migration may have contributed to this, but a further and possibly more important reason for the closing of these gaps may have been a form of policy intervention which, while not usually going under the heading of regional policy, can none the less have pronounced regional effects. General taxation and transfers under the social security system have an important impact on regional differentials and the form in which problems arise. To the extent that the tax system is progressive, there is a transfer from richer to poorer areas. Income maintenance expenditures may have an even larger effect in producing an automatic fiscal stabilization of the poorer regions, tending to rise, most obviously, as unemployment increases.

[12] For a more detailed discussion of the development of policy, but one limited to the nine countries of the EEC, see D.M. Yuill, K.J. Allen, and C.J. Hull (eds.), *Regional Policy in the European Community*, London 1980.

Other aspects of public expenditure may also be stabilizing. These various flows clearly mitigate the effects of regional disparities on individuals.

Estimates by the EEC suggest that this redistributive power is very significant (Table 14.6). For the four major countries, the Gini coefficient[13] of regional

TABLE 14.6. *Interregional redistributive effect of public finance*
(percentage reduction in Gini coefficient of regional income inequality)

	Revenue	Expenditure	Total
France (1969)	18.6	33.3[a]	51.9
Germany (1970)	-3.0	41.9[b]	38.9
Italy (1973)	-1.8	45.3	43.5
United Kingdom (1964)	-1.8	32.9	31.1
Switzerland[c] (1967)	-0.7	10.3	9.6

[a] 1970

[b] 1970 for consumption and investment; 1973 for transfers

[c] Excluding the social security system

Source: EEC, *Report of the Study Group on the Role of Public Finance in European Integration* (MacDougall Report), Brussels 1977, Vol. II.

income inequality is reduced by some 40 per cent relative to what it would have been without fiscal equalization – to set this figure in perspective, the equivalent reduction achieved by the direct tax and transfer system in the Gini coefficient for personal income distribution in the early 1970s in the United Kingdom and Sweden was, on average, of some 30 per cent.[14] Though the figures in this table suggest that this equalization comes about largely because of expenditure flows, with the tax system appearing actually regressive in four cases out of five, this finding is entirely due to the impact of indirect taxes (whose incidence is notoriously difficult to estimate). Personal income taxes have everywhere a pronounced redistributive effect. In so far as, in post-war Europe, both the degree of tax progressivity and the extent of social welfare expenditure have risen quite significantly and have, according to Chapter 7 above, contributed to diminishing household income disparities, they must have played a similar role in reducing regional inequality as well.

Though these various 'automatic' stabilizers mitigate the effects of regional disparities on incomes, they do not get at the root of the problem, which arises from structural changes and low productivity, at times combined with high 'efficiency wages'. Hence the need for action as well, in the form of specific regional policies. These have been followed by most European countries in the post-war period, with three different phases being identifiable – a first phase lasting until the second half of the 1950s, during which regional policy was more or less dormant; a second phase of very much more active regional policy spanning the 1960s and taking in, too, the early 1970s; and a third phase, from the oil crisis to the late 1970s, of consolidation and reappraisal in an environment which, as noted above, had become increasingly hostile to regional policy initiatives.

[13] For an explanation of the Gini coefficient see Ch. 7, n. 20.

[14] M.A. King, 'How Effective Have Fiscal Policies been in Changing the Distribution of Income and Wealth?', *American Economic Review*, May 1980.

The 1950s — dormant policies

That regional policy was on the whole dormant during the first policy phase is scarcely surprising. It was, after all, a time of recovery and reconstruction throughout Europe, a time when the emphasis was firmly on national growth and well-being with little interest in the 'luxury' of its spatial distribution. But the lack of action in the regional policy field was not solely due to the severity of national problems. The regional problem itself was very much less marked than it was later to become. In particular, traditional industries like coal-mining, shipbuilding, textiles, and iron and steel — all problem industries in subsequent years — were experiencing boom conditions as economies sought to catch up after the war, while the 'exodus from the land', although marked in some countries, was not as serious as was later to be the case. Finally, with the falling away of wartime and immediate post-war controls, there was a general faith in market forces and little support for intervention along regional policy, or any other, lines.

The result was that regional policy was decidedly low-key throughout the period. Most countries did not have an explicit policy, and those which did laid most emphasis on infrastructure provision. In Italy, for example, a special development agency, the Cassa per il Mezzogiorno, was set up in 1950 to encourage southern development by complementing the normal infrastructure activities of the state through so-called 'extraordinary interventions' wherever the standard state apparatus was shown to be inadequate or inappropriate.[15] In its initial phase the Cassa concentrated its resources on agricultural and more general infrastructure programmes (the provision of roads, harbours, airports, schools, and hospitals). During this period land reform was under way in the South (with large land-holdings being distributed amongst some 90,000 new peasant farmers), and, although not directly involving the Cassa, much 'extraordinary intervention' by the Cassa went towards supporting this land reform policy. Indeed, during its first ten years of existence some three-quarters of the Cassa's resources were devoted to agriculture. Through land reform and the infrastructure activities of the Cassa the aim was to change the socio-economic conditions of the Mezzogiorno so as to bring about spontaneous industrialization; and it was only when it was clear that this was not happening that, in 1957, a more direct strategy to promote industrialization was introduced.

In this phase, then, investment in infrastructure was the main component of policy in those countries where concern was being shown for the regional problem. Only in the United Kingdom were other aspects of regional policy prominent, and then only for a limited period. A regional problem in the United Kingdom had been evident since the 1920s, and a policy of taking 'work to the workers' had begun in 1934, only to be shelved with the outbreak of the war. After the war, most of the previous policy measures were retained (including government factory building in the designated Development Areas, the award of loans to industrial estate companies, and the offer of discretionary grants or loans to commercially viable projects), and, in addition, the system of Industrial Development Certificate (IDC) control was introduced in 1948. Under this system, all new projects above specified size levels were required to obtain IDC

---

[15] For an English-language survey of the Cassa's operations, see G. Podbielski, *Twenty-five Years of Special Action for the Development of Southern Italy*, Milan 1978.

approval as a legal prerequisite for application for local authority planning permission. By regulating development in the more pressured regions, IDC control had the objective of preventing overheating in those regions while at the same time helping to identify and divert 'mobile' industrial projects to the assisted areas. The prominence given to regional policy in the United Kingdom in the immediate post-war period was, however, short-lived. An external balance of payments crisis soon forced the Labour government to downgrade policy, and with a change of government in 1950 regional policy was placed firmly in the background until much later in the decade.

The 1960s – active intervention

As the 1950s progressed, the environment within which policy operated changed significantly, encouraging the pursuit of a more active regional policy. During this second policy phase (a phase which was to last until the early 1970s) increasing emphasis came to be placed, throughout Europe, on equality and on questions of distribution. At the same time as interest in the fate of the problem regions grew, the problem itself became more serious. The agricultural sector, as was noted earlier, went through a major technical revolution in many countries, leading to open unemployment and increasing underemployment in rural areas, and more significantly to massive migratory flows to major urban centres and the more prosperous regions. Many traditional industries also shed labour, particularly spatially concentrated activities like coal-mining, shipbuilding, and iron and steel. As well as creating unemployment, the difficulties experienced by such long-established industries fostered emigration to richer areas. As a result, there were serious problems of congestion and infrastructure provision in many of the major agglomerations – London, Paris, the Randstad, and the Milan–Turin–Genoa triangle in Northern Italy – and fears that the situation could only grow worse. Related to this, labour shortages in the prosperous regions tended to create inflationary pressures which, in some countries, were rapidly transmitted throughout the whole economy. In such a situation the case for regional policy was strong, and it was further strengthened by a general confidence at the time in government intervention; a conviction in many parts of Europe that the problems facing government could be solved if only the appropriate planning were undertaken and the correct policies adopted.

The first tentative steps towards a more active regional policy were taken in most countries towards the end of the 1950s, with financial incentives being provided to encourage firms to move to the problem regions. However, the incentives on offer were generally small-scale, were awarded only at the discretion of the administering authorities, and tended to have serious limiting conditions attached to them. From this quiet start, the role of incentives in regional policy grew rapidly. In the United Kingdom, for instance, expenditure on regional incentives rose more than twentyfold in the course of the 1960s, reflecting the introduction of free depreciation on plant and machinery expenditure and a 10 per cent plant and machinery grant in 1963, the move over to the nationally available, but regionally differentiated, Investment Grant on plant and machinery in 1966, and the introduction in 1967 of the Regional Employment Premium (a weekly labour subsidy to establishments in Development Areas of, initially, £1.50 for full-time men or 7 per cent of the average manual worker's wage, and less for other employees). In addition there was a rapid extension of the designated problem regions, especially after 1966.

But it was not only in the United Kingdom that regional incentives increased in importance. While 1957 is correctly viewed as the 'date of birth' of an incentive package in the Italian Mezzogiorno (capital grants, tax concessions, and soft loans being the main incentives on offer), it was only in 1965 that the available incentives became 'substantial' (incentive expenditure rising to some $250-300 million annually or nearly ½ per cent of GDP – a fivefold increase), and they were further strengthened in 1968 with the introduction of a very valuable concession on employer social security contributions amounting at first to 8.5 per cent of the wages and salaries over a ten-year period of additional labour employed, but rising to a 1979 level of some 27 per cent of the wages and salaries of any additional labour hired. In Ireland, too, the late 1960s saw a reorganization of the whole incentive system so as to make it both more effective (with the setting-up of a single body, the Industrial Development Authority, charged with the promotion of industrial development) and more attractive (the Industrial Development Authority being given responsibility for an incentive package based primarily on capital grants and aimed to be at least as valuable as others in Europe).

That regional incentives increased in importance in countries like Italy, the United Kingdom, and Ireland during the second policy phase is only to be expected; these were, after all, as was made clear in the previous section, the countries facing particularly severe regional problems. However, regional incentives also increased notably in other countries. In Belgium, for instance, minor regional aids (principally in the form of soft loans and loan guarantees), first introduced in 1959, rose significantly in value in 1966 and 1970 and were complemented by a capital grant scheme. In Denmark, the regional incentive package became substantially more attractive in 1969 (two years after problem areas were for the first time explicitly designated), when a 25 per cent investment grant was introduced and was further strengthened in 1971 when the loan guarantee system which had been the mainstay of the incentive package since its inception was replaced by a concessionary loan scheme. In Sweden, regional policy, having been inaugurated on an experimental basis in 1965, was put on to a more permanent footing in 1970, and, at the same time, the available aids were significantly expanded – the loans and grants previously on offer increasing in value by 50 per cent, while depreciation loans, loan guarantees, and relocation grants were introduced for the first time. And in the Netherlands, the floorspace-related and job-constrained incentives of the late 1950s and early 1960s gave way to the Investment Premium, a virtually automatic 25 per cent grant on fixed capital investment.

Even in Germany, thought by many to have little or no regional problem and a country with a strong free market philosophy, there was a major development in the regional incentives field. In 1969 a start was made on the harmonization of federal and *Länder* policies with the introduction of two new incentives – the federally awarded Investment Allowance (the base of the German incentive package) and the discretionary Investment Grant (half financed by the federal authorities and half by the *Länder*, but administered by the *Länder*). At the same time so-called 'maximum preferential rates' came into being, representing the maximum value of all public aids in the designated areas in net grant equivalent terms. That such steps were taken in Germany is particularly interesting. In the first place it emphasizes the strength of those forces leading to more active regional policy, since a change in the German constitution was in fact necessary to allow a joint federal/*Länder* initiative in what had previously been a policy area constitutionally reserved for the *Länder*. And secondly it shows that it is indeed possible to have harmonized incentives in a federal system – a lesson of considerable importance to those countries in Europe facing devolutionary pressures, as well as to the European Commission with its attempts to co-ordinate the regional incentive policies of member states.

Clearly, then, the second policy phase was one of considerable activity as far as regional incentives were concerned, with expenditure increasing greatly throughout Europe. At the same time, there were a number of related trends which contributed to the general strengthening of incentive policy. There was, for instance, a strong move towards capital grants during the period. By the late 1960s most European countries had a capital grant on offer as the base element of their regional incentive package, whereas a decade earlier capital grants were rare. The trend towards capital grants was, however, understandable in the context of the period. Capital grants are far more visible than other regional incentive instruments, can be pushed to very high values as a percentage of project costs, and, because of their great administrative flexibility, can be readily directed to meet regional policy objectives.

In contrast to capital grants, regional fiscal aids, if anything, lost popularity during the 1960s, perhaps primarily because, being administered by the national tax authorities, it often proved difficult to tailor them to meet regional objectives. In addition, they are of no value to firms not making profits (which may be the consequence of setting up in a new location, surely a prime justification for assistance), and their impact is much reduced by the fact that they are usually 'paid' through the tax system and hence normally with considerable delay. By the end of the second policy phase regional tax concessions were important only in France and Italy, and regional accelerated depreciation allowances only in Germany.

A further important trend of the 1960s was the introduction of regional labour subsidies in a number of countries – the Regional Employment Premium in the United Kingdom and the Social Security Concession in Italy being the two main ones. The move towards labour subsidies is readily explained. Such subsidies both gave the poorer regions a labour cost advantage (or at least reduced their high levels of 'efficiency wages') and helped to offset the capital orientation of most regional incentive packages. Indeed, given the strong economic arguments for operating policies which attempt to bring the nominal cost of labour in line with its opportunity cost, it is perhaps surprising that more labour subsidies were not introduced. Their prime drawback would seem to be their expense. In 1977, over $1 billion (or ½ per cent of GDP, and considerably more than was spent *in total* on the remaining elements of the southern incentive package) was forgone by the Italian social security authorities in respect of the Mezzogiorno Social Security Concession, while expenditure on the British Regional Employment Premium had reached some $400 million annually (i.e. some two-fifths of British regional incentive expenditure) when it was withdrawn in 1976 as part of a series of public expenditure cuts.

Related to the trends discussed so far, there was a move in a number of the larger European countries away from discretionary assistance and towards more 'automatic' incentives i.e. incentives available at fixed rates and awarded more or less automatically if the conditions of the award were met. A whole range of such incentives was introduced in the latter half of the 1960s – the Investment Allowance in Germany, the Investment Premium in the Netherlands, the Investment Grant and Regional Employment Premium in the United Kingdom, and the Social Security Concession in Italy; while the Regional Development Grant in France was administered in a more automatic fashion from 1964 onwards. Obviously such incentives are far more visible than assistance couched in 'up to' terms, and where the decision whether or not to make an award is at the discretion of the administering body. As such they are more likely to be taken into account by a firm making an investment/location decision than are discretionary aids.

Despite this trend towards more automatic assistance, discretionary incentives remained an important part of most aid packages. In the larger countries they were used to 'top up' the automatic base of the incentive system and were viewed as being extremely useful in tailoring the regional incentive package as a whole to the needs of both applicant firms and recipient regions. The British incentive package introduced in 1972 followed this approach explicitly, discretionary Selective Financial Assistance being awarded on top of a predictable and visible base in the form of the Regional Development Grant and the Regional Employment Premium. Of the larger European countries, it was only in Italy that total reliance was placed on automatic measures, a reflection certainly of the severity of the regional problem in the Mezzogiorno but perhaps also a consequence of the Italian administrative system. In the smaller countries (for example Belgium, Denmark, and Ireland) a very strong element of discretion was retained, due primarily to the fact that relatively few cases passed through the incentive system, thus making 'real' discretion feasible.

In addition to these various trends in incentive policy, the second phase saw increasing emphasis being laid on other aspects of regional policy. The operation of disincentives or controls in the pressured regions is of special note. These policies, which can be viewed as the reverse side of the coin from incentives in the problem regions, have been of particular importance in France and the United Kingdom. Although, as we have seen, the British system of IDC control came into force in 1948, it lay more or less dormant for most of the 1950s and really began to bite significantly only in the 1960s, especially after the lowering of the floorspace exemption limit (below which an IDC is not required) in the Midlands and in the South-East from 5,000 square feet ($465m^2$) to a mere 1,000 square feet (93 sq.m.) in 1965. Not only was the coverage of the control widened at this time, but the stringency with which it was implemented also increased. The percentage of IDC applications refused in the Midlands and the South-East averaged around 22 per cent during the 1960s, compared to just 10 per cent in the previous decade. In addition to a strengthening of IDC control, 1965 saw the introduction of a similar control on the office sector, the Office Development Permit – a result of increasing congestion in the prosperous regions and the growing feeling that the office sector could play an important role in regional development.

In France, locational control in the Paris region through a system of permits (the *Agrément*) was among the first regional policy measures in the mid-1950s. Applied initially to the manufacturing sector, the coverage of this control was widened to include the office sector in 1958, and it was augmented by the introduction of the *Redevance*, a type of 'congestion tax', in 1960. Perhaps more so than in Britain, the French measures linked the problems of congestion in the pressured regions to the lack of employment opportunities in the problem regions, it being felt that by using controls to steer projects from the pressured to the problem regions, a 'simultaneous solution' to both of these problems could be achieved.

As the 1960s progressed, fears of congestion in major urban centres led to demands for control policies elsewhere in Europe; and in the early 1970s, schemes were introduced in Italy (Authorization, 1972) and the Netherlands (Selective Investment Regulation, 1974). Neither of these schemes has had a significant impact, however, a major explanatory factor here being that these controls were introduced around the time of the downturn of the European economy in 1973-4, a downturn which saw fears of congestion rapidly recede and which also led to a significant decrease in the amount of mobile investment which could be 'pushed' by control policies to the problem regions. This point is taken up again below.

The discussion so far has covered incentives in the depressed regions and controls in the pressured regions, but there are four other aspects of regional policy in the 1960s which should be mentioned. First, there was a growing interest in the *use of state industry* to further regional development. In this regard the role of state industry in the promotion of the Mezzogiorno attracted particular attention. From 1957 onwards, the Italian state holding sector – a key component of the Italian economy, covering some 350 firms (including such famous names as Alfa Romeo, Alitalia, the Bank of Rome, and Italsider) and employing about 700,000 workers (or 5½ per cent of the labour force) – was obliged to have at least 40 per cent of its total investment in the Mezzogiorno (60 per cent since 1971) and to place at least 60 per cent of its new investment there (80 per cent since 1971). Even though these percentages have in practice been applied only to potentially mobile investment, they have had a significant impact, with state holding employment in the Mezzogiorno more than doubling since their introduction (so that it now accounts for over one-quarter of all state holding employment).

Secondly, despite the increasing emphasis on incentive policy, *infrastructure investment* remained of importance in a number of countries, especially in rural and sparsely populated areas. However, in the course of the 1960s it came increasingly to be viewed as necessary for the development of a region rather than sufficient in itself to bring about development.

Thirdly, *government office dispersal* was encouraged in a number of countries, in particular in the United Kingdom. Other countries, too, actively considered the issue and towards the end of the phase were starting to take action. Perhaps the most noteworthy case of dispersal was the Danish decision in 1967 to move the regional incentive administration to Silkeborg in Jutland – a just reward perhaps for its advocacy of the transfer from Copenhagen of government offices!

A final aspect of regional policy during the 1960s which must be commented on concerns *area designation*. The mid-1960s saw great interest in most European countries in the use of 'growth poles' to stimulate development. They were seen as a way of settlement restructuring, of providing external economies for firms locating in the poles, and of creating economies of scale as regards infrastructure provision. The concept was a strong element of French regional policy, but was perhaps taken furthest in Italy with the plan to create an interrelated industry complex at Bari–Taranto. This plan was widely admired, but in the event came up against serious practical difficulties. In particular, there were major problems in identifying suitably interrelated industries at the highly disaggregated level demanded and in developing the linkages between such industries 'on the ground'. And it was at the practical level, too, that the growth pole concept itself tended to founder, it often being politically inexpedient – not to say dangerous – to explicitly select poles on which growth would or would not be concentrated. In addition, there was growing concern about undesirable 'backwash' effects, and the negative impact which growth poles tended to have on their economic hinterlands. In this regard, developments in France are especially interesting. Following the designation of eight growth poles (*Métropoles d'équilibre*) scattered throughout the country (as countervailing weights to the pull of Paris), a policy for 'medium-sized towns' was adopted in an attempt to stabilize the economic hinterlands of these growth poles – and in the 1970s a policy in favour of 'natural local regions' was introduced, aimed specifically at the problem of rural depopulation. In other countries, too, the growth pole concept has gone out of fashion. In the late 1970s only in Germany and the Netherlands were growth poles designated as part of regional incentive policy; and in both countries the number of poles designated (some 300 in Germany and over 40 in the Netherlands) was such as seriously to reduce the theoretical benefits of the policy.

The post-1973 period

From the above review, it is clear that the second phase of regional policy in Europe – beginning in the late 1950s and lasting until the early 1970s – was a very active one. Not only was there a heavy emphasis on regional incentives, and especially on capital grants, but considerable use, too, was made of other elements of policy: controls and disincentives, state industry, and infrastructure investment. It was noted earlier that this activity can be attributed to an economic and political environment which was highly favourable to regional policy initiatives. This environment changed markedly as a consequence of the oil crisis of 1973–4. No longer was overheating and the threat of congestion in the pressured regions a problem; no longer was unemployment and underemployment limited to the traditional problem regions; no longer was economic growth taken for granted; and no longer was there the confidence that there had been in the ability of government to solve problems. The conditions which had spawned a period of very active regional policy disappeared, to be replaced by widespread high levels of unemployment, inflation, industrial overcapacity, increasing competition from low labour-cost countries, and public expenditure curtailment.

Given this far more hostile environment, regional policy was downgraded and few major innovations were launched, notwithstanding the growth of development agencies in some countries, a related move towards more selective aids, and the introduction of a number of small, 'gap-filling' schemes. Even the enlargement of the EEC in 1973 brought little change to the state of regional policy, despite the setting-up of the Regional Development Fund. The Fund was given too few resources, spread those resources too widely, and, of key importance, was used by member states to substitute for national awards in the problem regions rather than to supplement them.

Although there were few significant innovations in these years, there were no major cutbacks, except in the United Kingdom, where the Regional Employment Premium was dropped and the Regional Development Grant withdrawn from the mining and construction sectors, as part of a series of public expenditure cuts in 1976, and where a number of major changes in the regional policy sphere followed the election of a Conservative government in May 1979. Thus, the United Kingdom assisted areas were to be cut back dramatically so that, by August 1982, they would hold under 30 per cent of the national population (as against 43 per cent in June 1979); the Regional Development Grant was to be reduced from 20 to 15 per cent in the Development Areas, and to be withdrawn completely from the Intermediate Areas; and Selective Financial Assistance was to be limited to projects in need. As a result it was hoped to reduce regional policy expenditure by some two-fifths (i.e. about $½ billion) while at the same time making policy more cost-effective by concentrating it on the areas of greatest need.

But apart from these changes, changes which perhaps herald a new policy phase in the United Kingdom, there have, as already noted, been no significant policy cutbacks in Europe. Rather, the period has been one of consolidation, at least as far as regional incentives are concerned. These have remained important in the late 1970s, as can be seen in Table 14.7. Though the data shown cover 90 per cent of all regional incentive expenditure in the EEC countries, they

TABLE 14.7. *Regional incentive expenditure, 1979*

	Total		$ per head in designated problem regions[a]
	$ million	Per cent of public expenditure	
France	635	0.2	32
Germany	1,129	0.3	51
Italy	2,514	1.7	129
United Kingdom	1,169	0.7	46
Great Britain	988	..	41
Northern Ireland	181	..	113
Belgium	215	0.4	55
Denmark	48	(0.2)	30
Ireland	431	(6.2)	130[b]
Netherlands	202	0.2	53

Note: the figures in all cases cover expenditure commitments; for exact coverage, see the original source.

[a] The figures use the percentage of the national population contained within the designated problem regions. This is an approximation since some incentives are available only to parts of the problem regions

[b] Per head of total population since the whole of Ireland is viewed as a problem region by the EEC

Sources: D.M. Yuill and K.J. Allen (eds.), *European Regional Incentives 1981*, Glasgow 1981; OECD, *National Accounts of OECD Countries, 1976* and *1962-1979*.

must, for a number of reasons, be treated with caution. Thus, appropriate statistical information on fiscal aids is not always available (the Italian tax concessions are, for instance, excluded), and when available is not always in the most relevant form. Similarly, the subsidy element of soft loans is rarely identified, with the result that the soft loans on offer in the United Kingdom and Denmark are shown in the table in terms of gross expenditure rather than the net grant equivalent of that expenditure (thus overstating their importance). In addition, information tends to be in terms of expenditure committed rather than actually made, and there are differences between schemes and packages regarding the extent to which funds committed are actually spent. These and related difficulties are obviously compounded when making international comparisons. As a result, any discussion of the figures must, of necessity, be somewhat tentative.

As they stand, the data suggest that Italy is by far the largest spender in absolute terms and Ireland in relative terms – though the Irish figures are in fact national rather than purely regional, as a consequence of the fact that all of Ireland is viewed as a problem region for EEC regional policy purposes. Elsewhere, expenditure lies between ¼ and ½ per cent of total public spending. Dividing expenditure by the population of the standard recipient regions produces three clear groups. At the top, with average regional incentive expenditure per head in 1979 of over $100, are the whole of Ireland (both North and South) and the Mezzogiorno, generally recognized to be the three worst-off parts of the EEC. Next comes a middle group consisting of the German, British, Belgian, and Dutch problem regions with expenditure per head of $40 to $50. Finally, the French and Danish figures bring up the rear.

Although regional incentive expenditure showed no real signs of decline towards the end of the 1970s (except in the United Kingdom), regional policy certainly suffered in other respects. Increasing pressure was, for instance, brought to bear for the abandonment or relaxation of disincentive policies. The conditions under which such policies can best operate no longer prevailed. Generally high levels of unemployment and problems in the major cities in the prosperous regions removed the rationale for this type of policy, while a lower volume of mobile investment reduced the potential for controls to have a positive impact. Under such conditions, the danger of disincentive policies was that projects discouraged from locating in prosperous areas would be abandoned rather than relocated elsewhere. As a result, disincentive measures were considerably relaxed in terms of their exemption limits, their geographic coverage, and the proportion of applications refused. By the late 1970s, however, only one disincentive policy, the British Office Development Permit, had been abolished, although the others were largely dormant.

At the same time as control policy became ineffective, government office dispersal met with increasing opposition, while fiscal incentives 'lost their bite' due to the generally lower levels of taxable profits in many countries. Most important, however, there was a growth of micro-policy nationally which served to cut into the advantage offered by regional aid. Some of these micro-policies aimed to generate economic activity throughout the country (for instance, the WIR scheme introduced in the Netherlands in May 1978[16]); some attempted

[16] The WIR (*Wet Investeringsrekening*) or Investment Account Scheme is an auto-

to help sectors experiencing particular difficulties (aids to the steel industry, to shipbuilding, and to textiles could be found in most European countries); and some tried to solve spatial problems other than those found in the traditionally designated problem regions (inner city problems in the United Kingdom, for example).

But whatever their aim, these policies, as mentioned earlier, made serious inroads into the policy differential in favour of the problem regions. They meant that although regional policy (and in particular regional incentive policy) had not changed significantly during the third policy phase (except in the United Kingdom), there had been a definite lowering of regional policy in the national list of priorities. More and more there was a questioning of the role regional policy had to play under current (and future) economic conditions.

III. Policy Effects[17]

Until the mid-1970s there was little study of the effects of regional policy in the sense of separating out and quantifying the impact of policy from those other forces acting on the performance of the assisted areas. Rather, the majority of studies either discussed the amount of, say, employment associated with (as opposed to induced by) regional measures, or were of the 'micro', questionnaire nature, whereby, for example, firms were asked to define and rank the various factors, including policy, which influenced their decision to move into the assisted areas. The lack of evaluation research can be attributed to a number of factors. First, as noted in the previous section, policy only became active in the 1960s and, for most of that decade, its justification was 'self-evident'. Second, there was no appropriate statistical base for evaluation studies, particularly those involving time-series analysis. Finally, an appropriate analytical framework for evaluation was slow in developing, related, amongst other things, to the late emergence of economic as opposed to social and political justifications for policy. Even in the United Kingdom, with its long academic tradition of regional studies and with its very active and long-standing policy, there was virtually no evaluation work, leading to a comment by the 1972 House of Commons Expenditure Committee which, in fact, sums up well the position at that time throughout Europe. 'There must be few areas of government expenditure in which so much is spent but so little known about the success of the policy. The most our witnesses could say was that . . . the situation was better than it would have been without the incentives and controls of some sort of regional policy.

---

matic, item-related aid covering almost all types of fixed investment and taken in the form of reduced tax payments when profits are made and negative tax payments when there are losses (or insufficient profits). It consists of a basic (national) premium plus (as at January 1981) six additional premiums – a small-scale allowance, a large project allowance, a physical planning allowance, an environmental allowance, an energy-saving allowance, and a special regional allowance. For more details on this last allowance and on other regional incentive schemes, see D.M. Yuill and K.J. Allen (eds.), *European Regional Incentives 1981*, Glasgow 1981.

[17] The evaluation research cited in the bibliography has been of considerable assistance in the preparation of this section.

Yet no one could say whether this effect was a major or a minor one.'[18] In the later 1970s, the situation, of course, changed markedly. In particular, the environment in which policy had to operate became more hostile, making policy evaluation something of a necessity. At the same time, data availability had improved so that meaningful evaluation had become possible.

It is fitting to begin an examination of evaluation studies with the United Kingdom, since it was here (goaded, perhaps, by the observations of the Expenditure Committee) that much of the initial progress was made in the application of techniques to isolate and measure the impact of regional policy. Much of the pioneering work in this field was done by Moore and Rhodes.[19] Their basic approach, and the approach subsequently adopted by a number of other researchers both in the United Kingdom and elsewhere in Europe, involved identifying a hypothetical 'policy-off' position (i.e. the situation which would have occurred in the absence of regional policy) and then attributing the difference between this position and the actual 'policy-on' position to policy itself. A key aspect of this approach is obviously identifying how the variable under study (normally employment, but also investment and the movement of firms) would have behaved under the assumption that there had been no regional policy. Though the techniques which allow such estimates to be made are inevitably imperfect and any results obtained must be treated with caution, some confidence can be expressed in many of the findings, in so far as results from a variety of approaches have tended to display a considerable degree of harmony.

In Great Britain, for example, there is general agreement that policy as a whole, as well as each of its major instruments, has been effective in terms of stimulating employment, investment, and the movement of firms into the assisted areas. The seminal study by Moore and Rhodes[20] focused on the effect of policy on employment using a 'shift–share' approach. The authors estimated that some 150,000 manufacturing jobs (12 per cent of employment in this sector) could be directly attributed to the operation of regional policy in the 1963–71 period, and that, after allowing for multiplier and other effects, a total of 220,000 jobs were created by policy in this period. A later study,[21] covering the 1960–76 period, identified a *direct* policy effect of 282,000 jobs (and a *total* policy effect of 540,000 jobs), but with a tailing off in the later years — only 17,000 jobs per annum being created in the 1972–6 period compared with 26,000 jobs per annum from 1968 to 1971. This reduction in the impact of policy was attributed in part to a weakening of policy and the secular decline of manufacturing industry. Another study,[22] using an analysis of variance approach, estimated a policy effect of around 100,000 jobs for the 1963–71 period — a result not too dissimilar from the 150,000 noted above once account is taken of

[18] House of Commons Expenditure Committee, *Regional Development Incentives: Report* (HC 85), HMSO, London 1973, para. 116.

[19] B.C. Moore and J. Rhodes, 'Evaluating the Effects of British Regional Economic Policy', *Economic Journal*, March 1973.

[20] Ibid.

[21] B.C. Moore, J. Rhodes, and P. Tyler, 'The Impact of Regional Policy in the 1970s', *Centre for Environmental Studies Review*, Vol. 1, 1978.

[22] T.W. Buck and M.H. Atkins, 'The Impact of British Regional Policies on Employment Growth', *Oxford Economic Papers*, March 1976.

differences in coverage and comprehensiveness. However, not only was the statistical significance of many of the components disappointing, but, in contrast to other studies, it was found that the impact of policy deteriorated in the 1967–71 period despite the fact that policy was more active then than in the preceding years.

Similarly, substantial policy effects have also been found on investment. Moore and Rhodes,[23] again using shift-share, estimated that actual investment in the Development Areas was, by 1970, 30 per cent above what it would have been had policy remained passive – suggesting extra investment of between £300 million and £400 million ($720 to $960 million). A similar study for Scotland[24] concluded that regional policy generated £220 million ($600 million) of investment between 1960 and 1971, amounting to some 13 per cent of total investment in Scotland over this period. Other studies have revealed an investment shift towards the Development Areas. One study suggests a substantial switch equal to about 12 per cent of the national investment of an average industry,[25] while another detects a shift of over 7 per cent to the Development Areas by 1975.[26] This latter study not only attributes an increase of between 4 and 8 per cent in total United Kingdom investment to regional policy, but also shows that the trend in the policy effect on investment has been maintained into the 1970s, unlike that noted for employment.

The third main focus of British evaluation studies has been on the movement of firms, mainly through the use of regression analysis. One study[27] suggested that 84 to 87 per cent (943 to 978) of all moves into the Development Areas in the 1960–71 period were due to regional policy, and, after adjusting for the number of years any given policy measure was in operation during the study period, attributed 45 to 46 moves per annum to IDC control, 36 to investment incentives, 26 to 40 to the Regional Employment Premium, and some 13 to 15 moves to non-policy factors. An alternative approach,[28] which separated out the *generation* of movement from the *share* going to the Development Areas, found a much lower policy impact – with policy inducing around 50 per cent of the moves into the Development Areas over the 1961–71 period, some 40 per cent of all the moves taking place. The major role of IDC control and investment incentives in diverting firms to the Development Areas was again confirmed, but doubt was cast on the effectiveness of the Regional Employment Premium.

As in Great Britain, studies of the effects of regional policy in the Netherlands are in broad agreement that policy has been effective. Studies using the

[23] Moore and Rhodes, 'Evaluating the Effects'.

[24] H.M. Begg, C.M. Lythe, and D.R. McDonald, 'The Impact of Regional Policy on Manufacturing Investment: Scotland 1960–1971', *Urban Studies*, June 1976.

[25] This unpublished study, by Gleed and Lund, is discussed in B. Ashcroft, 'The Evaluation of Regional Economic Policy: The Case of the United Kingdom', in K.J. Allen, *Balanced National Growth*, Lexington 1979, p. 269.

[26] R.D. Rees and R.H.C. Miall, 'The Effects of Regional Policy on Manufacturing Investment and Capital Stock within the UK', *Government Economic Service Working Paper* No. 26, HMSO, London 1979.

[27] B.C. Moore and J. Rhodes, 'Regional Economic Policy and the Movement of Manufacturing Firms to Development Areas', *Economica*, February 1976.

[28] B. Ashcroft and J. Taylor, 'The Movement of Manufacturing Industry and the Effect of Regional Policy', *Oxford Economic Papers*, March 1977.

regression residual[29] to identify the policy effect on employment suggested that during the 1950s and 1960s regional policy could tentatively be regarded as having been effective in roughly half of the Dutch assisted areas, while another employment-based study,[30] focusing on the Northern Development Area (the main assisted area), estimated that policy created 25,000 jobs in the 1960-7 period, equivalent to 42 per cent of the net increase in employment in this area. For investment, the investment-distribution component of a sixty-three-equation regional economic model was used to assess the impact of regional capital grants and it was found that these were responsible for 17 per cent of total investment in the Northern Development Area in the period 1960 to 1974.[31] It was felt, however, that the relative effectiveness of regional grants had declined in the 1970s, due in particular to higher unemployment in the west of the country. The concluding section returns to the effectiveness of regional policy in periods of high national unemployment.

In Germany, the pattern of results, at least for investment, does not suggest that policy has had a very significant effect. Two studies,[32] for example, conclude that while investment incentives did have an overall positive effect on investment in the assisted areas, the total investment induced by policy over the 1969-73 period was not much higher than the amount of the subsidy. Similarly, another study[33] where regional incentives entered the regression model in different forms (e.g. as a dummy variable or measured according to their volume) found a significant policy effect on investment in only one sector. However, in contrast to these results, a study of the employment effects of regional policy[34] suggested that policy induced between 57,000 and 110,000 manufacturing jobs in the assisted areas in the 1971-3 period.

Finally, in Italy, a study combining shift-share and regression modelling found a substantial employment effect.[35] For the Mezzogiorno, it was estimated that regional investment incentives generated between 79,000 and 124,000 manufacturing jobs over the 1953-71 period. It was further estimated that some 13 per cent of manufacturing employment in the Mezzogiorno in 1971 could be attributed to the impact of regional investment incentives.

That the various studies mentioned above have generally shown regional policy

[29] N.D. Vanhove, 'De doelmatigheid van het regionaleconomisch beleid in Nederland' (The Efficiency of Regional Economic Policy in the Netherlands), Ph.D. Dissertation, Ned. Economische Hogeschool, 1961; J.J. van Duijn, 'De doelmatigheid van het regionaleconomisch beleid in Nederland in de jahren zestig' (The Efficiency of Regional Economic Policy in the Netherlands in the 1970s), Tijdschrift voor Economisch en Sociale Geografie, 1975.

[30] J. Paelinck, Hoe doelmatig kan regionaal en sectoraal beleid zijn? (How Effective can Regional and Sectoral Policy be?), Leiden 1973.

[31] A van Delff, B.A. van Hamel, and H. Hetson, 'Een multi-regionaal model voor Nederland', (A Multi-Regional Model for the Netherlands), Centraal Planbureau Occasional Papers, No. 13, 1977.

[32] H.M. Bölting, 'Wirkungsanalyse der Instrumente der regionalen Wirtschaftspolitik', Beiträge zum Siedlungs- und Wohnungswesen und zur Raumplanung, 1976; E. Recker, 'Erfolgskontrolle regionaler Aktionsprogramme durch Indikatoren', Forschung zur Raumentwicklung, 1977.

[33] W. Erfeld, 'Determinanten der regionalen Investitionstätigkeit in der Bundesrepublik Deutschland', Dissertation, Münster, 1979.

[34] Recker, 'Erfolgskontrolle'.

[35] A. Del Monte, Politica regionale e sviluppo economico, Milan 1977.

to have had a significant positive effect is hardly surprising. Most relate, after all, to the period when regional policy was at its most active and when external forces, in particular tight labour market conditions in the more prosperous regions, were reinforcing the effectiveness of policy. In this regard, it is interesting to note that the most up-to-date results tend to show a weakening policy impact.

Conclusions

This chapter has identified three broad phases of regional policy in Europe in the post-war period. In the first phase, lasting until the second half of the 1950s, there was virtually no regional policy in operation and there was no attempt to evaluate what policy there was. This was not, however, surprising given the emphasis throughout Europe on national recovery and reconstruction, and the feeling that any regional problems that existed were simply a short-run result of the recovery and reconstruction process.

In the second phase, covering approximately the period 1960 to 1973, regional problems became more prominent. This was partly because the problem itself intensified, either because of strong economic forces which tended to concentrate activity in richer areas (e.g. in Italy), or following substantial downturns in a number of key traditional industries like shipbuilding, mining, and textiles (e.g. in the United Kingdom). But it was also due to the prevailing climate of buoyant national economic growth which allowed and indeed encouraged greater concern about the problem of regional disparities. The consequence was that throughout this second phase there was a major interest in and growth of regional policy, and especially regional incentive policy. Policy evaluation remained rare, however, and indeed it was only towards the end of this phase that the first tentative attempts at evaluation took place.

In the third phase, from the oil crisis to the end of the period under review, there was a noticeable change in the environment in which policy operated. Unemployment became a national rather than simply a regional problem and was accompanied by high levels of inflation and sluggish economic growth. As a result, specifically regional problems and policies became of less importance, although expenditure on regional policy remained historically high, major cutbacks occurring only in the United Kingdom. At the same time, interest in policy evaluation grew markedly. It is thanks to this increased work on the impact of policy that some tentative conclusions can be ventured on the effects of government intervention in this area. Very broadly, most of the available evidence suggests that policy action has had a measurable and positive impact on problem regions. Not only have income differentials between regions been reduced somewhat through the period due to migration and the equalizing role of government expenditure and taxation flows, but investment and employment have also risen in underprivileged areas, above the levels they would otherwise have reached, because of specific policy measures designed to stimulate activity there. That results have not, perhaps, been as large as might *ex ante* have been hoped for, particularly for unemployment,[36] may partly stem from

---

[36] It should be noted that if the regional policy effect on unemployment is examined,

the strength of the centripetal forces which were at work in pulling industry towards the richer regions of a country (and, increasingly, of Europe). But partly, also, the successes of policies have been impaired by the general deterioration in the macroeconomic climate that intervened after the oil crisis. Indeed, as was noted in the previous section, empirical work has tended to suggest that, after the heyday of the 1960s, the impact of policies weakened somewhat. In view of this, there must be some concern about the justification for regional policy under the foreseeable economic conditions of the 1980s. Is regional policy still worth while?

During the second policy phase there were three clear justifications for regional policy in general and for a policy of taking the 'work to the workers' in particular – social, political, and economic. The first recognized the many social problems which can be created by massive migratory movements and by the selective nature of migration. Moreover, it reflected the desire to preserve regional cultures and identities, and stressed the need for equity between regions as well as between individuals. The political justification pointed to the serious political consequences which can arise if no response is made to significant economic disparities between regions. The movements for greater autonomy and even separation in France, the United Kingdom, Belgium, and Spain are clear examples of the inherent political dangers of spatial grievances. The economic justification emphasized the misallocation and under-utilization of resources which would occur in the absence of policy. On the one hand, policy allowed resources in problem regions, and especially human capital resources, to be utilized, which might otherwise remain redundant; and on the other, it helped take the economic 'heat' out of the more pressured parts of the country and thus permitted the national economy to be run at a higher level of demand pressures than would otherwise have been the case. Since in addition to these general justifications for policy there were more specific justifications in particular countries (for example, military considerations, and especially the desire to avoid the depopulation of sensitive border areas in Germany and Norway, and regional planning priorities in the Netherlands) the overall case for policy was both strong and clear.

Under the economic conditions pertaining since 1973, some of the above justifications have undoubtedly been weakened. In particular, the economic justifications for policy came under considerable pressure. While, in the 1960s, regional policy operated to complement market forces, the pursuit of an active policy under conditions of low rates of investment and growth, high levels of unemployment, and a relative and often absolute decline in the manufacturing sector has been thought by some to be the equivalent of 'pushing on a string'. Not only have low levels of economic growth and high rates of unemployment nationally shifted the attention of policy-makers towards the *level* of economic activity rather than its spatial distribution, but, in the face of the problems

---

an effective policy and little change in unemployment can be entirely compatible. Thus, while regional policy influences the demand for labour by creating or maintaining jobs, it is also likely that policy will add to the regional supply of labour in terms of higher activity rates and lower out-migration. Indeed, some researchers (e.g. Moore and Rhodes) suggest that the major effect of regional policy is in reducing 'forced' out-migration.

confronting the manufacturing sector – the prime target of regional policy effort up until now – questions have been raised about the potential of policy both to attract industry to the problem regions and to encourage the expansion of the firms already there. In a situation where regional problems are falling in the hierarchy of national policy priorities and where there are doubts about the potential effectiveness of policy, does regional policy have a role to play in the 1980s?

While the economic justification for policy propounded in the 1960s has certainly become less convincing, an economic case for policy can still be made based on the differing opportunity costs of labour (shadow wage rates) in the problem and non-problem regions. Moreover, the social and, particularly, political justifications remain strong. Regional aspirations, fired during the 1960s, are still at a high level in many European countries. Even more important, however, as far as the case for policy is concerned, are a number of emerging trends which suggest a continuing need for regional policy in the 1980s.

It can, for example, be argued that if further steps are taken within the EEC along the road to a common European currency, then there will be an obvious need for policy. Indeed, unless policy is strengthened so as to allow regions and countries to be compensated for the absence of any exchange rate mechanism it is difficult to imagine much progress towards economic and monetary union being made. A further justification for policy lies in the fact that the problems facing the depressed regions are likely to increase in future years, given their peripheral location *vis-à-vis* the main European countries and the significance of this in an era of high transport and energy costs. But perhaps the most significant argument rests on changes which are likely to be felt in the problem regions over the 1980s as a result of movements in the international division of labour. As low labour-cost countries become industrialized, the European economies will have to keep upgrading their technology and human capital if they are to maintain their comparative advantage and competitive position. However, if this strategy is followed, the likelihood is that the more prosperous regions will adapt most readily, in view of their already significant (and growing) functional and qualitative superiority. But not only do the traditional problem regions have less potential to increase the technological and human capital inputs of their products, they also are the regions most likely to be damaged by increased competition from the developing world, since a major feature of many of them is their concentration on routine production processes and the production of goods already at a mature stage in the product life cycle. In short, the traditional problem regions are likely to lose out, both to the more prosperous parts of their own countries, and to the newly industrializing countries, if no corrective action is taken.

Appendix: Sources of Regional GDP and Unemployment Data

A variety of private and official, national, and international sources was used to construct Tables 14.1, 14.2, 14.5, and Fig. 14.1. This inevitably means that (as already mentioned in the text) many of the figures shown are not strictly comparable across countries, a problem which is particularly acute for the unemployment data. The major common sources that were used were three EEC publications providing reasonably homogeneous statistics for member countries: CEE, *Statistiques régionales, 1972*; Eurostat, *Regional Statistics, 1970–1977*; and EEC *The Regions of Europe*, Luxembourg 1981. The following sources were also used:

Germany: Statistisches Bundesamt, *Statistisches Jahrbuch, 1967* and *1980*.
Italy: ISTAT, *Annuario di statistiche del lavoro, 1971*, and *Bollettino mensile di statistica*, June 1980.
United Kingdom: CSO, *Regional Statistics, 1975, 1979*, and *1980*; W. Molle, *Regional Disparity and Economic Development in the European Community*, London 1980.
Spain: Instituto nacional de estadística, *Annuario estadístico de España 1977* and *1979*; Banco de Bilbao, *Renta nacional de España y su distributión provincial, 1955–1975*, Bilbao 1978.
Austria: Österreichisches statistisches Zentralamt, *Statistisches Jahrbuch, 1976* and *1979*; H. Seidel, F. Butschek, and A. Kausel, *Die regionale Dynamik der österreichischen Wirtschaft*, WIFO, Vienna 1966; WIFO internal estimates.
Belgium: Institut national de statistique, *Annuaire de statistiques régionales, 1979*.
Finland: Central Statistical Office of Finland, *Statistical Yearbook of Finland, 1979*; Planning Division, Ministry of Labour, *Labour Report, 1978–4*.
Greece: National Statistical Service of Greece, *Statistical Yearbook of Greece, 1978*; C.L. Papageorgiou, *Regional Employment in Greece*, National Centre of Social Research, Athens 1973.
Ireland: EEC, *Regional Development Programme – Ireland 1977–1980*, Brussels 1978.
Norway: Statistik Sentralbyrå, *National Accounts by County, 1973*, and *Arbeidsmarkedstatistikk, 1978*.
Portugal: OECD, *Regional Problems and Policies in Portugal*, Paris 1979; M.M. Lobo da Conceiçao, 'Consideraçoes sobre o projecto "Repartiçao regional do producto: ensaio para 1970"', Instituto nacional de estatistica, *Estudos 48*, 1975.
Sweden: Statistika Centralbyrån, *Statistik årsbok, 1979*, and *Arbetskraftsunderökningarna, 1977*.
Switzerland: Union Bank of Switzerland, *Switzerland in Figures, 1978*.

Bibliography

There have, over the years, been a considerable number of international studies on regional problems and policies in Europe. Amongst these, one would mention K.J. Allen *et al.*, *Regional Incentives in the European Community: A Comparative Study*, Brussels 1979; R. Wettmann and W. Nicol, *Deglomeration Policies in the European Community: A Comparative Study*, Brussels 1981; D.M. Yuill, K.J. Allen, and C.J. Hull (eds.), *Regional Policy in the European Community*, London 1980; W. Molle, *Regional Disparity and Economic Development in the European Community*, London 1980; N. Vanhove and L.H. Klaassen, *Regional Policy: A European Approach*, London 1980; A.J. Brown and E.M. Burrows, *Regional Economic Problems: Comparative Experiences of Some Market Economies*, London 1977; OECD, *Regional Problems and Policies in OECD Countries*, Paris 1976; J.L. Sundquist, *Dispersing Population: What America can Learn from Europe*, Washington 1975; H.D. Clout (ed.), *Regional Development in Western Europe*, London 1975; N.M. Hansen (ed.), *Public Policy and Regional Economic Development*, Cambridge,

Mass. 1974. The first two of these works are published as part of the European Commission's Regional Policy Series, a series containing a number of relevant publications. Also of interest is the OECD series on Regional Development Policies, which contains not only individual country studies but also more general cross-country overviews.

At the national level, a vast amount has been written on regional problems and policies in most European countries. The most important references can be found in a set of national bibliographies compiled under a common format and recently published: see K.J. Allen (general editor), *Regional Problems and Policies in the European Community: A Bibliography*, London 1978.

Turning from publications on regional problems and policies generally to evaluation research, most are of British origin (see Section III for a review of individual country studies). Extremely useful overviews of British research are B. Ashcroft, 'The Evaluation of Regional Economic Policy: The Case of the United Kingdom', in K.J. Allen (ed.), *Balanced National Growth*, Lexington 1979, and J. Marquand, 'Measuring the Effects and Costs of Regional Incentives', *Government Economic Service Working Paper*, No. 32, HMSO, London 1980. At the international level, the following overview reports are available: B. Ashcroft, 'The Evaluation of Regional Policy in Europe: A Survey and Critique', *Studies in Public Policy*, No. 68, Centre for the Study of Public Policy, Glasgow 1980; W. Nicol, 'An Appreciation of Regional Policy Evaluation Studies: A Comparative Study', International Institute of Management, Wissenschaftszentrum, Berlin 1980.

PART III

COUNTRY EXPERIENCE

15

France*

CHRISTIAN SAUTTER**

Introduction

The French economy is full of paradoxes. At the beginning of the post-war period, the country was beset with numerous handicaps — in particular, the difficult legacy of a very poor industrial and demographic performance between the wars and of a society troubled by repeated crises. Yet despite such obstacles, growth was rapid (4.7 per cent per annum from 1952 to 1979) (Table 15.1), and

TABLE 15.1. *Longer-term trends*

	1952–79	1952–59	1959–69	1969–73	1973–79
	average annual percentage changes				
GDP	4.7	4.2	5.7	5.6	3.0
Inflation[a]	5.5	3.3	3.9	6.2	10.7
Employment	0.4	−0.2	0.7	0.9	0.3
	1952–79	1952–59	1960–69	1970–73	1974–79
	percentages				
Investment ratio[b]	(21.8)	(16.8)	22.2	24.3	22.5
Unemployment rate[c]	2.6	2.0	1.8	2.6	4.5
	$ million, annual averages				
Current balance	−645[d]	(67)[e]	−288	45	−1,699

[a] Consumer prices
[b] Gross fixed investment in per cent of GDP at constant prices
[c] In per cent of the labour force
[d] 1960–79
[e] With non-Franc Area countries

Sources: OECD, *National Accounts of OECD Countries, 1950–1979*; OECD, *Manpower Statistics, 1950–1962*; OECD, *Labour Force Statistics* (various issues); OECD, *Economic Outlook*, July 1971; OECD, *Balance of Payments Statistics, 1950–1961* and *1960–1977*: J.-J. Carré, P. Dubois, and E. Malinvaud, *French Economic Growth*, Oxford 1976; C. Sorrentino, 'Methodological and Conceptual Problems in Measuring Unemployment in OECD Countries', *mimeo*, OECD, Paris 1976.

what is more, accelerating and becoming steadier between the 1950s and the 1960s even though the reconstruction period had come to an end and protectionist barriers had been removed at a stroke in 1958. An annual growth

---

* As for other country chapters, editorial policy has imposed the use of internationally standardized statistics, which at times differ from national concepts and figures.

** Ecole des hautes études en sciences sociales, Paris and Centre d'études prospectives et d'information internationales (CEPII), Paris. The views expressed are those of the author and are not necessarily shared by the CEPII. This chapter was completed in January 1981.

rate of just over 4 per cent from 1952 to 1959 gave way to one of close to 6 per cent between 1959 and 1973. The first oil shock of 1973 was to put an end to this golden age of rapid growth in France and in other Western nations.

Inflation followed a somewhat different path to that of output. Price pressures were uneven in the first full decade of the period – after rising by 15 per cent per annum between 1950 and 1952, the consumer price index was nearly stable for the five years to 1957, only to rise by over 20 per cent in 1958-9 in the wake of two substantial devaluations. Trends through much of the 1960s were steadier, but 1968 clearly marked a turning-point. From then on inflation rose in stages. Each new external shock was to take it to a higher level, and the policy of stabilization contained in the 1976 Barre Plan did not bring about any clear deceleration.

These growth and inflation trends were largely the result of changing economic behaviour and economic policies. The main dates which mark the post-war period are 1945, 1958, 1968, 1973, and 1976. The year 1945 and those immediately after it were crucial. This period saw a marked change in attitudes, made possible by the rise of a new generation of entrepreneurs, civil servants, and trade unionists (many stemming from the resistance movement), whose forward-looking outlook on both social and economic matters stood in sharp contrast to the immobility and defeatism of much of the interwar period. It was in the years 1945-7 that, paradoxically, a hitherto profoundly divided society forged a particularly strongly held consensus which was to last through to the late 1970s. According to this consensus view, which was more often implicit than not, the growth of national income reduced social tensions. It was understood that in a non-zero sum game all players could expect to make a gain without jeopardizing their previously acquired positions. The lasting nature of this belief is illustrated by the country's reactions when serious difficulties arose in 1968 – the almost unanimous reflex was to go for 'Japanese-style' growth. Even after the oil crisis of 1973, the Seventh Plan (1976-80) advocated rapid growth to prevent unemployment, but also to keep inflation from rising.

Sapped by colonial wars and a number of imbalances, the Fourth Republic disappeared in 1958. That year saw the implementation of the Rueff Plan, which was to change profoundly the direction of the French economy – in particular, the widespread indexation of most forms of revenue on prices was abolished and the protectionist barriers surrounding the economy were dismantled. The plan was to usher in what then appeared as a very favourable period (1959-67). On the political side, the Algerian war was brought to an end in 1962. On the economic side, the growth of investment gathered momentum, and for the first time since the war there was a rise in the labour supply. The growth of output thus accelerated while inflation was neither too rapid nor too persistent, despite the 1957-8 devaluations and the surge in demand pressures which followed the repatriation of French nationals from Algeria. Though a stabilization plan had to be imposed in 1963, it operated in the desired manner – its effects were largely concentrated on prices rather than on quantities.

This period was interrupted by the *événements* of 1968. The disturbances were triggered off by increased numbers of students, born in the immediate post-war years, entering the rigid university structures of the day. The young workers belonging to this age-group were at the same time discovering income differentials and power structures developed during the 1950s, if not earlier. Economic progress and social immobility are not necessarily incompatible — indeed, the opposite may be true. In France as in other countries, for instance Japan, full employment and rapid increases in purchasing power during the 1960s had maintained an implicit consensus which prevented wider issues being raised, at least for a time. The crisis was defused by a few urgent social reforms (e.g. large increases in minimum wages and a university reform), and the economy entered a period of feverish growth greatly facilitated by another sharp devaluation in 1969 and accompanied by much higher inflation.

The oil shock of 1973 struck an economy in disequilibrium. The stagnation in the Western world which followed it did away with a condition vital to the pursuit of high domestic growth – that of rapidly growing world demand. Above all, the terms of trade shift implied that a newcomer (OPEC) could now lay claim to a share in national income, the distribution of which had been subject to increasing tensions since 1968. After initial policy hesitations, which led to stop–go developments, a new approach was felt to be essential. This need was to be fulfilled by the 1976 Barre Plan. Following a long period in which short-run demand management had dominated economic policy, this plan put forward a set of medium- rather than short-term aims. The plan's main object was to adapt the French economy to a new world of expensive oil, increased competition, and slower growth. Its disappointing outcome leads one to ask whether it was ever directed at, or capable of dealing with, the imbalances revealed and subsequently heightened by the 1968 crisis.

Though growth appeared exceptionally steady (at least between 1959 and 1973), the economy was transformed through a series of qualitative leaps from one decisive threshold to the next. Between 1952 and 1979 real GDP increased 3½ times, the share of agriculture in total employment fell from nearly 30 to less than 10 per cent, and the economy was opened up to the outside world (the share of foreign trade in GDP rising from some 13 to 21 per cent in current prices and by more in constant prices). In one generation the French economic horizon, hitherto limited to the colonial empire, widened to include Europe and eventually the world. The major role in these changes was probably played by those in the private (corporate) sector, whose decisions determined the trend of investment, prices, wages, or productivity. Yet special emphasis must also be put on the role of the state in its triple function as a producer (the nationalized sector was both large and dynamic throughout the period), as a redistributor of income, and as a regulator of economic activity.

The chapter's first section covers the period 1945–68 and deals mainly with the reasons for the sudden leap which took place after the liberation, for the acceleration which occurred after 1959, and for the steadiness of growth in the 1960s. The second section covers the period 1968–1979. It discusses first the growing tensions surrounding the distribution of national income and then the problems posed by the first oil shock. It concludes with a brief comparison between the Barre Plan of 1976 and the Rueff Plan of 1958, since, to some extent at least, the situation of the mid-1970s had similarities with that of 1957-8 — major economic and social reforms were necessary on both occasions in order to move on to a new and different growth path.

In France, and probably elsewhere too, it would seem impossible to make a purely economic analysis of post-war growth which would provide a full account for why growth was rapid at the outset and why it eventually slowed down. Important social and political events occurred at each major turning-point which economists cannot explain, but which they cannot ignore either. It is not by accident that the basic work by Carré, Dubois, and Malinvaud on French economic growth ends with a 'questionnaire to our sociologist colleagues'.[1] The essay character of the pages that follow is explained both by the limits of economic analysis and the brevity of this chapter.

I. From 1945 to the Social Crisis of 1968

Growth and transformation

The French growth rate from 1952 to 1973 seems exceptional when compared with that of most other Western countries, or with that recorded in the interwar period, the more so if one bears in mind the unfavourable demographic conditions which prevailed until the early 1960s.

Between 1952 and 1973[2] GDP grew at an annual average rate of 5.2 per cent – a performance below that of Japan (9.6 per cent over the same period), but close to those of Germany and Italy (5.7 and 5.4 per cent respectively), and well ahead of the 3.5 per cent recorded by the United States and the 3.1 per cent of the United Kingdom. And unlike Germany or Italy, French growth actually accelerated in the second half of the period (Table 1.6).

The contrast with earlier periods is particularly striking. Between the beginning of the century and the 1929 peak, French growth, at 1.6 per cent per annum, had been sluggish relative not only to that of the United States (3.5 per cent), but also to those of Italy and Germany (2.2 and 2.0 per cent respectively). Among the major countries, only the United Kingdom grew more slowly in this period (1.1 per cent).[3] In the interwar years France was similarly one of the slowest-growing countries in Europe. It is true that during the 1920s, which included a natural catch-up following the war, growth reached nearly 5 per cent per annum, but then output fell by 11 per cent in the depression (1929–32) and did not reach its 1929 level till ten years later.

This acceleration is the more striking since, unlike West Germany, France did not initially have the advantage of an abundant and skilled labour force. Between 1946 and 1962, the active population grew very slowly (0.1 per cent per annum), mainly a reflection of the demographic stagnation of the interwar period. Though net immigration was substantial, particularly from 1955 onwards, it did no more than compensate for the effects of falling participation rates. The year 1962, however, marked a turning-point. In the following fifteen years the labour force grew at rates unprecedented since the beginning of the century (nearly 3

---

[1] J.-J. Carré, P. Dubois, and E. Malinvaud, *French Economic Growth*, Oxford 1976.

[2] Growth was very rapid in the years 1946–52 (nearly 8 per cent per annum according to figures presented in A. Maddison, 'Phases of Capitalist Development', *Banca Nazionale del Lavoro Quarterly Review*, June 1977), but this largely reflected the reconstruction process.

[3] Data from Maddison, 'Phases of Development'.

million people or 0.8 per cent per annum).[4] The reasons for this sharp change in trend are to be found partly in a temporary acceleration due to the 1962 influx into the labour force of nearly 300,000 French nationals repatriated from Algeria, and, more importantly, in two longer-run phenomena — the generations born during the years of high birth rates after the war reached working age, while female activity rates, which had been falling for a century, began to pick up. From then on the available labour force increased rapidly despite falling participation rates among both the old and the young.

With rapid growth throughout the 1950s and the 1960s came major changes in the sectoral distribution of the labour force, in the weights of various industrial branches, in the structure of foreign trade, and, of course, in living conditions. French industry, in particular, saw changes of such a drastic nature as to merit the term transformation.

Despite the stagnation in overall employment, large-scale labour movements took place between sectors. There was, in particular, a very sizeable shift out of agriculture (1.8 million people from 1949 to 1962, or one-third of initial farm employment) which supplied the rising needs of the manufacturing sector (170,000), the construction sector (550,000), and above all, the tertiary sector (over 1 million). Employment growth in industry may have been relatively modest, but its reorientation from light industry towards the production of machinery and consumer durables was significant (Table 15.2). The textile, clothing, and leather industries lost a fifth of their labour force between 1952 and 1959, while the heterogenous group of mechanical and electrical industries increased its labour force by 15 per cent and the basic industries' sector by 6 per cent. These changes continued along the same lines during the 1960s and indeed also in the 1970s.

TABLE 15.2. *Industrial employment structure*[a]
(percentage shares in total)

	1952	1959	1966	1966[b]	1973[b]
Mining and public utilities	7.2	6.7	5.7	7.8	6.1
Food and beverages	11.4	11.8	11.0	9.0	8.3
Basic industries[c]	14.2	15.1	15.7	18.4	19.6
Mechanical and electrical industries[d]	27.2	31.3	34.3	35.3	39.3
Textiles, clothing, and leather	26.5	21.4	19.1	17.8	14.5
Wood, paper, and miscellaneous industries	13.5	13.5	14.2	11.7	12.2
Total (in thousands)	5,690	5,676	5,987	5,459	5,949

[a] Excluding construction
[b] Employees only
[c] Steel, non-ferrous metals, chemicals, and building materials
[d] Mechanical engineering, electrical engineering, and transport equipment
Sources: J.-J. Carré, P. Dubois, and E. Malinvaud, *French Economic Growth*, Oxford 1976; OECD, *Labour Force Statistics, 1965–1976*.

[4] F. Eymard-Duvernay, 'Combien d'actifs d'ici l'an 2000?', *Economie et statistique*, October 1979.

TABLE 15.3. *Foreign trade structure*
(percentage shares in total)

	1952–54	1958–60	1968–70	1977–79
Imports				
From the Franc Area	24.7	18.2	9.8	2.8
From the EEC	21.2	30.4	54.6	50.4
From other countries	54.1	51.4	35.6	46.8
Exports				
To the Franc Area	38.4	26.2	12.0	5.1
To the EEC	25.3	32.6	52.5	52.1
To other countries	36.3	41.2	35.5	42.8
Primary products	31.4	26.9	26.9	23.8
of which: Agricultural products[a]	12.9	12.7	16.3	14.5
Manufactures	68.6	73.1	73.0	76.2
of which: Chemicals[b]	7.7	8.5	10.4	11.6
Semi-manufactures[c]	33.6	31.1	22.1	19.1
Machinery and transport equipment[d]	17.5	24.0	31.3	36.3
Export performance[e]	8.9	8.9	8.4	10.0

[a] SITC 0+1
[b] SITC 5
[c] SITC 6–68
[d] SITC 7
[e] Share in the exports of manufactures of the 12 major exporting countries.
Sources: OEEC, *Statistical Bulletins, Foreign Trade, Series IV* and *Series B* (various issues);
OECD, *Statistics of Foreign Trade, Series A* and *Series B* (various issues); NIESR,
Economic Review (various issues).

Further evidence of the industrial transformation can be found in the geographical and commodity reorientation of trade flows (Table 15.3). Between the
early 1950s and the late 1970s, the weight of the Franc Area in French exports
declined from nearly 40 to barely 5 per cent, and from 25 to 3 per cent in imports — the countries of the EEC, with which France did less than one-quarter of
its trade in 1952-4, accounted for one-half by the late 1970s. There was a similar
sharp change in the commodity composition of trade. Agricultural products remained an important and relatively stable element of the country's exports,
but there were marked declines in the importance of other primary products and
semi-manufactures whose combined share over the 25 years fell from 52 to 28
per cent, while the proportion of exports of machinery and transport equipment
doubled. Interestingly, perhaps, this very pronounced transformation was
accompanied by great stability in export performance. France's share in the
manufactured exports of the twelve major exporting countries remained virtually
unchanged over a quarter of a century, in sharp contrast to what happened for
other major competitors — sharp losses in the United Kingdom and in the
United States, sharp gains in Germany, Italy, and, of course, Japan.

Inevitably, this transformation was accompanied by significant changes in
living conditions. The urban population increased from 59 per cent of the total
in 1954 to 70 per cent in 1968. Household consumption turned towards durables

and by the early 1970s the numbers of refrigerators, television sets, washing machines, and cars were nearing saturation level. The housing stock was increased and improved – of the 350,000 main dwellings built each year from 1962 to 1968, 200,000 were accounted for by the increase in the number of households and 150,000 replaced dwellings which had become uninhabitable. There was also a boom in purchases of holiday homes (from 450,000 in 1954 to 1.7 million in 1975). But the improvement in living standards did not do away with the inequality of income distribution any more than it soothed social tensions, as the events of 1968 were to show.

Changes in attitudes – 1945 to 1947

'It was obvious to everyone that France had emerged from the war seriously weakened. Less well known, or less willingly acknowledged, was the weakness from which she was already suffering when war broke out. This, no less than military or moral shortcomings, explained her sudden collapse . . . By 1938 the country was exhausted: it had lost a third of its investment capacity in a decade of crisis and social change.'[5] This was the picture of France as seen by Jean Monnet, which he divulged to a new generation of industrialists, trade unionists, and officials inflamed by the 'patriotic zeal of the liberation'. For a short while (1946–7) these new leaders worked together, not to rebuild the country as it had been but to modernize it. A major instrument of this task was the development of a plan which de Gaulle approved on 3 January 1946. The plan had four objectives – (a) to increase domestic production and foreign trade, particularly in those sectors in which France was already in a favourable position; (b) to increase productivity; (c) to ensure full employment; (d) to raise the standard of living and to improve living conditions.[6]

The major features of the First Plan (1947–52) were detailed investment and output programmes, which were largely achieved, for six basic priority sectors (coal, electricity, steel, cement, agricultural machinery, and transport) and a number of structural reforms. In the economic field these were the nationalization of the central bank and of the four major clearing banks, of public utilities, of coal-mining, and of the Renault factories. In the social sphere, the period saw the creation of the social security system and the setting-up of 'Enterprise Committees'.[7] The First Plan was followed by many others, but precise and rigid planning was discontinued, in favour of broader and increasingly vague targets which were only infrequently met.[8] Even in areas such as social infrastructure, for which the government was directly responsible, planned levels of expenditure were not always achieved because public investment turned out, in practice, to be the most flexible part of the budget and was consequently often changed for short-run demand management purposes. Shortfalls also occurred for the investment of public corporations or of sectors heavily dependent on government support, such as steel. As for private productive investment by firms

---

[5] J. Monnet, *Memoirs*, London 1978, pp. 232–3.

[6] Ibid., p. 240.

[7] These are advisory bodies with equal union and management representation.

[8] Carré *et al.*, *French Growth*, Ch. 14; P. Dubois (ed.), *La planification française en pratique*, Paris 1976.

less dependent on public aid, there is little evidence suggesting that it was directly influenced by the various plans, though indirect favourable effects may well have occurred.

But a discussion of French planning conducted in terms of achievements or shortfalls with respect to targeted levels misses what was probably the essential contribution, in particular of the early plans, to the resurgence of the country. The First Plan was more than a mere document outlining some hopes, or a collection of urgent investment programmes. It was a shared belief that growth, productivity, and the opening to the outside world would make possible a non-zero sum game for all. Though social tensions remained high in subsequent years, they worked themselves out in the sharing of the 'surplus' generated by growth. Both the major social partners were able to hold on to acquired advantages, while at the same time gaining increased spending-power or self-financing possibilities. What is more, the First Plan and those which followed made the idea of an opening to foreign competition acceptable to a country with deeply protectionist reflexes.

Thus, the 1945-7 period was of paramount importance for understanding the subsequent course of the French economy. During those years a change in attitudes was achieved which pulled the country out of the stagnation of the 1930s. Productivity and investment became positive notions because they promoted growth and growth itself was seen as mollifying social antagonisms. Indeed, this belief in the virtues of growth permeated French economic thinking even after the 1973 crisis. Both the preparatory work for the Seventh Plan (1976-80) and the joint electoral programme of the left-wing parties for the 1978 parliamentary elections were still influenced by hopes of rapid growth.

Changes in policies – the Rueff Plan of 1958

A second major turning-point in post-war economic history was the 1958 Rueff Plan[9], which was made possible by political changes and necessary by the inflationary and external difficulties the country was facing. Thus, the current account deficit in 1956-7 had averaged $1 billion (a very high figure for the time), while inflation in 1958 had accelerated to 15 per cent. Moreover, France had signed the 1957 Treaty of Rome which was to open its borders to what was feared would be an invasion of cheaper and better German industrial products. The plan, which was put into action at the very end of 1958, was inspired by an unswerving liberalism.

At home, a major aim was the abolition of a widespread system of indexation and subsidies. Thus, cross indexations were abolished (e.g. the indexation of agricultural on industrial prices), though direct indexations within a sector were to remain (e.g. farm rents remained indexed to the price of wheat and minimum wages to consumer prices). Drastic changes also took place in public sector transactions. Subsidies were cut sharply, with, as an inevitable consequence, a rapid rise in food and nationalized industries' prices. Cuts were also made in the welfare field, with declines in social transfers, family allowances, repayments of medical charges, and ex-servicemen's pensions. On the revenue side, corporate taxation was increased, but the effects of this measure were largely offset by

---

[9] A. de Lattre, *Politique économique de la France depuis 1945*, Paris 1966.

more generous depreciation allowances and, in late 1959, by the substitution of the old straight-line depreciation system with a system designed to encourage early depreciation.

Abroad, the aim was to put an end to growing balance of payments difficulties, which were occurring despite protection, and to take a gamble on the virtues of free trade in a stable and fast-growing world economy. A sharp devaluation (17.5 per cent) not only brought French prices into line with those of foreign competitors but provided French firms with a clear competitive advantage. This was felt necessary in view of the sudden opening of the economy which had been decided upon, and which implied a 90 per cent liberalization of trade accompanied by the return to convertibility with all the countries of Western Europe.

The effects of the Rueff Plan were deep and lasting. Its main results were a shift in income distribution from labour to capital and a shift of output from the economy's sheltered sectors towards manufacturing. The first effect was largely obtained thanks to near-stagnation in real wages in 1958-9. This stagnation did not result, however, from any slowdown in economic activity and concomitant rises in unemployment. On the contrary, growth accelerated and unemployment declined at least in 1959, but the cost of living was also deliberately and sharply increased. The absence of reaction on the part of trade unions is probably to be ascribed to the political context of the early days of the Fifth Republic.

The shift into the tradeable sector was made possible by devaluation. The latter was not considered merely as a measure imposed by outside circumstances and designed to eliminate a price gap built up over the preceding years. It was meant to be an 'offensive' devaluation which was expected to have structural effects.[10] It was 'offensive' because its aim was to give French industry a competitive advantage for some years to come. Its structural aspect was the increase in outlets which the gain in competitiveness was to provide (between 1959 and 1961 the surplus achieved on goods and services transactions with the rest of the world was close to 2 per cent of GDP). This increase in outlets mainly benefited the manufacturing sector and led to an investment boom in the years 1960-2 in exporting industries.[11] By 1963, the competitive advantage had disappeared because French inflation had been more rapid than that abroad. The economy in 1963, however, was very different from that of 1959. In the interim the size and productivity of its industry had been sharply increased by capitalizing on a transitory competitive advantage.

With the Rueff Plan, France entered a period of much more rapid and smooth growth as compared with the 1950s (Fig. 15.1). Both by historical and international standards, the steadiness of output trends was exceptional. Some of the more important reasons for this are to be found in the income formation process on the one hand and in the formulation of economic policies on the other. Throughout the 1960s and until the mid-1970s, demand management policies were always applied in a very gradual fashion. Despite continuing inflationary tendencies and the reappearance, after 1962, of threats to the balance of

---

[10] J. Mistral, 'Vingt ans de redéploiement du commerce extérieur', *Economie et statistique*, October 1975.

[11] Investment was also helped by the fiscal incentives which had been recently introduced.

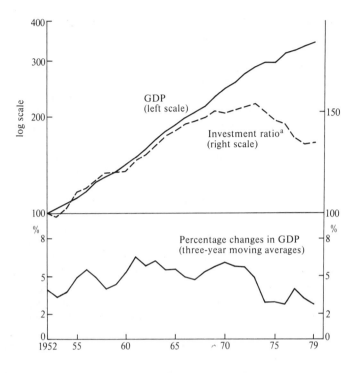

FIG. 15.1. *Output and investment trends, 1952–1973* (indice: 1952 = 100)
[a] Gross fixed investment in per cent of GDP at constant prices
Source: OECD, *National Accounts of OECD Countries, 1950–1979.*

payments, the government did not engage in stop-go policies. The September 1963 stabilization plan was moderate compared with the 1958 Rueff Plan or German and Italian policies in the mid-1960s. The whole period can be charac- terized as one of successful 'fine tuning' which accepted a moderate rate of in- flation, and, in 1969, a devaluation, as the price to pay for a continued low level of unemployment and a rapid rise in output.

At the same time, the development of labour's purchasing power was excep- tionally steady from 1959 onwards. Partly this was due to the relative steadiness in the distribution of primary incomes, to which a logical counterpart was the stability in the self-financing ratio of the corporate non-agricultural sector.[12] It was also partly due to the smooth and continuous growth in public sector trans- fers to households. As a result, private consumption and residential construction also rose steadily — both at the beginning and at the end of the period these two components represented two-thirds of total domestic demand.

On the supply side, regular increases in both domestic and foreign demand, continuing pressure on production costs, and the acceptance by wage-earners of the efforts to modernize provided three powerful reasons why companies

[12] OECD, *Economic Survey of France, 1975.*

committed themselves to a continued investment effort. Though, traditionally, investment is a relatively volatile element of demand, corporate sector gross fixed capital formation also grew very steadily between 1959 and 1973 — having accounted for 35 per cent of cyclical fluctuations from 1949 to 1962 it accounted for only 17 per cent from 1958 to 1975 (including therefore the 1974-5 recession).[13] Demand and supply thus grew regularly and simultaneously in a virtuous circle of steadily rising productivity and spending-power (which in France goes under the name of 'fordism'. The term comes from the pre-war motor magnate who, it is said, had decided to give his workers real wage increases so that they would increase their productivity ('taylorism') and could then buy the vehicles they had produced). Be this as it may, there is no doubt that in the most dynamic sectors of the French economy, the machinery and durable consumer goods industries, a process was at work in which these branches were creating their investment goods and their outlets at one and the same time. Mass production and mass consumption developed each other and pulled each other along.

The nature of the growth process

In trying to account for France's rapid growth from the end of the war to the late 1960s or early 1970s, the text has so far privileged an explanation which runs from changes in attitudes, in policies, and in expectations to changes in demand, particularly investment, which then call forth their own supply. Growth is thus led neither by a detailed planning policy nor by a spontaneous surge made possible by supply side factors. The role of policies was that of creating a favourable environment, in particular for the economy's tradeable sector. Though planning and industrial policies were at work through the period, their contribution is best seen not as achieving precise targets in priority sectors within manufacturing, but rather as creating conditions for rapid growth in the profits and investment of the manufacturing sector as a whole. As for supply factors, these are seen at best as having only played a permissive role.[14]

Yet an alternative explanation, stressing the importance of hidden labour reserves, could also be advanced. Having fallen behind other countries in the 1930s, it could be argued that France, not unlike Japan or Italy, for instance, embarked in the 1950s on a period of 'extensive' growth characterized by the use of unemployed or underemployed labour, a relatively moderate growth of productivity, and an even slower growth of real wages, wage claims being dampened by the presence of surplus labour. The existence of an abundant agricultural labour force after the war and the rapid rural exodus which followed might provide evidence supporting such an interpretation. It does not appear, however, that such a model is applicable to French post-war experience. The stagnation in industrial employment and the rundown of sectors employing

[13] J.M. Chanut and G. Laroque, 'Point de vue sur les fluctuations macroéconomiques de 1949 à 1975', *Economie et statistique*, June 1979.

[14] Very indirect evidence for this can be found in 'growth accounting' estimates made by E. Denison (*Why Growth Rates Differ*, Brookings Institution, Washington 1967) and Carré et al. (*French Growth*), which both suggest, once put on a comparable basis, that factor inputs can only account for some 50 per cent of the growth achieved by the economy over the periods 1950–62 and 1951–69 respectively.

unskilled labour (e.g. textiles, clothing, or leather) have already been dealt with. It is true that industries requiring a skilled labour force, such as machinery and consumer durables, increased their employment quite sharply (2 per cent per annum from 1952 to 1966); and that the length of the working week remained virtually stable and at a high level (−0.2 per cent per annum from 1952 to 1966). But the increase in hourly productivity in these same sectors was rapid (3.9 per cent per annum), led no doubt by a fast growth in fixed capital investment (5.6 per cent per annum).

Generally, the capital-intensive nature of growth is underlined by the priority given to productivity and capital formation in the First Plan and by the high levels of investment throughout the 1950s. The investment effort was 'systematically higher than before the war, except for the three years 1929, 1930 and 1931. Over the whole period 1949–63 the average investment ratio was over 20 per cent whereas from 1896 to 1913 it was 14.9 per cent, and from 1922 to 1938 it was 16.1 per cent.'[15] The authors of this quotation, as well as pointing out the sheer size of the investment effort, insist upon the importance given to equipment as compared with building (an indicator that investment was concentrated on increasing productivity), and stress the effect that modernizing the capital stock must also have had on output per worker.

Lastly, the wage formation process during the 1950s and later does not follow the dualist model developed by Lewis.[16] There was no 'modern' sector on the one hand, with real wages following increases in productivity, and a 'traditional' sector on the other, in which wages were not based on performance in the sector, but on incomes in an agricultural sector with surplus labour. A striking fact which it is difficult to explain is the great stability of wage differentials by sector, sex, or qualification during the 1950s and 1960s.[17] Closer analysis shows that there is a gap between the high-wage unionized and concentrated industries, which seem little affected by the state of the labour market and play a leading role in wage negotiations, and low wages in non-unionized and dispersed sectors.[18] But the differences between the two are not sufficiently significant to allow the conclusion that one is in the presence of a dualist model of development.

This relative constancy of differentials was not the result of a 'ratchet effect' following the institution of a minimum wage in 1950. The latter barely kept in line with price increases, and fell relative to other incomes until 1968. In fact, the wage formation process before 1968 does not raise many difficult questions.[19] The elasticity of nominal wages with respect to consumer prices moved from 0.77 between 1947 and 1958 to 0.4 between 1959 and 1967, while the

[15] Carré et al.. French Growth, p. 117.

[16] W.A. Lewis, 'Development with Unlimited Supplies of Labour', Manchester School, May 1954.

[17] Carré et al., French Growth, pp. 421–30; INSEE, 'Fresque historique du système productif', Collections de l'INSEE, série E, No. 27, 1974; see also Ch. 7 above.

[18] J.J. Silvestre, 'La dynamique des salaires nominaux en France: étude sectorielle', Revue économique, May 1971.

[19] R. Boyer, 'Les salaires en longue periode', Economie et statistique, September 1978; for a shorter version in English, see 'Wage Formation in Historical Perspective: The French Experience', Cambridge Journal of Economics, September 1979.

very low level of unemployment had an insignificant influence before as well as after 1968. Yet wages exploded in 1968, a year which marks a new turning-point in French post-war economic history.

II. From the Social Crisis of 1968 to the Second Oil Shock

Feverish growth, 1968-73

The rapid growth process of the 1950s, and the even faster growth of the 1960s, had been superimposed on a society which had remained very rigid. The origins of the 1968 social crisis are to be found in the growing perception, most marked in the wave of young people reaching working age, of this gap between an inflexible and archaic social structure and economic structures which had undergone radical changes. Three points in particular are worth noting:

(i) Wage differentials had remained high and had been aggravated by the growing gap between the minimum wage and the average wage.[20] Though knowledge of non-wage incomes was scanty, it was generally felt that the overall distribution of incomes was unfair;

(ii) Despite rapid growth the working day had remained long compared with that of virtually all other industrialized Western European countries;[21]

(iii) More generally, the shop-floor hierarchy, conveyor-belt production, and the growing demands for shift-work were becoming progressively less acceptable to the new generations.

In addition, unemployment had begun to rise. The movement was not widespread, but reflected important qualitative changes in the labour market. Employers were becoming more selective. The influx of young people into the labour force, the increase in the female working population, and new changes in industrial structure which had begun in the mid-1960s (e.g. increased concentration into groups of international size, a movement of firms towards the west coast of France where labour was cheaper and more abundant) all combined to alter the way in which the labour market operated. The rise in unemployment was one aspect of this change.[22] Although job creation accelerated from 0.6 per cent per annum between the 1959 and 1963 peaks, to 0.8 per cent from 1963 to 1965, and 0.9 per cent per annum from 1969 to 1973), unemployment doubled between the 1963 low point of 1.3 per cent of the labour force and the 1973 level of 2.7 per cent.

The 'Grenelle Agreements' of June 1968 which brought the May events to an end contained four major decisions:

[20] The ratio between the ninth and the first (or lowest) decile in the wage distribution had actually risen between 1950 (when it stood at 3.4) and 1960 (3.8). It then remained stable until 1968 and only came down after the Grenelle Agreements (to 3.6 in 1973).

[21] EEC data (published in INSEE, *Données sociales*, 1978) show that in 1972 French full-time wage earners in industry worked 1957 hours a year as agains 1767 in Germany and 1670 in Italy.

[22] R. Salais, 'Analyse des mécanismes de détermination du chômage', *Economie et statistique*, October 1977.

(i) The minimum wage was raised by 35 per cent, thus suddenly closing the gap with average real wages that had appeared and grown since 1961;

(ii) Other wages also rose considerably (from 10 to 15 per cent);

(iii) The length of the working week was cut;

(iv) Qualitative improvements in working conditions were made via, for instance, the creation of trade-union cells within firms and the trend towards monthly wage payments.

Despite the sharp jolt, growth apparently remained as rapid and steady as before, helped no doubt by a new large devaluation. The 1969 devaluation and that of 1958 had many features in common. The devaluation was again an 'offensive' one, aimed not only at closing the price gap which had developed since 1963 and particularly following the 1968 wage increases, but also at anticipating future inflation. Not unlike the post-1958 experience, exporting industries recorded a new investment boom between 1969 and 1971, just at a time at which capital accumulation was slowing down elsewhere, notably in Germany and Japan. There was, however, a difference in firms' reactions.[23] While in 1959 the volume of exports had risen sharply, in 1969 it was profits which rose since export prices in foreign currencies remained unchanged. Thus the profitability of the manufacturing sector increased and the investment boom which followed was as much due to this profit effect as to a demand effect.

But this period saw a fundamental change intervening in the wage and price determination mechanism. From then on wages and prices were to be indexed on each other in a system which has been called 'monopolistic regulation'[24] and whose essential features are:

(i) Nominal wage increases are barely affected by unemployment levels and depend on previous rises in the cost of living (the two crucial parameters being the wage elasticity with respect to prices and the lags in the response mechanism). This largely results from collective wage negotiations in key sectors and the indexation of the minimum wage not only on consumer prices, but partly also on the country's real growth;

(ii) Prices are determined by a mark-up on production costs, with imbalances between demand and supply playing a diminishing role;

(iii) Monetary policy is permissive.

Such a mechanism could be unstable. The wage–price spiral does not degenerate into self-propelled and ever increasing inflation if three conditions are fulfilled: (a) the lag between price rises and wage rises remains sufficiently long; (b) rapid growth guarantees 'automatic' increases in the purchasing power of wages while at the same time maintaining profit margins; (c) there are no disturbances from the outside. Until 1973, the first two conditions were broadly met, and, if anything, the existence of an international inflationary environment

[23] Mistral, 'Vingt ans de redéploiement'.

[24] J.P. Benassy, R. Boyer, and R.M. Gelpi, 'Régulation des économies capitalistes et inflation', *Revue économique*, May 1979; see also Ch. 2 above.

in which price competition was probably somewhat weakened provided a favourable background. But the 1973 oil shock upset the balance of this feverish growth trend.

From the first oil shock to the end of the decade

The quadrupling of oil prices in 1973 introduced a double disturbance: the shift in income distribution towards OPEC stirred up existing inflationary tensions, while a medium-term deceleration intervened in the economic growth of the Western world. Major breaks in the trend appeared between the 1973–9 period and the earlier years of high growth (Table 15.1):

(i) The growth rate of output was nearly halved and expansion was less regular; France none the less remained ahead of the European OECD average (3.0 as against 2.4 per cent) and in contrast to most other countries did not experience an actual fall in output in either 1974 or 1975;[25]

(ii) Inflation nearly doubled on average and hardly slowed down throughout the period; but as in the 1960–73 years, France's rate of consumer price increases remained very close to the European OECD average;[26]

(iii) The growth of employment decelerated (Table 15.4); the manufacturing sector actually shed labour, tertiary employment continued to grow at roughly similar rates, while the rural exodus slowed down somewhat;

TABLE 15.4. *Changes in employment*
(average annual change in thousands)

	1963 to 1969	1969 to 1973	1973 to 1979
Agriculture, forestry, fishing	−130	−153	−78
Industry[a]	64	78	−100
Other sectors	227	263	229
Total	161	188	52

[a] Including construction
Source: OECD, *Labour Force Statistics* (various issues).

(iv) Unemployment more than doubled between 1973 and 1979 (from 2.6 to 5.9 per cent of the labour force), and this despite a complete halt to net immigration, falling participation rates among the young and the old, and a deceleration in productivity growth;

(v) The current account of the balance of payments was in deficit between 1973 and 1977; a surplus was only re-established in 1978–9 on the eve of the second oil shock (Table 15.5); in contrast to most other European countries, however, the budget deficit remained moderate.

[25] In fact, France is the only country in Europe, apart from Norway, which did not experience a fall in output on a year-to-year basis over the whole post-war period between 1945 and 1979.

[26] Between 1960 and 1973, French prices rose by 4.6 per cent per annum and European ones by 4.5 per cent: between 1973 and 1979, the respective figures were 10.7 and 10.9 per cent.

TABLE 15.5. *Selected financial indicators*

	General government net lending[a]	Current balance[b]
Average 1970–73	0.8	–
1974	0.6	–6.1
1975	–2.2	–0.1
1976	–0.5	–5.9
1977	–0.8	–3.0
1978	–1.8	3.7
1979	–0.8	1.2

[a] In per cent of GDP at current prices
[b] $ billion
Sources: OECD, *National Accounts of OECD Countries, 1962–1979*, and *Economic Outlook*, July 1981.

Looking at these main indicators, the break is clear. Paradoxically, however, and despite sharp changes in the international environment and in policies, following the adoption of the Barre Plan, economic behaviour seems to have changed very little, be this on the supply side of the economy or in inflationary attitudes and income distribution struggles. A brief look at the investment and inflation experience of this period will illustrate the point.

The volume of productive investment in the economy's tradeable sectors (energy and manufacturing) was in 1979 below the 1970 level, having fallen by 1.2 per cent per annum between 1973 and 1979. This level, however, remained above that needed to simply replace worn-out machinery and equipment. It even exceeded what would have been required to sustain a growth rate cut by half, on the assumption of unchanged capital–output and scrapping ratios. This relatively optimistic statement must, however, be qualified by two sets of considerations. First, industrial investment in this period included large investment programmes in nationalized industries (with relatively high capital–output ratios), such as nuclear energy, telecommunications, etc. The decline in private industrial investment was, thus, more pronounced than would appear from the global figures. Second, the crisis probably led to accelerated scrapping of machinery and some increases in capital–output ratios as a result of investment in energy-saving equipment about which little information is available.

Though industrial productivity growth decelerated (by one-third), the slowdown was moderate if compared to the much more pronounced drop in the growth rate of industrial output, which fell by two-thirds. Estimates of total productivity, obtained by weighting the contributions of labour and capital, indicate a deceleration of only one-quarter, *after* adjustment for the persistent under-utilization of production factors (Table 15.6). And OECD estimates comparing the years 1973–7 with the period 1963–73 confirm that the slowdown in French industrial productivity growth was the least marked among the major Western economies.[27]

The relative resilience of investment and the only modest slowdown in

[27] OECD, *Economic Outlook*, July 1979.

TABLE 15.6. *Components of growth in manufacturing*
(average annual percentage changes)

	1963–73	1973–79
Value added	7.2	2.5
Gross fixed investment	6.4	−1.2
Capital stock	5.9	4.0
Employment	1.1	−1.3
Man-hours	0.4	−2.3
Capital–labour ratio	4.9	5.3
Hourly productivity	6.8	4.8
Capital productivity	1.2	−1.5
Total factor productivity	5.1	2.9
(adjusted for under-utilization		
of resources)	(4.9)	(3.7)

Source: P. Dubois, 'La rupture de 1974', *Economie et statistique*, August 1980.

productivity growth both suggest that by the end of the decade, at least in manufacturing and probably in the economy as a whole, a large growth potential still existed. And this conclusion is reinforced by the presence of an abundant labour supply — through the late 1970s the labour market saw a large influx, resulting from the high birth rates which had occurred from the end of the war to the mid-1960s, and only relatively small withdrawals, in view of the low numbers born during World War I.

On the inflation side, the French economy entered the 1974-9 period in conditions of rapid growth and strong inflationary tendencies surrounding the division of national income. This unbalanced situation was aggravated by the oil shock. The latter implied a sudden shift of real disposable income to the outside world in view of a lasting deterioration in the terms of trade. This shift can be put at over 2 per cent of GDP in 1974 and was still of the order of 1 per cent in 1978-9.[28] In an economy in which tension and conflict over the distribution of national income had been common, even down to tenths of percentage points, a shortfall in the 'surplus' to be distributed was bound to be very disruptive.[29]

The definition of 'surplus' retained in this context is what is left over from a given GDP once the maintenance of the existing factors of production has been assured. This maintenance, in turn, implies the constancy of the real purchasing power of both employees and self-employed and a sufficient level of depreciation allowances to ensure a renewal of the capital stock at replacement costs. Until the oil shock the share of the 'surplus' so defined was roughly constant

[28] The terms of trade shift is here measured as:

$$\text{T of T} = (X-M) - \frac{1}{p'}\,(p_x X - p_m M),$$

where X and M stand for constant price exports and imports of goods and services, p_x and p_m for their respective price indices and p' for the implicit deflator of total domestic demand.

[29] Though, of course, other countries such as Japan were able to cope successfully with much larger adjustments: C. Sautter, 'L'adaptation du Japon au ralentissement de la croissance et à la ponction extérieure', *Revue économique*, November 1979.

(and on average equal to 27.8 per cent of GDP over the years 1963-73). Between 1974 and 1979, the 'surplus' fell to 24.5 per cent of GDP as a result of the deceleration in output and productivity growth. And in addition to this 3.3 per cent decline came a terms of trade deterioration equivalent to some 1.4 per cent of GDP on average (Table 15.7).

TABLE 15.7. *Distribution of economic 'surplus'* [a]
(percentage shares in total)

	1960–67	1968–73	1974–76	1977–79
Change in real wages[b]	7.6	8.2	8.6	5.9
Change in real entrepreneurial income[c]	4.1	3.3	−0.5	1.8
Direct taxes less subsidies	53.4	46.9	48.7	50.0
Net operating surplus of corporate sector	28.4	31.7	26.9	27.5
Other[d]	7.4	10.9	10.0	9.7
Terms of trade changes	−0.9	−1.0	6.3	5.1
Total economic 'surplus'	100.0	100.0	100.0	100.0
'Surplus' in per cent of GDP	27.4	28.3	24.9	24.0

[a] For definition, see text
[b] Compensation of employees deflated by implicit private consumption deflator
[c] Entrepreneurial income deflated by implicit private consumption deflator
[d] Other primary incomes of households, general government, and financial institutions
Source: author's calculations based on data in INSEE, 'Rapport sur les comptes de la nation', *Collections de l'INSEE*, série C (various issues).

Between 1974 and 1976, the terms of trade shift was borne in almost equal parts by the corporate and the self-employed sectors — indeed the latter's real incomes were in 1976 below those of 1973. The purchasing power of dependent employees on the other hand went on rising at roughly the same rate as that experienced in the years 1968-73, despite the reduction in the 'surplus'. The situation was modified in 1977-9, when the burden of the loss in real income arising from the deterioration in the terms of trade was more equitably distributed between the three groups. In fact, the shares of wages and salaries, corporate profits, and self-employed incomes returned in this period to close to the values observed in the 1960s.

It is not easy to link in any rigorous way these variations in the distribution of the 'surplus', which must have reflected the changing bargaining strength of the various social groups and of the government over this period, with the trend of inflation. It would appear, however, that some deceleration in underlying pressures took place and that the economy faced the second oil shock of 1979 with a lower inflationary potential than had been the case in 1973. It is true that consumer price rises accelerated from a trough of some 9 per cent in 1978 to double-digit figures in 1979-80. But this result was strongly influenced not only by the second increase in oil prices, but also by the freeing of prices of manufactures from controls (which shortened the lag between cost and price increases), and by a sharp rise in public enterprise prices (40 per cent in two years), following the spring 1978 parliamentary elections. It is difficult, in these circumstances, to disentangle the contributions of these various factors to inflation on the one hand, and a possible change in the wage and price formation process on the other. It is hence equally difficult to assess the likely effects of the Barre Plan, one of whose essential aims had been that of curbing inflationary pressures.

The Barre Plan

While Germany had started to tackle inflationary excesses in the spring of 1973, six months before the first oil shock, in France it was not until autumn 1976, and following three years of stop–go policies, that an overall plan was drawn up to deal with an inflationary spiral deeply rooted since 1968 and aggravated in 1973.[30] The seriousness of the economic problems the country faced was not dissimilar to that of 1958, and a comparison can be drawn between the Rueff and Barre Plans. Inflationary tensions were deeper and more serious in 1976 than in 1958 – the elasticity of wages with respect to prices and that of prices with respect to wages were close to unity, and the rise in oil prices was transmitting powerful shocks from the outside. But up to a point at least a similar medium-term problem presented itself on both occasions – how to launch the French economy on to a different growth path. In 1958 this was towards rapid growth open to an expanding and balanced world economy. In 1976, it was towards slower growth in a world economy which had decelerated and become unbalanced.

The Barre Plan was primarily a 'plan of rejection' – rejection of nominal and hence real devaluation of the franc; refusal to prop up demand by means of a budgetary deficit. The rejection of devaluation, which was diametrically opposed to the strategy of the Rueff Plan, was defended on the strength of two arguments. First, it was felt that depreciation of the currency had become hazardous and possibly harmful in conditions in which price-inelastic oil imports had grown in volume, world demand was low, and unstable foreign currency markets were likely to magnify the short-run negative effects of the 'J-curve'. Second, it was argued that in order to break the wage–price spiral the safety valve of periodic devaluations had to be done away with. As to the refusal to increase the budget deficit, which had risen steeply elsewhere in the later 1970s, for instance in Germany and Japan, this was motivated by the presence of a new 'external constraint'. Henceforth, it was argued, the French economy could no longer grow at its potential maximum speed, but only at a rate compatible with current balance of payments equilibrium in the medium term. A policy which propped up demand would inevitably result in higher external deficits; only a supply-oriented policy could ease the external constraint. In any case, as household consumption grew at a relatively rapid rate until 1979, as a result of continuing increases in real wages and transfers, any additional support to demand seemed unnecessary.

On the wages and prices front the plan's main measures were a review of the so-called 'EDF (*Electricité de France*) Agreement', and the July 1978 freeing of industrial prices. The 1969 'EDF Agreement' had institutionalized the indexation

---

[30] B. Balassa, 'Assessment and Prospects of the Barre Policies' (provisional title), in American Enterprise Institute, *The Political Economy of France* (forthcoming).

of wages to the cost of living, to the performance of the firm, and to national economic growth. The effects of the suppression of this virtually automatic indexation system were, however, limited, since the Electricity Board was not really a 'leading' sector for wage negotiations. The 'leading' sectors were in the car, mechanical, and electrical construction industries which, on the contrary, benefited from the freeing of prices in 1978 and largely escaped credit controls (since export credits were exempted). Monetary policy was supposed to be restrictive but turned out in fact not to be very severe, largely because of the exceptions made for exports, energy-saving investment, and housing construction. From 1976 to 1979 money supply (M_2) grew at approximately the same rate as nominal GDP and the economy's liquidity ratio remained at the same level for three years.

The freeing of industrial prices did not mean that government intervention in the economy suddenly diminished. On the contrary, 'supply' policies continued in the form of both general and selective measures. The former took largely the form of fiscal incentives to investment, including, in addition to corporate tax concessions and subsidized loans, income tax credits on limited purchases of French shares. Semi-generalized measures in favour of the tradeable sector were taken by prolonging a supply policy instituted and put into practice towards the end of the 1960s.[31] This included the already mentioned freeing of industrial prices, and the absence of controls on export credits. Finally, large-scale sectoral programmes were undertaken by public corporations in areas such as nuclear energy and telecommunications; committees were created with considerable financial means at their disposal to help industrial restructuring, and one particular such committee was entrusted with the task of supporting six 'strategic industries': off-shore technology, office information systems, electronics, the development of robots, bio-industries, and energy-saving equipment. To a certain extent a move was made away from generalized blanket support to the whole of industry towards the encouragement at the margin of upstream sectors and branches in need of redeployment.

The Barre Plan differed from the Rueff Plan in that it was unable, or did not want, to break with the past. The international climate had narrowed the scope for manœuvre, while socio-political considerations prevented the adoption of decisive policies on the prices and wages front. Though claiming to be liberal, as did the Rueff Plan of 1958, the Barre Plan's liberalism was of a more moderate kind.

Conclusions

This chapter opened by arguing that France's post-war economic history was full of paradoxes. Perhaps the major one, often alluded to in the preceding pages, was the contrast between a growth process which was not only rapid but also very smooth by international standards (even in the 1950s and the 1970s, let alone the 1960s), and rather violent social and political changes which find few parallels in Europe. Despite two long and costly colonial wars between the early 1950s and the early 1960s, and two major social and political crises in 1958 and

---

[31] R. Courbis, *Compétitivité et croissance en économie concurrencée*, Paris 1975.

1968 (as well as a sudden influx of nearly 1 million people in 1962), the growth momentum was not interrupted. While for a neo-classical economist this might be confirmation of the inherent stability of a capitalist system, a much more plausible explanation is that of the creation of a tacit consensus, reached in the early post-war years, on the virtues of rapid economic growth. Once started, this consensus was self-sustaining, since growth allowed a general expansion of the 'surplus' to be distributed in which everybody, or nearly everybody, could partake. Social conflicts remained, of course, but apart from brief and sometimes violent explosions, were defused by rising income levels.

Growth was rapid, therefore, because of this consensus in favour of investment and productivity, not because of largely predetermined supply factors. And growth was smooth because the regular increase in purchasing power nourished a steady rise in household consumption, while the recourse to devaluation avoided the sudden 'stops' which would have been imposed by a deflationary policy. But it is clear that a growth process largely based on such factors is essentially fragile. The difficulties which the French economy increasingly faced from the late 1960s onwards cannot be explained away either by the sudden increase in oil prices or by the gradual disappearance of some of the driving forces behind the growth of the 1950s and 1960s. At the heart of the growth process lie not only investment, technical progress, or labour, but also the distribution of the 'surplus', in other words the real wage-productivity-profitability nexus. Once this distribution is subject to increasing pressures, the mechanism's smooth workings are endangered.

This is what happened from the late 1960s onwards — rising tensions generated by an unequal income distribution pushed the rate of inflation up in stages, while at the same time the speed of the industrial transformation was creating a new problem in the form of a slowly rising level of 'structural' unemployment. Even if the Bretton Woods monetary system had not collapsed, even if energy had remained cheap, the rapid growth of the French economy would have imposed a number of structural changes which were only hesitantly undertaken after 1968. Amongst these should be mentioned a narrowing of income disparities, a shortening of the working week, the redeployment of resources towards the manufacturing sector and, within that sector, to branches with high value added or a high economic surplus (i.e. containing a high proportion of skilled labour and heavily involved in research and development).

From 1974 onwards, a balance of payments constraint in a world of slower growth overshadowed the possible 'physical' constraints of limited labour and saving resources. Thanks to demographic increases, the continuing high level of savings,[32] and opportunities offered by a third industrial revolution geared to electronics, the growth potential remained almost certainly in the region of 4 to 5 per cent per annum. The rapid change in specialization in the 1970s towards upstream activities, combined with a withdrawal from sectors in which world demand was stagnant (which placed France second after Japan and ahead of

---

[32] The household saving ratio stood on average at 15.4 per cent of disposable income in the period 1959–68, 16.4 per cent in 1969–73, and 17.3 per cent in 1974–9; INSEE, 'Rapport sur les comptes de la nation', *Collections de l'INSEE*, série C, Nos. 86–7, 1979.

Germany[33]), the leading role played by nationalized industries, and the ambitions of the energy programme show that the French economy still has considerable industrial vigour with which to face the 1980s.

But the macroeconomic projections made in preparation for the Eighth Plan (1981-5) show how difficult it will be to bring the growth rate close to its 4 to 5 per cent potential in the foreseeable future given the expected international climate.[34] And this in turn will lead to increasing unemployment at least until the demographic turn-around of the mid-1980s, when the number of school-leavers reaching working age will begin to decline. The much discussed studies made for the Eighth Plan demonstrate that partial solutions are possible, entailing, however, redistributions of income, jobs, and power. A reduction in working hours could be one powerful means of reconciling rapid technical progress and industrial adaptability (i.e. a considerable increase in hourly productivity), with the slower growth of production resulting from the stagnation in the world economy. But for this to be successful production methods and the distribution of income would have to change fundamentally. Equipment and machinery would have to be used to their maximum, and the inevitable drop in real wages which would be untenable for blue as well as white collar workers would have to be compensated for by a redistribution of income.[35]

The problem is not simply an issue of economic policy, of effectively combining a moderately restrictive monetary stance and rigorous budgetary management, of using the nationalized industries as leading sectors or stimulating private initiative. The real problem is that of transforming the implicit consensus which had backed rapid growth for thirty years into a new consensus designed to maintain France's position in a fiercely competitive and energy-constrained world, and to ensure forms of work-sharing at home that preserve full employment for the new generations of entrants into the labour markets.

Bibliography

The single most important book on the French economy, which has often been referred to in the preceding pages, is J.-J. Carré, P. Dubois, and E. Malinvaud, *French Economic Growth*, Oxford 1976, a work which covers not only the post-war period, but also the country's economic history since the beginning of the century. A very interesting survey can also be found in R. Courbis, *Compétitivité et croissance en économie concurrencée*, Paris 1975. An analysis of the 1950s and 1960s is contained in INSEE, 'Fresque historique du système productif', *Collections de l'INSEE*, série E, No. 27, 1974, while an account of the 1970s can be found in R. Boyer and J. Mistral, *Accumulation, inflation, crises*, Paris 1978.

More detailed material is contained in INSEE, 'Rapport sur les comptes de la nation', *Collection de l'INSEE*, série C, which is the equivalent of an annual

[33] G. Lafay and M. Fouquin, 'Spécialisation et adaptation face à la crise', *Economie prospective internationale*, January 1980.

[34] Commissariat au Plan, *Rapport de la comission du developpement du VIIIe Plan*, Paris 1980.

[35] G. Oudiz, E. Raoul, and H. Sterdiniak, 'Reduire la durée du travail: quelles conséquences?', *Economie et statistique*, May 1979.

economic survey. The INSEE publication, *Donées sociales*, issued every three years, complements the picture by providing wider background material. The monthly INSEE review, *Economie et statistique*, as well as the brief annual OECD *Economic Surveys*, provide further analysis of trends and policies.

On economic policy, A. de Lattre, *Politique économique de la France depuis 1945*, Paris 1966, is a comprehensive survey up to the mid-1960s. The planning experience is covered in a very interesting book by C. Gruson, *Origines et espoirs de la planification française*, Paris 1968, while monetary policy is analysed in J.-H. David, *La politique monétaire en France*, Paris 1974, and OECD, *Monetary Policy in France*, Paris 1974.

16

West Germany*

KLAUS HINRICH HENNINGS**

Introduction

Like other European economies, West Germany[1] has experienced almost uninterrupted growth since the war. The pace of expansion was both smoother and
more rapid than in any other period of German history. Though there were
cycles in the post-war period, these were in no way comparable to the much
more pronounced fluctuations of pre-war years. The 5 per cent annual output
growth that was recorded between 1950 and 1979 was well above the 2½ to 3
per cent rates witnessed in the second half of the nineteenth century or in the
first half of the twentieth century.[2] Contrary to the experience of other industrialized economies, however, a distinct long-term decline in the post-war
trend growth rate set in before the outbreak of the oil crisis and the ensuing
deceleration in the Western world (Fig. 16.1).

To understand both the rapid rise of prosperity and the decline in the pace
of economic development, it will be convenient to distinguish four periods
which more or less coincide with the three and a half decades since 1945 (Table
16.1). The years between 1945 and the early 1950s were dominated by the
attempt to rebuild and reconstruct. In a sense, the West German economy was
'created' in those years, and thus the foundation laid for what was to follow.
The 1950s saw the gradual integration of Germany into the Western world,
culminating in the creation of the EEC. The economic consequences of this
process were rapid export-led growth and a high degree of stability — business
cycles were mild, and the ability of the system to adapt to changing circumstances high. In the 1960s, growth was less rapid, more cyclical, and increasingly
constrained by limited labour supply, despite a substantial inflow of foreign
workers. By now a very open economy, Germany had to deal with a series of
external shocks, most of which took the form of large capital inflows due to
speculation on the Deutschmark (DM) exchange rate. One consequence of these
recurrent shocks was increased inflation. The attempt to preserve price stability
in the face of imported inflation led the authorities to apply stop–go policies
which worked, but worked so well that they contributed to the breakdown of
the consensus which had characterized economic policy-making in the 1950s
and 1960s.

* As for other country chapters, editorial policy has imposed the use of internationally
standardized statistics which at times differ from national concepts and figures.

** University of Hanover. The author is grateful for critical comments and suggestions to
Professor K. Borchardt of Munich University.

[1] More often than not the term 'Germany' will be used in what follows rather than the
more correct 'West Germany', let alone the cumbersome official denomination 'Federal
Republic of Germany'. No political intentions are, of course, implied.

[2] W.G. Hoffmann, *Das Wachstum der deutschen Wirtschaft seit der Mitte des 19. Jahrhunderts*, Berlin 1965.

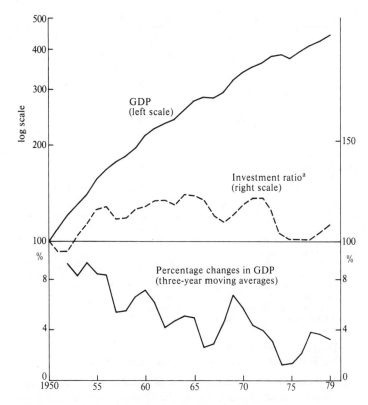

FIG. 16.1. *Output and investment trends, 1950–1979* (indices: 1950 = 100)
[a] Gross fixed investment in per cent of GDP at constant prices
Source: OECD, *National Accounts of OECD Countries, 1950–1979.*

The 1970s, finally, witnessed a change in both the external and internal environment. The oil shock, and perhaps even more the collapse of the post-war international monetary system, created a need for structural adjustment, which, however, was difficult to effect. The result was slower growth, sizeable unemployment, and a higher rate of inflation. While it is difficult to ascribe the deceleration in growth to any one cause or group of causes, it is the main contention of the discussion which follows that the difficulties the economy had to face in the 1970s were to a large extent the result of the particular form growth took in the 1950s and 1960s, and that the way in which the economy reacted to external shocks in the 1970s had much to do with what might be called the breakdown of the post-war consensus among social groups powerful enough to affect the economy by their changed behaviour.

Each of these periods will be taken up in turn in the discussion. First, however, it is necessary to consider briefly some institutional features which are important for the analysis that follows. Three in particular will be discussed:

(i) Post-war decentralization;

TABLE 16.1. *Longer-term trends*

	1950–79	1950–60	1960–70	1970–79
	average annual percentage changes			
GDP	5.3	8.0	4.7	2.9
Inflation[a]	3.1	1.9	2.6	4.5
Employment	0.6	2.1	0.1	−0.5
	1950–79	1950–60	1961–70	1971–79
	percentages			
Investment ratio[b]	(22.9)	(22.5)	24.0	22.2
Unemployment rate[c]	2.4	3.8	0.6	2.4
	$ million, annual averages			
Current balance	1,643	838	760	3,609

[a] Consumer prices
[b] Gross fixed investment in per cent of GDP at constant prices
[c] In per cent of the labour force

Sources: OECD, *National Accounts of OECD Countries, 1950–1979*; OECD, *Manpower Statistics, 1950–1962*; OECD, *Labour Force Statistics* (various issues); OECD, *Balance of Payments Statistics, 1950–1961* and *1960–1977*; OECD, *Economic Outlook*, July 1981; IMF, *International Financial Statistics* (1980 Yearbook); C. Sorrentino, 'Methodological and Conceptual Problems in Measuring Unemployment', *mimeo*, OECD, Paris 1976.

(ii) The role of the central bank;
(iii) The importance of a liberal economic constitution.

First, West Germany is a much more decentralized state than pre-war Germany ever was. There is much diversity among the Country's *Länder* and none of them dominates the federation as Prussia had dominated the German Reich. Moreover, the *Länder* are not only formally independent states; the constitution provides them with sufficient economic power to be able to pursue (within limits) their own policies. *Länder*, as well as local authorities, have their own tax incomes, and are responsible for a sizeable part of public spending (Table 16.2). This creates a number of obstacles to effective and timely fiscal policy action. On the revenue side, changes in taxation require, as a rule, legislation and the agreement of all concerned, which makes for delays. There are provisions for non-legislative changes in taxation, but they have never been used for political reasons. On the expenditure side, a large part of public current expenditure, and an even larger one of public investment, is controlled by *Länder* and local authorities; especially the latter have at times proceeded with their plans irrespective of the stance of federal fiscal policies. On the whole, therefore, fiscal policies are difficult to use as tools of demand management. When they were used, they proved to be more effective for stimulating than for restricting demand; yet the lags involved turned out to be so long that the effect was often pro- rather than counter-cyclical.

Another aspect of decentralization is the existence of separate and autonomous public authorities established by an act of parliament which grants them independence and at the same time assigns them specific tasks which they have to pursue irrespective of government orders. The prime example of this kind of institution is the Deutsche Bundesbank. Although required to co-operate with

TABLE 16.2. *Share of various levels of government in public
expenditure and revenues, 1977*
(percentages)

	Expenditure	Revenues	Tax element[a] in total revenues (percentage)
Federal government	26.4	24.0	95.7
Social security funds	31.3	32.4	83.3
Länder	24.5	24.4	69.8
Local authorities	16.3	16.9	35.9
Other public authorities	1.5	2.3	34.5

[a] Including social security contributions
Source: Statistisches Bundesamt, *Statistisches Jahrbuch, 1980*.

the (federal) government, the Bundesbank can and has pursued its own policies, at times against the wishes of Bonn, or even more so of *Länder* governments. This is not the place to discuss the constitution and organization of the Bundesbank in detail,[3] but it is important for what follows to note that it is charged primarily with safeguarding the value of the currency (which is interpreted as keeping the rate of inflation down). The determination of the exchange rate, by contrast, is not one of its tasks but rather the prerogative of the federal government. Nor is the Bundesbank obliged to finance government operations; on the contrary, there is an absolute limit to the amount of Bundesbank lending to the government.

The dispersion of authority that goes with federalism, the deliberate decentralization of economic decision-making powers and emphasis on the due process of law (which allows the autonomous authorities discussed above to stand up to the government in court, if necessary), are all instances of the turn towards a liberal political constitution which characterizes post-war Germany and which has a counterpart in a system of economic institutions which stress decentralization, reliance on market processes, and a belief in competition. The creation of such institutions was greatly helped by the adoption, from 1948 onwards, of a concept known as *Soziale Marktwirtschaft* as a guideline for economic policy-making. The concept consists of a combination of policy proposals designed to further competition with policy proposals designed to correct the outcome of the market process, or, to use another formula which needs to be filled with empirical detail, to use as much competition as possible, and as much planning as necessary.[4] Macroeconomic demand management is certainly not ruled out by this set of ideas (although it took some time before it was

[3] Such an analysis will be found, e.g., in K. Holbik (ed.), *Monetary Policy in Twelve Industrial Countries*, Federal Reserve Bank of Boston, Boston 1973, Ch. 5.

[4] For a more detailed discussion of the concept, see R. Blum, *Soziale Marktwirtschaft*, Tübingen 1969. For an analysis of how it has been applied, see H. Lampert, *Die Wirtschafts- und Sozialordnung der Bundesrepublik Deutschland*, Munich 1978 (6th edn.), and D. Cassel, G. Gutmann, and H.J. Thieme (eds.), *25 Jahre Marktwirtschaft in der Bundesrepublik Deutschland*, Stuttgart 1972. A much more critical assessment is offered by M. Welteke, *Theorie und Praxis der Sozialen Marktwirtschaft*, Frankfurt 1976.

generally accepted); nor are government regulations or intervention in markets in which competition is limited, such as agriculture, housing, or transport. In fact, a large array of pragmatic policies can be subsumed under the concept as long as the general principle of promoting competition is not violated. What *Soziale Marktwirtschaft* meant and means in practice is therefore best seen by studying economic policy-making in action.

It is important, however, to appreciate the role the concept as such has played in the formulation of economic policies from 1948 onwards. For most of the period since then, it was the declared set of principles by which all governments (whether led by Christian Democrats, or by Social Democrats) vowed to abide. In consequence, a semantic uniformity of interests among all parties was created which helped to focus policy debates on the best means to achieve given ends, which tended to exclude for a long time discussion about and between radically different approaches, and which reinforced the consensus in economic matters which characterized economic policy-making in the country. In practice, of course, the actual policies adopted by various governments have often differed from the ideal concept. The latter, in turn, has quite frequently been in danger of being turned into a cult – with high priests, long-winded incantations, a common creed, a vigorous group of missionaries in heathen countries, and dogmatic theologians in universities. Yet in spite of all this the concept has played an important role for Germany's economic development. On the one hand it has been flexible enough to allow differing interpretations over time; on the other it has provided an important element of continuity in economic policy-making – the idea that policy should promote vigorous competition.

I. Reconstruction, 1945–1950

In order to understand German economic developments from the 1950s onwards it is necessary to discuss briefly the years immediately after World War II, because it was in those years that the basis was laid for what was to follow. The difficulties of that period have often been described;[5] what should be pointed out here is that the situation, desperate though it was, also provided opportunities and that these were seized.

Early opportunities

At the end of the war, the German economy disintegrated into local and regional sub-economies, with output in 1946 down to perhaps about a quarter of its pre-war level.[6] This was not so much due to wartime damage of industrial capacity as to a number of bottle-necks. There had, of course, been widespread destruction,

---

[5] One of the best descriptions is G. Stolper, *German Realities*, New York 1948. An excellent economic analysis can be found in H.C. Wallich, *Mainsprings of the German Revival*, New Haven 1955.

[6] Few reliable statistical data are available on a consistent basis for the period. The figure given in the text comes from G. Stolper, K. Häuser, and K. Borchardt, *The German Economy: 1870 to the Present*, London 1967.

but it has been estimated[7] that wartime investment had increased the industrial capital stock by more than the extent of wartime damage. Even if post-war reparations, forced dismantling, and disinvestment for other reasons, are taken into account, industrial capacity in the aggregate was probably some 10 per cent larger than it had been in 1936. In individual industries, however, the situation was much worse. Basic sectors such as coal-mining, iron and steel production, electricity generation, and above all transportation had been seriously affected by wartime destruction and post-war disintegration. The breakdown of the communications system, in particular, meant that most economic transactions had been reduced to barter.

The reintegration of local sub-economies was a slow process hampered by administrative chaos and the continued lack of transport facilities. But it did provide opportunities for the enterprising, precisely because it was not planned or directed. West Germany had inherited more than 60 per cent of the industrial capacity of the former Reich and an even higher share of its capital goods industries, but had lost access to the agricultural surpluses of East Germany. These structural imbalances and bottle-necks compelled a reorientation of economic activities which represented an obvious burden, yet also offered the opportunity to create new economic structures unhampered by the legacy of history.

Similarly, the widespread destruction of German towns and cities turned (with hindsight) into an advantage. The discomfort created by the fact that only every third family had a home after the end of the war made for a huge demand for housing which became a mainstay of the investment booms which followed in the 1950s. Here, too, the selective nature of damage and destruction made for profitable investment opportunities and a low incremental capital-output ratio.

Finally, the fact that millions of Germans fled before the advancing Russian army, or were later forcibly evicted from areas east of the Oder–Neisse demarcation line, presented problems as well as advantages. The influx of so many people (about 10 million, or a quarter of the population) was a severe strain on resources already stretched to the limit, and worsened both the housing shortage and the already precarious provision of food. Yet it was also to provide the economy with a cheap, mobile, and often highly trained labour force, as well as with a pool of entrepreneurial talent.

Economic reforms

Although production grew from late 1945 onwards, and there was some economic development and reconstruction, albeit uneven and unbalanced, the major obstacle to progress became increasingly the way in which the economy was administered. This bottle-neck was removed in 1948 by three interrelated major policy decisions: the announcement of the Marshall Plan, a monetary reform, and a partial dismantling of wartime controls. These measures were linked by the decision to create a West German state, and thus to accept the partition of the country which had of course begun much earlier. Together, they amounted

---

[7] See R. Krengel, *Anlagevermögen, Produktion und Beschäftigung der Industrie im Gebiet der Bundesrepublik von 1924 bis 1956*, Berlin 1958.

to a reform of the economic constitution; what is perhaps even more important is that they changed fundamentally the attitudes and expectations of the population.

Foreign aid had already played an important role in the years immediately after 1945, in particular by averting food crises. Between 1945 and 1948 some two-thirds of German imports were financed by largely American help.[8] The Marshall Plan first supplemented and later supplanted such aid. Food and animal feeds accounted for a large proportion of total deliveries, but investment goods became progressively more important and helped remove many of the bottle-necks which throttled production.

Yet the political and psychological impact of the Marshall Plan was even greater, and probably accounts for the fact that the plan seems to have been more successful in Germany than in countries like Britain or France which received more than twice as much in aid. The inclusion of Germany in the European Recovery Programme (and the membership in the OEEC which this entailed) was the first step towards the integration of the economy into the network of Western trade. In political terms, the decision to create a West German state firmly integrated the country into the Western alliance and thus ended a long period of uncertainty. It represented a change of policy away from plans to reduce Germany to dismembered agricultural mini-states and towards its acceptance as a member of the post-war Western community. Finally, the country's participation in Marshall Aid prejudged a number of features of the economic constitution of the new state. In particular, the Marshall Plan implied a private ownership economy, and thus in effect put an end to debates on other forms of economic organization which had been proposed.

The monetary reform which was planned in close conjunction with the Marshall Plan, and under equally close supervision of the United States authorities, had similar effects. The scarcities which had prevailed after 1945 had required a continuation of the stringent system of wartime rationing and price controls. Yet sanctions had become less strict, and repressed inflation came increasingly into the open. Banknotes lost their role as medium of exchange, barter was widespread, and black markets threatened to engulf 'official' markets. In addition, the whole system of administrative allocation and control was endangered. The June 1948 reform drastically reduced both the money supply, by creating a new currency, and the level of public and private debts.[9] Though prices rose rapidly in the second half of 1948, the reform succeeded in curbing inflation by 1949 and in redistributing the burden of the war effort by destroying almost all monetary wealth.

The reform was accompanied by the abolition of rationing, and the revocation of price controls on consumer goods, though not on capital goods or on incomes.

---

[8] F.-W. Henning, *Das industrialisierte Deutschland, 1914 bis 1972*, Stuttgart 1974, p. 209.
[9] The monetary reform is analysed in detail in H. Möller, 'Die westdeutsche Währungs-reform von 1948', in Deutsche Bundesbank (ed.), *Währung und Wirtschaft in Deutschland, 1876-1975*, Frankfurt 1976; see also R. Richter (ed.), 'Currency and Economic Reform: West Germany After World War II', *Zeitschrift für die gesamte Staatswissenschaft*, September 1979.

This meant that households bore the brunt of the rise in prices which followed the monetary reform. Despite the initial social unrest this measure caused, the policy was pursued in order to accomplish a reversal in the existing set of priorities. Whereas before 1948 investment goods industries had been accorded precedence in an attempt to overcome sectoral shortages, it was felt that now consumer goods industries should be free to expand in response to demand.

By 1950 recovery from the ruins of World War II was well under way and some major decisions had been taken which were to determine the future course of events. For this reason, the 1948 monetary reform and the abolition of price controls have often been hailed as the parents of the German economic 'miracle' (with the Marshall Plan being cast in the role of midwife). Yet 1948 does not mark the dawn of an era of unlimited private initiative. The economic policies pursued by the government of the newly created state conformed as little to the ideals of an old-fashioned liberal economic policy as had the policies of the occupying powers in the three Western zones before 1948. Nor did economic growth start in 1948. The increase in production had begun well before and indeed faltered (temporarily) thereafter. The importance of the monetary reform and the (after all only partial) abolition of wartime controls was rather that, like the inclusion of West Germany in the European Recovery Program, they changed the outlook of the population, raised expectations, and released energies, and thus put an end to the despondency which had prevailed in the years immediately after 1945.

II. Export-led Growth, 1950–1960

The 1950s were a decade of unprecedented growth. Income per head more than doubled, food supplies became plentiful, the housing shortage eased, and an ever-increasing variety of consumer goods became available. In 1945 the belief was widespread that it would take a generation at least to rebuild Germany. To all intents and purposes, the period of reconstruction came to a close in 1955 if not earlier. After the horrors of war and the uncertainty of the post-war years Germans sought economic security as well as self-respect in economic success. One reason why this success was possible was that there existed a broad consensus beyond ideological divisions and conflicts that economic growth was to be accorded first priority, since it could be relied upon to solve a number of potentially divisive issues such as the integration of several million refugees from the East or the distribution of the costs of the lost war and the post-war occupation. Rapid growth, rising employment, and a low rate of inflation in turn cemented this consensus, which found its expression, among other things, in the gradual acceptance of the *Soziale Marktwirtschaft* concept by all parties in parliament, as well as by both sides of industry.

Growth and cycles

The growth of output between 1950 and 1960 (at some 8 per cent per annum) was the fastest in Europe in the period. It was accompanied by a rapid reduction in unemployment, by a very low rate of inflation (second only to those of Portugal and Switzerland), by a continuous surplus on the current account of the balance of payments from 1951 onwards, as well as by a near trebling in

Germany's share in world exports of manufactures. By 1960, Germany's GDP was again the largest in Europe and so were its foreign currency reserves, while unemployment had come down to less than 1 per cent of the labour force. Not even the Japanese economy could muster quite such an impressive achievement over this decade.

As in other industrialized countries, there were cyclical fluctuations, but these were relatively mild and never involved declines in output. Each cycle lasted for roughly four years and coincided, by and large, with similar cycles in the United States. The first of these cycles was engendered by the wave of speculative buying which preceded the Korean War in 1950. Since Germany was not allowed to turn to war production, and had unused capacities, it could satisfy export demand, and experienced the first of many export-generated booms. The upswing ran into difficulties at the turn of 1950–1 when bottle-necks, particularly in coal-mining, iron and steel production, and electricity generation, appeared. The next boom began early in 1954 under the influence of the abolition of many import controls and an upswing in the American economy, and lasted until restrictive monetary policies broke its impact at the end of 1955. The downswing extended into the first few months of 1959. Another boom in the United States and the almost complete abolition of re-strictions on capital flows in December 1958 led to a renewed upswing early in 1959 which lasted until the first quarter of 1961.

Structural change was rapid (Table 16.3). As elsewhere in Europe, agricul-tural employment diminished sharply (from 25 to 14½ per cent of the labour force), and this shift in resources was a major source of productivity growth. Within industry, consumer goods and such heavy basic sectors as mining and iron and steel, which had dominated the German economy in the interwar years, lost their leading role. Chemicals, machinery, and automobile manu-facturing assumed a dominant position, accounting between them for about 40 per cent of all employment, and similar shares in total production, and capital formation. These industries were also among those which had the highest share of exports in total sales and experienced rapid productivity gains suggesting that the exploitation of scale economies played a role in their expansion.

A further and very important factor in growth was a flexible labour supply. Throughout the 1950s, demand for labour rose rapidly (total employment in-creased by some 2 per cent per annum), while hours worked fell drastically, and the participation rate ceased to rise in 1957. Demand for labour was, there-fore, very largely demand for additional employees. This did not create ten-sions, however, because of the presence of several sources of labour – in par-ticular the rural exodus and structural unemployment which in the early 1950s was still sizeable (the unemployment rate stood at some 7 per cent in 1950). In addition, more than 2½ million Germans (or 10 per cent of the West German labour force) left East for West Germany between 1949 and 1961, and increased the pool of those in search of work. As most of them were able-bodied, well educated, and in their prime, the human capital they represented added signi-ficantly to the manpower available to the economy. In brief, therefore, labour supply was flexible and plentiful, and the virtual absence of regional policies per-mitted great changes in the regional distribution of the labour force.

But abundant labour is basically only a permissive factor. To explain the very

TABLE 16.3. *Structural changes*
(percentage shares in total)

	1950-54	1955-59	1960-64	1965-69	1970-74	1975-79
GDP[a]						
Agriculture	..	..	4.4	3.8	3.4	3.1
Industry	..	..	50.8	51.6	52.4	50.3
Employment[b]						
Agriculture	22.2	17.0	12.4	10.0	7.7	6.6
Industry	44.0	47.4	48.2	48.2	48.2	45.3
Exports in total sales[b]						
Manufacturing	10.9	14.5	15.1	18.3	21.1	24.0
Basic goods	12.1	15.0	15.3	18.5	21.7	23.3
Iron and steel	15.3	19.2	20.5	25.0	29.5	32.1
Chemicals	16.8	22.1	23.8	28.8	32.8	33.9
Investment goods	20.6	25.1	24.7	28.9	31.2	34.4
Machinery	28.5	29.2	30.5	36.1	39.1	43.5
Road vehicles	19.5	33.7	33.4	40.2	42.1	39.4
Electrical engineering	13.8	18.8	18.0	21.4	23.4	27.7
Data processing	..	..	..	..	49.5	50.4
Consumer goods	5.5	7.2	7.3	9.3	11.2	13.5

[a] Value added in GDP at constant (1970) prices
[b] Before 1960 excluding Saarland and West Berlin
Sources: Sachverständigenrat, *Gutachten 1976/77* and *1980/81*; Statistisches Bundesamt, *Statistisches Jahrbuch* (various issues); W. Glastetter, *Die wirtschaftliche Entwicklung der Bundesrepublik Deutschland im Zeitraum 1950 bis 1975*, Berlin 1977.

rapid growth of the economy in these years it is necessary to look in addition at the performance of the two most buoyant demand components — exports and investment. The role of exports was clearly linked to the cyclical story already mentioned above. That of investment was influenced by the posture of economic policies.

The role of foreign trade

One of the outstanding features of the period is the extent to which the role of foreign trade increased. Within a decade, the share of exports in GDP rose from 9 to 19 per cent (and that of imports from 10 to 16½ per cent). To some extent this was the result of determined efforts by German firms. It was natural for them to seek markets abroad after they had lost so much of their domestic outlets by the partition of Germany into two separate states with little trade between them; and in view of the costs involved in establishing a presence in foreign markets it was probably also rational to adopt a pricing policy which attempted not to transmit the full extent of domestic cost increases to export prices. But whatever the role of these factors, there were also structural reasons which help to explain the export success. German industry had traditionally had a comparative advantage in investment goods. The needs of reconstruction in the post-war period both at home and abroad made for high demand, and probably also for scale economies; the transfer of so much human capital into West Germany and the high degree of factor mobility made it possible to take advantage of this situation. As a consequence, a high proportion of Germany's exports were goods with income elasticities above unity. In addition, integration in Western Europe meant that German markets grew rapidly.

Buoyant export demand played a very important role in the cyclical behaviour of the economy (Table 16.4). Every boom seems to have been started

TABLE 16.4. *Cyclical developments*

	Growth of final demand[a] (annual percentage changes)	Percentage contribution to growth of final demand		
		Exports of goods and services	Gross fixed investment	Private consumption
1951	23.3	28.5	16.1	39.6
1952	14.2	17.2	20.3	41.9
1953	7.6	27.3	30.4	63.8
1954	9.9	32.6	22.1	35.7
1955	16.1	19.5	28.8	38.7
1956	11.2	30.7	19.9	49.6
1957	10.2	34.2	5.7	43.7
1958	6.6	9.3	20.9	57.1
1959	9.6	25.2	28.6	34.7
1960	13.0	23.2	22.3	33.8
1961	8.9	8.1	31.6	52.0
1962	9.0	8.7	26.9	47.0
1963	6.2	22.1	18.5	46.0
1964	10.0	17.4	31.1	37.1
1965	10.4	14.2	15.9	46.8
1966	6.1	33.7	12.8	52.3
1967	0.7	182.8	−228.6	173.2
1968	9.0	25.9	11.3	34.4
1969	12.9	20.8	23.8	36.8
1970	14.0	15.6	34.0	36.6
1971	12.7	17.1	28.4	44.1
1972	9.2	18.0	17.7	47.9
1973	11.5	27.6	9.8	38.6

[a] GDP plus imports of goods and services at current prices
Source: Sachverständigenrat, *Gutachten 1976/77* and *1980/81*.

by a more than proportional increase in exports, which led first to an increase in investment, and then to an increase in consumption. It is the succession of these four-to-five-years export-led upswings (1950-51, 1954, 1959) and of the optimistic expectations they engendered which together amount to a pattern of export-led growth.

That again and again the initial stimulus for an upswing came from export demand is explained by the low rate of inflation together with high productivity growth and lagging increases in wages. The rate of inflation was low because budget surpluses neutralized the inflationary consequences of persistent export surpluses in a regime of fixed exchange rates. In addition, monetary policy adopted a determined anti-inflationary stance, mindful of the fact that most Germans had lived through two major inflations which had destroyed all monetary wealth in their lifetime, and hence tended to judge their governments by their success in keeping prices stable.

More importantly, wage increases lagged behind output increases by about a year. As a consequence, firms found their profits rising in the early stages of an upswing, and could use them to initiate and finance new investment. The productivity gains were distributed in the form of higher wages only in the later phase of an upswing. Thus the wage lag (and the corresponding cyclical movement of profits) helped to finance first the investment boom, and then the consumption boom. Indeed, an upswing typically ended when the increase in domestic demand generated by wage increases resulted in inflationary tendencies which prompted monetary policy to adopt a restrictive stance. The wage lag was due primarily to institutional factors, though abundant labour supplies contributed as well. Good industrial relations and strict adherence to labour and trade union legislation ensured that unions needed hard evidence before they put up new wage claims. This recognition lag was further prolonged by the fact that wage agreements could not be scrapped without incurring heavy penalties and usually lasted for more than a year. It is also true to say that in the 1950s (and in the 1960s) the unions put security of employment and other policy aims such as the achievement of co-determination legislation before wage increase maximization. The charge that their behaviour was too docile therefore misses the point; nor does it take into account that they were (and are) all too aware of the macroeconomic consequences of their actions (there are only sixteen trade unions). That German workers did not lose out in the long run is shown by the fact that real wages increased quite substantially. Nevertheless, the inequality of income and wealth probably increased. That this did not lead to much conflict is yet another indicator of the presence of a broad consensus about priorities — first came reconstruction, then the consolidation of what had been achieved.

Economic policies

The major role performed by economic policies in this period was that of furthering capital formation. It was seen above that the profits generated by rising exports and lagging wages contributed to high rates of investment, but the demand for capital was particularly large while its supply was much less plentiful. The reconstruction of industry, the rebuilding of cities, and the alleviation of the housing shortage in the industrial centres where employment grew so rapidly made for strong investment demand. So did the fact that consumer demand expanded (thus generating a derived demand for investment) once incomes began to rise and were expected to rise still further. The influx of so many more Germans finally added a demographic component to both the demand for consumer goods and the expectation of a permanent increase in that demand. By contrast, the supply of capital presented a problem. Private savings were small. They rose of course as incomes rose (from 3 to 9 per cent of household disposable income), but not by nearly enough to meet the demand for capital.

The gap was narrowed by tax policies which favoured savings, particularly in the corporate sector.[10] Liberal depreciation allowances, the permission to revalue

---

[10] Fiscal policies in this period are discussed in detail in F.G. Reuss, *Fiscal Policy for Growth without Inflation*, Baltimore 1963.

existing capital stocks in connection with the monetary reform discussed above, tax exemptions, and various other means favoured the retention of profits, and also provided direct investment incentives. Most of these measures were constructed so as to subsidize the reinvestment of profits already earned. As a result, at least 60 per cent of gross investment was financed out of depreciation and retained profits throughout the decade.

A second important source of savings for capital formation was the public sector. Old-fashioned budget principles and 'sound' fiscal policies led the government to save for the eventuality of, first, increased payments to the occupying forces, and, later, the military expenditure which would follow from the projected joining of the European Defence Community and later NATO. These budget surpluses were increased by fiscal drag, which raised tax receipts by more than was expected or planned to meet government expenditures. Indeed, in the 1950s budget surpluses contributed more to the financing of gross investment than did personal savings.

Thus the rate of capital formation was high primarily because there were large government surpluses and because economic policy favoured business sector self-financing. Both sets of policies can be viewed as involving forced savings which reduced the real consumption possibilities of private households. The tax advantages granted to the business sector certainly reduced disposable incomes. So did the extremely low levels of social security payments (which are understandable if one remembers the huge obligations West German society had to shoulder as a result of war and partition).

While these policies were largely successful in furthering investment and growth, they did lead to a number of problems. In particular, they reinforced income maldistribution – in the 1950s the degree of inequality may have been greater than before the war – and the share of wages in national income actually fell if corrected for the declining number of self-employed. Difficulties were bound to emerge once these growing inequalities began to be perceived as the consequences of producer-oriented policies promoting the accumulation of real capital. A further problem stemming from these policies was that the reliance on a high degree of self-financing inhibited the development of an efficient capital market. The latter remained small, and was in addition subject to administrative controls in order to channel subsidies to the housing sector, and maintain a 'cheap money' policy for investment purposes. As a result, bank lending became an increasingly important source of both short-term and long-term credit for the corporate sector, which used banks for the interim financing of investment projects which were ultimately financed out of the profits they generated. German banks had traditionally been closely involved with business and commerce; these ties were made stronger by the ways used to increase capital formation in the 1950s, and gave banks the strong position in the German economy which was later to become a controversial issue.

Structural policies were used sparingly. Where they were pursued (e.g. in agriculture or coal-mining), they were used to improve performance and not to save jobs. Public investment occurred primarily in areas where there was high demand for public goods such as transport, energy generation, or housing construction, and more often than not in response to market signals such as shortages or rationing. In addition, there was a general policy of promoting competition.

Thus, for instance, almost all the price and wage controls which had remained in force in 1948 were gradually dismantled in the following five years. Similarly, restrictions on foreign trade were eased, and finally totally abolished in 1958 when the DM became fully convertible. Yet it should be emphasized that these measures were taken only when the time was ripe for them. In particular, the liberalization of foreign trade came after Germany had had a positive balance of trade for some time.

All this was in keeping with the *Soziale Marktwirtschaft* concept: the accent was on the market as the prime mechanism of allocation, and on private initiative as the main motive force. That these policies were on the whole producer-oriented rather than consumer-oriented should not detract from the fact that their aim was to overcome inherited structural imbalances and to create competitive markets. Demand management policies, on the other hand, were hardly needed nor used. As will be seen below, this was to change in the 1960s.

III. The Conflict between External and Internal Balances, 1960-1970

Growth in the 1960s was somewhat less rapid than it had been in the 1950s and more in line with what was recorded elsewhere in Europe. It was high enough, however, to ensure full employment and attract a large number of foreign workers. As in the 1950s, growth was primarily based on exports, but unlike the 1950s persistent export surpluses generated 'imported' inflation and pressures for revaluation. In the conflict between internal and external stability, successive governments chose to strive for the former. But by giving priority to internal stability, Germany not only undermined the international monetary system as it had been conceived in Bretton Woods; it also unleashed forces which helped to destroy the consensus that had been an important element in the development of the economy in the post-war period.

Growth and cycles

A major reason for lower growth in the 1960s was a reduction in the elasticity of labour supply Throughout the decade, the labour force was virtually constant. Though population increased, the participation rate fell as the age structure of the population changed, as longer periods were spent on education and training, and as a more flexible retirement age was introduced towards the end of the decade. Moreover, the building of the Berlin wall in 1961 put an end to immigration from East Germany which in previous years had been a major source of manpower. In an attempt to alleviate the labour shortage, German firms began to recruit foreigners in larger numbers. In 1960 barely 250,000 foreigners were working in West Germany; by 1970 their number had risen to 1.8 million (almost 7 per cent of the labour force). Most of them came from Mediterranean countries, were less skilled, and required more training than the Germans who had come before 1961. This reduced the growth of labour productivity as well as occupational mobility, and generally made the labour market much less flexible than it had been in the 1950s.

The scarcity of labour and the slower growth of labour productivity induced firms to introduce more capital-intensive methods of production. Capital formation increased, with the share of investment rising to 25 per cent in some years. Much of this investment was used for capital deepening – the capital-output ratio, which had fallen in the 1950s, rose in the 1960s – and occurred in industry which continued to expand relative to other sectors. Throughout the 1960s, it provided almost half of all employment in the economy, and generated more than half of all output – the highest ratios in Europe in the period. This expansion was based on the continued export success of its key branches (Table 16.3). Much of investment was therefore directly or indirectly export-induced, and growth continued to be export-led. But investment was also high because firms again and again found their optimistic expectations justified. That the DM was undervalued throughout the 1960s was an important element in this situation.

Because growth was export-led and export-oriented, the dependence of several key sectors on foreign demand increased. Investment goods accounted on average for more than half of total exports and basic goods for another quarter. This dependence is an important reason for the markedly more cyclical nature of the growth process in the 1960s. Three major cycles occurred in the decade – a first one from 1958 to 1963 with a peak in the first half of 1961; a second one from 1963-4 to the recession of 1967, and a third one from the 1968 boom to the late 1971 trough.

All three cycles followed the pattern of the 1950s[11] – they typically began with an increase in export demand which led, after about half a year, to an increase in production, first in export industries and then in those whose inputs were required for the production of exports. After a year or so, investment orders rose. Productivity lagged somewhat behind production, and wage increases typically lagged about a year behind productivity increases. As in the 1950s, this wage lag generated high profits in the first phase of the boom which induced firms to invest; towards the end of the boom high profits led to some wage-push and increased incomes stimulated consumer demand; but the wage lag implied that private consumption reached its peak only after total production and capacity utilization had reached their peak, so that the consumer boom did not lead to a disproportionate increase in imports. Nor did it create much inflationary pressure – consumer prices typically rose only a year after consumer spending had begun to rise. By the standards of the 1970s the overall rate of inflation was very low. In no year did consumer prices rise by more than 4 per cent, and their average increase through the decade was only 2½ per cent.

Inflation and undervaluation

Yet inflation was higher than it had been in the 1950s, and was viewed with concern. As has been pointed out above, most people had experienced already two hyperinflations (one open, one repressed; but both destructive), and were extremely wary of anything that looked like the beginning of a third. The point cannot be stressed enough. A low rate of inflation was not just a policy aim

[11] The cyclical pattern of the economy has been analysed by H. Giersch, *Growth, Cycles and Exchange Rates: The Experience of West Germany*, Stockholm 1970, and by P.A. Klein, 'Postwar Growth Cycles in the German Economy', in H.W. Schröder and R. Spree (eds.), *Historische Konjunkturforschung*, Stuttgart 1981. For the 'wage lag' see W. Noll, 'Lohn-lag und Zyklenbildung', *Schmollers Jahrbuch*, No. 1, 1970.

among several which could be 'traded-off' – price stability was an important element of the post-war consensus which characterized German society, and was valued as such. Unfortunately, however, inflation was almost unavoidable. Continued balance of payments surpluses under fixed exchange rates implied continued increases in the money supply. In the 1950s these had been offset by persistent budget surpluses. But in the 1960s such surpluses virtually disappeared as the central government stepped up its military outlays and local authorities their investment expenditure. Moreover, the pressures on the balance of payments and on the currency became stronger as international capital mobility grew and the DM became increasingly undervalued in relation to other currencies.[12]

When the exchange rate of the newly created DM was fixed in 1948, the parity chosen was probably a reasonably accurate reflection of its international purchasing-power. In line with other European currencies the DM was devalued in 1949 against the dollar, but at a lower rate. The 1950 balance of payments deficit led to demands for a further devaluation which subsided only when the series of balance of payments surpluses began in 1951. In the next few years foreign reserves accumulated, but this was considered necessary in view of their low level, the growing importance of foreign trade, and the world-wide dollar shortage. Moreover, the balance of payments with some of Germany's major trading partners, notably France, was still in deficit, so that it was difficult to say that the exchange rate (measured in terms of dollars) was wrong. Nevertheless it is probably true that from the mid-1950s onwards the DM was below the level compatible with external stability (Fig. 16.2). After all, the government gradually revoked all measures to promote exports, and encouraged capital outflows. Revaluation was first discussed in 1957, after the outbreak of the Suez War had led to speculation in favour of the DM, but was rejected because it was feared that the introduction of complete convertibility, scheduled for 1958, would result in a reduction of reserves. It did not. On the contrary, continuing balance of payments surpluses led to renewed and repeated international speculative bouts which eventually forced two revaluations (in 1961 by 5 per cent and in 1969 by 9.3 per cent).

In spite of these revaluations the DM remained undervalued. Current surpluses continued through most of the decade and the level of reserves nearly doubled between 1960 and 1970. Indeed, the DM could not but be undervalued as long as German prices rose by less than those of other major trading countries. This reinforced speculation and led to 'imported' inflation. The undervalued currency and the accumulation of reserves created inflationary pressures not only via money supply increases but also via the additional demand for German goods. There was, in other words, a direct effect on the price level in addition to the indirect effect working through the creation of central bank money. This was not seen at first and the Bundesbank's response up to the mid-1960s concentrated on counteracting the increases in money supply which resulted from persistent export surpluses.

---

[12] 'Undervaluation' is not always easy to define; it is being used here because it was a key concept in economic policy debates in Germany; see O. Emminger, 'Deutsche Geld- und Währungspolitik im Spannungsfeld zwischen innerem und äusseren Gleichgewicht 1948–1975', in Bundesbank (ed.), *Währung und Wirtschaft*, and other contributions in the same volume.

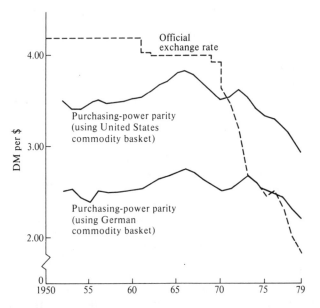

FIG. 16.2. *Official and purchasing-power dollar exchange rate* (DM per United States dollar)
Sources: IMF, *International Financial Statistics* (1980 Yearbook); Statistisches Bundesamt,
Statistisches Jahrbuch (various issues).

There has been controversy about the Bundesbank's ability to sterilize the inflow of foreign funds.[13] On the basis of the available evidence it would seem safe to say that, on the whole, it managed to reduce the domestic supply of central bank money to such an extent that its growth rate supported no more than a moderate rate of inflation (Table 16.5). But that is not to say that the Bundesbank effectively controlled the money supply. Any attempt to reduce the money supply increased interest rates and induced an inflow of foreign funds which tended to defeat the restrictive stance of monetary policy. Restrictive monetary policy measures could be used effectively only as long as the higher interest rates they generated remained below those of other major countries. In practice this meant that the Bundesbank could control the money supply only as long as foreign interest rates were rising, and that the conduct of monetary policies was difficult at best. In particular, the offsetting capital flows induced by Bundesbank attempts to reduce the growth rate of the money supply lengthened the time-lag which elapsed before policy measures became effective, and also required larger policy changes than would otherwise have been the case. Similarly, as the size of the Eurodollar market increased and more foreign

[13] Most of the contributions will be found in the following: R.J. Herring and R.C. Marston, *National Monetary Policies and International Financial Markets*, Amsterdam 1977 (especially Chs. 5 and 6); H.A. Poniachek, *Monetary Independence under Flexible Exchange Rates*, Lexington 1979 (especially Chs. 5 and 7); and N. Thygesen, 'Monetary Policy, Capital Flows and Internal Stability: Some Experiences from Large Industrial Countries', *Swedish Journal of Economics*, March 1973; see also Ch. 11 above.

TABLE 16.5. *Changes in bank liquidity*
(DM million)

	Change in bank liquidity	Due to changes in:			
		foreign reserves	fiscal policy measures	monetary policy measures[a]	other factors
1955	−1,307	2,026	−2,049	−514	−770
1956	1,507	5,689	−1,855	−1,232	−1,095
1957	−1,179	8,062	−561	−4,813	−3,867
1958	627	5,503	−1,816	−1,736	−1,324
1959	−293	3,388	−3,249	93	−525
1960	−797	10,748	−5,312	−5,336	−897
1961	490	5,575	−5,095	2,891	−2,881
1962	−1,056	−515	1,109	−452	−1,198
1963	1,276	2,420	1,588	−1,166	−1,566
1964	−3,316	−481	390	−2,154	−1,071
1965	−3,665	−1,098	1,125	−1,021	−2,671
1966	−242	1,906	690	−1,028	−1,810
1967	7,195	−206	980	4,121	2,300
1968	5,201	9,009	−2,467	−3,370	2,029
1969	−14,540	−9,337	469	−4,709	−963
1970	4,161	19,924	−2,276	−12,757	−730
1971	−3,118	14,783	−4,724	−9,264	−3,913
1972	−5,179	16,905	3,921	−20,281	−5,724

Note: there are three breaks in series: between 1956 and 1957, 1961 and 1962, and 1967 and 1968.
[a] Effect of open market operations and changes in minimum reserves
Source: Deutsche Bundesbank, *Monatsberichte* (various issues).

portfolio investments were placed in Germany as a hedge against inflation (and with the long-term prospect of a possible revaluation), stronger measures had to be introduced. Thus the Bundesbank repeatedly used discriminatory minimum reserve rates (both average and marginal ones) on non-resident deposits, and tried to induce German banks to invest in foreign currencies (i.e. to re-export the capital inflow) by offering profitable swap rates, and by allowing such investments to be deducted from the deposits on which minimum reserves were calculated.[14]

The relative success of monetary policy in sterilizing the continuing inflows of capital had two major consequences. Firstly, because the DM remained, on balance, undervalued, exports were larger than they would otherwise have been and growth was stimulated by foreign demand. Secondly, the preference for internal over external stability (implicit in the reluctance to revalue) encouraged the almost certainly unintended emergence of huge speculative capital flows which ultimately contributed to the disappearance of the post-war international

[14] O. Emminger, 'The D-Mark in the Conflict between Internal and External Equilibrium, 1948–75', *Princeton Essays in International Finance*, No. 122, 1977; see also OECD, *Monetary Policy in Germany*, Paris 1973.

monetary order.[15] When this happened in the 1970s and the DM was forced to float upwards, the presence of too large an export sector, hitherto a factor making for growth, turned out to be an obstacle to rapid expansion. But before turning to this last troubled decade, mention must be made of some other changes in policies and attitudes that characterized the latter part of the 1960s and possibly also contributed to the difficulties of the 1970s.

Changes in policies and attitudes

While monetary policy was very active, fiscal policy through most of the decade followed the pattern established in the 1950s and was mainly used to encourage saving and investment. But policies turned out increasingly to be pro-cyclical,[16] particularly in 1965-6 when a pre-election spending spree by the federal government coincided with a substantial increase in local authority expenditure. As both came in the wake of a large tax cut, the Bundesbank felt obliged to intervene, was able to do so because of a rise in foreign interest rates, and, by fully using its instruments, engineered the 1967 recession — output actually fell and unemployment rose considerably, but the rate of inflation came down to 1½ per cent.

The recession coincided with an end to almost twenty years of Christian Democrat rule, and the coming to power of the Social Democrats as junior partners in a coalition government. With the change in government came a change in attitudes to fiscal policies at least at the federal level. The upswing which began in mid-1967 was the result of a textbook combination of monetary and fiscal policies, helped by another increase in export demand. More importantly, the recession led to legislative efforts to improve the range of policy instruments available for stabilization policies. With the *Stabilitätsgesetz* (Stabilization law) of 1967 the government for the first time officially accepted responsibility for demand management. Hailed at the time as the macroeconomic counterpart to the legislation which in the 1950s had provided the (microeconomic) basis for the competitive order, the act provided two kinds of measures. The federal government was empowered to use some automatic policy instruments such as a temporary surcharge on certain taxes without prior legislation (and hence without prior agreement by other levels of government); and a number of institutions were created which, it was hoped, would improve the co-ordination of fiscal policies, and in particular reduce the danger of unco-ordinated and excessive changes in public expenditure. Although it cannot be denied that a certain amount of co-ordination was achieved, the act did not improve fiscal policies as much as it had been hoped. The main reason was that its provisions were not used because it was politically more acceptable to use *ad hoc* measures which required the consent of all concerned.

---

[15] It should be added that Germany was not the only culprit (see, for instance, M. Michaely, *The Responsiveness of Demand Policies to Balance of Payments: Postwar Patterns*, NBER, New York 1971); but as the country with the largest and most persistent balance of payments surplus it contributed substantially to the demise of the system by not abiding by the rules of the game.

[16] B. Hansen, *Fiscal Policy in Seven Countries, 1955-1965*, OECD, Paris 1969; D. Biehl et al., *Konjunkturelle Wirkungen öffentlicher Haushalte*, Tübingen 1978.

The *Stabilitätsgesetz* also created what is known as the *Konzertierte Aktion* (Concerted Action) – a conference of representatives of trade unions and employer associations, of government and Bundesbank officials, and of independent experts[17] which meets two or three times a year to consider the state of the economy and exchange information about possible future developments. The aim had originally been to set guidelines for wage increases. For obvious reasons this was not achieved. Nevertheless the exchange of information has in all probability reduced uncertainty on both sides of industry about the future course of government policies and Bundesbank actions. This has had an important bearing on stabilization policies in the 1970s when wage conflicts became much more prominent than they had been in the 1950s or 1960s.

The measures which had been taken to end the 1967 recession were successful, but turned out to have been too strong, because they coincided with yet another increase in foreign demand which was unusually large. The result was a boom which rapidly increased production, employment, and capacity utilization. The unexpected speed of the upswing generated large profits, all the more so as the trade unions had been deliberately moderate in their wage demands in order to help overcome the recession, and as a revaluation was shunned until late 1969 despite record speculative inflows. The profit 'explosion' generated as usual high investment ratios and high wage demands. What was new, indeed unprecedented, was the social unrest on the shop-floor which erupted in a series of wildcat strikes in the autumn of 1969. These unofficial strikes forced trade union leaders to re-establish authority over their members by much more aggressive wage bargaining than both sides of industry had become accustomed to (Fig. 16.3). At the same time, the employers were much less prepared to yield than usual. The stage was thus set for an intensification of wage conflicts. The intransigence shown by both sides of industry on this occasion was but one manifestation of the breakdown of the political and social consensus which had dominated German economic life after 1945.

By the end of the 1960s, the economy had lost some of the stability and flexibility of earlier years. To a large extent this resulted from changes in attitudes. Political and economic reconstruction had clearly come to an end and the idea gained currency that the time had come to enjoy the fruits of the years of hard work. Growth was no longer an aim beyond dispute. While much of the debate on the 'quality' of growth remained ineffectual, there can be little doubt that the distribution of the benefits of economic growth was given much more attention than in the 1950s or the early 1960s. Redistribution became the watchword, and with it a critical attitude towards the working of the free market, and thus the concept of *Soziale Marktwirtschaft*. It was certainly not by chance that the Social Democrats formed the government after the 1969 elections – they embodied this critical attitude, advocated reform policies, and seemed to care more about the distribution (and redistribution) of income and wealth.

[17] The most important of these independent experts are members of the Sachverständigenrat and their staff. The Sachverständigenrat was created in 1963 on the model of the American Council of Economic Advisers; but with a different constitution. It consists of five independent members (usually academics drawn from universities and research institutes) who have to report annually on the state of the economy, and who should propose policy alternatives. The federal government is obliged by law to comment on their analysis.

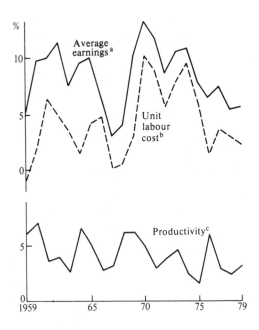

FIG. 16.3. *Average earnings, unit labour costs, and productivity* (annual percentage changes)
[a] Average gross hourly earnings in industry
[b] In the whole economy
[c] GDP per employed
Sources: Bundesministerium für Arbeit und Sozialordnung, *Statistisches Taschenbuch, 1980*; Sachverständigenrat, *Gutachten 1976/77* and *1980/81*.

IV. Stagflation and Structural Problems, 1970-1979

For Germany, as for other industrialized economies, the 1970s were a difficult period. Growth was lower, unemployment and inflation higher. The recession of 1975 was severe enough to bring back memories of the 1930s. Worse still, it seems to have changed the long-term outlook of decision-makers in government, industry, and trade. Recovery there was, but it was slow and insufficient to restore full employment. Though the economy fared better than most other European countries, for most Germans the rate of inflation, the lower growth of incomes, and the increased risk of unemployment were bad enough. Towards the end of the 1970s the outlook turned into guarded optimism, mixed with concern over the needs for structural adjustment which became increasingly apparent in the wake not only of the oil price rise but, more importantly, of the floating and consequent appreciation of the DM.

Growth and cycles

Throughout the 1970s, growth was no higher than in other large industrialized countries, and sometimes lower. In the first half of the decade the main obstacle to higher growth was, as in the 1960s, shortage of labour, especially qualified labour. Investment was high (the share of gross investment in GDP was close to one quarter between 1970 and 1973), but investment requirements were higher still. The large investment effort of the previous two decades called for increased replacement, and the shortage of labour for increased substitution of labour by capital. In the second half of the decade, growth was even lower than in the first half, but for different reasons. High unemployment, a sizeable margin of unused capacities, and low investment point to a lack of demand rather than to supply barriers.

A similar picture emerges when one looks at employment. Over the decade as a whole employment increased only slightly. Mainly for demographic reasons, the participation rate fell, though less so than in the 1960s. In the first few years of the decade the employment of foreign workers increased, reaching almost 2½ million (10 per cent of the work-force, and more than 11 per cent of dependent employment). For cyclical reasons the recruitment of (non-EEC) foreign workers was prohibited in 1973, but numbers declined only slightly (to less than 2 million in 1979 or 7.5 per cent of the work-force), partly because of the falling participation rates of Germans, partly because of a continued decline in hours worked (from 44.0 hours per week in 1970 to 41.9 hours in 1979 in industry). To all intents and purposes, therefore, there was a marked scarcity of labour until 1973. In 1974, the situation changed – unemployment rose and vacancies fell. To the end of the decade, unemployment remained high, especially among the less qualified and the elderly.

Cyclical fluctuations were marked in the first half of the 1970s. The decade began with the downturn of a cycle which had begun in 1967–8. Events followed the traditional pattern except that the rate of inflation did not abate as usual. Another upswing developed in 1972, once again accompanied by an increase in exports, although internal demand, as in 1968, played a larger role than usual. The turning-point came early in 1973, and was brought about by a combination of monetary and fiscal policies. The Bundesbank had regained its ability to control the money supply after the move to a floating exchange rate, and used it immediately by applying a severe credit squeeze in order to reduce an unprecedented rate of inflation. Fiscal policies were also shifted into a restrictive stance because it was feared that the upswing could endanger the 'social peace' and further intensify wage conflicts. What might well have been a normal recession then turned into a very severe one under the influence of the rise in oil prices and the ensuing slowdown in world trade, as well as of an unexpected rise in household savings. A relaxation of policies and a rise in foreign demand generated an upswing in the second half of 1975, but this was not followed by a very marked increase in investment demand, and faltered towards the end of 1977. It was followed by a 'mini' decline which lasted until the middle of 1978 and by a 'mini' upswing which came to an end early in 1980, both characterized by low capacity utilization and sluggish investment.

The pattern of developments as described above diverged in many respects from the pattern that had shaped the cycles and trends of the 1950s and 1960s. Thus, fiscal policy came to play a much more active role, wage negotiations and the movement of labour costs were of crucial importance, notably in the first half of the decade, while a low rate of investment in the second gave rise to worries about the capacity of the economy to overcome structural problems. In addition, the whole period was overshadowed by the move to floating exchange rates, whose longer-run consequences were probably larger than even those of the oil price rises.

The move to floating and the role of policies

The 1969 revaluation had given Germany a temporary respite – much of the speculative capital inflow was. withdrawn. But the lull was of only short duration. In view of a relatively high rate of inflation, the Bundesbank stuck to a restrictive policy and inflows resumed in the early 1970s at an increasing rate in spite of all endeavours to deter them (e.g. a licensing system for non-resident purchases of domestic money-market paper or a cash deposit scheme on foreign non-bank lending). The Bundesbank was again overwhelmed in May 1971 and the government agreed to a temporary floating of the exchange rate, which was then frozen, at a higher value, at the Smithsonian Agreements of December 1971. Predictably, speculation continued, and massive inflows of capital swelled the money supply until the exchange rate was again allowed to float, this time for good, in March 1973. By then, however, the damage was done. The money supply had been greatly increased, and inflation was close to double digits. Worse still, the attempts at direct controls of capital flows furthered the integration of international capital markets, taught German non-bank firms to use such markets, and thus eroded Bundesbank control over the money supply.

When the Bundesbank was freed of the shackles into which the fixed exchange rate system had turned, it made full use of its newly gained powers. The restrictive stance initiated in 1973 continued through most of 1974. As in 1966–7, monetary policy succeeded in reducing the rate of inflation at the price of an increase in unemployment. This time, however, the recession was much more severe than in 1967, and recovery took much longer. One reason for both these phenomena may well have been the continued appreciation; between 1972 and 1979 the DM's effective exchange rate was revalued by as much as 39 per cent.

Another reason for both the recession's severity and the recovery's faltering pace may be found in the stance of fiscal policies. With the change of government to the Social Democrats in 1969, Keynesian demand management had become acceptable, and fiscal policies were used for stabilization purposes much more than before. Unfortunately, however, the use made of these instruments was not always very fortunate. For one thing, the stop–go nature of fiscal policy changes created uncertainty, led firms to believe that measures were only temporary and hence not worth adjusting to, and forced the hand of the authorities (as in 1972, when a temporary and repayable surcharge had to be released at an inopportune time). For another, the Social Democrats had won the election with the promise of reforms which could be seen as attempts to strengthen the position of wage earners and employees *vis-à-vis* employers and the recipients of non-wage incomes. The combined effects of all this were rapidly expanding budgets and a decline in private investment. That between 1973 and 1979 no less than twelve programmes for the improvement of employment, growth, investment, or the alleviation of unemployment and regional and structural problems were announced does not change that verdict much. Admittedly some of them were not without effect; in particular, the measures decided at the Bonn summit were instrumental in the 1978–9 upswing. But there is evidence that the basic idea of all such measures, in so far as they tried to affect investment, was wrong – attempts to change the temporal distribution of investment do not leave the total amount of planned investment unaffected. Indeed, the net effect of fiscal policy, particularly in the period after 1973, seems to have been to deter investment.[18]

Wages and profits

The low rate of investment was clearly one of Germany's major problems in the post-1973 period. The reasons for this decline, which was larger than in a number of other industrialized countries, are complex. The most promising explanation seems to be a combination of various factors: a decline in profitability, combined with changed expectations, and uncertainty about the long-term effects of the DM's appreciation which followed the move to floating exchange rates.

Measures of profitability are notoriously unreliable and difficult to interpret; but most of the available estimates show a more or less marked fall in the 1970s.[19] There is also evidence that the rate of return of real capital fell below the yield that could be earned by investing in financial assets. Firms often preferred to invest on the capital market rather than in capital goods – the average indebtedness of firms increased and so did German firms' investment abroad. The decline in profits had not set in suddenly. A gentle downward trend was already apparent in the 1960s. But it became more pronounced in the 1970s largely as a result of increased wage pressures in the first half of the decade and the appreciation of the currency in the second.

As pointed out above, the labour market in the early 1970s had been characterized by excess demand. This would have made for large wage claims even if the trade unions had not been jolted by the wildcat strikes in the autumn of 1969 and the obviously changed mood of their members. As it was, trade-union negotiators became much more aggressive. Closely allied with the party in power which emphasized full employment as a prime policy aim much more than previous governments had done, they had every right to assume that they would not jeopardize employment by asking for high wage increases. In view of the higher rate of inflation, they also insisted that contracts run for shorter periods. At the same time, employers had no good reason to withhold wage increases or to resist shorter agreements. The outlook was favourable and the chances high that increases in labour costs would be handed on in the form of higher prices. Expectations turned out to be correct in 1970-1, and a wage conflict was avoided. But when unions tried to repeat their performance in the 1972-3 upswing the Bundesbank became convinced that inflationary expectations

---

[18] See K.H. Oppenländer, 'Einige Gedanken zu den Ursachen der aktuellen Investitionsschwäche in der Industrie der Bundesrepublik', in A.E. Ott (ed.), *Gegenwartsprobleme der Wirtschaft und Wirtschaftswissenschaften*, Tübingen 1978.

[19] See T.P. Hill, *Profits and Rates of Return*, OECD, Paris 1979, and E. Altvater, J. Hoffmann, and W. Semmler, *Vom Wirtschaftswunder zur Wirtschaftskrise*, Berlin 1979. Estimates which can be obtained from Bundesbank data show similar tendencies. The exception is provided by estimates of the own rate of return of the private corporate and non-corporate sector provided by K. Conrad and D.W. Jorgenson, *Measuring Performance in the Private Economy of the Federal Republic of Germany, 1950–1973*, Tübingen 1975.

were rising and that strong measures were required to eradicate them. At the same time, employers realized that increased labour costs endangered exports, that the upswing was less pronounced than usual, and that profits suffered, and curtailed their investment orders. It would be wrong to attribute the slow growth of investment to trade-union behaviour alone, but it cannot be denied that increased labour costs did play a role in this context.

The restrictive policy which the Bundesbank pursued throughout 1974 (and, possibly, the change in the stance of fiscal policy) exorcized whatever inflationary expectations the oil price rise had created, and made it clear that the authorities would pursue rigorous anti-inflationary policies. This seems to have persuaded the trade unions (and if not, rising unemployment did) to moderate their wage demands, and convinced employers that they could not count on the Bundesbank automatically underwriting whatever increase in the money supply was required to validate the wage increases they had granted. The result of this learning process on both sides of industry was that inflationary expectations were broken. Yet unit labour costs continued to increase by more than did productivity. This lowered profits which in any case were affected by structural problems revealed by the appreciation of the DM exchange rate.

Structural problems

Until the early 1970s, the undervaluation of the DM had favoured tradeable goods production at the expense of non-tradeables. From this, manufacturing industry benefited more than other sectors of the economy, and within industry those branches of manufacturing which used relatively low-skilled labour-intensive technologies to produce products which were technologically relatively mature, such as the automobile industry. These industries were able to absorb increases in labour costs because inflation at home was lower than in those economies to which they sold an ever increasing proportion of their products; and as long as an increased supply of labour was available to them there was no need to switch to more capital-intensive technologies. With an appreciating DM, however, they lost much of their competitiveness in foreign markets, and were no longer able to absorb rising labour costs. The results were lower profit margins, and in the short run lower capacity utilization, unemployment, and a revision of investment plans which amounted to a reduction in planned expansion.

In the long run, the appreciation of the exchange rate since 1973 revealed a specialization pattern which was not well adapted to the cost conditions and factor price relations appropriate to a highly industrialized economy rich in human and physical capital. This is borne out by a number of facts. First, some industries suffered a reduction of competitiveness not only abroad, but also at home: in the 1970s imports from developing countries increased rapidly in labour-intensive and technologically unsophisticated products. Secondly, there is indirect evidence for obsolescence due to structural adaptation. Direct foreign investment by German firms increased considerably in the later 1970s, and it is well known that some industrial activities were relocated to countries with lower unit labour costs. It has also been argued that the high level of unemployment was due to obsolescence.[20] While it is true, however, that the relative decline of

[20] See especially H. Giersch (ed.), *Capital Shortage and Unemployment in the World Economy*, Tübingen 1978.

the manufacturing sector contributed much to unemployment, it is not immediately obvious that it also contributed to its persistence. There is, finally, evidence which can be interpreted as structural change in response to changes in cost conditions and in factor prices caused by the appreciation as well as the increase in unit labour costs. Manufacturing industry grew less rapidly than other sectors of the economy and there seems to have been a shift from the production of tradeables to the production of non-tradeables, the service sector of the economy having grown much more rapidly in the later 1970s than any other.

The increase in unemployment in the second half of the 1970s is therefore in part the by-product of structural change which was triggered off by external changes which altered the appropriate specialization pattern of the economy. In the 1950s and 1960s growth was rapid enough to prevent a high labour turnover due to structural change from turning into persistent unemployment. In the 1970s growth was sluggish, and so workers made redundant did not immediately find new jobs. Slow growth is of course not the only reason why structural change was slow. It is difficult at the best of times to predict the shape of things to come, and much more difficult when the situation is changing rapidly and there is uncertainty about the future course of events, as there was in the second half of the 1970s.

Other factors also explain the low rate of investment after 1973. There was the demographic factor of a decline in the population which translates easily into a long-term decline in the growth rate of demand. One can also point to a certain degree of market satiation with products which had in the past provided much of the growth of output, especially durable consumer goods. There was the uncertainty created by high public expenditures which at times crowded out private expenditures; and the consequences which, it was feared, would flow from the large increase in the public debt which accompanied the rise in public spending. Moreover, households reacted to increased unemployment with increased savings, thus reducing demand. All these factors translate into the argument that fears of a lower growth rate of demand in the future induced producers to reduce their investment plans.

Yet another factor which caused uncertainty and required structural adaptation was the rise in oil prices. Germany adapted to this better than most other European countries. The large current account surplus and the DM's appreciation helped to cushion the direct impact. Moreover, the very restrictive monetary policy stance of 1974 made it clear that the OPEC decision represented a change in the *relative* price of energy inputs. Although industrial production increased considerably between 1973 and 1979, the volume of oil imports actually fell. It was only in 1979 that a (further) rise in oil prices caused a German balance of payments deficit. Yet this was due less to the rising cost of the oil bill than to changes in the competitiveness of German industries.

In the past, the international commodity terms of trade had favoured Germany. Although the volume of imports grew faster than that of exports, the foodstuffs and raw materials which accounted for most of Germany's imports were cheaper than the manufactured products which made up the bulk of German exports. The 1970s, however, saw some deterioration in the terms of trade (even excluding oil). At the same time, the share of manufactured products in German imports rose considerably, suggesting a loss of competitiveness at home (as pointed out above), and the need for structural adaptation especially in industries with a high export share.

By way of conclusion it should be added that there is a considerable diversity of opinion among German economists about the correct diagnosis of what went wrong in the 1970s. While many would subscribe to the view that structural change and obsolescence were the main problem, others would put more emphasis on insufficient demand, and yet another group would point to rigidities in the labour market as the main obstacle to full employment and prosperity. However, while it may well be true that aggregate demand was lower than it could have been, it is not at all certain how it could have been increased. Fiscal policy was moderately expansionary in the late 1970s and so was monetary policy until 1978. What was missing from the traditional pattern of things was a strong increase in export demand, and a rise in investment. Neither seemed to behave in their traditional manner — precisely one of the points made by the 'structuralist' explanation. Similarly, few would deny that the labour market was more rigid in the 1970s than it had been in the 1960s and especially in the 1950s. Yet these rigidities would be of little consequence if there were not the need for structural change.

Conclusions

Seen in comparative perspective, the development of the German economy in the thirty years to the end of the 1970s can broadly be described as a 'success story'. In the 1950s, the economy grew extremely rapidly and achieved in a few years a return to levels of economic strength which, at the end of the war, would have seemed out of reach even to the most optimistic. In the 1960s, it consolidated this strength by acquiring a powerful position in world markets, exemplified by the persistent export surpluses and continued upward pressures on its currency. Even in the 1970s, despite the difficulties and problems mentioned in the last section, the economy's performance in terms of inflation, unemployment, and even growth was enviable by the standards of most other European countries.

A number of factors contributed to these achievements. At the outset, the decision, taken in the late 1940s outside Germany, to help its reconstruction and to integrate the country into the Western alliance was particularly crucial in changing expectations, in strengthening business confidence, and in forging a consensus which put economic success at the top of the population's aims. This confidence and the consensus spurred growth over the following quarter of a century. In addition, a flexible labour market allowed rapid structural changes, a high degree of competitiveness, and relatively large profits. The resulting high levels of exports and investment reinforced each other in a textbook-like case of export-led growth.

If these were indeed the engines of development, some slowdown was probably inevitable. Elastic labour supplies could not be forthcoming for ever, and indeed the labour market tightened progressively. As for optimistic expectations and consensus, these are intrinsically fragile factors and could well swing in an opposite direction or break down, as they did from the late 1960s onwards.[21] It

---

[21] Of course, West Germany is not the only country which experienced social and

is a further measure of the success of the economy that despite such changing circumstances as well as three, admittedly insufficient and belated, revaluations of the currency, the unavoidable deceleration occurred comparatively smoothly through the 1960s and the early 1970s.

The later 1970s were more difficult years. Not only did Germany have to face changed terms of trade and a world slowdown, but also a loss of competitiveness brought about by its own earlier export successes. And in addition, business expectations, as elsewhere in the Western world, were shaken by the new experience of stagflation and the inability of governments to end it; while the social cohesion of the earlier years gave way to (by German standards) more antagonistic relations between the social partners. But in comparative terms, German policies and performance still remained an example for the rest of Europe.

Looking at the period as a whole, one is struck, perhaps, by the apparent absence of government. Once the essential reforms of the early post-war years had been accomplished, economic policy-making was much less in evidence than in most of the other major European countries. Demand management was not resorted to until the late 1960s and its story since then was, at best, only a qualified success. Fiscal policies were little used for demand management purposes until the early 1970s when, paradoxically, their comparative advantage in a regime of floating exchange rates was declining. Monetary policy was used extensively and reasonably successfully in the 1960s in trying to stave off re-valuations, but its overwhelming aim was the control of inflation. Selective or structural policies were, in principle, shunned for ideological reasons. But while this does suggest that Germany was economically much more liberal than most of its neighbours, it is far from correct to conclude that the state was absent. Industrial and regional policies were resorted to in practice more frequently than is often thought;[22] public expenditures (and revenues) were, as a percentage of GDP, higher in the late 1970s than in any other major OECD country, suggesting that the redistributive role of the government was considerable. Even at the macroeconomic level, whatever the cyclical shortcomings of particular measures, the presence of an armoury of fiscal and monetary instruments which could in principle be used might well have reinforced business confidence.

Turning now to briefly look at the 1980s, it could be argued that there are similarities with the situation as it was at the beginning of the 1950s — on both occasions, high investment and structural change were required. Then there was the prospect of rising domestic demand and the possibility of an expanding export market. At the beginning of the 1980s, the outlook is not quite as favourable. Yet, as thirty years earlier, the situation presents both problems and opportunities.

Among the problems, rising unemployment is probably the major threat.

---

political changes towards the end of the 1960s: see, for instance, C. Crouch and A. Pizzorno (eds.), *The Resurgence of Class Conflict in Western Europe since 1968*, London 1978.

[22] For a discussion of Germany's industrial policies, see W.M. Corden and G. Fels (eds.), *Public Assistance to Industry*, Trade Policy Research Centre, London 1976, and J.B. Donges, 'Industrial Policies in West Germany's not so-Market-oriented Economy', *The World Economy*, September 1980.

Combined with lower growth it could mean more social conflict and thus impede the necessary structural change. If there are nevertheless good reasons for the guarded optimism which seems to be the prevailing mood at the beginning of the decade, these stem from the stability of West Germany's political institutions and processes, and the resources (both physical and human) the country can rely on. In this respect the situation is quite different from what it was in the 1950s. There are less optimistic expectations about the future, and there is the inflexibility which comes with established positions; but there is also the confidence which has grown out of the experience of thirty years of increasing prosperity.

Bibliography

The English-language literature is not particularly rich in works on the German economy. This bibliography therefore also includes works written in German.

Post-war developments are analysed in historical perspective in G. Stolper, K. Häuser, and K. Borchardt, *The German Economy: 1870 to the Present*, London 1967. W.G. Hoffmann, *Das Wachstum der deutschen Wirtschaft seit der Mitte des 19. Jahrhunderts*, Berlin 1965, is an indispensable source of data, but no more. Interesting hypotheses about long waves of economic activity are put forward by H.H. Glismann, H. Rodemer, and F. Wolter, 'Zur Natur der Wachstumsschwäche in der Bundesrepublik Deutschland', and 'Lange Wellen wirtschaftlichen Wachstums', *Kieler Diskussionsbeiträge*, Nos. 65 and 74, Institut für Weltwirtschaft, Kiel 1978 and 1980 respectively.

A good attempt at a quantitative and comparative analysis of the post-war period as a whole can be found in K.W. Schatz, *Wachstum und Strukturwandel der westdeutschen Wirtschaft im internationalen Vergleich*, Tübingen 1974. H. Winkel, *Die Wirtschaft im geteilten Deutschland, 1945-1970*, Wiesbaden 1974, gives a very conventional account, while E. Altvater, J. Hoffmann, and W. Semmler, *Vom Wirtschaftswunder zur Wirtschaftskrise*, Berlin 1979, provide an analysis written from a Marxist standpoint. A useful compendium of statistical data can be found in W. Glastetter, *Die wirtschaftliche Entwicklung der Bundesrepublik Deutschland im Zeitraum bis 1975*, Berlin 1977. For more than purely economic trends, see R. Löwenthal and H.-P. Schwarz (eds.), *Die Zweite Republik*, Stuttgart 1974 (an unusually informative collection of papers discussing political, sociological, and economic trends), and Komission für den Wirtschaftlichen und sozialen Wandeln, *Wirtschaftlicher und Sozialer Wandel in der Bundesrepublik Deutschland*, Göttingen 1977 (a summary of a massive research programme on economic and social change in the country). Finally R. Dahrendorf, *Society and Democracy in Germany*, New York 1967, presents an excellent sociological analysis of German society and its traditions.

The *earlier part of the post-war period* is surveyed in two excellent accounts by W. Abelshauser, *Wirtschaft in Westdeutschland, 1945-1948*, Stuttgart 1975, and H.C. Wallich, *Mainsprings of the German Revival*, New Haven 1955. A useful collection of papers for the years before 1960 can be found in R. Richter (ed.), 'Currency and Economic Reform: West Germany after World War II', *Zeitschrift für die gesamte Staatswissenschaft*, September 1979. The cyclical experience of *the 1950s and 1960s* is looked at in W. Vogt, *Wachstumzyklen der westdeutschen Wirtschaft*, Tübingen 1968, and, especially, in an excellent analysis by H. Giersch (a former president of the Sachverständigenrat), *Growth, Cylces and Exchange Rates: The Experience of West Germany*, Stockholm 1970.

E. Sohmen, 'Competition and Growth: The Lesson of West Germany', *American Economic Review*, December 1959, and H. Arndt, 'Competition, Price and Wage Flexibility, and Inflation: The German Experience', *The Antitrust Bulletin*, No. 17, 1972, analyse special aspects of developments in the 1950s and 1960s. The German balance of payments is discussed by W.P. Wadbrook, *West German Balance of Payments Policy*, New York 1972, and in two thought-provoking papers by C.P. Kindleberger, 'Germany's Persistent Balance-of-Payments Disequilibrium', in R.E. Baldwin *et al.*, *Trade, Growth and the Balance of Payments*, Chicago 1966, and 'Germany's Persistent Balance-of-Payments Disequilibrium Revisited', *Banca Nazionale del Lavoro Quarterly Review*, June 1976. Papers surveying some aspects of the experience of *the 1970s* can be found in N. Kloten *et al.*, *Zur Entwicklung des Geldwertes in Deutschland*, Tübingen 1980, while the problems of structural change are discussed in H. Giersch (ed.), *Capital Shortage and Unemployment in the World Economy*, Tübingen 1978, and G. Fels and K.D. Schmidt, *Die deutsche Wirtschaft im Strukturwandel*, Tübingen 1980.

On *economic policy*, the standard exposition of the *Soziale Martwirtschaft* concept, in both theory and practice, is G. Gutmann *et al.*, *Die Wirtschafts-verfassung der Bundesrepublik Deutschland*, Stuttgart 1976. A number of important analyses of policy issues can be found in Deutsche Bundesbank (ed.), *Währung und Wirtschaft in Deutschland, 1876-1975*, Frankfurt 1976, and in D. Cassel, G. Gutmann, H.J. Thieme (eds.), *25 Jahre Marktwirtschaft in der Bundesrepublik Deutschland*, Stuttgart 1972. Surveys of monetary policy are contained in OECD, *Monetary Policy in Germany*, Paris 1973, and S.F. Fowen, A.S. Courakis, and M.H. Miller (eds.), *Monetary Policy and Economic Activity in West Germany*, London 1977.

The most comprehensive analysis of current developments is provided by the Sachverständigenrat in their annual *Gutachten*. The *Annual Report* by the Deutsche Bundesbank is another valuable source, but concentrates on monetary policy. Short summaries are provided by the OECD in their annual *Economic Surveys*. In addition, there are regular assessments by the five main German economic research institutes (Deutsches Institut für Wirtschaftsforschung, Berlin; HWWA-Institut für Wirtschaftsforschung, Hamburg; IFO-Institut für Wirtschaftsforschung, Munich; Institut für Weltwirtschaft, Kiel; and Rheinisch-Westfälisches Institut für Wirtschaftsforschung, Essen).

17

Italy[*]

GUIDO M. REY[**]

Introduction

The growth of the post-war Italian economy has generated numerous and diverse interpretations which have reflected the contradictions of the country's development.[1] The aim of this chapter is certainly not to prove that these contradictions did not exist. On the contrary, it will try to illustrate how the economy evolved precisely because of such contradictions and how deceptive it is to look for a global model capable of providing a unique explanation for what happened.

One of the more controversial issues in the economic policy debate during the period has been centred on the merits of foreign trade and on the role of foreign versus domestic factors in stimulating growth. The arguments between the advocates of free trade and those of protectionism were particularly animated in the period in which Italy was involved in repairing the material and moral damage caused by World War II. They reappeared in the mid-1950s, when the decision to join the EEC was taken, and they emerged again in the second half of the 1970s, when the sudden change in the international terms of trade between primary products and manufactures seemed to jeopardize one of the elements which had favoured Italian industrial development until then.

The essential element of the initial debate was whether or not Italian industry was capable of competing on world markets. The advocates of international economic integration believed, and still believe, that the external stimulus would push the Italian economy along a path of sustained development while at the same time anchoring the country to the Western democracies. In particular, the decision to participate in the early post-war liberalization of international trade was based on the idea that there would be sufficient outlets for exports to compensate imports thanks to a largely unsatisfied and stable world demand for the traditional textile and foodstuff sectors. It was also felt that the problems which competition could create were likely to be limited to the metal-working industries and to some areas of the chemical sector where protection had been particularly high. Finally, the resumption in the international movements of labour

---

* As for other country chapters, editorial policy has imposed the use of internationally standardized statistics which at times differ from national concepts and figures.

** ISTAT, Rome. The views expressed are those of the author and do not necessarily reflect those of ISTAT.

[1] Numerous references to the various interpretations that have been given of post-war Italian economic developments can be found in P. Ciocca, R. Filosa, and G.M. Rey, 'Integrazione e sviluppo dell'economia italiana nell'ultimo ventennio: un riesame critico', in Banca d'Italia, *Contributi alla ricerca economica*, No. 3, 1973 (an abridged version of which has appeared as 'Integration and Development of the Italian Economy', *Banca Nazionale del Lavoro Quarterly Review*, September 1975), and in A. Graziani, *L'economia italiana dal 1945 ad oggi*, Bologna 1979 (2nd edn.).

and capital would have favoured Italy, thanks to traditional emigrant remittances on the one hand, and an inflow of foreign funds on the other because of an expected rate of return above that recorded in competing countries.

Conversely, the opponents of this view feared, and still fear, that the balance of payments constraint would impose a deceleration in the country's growth in order to limit imports to a level compatible with the value of exports. Above all, they feared that the international division of labour would confine Italian industry to sectors with relatively low productivity growth and with limited scope for capital accumulation which would have aggravated the problems of employment and the North–South divide.

The choice which was made is well known. Italy joined the United States-inspired movement towards free trade at the turn of the 1940s and was an important force behind the creation of the EEC in the late 1950s. A necessary initial ingredient of this policy was the stabilization of prices and wages, even at the cost of some temporary underemployment of resources, and the avoidance of overly expansionary policies. The overall results of this strategy were positive. Italy's growth rate was among the highest in Europe and so was its rate of investment (Fig. 17.1). The balance of payments was usually in surplus, industrial employment grew, and a systematic process of industrialization was pursued.

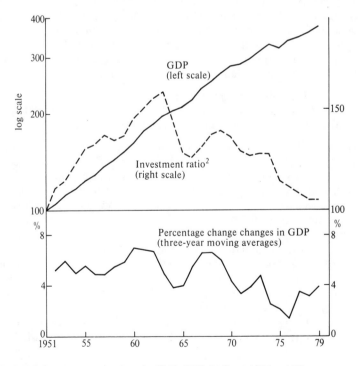

FIG. 17.1. *Output and investment trends, 1951–1979* (indices: 1951 = 100)
[a] Gross fixed investment in per cent of GDP at constant prices
Source: OECD, *National Accounts of OECD Countries, 1950–1979.*

Income distribution saw a shift in favour of labour and, within the personal sector, a clear movement towards greater equality, at least in the 1970s.

It is true, however, that a number of problems and difficulties were not solved. Among these one can list the economic and social gap between the industrialized North and the agricultural South which has remained almost unchanged over the last thirty years, the backwardness of the agricultural sector, the continuing high rate of open unemployment, and the inflationary pressures of the 1970s. The public sector deserves special mention as an increasingly intrusive recipient of household savings and at the same time an inefficient user of these resources. Finally, it is worth remembering that income and wealth inequalities remain large; that the capital per worker endowment and therefore the productivity of Italian labour have been consistently below those of other industrialized countries; and that, increasingly through the period, economic life was dominated by political forces, particularly in the areas of industrial relations and wage negotiations.

This contradiction between on the one hand rapid growth, and on the other continuing structural problems is best shown by the gap between Italy's per caput income and that of other developed countries (with Italy still only at some 55 per cent of the other EEC members' level in the late 1970s) or by a series of indicators of development which have always relegated the economy to an intermediary ranking in a world league table – a relatively low position in the Western industrialized world or a relatively high one among developing countries.

In an analysis of economic expansion over a long time-span, a subdivision of the period seems essential, even if such subdivisions are always subjective, the demarcation lines often artificial, and the periods chosen shade into each other (Table 17.1). The subdivision proposed is as follows:

    (i) 1951–63, or the years of rapid development;[2]
    (ii) 1963–69, a period in which earlier growth was not consolidated;
    (iii) 1969–79, a decade of slowdown and recurrent crises.

The years to 1963 can be further subdivided into two phases: a first one, from 1951 to 1958, characterized by a development which was largely internal in origin, and a second one from 1958 to 1963, in which growth accelerated and was stimulated by European integration. The intermediary period (1963–69) was one in which expansion remained relatively rapid and prices relatively stable, but investment stagnated as firms used more efficiently the capital equipment previously installed. Finally, the 1970s saw a halving in the growth rate and a sharp acceleration in inflation. Two distinct elements contributed to the difficulties of this period. The first, of internal origin, was the crisis in industrial relations which was particularly acute in the early 1970s. The second, of external origin, developed from 1973 and was sparked off by the oil shock and the shift in the international terms of trade.

The brevity of the text that follows inevitably implies that a full discussion of these various periods is impossible. Only a few selected features will be touched

---

[2] 1951 is chosen because it is the first post-war year for which full national accounts statistics are available. It is also a year in which the reconstruction period may be safely said to have come to an end.

TABLE 17.1. *Longer-term trends*

	1951–79	1951–63	1963–69	1969–79
	average annual percentage changes			
GDP	4.8	5.8	5.3	3.3
Inflation[a]	6.1	2.7	3.4	12.2
Employment	0.2	0.1	—0.4	0.6
	1951–79	1951–63	1964–69	1970–79
	percentages			
Investment ratio[b]	(22.8)	(24.4)	24.2	21.1
Unemployment rate[c]	6.3	6.7	5.3	6.2
	$ million, annual averages			
Current balance	589	65	1,919	471

[a] Consumer prices
[b] Gross fixed investment in per cent of GDP at constant prices
[c] In per cent of the labour force

Sources: OECD, *National Accounts of OECD Countries, 1950–1979*; OECD, *Labour Force Statistics, 1968-1979*; OECD, *Balance of Payments Statistics, 1950–1961* and *1960–1977*; OECD, *Economic Outlook*, July 1981; IMF, *International Financial Statistics* (1980 Yearbook); C. Sorrentino, 'Methodological and Conceptual Problems in Measuring Unemployment', *mimeo*, OECD, Paris 1976; ISTAT, *Annuario di contabilità nazionale, 1978* (Vol. 1).

upon which, it is felt, are important for an understanding of Italian economic developments. But the choice of such features is, of course, subjective and their treatment at times compressed by the editorial constraints of space.

I. The Years of Rapid Growth, 1951–1963

The years 1951–63 saw an unprecedentedly high growth rate (close to 6 per cent per annum),[3] accompanied by profound structural transformation (Table 17.2). In particular, the weight of agricultural employment, which was still above 45 per cent at the beginning of the period, making Italy only a semi-industrialized country at best, had shrunk to 28 per cent by 1963 – a year in which Italy achieved, for the first time in its modern history, a situation close to full employment. This process was accompanied by massive emigration and urbanization, largely from rural areas in the South to the North's urban conurbations. Yet despite such sharp and, in many ways, disruptive social changes, cyclical fluctuations were mild and price inflation very subdued. At a macroeconomic level, therefore, this period was one of relatively smooth and favourable developments without great discontinuities. Yet a subdivision into two phases may still be desirable so as to emphasize the different roles played by domestic and external forces at various points of time. The years from 1951 to 1958 saw growth largely spurred by forces of internal origin; the subsequent 1958–63 period

[3] In the previous period of rapid expansion, the 1920s, Italian output had not grown by much more than 3½ per cent per annum.

TABLE 17.2. *Structural changes*
(percentages)

	Agriculture	Industry	Services
Employment shares			
1951	46	27	27
1958	36	32	32
1963	28	37	34
1969	22	39	39
1979	15	38	47
Output shares − constant (1970) prices			
1951	(15)	(31)	(54)
1958	(13)	(36)	(51)
1963	10	41	49
1969	9	43	48
1979	7	43	50
Output shares − current prices			
1951	(20)	(40)	(40)
1958	(16)	(39)	(45)
1963	12	42	46
1969	9	42	48
1979	7	44	49

Sources: OECD, *National Accounts of OECD Countriês, 1962–1979*; OECD, *Labour Force Statistics, 1968–1979*; ISTAT, *Annuario di contabilità nazionale, 1978* (Vol. 1).

witnessed an accelerated expansion and international integration stimulated by membership of the Common Market.

1951–58 − demand, output, and policies

The most notable development in the 1950s was the very rapid growth of fixed investment achieved by both the public sector and private entrepreneurs (Table 17.3). Between 1951 and 1958 gross capital formation rose by 10 per cent per annum, with the investment share increasing from 18 to 24 per cent of GDP. Within this total, the most dynamic component was residential construction − a reflection partly of reconstruction and urbanization needs and partly of large public financial help. Conversely, private consumption remained subdued in line with the moderate growth of real wages. The latter reflected a situation of excess supply on the labour market and the acceptance by the weak Italian trade unions of the time of a wage policy which clearly favoured the process of industrialization.

Exports were the other most dynamic component of demand, with invisible receipts rising particularly rapidly thanks to tourist earnings and migrants' remittances. Yet despite such growth, the current balance was in (declining) deficit virtually throughout the period, and the trade deficit corresponded to as much as 3 per cent of GDP. The reason for this lay in the sustained growth of imports pulled in by the buoyant development of domestic demand. The balance of payments, however, did not represent a constraint on growth in the period. The current deficit was amply covered by capital inflows (aid at first, direct investment later), and the level of international reserves, low at the outset ($0.8 billion), had trebled by 1958.

TABLE 17.3. *Growth of GDP and selected demand components, 1951–1963*
(average annual percentage changes)

	1951–63	1951–58	1958–63
GDP	5.8	5.3	6.6
Private consumption	5.5	4.5	7.0
of which: durables	8.9	5.0	14.5
Gross fixed investment	9.9	9.8	10.1
of which: residential construction	12.8	15.5	9.0
machinery and equipment	9.3	6.0	14.0
of which: agriculture	8.3	10.0	5.8
industry	9.1	7.1	12.1
Exports of goods and services	13.2	12.9	13.7
of which: goods	11.9	8.8	16.3
Imports of goods and services	13.6	9.4	19.8
of which: goods	12.9	7.2	21.3

Sources: OECD, *National Accounts of OECD Countries, 1950–1968* and *1950–1979*;
ISTAT, *Annuario di contabilità nazionale*, 1978 (Vol. 1).

The least satisfactory aspect of the economic performance of these years is to be found in the employment field. Overall employment rose very little, and (according to internationally comparable estimates) the rate of unemployment barely declined from 8 to 7½ per cent of the labour force, despite a net emigration flow equivalent to perhaps 5 per cent of the labour force. Though jobs were created in industry and services (1¼ and 1 million respectively), 1¾ million people left the land.

Despite, or perhaps because of, this exodus, agricultural productivity rose rapidly (6¼ per cent per annum), helped also by substantial government aid. Thus, the volume of agricultural investment virtually doubled in the period. Southern agriculture was particularly helped, both directly via the creation of the Cassa per il Mezzogiorno (the Development Fund for the South), and indirectly via agrarian reform. Overall, agriculture played an important role in the growth process of this period – it supplied much of the labour which the manufacturing and construction sectors required; it provided a sustained demand for industrial output, following the increase in the use of fertilizers, the spread of mechanization, and the extension of land reclamation; and it maintained a surplus in the trade balance for foodstuffs.

More controversial were the results of the expansion of the services sector. The low growth of productivity and the inflation potential which are inherent in this branch in any country were made worse in Italy by a pronounced lack of competition, by speculation in housing, and, more generally, by the widespread inefficiencies typical of the tertiary sector of a relatively backward country. As a result, the terms of trade between services and industry (excluding construction) rose by nearly 6 per cent per annum.[4]

Over the period, economic policy favoured, more or less consciously, selective

---

[4] In comparison, and over the same period, they were rising by only 3¼ to 3½ per cent per annum in Germany and France, while being virtually stable in the United Kingdom.

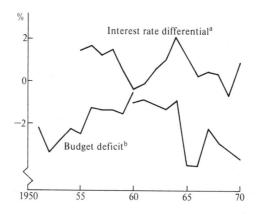

FIG. 17.2. *Indicators of policy stance* (percentages)
[a] Difference between long-term government bond yields in Italy and the average of similar long-term rates in France, Germany, the United Kingdom, and the United States
[b] General government net lending in per cent of GDP; break in series in 1960
Sources: OECD, *National Accounts of OECD Countries, 1950–1968* and *1950–1979*; ISTAT, *Bollettino mensile di statistica*, July 1981; IMF, *International Financial Statistics* (1980 Yearbook).

intervention in specific areas (e.g. agriculture, housing, the South, energy, iron and steel), but followed otherwise an overall cautious stance with only modest expansionary effects. Fiscal policy was entirely directed towards containing the budget deficit — a policy which met with some success, since the latter fell from a peak of 3.2 per cent of GDP in 1952 to 1.3 per cent in 1958. This prudent budget policy was accompanied by an equally cautious monetary policy. The growth in money supply largely followed that of current price output, and interest rates were kept at a high level, if seen relative to virtual price stability at home and interest rate levels abroad (Fig. 17.2).

Yet such relatively high interest rates did not seem to check investment. Partly, this may have resulted from the elimination of uncertainty which a stable interest rate policy signified. Credit supply responded flexibly to variations in demand without giving rise to rationing phenomena. More importantly, however, most investment was financed from internal funds. This was even true of the interest-rate-sensitive residential construction sector whose self-financing ratio was as high as 80 per cent and which, in addition, benefited from public financial help.

1951–58 – domestic-led growth

These high self-financing ratios point to the presence of high profits. Data on the latter are not always easily forthcoming, but according to the figures assembled by Hill for ten OECD countries,[5] it would appear that in the mid-1950s the share of profits in industrial value added was in Italy second only to that of Germany. More interestingly, perhaps, while employee compensation rose, as a percentage of national income, by some two percentage points between 1951

[5] T.P. Hill, *Profits and Rates of Return*, OECD, Paris 1979.

and 1958, adjusting for the rising number of employees results in a decline of roughly 1 percentage point. These rather favourable profit developments were, of course, the counterpart to the relative wage sluggishness mentioned above. Excess supplies of labour implied an income distribution shift towards capital. Optimistic expectations buttressed by an accommodating monetary policy meant that increased profits were reinvested.[6]

High investment, in turn, allowed large productivity gains which moderated the rise in employment and further restrained the rise in wages. Unit labour costs as a result hardly rose (1 per cent per annum in industry, excluding construction, between 1951 and 1958), allowing a continued fall in export prices on the one hand, and further rises in profits on the other. Though consumption was inevitably sacrificed, the rapid rise in investment maintained growth at high levels.

In this interpretation, the mainsprings of growth come mainly from internal forces, particularly from the 'virtuous circle' of high investment–high productivity gains–high profits–high investment. An alternative explanation has, however, also been put forward which privileges the role of foreign trade in this period and argues that Italian growth was export-led and that the changes in the country's industrial structure were determined by foreign demand.[7] Yet the evidence for such a thesis does not seem very conclusive.[8] Merchandise exports, as was seen above, grew less rapidly than investment; the share of exports in total manufacturing value added rose only by 2¼ percentage points over the period (from 7.1 per cent in 1951–2 to 9.4 per cent in 1957–8), and the commodity composition of trade did not change drastically – on the contrary, the shares of both exports and imports of consumer goods remained stable, while those of investment goods rose, confirming the thesis that domestic expansion in a particular area stimulates not only imports but also exports.[9] If one looks at individual sectors, the metal-manufacturing branch (one-quarter of total manufacturing) shows, for instance, that in the early part of the period imports were rising while exports were declining, and that it was only in the later 1950s that this tendency was reversed – again prima-facie evidence that domestic demand led the way and that later export successes were based on earlier increases in production and scale economies made possible by rising outlets at home.

In conclusion, therefore, it would seem that this period saw a sustained development largely of internal origin, even though the contribution of external demand accelerated through time. This process occurred in the absence of pronounced cyclical fluctuations and was supported by relative monetary stability. But it kept alive many of the structural contradictions and problems in existence

---

[6] There are similarities in this mechanism with the dual economy model postulated by C.P. Kindleberger (*Europe's Postwar Growth*, Cambridge, Mass. 1967).

[7] See, in particular, A. Graziani *et al.*, *Lo sviluppo di un'economia aperta*, Naples 1969, for whom export-led growth is made a function of dualism, and A. Lamfalussy, *The United Kingdom and the Six*, London 1963, for whom it was a function of low wages and an undervalued currency. For an econometric study supporting the export-led thesis see R.M. Stern, *Foreign Trade and Economic Growth in Italy*, New York 1967.

[8] For more detail see Ciocca, Filosa, Rey, 'Integration and Development'.

[9] S.B. Linder, *An Essay on Trade and Transformation*, Stockholm 1961.

at the beginning of the 1950s. The technological backwardness of much of the manufacturing sector remained substantial; agricultural productivity was low when compared to that of other European countries, and many branches of the services sector were still at pre-industrial levels of development and efficiency.

It is with this contradictory background – a dynamic rapidly growing economy on the one hand, yet one fettered by numerous elements of backwardness – that Italy was going to face the difficult confrontation with the other more developed partners of the EEC.

1958–63 – the economic 'miracle'

The five years from the mild slowdown of 1958 to the boom of 1962–3 must be considered absolutely exceptional from all angles. Growth was extremely rapid (6½ per cent per annum), with investment rising at 10 per cent and reaching a share in national income of over 26 per cent – one of the highest levels recorded by any European country in the post-war period (Table 1.5). At the 1963 peak, Italy enjoyed for the first time in its modern history a situation of full employment, within the limits in which it is possible to speak of full employment in a dualistic economic system. And it is during this period that the structure of output evolved towards a composition which reflected the country's newly found position as an industrial economy. The share of industry in constant (1970) prices rose from 36 to 41 per cent, while that of agriculture declined by as much as 3 percentage points. These shares were to change relatively little in the following fifteen years – by less, in any case, than in the brief period under consideration.

There are both marked similarities and sharp differences *vis-à-vis* the earlier years in the contribution of various expenditure components to growth. As in 1951–8, investment rose extremely rapidly, but whilst residential construction and agriculture had been the most dynamic elements in the 1950s, this role was now taken by investment in machinery and equipment, particularly in industry (Table 17.3). And whilst exports of goods and services remained the single fastest-growing major element of total demand in both sub-periods, the rate of growth of merchandise exports now outstripped that of invisibles. A third, and very noticeable change from the 1951–8 years is to be found in the sharp acceleration in the growth of private consumption, particularly marked for durable purchases, whose level doubled in five years.

The buoyant growth rates of output and investment were accompanied by an acceleration in the growth of productivity to 7 per cent per annum for the economy as a whole and to over 8 per cent in manufacturing alone. Despite this surge in productivity growth, employment in industry and services both rose. The increase was on this occasion insufficient, however, to absorb an accelerated decline in the agricultural work-force, and total employment fell, therefore, if only slightly. A situation of virtual full employment was none the less achieved thanks to a fall in participation rates[10] and to an acceleration in the emigration movement to some 280,000 per annum. More importantly, overall full

---

[10] This was partly due to a decline in female activity rates consequent upon massive urbanization – women who had usually been counted as members of the labour force in agriculture, even if they only worked on a very part-time basis, were unable to find jobs in towns.

employment reflected an imbalanced situation between northern and southern Italy. In the 'industrial triangle' of the North (Piedmont, Liguria, and Lombardy), the rate of unemployment had, by 1963, fallen to barely 1½ per cent, while it was still above 3 per cent in the South. In addition, a pronounced scarcity of skilled workers meant that sectoral bottle-necks became progressively more pronounced as the boom gathered strength.

One of the factors that made this boom possible was the more expansionary stance of economic policy. On the monetary policy front the monetary base rose at 13 per cent per annum between 1958 and 1962, as against a growth of current price GDP of 9½ per cent, while interest rates fell gradually, at a time at which inflation was accelerating. On the fiscal policy side, the earlier aim of containing budget deficits gave way to a somewhat more relaxed attitude. In both cases policies seem to have become more pro-cyclical as time went by. Thus, in late 1962, at a time of peak pressures on capacity, the Bank of Italy lowered minimum reserve requirements and facilitated short-term capital inflows.[11] And throughout the years 1960-2, public enterprise investment rose very rapidly and clearly contributed to the acceleration in economic activity.[12]

An even more important reason for growth in this period is, however, to be found on the external side. Italy's entry into the Common Market seems to have had positive effects on the economy going beyond those recorded in other member countries.[13] The modernization of the industrial apparatus and relatively low wage levels had made protection superfluous and had put the country in a favourable position for benefiting from an enlargement of markets: indeed, the reduction in customs barriers stimulated efficiency. More importantly, entrepreneurial expectations seem to have been strengthened. As a result, investment was stimulated, supply increased, economies of scale were probably achieved, and Italy benefited from such 'dynamic' effects more than from simple trade creation or diversion.

With integration in the EEC area went a step jump in the shares of foreign trade in output. The combined share of exports and imports of goods and services in current price GDP, which had risen from 23 to 24½ per cent between 1951-2 and 1957-8, increased to 29½ per cent in the next five years. It is in this period that the structure of trade took the composition that was to remain dominant until the oil crisis. On the exports side, manufactures rose to 78 per cent of the total, while the share of foodstuffs declined. On the imports side, the latter increased sharply, and the trade balance in agricultural products swung into large deficit in 1960, a deficit that was to continue through the next twenty years. Otherwise, however, most sectoral trade balances for industrial products remained in rough equilibrium, with the only major exception provided by the surplus on clothing.

Successful international integration was not fully paralleled by a similar process of integration at home. But Southern Italy, which had lost ground in the 1950s relative to the rest of the country (Table 14.3), benefited from a shift in government priorities in the late 1950s. It was realized that a strategy for

[11] OECD, *Monetary Policy in Italy*, Paris 1973, p. 37.
[12] B. Hansen, *Fiscal Policy in Seven Countries, 1955-1965*, OECD, Paris 1969, p. 307.
[13] See Ch. 8 above.

development could not be based solely on infrastructure investment, agrarian reform, and emigration but had to pass by a policy of moving jobs to people. A concerted, government-led effort began to encourage industrial investment in the area, with an array of incentives and subsidies designed to stimulate the relocation of industry. Spearhead of the new policy were the nationalized corporations (which are particularly important in Italy, accounting, for instance, for some 8 per cent of total value added in 1979), which were instructed to concentrate in the South 60 per cent of their capital formation. Largely as a result, industrial investment rose by 25 per cent per annum between 1958 and 1963, as against a national figure of 12 per cent. It is true, however, that the capital-intensive nature of much of this investment meant that industrial (and overall) employment fell through the period.

1958-63 – problems and policies

This story of broad successes is, however, marred by the appearance in the early 1960s of two problems which had not been encountered in the 1950s – price inflation and the emergence of a balance of payments deficit. Prices had remained virtually stable since the Korean War period. Between 1951 and 1961, consumer price inflation had been only 2 per cent per annum. In 1962, however, consumer prices rose by 4.7 per cent and in 1963 by 7.5 per cent – well above the 3¾ per cent recorded at the time by EEC partner countries. At the root of the initial inflation were foodstuff prices and rents (in 1962 the implicit price deflator for value added in agriculture rose by 11 per cent; that for services by 7 per cent). Soon, however, inflation spread, particularly in the tertiary sector, but also to the labour market. The achievement of virtual full employment and the appearance of excess demand pressures coincided with the renewal of three-year wage contracts and resulted in a two-digit increase in contractual wages. In industry (excluding construction) average earnings per employee, which had already risen by 14 per cent in 1962, rose by a further 20 per cent in 1963, and unit labour costs jumped by 15 per cent in that year.[14]

Domestic inflation led to a sharp loss in competitiveness (import unit values had remained stable between 1958 and 1963), and, combined with excess demand, to a marked deterioration in the balance of payments. The trade deficit trebled between 1961 and 1963, reaching in that year the equivalent of 3.6 per cent of GDP, and the current account recorded a $¾ billion deficit for the first time since 1956. The situation was further aggravated by a concomitant increase in illegal capital exports (from some $0.3 billion in 1961 to as much as $1½ billion in 1963). Inflation and the precarious current account position played some role in this outflow, which had also been facilitated by an expansionary monetary policy, but the primary cause is to be found in political factors (the coming to power of a centre-left government which nationalized electric energy and tried to enforce tax payments on dividends).

The inevitable policy reaction came in late 1963 and was particularly sharp on the monetary side – the monetary base remained virtually constant in the three quarters to mid-1964. Fiscal policy was tightened in early 1964, mainly via

---

[14] A. Fazio, 'Inflation and Wage Indexation in Italy', *Banca Nazionale del Lavoro Quarterly Review*, June 1981.

an increase in taxation. The combined effect of these policy measures was rapid and substantial – inflation decelerated to rates similar to those of Italy's main competitors already by the end of 1964, the current account was back in substantial surplus in that year ($0.6 billion), and illegal capital exports were cut down sharply. It is true, however, as will be seen in the next section, that growth slowed down, that the investment ratio fell, never to recover its 1963 level, and that Italy was ushered into a period of faltering economic performance.

This episode of policy stringency has generated an abundant literature[15] which has often argued that the measures were belated and were applied too harshly. On the first issue, there would seem to be a general consensus – as mentioned earlier, both fiscal and monetary policies remained expansionary and therefore acted pro-cyclically until early 1963. The second issue turns on whether the economy was already slowing down in the course of that year. The evidence on this point is more mixed, though it would seem that activity had begun to weaken before restrictive measures were imposed. While, with the benefit of hindsight, it could therefore be argued that monetary policy, in particular, may have been guilty of 'overkill', such a judgement can be questioned. It forgets, for instance, that the statistical information available at the time was scanty, sometimes unreliable, and often issued only with long lags. More importantly, it glosses over the fact that the policy issue confronting the authorities was not merely that of controlling a cyclical fluctuation in activity, but that of curbing a major speculative run on financial markets which was endangering the level of reserves and possibly the value of the currency. Fine tuning in the circumstances may well have proved ineffective.

The year 1963 was to prove an important dividing-line for Italian post-war economic developments. Up to then, rapid growth had been led primarily by a process of capital accumulation favoured by the profit situation, and had been accompanied by large productivity gains, restrained wage rises, and rapid international integration. Some of these forces remained at work through the remainder of the 1960s; others, however, lost in importance. The years up to 1963 had also been characterized by massive and unplanned internal migration with substantial social costs which became fully apparent only at the turn of the 1960s, a decade later. It is the relative neglect of these costs in the years of the so-called 'miracle' that in many ways is the biggest blot on the history of this period.

II. The Years of Stabilization, 1963–1969

From the balance of payments crisis of 1963 to the industrial relations crisis of 1969, the Italian economy grew at a rate that was still relatively rapid both by historical standards and in comparison with other countries in Europe at the time. There was a deceleration from the buoyant tempo of 1958–63, but this was to some extent inevitable if a repetition of the excess demand pressures of

---

[15] See, for instance, Bank of Italy, *Annual Report, 1962, 1963*, and *1964*; F. Modigliani and G. La Malfa, 'Inflation, Balance of Payments Deficit and their Cure through Monetary Policy: The Italian Example', *Banca Nazionale del Lavoro Quarterly Review*, March 1967, or, for a survey, V. Valli, *L'economia e la politica economica italiana (1945–1979)*, Milan 1979 (2nd edn.).

1962-3 was to be avoided. Moreover, prices were relatively stable and the current account of the balance of payments in massive surplus. Yet in many ways this period can be described as one of lost opportunities. Rather than using the breathing-space provided by a moderation in demand pressures and by a healthy balance of payments to consolidate the achievement of the previous decade and a half, the economy remained in a state of disequilibrium. On capital markets, speculative investment abroad was preferred to productive investment at home; on labour markets, employment declined further while emigration continued; in the public sector policy remained timid and often incoherent.

From recession to the 'Hot Autumn'

The years 1964-5 saw pronounced slowdown as a result of the 1963-4 restrictive measures — domestic demand grew by only ½ per cent per annum. Thereafter, growth picked up and was quite rapid, but the large gap between actual and potential output which had appeared in 1964-5 was only partially and very slowly reabsorbed.[16] The most notable feature of the period was the weakness of investment. As a share of GDP, gross fixed capital formation fell back to 24 per cent, or close to the European average of the time. Industrial investment was barely back to its 1963 level in 1969; manufacturing investment fell by nearly 3 per cent per annum. On the domestic side, it was really only private consumption which, helped by an increase in transfer incomes, grew at a rate (5½ per cent per annum) equal to that of the 1951-63 period.

Exports were, thus, the most rapidly growing single major demand component: 12½ per cent per annum for goods and services, over 15 per cent for goods only. The reasons for this pronounced success were partly of a demand-pull nature — European imports were growing rapidly in this period and shifted towards Italian products whose relative competitiveness was sharply increasing.[17] But supply-push was probably more important — exports played a compensating role for the weakness of internal demand, particularly in 1964-5, when the cumulative 1 per cent growth of domestic demand was matched by a 33 per cent growth in sales abroad. As a result, the external component came to represent as much as 30 per cent of overall demand for industry, with peaks of over 40 per cent in the mechanical and transport equipment sectors.

Though imports grew at double the rate of domestic demand, the trade balance was actually in surplus in most years of the period. As for the current account, it averaged $2 billion per annum, a figure well above that of any other European country at the time (Germany was averaging $1 billion) and second only to that of the United States. This represented as much as 2¾ per cent of GDP. Yet reserve accumulation was only modest ($1½ billion from 1963 to 1969), largely because illegal capital exports continued ($5½ billion over the same period).

The improvement in competitiveness was helped by the subdued movement

---

[16] For an estimate of Italian potential output, see OECD, 'The Measurement of Domestic Cyclical Fluctuations', *OECD Economic Outlook – Occasional Studies*, July 1973.

[17] By 4 percentage points on a unit current cost basis and by 10 percentage points on an export average value basis; OECD, 'The International Competitiveness of Selected OECD Countries', *OECD Economic Outlook – Occasional Studies*, July 1978.

of prices and by further substantial gains in productivity. Even though activity slowed down, capacity utilization decreased, and investment stagnated at best, industrial productivity rose at over 6 per cent per annum, close to the 6½ per cent recorded in 1958-63, a time of much more rapid output and investment growth (Table 17.4). And unit labour costs remained virtually stable – a performance even better than that of either the 1950s or the years of the 'miracle'.

TABLE 17.4. *Productivity trends*[a]
(average annual percentage changes)

	1951–79	1951–58	1958–63	1963–69	1969–73	1973–79
Total	4.6	4.7	7.1	5.7	4.4	1.5
Agriculture	6.0	6.2	7.3	7.5	4.8	4.1
Industry	4.7	4.6	6.6	6.2	4.5	1.9
Services	2.2	1.4	4.9	3.0	2.6	–

[a] GDP per employed

*Sources:*OECD, *National Accounts of OECD Countries, 1962-1979*; OECD, *Labour Force Statistics, 1968-1979*; ISTAT, *Annuario di contabilità nazionale, 1978* (Vol. 1).

Both these results were achieved, however, by a compression of wage increases, and by a policy of ruthless rationalization on the factory floor, with employers sharply improving the utilization of the equipment which had been installed earlier. As a result, employment declined further, unemployment increased again even though large emigration continued, and the share of employee compensation in national income actually fell sharply despite a further shift in the composition of total employment away from independent workers to wage and salary earners.

Both the worsening of working conditions on the factory floor and the shift in income distribution away from labour must have contributed to the autumn 1969 industrial relations crisis. Other factors at work were probably the increasing politicization of the trade union movement and the resentment and frustrations felt in the urban conurbations of the North not only on account of an inadequate social infrastructure, but also because of the absence of concerted policies to overcome it despite repeated promises. The occasion for increased conflict was the renegotiation of the three-year wage contracts which, in 1969, covered almost all industrial and agricultural workers. An idea of the bitterness of the strikes is provided by the 8 per cent drop in industrial production between the third and fourth quarters of 1969 and by the number of workdays lost on account of strike activity: 3.1 per employee in 1969 as against 1.8 in 1962 (the previous peak year), and as many as 25.6 in manufacturing as against 14.2 in 1962 or 4.8 in 1963. The major consequence of this brief but intense period of conflict – a radical change in the industrial relations climate – was to be felt in the following decade.

The lost opportunity

An assessment of these years must begin with an examination of economic policies. These were dominated by debates about the relative effectiveness of monetary and fiscal policies or between defenders of longer-run structural intervention and proponents of short-term counter-cyclical stabilization. Yet these debates, in which the views of Keynesian demand management prevailed, often ignored the institutional reality of the economy and, in particular, the lack of flexibility of the public sector. Widespread tax evasion, an inefficient administration, an anachronistic budget system, long lags between policy decisions and expenditure flows, the accumulation of unused appropriations for capital projects because of bureaucratic impediments, were all characteristics of Italy's public finance system which made timely (or even structural) intervention most difficult.

As a result, and though it was felt that more expansionary policies were perhaps necessary to move the economy out of the 1964-5 slowdown, the expected effects of the measures that were adopted was usually overestimated. It was really only in 1965 that, thanks partly to a reduction in employers' social security contributions, a sizeable stimulative impact was achieved.[18] Otherwise, however, budgetary policy was weak and ineffective despite an increase in the budget deficit. So too was monetary policy, though in a sense this was not unexpected. As is well known, monetary measures are much less effective in stimulating than in restricting an economy. Moreover, given that the primary target 'assigned' to monetary policy was the balance of payments, it was difficult for the central bank to simultaneously pursue internal equilibrium as well.

The lack of sufficiently expansionary economic policies may have been one of the cyclical reasons for what was probably the most important and least well-understood phenomenon of this period – the stagnation of investment. In the presence of a relatively cautious attitude by the authorities and a deceleration in the growth of domestic demand, unused capacity margins rose with predictable effects on business investment propensities. In addition, a stock adjustment mechanism may have played some role in the wake of the massive investment effort of the early 1960s. But other more structural forces were probably also at work. Political uncertainties, for instance, may have been important. Though the industrial relations conflicts of 1962-3 had given way to a period of trade-union weakness, the accession of a centre-left government first and political instability later probably depressed entrepreneurial confidence.[19]

Despite favourable productivity and unit labour cost trends, the share of profits in value added had begun to decline already in the early 1960s, and the mid-1960s recovery was insufficient to restore profitability to earlier levels (Fig. 17.3). This was particularly true in manufacturing and largely reflected the country's opening to foreign trade. In a fixed exchange rate system, the tradeable sectors of the economy were no longer able to pass on to prices even very modest cost increases. Elsewhere, profitability was probably less eroded, but profits did not find their way into productive investment as they had done in the 1950s.

This raises another important problem – the diversification of financial

[18] The largest in both Hansen's calculations for 1955–65 (Hansen, *Fiscal Policy*) and in similar Italian calculations for 1952–69 (G. Bognetti, 'Analisi quantitativa delle strutture e delle tendenze del bilancio pubblico italiano dal 1951 al 1969', in V. Balloni (ed.), *Lezioni sulla politica economica in Italia*, Milan 1972).

[19] P. Sylos Labini, *Sindacati, inflazione e produttività*, Bari 1972.

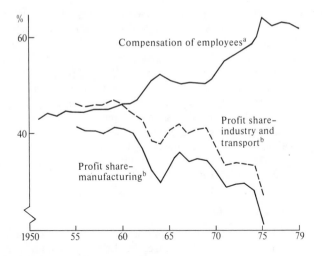

FIG. 17.3. *Indicators of profitability* (percentages)
[a] In per cent of national income
[b] Gross operating surplus in per cent of gross value added
Sources: T.P. Hill, *Profits and Rates of Return*, OECD, Paris 1979; OECD, *National Accounts of OECD Countries, 1950–1979*.

resources that took place in the period. Financial wealth, which had been destroyed by war and subsequent inflation, had been rebuilt and was used in a variety of ways in these years. At the industrial level, there was a rise in the degree of oligopoly, with numerous small and medium-sized firms taken over by larger competitors. In the tertiary sector, there was renewed speculation in residential construction. In contrast to the 1950s, however, large resources were, on this occasion, devoted to the building of luxury houses and holiday homes. An increased budget deficit also provided an outlet for investment in public sector bonds.

But the most important form of diversification took place in favour of foreign assets which ensured the requirements of anonymity and tax exemption which the Italian middle class had traditionally felt were part of its prerogatives. Yield differentials played hardly any role in these outflows, nor did political fears, after the 1962–3 episode, though the limited range of financial assets which Italian intermediaries were capable of offering was probably important. It is in these often wasteful flows of funds that is to be found one of the major reasons of the lost opportunity of these years – the surplus which had been accumulated up to 1963 was squandered in conspicuous and speculative forms of consumption and investment. Italy, a country which by the standards of Western Europe was still relatively poor and underdeveloped, exported in those years both labour and capital – net emigration was equivalent to some 3½ to 4 per cent of the labour force; the transfer of resources abroad to close to 3 per cent of GDP.

The disappointment was the greater in view of the promises which the new reformist government experiment had held forth. It is true that this experience saw the first sharp increase in welfare expenditure. Public spending rose rapidly from 1965 and in the late 1960s was equivalent to 35 per cent of GDP as against

30 per cent in 1960–1. Social security benefits increased their share from 9½ to 12½ per cent of GDP over the same period. But in other areas achievements fell well short of promises.

The problem of the South, the backwardness of agriculture, the inefficiencies of the administration, tax evasion, land and building speculation, the non-existence of a market for risk capital, the absence of anti-monopoly legislation, etc., were all items on the programme of reforms which were systematically spelt out but were also, and with as much regularity, ignored in practice. But above all, the major mistake of the period was the absence of an adequate expansionary policy. This in turn depressed productive investment, whose place was taken by a short-sighted policy of rationalization, one of whose main consequences was the 'Hot Autumn' of 1969.

III. The Years of Crisis, 1969–1979

As elsewhere in Europe, but probably more so, the 1970s were marked by a very significant deterioration in performance. In the early years of the decade, the economy had to absorb the serious consequences which the 'Hot Autumn' had on productivity and inflation, a task made more difficult by the concomitant international monetary crisis. In the mid-1970s, the increase in oil prices hit with particular force a country highly dependent on imported energy. And in the late 1970s, the scenario repeated itself with the difference that the intervening years had seen a painful adjustment process which had increased the fragility of the economy. It is true that, in a sense, these various shocks can be considered exogenous, particularly the breakdown of the Bretton Woods system and the changes in the terms of trade between oil and manufactures. But their negative effects were probably amplified in Italy by the weaknesses inherited from the past.

From the industrial relations crisis to the first oil crisis

The first four years of the 1970s were marked by the effects of the change in labour relations resulting from the 'Hot Autumn' of 1969 and from the change in international monetary relations which occurred after the Smithsonian Agreements of late 1971. For Italy, the more significant of these two changes was clearly the first, which, in fact, conditioned the behaviour of the economy throughout the decade. The immediate effect of the strike wave was a very sharp increase in labour costs. Average employee compensation rose by 15 per cent in 1970, as against an annual rise of 8½ per cent in the 1963–9 period. In industry, the increase was as high as 19 per cent. But however disruptive this may have been, the strikes' consequences on the length of the working week and on labour relations on the factory floor were even more important. The unions had obtained not only large wage increases but also substantial reductions in hours worked and, in particular, in overtime work. Between 1966–8 and 1972–4, the number of hours worked by an employee in industry had fallen by 12 per cent. In addition, a new labour law (the *Statuto dei lavoratori*) had drastically limited the scope of employers in dismissing workers, had reduced within-firm labour mobility, and had virtually eliminated the possibility of controlling absenteeism.

The consequences for output, productivity, and unit labour costs were substantial. The increasing rigidity of the labour force reduced the elasticity and flexibility of supply, and curtailed the use of capital equipment. This was particularly so in large firms whose productive processes were more rigid and whose labour force was more unionized. Overall productivity growth decelerated from 5¾ to 4½ per cent per annum between 1963-9 and 1969-73, and the drop was even more pronounced in manufacturing – from 6½ to 5 per cent. Given the concomitant increases in the wage bill, unit labour costs in industry, which had been virtually stable in the second half of the 1960s, shot up to a 10 per cent annual rate of increase in this period. Inflation inevitably accelerated, with the rise in the implicit GDP deflator more than doubling to 8 per cent per annum, as against 3½ per cent in the previous six years. Consumer prices increased at a double-digit rate in 1973 for the first time since 1951. The acceleration in inflation in 1972-3 was helped by the boom in primary product prices begun in 1972. This led to a 9 per cent deterioration in the domestic terms of trade between industrial and agricultural products.

But international developments had already had earlier and more important consequences for the economy in the wake of the Smithsonian Agreements. These had implied for Italy a 7 per cent appreciation *vis-à-vis* the dollar. Though in effective terms the lira's value had been altered only little, in real terms (i.e. adjusted for inflationary differentials), the currency became progressively overvalued between 1971 and 1973. This resulted in a deterioration in competitiveness best shown by the loss in market shares of Italian exports abroad[20] and even more by the very sharp rise in import penetration – the share of imports of manufactures in GDP rose by 3½ percentage points between 1969 and 1974, or by more than in the preceding ten years despite the trade creation effects of the EEC in the early 1960s.

The inevitable deterioration in the current account (a $5 billion swing between 1969 and 1973 equivalent to more than 4 per cent of GDP), combined with a new international loss of confidence in the dollar, led to a speculative crisis in Italy in early 1973. After an intermediate period with a dual foreign currency market, the lira was devalued by about 15 per cent *vis-à-vis* the dollar and by some 10 per cent in effective terms.

Devaluation came too late, however, to provide much of a boost to either profits or demand. The latter had been sluggish over this period, partly because of a restrictive policy stance in 1970 (in response to renewed speculative capital outflows), partly because of more pessimistic entrepreneurial expectations (as a result of the labour disputes), and partly because of the loss in competitiveness (which was depressing exports and boosting imports). Investment was particularly weak. Despite a sharp, devaluation-induced rise in 1973, its GDP share for the period as a whole fell below even the depressed level of the years 1964-9.

To some extent this was due to a decline in residential construction as a result of restrictions imposed on building activities in large cities and rent freezes. But the major reason was the sluggishness of industrial investment, particularly in the private sector where capital formation was virtually stagnant (Table 17.5). The

[20] NIESR estimates show that after virtually uninterrupted growth from 1950 to 1969, the share of Italian manufactured sales in the exports of the twelve more important exporting countries fell between 1969 and 1974.

TABLE 17.5. *Growth of GDP and selected demand components, 1969–1979*
(average annual percentage changes)

	1969–79	1969–73	1973–79
GDP	3.3	4.3	2.6
Private consumption	3.3	4.9	2.2
Gross fixed investment	0.4	2.0	−0.7
of which: general government[a]	2.5	2.5	2.5
of which: industry	−0.3	5.4	−4.6
manufacturing[b]	—[c]	8.6	−6.4[c]
Exports of goods and services	7.9	6.7	8.7
Imports of goods and services	6.5	9.8	4.3

[a] Deflated by implicit gross fixed investment deflator
[b] Including mining
[c] 1969–78 and 1973–78
Sources: OECD, *National Accounts of OECD Countries, 1962–1979*; ISTAT, *Bollettino mensile di statistica*, July 1981.

decline in profitability had accelerated, as firms were under pressure from the labour costs side on the one hand, and the rise in import penetration on the other. Rather than increase productivity by raising the capital–labour ratio, entrepreneurs, particularly in medium-sized and small firms, often preferred to decentralize their productive activities towards smaller-scale establishments or even self-employed operators working at home in order to depress their wage bills and circumvent trade-union restrictions.

The only major autonomous demand component that was at all buoyant was the investment activity of the public sector. Industrial investment by public corporations rose substantially (15 per cent per annum), particularly in the South. Yet often the very large projects that were being carried out were financed by subsidized loans. Such initiatives, which were frequently designed to support effective demand, were to encounter serious financial difficulties in the following period when the deceleration in growth was even sharper.

A further and more structural consequence of the 'Hot Autumn' was a marked redistribution of income towards labour and against capital. Employee compensation which, as a share of national income, had risen by 7 percentage points between 1951 and 1969, jumped by an equivalent amount in the four years from 1969 to 1973. This changed profoundly the flow of funds matrix of the economy. The traditional savings surplus of the household sector rose to over 74 per cent of total national savings in 1970 and to 91 per cent in 1973. At the same time, the ratio between corporate indebtedness and corporate savings went from 1.4 to 1.6, while the public sector deficit increased. In addition, household wealth, which had traditionally financed residential construction, was increasingly invested in short-term assets, thus creating the need for substantial financial intermediation between the sources of short-term funds on the one hand and the requirements for longer-term productive investment on the other.

The economic policy strategy of this period was designed to increase government intervention so as to offset some of the unfavourable consequences of the industrial relations crisis. The already mentioned rise in public investment was part of this policy. Another was a substantial increase in transfer payments, particularly for pensions, meant to help social categories not protected by unions. The measures approved took the form of increases in minimum retirement benefit levels, extensions of eligibility, and social assistance to the aged population in poverty. The result of these various interventions was, however, to swell the public sector deficit, well before similar increases occurred elsewhere in Europe after the oil crisis. As a percentage of GDP, general government net lending went from 3.1 per cent in 1969, to 7.0 per cent in 1973 – the highest figure in Europe at the time.

In summary, this period saw a further worsening in Italy's economic performance. Growth was slower than in the 1960s, investment stagnated, employment fell, and inflation accelerated. Much of this was due to the immediate effects of the 'Hot Autumn' which squeezed profits and diminished Italy's competitiveness. The subsequent breakdown of the international monetary system and the effects of the world boom in commodity prices worsened an already difficult situation.

Economic policy attempted to compensate for lower private demand by injecting purchasing-power into the economy, and to offset the loss in competitiveness by devaluing the currency. Both measures met with only a limited degree of success and created serious problems for the future. The effects of rising public expenditure on output growth were modest, while the increase in the public sector's deficit was large. The improvement in competitiveness was temporary, as the increased indexation of all revenues eroded Italy's price advantage, but the acceleration in inflationary expectations was pronounced. Nor, of course, did the period see any solution to Italy's numerous structural problems – the need for industrial change away from traditional activities, reform of the civil service, control of monopolies and of financial concentrations, etc. On the contrary, if anything, two new structural problems were superimposed on the old ones – an increasingly rigid labour market as a consequence of trade-union action and an increasing rigidity in the formation of personal incomes as a consequence of the spread of subsidies and transfers from the public sector. Both were to make the adjustment to the oil crisis much more difficult than it might otherwise have been.

From the first to the second oil crisis

As in most other European countries, the six years from the first to the second oil crisis were dominated by inflation. In Italy this was particularly rapid – some 16 per cent per annum for consumer prices, or a rate only just below those of Spain, Portugal, Turkey, and Iceland. All sectors of the economy contributed to the inflationary spiral – firms by defending their market power via increasing recourse to cartels, and unions by supporting progressively more rigid forms of indexation, while the public sector tried to maintain an artificial consensus by an increasingly indiscriminate use of subsidies and other forms of help to numerous pressure groups. Partly as a result, the growth rate of output fell sharply, investment declined, the public sector's deficit rose to an average 9 per cent of GDP, the currency was devalued by over 40 per cent in effective terms, and the deceleration in inflation that took place elsewhere in Europe through the period was only very minor (consumer prices were still rising by nearly 15 per cent in 1979). When the second oil crisis struck, Italy was ripe for a renewed upward jump in the rate of price increases to over 20 per cent.

Given the country's heavy dependence on oil (70 per cent of energy needs), the terms of trade deterioration was particularly pronounced: 21 per cent between 1972 and 1974 or the equivalent of some 4½ per cent of GDP,[21] more than any other European country with the exception of the United Kingdom. The inevitable effect on prices of a more than doubling in two years of import unit values was magnified from 1975 onwards by a reform in Italy's wage indexation mechanism (the so-called *scala mobile*). This had been in existence since the early post-war period, but had lost some of its importance at the time of the large wage increases in the early 1970s. It was, however, reinforced and extended in 1975 under the pressure of both unions, which wanted to protect their members from accelerating inflation, and employers, who preferred the certainty of a rigid indexation system to the unpredictability for their wage bills of uncoordinated firm or even plant and section bargaining. The effect of the reform was to provide on average 75 to 80 per cent cover against increases in the cost of living (though for some categories of workers, this cover was actually above 100 per cent!). As a result, while the *scala mobile* had been responsible for perhaps one-quarter of the 20 per cent annual increase in hourly industrial wages between 1969 and 1974, its contribution rose to nearly 60 per cent of the recorded 22 per cent rise between 1975 and 1979.[22]

The other major consequence of the terms of trade deterioration was on the balance of payments. The current account, as in most other countries, swung into massive deficit in 1974 ($8 billion or 4¾ per cent of GDP). On the one hand, this added fuel to speculation against the lira, which dropped sharply in 1973-4 and again at the turn of 1975. On the other, it required a shift in resources and a reduction in internal absorption to pay for higher-priced imports. In this respect the economy was successful. By 1979, the current account was back in substantial surplus ($5 billion) thanks to a drastic reduction in the growth of domestic demand. While GDP expanded at the already sluggish annual rate of 2.6 per cent between 1973 and 1979, internal demand grew by only 1.4 per cent (a sharp slowdown if compared to the 5 per cent of the years 1969-73).

As had been the case since 1963, this deceleration was mainly due to investment. Gross fixed capital formation actually fell in the period, with industrial investment particularly weak. As in the previous period, government investment was the only major component which showed relative buoyancy, in contrast to experience almost everywhere else, where public expenditure cuts were being concentrated on the capital side. But the overall investment ratio had by now come down to only 20 per cent on average and to as little as 19 per cent in 1978-9 – a figure that had not been recorded since 1951-2. While Italy in the early 1960s had been a country with one of the highest investment shares in Europe, by the late 1970s this share had come down to the levels recorded by the United Kingdom.

As domestic demand stagnated, exports boomed, confirming the presence of an inverse relationship between the two variables. After a period of losses in

---

[21] According to OECD estimates of the income effect of the terms of trade change.
[22] Fazio, 'Inflation', p. 160.

markets abroad, Italy regained market shares while the growth of import penetration slowed down. Though domestic inflation had been rapid, the advantages of depreciation were not entirely lost – according to the IMF, relative unit labour costs, adjusted for cyclical fluctuations in productivity, fell by 15 per cent over the period. Since the decline in relative export unit values was of only 2½ per cent, profit margins in the tradeable sector, seriously eroded between 1969 and 1973, must have seen some rise.

But the overall profit situation improved only little. The continuing restraining effect of union action on overtime work, on labour mobility, and on a flexible within-firm use of the labour force, combined with low investment, meant that the scope for productivity advances was limited. In addition, employment was defended unconditionally so that Italy, almost alone in Europe, saw a sizeable increase in employment in these six years after having witnessed declining employment levels since 1961. As a result, overall productivity growth, at barely 1½ per cent per annum, showed one of the sharpest slowdowns in Europe. Yet relatively rapid population growth, a return flow of migrants and, for the first time since the early 1960s, a rise in female participation rates, meant that unemployment also edged up to reach, by 1979, 7½ per cent of the labour force and as much as 25 per cent among the young.

Economic policy curbed demand growth via both monetary and fiscal stringency. On the monetary side, interest rates were kept at consistently high levels (the prime rate oscillated between 15 and 19 per cent), and ceilings were repeatedly placed on bank credit. On the fiscal side, direct taxation was increased sharply thanks to the introduction of a pay-as-you-earn income tax system, a crackdown on tax avoidance, and the workings of fiscal drag in a situation of rapid inflation, progressive tax rates, and virtually no indexation of tax brackets. Indeed, the rapid rise in the importance of direct taxes in total government revenues probably contributed, together with the egalitarian wage policies of the trade unions, to bring about a remarkably swift equalization of post-tax incomes.

In addition to a restrictive role and to a contribution to income equality, the public sector intervened on the expenditure side in a much more *ad hoc* way. Its principal role in the period seems to have been that of offsetting losses incurred because of the economic crisis – it compensated for the real income losses suffered by the unemployed, for the falls in profits of the corporate sector, and even for the earlier planning mistakes made by large private and public firms. This led to a systematic distortion in the composition of public spending which privileged transfers to households and enterprises, but also interest payments since the size of the public debt grew, as did, of course, interest rates (Table 17.6).

The late 1970s were thus difficult years for the economy. They saw an increasing rigidity in public expenditure coupled with a weakening of the demand management role which the public sector could play in view of a concomitant regional devolution of many expenditure flows. To this were added an above average rate of inflation and a below average rate of investment as well as the legacy of numerous structural problems, few of which had been tackled since Italy had become an industrialized economy in the late 1950s or early 1960s. The only positive note was to be found in export successes often achieved in

TABLE 17.6. *Structure of government revenues and expenditures*
(percentages)

	1960–61	1969–70	1978–79
Total revenues (in per cent of GDP)	29.1	31.2	36.4
shares of: Direct taxes	17.9	18.9	27.3
Indirect taxes	41.7	36.6	26.9
Social security contributions	28.7	33.7	35.3
Total expenditures (in per cent of GDP)	30.1	34.6	46.0
shares of: Consumption	42.3	40.5	34.8
Investment	11.8	8.8	6.7
Social transfers	32.4	35.8	35.0
Interest payments	5.0	5.0	12.7
Subsidies to producers	3.8	4.7	5.8
General government net lending (in per cent of GDP)	−0.9	−3.3	−9.6

Sources: ISTAT, *Bollettino mensile di statistica*, July 1981; OECD, *National Accounts of OECD Countries, 1950–1979.*

what has been called the 'submerged economy' – small firms operating in semi-legal status to avoid trade-union restrictions and government taxation. Seen in a comparative perspective, Italy probably did less well than many of its competitors – a reflection, partly, of greater vulnerability to oil price rises and slowdowns in the growth of world trade, but more importantly, of longer-run unresolved problems and fragility.

Conclusions

Looking at Italian economic history over a thirty year time-span, a key development was clearly the growth of the industrial sector at the expense of agriculture. Within little more than a generation, Italy was transformed from an only partially developed to a much more mature economy. And the process of industrial growth itself saw the rise of relatively advanced sectors (chemicals, transport equipment, engineering) at the expense of traditional, labour-intensive branches such as textiles or food products.

There was no single engine of growth behind this development. Until the early 1970s, the major factors were high rates of investment and of productivity growth, stable terms of trade between industrial products and raw materials, and relatively low wage costs made possible by an excess supply of labour. These factors interacted among each other to produce a largely, though not entirely, domestically generated growth process. From the early 1970s onwards, most of these forces weakened. The social costs of the earlier transformation of the country led to a changed climate of labour relations, with negative effects on productivity, wages, and investment, while the oil crisis seriously affected a country heavily dependent on imported energy. Growth was now much lower and led by either public sector intervention or exports.

The second major component of the growth process over the three decades is to be found in foreign trade and in the integration of the economy into Western Europe. The contribution of external forces was varied – a rapid growth of exports which at times (the mid-1960s, the latter 1970s) represented the most dynamic demand component, a continuous supply of cheap raw materials (at least until the mid-1970s), the availability of technology, which boosted productivity, and the impact of competing products, which limited the scope for restrictive practices at home.

International economic integration, however, also brought out some of the country's weaknesses. Successful integration required continuous flexibility and the acceptance of uncertainty. Italian society tried to refuse both in the 1970s. The devaluation that inevitably followed was largely offset by accelerated inflation, while the difficulties which worsened terms of trade and lower growth implied for incomes stimulated calls for increased government aid in the form of transfers and subsidies financed by rising budget deficits and monetary creation.

This leads to a consideration of a third element in the growth process – the role of the public sector and of economic policies. A number of critical references to this have been made in the preceding text, but an objective judgement must bear in mind the diversity in the forms of public intervention, and the role of the state not only in the traditional monetary and fiscal areas, but also in industry and in finance. Particularly in the 1950s and in part of the 1960s, these various branches of the government machine facilitated the growth process by broadly permissive macroeconomic policies, by the strengthening of several crucial industrial sectors (e.g. steel or energy), by the financing of a substantial housing and infrastructure effort, or by the pursuit of a relatively successful process of development and industrialization in the South. It is true that in the 1970s public sector operations increasingly took the form of hand-outs to pressure groups with diminishing attention paid to economic efficiency, but this was often done in an attempt to remedy many of the mistakes made by private enterprise.

Turning to a brief look at the 1980s, the weaknesses which the economy has accumulated through the last decade, and which are best illustrated by two indicators – a record budget deficit and a record rate of inflation – will inevitably condition economic developments and policies for a number of years. Integration within the EEC presents a further constraint. Protectionism is no longer possible, while successful devaluations are difficult even if exchange rate flexibility is maintained. This implies that, despite the domestic needs of the economy, Italy may have to grow at rates close to those of its partners, unless its productivity performance improves drastically. Yet on the domestic side demand will be limited by the requirements of the balance of payments on the one hand, and by the necessity to reduce the public sector deficit on the other. In conditions of relatively subdued domestic demand growth, neither investment nor productivity are likely to be at all buoyant.

More satisfactory developments could be obtained via a supply-oriented policy, particularly in the service sector where inefficiencies are widespread and whose excessive rents and financial costs represent a heavy burden for households and firms. But this would require structural reforms, necessary also to improve the functioning of the public sector, to reduce youth unemployment, to pursue southern development, notably in the area's large urban conurbations, etc. Unfortunately, the history of the last thirty years has shown that

Italy has usually chosen the road of short-run stop-gap measures rather than the much more difficult, but also more rewarding, one of longer-run structural reforms.

Bibliography

Ample bibliographies on Italian economic developments for the three decades here examined can be found in V. Valli, *L'economia e la politica economica italiana (1945-1979)*, Milan 1979 (2nd edn.), and for the period to the early 1970s in P. Ciocca, R. Filosa, and G.M. Rey, 'Integration and Development of the Italian Economy, 1951-1971', *Banca Nazionale del Lavoro Quarterly Review*, September 1975. One of the best post-war surveys is to be found in a collection of articles edited by A. Graziani, *L'economia italiana dal 1945 ad oggi*, Bologna 1979 (2nd edn.).

Several works cover the whole or parts of the post-war period. In English one can mention D.C. Templeman, *The Italian Economy*, New York 1981; E. John, *Italy in the 1970s*, London 1975; K.J. Allen and A. Stevenson, *An Introduction to the Italian Economy*, London 1974; G. Podbielsky, *Italy, Development and Crisis in the Post-war Economy*, Oxford 1974; G. Fuà, *Notes on Italian Economic Growth*, Milan 1964. In Italian, the already cited work by V. Valli, and M. D'Antonio, *Sviluppo e Crisi del Capitalismo Italiano*, Bari 1972.

The problems of the 1960s are discussed in P. Sylos Labini, *Sindacati, inflazione e produttività*, Bari 1972. Those of the 1970s have generated a very ample literature; worthy of notice are: G. Franco, *Sviluppo e crisi dell'economia italiana*, Milan 1975 (a collection of essays dealing, in particular, with the labour market, industrial structure and dualism, and monetary policy); G. Nardozzi, *I difficili anni 70 – I problemi della politica economica italiana: 1973-1979*, Milan 1979 (whose articles concentrate on labour costs, public finance, and balance of payments problems); G. Carli (ed.), *Sviluppo economico e strutture finanziarie*, Bologna 1977 (which looks at the relationships between the financial sector and enterprises); and G. Fuà, *Occupazione e capacità produttive: la realtà italiana*, Bologna 1976.

On more specific topics, Italy's *external economic relations* are treated in G. Basevi and A. Soci, *La bilancia dei pagamenti italiana*, Bologna 1978; F. Masera (ed.), *Bilancia dei pagamenti e sistema monetario internazionale*, Milan 1975; and F. Onida, 'Italian Exports and Industrial Structure in the 1970s', *Banco di Roma Review of Economic Conditions in Italy*, February 1980.

Labour market and labour cost problems are examined in B. Jossa and S. Vinci, 'The Italian Economy from 1963 to Today: An Interpretation', *Banco di Roma Review of Economic Conditions in Italy*, February 1981; V. Conti and R. Filosa, 'Accumulazione, produttività e costo del lavoro nell'industria manifatturiera: un'analisi disaggregata', Banca d'Italia, *Contributi alla ricerca economica*, No. 6, 1976; B. Contini, *Lo sviluppo di un'economia parallela*, Milan 1979 (which looks in particular at Italy's 'black economy') and 'The Labour Market in Italy', *Banco di Roma Review of Economic Conditions in Italy*, No. 2, 1979. An interesting debate on the problems of indexation, with contributions from G. Faustini, L. Spaventa, R. Filosa, and I. Visco, can be found in several 1976 and 1977 issues of *Moneta e Credito*.

On *economic policy* in the 1960s, see G. Fuà and P. Sylos Labini, *Idee per la programmazione economica*, Bari 1963. The 1970s are treated in F. Reviglio, *Spesa pubblica e stagnazione dell'economia in Italia*, Bologna 1977; P. Ranci (ed.), *Moneta e politica monetaria in Italia*, Milan 1977; A. Pedone, *Evasori e tartassati,* Bologna 1979; F. Caffè (ed.), 'L'economia degli anni settanta', *Note Economiche*, No. 5–6, 1980 (a collection of articles with particular reference to the domestic and international monetary problems), and in a special number of *Banco di Roma Economia Italiana*, No. 2, 1979 devoted to the 'crowding out' issue.

Finally, a brief account of *southern problems* can be found in A. Graziani, 'The Mezzogiorno in the Italian Economy', *Cambridge Journal of Economics*, December 1978, while the social and political forces which generated and accompanied Italy's *inflation* in the 1970s are treated by M. Salvati, *Alle origini dell'inflazione italiana*, Bologna 1978.

18

United Kingdom*

Introduction

It would be generally agreed that the United Kingdom's economic performance in the post-war period can only be described as poor, at least by comparison with that of other industrialized economies. Thus, Britain's growth rate was the slowest in Western (and Eastern) Europe over the three decades, its inflation rate among the highest, and its balance of payments difficulties almost endemic. *Vis-à-vis* the pre-war period the record is somewhat better, particularly in the fields of investment, which was much higher in the 1950s and 1960s, and unemployment, which was much lower, but there was very little acceleration in growth (in both periods GDP expanded by some 2½ per cent per annum), in contrast to what happened elsewhere in Europe.

On the face of things, in 1950 the economy was relatively favourably placed both to take advantage of beneficial developments in world trade and in technological innovation and to cope with any external disruptions – per caput incomes were the highest in Europe (if one excludes Sweden and Switzerland which had remained neutral during the war); the share of world trade in manufactures (at over one-quarter) was close to that of the United States; the production structure was heavily concentrated in capital goods industries (a sector with a great potential in view of the ensuing worldwide investment boom); and there was probably a greater degree of consensus in British society, now buttressed by a novel and advanced welfare state, than at any time in the pre-war period. Yet during the next thirty years growth was consistently and significantly lower than that of apparently less favourably placed economies, and by the end of the period the country found itself, despite the further benefit of approaching self-sufficiency in oil, with unemployment at levels not seen since the 1930s, persistently high inflation rates, and with all policy options other than severe deflation apparently either closed or deliberately rejected (Fig. 18.1).

There has been no lack of hypotheses to account for this failure. Some of these hypotheses have been specific and capable of empirical testing. Among them are the suggestions that the existence of the Sterling Area and sterling's status as an international trading currency for much of the period both exacerbated cyclical balance of payments problems (because of the associated short-term capital flow crises) and at the same time restricted exchange rate policy by making the maintenance of a fixed parity a central aim of economic policy. In this group of testable hypotheses could also be placed the suggestion that the existence in the United Kingdom of a small and efficient agricultural sector

---

* As for other country chapters, editorial policy has imposed the use of internationally standardized statistics which at times differ from national concepts and figures.
** University of Leeds.

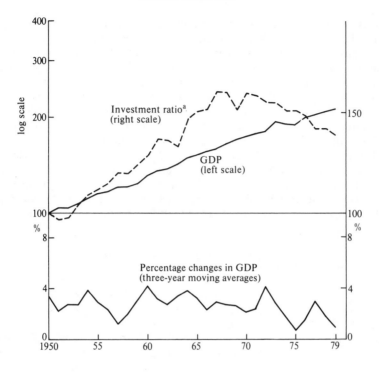

FIG. 18.1. *Output and investment trends, 1950–1979* (indices: 1950 = 100)
[a] Gross fixed investment in per cent of GDP at constant prices
Source: OECD, *National Accounts of OECD Countries, 1950–1979.*

meant that there was not available a pool of relatively low-productivity labour
which could transfer (or be transferred) into a relatively high-productivity manufacturing sector. Less directly verifiable possible explanations include the suggestion that the attempt to 'fine tune' the economy, together with the balance
of payments sensitivity already noted, led to frequent changes between expansionary and contractionary periods which in turn led to excessive caution in
capital formation and thus to a reduction in the underlying rate of growth of
productivity. At the other end of the spectrum lie suggestions which, however
plausible on the basis of casual impressions, are difficult or impossible to explore
systematically. These include propositions that the structure of trade unions is
too fragmented and/or that its foundation on a craft rather than an industry
basis is harmful; that industrial management is poorly trained and/or insufficiently
motivated; that while the British are 'good' at fundamental research they are
'bad' at consequential industrial development; that the social and educational
system is somehow inimical to the pursuit of economic growth.

It would be highly convenient if, by a judicious selection from amongst these
diverse but by no means incompatible hypotheses, one could arrive at a coherent
and empirically supported account of Britain's relative economic decline. As the
following narrative shows, however, such a unified account is in reality impossible

and its pursuit is more likely to obscure than to clarify the complex of causes underlying the country's poor performance. Indeed, the mistaken belief that there must ultimately be a single underlying cause has almost certainly itself been a contributory factor by leading successive governments to adopt or to reverse wholesale economic policies on the grounds that the identification of a single cause leads to the adoption of a single policy panacea. The successive failures of these panaceas have not, unfortunately, led to the abandonment of the search in favour of a more pragmatic and less unitary approach to the problems of an advanced industrial and highly open economy.

This chapter is broadly structured around major economic policy attempts at improving performance. Though history cannot easily be divided into clearly defined epochs, in the case of the British economy and its management quite clear eras can in fact be discerned even if their precise dates of beginning and ending remain a matter of debate (Table 18.1). Broadly, one may speak of the

TABLE 18.1. *Longer-term trends*

	1950–79	1950–64	1964–73	1973–79
	average annual percentage changes			
GDP	2.6	2.9	3.0	1.3
Inflation[a]	6.6	3.3	5.9	15.6
Employment	0.4	0.8	–	0.1
	1950–79	1950–64	1965–73	1974–79
	percentages			
Investment ratio[b]	18.0	15.6	20.3	18.8
Unemployment rate[c]	3.2	2.5	3.2	5.1
	$ million, annual averages			
Current balance	−373	270	116	−2,691

[a] Consumer prices
[b] Gross fixed investment in per cent of GDP at constant prices
[c] In per cent of the labour force
Sources: OECD, *National Accounts of OECD Countries, 1950-1979*; OECD, *Manpower Statistics, 1950-1962*; OECD, *Labour Force Statistics* (various issues); OECD, *Balance of Payments Statistics 1950-1961* and *1960-1977*; OECD, *Economic Outlook*, July 1981; IMF, *International Financial Statistics* (1980 Yearbook); C. Sorrentino, 'Methodological and Conceptual Problems in Measuring Unemployment', *mimeo*, OECD, Paris 1976; CSO, *Economic Trends* (Annual Supplement, 1981).

era of the 'stop–go' cycle and of demand management (from about 1950 to the early 1960s), of the era of growing incompatibility of macroeconomic policy aims and of novel structural policies (roughly, the 1960s and early 1970s), and of the period of high inflation and reactions to the oil crisis and ensuing world slowdown (the years 1974-9). These divisions are by no means hard and fast, but they serve to focus attention on the ways in which economic policies changed in the thirty years in response to changes in both the external environment and in internal factors.

I. The Era of Demand Management, 1950–1964

By 1950 the British economy had largely recovered from the problems left by the war. The structures of demand and production had returned to a peacetime footing, the traumas associated with the nationalization of a number of major industries (coal, the bulk of the steel industry, railways, long distance road haulage, electricity, and gas) had faded, and the much feared post-war inflation had not occurred despite a 30 per cent devaluation against the dollar in 1949. Perhaps most important, the broad principles of 'Keynesian' control of aggregate demand as the basis of macroeconomic management had been accepted by both major political parties, and the principal task for policy was henceforth to be the 'maintenance of a high and stable level of employment' (to quote the official 1944 White Paper on employment policy). Yet from then on, for the next decade and a half, the story was one of successive (if small) cycles, with demand management apparently incapable of fine tuning the economy. More importantly, perhaps, these cycles were accompanied by an underlying comparative deterioration in performance most apparent on the productivity and competitiveness fronts.

The story of 'stop–go'

The years 1950–64 were marked by a succession of swings in economic policies and activity prompted by inflationary and/or balance of payments crises on the one hand and increases in unemployment and spare capacity margins on the other (Fig. 18.2). The first of these cycles followed on the outbreak of the Korean War in mid-1950. This led to a worldwide surge in industrial production, to hugely increased demand for raw materials, and thence to very large increases in commodity prices. United Kingdom import unit values rose by nearly one-half between mid-1950 and mid-1951 (an increase comparable to the 50 per cent experienced between mid-1973 and mid-1974), generating both renewed inflationary pressures at home and a marked deterioration in the balance of payments. The problems facing the economy were further exacerbated by the commitment, again associated with the Korean War, to increase defence expenditures as a proportion of national product.

In 1951 consumer price inflation reached 10 per cent while the current account deficit amounted to some 3 per cent of GDP. Furthermore there was heavy speculation against sterling, attributable to doubts about exchange rate policy and to continuing uncertainty about the pound's convertibility. The policy response was to tighten import controls – the spring 1952 budget resisted the temptation to deflate generally, though hire-purchase controls were tightened and Bank Rate was raised for the first time since the war, from 2 to 2½ per cent. Partly in consequence, but mainly because of the post-Korean War fallback in world commodity prices, the current balance moved back into surplus in 1952 and slack home demand became the main concern. The 1953 budget was thus an expansionary one: both income and indirect taxes were cut and growth accelerated. Moves towards the dismantling of controls continued, and by the end of the year, only about half of non-Sterling Area imports were still restricted. Consumer rationing also diminished and finally ended in mid-1954.

Allowing for the after-effects of the Korean War, the first years of the

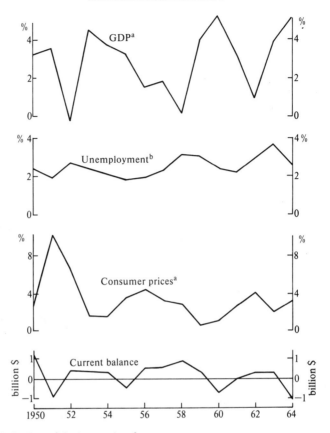

FIG. 18.2. *Indicators of the 'stop-go' cycle*
[a] Annual percentage changes
[b] In per cent of the labour force
Sources: OECD, *National Accounts of OECD Countries, 1950-1979*; OECD, *Balance of Payments Statistics 1950-1961* and *1960-1977*; C. Sorrentino, 'Methodological and Conceptual Problems in Measuring Unemployment', *mimeo*, OECD, Paris 1976; IMF, *International Financial Statistics* (1980 Yearbook); CSO, *Economic Trends* (Annual Supplement, 1981).

Conservative government were thus ones of apparently controlled but continued expansion. Contemporary comment was largely complacent – there seemed no reason why this steady growth with full employment should not continue indefinitely, with perhaps the occasional touch on the demand management 'brake' or 'accelerator' to neutralize minor unforeseen disturbances. In fact, however, as was to happen over and over again in the next decade, the expansion rapidly got out of hand and policy went into sharp reverse – without this repeated experience shaking, at least, for a good number of years, the underlying faith in the adequacy of fine tuning of demand.[1]

[1] J.C.R. Dow, *The Management of the British Economy, 1945-60*, NIESR, Cambridge 1964, Ch. XV.

After the expansionary budget of 1953, that of 1954 was a 'no change' one. Though output was rising rapidly, the current balance nevertheless remained in surplus and the rate of price inflation was below 2 per cent. By early 1955, there were few visible signs that the economy was 'overheating'. Such worries as there may have been were allayed by a rise in Bank Rate to 4½ per cent, and hire-purchase controls (which had been abolished in mid-1954) were reintroduced. With hindsight, it is clear that the fiscal expansion in the budget of spring 1955 was an error, and cynical observers were quick to point out that a general election was to be held in May. But given the absence of clear signs at the time of over-expansion and the fact that restrictive credit measures had already been taken, it is at least arguable that the budget income tax cut was merely overconfident rather than a deliberate mismanagement of the economy for electoral gain. At all events, by the summer (and following the return of the Conservatives with an increased majority) the evidence of excessive demand pressure was unmistakable. Unemployment fell to below 1 per cent (on United Kingdom definitions), rates of both price and wage inflation were increasing, and, most significantly, the balance of payments moved into clear deficit on current account. Policy consequently took a marked — though not dramatic — deflationary turn. As so often during this period, however, it is difficult to tell, even with the benefit of hindsight, whether the policies moderated the expansionary forces in the economy or exacerbated a downturn which was coming anyway.[2]

Although the volume of world trade continued to grow quite substantially through 1956 and 1957 (as did British exports), both public spending and private fixed investment slowed down, and stockbuilding fell sharply. In 1958 world economic developments compounded the domestic deflationary influences. World trade fell, partly reflecting the United States recession, and British merchandise exports dropped by over 4 per cent. Private fixed investment came to a standstill and public expenditure continued to fall. Despite these more or less exogenous depressing factors, the 1956 budget measures were very mildly deflationary, those of 1957 and 1958 only very cautiously expansionary. Meanwhile Bank Rate was raised from 4½ per cent to the record level of 7 per cent by the autumn of 1957, hire-purchase controls were tightened further in 1956, and attempts to restrain bank lending were made in 1956 and again in 1957.

Policy in this period was, however, strongly influenced by events which had nothing to do with the state of the domestic economy. The Suez crisis of late 1956 and a 'confidence' crisis in 1957 both provoked speculation against sterling and runs on the gold and foreign currency reserves. The Suez crisis was weathered effectively by means of borrowing, largely from the IMF, but the 1957 crisis was not so easily resolved. The convertibility issue, which had raised acute problems in the late 1940s, had been resolved *de facto* in 1955 when the Bank of England began to intervene in the market for 'transferable' sterling. 'Transferable' sterling was sterling which could be used in international trading *except* with dollar countries. Such sterling could inevitably be exchanged for dollars on unofficial markets, though equally inevitably only at a disadvantageous rate compared to the official parity. Convertibility was thus to be had, at a price; for the Bank of

---

[2] Ibid.; see also G.D.N. Worswick, 'Fiscal Policy and Stabilization in Britain', in A. Cairncross (ed.), *Britain's Economic Prospects Reconsidered*, London 1971.

England to intervene in these markets involved not only the official recognition of the *de facto* convertibility but, much more importantly, official involvement with the market value of sterling. By extension, this in turn meant that the exchange rate question was no longer to be regarded as utterly closed.[3] In consequence, when there was a bout of general speculation about European par values in 1957, the pound was no longer immune, despite the fact that, largely because of the relatively depressed state of the domestic economy, the current account was in comfortable surplus. It was reaction to the speculation against sterling which this realization provoked which was the proximate cause of the rise in Bank Rate to 7 per cent, and also the cause of firm recommitment to the defence of the parity.

The 1957 policy reaction is also interesting in that it led to explicit official pronouncements (though little action) on the latterly central issues of inflation and monetary control. Pressure against sterling was correctly attributed to the relatively rapid rise in domestic costs of production. With a clarity which was less apparent during the corresponding debate on the 1970s, the question was posed directly in terms of 'cost–push' and 'demand–pull' explanations of inflationary pressure. The then Chancellor spoke in terms of restraint on public spending and on bank lending and suggested that as long as it was believed that the authorities were prepared to see the necessary finance produced to match the upward spiral of costs, inflation would continue.

The next few years – up to 1964 – saw a rather more regular alternation of the periods of expansion and stagnation coupled with the attempt to dampen these fluctuations by means of counter-cyclical demand management policy. On this front there is little to say of more than parochial interest. The already noted stagnation of the economy by 1958 led to expansionary measures in 1958 and, on a more substantial scale, in 1959. By 1960 there were clear signs of overheating and the current account moved into deficit. Policy duly went into reverse in 1960, but a substantial restrictive shift was delayed until July 1961 and was then a crisis reaction to the balance of payments situation and the associated shift in confidence in sterling (to some extent provoked by DM and guilder revaluation). Again, external forces compounded the slowdown in the economy – the volume of exports of goods rose by only about one per cent in 1962. A broadly neutral budget in 1962 was thus followed by a substantially reflationary one in 1963. Once more the economy was set on a path of growth; once more the growth got out of hand: 1964 saw another balance of payments deficit emerge as unemployment fell towards 1½ per cent and the scene was set for another round of restrictive demand management measures.

Successes and failures

Thus apart from alarums and excursions associated with speculation in and about sterling, the years 1950-64 were very largely years of cyclical growth accompanied by a policy of short-term demand management whose primary aim was to eliminate or at least moderate such fluctuations. As the preceding narrative has shown, this policy consisted predominantly in the use of fiscal

---

[3] M.F.G. Scott, 'The Balance of Payments Crisis', in G.D.N. Worswick and P. H. Ady (eds.), *The British Economy in the 1950s*, Oxford 1962.

instruments with the exchange rate taken as a datum. Fiscal policy in turn meant very largely changes in tax rates since public spending, it was argued, should be determined by longer-term social and economic considerations rather than by short-run economic management needs and was, in any case, difficult to alter at short notice. Monetary policy played a subsidiary role, employed as an additional influence on consumer demand through changes in consumer credit regulations and instructions to the commercial banks on lending. This subsidiary role was reinforced by the findings of the very influential Radcliffe Report on monetary policy in 1959.[4] Its broad conclusion (to the government's disappointment) was that attention could only realistically be paid to a rather general concept of 'liquidity' in the economy, and then only as one among many factors influencing aggregate demand. No specific role − certainly not that of the control of a particular monetary aggregate − was either found or foreseen for monetary policy as a specifically counter-inflation weapon. The role of monetary policy was, however, more important on the external side, with changes in Bank Rate designed not only to moderate short-term external capital flows but also to indicate the determination of the authorities to protect the level of reserves.

That this general approach happened to coincide very largely with a period of Conservative administration is not important: there is every reason to suppose that a Labour administration would have acted in much the same way. That the approach should have had such a long and largely uncontroversial run is, even with hindsight, not immediately explicable. There were probably both positive and negative reasons. On the negative side, the rejection by the Conservative party of a full *laissez-faire* approach and by the Labour party of a centrally planned strategy, together with the explicit rejection of exchange rate policy, apparently left little alternative to the management of aggregate demand as the mainstay of economic policy. On the positive side, there was some evidence (which the passage of time has not weakened) that − almost fortuitously − the achievement of the 'correct' level of domestic demand in relation to domestic supply would, *at that time*, have procured a tolerable rate of price inflation and balance on external account as well as full employment. There was, that is to say, no apparent *fundamental* conflict between the objectives of full employment, balance of payments equilibrium, and (relative) price stability at the existing parity.

Contemporary criticism of macroeconomic policy was thus concentrated almost exclusively on the size and timing of demand management adjustments rather than calling into question the correctness of the underlying strategy.[5] Whether the policy did in fact succeed in dampening the cycles or whether it may not actually, if unintentionally, have contributed to them is still a matter of debate. Successful demand management requires that policy-makers should anticipate exogenously induced cyclical fluctuations − that is, both forecast such changes and forestall them by appropriate policy adjustment. These two requirements were satisfied, if at all, only spasmodically during the whole of

---

[4] *Committee on the Working of the Monetary System, Report* (Radcliffe Report), Cmnd. 827, HMSO, London 1959.

[5] M.J.C. Surrey, 'Assessing the Economy', in D. Morris (ed.), *The Economic System in the UK*, Oxford 1979 (2nd edn.).

the post-war period, but particularly during the 1950s and 1960s. The Treasury did not have anything like a formal statistical model of the economy until the mid-1960s, and did not have a fully-fledged econometric model until the very end of the 1960s. But useful projections could be and were made none the less.

A more compelling criticism of what came to be known as 'stop-go' demand management is that policy-makers based their decisions (via currently available indicators) on what had already happened to the economy rather than on what was likely to be happening in the future when policy changes had their effects.[6] There was thus a strong possibility that, for example, deflationary tax changes announced in response to adverse trade figures and low unemployment figures might in practice serve only to exaggerate a slowdown (and balance of payments improvement) which would have taken place anyway. At all events, the alternation of periods of expansionary fiscal and monetary measures (1953, 1955, 1958-9, 1962-3) and contractionary measures (1951-2, 1956-7, 1960-1) led to a widespread belief that the authorities were at best incapable of fully stabilizing the economy and at worst actively contributed to destabilizing forces. Those who took the latter view further argued, as Britain's relatively slow rate of growth became apparent, that this failure too was partly attributable to government policy in that the alternation of periods of rapid expansion and stagnation reduced entrepreneurs' confidence in the likelihood of sustained and steady expansion of demand and so reduced the rate of investment in new plant, machinery, and buildings, hence further lowering the underlying rate of growth of technical progress and of output per head.

Yet almost the opposite argument is also tenable. Even if, *ex post*, policy may have been destabilizing, the belief that governments were trying to smooth cyclical fluctuations may have led (at least initially) to stabilizing private behaviour.[7] Thus, investment which, as noticed above, was high by pre-war standards, might actually have been boosted by the (not entirely mistaken) perception that full employment and perhaps growth were to be pursued over the medium term.[8] It should also be noted that by the standards of both the pre-war period and the post-war performance of other countries, British cyclical fluctuations were relatively modest in these years – the gap between actual and potential output was never very large (Table 10.4), the annual swings in unemployment never above 1 percentage point of the labour force.

But whatever the merits and demerits of cyclical stabilization policy, the reliance on one policy instrument to achieve all the main economic objectives simultaneously was ultimately doomed to failure. It was largely fortuitous that for quite a long period it so happened that the pressure of demand required to produce a relatively low level of unemployment at the given exchange rate should have proved consistent with both a fairly modest rate of domestic cost and price inflation and with a tolerable balance of payments position (taking one year with another).

With the hindsight of the early 1980s, it is possible to say, paradoxically,

---

[6] Worswick, 'Fiscal Policy'.

[7] M.N. Baily, 'Stabilization Policy and Private Economic Behavior', *Brookings Papers on Economic Activity*, No. 1, 1978.

[8] See Chs. 1 and 10.

that the era of demand management or fine tuning was both a success and a failure. The successes were that unemployment never reached the levels of the 1920s and 1930s, nor those to be experienced in the 1970s; the rate of retail price inflation averaged only about 3 per cent a year, and real output per head and real incomes rose progressively, if erratically. The failures were that real economic growth was increasingly recognized as being slow compared with growth in other Western European economies, and that the rate of cost inflation coupled with a relatively low trend rate of productivity growth and a fixed exchange rate was leading to a progressive loss of international competitiveness.

Emerging problems

These problems, however, were only dimly perceived in the 1950s even though they were becoming increasingly significant. On the external side, the balance of payments was, of course, a constant source of concern (though largely because of the existence of the Sterling Area and of external sterling balances), while the longer-run loss in competitiveness was not at the centre of the economic debate. In the early 1950s overseas holdings of sterling were perhaps four times as large as official reserves, and the same remained true in the mid-1960s, a reflection on Britain's incapacity to increase its level of reserves despite a small current account surplus. Indeed, the United Kingdom was through these years the only European country which was a major exporter of long-term capital on a net basis.[9]

The Sterling Area existed on the understanding that member countries would hold their external reserves in sterling while Sterling Area convertibility meant an obligation to provide non-sterling foreign exchange in return for sterling as the need arose, together with access to the London capital market for member governments, but not for non-members.[10] The existence of large sterling holdings, together with the importance of sterling as a trading currency even outside the Sterling Area, meant that Britain was quite exceptionally at the mercy of large inflows and outflows of short-term capital. Since such flows were predominantly governed by relative short-run interest rates and by expectations about possible changes in exchange rates, interest rate and exchange rate policy were to an unparalleled degree governed by capital account considerations. Most importantly, any expectation of devaluation was likely to lead to large outflows of short-term capital and to unsustainable falls in the reserves. In turn this meant that any deterioration in the current account, however insignificant in itself, was likely if it led to the slightest suspicion of devaluation to become magnified out of all proportion in terms of the overall effect on the reserves. Economic policy thus became increasingly directed towards external equilibrium and towards the preservation of somewhat vaguely defined 'confidence'.

The crucial underlying reason why this 'confidence' was gradually dwindling was to be found in the United Kingdom's poor competitive record over this period (Table 18.2). Though price inflation was very moderate (by later standards), it was well above that of the two major competing countries (the

[9] UNECE, *Economic Survey of Europe in 1971*. Pt. 1, New York 1972, p. 37.

[10] Scott, 'Balance of Payments Crisis'; see also S. Strange, *Sterling and British Policy*, Oxford 1971.

TABLE 18.2. *Indicators of competitiveness*
(average annual percentage changes)

	1950–54	1954–59	1959–64
Relative costs[a]	..	−2.6	1.0
Relative export prices[b]	−1.4	−1.3	−0.8
Relative export profitability[c]	−0.1	−0.6	−0.6
Relative import prices[d]	0.9	−2.2	−0.6
Export performance[e]	−5.5	−2.5	−3.2

[a] Unit labour costs in manufacturing in seven countries (weighted by 1960 export values), divided by United Kingdom unit labour costs

[b] Industrial countries' export unit values, divided by United Kingdom export unit values

[c] United Kingdom export unit values divided by wholesale prices of manufactures

[d] United Kingdom import prices of manufactures divided by wholesale prices of manufactures

[e] Share in exports of manufactures of the twelve major exporting countries; changes between end-years in percentage points

Sources: CSO, *Economic Trends*, May 1967 and various issues; IMF, *International Financial Statistics* (1980 Yearbook); Board of Trade, *Board of Trade Journal* (various issues); NIESR, *Economic Review* (various issues).

United States and Germany). Export price competitiveness was declining rapidly and Britain's share of world trade in manufactures fell uninterruptedly from over 25 per cent in 1950 to barely 14 per cent in 1965. No doubt some of this loss was inevitable as Germany and Japan, in particular, regained their pre-war markets, and some of it reflected sluggish growth in Sterling Area countries, but, on the other hand, the relatively favourable commodity composition of British exports at the start of the period should, *ceteris paribus*, have allowed a more satisfactory performance.

The second major area in which the United Kingdom's record was disappointing was that of growth. Though full employment was maintained and output grew at some 3 per cent per annum, this was not only well below the rates achieved by such 'catching up' countries as Germany and Italy, but also below what France was recording at the time (5 per cent), or even Scandinavia (4 per cent on average). Low output growth was accompanied by low productivity growth (only half the rate of OECD Europe), by a low share of investment in output (15 per cent against the European average of 20 per cent), and by much the lowest share of profits in value added (at least for those countries for which comparable figures for the industrial and transport sectors are available).[11]

It seems clear that these two areas of difficulty were interrelated: low productivity growth and low competitiveness interacted with each other.[12] The former meant that British goods were losing their competitive edge in terms of both price and non-price factors. The latter implied progressively more pronounced sterling crises and 'stop' policies, thus curtailing or preventing investment upswings. But it is more difficult to pinpoint the underlying reasons for the *malaise*. Trade unions, often blamed for much that went wrong in

[11] T.P. Hill, *Profits and Rates of Return*, OECD, Paris 1979.

[12] R.C.O. Matthews, 'Foreign Trade and British Economic Growth', *Scottish Journal of Political Economy*, November 1973.

Britain in the post-war period, seemed in fact to acquiesce at the time in the general climate of prosperity. According to an American observer, however, the collective bargaining and industrial relations system 'Through a self-reinforcing mechanism whose elements include the creation and prolongation of occupational shortages, makework rules, low basic rates of pay, and excessive overtime or restriction of output (and sometimes labor) under incentive systems . . . tended to depress capital-labor and output-capital ratios and also, thereby, investment'.[13]

A relatively rigid and rigidly demarcated labour market was probably one major reason. Another perhaps equally important one was an all-pervasive attitude on the part of unions, employers, and government alike made up of a mixture of sluggishness and complacency. The former may have been a reaction to war and the establishment of the welfare state; the latter may have reflected the continued belief that the country was not only the richest in Europe but also a major imperial power. Indeed, the legacy of empire lies behind a number of the economic problems of the period — long-term net outflows of funds depressed the capital account of the balance of payments; the size of defence expenditure worsened the current account and 'crowded out' civilian investment and exports in capital goods sectors; the overhang of sterling balances magnified the various external crises; the allocation of a significant research and development effort into a few largely military sectors led to a waste of scarce human and capital resources in fields in which United States superiority was unchallengeable;[14] the continuation of imperial preference probably slowed down the necessary restructuring of British industry. It was only after the Suez episode that the country began to realize how limited its political influence was; and it was only after several years of successful integration and rapid economic growth by the Common Market countries that Britain became aware of its loss of economic pre-eminence in Europe.

II. The Search for New Policies, 1964-1973

Britain entered the 1960s with a growing realization that its economic performance was unsatisfactory both in absolute terms and relative to what was happening abroad, that the inflation rate (though low by later standards) was somewhat higher than in competing countries, and that demand management under a fixed exchange rate had solved neither these longer-term problems nor those of short-term stabilization. There was, in consequence, a search for policies that could attack the growth-inflation-competitiveness nexus and the years from the early 1960s to the early 1970s saw a succession of uncoordinated attempts to implement new and sometimes radical solutions to the country's economic problems. Some of these were of major importance — in particular devaluation in 1967, but also the earlier introduction of incomes policies and the later move to a floating exchange rate. Others were of perhaps lesser significance, at least with the benefit of hindsight, e.g. the adoption of indicative planning in

---

[13] L. Ulman, 'Collective Bargaining and Industrial Efficiency', in R.E. Caves and Associates, *Britain's Economic Prospects*, Brookings Institution, Washington 1968, p. 360.

[14] C. Freeman, 'Technical Innovation and British Trade Performance', in F.T. Blackaby (ed.), *De-industrialisation*, NIESR, London 1979, pp. 66-8.

the early part of the period, or the (very partial and temporary) rejection of interventionism in favour of a more *laissez-faire* attitude in the latter part, but they all testified to a new and more structuralist outlook on the economy and contrasted strongly with the previous decade's attitude of relative complacency and fine tuning.

The story of the period begins with a 'dash for growth' and ends with a 'dash for growth', the former largely induced by a combination of electoral consider-ations and rising unemployment, the latter more a function of high unemploy-ment alone (Fig. 18.3). Growth in 1964 was above 5 per cent, in 1973 above 7

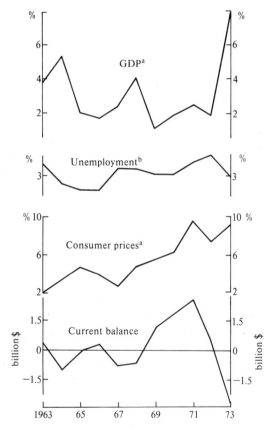

FIG. 18.3. *Economic trends, 1963–1973*
[a] Annual percentage changes
[b] In per cent of the labour force
Sources: OECD, *National Accounts of OECD Countries, 1950–1979*; OECD, *Balance of Payments Statistics, 1960–1977*; OECD, *Economic Outlook*, July 1981; IMF, *International Financial Statistics* (1980 Yearbook).

per cent. In between were years of relatively sluggish expansion (2½ per cent per annum on average), imposed at first by balance of payments constraints, then by the restrictive policies that followed devaluation, and in the early 1970s by attempts to curb inflation. Unemployment rose through the period, inflation accelerated to nearly 10 per cent, and profitability fell to new lows. Yet a few positive features emerged — productivity growth which had been very slow until then accelerated somewhat (from 2 to 3 per cent per year for the economy as a whole, from just over 2 per cent to nearly 4 per cent in manufacturing), and the current account was in very large surplus between 1969 and 1971.

Policies for incomes

The search for new policies that would ultimately allow Britain to grow faster began with an attack on the rate of inflation and, in particular, on wage inflation. Incomes policies were introduced not so much as a way to reduce inflation *per se*, since this had not been seen as a serious worry for policy-makers in the 1950s, but on somewhat more complex grounds. The basic reasoning was this: since the early 1950s, the United Kingdom's inflation rate had been somewhat higher than those of its major competitors; given the aim of maintaining a fixed exchange rate, this meant that exports became progressively either less price competitive or less profitable or both, while, correspondingly, import penetration tended to grow; it followed that the balance of payments constraint would become steadily more restrictive, and the expansion of demand and output steadily less feasible. The main possible ways out of this vicious circle were to abandon the fixed exchange rate (ruled out by political decision), to increase productivity (attempted with dubious success as described below), or to reduce the rate of wage inflation. The last could be achieved either — perhaps — by deflation and an increase in unemployment (a process which was likely to run counter to the attempt to raise the growth rate), or by attempting to influence wage bargaining directly. The latter might be achieved by reforming the legal aspects of industrial relations (dubious and, though later attempted, stubbornly and successfully resisted), or by means of a centrally imposed intervention in wage bargaining — more loosely, by means of an incomes policy.[15]

The first serious attempt at an incomes policy came with the 1961 crisis, when the Conservative government introduced a mandatory (but not legally enforceable) six-month 'pay pause' for the public sector. Between then and the late 1970s, incomes policies in some shape or form were in almost continuous operation. Immediately following the pay pause there was a series of policies based on voluntary compliance with a 'norm' for wage increases related to the contemporaneous target rate of economic growth (see below). There were provisions for 'exceptional' above-norm increases on grounds of, for example, above-average increases in productivity, labour mobility, or relatively low pay. These exceptions were 'policed' — or at least monitored — by a special central institution: between 1962 and 1964 the National Incomes Commission and between 1965 and 1970 the National Board for Prices and Incomes.

In practice there was — and remains — considerable doubt about the effectiveness of incomes policies of this kind in restraining the rate of growth of money wages below what would otherwise have happened.[16] Grounds for 'exceptional'

[15] F.T. Blackaby, 'Incomes Policy', in F.T. Blackaby (ed.), *British Economic Policy, 1960-74*, NIESR, Cambridge 1978.
[16] See Ch. 12.

increases were easy to find and exploit, so that the 'norm' tended to become regarded as a minimum entitlement, and the voluntary nature of the policies meant that they relied heavily on the usually half-hearted acquiescence of the trade unions. In fact the only period during the 1960s when incomes policy had a marked effect on the rate of pay inflation was during the *statutory* and universal (no exemptions) policy of 1966-7, when there was a six-month freeze followed by six months during which only increases on very exceptional grounds were permitted. But the main purpose of this rigid policy (which was inherently only maintainable for a relatively short period) was to boost overseas 'confidence' and, probably, to contribute through real wage reductions to a general policy of deflation in response to the balance of payments crisis of July 1966.

The return after mid-1967 to a voluntary norm-based policy in practice meant a gradual crumbling of incomes policy, which was finally (though only temporarily) abandoned on the return of the Conservatives to power in 1970. The pattern of crisis followed by statutory freeze, giving way to progressive relaxation and final abandonment, was repeated in 1973-4 and again in 1975-8: again only the initial freeze or statutory maximum increase had perceptible effects on the rate of cost-inflation, and they were by their nature only temporary. The question of whether it would be possible to devise a flexible but effective long-term incomes policy in the context of British bargaining institutions and practices remains open.

Policies for growth

A second general area of concern about economic policy was Britain's comparatively poor performance in terms of economic growth. During the 1950s this problem had scarcely been recognized. Governments were, it is true, aware that a higher rate of productive investment was somehow better than a lower one and had sporadically considered and changed various aspects of the taxation allowances made for investment. But the conventional wisdom was that firms' investment plans were influenced far more by expectations of future levels of demand than by immediate financial considerations. It followed that the only way in which the overall level of private sector investment could be raised was by positively affecting these expectations. Negatively, as already noted, this led to criticism of demand management on the grounds that it had in practice contributed to, rather than moderating, fluctuations in the growth of demand which tended to depress the state of confidence and consequently the rate of new investment.[17] More positively, there was a growing belief (mainly but not exclusively in the Labour party) that there was something to be learned from the French model of 'indicative' planning.

An indicative plan is effectively a set of projections of demand for the outputs of different industries based on an assumed overall rate of growth of the economy. This, it was held, would provide information of a consistent kind which no individual industry (or firm) could provide for itself and thus directly reduce uncertainty about the future. In addition, and perhaps more importantly, if it could also be shown that a higher rate of growth were feasible (in the sense

---

[17] W. Beckerman, 'Demand, Exports and Growth', in W. Beckerman and Associates, *The British Economy in 1975*, NIESR, Cambridge 1975.

of demonstrating that such a higher rate would not involve insurmountable constraints on individual industries or on the economy as a whole), then a plan of such a sort would be self-fulfilling – more unkindly, would be a successful confidence trick.[18]

The machinery for such planning was initiated in 1962 by the setting up of the National Economic Development Office (NEDO). The initial chosen 'feasible' growth rate was 4 per cent per annum over a five-year period (later revised to 3.8 per cent) – a rate thought to be sufficiently higher than the past trend of some 2½ to 3 per cent as to make the exercise worthwhile, yet not so high as to be quite unrealistic. In the event (for reasons explained below), the National Plan was quickly overtaken by short-term crises and policy responses, and the whole notion of indicative planning was totally discredited after 1966.

Another aspect of concern with the supply side of the economy related to the availability of labour to the manufacturing sector. It was argued that in many other European economies, there existed large agricultural sectors in which both the level and the rate of growth of productivity were relatively low, and where the movement of labour into the manufacturing sector (with relatively high levels of productivity and productivity growth) was both easy and beneficial. Britain, by contrast, had already contracted its agricultural sector to a much greater degree, so that no such pool of labour available to move into manufacturing existed. There was, however, a large and growing service sector in which, because of the limited possibilities for economies of scale, productivity growth was believed to be low (a belief difficult to prove because of the problems of measuring productivity in services). The Selective Employment Tax was thus introduced (in 1966) to tax, on a per caput basis, employment in services but not in manufacturing (indeed there was a slight subsidy in the latter case). How successful the tax was is, of course, difficult to ascertain. It was probably too small to have a marked impact on the sectoral distribution of labour. Within the services sector there seems to have been some acceleration in the rate of growth of productivity as well as some additional inflation.[19] But manufacturing, which was supposed to benefit from an increased availability of labour, in fact recorded a significant 'shake-out' of workers in those years – productivity growth accelerated, but for reasons almost opposite to the ones that had been predicted.

The supply of labour to the manufacturing sector again became a policy issue in the later part of the 1970s. This time the proposition was that the growth of the public sector had starved manufacturing of labour;[20] again, the assumption of an unfulfilled demand for labour in manufacturing industry was not demonstrated. The argument was overtaken by a more widespread preoccupation with the size of the public sector which, for various reasons discussed later, played a predominant part in the discussion of policy in the late 1970s.

[18] P.D. Henderson, 'Planning and the Machinery of Policy', in P.D. Henderson (ed.), *Economic Growth in Britain*, London 1966.

[19] W.B. Reddaway and Associates, *Effects of Selective Employment Tax, Final Report*, University of Cambridge Department of Applied Economics, Cambridge 1973.

[20] R. Bacon and W. Eltis, *Britain's Economic Problem*, London 1978 (2nd edn.).

Policies for the balance of payments

By the mid-1960s the problem of sterling had, paradoxically, both intensified and eased. The growing incompatibility at the fixed exchange rate of $2.80 of internal and external balance together with the overriding apparent importance of preserving the parity had imparted an increasingly deflationary bias to economic policy – a bias, many argued, that could only be eliminated by devaluation.[21] At the same time, the decline of the Sterling Area and the falling significance of the pound as an international trading currency made the objections to a change in attitude towards the exchange rate less powerful.

The parity was clearly on the agenda for the incoming Labour government of 1964. In addition to political and longer-term economic considerations, the new government took office as the scale of the 1964 balance of payments deficit was becoming apparent. Action of some kind was clearly needed and devaluation was on purely economic grounds a strong candidate. The decision to maintain the parity at all costs and thus to deflate in 1965-6 thus needs a good deal of explaining. It seems clear that the advice which the government was receiving from its economic advisers was broadly in favour of devaluation and that its rejection was based on political and historical aspects, not on economic grounds.[22] In particular, the fact that it had been Labour governments which had devalued in 1931 and 1949, together with the irrational adoption during the 1950s of the value of the exchange rate as a symbol of national economic standing, led to the feeling that devaluation was to be considered only as a last resort and, even then, as an admission of defeat. In the longer term the National Plan and the pursuit of an incomes policy would solve the underlying problems of growth and competitiveness; in the short run, deflation and high interest rates, in the conventional way, would solve the immediate balance of payments problem. The one innovation was a temporary 'Import Surcharge' of 15 per cent (soon reduced to 10 per cent) on imports of manufactured and semi-manufactured goods.

In fact the 'new' policies palpably failed to show signs of working effectively – in the case of the National Plan largely because of the choice of deflation over devaluation itself. The worsening of the underlying problem simply pushed the government into further deflation and a crisis pay freeze in July 1966. The inevitable adjustment of the exchange rate finally took place in November 1967 in the form of a step devaluation from $2.80 to the pound to $2.40. The new peg was maintained until the Smithsonian realignment of exchange rates in December 1971 (with the exception of a brief period of floating in the autumn of that year); the Smithsonian parity of $2.60 was maintained until the final decision to float in June 1972.[23]

Devaluation was, on the face of things, highly successful: the balance of payments on current account moved from deficits of about $¾ billion in 1967 and

[21] A. Graham and W. Beckerman, 'Economic Performance and the Foreign Balance', in W. Beckerman (ed.), *The Labour Government's Economic Record, 1964-1970*, London 1972.

[22] Ibid.; see also R.H.S. Crossman, *Diaries of a Cabinet Minister*, London 1977, various entries for 1964-7.

[23] J.H.B. Tew, 'Policies aimed at Improving the Balance of Payments', in Blackaby (ed.), *British Economic Policy*.

again in 1968 (the 'J-curve' effect) steadily towards a surplus of over $2½ billion by 1971 (Table 18.3). There is, however, room for considerable doubt about the extent to which this improvement was attributable to the devaluation. Steady

TABLE 18.3. *Indicators of performance: pre- and post-devaluation*

	1959–63	1963–67	1967–71
	average annual percentage changes		
Relative costs[a]	..	−0.1	0.8
Relative export prices[b]	..	−0.9	0.4
Relative export profitability[c]	−0.3	−0.8	0.2
Relative import prices[c]	−1.0	−0.5	−
	1960–63	1964–67	1968–71
	percentages, annual averages		
Export performance[c]	15.7	13.5	11.1
Import penetration[d]	5.3	7.0	8.5
Investment ratio − total[e]	17.3	19.7	20.6
− manufacturing[e]	4.0	3.9	4.2
Profit rate[f]	12.5	11.3	9.5

[a] Unit current costs in manufacturing in thirteen countries divided by United Kingdom unit current costs in manufacturing (in common currency)
[b] Manufactured exports average values in thirteen countries divided by United Kingdom manufactured exports average values (in common currency)
[c] See notes to Table 18.2
[d] Imports of manufactures in per cent of GDP at constant prices
[e] Gross fixed investment in per cent of GDP at constant prices
[f] Real pre-tax rate of return on trading assets of industrial and commercial companies
Sources: OECD, 'The International Competitiveness of Selected OECD Countries', *OECD Economic Outlook − Occasional Studies*, July 1978; OECD, *National Accounts of OECD Countries, 1950–1979*; IMF, *International Financial Statistics* (1980 Yearbook); CSO, *Economic Trends* (Annual Supplement, 1981); NIESR, *Economic Review* (various issues); Bank of England, 'Measures of Real Profitability', *Bank of England Quarterly Bulletin*, December 1978.

domestic deflation had taken place: registered unemployment rose from 500,000 in 1967 to over 700,000 in 1971, and the volume of world trade in manufactures increased at a rapid rate − by over 50 per cent between 1967 and 1971. On the other hand, a number of studies which have tried to allow for these favourable influences have none the less obtained estimates suggesting a significant effect stemming purely from devaluation − between $1 to $2½ billion in 1970; or figures accounting for 40 to 90 per cent of the improvement in the current account between 1967 and 1970.[24] A more serious criticism of devaluation is probably that its effects were short-lived. There seems little doubt that the increase in import prices induced by the parity change, and the subsequent wage-price spiral, played a significant part in the acceleration of retail price inflation from 2½ per cent in 1967 to 9½ per cent in 1971. More importantly, the breathing space which a favourable balance of payments position had provided was not used. Policies were restrictive, given the overriding need to make

[24] Ibid., p. 355.

devaluation work, but restriction was probably carried on for too long. Real wages suffered, thus laying the ground for the wage 'explosion' of 1969-70, while profitability did not improve, and investment, therefore, rose only little. By 1971 a good deal of the competitive advantage conferred by devaluation had already been eroded.

Policies in disarray

At the beginning of the 1970s, then, the British economy was by most standards in a sorry state. The growth rate had fallen to 2 per cent per annum or less, unemployment was around three-quarters of a million, price inflation was approaching 10 per cent a year, and the balance of payments – although in healthy surplus – was threatened by the erosion of competitiveness. Nor was this gloomy picture attributable to any great extent to wrong policy decisions, which would have been reversible. Rather, it seems that few if any of the policy instruments – whether old or new – had had much effect on the development of the economy. Demand management was clearly considered insufficient, the various attempts to increase the underlying rate of growth of productivity appeared to have had little or no impact, incomes policies had proved to have had at best very short-lived effects on inflation, and exchange rate adjustment had turned out not to be the panacea which it had widely been expected to be.

Some at least of this seems to have been recognized by the incoming Conservative administration of 1970. At all events, the approach to both industrial policy and to pay bargaining was distinctly *laissez-faire* while, on the more active side, there were commitments to reform the laws relating to trade unions, to make a determined attempt to join the EEC, and to introduce a more flexible framework for the operation of monetary policy (itself to be given, partly at the instigation of the IMF, greater prominence). Not all of this, of course, could be done at once, though the machinery to monitor pay settlements was immediately wound up, there were numerous piecemeal withdrawals of various government interventions in the conduct of private industry, an Industrial Relations Bill was introduced, direct controls over consumer credit and bank advances were abolished, and the move towards the introduction of VAT was begun. But the management of the economy at large soon posed familiar problems and led to familiar policy responses. Unemployment began to rise sharply – to nearly one million in the winter of 1971-2 – without any perceptible abatement in the rate of pay increases, and this, together with the proposed legislation in the field of industrial relations and the attempt to moderate wage settlements in the public but not in the private sector, generated a distinct increase in industrial unrest, leading, amongst other things, to the collapse of the government's own attempts to moderate public sector pay settlements in the face of a bitter strike by the miners in the winter of 1971-2.

By the spring of 1972, economic policy – such as it was – was in complete disarray, and there was something of a volte-face, or 'U-turn'. On the counter-inflation front, policy changed first to one of tripartite negotiation with the trade unions and the employers' federation and then, when that failed after about six months, to one of statutory intervention: a ninety-day complete freeze of wages, succeeded by a six-month period of a maximum award for any one employee, followed by a period of effective indexation of wages to prices.

On the macroeconomic front the new policy was partly familiar — very substantial fiscal and monetary reflation — and partly novel: it was announced that the parity of sterling would not be defended if the balance of payments consequences of the reflationary measures led to downward pressure on the exchange rate.[25]

Again, however, the change in policy towards sterling did not prove to be quite the panacea that many had supposed. The case for the move to a floating rate had been based on the supposition that such a rate would have 'accommodated' the gradual but persistent excess of British cost inflation over that of competitor countries and so have avoided the growing incompatibility of internal and external equilibrium of the 1950s and early 1960s. This case left out of account the indirect effects on domestic costs of the rise in import prices following depreciation. If workers bargained effectively in real terms and were not subject to 'money illusion' then ultimately total domestic costs would rise sufficiently to nullify the initial competitive advantage gained by the depreciation. Whether or not this was strictly the case (an issue which is still empirically debated), a downward movement in the exchange rate would certainly add to cost-inflationary pressures. In the event, the matter was resolved by the introduction of wage indexation shortly before the oil price rises of 1973-4. Under these conditions a floating exchange rate could contribute nothing to what now became the most pressing problem of policy — that of controlling the inflation rate.

The story of this period is thus one which started with great hopes for the two major issues that had to be tackled — growth and competitiveness — and ended in complete disarray with stop–go policies being compounded by 'U-turns' in the management of the economy. Initially, it was felt that growth was supply constrained and that policies encouraging investment and freeing labour for more productive uses would allow an acceleration. When these notionally 'supply-side' policies failed, there was a reversion to the belief that a sustained expansion of demand would stimulate investment and so provide indirectly for faster sustainable growth. The old stumbling-block for such a policy, the balance of payments constraint, was removed by abandoning the commitment to a fixed exchange rate (though world-wide developments made this abandonment inevitable in any case). But a floating exchange rate made the inflation problem far less tractable: the inflationary impact of the OPEC and other commodity price rises put the seal on the arrival of inflation as the number one priority of policy. With the failure, real or apparent, of 'orthodox' policies to solve the economic management problems of the 1960s and early 1970s, the way was open for a different approach and for the later 1970s 'monetarist experiment'.

III. The Years of Crisis, 1973–1979

The commodity price boom and the oil crisis hit the United Kingdom with particular force — OECD estimates put the income effect of the terms of trade deterioration between 1972 and 1974 at some 5½ per cent of GDP, by far the largest figure in Europe. In addition, the economy's fragility was increased by

[25] F.T. Blackaby, 'Narrative, 1960–74', in Blackaby (ed.), *British Economic Policy*.

the after-effects of the significant overheating of demand of 1973, by a damaging miners' strike in early 1974, and by an indexation system that ensured a rapid propagation of external inflationary impulses. It is perhaps not surprising that, in the circumstances, Britain's economic performance deteriorated very sharply in 1974–5. The rate of inflation and the current account deficit were the highest in Europe, the decline in output the most pronounced outside Switzerland. There was some partial recovery in the years that followed, but inflation proved stubborn, unemployment rose steadily, and growth was very low (Table 18.4). The whole industrialized world experienced similar developments, but Britain's worsening was probably more marked than that of most other European countries, and this despite the achievement of near self-sufficiency in oil by 1979.

TABLE 18.4. *Macroeconomic indicators*

	1973–79[a]	1974	1975	1976	1977	1978	1979
	annual percentage changes						
GDP	1.3	−1.2	−0.8	4.2	1.0	3.6	0.9
Gross fixed investment	−0.6	−2.7	−1.0	1.1	−2.7	3.5	−1.4
Productivity[b]	1.2	−1.6	−0.3	4.9	0.7	3.5	0.3
Inflation[c]	15.6	16.0	24.2	16.5	15.9	8.3	13.4
Effective exchange rate	−4.0	−3.1	−7.7	−15.4	−5.0	1.4	7.6
	percentages						
PSBR[d]	8.1[e]	6.1	10.1	8.4	5.5	7.3	11.0
Export performance[f]	9.3[e]	8.8	9.3	8.8	9.4	9.5	9.7
Import penetration[g]	13.8[e]	12.8	12.1	12.6	13.7	14.7	16.8

[a] Average annual percentage changes
[b] GDP per employed
[c] Consumer prices
[d] In per cent of GDP at current prices
[e] Annual averages, 1974–79
[f] Share of exports of manufactures of the twelve major exporting countries
[g] Imports of manufactures in per cent of GDP at constant prices
Sources: OECD, *National Accounts of OECD Countries, 1950–1979*; OECD, *Labour Force Statistics, 1968–1979*; IMF, *International Financial Statistics* (1980 Yearbook); NIESR, *Economic Review*, August 1981.

Muddling through, 1974–75

The immediate reaction to the crisis concentrated on the planned reduction in oil supplies. In particular, a three-day working week was mandatory from 1 January 1974 in order to reduce the demand for energy, and a set of deflationary measures (mainly very substantial cuts in public expenditure plans for 1974/5) was announced in December 1973. In fact, the threat of reductions in oil supplies was largely unrealized and the three-day week ended early in March. More considered appraisal of the economic consequences of the oil price rise was complicated by the miners' actions in support of a pay claim, which took the form of an overtime ban from mid-November 1973 and an all-out strike from early February to mid-March, when a new Labour government significantly increased the original pay offer.

As elsewhere, the new government was faced by a simultaneous inflationary and deflationary shock. In two respects, however, the United Kingdom was rather better placed than the majority of other oil-importing countries. In the short term, the continued even though diminished importance of London as a financial centre meant that Britain was likely to benefit disproportionately from the recycling of OPEC petro-dollars. Secondly, the prospect of North Sea oil meant that the balance of payments deterioration would eventually disappear; in addition, this prospect further added to the attractiveness of London as a home for OPEC funds. Given that the balance of payments situation, in these circumstances, did not seem as precarious as in other countries, it could be argued that Britain was ideally placed to follow the appropriate response to the price-inflationary and demand-deflationary effects that were occurring. This response would have been to treat the oil price rise as similar to an exogenous increase in indirect tax and thus to offset its effect on the domestic price level by reducing non-oil indirect taxes. This would have neutralized the imported inflation effect and the impact on real incomes, output, and employment while leaving the *relative* price of oil to other goods still (desirably) sharply higher.

Partly perhaps because most other major countries were rapidly moving into a restrictive posture, the new Labour government failed to adopt this approach. Indeed, it failed to develop a coherent policy response to the crisis at all. It was immediately confronted with enormous external trade deficits, deepening recession, and a worsening rate of inflation. Any attempt to prevent the recession by reflationary action was likely to add to inflationary pressures both directly (it was still believed) and, given the floating exchange rate, indirectly by worsening the non-oil balance of payments deficit, increasing the downward pressure on the pound, and so raising import costs in sterling terms. On the other hand, any attempt to control the rate of inflation directly by means of an extended period of effective severe restraint on pay increases (even if that had been a practical proposition in political terms) would be likely to have cut private consumption without a prompt compensatory increase in exports and would, therefore, have deepened the recession. In fact the government's response to the incomes policy question was as perverse as it could be. Stage III of the outgoing Conservative government's incomes policy had effectively indexed money wages to the index of retail prices by means of 'threshold' payments awarded to the greater part of the work-force as the price index reached specified levels. In the circumstances, when import prices were rising no faster than domestic money wages, this policy was eminently sensible; any underlying increase in output per head would have automatically led to a gradual reduction in the rate of inflation. The oil price rise, however, promptly made this mechanism work in a positively perverse way — the possibility of a wage-price spiral consequent on the OPEC price increase was now a legislated certainty. Why Stage III was not immediately abandoned remains for the time being a mystery.

The economy muddled through 1974 in a fashion which in effect made the worst of every possible world. The March budget, though complex, was broadly neutral in demand terms. Subsidies on foods were increased, presumably in an attempt to offset the price inflationary effect of the oil price rise, but at the same time this downward influence on the general price level was offset by increases in nationalized industries prices. Similarly, later in 1974 the standard rate of VAT was lowered from 10 to 8 per cent, but the nationalized industries were told that their future subsidies were to be phased out, with the corollary of further price increases. Finally, by the end of the year, the rigid wage-index-ation of Stage III was abandoned and a less formal approach, the 'Social Con-tract', was adopted. This was a purely voluntary agreement between the govern-ment and the Trades Union Congress to moderate wage claims, but, self-defeatingly, it allowed compensation for price increases.[26]

These various policy vacillations inevitably led to a severe domestic crisis in 1975. Again, it is hard to make sense of official policy reaction. Against a back-ground of falling real output and rapidly rising unemployment, the spring budget was significantly contractionary, and, moreover, despite an accelerating rate of inflation, was so largely by means of increases in indirect taxes and duties which themselves were estimated to add nearly 3 per cent to the retail price index. After two years of statutory incomes policy, pressures for the correction of 'anomalies' and consequential readjustment of differentials were very great, and the 'Social Contract' demonstrably failed to contain them — in the second quarter of 1975 average earnings were 28 per cent higher than a year earlier and retail prices 24 per cent higher. Inevitably, the inflation problem came to dominate all others, particularly unemployment (which rose rapidly towards one million during the first half of 1975) and the balance of payments (where the current account, although still in substantial deficit, was beginning to im-prove as the domestic recession deepened).

Anti-inflationary policies, 1976–79

The later 1970s were characterized by a determined if ineffectual attempt to come to grips with inflation. 1976 marked a very clear turning-point. This was the adoption of a highly orthodox policy of deflation which, for a variety of reasons, was presented by both the then Labour administration and the new Conservative administration as a 'new' or 'fresh' policy based on control of the money supply, variously conceived. The point of departure was a 'Letter of Intent' to the IMF in late 1976 as a condition of an IMF loan following a serious sterling crisis. The Letter of Intent contained commitments about the conduct of economic policy in the form of targets for the level of the Public Sector Borrowing Requirement (PSBR), the rates of growth of domestic credit ex-pansion and of the broadly defined money supply (sterling M_3), and the appro-priate level of the exchange rate. These commitments, perhaps to the authorities' relief, largely precluded discretionary fiscal, monetary, and exchange rate shifts.

Two features of the 'new' casting of policy in terms of monetary targets were particularly significant. First, there was the introduction of the concept of the PSBR as a (or the) major determinant of the rate of growth of the money supply rather than as a given datum or base for the operation of monetary policy in terms of the relative proportions to be financed by monetary expansion and by borrowing from the non-bank private sector. This, secondly, meant that the determination of the PSBR (fiscal policy) was to be governed primarily in terms

    [26] R.F. Elliott and J.L. Fallick, 'An Overview', in J.L. Fallick and R.F. Elliott (eds.), *Incomes Policies, Inflation and Relative Pay*, London 1981.

of its monetary implications. Thus the presentation of government policy in terms of firm monetary control in practice meant simply a new name for an orthodox, and increasingly severe, fiscal deflation via public expenditure curbs in order to reduce the PSBR. It is worth noting that the other commitment to the IMF in the Letter of Intent − to manage the exchange rate so as to preserve competitiveness − was quietly ignored. In fact North Sea oil together with relatively high interest rates (themselves a concomitant of a restrictive monetary policy) served to produce an exchange rate high enough by 1979 to have reduced price competitiveness by some 15 per cent compared with 1975.

Initially, however, the 'conversion' to monetarism was pragmatic. It went hand in hand with incomes policies and was seen more in terms of substituting a new target for the old exchange rate parity in a world of floating rates, than as a quest for ultimate salvation. Initially, too, the combination of orthodox deflation and wage restraint was very successful. Consumer price inflation was reduced from nearly 25 per cent in 1975 to just over 8 per cent in 1978, and this despite a very sharp exchange rate depreciation in 1976. Much of the credit for this must go to the attempt to operate a 'consensus' incomes policy for which a prima-facie judgement of success can be made. Even this policy, however, proved unsustainable, and it was effectively abandoned some time before the Labour party lost power in 1979. The reasons for the collapse of the incomes policy and for the acceleration in wage inflation in the autumn of 1978 remain obscure. Neither a monetarist nor a cost−push interpretation would have predicted such an outcome given that, at the time, monetary targets were in place, inflation was visibly decelerating, and real incomes were rising (thanks partly to budgetary tax cuts).

A second area of (very partial) success was on the foreign trade front. Not only, of course, did the importance of the 'oil deficit' diminish substantially thanks to North Sea production, but Britain, for the first time since 1950, began to gain market shares abroad. To some extent this may have been due to Common Market effects and to the sluggishness of world trade (United Kingdom exports seem to fare relatively better when world growth is relatively slow), but it may also have reflected an improvement in competitiveness consequent upon depreciation. But while export performance was improving, import penetration rose very sharply despite what should have been an equal improvement in price competitiveness. Hence scepticism about the effectiveness of exchange rate depreciation was strengthened and the search for an effective anti-inflationary policy reinforced.

Only a rather tentative assessment of policy in the later 1970s can be offered. The breakdown of the 'consensus' incomes policy of 1976-7 paved the way for the election in 1979 of a Conservative administration giving the battle against inflation by 'monetarist' means clear priority over all other economic objectives. This policy was enshrined in a Medium Term Financial Strategy which placed reductions in the PSBR at the centre of the stage. The first showing of this strategy was not convincing. The effect of falling real income on tax revenues and social security expenditures made reductions in the PSBR much harder than anticipated to achieve: the net effect on the PSBR of reductions in public expenditure were, after the effects of the induced fall in output, incomes, and employment, much smaller than the gross effects. Partly in consequence, and

partly because of reluctance to control bank lending, targets for the rate of expansion of the money supply were not met; whether or not as a result, inflation
remained stubbornly high. The expected achievements of policy remained unfulfilled hopes, amounting to little more than a vague belief that mass unemployment would induce a 'new realism' in British industry, whose unspecified
benefits would far outweigh the very tangible costs incurred.

Conclusions

The preceding text has deliberately concentrated on economic policy, more so
than other country chapters in this book. In the British context this is understandable. Over the thirty years of the period United Kingdom economic history
reads as a constant pursuit of a simple but chimerical policy solution to the
country's problems. Virtually every kind of macroeconomic option was ex-
plored, from demand management under a fixed exchange rate, through indicative planning and incomes policies, to devaluation; from devaluation to a
floating exchange rate and a deliberate attempt at a more passive, market-
oriented, role for government, and back to incomes policy and conventional
though increasingly deflationary fiscal and monetary management. Abstracting
from short-run fluctuations, none of these changes seems to have had much
effect on underlying structural trends. Britain started the period as one of
Europe's most prosperous and strongest countries, and ended it as one of the
most fragile.

One reason for this disappointing performance may, in fact, have been the
frequency and violence of the policy changes themselves: the disruptive jerks
from one remedy to the next, the dogmatism with which many of the 'solutions'
were introduced, the associated belief in the application of one 'true cure'
rather than a belief in balance and eclecticism. There was never a period when it
was recognized that Britain's economic problems had many dimensions and
needed a variety of simultaneous policy initiatives, not a sequence of policy
initiatives. But other factors were also at work. Attitudes were no doubt important – in the 1950s there may have been complacency on the part of both
government and management; by the 1970s this had been eclipsed or superseded,
according to many, by the deep and entrenched conservatism of the trade
unions. But these remain impressions, remarkably difficult to pin down in terms
of clear-cut evidence on cause, consequence, or cure.

Throughout the period, the labour market was probably less flexible than it
was on the continent, partly perhaps because of an inherent lower overall supply
elasticity of labour, but more importantly because of man-made obstacles to
geographical and occupational mobility and to technological advance. An inflexible labour market, in turn, became a persistent source of cost–push inflationary pressures and hence of perennial difficulties on the competitiveness front.

By the end of the 1970s there was a widespread feeling, intensified by the
failure of North Sea oil to alleviate rather than exacerbate the economic problem, that the British economy had reached some sort of unprecedented crisis
point. And as so often before, a new simple 'solution' was advanced and adopted.
'Monetarism' was to be the answer not only to the immediate problem of inflation but also to the problems of growth and efficiency. The experience of the

early 1980s hardly augurs well. The chosen instrument of monetary policy has been fiscal deflation: the first impact of the policy has been severe depression of demand, output, and employment. So far, the 'new' policy has led the economy not only into further relative decline but into absolute recession with few, if any, signs of the hoped-for benefits in the form of lower inflation and increased competitiveness on the scale needed to reverse the depression. The managers of the British economy appear to have learned nothing from, and forgotten everything of, the experience of the last thirty years.

Bibliography

The bibliography of Britain's economic record over the three decades since 1950 is immense: few other countries seem to have aroused nearly as much analysis and debate. The following brief note can only be taken as an introductory guide.

For a general narrative guide with a historical flavour, see J.F. Wright, *Britain in the Age of Economic Management*, Oxford 1979; and, for a longer historical perspective, R.C.O. Matthews, 'Why has Britain had Full Employment since the War?', *Economic Journal*, September 1968, and 'Foreign Trade and British Economic Growth', *Scottish Journal of Political Economy*, November 1973.

The experience of the 1950s and 1960s is narrated and analysed in: G.D.N. Worswick and P.H. Ady (eds.), *The British Economy in the 1950s*, Oxford 1962; J.C.R. Dow, *The Management of the British Economy, 1945–60*, NIESR, Cambridge, 1964; and W. Beckerman (ed.), *The Labour Government's Economic Record, 1964–1970*, London 1972. The 1960s and the first half of the 1970s are covered by F.T. Blackaby (ed.), *British Economic Policy, 1960–74*, NIESR, Cambridge 1978. The problems of the later 1970s are too recent to have yet received dispassionate attention, but much interesting analysis is contained in: M. Posner (ed.), *Demand Management*, NIESR, London 1978; F.T. Blackaby (ed.), *De-industrialisation*, NIESR, London 1979; and R. Major (ed.), *Britain's Trade and Exchange-Rate Policy*, NIESR, London 1979. There are two Brookings Institution surveys of many of the issues: R.E. Caves and Associates, *Britain's Economic Prospects*, Washington 1968, and R.E. Caves and L.B. Krause (eds.), *Britain's Economic Performance*, Washington 1980. A British response to the first of these surveys is A. Cairncross (ed.), *Britain's Economic Prospects Reconsidered*, London 1971.

Interpretations of Britain's comparatively low rate of *economic growth* are usefully surveyed in W. Beckerman (ed.), *Slow Growth in Britain*, Oxford 1979; two explanations not covered there are by N. Kaldor, *Causes of the Slow Rate of Economic Growth of the UK*, Cambridge 1966, and by A. Glyn and B. Sutcliffe, *British Capitalism, Workers and the Profits Squeeze*, London 1972. *Inflation* is treated from the labour market angle by J.L. Fallick and R.F. Elliott (eds.), *Incomes Policies, Inflation and Relative Pay*, London 1981, and from a combination of labour market and monetarist viewpoints in M. Parkin and M.T. Sumner (eds.), *Inflation in the United Kingdom*, Manchester 1978. *Monetary policy* in the latter 1970s is analysed in House of Commons Treasury and Civil Service Committee, *Monetary Policy, Third Report*, HMSO, London 1981; see also M.J. Artis and M.K. Lewis, *Monetary Control in the United Kingdom*, Oxford 1981. *Balance of payments and exchange rate* problems are briefly surveyed in A.P. Thirlwall, *Balance of Payments Theory and the UK Experience*, London 1980; a more detailed study of recent problems is in the already quoted volume edited by Major.

19

Spain*

EDUARDO MERIGÓ**

Introduction

At the beginning of the 1950s, two important characteristics made Spain a country very different from the other major economies of Western Europe — relative underdevelopment and the institutional background of an authoritarian regime.

Despite a period of growth and industrialization begun in the years of neutrality during World War I and pursued in the 1920s, depression, political upheavals, and the civil war had meant that in 1940 Spain was economically more backward than ten years earlier. The proportion of the active population engaged in industrial activities had declined to 22 per cent (the level of 1920), while that in agriculture had risen to over 50 per cent. Although the latter share declined during the period of post-war reconstruction, it was still higher in 1950 than in 1930.[1] Yet at the same time, agricultural production was 20 to 30 per cent lower in the 1940s than in the 1920s. Output only recovered pre-war levels during the 1950s, and it was not until the 1960s that the same could be said of productivity. Overall output, which had fallen by 25 per cent during the 1930s, grew at an annual rate of only 1¼ per cent in the 1940s. Consequently, by 1950, it was still some 10 per cent below its 1930 level. And GDP per caput, at $300 in 1954, the first year for which comparable data are available, was barely 40 per cent of the average for OECD Europe.

A second, and perhaps more important, aspect of the situation at the beginning of the 1950s was the institutional background. The Spanish regime had established the institutional pattern of a corporate state superimposed on an administration which was basically Napoleonic, highly centralized, and rather inefficient. The absence of democracy was thus apparent not only in the suppression of human rights and democratic political processes, but also in the existence of a number of institutions and a legal system without equivalent in other Western market economies.

Key elements in the system were vertical trade unions and a single authority controlling the public enterprise sector. The former stemmed from the 1939 'Basic Labour Law' which had made labour and employers' unions illegal and had provided for the compulsory affiliation of both workers and employers to a National Trades Union Organization. The organization was designed to be an instrument at the service of the state, through which the latter would realize its economic policy. The state itself was defined as a 'gigantic Trade Union'. The

---

* As for other country chapters, editorial policy has imposed the use of internationally standardized statistics which at times differ from national concepts and figures.

** Madrid.

[1] These various figures can be found in J. Prados Arrarte, *La economía española en los próximos veinte años*, Madrid 1958.

same law made strikes illegal but also made it virtually impossible for employers to dismiss workers or to resort to temporary recruitment. In essence, it created a highly authoritarian and inflexible system of labour relations. Public enterprises were, on the other hand, controlled by the National Institute for Industry (INI) which had been created under a distinctly fascist inspiration and with objectives and management criteria which responded very closely to the fascist pattern. Industrial development at all costs, with clearly autarkic connotations, was of paramount importance, whilst political considerations of national defence or prestige took precedence over economic efficiency.

But the control of economic activity went beyond these two institutions. During the 1940s, many mechanisms typical of a war economy — such as price controls and rationing — were not only maintained but even reinforced and generalized. Foreign trade was regulated by quantitative controls on imports and exports. The creation of new industries required specific authorization. Certain types of agricultural production, such as cereals, were controlled by assigning specific areas to that purpose. Housing policy was carried out through highly complicated support and control mechanisms, and a large share of financial resources was either directly channelled through official credit institutions or subject to complex regulations which assigned them to specific needs.

These anti-capitalist aspects of the regime were strongly mitigated, however, by the very favourable fiscal treatment given to high personal incomes and profits. This characteristic was maintained throughout the entire lifetime of the regime. Thus, the GDP share of government revenue represented by direct taxes was lower than in any comparable country from the mid-1950s to the mid-1970s and so was the share of transfer payments to households.[2]

It would be difficult, however, to understand Spanish economic performance in the first two decades of the post-war period without taking one further factor into account: the fascist, nationalistic ideology considered economic growth as an essential aim. Its purpose may well have been power rather than welfare, but the growth objective was patently clear. The authoritarian nature of the regime, together with a regressive fiscal system, made it possible to generate a fairly high level of capital accumulation which, despite an inefficient allocation of resources, permitted, in the early stages, relatively high output growth rates.

Table 19.1 summarizes the most relevant data regarding economic developments in Spain during the past three decades. It shows very rapid growth but also a number of weaknesses, which provided the limits to such growth and made periods of structural adjustment necessary. This is not uncommon, but the interesting, differentiating feature in the Spanish case is that the structural weaknesses, although economic in nature, were strongly linked to political factors. The story repeats itself twice during the period under consideration. The years 1959–60 were ones of stagnation as a result of structural adjustment after a decade of growth on an autarkic, highly *dirigiste* basis. The period of adjustment was short but intense and might be interpreted as purely conjunctural rather than structural. However, the changes in economic policy were far-reaching, coinciding with the entry of Spain into certain major economic institutions (IMF, IBRD, and OECD), and were preceded by a sweeping change in the

---

[2] OECD, *Public Expenditure Trends*, Paris 1978.

TABLE 19.1. *Longer-term trends*

	1950–79	1950–59	1959–73	1973–79
	average annual percentage changes			
GDP	(5.5[a])	(5.4[b])	6.9	2.8
Inflation[c]	8.5	5.7	6.5	17.9
Employment	0.4	0.8[d]	0.9[e]	−1.4
	1950–79	1950–59	1960–73	1974–79
	percentages			
Investment ratio[f]	(20.9)[g]	(15.8)[h]	21.4	21.9
Unemployment rate[j]	(3.1)[k]	(1.9)[m]	(2.5)	5.3
	$ million, annual averages			
Current balance	−407[g]	−47[h]	31	−1,787

[a] 1949–79
[b] 1949–59
[c] Consumer prices
[d] 1950–60
[e] 1960–73
[f] Gross fixed capital formation in per cent of GDP at constant prices
[g] 1954–79
[h] 1954–59
[j] In per cent of the labour force
[k] 1956–79
[m] 1956–59

Sources: OECD, *National Accounts of OECD Countries, 1950–1979*; OECD, *Manpower Statistics, 1950–62*; OECD, *Labour Force Statistics* (various issues); OECD, *Balance of Payments Statistics, 1950–1961* and *1966–1977*; OECD, *Economic Outlook, July 1981*; IMF, *International Financial Statistics* (1980 Yearbook); UNECE, *Some Factors in Economic Growth in Europe during the 1950s*, Geneva 1964.

composition of the government which weakened the influence of the fascist doctrine.

The second, much deeper and still unresolved adjustment period occurred after the oil crisis of 1973. The period undoubtedly shows features which are common to all industrialized countries, but five years of uninterrupted recession were not simply the result of the oil crisis. The end of the Franco regime (Franco died in November 1975), the period of transition towards democracy (the first free elections were held in June 1977), and the adoption of a constitution (approved in 1978) coincided not only with the oil crisis, but also with an institutional structure which was creaking at the seams, unable to function in a country in which output had increased by nearly five times in thirty years.

The analysis presented in the following three sections will focus on these two particularly important periods of adjustment and on the forces that made them necessary. The 1950s, a decade of rapid growth for both economic and socio-political reasons, led to the crisis and Stabilization Programme of 1959 (Fig. 19.1). The years from 1960 to 1973, apparently a period of smooth and high rates of expansion, none the less created problems and difficulties which would have erupted even in the absence of the oil crisis. The combination of the latter with a radical change in regime ushered in a prolonged period of economic

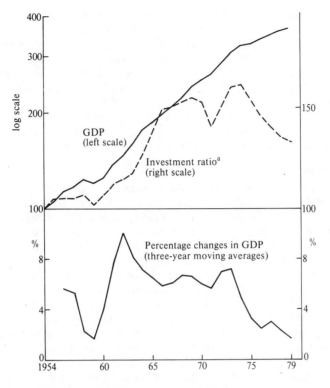

FIG. 19.1. *Output and investment trends, 1954–1979* (indices: 1954 = 100)
[a] Gross fixed investment in per cent of GDP at constant prices
Source: OECD, *National Accounts of OECD Countries, 1950–1979*.

malaise as a result of which Spain entered the 1980s in a prevailing mood of profound pessimism.

I. Unbalanced Growth, 1950–1959

Economic developments during the 1950s were a continuation of the pattern of growth witnessed in the 1940s, without significant qualitative changes. The international context, however, was much more favourable, and the domestic economy moved away from the task of mere reconstruction towards accelerated industrialization.

The growth of output, at some 5½ per cent per annum during this period,[3]

[3] A note on the availability and accuracy of statistics is obligatory in any analysis of the Spanish economy, particularly in the post-war period. National accounts were simply non-existent until the mid-1950s and can only be regarded as reasonably accurate since 1970. The first statistical bulletin of the Bank of Spain appeared only in 1960. Indicators of prices, unemployment, or even active population are either utterly misleading or inaccurate. Although, in particularly relevant cases, the shortcomings of the data will be mentioned, it should be remembered that, at least with regard to the period 1950–9, one is dealing with informed guesses (very often from private sources) rather than with proper statistics.

was close to the average of other European countries in the 1950s. Statistical shortcomings make it particularly difficult to estimate the rate of investment which made such a rate of growth possible, since investment data were among what were probably the most inaccurate of contemporary Spanish statistics. The rough estimate of 16 per cent shown in Table 19.1 is significantly lower than the average of other West European countries in the decade under consideration. But the low incremental capital–output ratio is not surprising in view of the depressed salary levels and the excessive supply of labour in agriculture, where productivity could be increased with very little investment by simply transferring underemployed workers to the labour-intensive services sector.

Factors in growth

Most Spanish economists agree that the financial and human resources transferred from agriculture provided the basis for the economic 'take-off' of the 1950s – a finding in line with the pattern in most countries at the same stage of economic development.[4] On the labour side, agriculture, whose employment fell by close to half a million over the decade, supplied some of the rising manpower needs of industry. More importantly, the continued excess supply of labour in the countryside, together with the political situation, depressed the levels of agricultural wages – these fell steadily in real terms through the 1940s (from 73 per cent of their 1936 level in 1941 to as little as 53 per cent in 1951) and rose only modestly in the 1950s (they were back to the 1936 figure in 1959). Indirectly, this must have contributed to dampening wage pressures in the industrial sector.

On the financial side, although agriculture accounted for one-third of total output over the decade, its share in total investment was of only some 10 per cent.[5] The financing capacity of the agricultural sector, defined as the difference between agricultural savings and investment, amounted to 16 per cent of agricultural output and to as much as 25 per cent of gross fixed investment in the non-agricultural sectors. These percentages were even higher in the 1940s but declined steadily during the 1950s and became insignificant in the late 1960s.

The financing capacity of the agricultural sector was particularly high in the first two decades of the post-war period, partly because, as was seen, investment in the sector was limited, but also because consumption levels among the agricultural population were particularly low. The latter is explained not only by the already mentioned excess supply of labour, but also by the structure of property and employment. Taking agriculture as a whole, Spain and Portugal headed the list of European countries in terms of land concentration, with 1 per cent of the number of holdings occupying 50 per cent of the land. Arable land was more evenly distributed, but the structure of holdings was still considerably biased in favour of the largest ones. In 1962, 27 per cent of arable land was occupied by holdings of more than 100 hectares, whilst the proportion in the EEC at the time was 11 per cent.[6] Largely for this reason, the share of salaried

    [4] J.M. Naredo et al., La agricultura en el desarrollo capitalista español (1940-1970), Madrid 1975.

    [5] UNECE, Some Factors in Economic Growth in Europe during the 1950s, Geneva 1964.

    [6] J.M. Naredo, La evolución de la agricultura en España. Desarrollo capitalista y crisis de las formas de producción tradicionales, Barcelona 1977.

employees in the agricultural labour force was close to 50 per cent in 1950 — well above the 30 per cent average for other European countries at the time.

The existence of a high financial surplus in agriculture does not, of course, necessarily imply that it will be used for investment in other productive sectors. The surplus could have been exported, hoarded, or invested in non-productive uses. In any case, as was seen, the resources generated in agriculture only accounted for a quarter of the investment in non-agricultural sectors. The following paragraphs will try to identify some of the factors which led to the increase in investment and output in industry — an increase which, though far from spectacular (the share of industry in total output only increased from approximately 30 per cent in 1950 to 34 per cent in 1959), provided the basis for the very rapid expansion of the 1960s.

The institutional background was important. The absence of trade unions, leading to low wages, the very low levels of direct taxation, the highly protectionist foreign trade policies, heavily favouring import substitution, and the investment drive by the public sector for the creation of basic industries, can generally be regarded as favourable for economic growth, at least in the early stages. These factors were only partly offset, again in the early stages, by the highly *dirigiste* attitudes of the administration, by the network of controls, and by the supply difficulties inherent in such a system.

A further powerful incentive for investment in the industrial sector may have come from relative price changes (Table 19.2). Already in the second half of the 1940s, prices rose more rapidly in industry than in the other sectors of the economy. This coincided with a slight improvement in investment from the very low levels of the early 1940s. The first half of the 1950s saw complete stagnation in agricultural prices (facilitated by the decline of real agricultural wages) and a continued rise in industrial prices. The trend was only partly reversed in the second half of the decade, as a result of the stabilization policies adopted at the end of the period.

These developments must have been helped by the already mentioned highly protectionist policies. As a result, the investment drive was almost exclusively geared to import substitution and there were no signs of export-led growth. The share in national income corresponding to exports, already low in 1951, declined steadily throughout the period, with only a modest rise in the stabilization

TABLE 19.2. *Sectoral value added deflators*
(indices: 1940 = 100)

	1945	1950	1955	1959
Agriculture	128	163	160	261
Industry	129	239	367	475
Services	141	231	307	406
Total[a]	134	219	297	399

[a] 1955 weights

Sources: M.J. González, *La economia política del Franquismo (1940–1970)*, Madrid 1979;
Ministerio de Hacienda, *Contabilidad nacional de España, 1954 a 1964*, Madrid 1969.

year of 1959 (Table 19.3). In absolute terms, non-food exports rose by less than 1 per cent per annum through the decade, confirming the inward nature of Spanish economic developments in this period. The national income share corresponding to imports remained roughly constant, at very low levels. The fact that it did not decline, in spite of import substitution efforts, is consistent with similar experience in other countries, as the rise in output generated new import demands.

TABLE 19.3. *Foreign trade structure*
(percentages)

	Imports			Exports		
	1950	1955	1959	1950	1955	1959
Share in national income[a]	10.5[b]	9.8	10.2	12.2[b]	7.1	6.4
Shares of:						
Food products	19	8	11	50	56	60
Raw materials and semi-finished products	62	62	65	27	31	27
Machinery and equipment	17	28	22	3	2	1
Consumer goods	2	2	2	20	11	12

[a] Goods only
[b] 1951
Sources: Ministerio de Comercio, *Información comercial española*, June 1961; Dirección general de aduanas, *Estadística del comercio exterior, 1963-1964.*

The composition of imports and exports is highly indicative of the structure of the Spanish economy at that time and of the developments discussed. As was appropriate in an essentially agricultural country, imports of foodstuffs were relatively low and exports high at the beginning of the period, and even more so at the end. Although agricultural output did not increase rapidly during the 1950s, it was substantially higher than in the previous decade, because of the easing of supply bottle-necks in agricultural inputs. More importantly, low wages kept the growth of domestic consumption below that of output during most of the decade, and permitted an increasing surplus of foodstuffs to be exported. This interpretation is confirmed by the extremely low share of consumer goods in total imports, although, in this case, it should be realized that strict import controls kept to an absolute minimum all imports which were not deemed to satisfy policy priorities. Conversely, the proportion of total imports taken up by machinery and equipment, which had been as low as 14 per cent on average during the 1940s, leapt to twice that figure in the mid-1950s. In addition, of course, one cannot overlook the fact that more than 60 per cent of Spanish imports were simply inputs for the productive sectors, particularly industry.

Bottle-necks

The balance of payments has always been regarded by Spanish economists as a major obstacle to growth. On the other hand, it might be considered that balance of payments problems are neither more nor less than the result of other more basic problems or of policy mistakes. In any case, it is clear that in the context of the economic isolation which Spain experienced during the 1940s, economic growth was hardly possible. The opportunity for take-off in the 1950s was provided by the initiation of United States aid, which began to enter in significant amounts in the early years of the decade. The second half of the 1950s saw a further development, which was to become the most important strategic factor permitting economic growth in Spain during the 1960s – the growth of tourism and the remittances of emigrant workers, as major foreign currency earners. As the trade balance deteriorated, however, with the investment boom of the mid-1950s, these factors were unable fully to offset the trade deficit, and, in the period 1955-8, the average current account deficit was close to $100 million.

The basic balance, however, remained in virtual equilibrium thanks largely to United States aid. In the circumstances it is difficult to understand why a balance of payments crisis led the government to adopt a series of measures in 1957 and 1958 which culminated in the Stabilization Programme of 1959. Two factors should be taken into account here: first, the extremely low level of Spanish reserves of gold and foreign exchange, which on a gross basis had fallen to $66 million in 1968 (the lowest figure in Europe, excluding Iceland); secondly, the lack of flexibility of the Spanish exchange control system and the inability to follow an adequate exchange rate policy. This provoked large short-term capital outflows in 1957 and 1958 which mainly took the form of under-recording of imports.

The other major permanent bottle-neck in the Spanish economy was inflation. The 1950s began with the highest rates of price rises recorded in the post-war period prior to the oil crisis (Table 19.4). The average rate of wholesale price inflation in 1950-1 was of the order of 23 per cent. The following four

TABLE 19.4. *Inflation in the 1950s*
(average annual percentage changes)

	1948–51	1951–56	1956–58	1958–60
Wholesale prices	17.3.	4.3	13.2	2.2
Consumer prices	8.7	2.1	12.2	4.1
Average wages	25.1[a]	3.1[b]	11.5	4.0

[a] Minimum wages, 1947–50
[b] Minimum wages, 1950–57
Sources: IMF, *International Financial Statistics* (1967/68 and 1980 Yearbooks); M.J. González, *La economia política del Franquismo (1940–1970)*, Madrid 1979; Ministero del Trabajo, *Reglamentaciones laborales* (various issues); H. París Eguilaz, *El desarrollo económico español: 1906–1964*, Madrid 1965.

years saw a very significant moderation of inflationary pressures with an average of only 3 per cent – one of the lowest rates in Spanish post-war history – but inflation resumed during the second half of the decade until the stabilization measures of 1959.

It would seem that both the inflationary spurt of 1949-51 and the stabilization of the following years can be attributed in part to supply developments. The 1940s had been a period of stagnation in output, which had created considerable supply bottle-necks. When these encountered rising demand pressures at the turn of the decade, an inflationary spurt was inevitable. The subsequent price deceleration seems to have been helped by the disappearance of one major supply constraint – electricity production rose thanks to the heavy investments made in the sector during the 1940s which matured at that time. The easing of import restrictions, as a result of the concession of United States aid, was also a significant factor.

There is little doubt, however, that subdued wage developments were at least as important as supply forces in terms of the achievement of price stability in 1951–5. The sudden increase in wages registered in 1956 (wage rates rose by over 14 per cent in that year), thanks to the political decision taken by the Falangist Minister of Labour of the time, was the main factor which sparked off a new round of inflation. While this was less pronounced than in the early 1950s, it was none the less substantial and represented a further reason for the 1958 crisis and the ensuing Stabilization Programme.

Economic policies and the Stabilization Programme

The role of policies until the late 1950s was limited. Monetary policies were virtually non-existent as the monetary authorities had neither the political will nor the instruments to carry out anything other than a permissive policy. The governor of the central bank was under the direct supervision of the Minister of Finance, who was himself controlled by the more political ministers, usually members of the Falangist party. Regarding the instruments, the central bank was practically unable to control the growth of monetary variables, because of the practice, initiated in 1917 and only ended in 1959, of financing budget deficits and extra-budgetary investment by the public sector, by issuing public debt which was automatically rediscountable at the central bank. Thus, what appeared in monetary statistics as central bank credits to private monetary institutions were, in fact, the result of the practice of rediscounting public debt previously purchased by these same institutions. As commercial banks had accumulated an increasing portfolio of such debt since the beginning of the decade, it was very difficult for the monetary authorities to control the growth of the monetary base. Although the last issues of rediscountable debt were made at the beginning of 1959, unused rediscount margins posed a threat to monetary stability during the whole of the 1960s.

The non-existence of an active monetary policy in an almost completely closed economy was, of course, as already mentioned, directly linked to the behaviour of the public sector. Here again, the lack of statistics makes detailed analysis impossible. Budgetary statistics are available, but the absence of information on the activities of a variety of autonomous public institutions, with their own revenue and expenditure and with access to central bank financing, either directly or through rediscountable debt issues, makes budgetary statistics irrelevant. Available estimates point to a rapid increase in public investment in the 1950s which, in view of the rigidity of the fiscal system, was directly or indirectly financed by monetary mechanisms.

Inefficient policies, the resumption of price inflation, and, even more, the balance of payments bottle-neck, made patent the impossibility of a country like Spain continuing to grow in autarkic conditions. Franco reacted to the difficulties building up on the economic front by appointing a new government in February 1957 – the most significant change was the nomination of two technocrats (belonging to the *Opus Dei* movement) to the economic ministries of Finance and Commerce. The influence of these men and many others at different government levels in promoting a change in economic policy from controls and the pursuit of autarky to the use of market mechanisms and liberalization was enormous. Its effects on the nature of economic policy, however, were not immediate, partly as a result of institutional inertia but also, perhaps, because there was not yet a sufficient awareness of the need for drastic adjustment.

The Ministry of Finance, through the Bank of Spain, initiated a contractionary monetary policy almost immediately, but its effects on the growth of the money supply only began to be felt during the autumn of 1957. Annual growth rates of money supply, which were over 20 per cent during the first half of 1957, declined to 17 per cent by the end of that year, and decelerated slowly to around 14 per cent by the end of 1958. The ministry also tried to use fiscal instruments for restrictive purposes. On the revenue side, the rigidity of the system made it impossible to increase tax pressure, and ministerial efforts were directed towards the completion of an urgent package of fiscal and budgetary reforms. The bases of assessment for taxation of industrial and commercial profits were altered and somewhat more stringent measures to combat tax evasion were adopted. On the expenditure side, an effort was made to consolidate the investment spending of autonomous institutions (until then almost completely uncontrolled) in a separate budgetary chapter. The budget deficit was contained in 1957 within the limits reached in 1956, and declined significantly in 1958.

The Ministry of Commerce acted on the exchange rate front. Spain had lived with a multiple-rate system since 1948. In 1957, the system was simplified and the rate, which was close to 40 pesetas per dollar for most imports and to 30 pesetas for most exports, was unified at 42 pesetas per dollar for both trade flows. A tourist rate was, however, fixed at 46 pesetas per dollar, and export taxes and subsidies were applied to various products. Though the average devaluation which was implicit in the reform was insufficient, there was an initial favourable influence on the trade balance. Since, however, domestic demand was still expanding and prices rising, this was gradually cancelled out. Instead of simply correcting the earlier mistake and applying a further across-the-board devaluation, the authorities took a series of measures in 1958, which led to the re-establishment of a multiple exchange rate system, with no less than ten different rates, ranging from 31 to 95 pesetas to the dollar. The disadvantages of the system were obvious, but the fact that it was re-established is indicative of the spirit that prevailed in the Spanish administration at that time. Similarly, the tightening of quantitative import restrictions (shortages of spare parts became acute, for example) and the proliferation of 'special export operations', of bilateral trade agreements, and of controls affecting current invisibles and foreign investment, indicate that although the system had reached its working limits, the Spanish political apparatus was incapable of reacting by itself, without being faced by a serious crisis.

The crisis came in the course of 1958. Its immediate origins were partly internal and partly external. Among the internal factors, one may cite a wave of illegal strikes in 1958, as a protest against inflation and the wage freeze. Informed public opinion also reacted with deep concern to the Treaty of Rome and to the generalization of internal convertibility of European currencies at the end of 1958. These internal factors might not have been sufficient, however, in the absence of a balance of payments crisis. This had been brewing for some time, but the situation became so acute towards the end of 1958 that the central bank's gold and foreign exchange reserves net of official short-term liabilities were reduced to virtually zero and were actually negative in the first half of 1959.

A wide-ranging Stabilization Programme was adopted by the government in July 1959.[7] A first series of measures was designed to eliminate remaining excess demand. The overall deficit of the public sector, initially budgeted at a figure close to the 1958 outcome, was substantially reduced by cutting expenditure and increasing revenue through new taxes (in particular on oil) and customs duties. Direct advances by the central bank to public institutions were frozen at their end-1958 levels and the government undertook to maintain the level of public spending for 1960 at its 1959 level, unless new taxes made it possible to do away with any recourse to central bank financing. In order to facilitate the control of monetary variables, the government further undertook to stop the issue of automatically rediscountable public debt stock, the discount rate was increased, and a 25 per cent import deposit was introduced.

These were largely conjunctural measures. The main interest of the Stabilization Programme, however, lies in the structural measures which it incorporated, at the insistence of the IMF and OEEC, and which provided the basis for Spanish economic growth during the following decade and a half. Possibly the most far-reaching reforms affected the foreign trade and payments system. The first steps were the suppression of price controls over freely imported goods in respect of which no profit margin was specified, and the suppression of the allocation procedure for freely imported raw materials. Multiple exchange rates were abolished and a single rate of 60 pesetas per dollar was introduced,[8] with only a very limited number of export taxes and import subsidies on a transitional basis. State trading in imports (very widespread in the past) was limited to agricultural products. A substantial share of imports (almost half) was liberated and a further substantial proportion brought under global import quotas. The accession of Spain to the European Monetary Agreement involved the suppression of bilateral agreements then in force with member countries. An amnesty was granted to Spanish residents holding foreign assets who repatriated them within six months. Finally, a new, much more liberal act on foreign investment was published.

The effects of the programme were substantial in a very short time. In spite of the sharp devaluation and the relaxation of price controls, the rise in prices was very limited. The shortage of raw materials and semi-finished goods which marked the preceding period disappeared almost immediately. The volume of bank credit remained well within the limits imposed and the budgetary results were very close to estimates. Even more striking was the improvement in the balance of payments, with the current account already back in surplus in 1959 and the trade deficit virtually eliminated in 1960. Though the lowering of

---

[7] The summary here presented is drawn from the thorough description of the programme presented in OEEC, *Economic Survey of Spain, 1960.*

[8] Amounting to an effective devaluation of the order of 20 per cent.

domestic demand pressures played some role, there is little doubt that the bulk of the improvement was due to the introduction of a realistic exchange rate. More importantly, the programme was also successful in a medium-term perspective – growth recovered rapidly in the course of 1960 and remained high over the next decade, suggesting that the programme's major achievement had been the removal of non-market obstacles.

The story of the 1950s is, thus, one of growth in an underdeveloped and highly controlled economy which reached its natural limits as the obstacles to growth stemming from a plethora of detailed controls became much more important than the possible earlier advantages of such a system. The removal of the most obvious of these obstacles set the stage for a similar experience in the following decade, with much more rapid growth for a much longer period of time, but with a more difficult and still unresolved outcome. One should recall that the essence of the regime and of its economic system had been untouched by the Stabilization Programme. The fiscal system remained weak and biased against the lower income groups. The system of labour relations had not changed, despite declarations of intent made in the programme. Public enterprises and the social security system, in spite of similar statements, remained in the same hands and with the same objectives. Technical problems had forced the regime to introduce market mechanisms in certain fields, but the reforms which should have accompanied the programme were of such political importance that the 'technocrats' who initiated the liberalization movement lacked the power and, possibly, the will, to pursue them.

II. The 'Miracle' Years, 1960–1973

The years from the Stabilization Programme to the outbreak of the first oil crisis witnessed very rapid growth of output (7 per cent per annum), a reasonable price performance (6½ per cent on average), and spectacular improvements in the balance of payments, and were accompanied by deep structural changes in the sectoral composition of output, exports, and employment. The change from a backward, largely rural economy to a fairly developed and industrialized one was no mean achievement and has often been referred to as the Spanish 'miracle', comparable to the so-called German, Italian, or Japanese 'miracles'. Yet a number of negative aspects remained or were even strengthened as the decade unfolded. These were largely a function of the rigidity and inadequacy of the political and institutional framework, which was still based on an ideology incompatible with the profound transformations that economic growth itself was bringing about in Spanish society.

Output growth and structural change

Growth of output was not only high, but also quite stable. With the single exception of 1960, no single year witnessed a GDP growth rate of less than 4 per cent. Cyclical fluctuations were, thus, relatively small. The growth in overall productivity was of the order of 6 per cent, with employment increasing less than the population in active age groups. Unemployment was low throughout the period, however, and the potential excess of active population was partly absorbed by emigration, which, for the period as a whole, may have amounted to as much as 6 per cent of the labour force. There was, however, a continuous decline in activity rates, partly as a result of emigration itself – emigrants often left the non-active members of their families in Spain – but also because lower retirement age and increased schooling were not offset by a significant increase in female activity rates, which remained amongst the lowest in Europe. As a result, although unemployment was low, the overall participation rate was also relatively low, indicating some form of disguised unemployment which presented serious potential dangers.

One of the major factors contributing to the acceleration in growth and productivity was the substantial increase in investment. The investment ratio, estimated at 16 per cent for the earlier period, rose to 21½ per cent, a figure closer to the European average. The fact that the growth rates of output and productivity were nearly 50 per cent higher than the European average for the period suggests that other factors played an even more important role.

One of these factors, no doubt, was the incorporation of technological progress, particularly in manufacturing. The growth of labour productivity in industry (excluding construction) was of the order of 8½ per cent per annum between 1960 and 1975. Such a high rate indicates substantial technical advances in Spanish industry during the period, achieved mainly as a result of two factors:

(i) A large share of total investment in machinery and equipment consisted of imports which, presumably, incorporated foreign 'best practice' techniques;

(ii) Foreign direct investment increased considerably during the period, with undeniable favourable effects on competition, the spread of advanced technology, and productivity.

A further very significant factor behind overall productivity growth was, of course, the large transfer of employment from low to high productivity sectors of the economy, with employment in agriculture declining from 41 to 23 per cent of the total. For the period 1960–75, the contribution of sectoral shifts to overall productivity growth has been put at some 15 per cent.[9]

Sectoral transfers of employment are rarely neutral in terms of localization, but in Spain, as in Italy, they implied internal migration of striking proportions. The share of Madrid, Barcelona, and Vizcaya (in the Basque Country), the provinces with the three largest cities in Spain, rose from 16 to 24 per cent of the population between 1955 and 1975. This reflected enormous regional imbalances and, had it not been for the fact that the capital, Madrid, is situated almost exactly in the geographical centre of the country, the shift towards the north of the peninsula would have been even more pronounced.

These internal migrations were accompanied by an unprecedented increase in urbanization. In 1975, about 50 per cent of the Spanish population lived in cities of over 100,000 inhabitants, as opposed to 30 per cent in 1940 – more than doubling in absolute terms, in view of overall population growth. The social problems that this type of change creates are well known. In Spain, they were aggravated by the insufficiency of public sector resources, particularly at

[9] Banco de Bilbao, *Renta nacional de España, 1955–1975*, Madrid 1978.

the local government level. This is yet another factor to be borne in mind when considering the socio-political and economic situation of Spain after the oil crisis.

The large employment and population changes so far discussed were, of course, related to very substantial changes in the structure of output (Table 19.5). Apart from an increase in the weight of construction, the striking development in terms of real output was the reduction of the share of agriculture from 22 to 11 per cent offset by a similar increase in the share of industry, with the services shares remaining constant throughout the period.

TABLE 19.5. *Structural changes*
(percentages)

	Agriculture	Industry[a]	Construction	Services
Employment shares				
1960	41	23	7	29
1975	23	27	10	40
Output shares — constant (1964) prices				
1960	22	29	5	43
1975	11	39	7	43
Output shares — current prices				
1960	23	31	5	41
1975	10	32	7	51
Memorandum item:				
Growth of labour productivity[b]	5½	8½	5	4

[a] Excluding construction
[b] Average annual percentage changes
Source: Banco de Bilbao, *Renta nacional de España y su distribución provincial, 1955–1975*, Bilbao 1978.

Developments were, however, substantially different if the structure of output at the beginning and at the end of the period are looked at in terms of current prices. The share of industry remained practically constant, the decline in the share of agriculture was even more acute, and the share of services increased to over 50 per cent. To some extent, this was almost inevitable in a rapidly expanding country, since the low growth of productivity in the services sector, coupled with the high growth of productivity in industry and a sharp rise in nominal incomes, provoked substantial changes in relative prices. There is little doubt, however, that inflation in the services sector was too high in Spain and that a substantial proportion of nominal output in that sector was constituted by an oversized and inefficient administration. In addition, relative income levels among certain professional categories were far too high in comparison with their counterparts in other countries, whilst blue-collar and rural incomes were too low, a situation necessarily related to the absence of free trade unions. One may add that inequalities in personal income distribution were among the highest in the OECD area already on a pre-tax basis, and that the almost total absence of an effective progressive income tax made the situation even worse on an after-tax basis.[10]

[10] M. Sawyer, 'Income Distribution in OECD Countries', *OECD Economic Outlook — Occasional Studies*, July 1976; see also Table 7.10 above.

To some extent, such inequalities may have contributed to the very rapid growth experienced in the 1960s. One factor to bear in mind is that the discussion so far has been limited to personal incomes, while the share of corporate profits in national income remained relatively low throughout the period. International comparisons in this respect are very misleading, because of structural differences and, particularly in the case of Spain, statistical difficulties. It seems beyond doubt, however, that self-financing among large Spanish corporations was low, while profits of individual entrepreneurs were high. Whatever the statistical shortcomings, it seems reasonable to suppose that the rewards to entrepreneurial activity were high during the period and that wealth and income inequalities combined with the prevailing 'growth spirit' and the absence of labour conflicts provided a favourable background to economic developments. These inequalities may, however, have contributed to the difficulties of the second half of the 1970s.

The balance of payments

It will be recalled that the main factor behind the 1959 Stabilization Programme was the balance of payments crisis, and that the main structural reforms undertaken by the programme concerned the external field. Judging from the results, the reforms were successful, and Spain recorded, on average, a small current account surplus during the period which, added to a steady and increasing influx of foreign investment, led to a substantial basic surplus and to a high level of reserves.

Averages for the period as a whole are not very meaningful, however. As Table 19.6 shows, after a surplus during the years immediately following the Stabilization Programme, the current account recorded substantial deficits which

TABLE 19.6. *Selected balance of payments items*
($ million, annual averages)

	1960–73	1960–62	1963–69	1970–73
Trade balance	−1,518	−287	−1,580	−2,333
Travel, net	1,191	348	1,016	2,131
Emigrants' remittances[a]	366	109	312	652
Current balance	31	222	−328	516
Foreign investment[b]	346	48	237	761
Basic balance	464	374	65	1,232
Change in reserves[c]	426	300	−30	1,317

[a] Including workers' earnings, net
[b] Direct, portfolio, and real estate investment by foreigners
[c] Increase = +

Sources: OECD, *Balances of Payments of OECD Countries, 1960–1977*; Ministerio de Comercio, *Balanza de pagos de España* (various issues).

led to a further (16.7 per cent) devaluation of the peseta in 1967. In 1970, however, a surplus was recorded again, and the following years were even somewhat embarrassing for the Spanish authorities as reserves increased considerably and there were upward pressures on the currency. The effective exchange rate for the peseta was allowed to appreciate by about 10 per cent between May 1970 and December 1973,[11] as a result of a policy which kept the peseta pegged to the dollar, but did not follow the latter in its two successive devaluations of 1971 and 1973.

Export performance was satisfactory during the period as a whole. Spain recorded significant gains in market shares only inferior, among OECD countries, to those of Japan and Italy. These gains in market shares were accompanied by appreciable changes with regard to markets of destination, with exports to the United States and non-OECD countries rising markedly faster than those to the traditional European outlets. Changes in the commodity composition of exports were even more striking. The share of agricultural products in total exports declined from 60 per cent in 1959 to 30 per cent in 1973, while the share of capital goods rose from a mere 1 per cent to 20 per cent. Exports of motor vehicles and ships, which were insignificant at the beginning of the period, accounted for more than 10 per cent of exports in 1973. As it later turned out, however, important structural weaknesses remained. Four groups of products (ships, footwear, electrical machinery, and rubber goods) represented nearly a quarter of all industrial exports. These and most other Spanish exports had a rather low technological content and a high labour content – a situation which made adaptation to the conditions that followed the oil crisis very difficult.

Perhaps one of the major policy mistakes which were made in the early 1960s was the maintenance of a high degree of tariff protection. Spain had, for political reasons, been kept out of the EEC, and, although a preferential trade agreement between Spain and the European Community was signed in October 1970, the reductions in import tariffs it implied were spread over a period of seven years and, on average, amounted to only 25 per cent. Thus, the Spanish authorities were confronted with a situation of a sizeable balance of payments surplus (largely due to tourism and foreign investment) and high tariff barriers. If, instead of opting for an appreciation of the peseta, they had followed a policy of unilateral or negotiated tariff reductions, with a lower value of the peseta, exports would have been encouraged, price distortions in the industrial sector would have diminished, and structural change might have been pursued more rapidly. As it was, however, the structure of Spanish imports was, at the end of the period, remarkably similar to what it had been during the 1950s, with food products accounting for 14 per cent of the total, consumer goods for only 9 per cent, and capital goods for 27 per cent.

The weaknesses just described, however, could hardly be considered as significant as they seem now with the benefit of hindsight, in a period overwhelmed by the rapid growth of foreign exchange receipts from tourism and emigrants' remittances. Net annual receipts from tourism rose from around $0.3 billion in the early 1960s to over $2 billion in the early 1970s, nearly offsetting the whole of the trade deficit. Emigrants' remittances rose from a mere $0.1 billion at the beginning of the period to nearly $1 billion in 1973, when not only the number of emigrants was at its peak, but the strength of the peseta and the booming real estate markets made it a sound investment to transfer emigrants' savings back home.

It is evident that the growth experience of the 1960s would have been quite

---

[11] Bank of Spain estimates.

different if the flows of foreign exchange from these two sources had been smaller, since the balance of payments would then have represented a constraint. Natural factors such as the geographical location of Spain, close to heavily populated countries with booming economies, were instrumental in both cases, but there were also important differences in both the causes and the effects of these flows. While emigrants' remittances reflected underemployment and poverty at home, together with full employment and prosperity in Europe, the growth of tourism was closely related to Spain's economic development during the period. The number of visitors rose from less than 1 million per annum in the early 1950s to approximately 6 million at the beginning of the 1960s, reaching a peak of 33 million in 1973. The number of hotel beds increased tenfold, many other accommodation facilities were constructed, a whole array of service establishments were built, and tourism became one of the country's major economic sectors. The way in which an entirely new entrepreneurial class appeared, catering for the new source of income, is highly indicative of the spirit of growth of the period. One of the economic advantages of tourism was that despite its localization in coastal areas, it countered, to some extent at least, the trend towards urbanization described above. There was also, however, a considerable cultural impact in the contact between the populations of the most developed countries of Europe and those of some of the most backward regions of Spain. The 'demonstration effect', with both its advantages and its disadvantages, was certainly closely related to the phenomenon of tourism in a country in which the press was censored and other media were under strict government control.

As in many other fields, the speed of the process (and the political conditions in which it occurred) created a number of well-known problems. Speculation, lack of planning and of municipal resources to provide adequate infrastructure were highly detrimental to the quality of many Spanish tourist resorts. The atomization of the sector and the lack of co-operation among small, individual entrepreneurs, together with financial dependence, placed much of the available capacity in the hands of tour operators, who imposed very low prices. Consequently, the sector was adversely affected by the large salary increases of the mid-1970s.

Economic policies

Reference was made in Section I above to the weaknesses of the fiscal system in the 1950s. These changed little in the 1960s. The size of the public sector remained small. Taking as an indicator the share of general government tax revenue in GDP, Spain recorded in the mid-1960s a figure of the order of 15 per cent — the lowest in the OECD area — as against ratios ranging from 17 to 21 per cent in other Mediterranean countries such as Turkey, Portugal, or Greece, let alone 27 per cent in Italy or 36 per cent in Sweden.[12] It is fashionable nowadays to argue that a large public sector is not necessarily indicative of social or economic well-being. There is little doubt, however, that, even though fiscal pressures increased by 8 percentage points between 1959 and 1973, government revenues were insufficient to cover welfare items widely regarded as basic needs, such as state education.

[12] OECD, *Revenue Statistics of OECD Member Countries, 1965-1979.*

This evidence is aggravated by an analysis of the sources of revenue. The share of direct taxes in total current revenues, which amounted to 29 per cent at the end of the 1950s, decreased steadily during the following decade, reaching its lowest point in 1973, at only 18 per cent. The failure, or the reluctance, of the regime to reduce fraud in corporate taxation and to establish a significant personal income tax system made it necessary to raise revenues by increasing indirect taxes and, particularly, social security contributions, which rose from 22 per cent of current revenue in 1954 to 36 per cent in 1973. Furthermore, the extreme centralization of resources and expenditure decisions undoubtedly had an adverse impact on the welfare effects of a given amount of expenditure. Throughout the period, the proportion of public expenditure devoted to local government was one of the lowest in OECD countries.[13]

The rigidity and obsolescence of the Spanish fiscal system had adverse effects not only on welfare but also on demand management. Budgets were approved for two-year periods, and the lack of information available to the budgetary authorities (particularly on the totally uncontrolled social security system), together with administrative inflexibility on the part of spending departments, made it very difficult to use fiscal policy for counter-cyclical purposes. An estimate of the economic impact of budget changes for the period 1959-69 gave almost neutral results for the sum of automatic and discretionary changes from the point of view of reducing cyclical fluctuations.[14]

Monetary policy, prior to the 1958-9 stabilization period, had been earlier described as 'non-existent'. The 1960s and the early 1970s witnessed a steady trend towards greater control of monetary variables on the part of the authorities. This trend, however, reflected two conflicting forces. On the one hand, it followed from a process of modernization by the central bank, which slowly acquired the instruments necessary for the monetary management of an increasingly more advanced and more complex economy. On the other hand, however, it reflected the continued resistance of the economic ministries and, particularly, of the Ministry of Finance, to following the path of liberalization laid out in the 1959 Stabilization Programme.

The first significant example of this dual approach was provided by the 1962 Credit and Banking Act, which gave the Bank of Spain greater power to control the banking system but, at the same time, placed it under the direct authority of the Ministry of Finance. An Institute of Medium- and Long-term Credit was created; official credit institutions were obliged to receive most of their finance directly from the Treasury, thus depriving them of financial autonomy; and the Ministry of Finance was given statutory powers to regulate the credit activities of commercial savings banks, by establishing coefficients of various kinds.

During the following years, the system became increasingly complex and regulated. Savings banks were obliged to invest 60 per cent of their resources in public debt or in authorized bonds (issued annually by large corporations). In addition, they had to allocate 7 per cent of their resources to housing loans and

[13] Banco de España, *Informe anual, 1980.*

[14] R. Bara, 'El cálculo del presupuesto según el modelo de Bent Hansen: su aplicación en España', *Hacienda pública española*, No. 14, 1972. The OECD, however (*Economic Survey of Spain, 1972*), using a similar approach, reached a somewhat more favourable verdict; see also Table 10.5 above.

23 per cent to various other preferential credit areas, leaving virtually nothing for discretionary use. Various kinds of reserve requirements were imposed on commercial banks, designed partly as instruments of monetary management and partly as a protective measure for depositors. However, a further requirement to invest a certain share of their resources (reaching 22 per cent in 1969) in public bonds, at extremely low rates, was due exclusively to the policy of channelling through official credit institutions a large proportion of the funds available in the system.

The overall importance of this complex set of intervention mechanisms was such that about 50 per cent of total financial resources was directed through various kinds of special channels during the 1960s. These channels implied not only a form of rationing, but also significant hidden subsidies, as interest rates bore little or no resemblance to those prevailing in free markets. The perverse effects of such subsidies on the allocation of resources were compounded by the fact that their importance could not easily be calculated, whilst their cost was not borne by the budget, but, rather, by other users of the financial system, either through abnormally high lending rates or abnormally low returns on savings. Needless to say, this system coexisted with a free market sector which was heavily interfered with. Interest rates were controlled throughout the period, although, in practice, black market rates became increasingly frequent.

There is little doubt that this system had as a result lower interest rates and longer terms applicable to selected investment projects as well as lower returns on savings, particularly on those of lower income groups. In this respect it was well in tune with the general pattern of the Spanish economy at the time. In theory, such a system had other notorious disadvantages. Apart from the allocation of huge resources to investments of highly dubious returns, it provided incentives to very capital-intensive projects in a country with an over-abundant supply of labour; it tended to discourage saving in the middle and lower income groups; and it hindered the appearance of genuine capital markets. As in many other fields, however, it is far from certain that orthodox economic analysis applied to individual aspects of the Spanish economy can explain the satisfactory global results. It might be maintained that, in a country like Spain, with a financial structure dominated by a few commercial banks and where markets were absent and sophisticated investors almost non-existent, the crude methods used did, in fact, force the system to provide the intermediation that rapid economic growth required at the time. Here again, however, it is hard to resist the impression that a system which probably worked well during most of the 1960s was becoming obsolete as a result of economic development itself, while the sclerosis of the regime made it impossible to carry out the necessary reforms.

It is this latter point which, in a sense, shows the limitations of the growth process of the 1960s. The 'miracle' years had resulted in a very rapid rise in living standards, but these developments had not been accompanied by a similar process of institutional change. The technocratic structures of the regime had become so accustomed to a world in which bureaucratic control was the rule and market freedom the exception, that when democracy arrived, they were to constitute a very serious obstacle to changes which, being belated, had become extremely urgent.

III. The Crisis Years, 1974-1979

The structural weaknesses accumulated in the 1950s and 1960s made Spain more vulnerable than most other major economies to the increase in oil prices which took place at the end of 1973. The proportion of total imports corresponding to energy products almost doubled in value between 1973 and 1974, the terms of trade deteriorated by some 20 per cent, and the current balance swung from a surplus of $0.5 billion to a deficit of $3.2 billion, equivalent to 4 per cent of GDP. The direct impact on domestic prices, measured by the GDP deflator, has been estimated at 7 percentage points for 1974 as a whole. However, the importance of the initial impact does not explain the consistent deterioration in most major economic variables for the rest of the decade. As shown in Table 19.1, output growth fell from 7 per cent per annum between 1959 and 1973, to a mere 2¾ per cent between 1973 and 1979. Employment declined by 1½ per cent per annum; unemployment rose to 8½ per cent of the active population by 1979; inflation accelerated to an average annual rate of 18 per cent, and investment declined steadily. Yet despite these fairly radical departures from earlier performance, the period was in fact dominated not so much by economic as by political events.

The unfolding of the crisis

The variable most relevant to an analysis of economic developments in these years is price inflation, since it is both a reflection of the most important underlying forces and a factor which helps to explain the changing attitude behind economic policy and the development of output and employment. As elsewhere, inflation was already accelerating in Spain towards the end of 1973, before the effects of the oil crisis were felt domestically. The government made a bold attempt, heavily criticized later, to compensate for part of the impact of the oil price rise by spreading it over a two-year period, thus avoiding the inflationary spurt it would otherwise have created. There were good reasons for and against such a policy decision, but they were never to be put to the test, for the events which followed had little connection with the policy decisions adopted.

There is little doubt that the most significant element in the economic history of the entire period was the wage explosion which occurred in 1974, immediately after the oil crisis. The figure shown in Table 19.7 is no more than an estimate, as Spanish statistics in this field are very poor. It is certain, however, that wages rose much more rapidly than the cost of living in 1974, 1975, and 1976. The fact that heavy demand pressures persisted through mid-1974 and that Spanish public opinion had not quite woken up to the oil crisis may have contributed to the relative ease with which such a wage explosion occurred. The year 1975, however, was one of very restrictive monetary policy, and by 1976 an atmosphere of crisis prevailed, ruling out any optimistic attitude on the part of entrepreneurs.

Institutional and sociological factors provide a much more serious explanation. There were no established channels for collective bargaining. The end of the Franco regime was close (Franco died at the end of 1975) and the earlier sensation of fear or indifference which had prevailed in the Spanish working class gave way to a surge of demands which ignored external economic circumstances and concentrated on the reaction to past grievances. Wage rates rose at a pace estimated as between 20 and 30 per cent per annum, with important collective agreements above 40 per cent. The depressed state of demand and price controls kept inflation well below such figures, at a fairly steady 17 to 18 per cent annual rate. As a result, profits declined sharply and the share of wages in national income rose by an astonishing 4 percentage points between 1974 and 1977.

TABLE 19.7. *Major macroeconomic indicators*

	1973	1974	1975	1976	1977	1978	1979
	annual percentage changes							
GDP	7.9	5.7	1.1	3.0	3.3	2.7	0.8
Gross fixed investment	14.3	6.6	−3.9	−2.0	−0.2	−1.1	−2.0
Inflation[a]	11.4	15.7	16.8	15.1	24.5	19.8	15.6
Wage rates	14	20	22	22	27	24	16
	percentages							
Wage share[b]	56.5	56.8	59.1	60.6	60.7	61.1	60.7
Unemployment rate[c]	2.5	2.6	3.7	4.7	5.2	6.9	8.5
	$ billion							
Current balance	0.6	−3.2	−3.5	−4.3	−2.5	1.6	1.1

[a] Consumer prices
[b] Compensation of employees in per cent of national income
[c] In per cent of the labour force
Sources: OECD, *National Accounts of OECD Countries, 1950-1979*, OECD, *Economic Outlook*, July 1981; IMF, *International Financial Statistics* (1980 Yearbook); author's estimates for wage rates, based on a variety of national sources.

Such developments, combined with political uncertainty and the institutional vacuum created by the necessarily slow process of profound constitutional and legal transformation, had strong depressive effects on investment. Gross fixed capital formation increased for the last time in 1974, as a result of the momentum acquired in 1972-3, but it fell by 4 per cent in real terms in 1975 and continued to decline during the next four years. Output did not fall, however, because the rise in real wages permitted fairly rapid increases in consumption in the first half of the period and export demand became a significant expansionary factor in the second. Nevertheless, the steady growth of the inactive age groups of the population, the return flow of emigrants, and the continued increases in productivity caused a steady increase in unemployment, which rose from a mere 2½ per cent of the labour force in 1973 to 8½ per cent in 1979.

The depressed state of demand, the impact of two devaluations, and the gradual decline in the real price of oil led to a considerable improvement in the balance of payments towards the end of the period. But even during the most difficult, initial years, foreign financing had been plentiful and the balance of payments was never a serious impediment to economic recovery.

Such is the story in a nutshell. A somewhat more detailed analysis of each of its major aspects is given in the following paragraphs, but it should be borne in mind that the close connections between institutional, political, and strictly economic factors makes it well nigh impossible to discuss economic developments in the period with the tools of normal business cycle analysis.

Economic policy reactions

The year 1974 was one of transition. In contrast to other countries, Spain had not taken restrictive economic measures during 1973 and the boom was clearly getting out of hand. When the oil crisis arrived, Spain was, with Sweden, one of the few countries which tried to spread its impact over a two- to three-year period. Indirect taxes were decreased to partly offset the impact on demand and prices, in the knowledge that the external financial position was sufficiently solid to withstand a fairly prolonged adjustment period, and the hope that, as it later turned out, the external economic situation would recover and the crisis could be smoothed over to some extent. As noted earlier, however, wage pressures rose sharply and the rate of inflation was accelerating when, in the spring of 1975, a very clear reversal took place in the policy stance. Both monetary and fiscal policy became highly restrictive and an attempt was made to control the growth of wages. The end of the Franco regime was near, however, and wage controls had practically no effect. Consequently, the restrictive monetary policy led, for the most part, to a reduction in price inflation at the expense of profits, with the share of employee compensation in national income rising from 57 per cent in 1974 to 59 per cent in 1975.

After Franco's death in November 1975, Spain entered a period of uneasy political transition which lasted until the first democratic general election in June 1977. During that period, it was hard to envisage anything other than a permissive economic policy, because governments lacked the political power to impose any kind of restrictive measures, and their efforts were directed towards the top priority task of ensuring a smooth transition. Meanwhile, the absence of legal collective bargaining procedures, together with the almost revolutionary spirit created by Franco's death, led to one of the most dismal climates for Spanish entrepreneurs, only partly offset by the accommodating economic policies, particularly in the pre-election period of the first half of 1977.

This being so, the first democratically elected government was confronted by galloping inflation, strong downward pressures on the peseta, and the virtual absence of an institutional framework on the economic front. The answer was a mixture of highly restrictive fiscal and monetary policies with a concerted income policy which significantly reduced wage and price increases. These measures, together with a 20 per cent devaluation of the peseta and an acceleration in the growth of foreign demand, led to a sharp swing in the current account, which moved from a deficit of over $4 billion in 1976 to a $1½ billion surplus in 1978, with reserves increasing by more than $4 billion in the latter year.

These measures were part of an economic package agreed between the government and the opposition parties in October 1977, denominated the 'Moncloa Agreements'. The package, valid until the end of 1978, included a number of institutional reforms and a fairly strict timetable for new legislation. There is little doubt that it constituted the best approach to the solution of Spanish economic and political problems at the time. The observer cannot help feeling, however, that its purpose was mostly to buy time until the new constitution was approved. This occurred in December 1978. Fresh elections were called for the spring of 1979 and the whole concerted approach to economic policy vanished. It is even doubtful whether there had ever been much confidence in it, for the savage monetary restrictions of late 1977 were either a miscalculation or due to a lack of conviction in the capacity of the left-wing parties to keep labour unions from violating the agreements. In any case, partisan politics gained ground in 1979 and a tight monetary policy was the main instrument used against price inflation in that year.

The vicious circle

Towards the end of the decade, the Spanish economy had reached a very uncomfortable position, with unsatisfactory developments for all the major economic variables. Inflation had stabilized at around 16 per cent per annum, wage rates were rising at a similar rate, unemployment was climbing steadily, investment was falling, and real output growing at a mere 1 to 2 per cent per annum. Until the oil price increases of the second half of 1979, the balance of payments situation could be regarded as satisfactory from a conservative point of view, since it showed a significant surplus on current account and large capital inflows. However, the surplus contributed to the vicious circle in which the economy was immersed as a result of a relentless pursuit of price stability through demand management measures in conditions of cost inflation and very low domestic demand. Indeed, the balance of payments surplus created upward pressures on the peseta, at a time at which the Spanish rate of inflation was significantly higher than that of its major competitors.

Between July 1977 and December 1979 the effective exchange rate of the peseta had appreciated by 11 per cent, while Spanish domestic inflation had been 20 percentage points faster than abroad. The new oil crisis complicated things further, but it is clear that, by the end of 1979, exports were ceasing to be an expansionary factor for Spanish output. Thus the very low level of domestic demand was inducing an appreciation of the exchange rate which, in turn, was cutting off the major expansionary force in the economy. The only other demand component which was growing at an above average rate — public consumption — was doing so at the expense of public investment, which remained stagnant or on the decline. At the same time, fiscal pressure increased rapidly during the period, with government current receipts rising from 23 per cent of GDP in 1974 to 28 per cent in 1979. The inadequacies of the Spanish fiscal system were mentioned earlier. According to most comparative criteria, fiscal pressure in Spain at the end of the 1970s would still be deemed low. However, its rapid increase in a period of economic slump and the allocation of its proceeds to public consumption and transfers were certainly a negative factor in the crisis of confidence affecting the Spanish entrepreneurial sector.

Monetary conditions were a further negative factor. Credit to the private sector rose much less rapidly than nominal GDP in 1977 and 1978 and only slightly more in 1979 (Table 19.8). Monetary policy was clearly constrained by two factors — the external surplus and the public sector deficit. As the target variable for monetary policy was money supply in its wider definition (M_3), and the autonomous factors mentioned above had an expansionary influence, the only recourse left to the central bank was a restriction of credit to the private sector. Money supply, which had been growing more rapidly than GDP

TABLE 19.8. *Growth of monetary variables and GDP*
(annual percentage changes)

	1973	1974	1975	1976	1977	1978	1979
GDP at current prices	20.6	23.2	18.0	20.2	26.9	23.5	16.7
Money supply (M 3)[a]	24.0	19.1	19.0	19.3	18.7	19.5	18.0
Credit to private sector[a]	27.6	25.7	21.9	23.4	22.8	13.8	16.9

[a] End-year to end-year

Sources: OECD, *National Accounts of OECD Countries, 1950-1979*; OECD, *Economic Survey of Spain* (various issues); Banco de España, *Boletín estadístico* (various issues).

at current prices during the whole of the previous decade, rose less rapidly than nominal GDP in every year except two after 1974.

To the vicious circle created by the external surplus was added, therefore, a dilemma for the public sector. Given the narrowness of financial markets, any rise in public expenditure had to be financed either through a further increase in the already growing fiscal pressure or through the monetary authorities. The latter, in order to achieve their monetary targets, had to further reduce credit to the private sector.

The reason for this dilemma was straightforward. The growth of the target monetary variable, which remained remarkably stable at around 19 per cent during six consecutive years, did not allow for any significant growth of real output unless inflation declined considerably. As inflation was not demand-induced but quite clearly cost-induced, the transmission mechanism from monetary tightness to lower prices was rather long-winded, particularly in view of the Spanish political and institutional system. Although the cost in terms of unemployment was very high, the results were not negligible as long as wage increases could be reduced to the rate of previous price inflation. Once this was achieved, however, it was difficult to obtain further progress through simple demand management measures. The situation seemed to correspond to a text-book case for incomes policies rather than to require further restriction.

There were probably two reasons why, after the 1977 'Moncloa Agreements', no fresh round of incomes policies was attempted:

(i) The wave of monetarism had made so many converts in Spain that it became difficult for governments to apply anything other than standard monetarist theory. The fact that there are enormous institutional and behavioural differences between Spain and the ideal free market economy on which the monetarist case is based did not seem to impress informed opinion;

(ii) Spanish politicians, who gave the world an example of peaceful transition from dictatorship to democracy, were finding it more difficult to achieve consensus in the economic field. The 'Moncloa Agreements' were clearly meant to carry the country through the pre-constitutional period, but, once the constitution was approved, partisan politics took over again.

Conclusions

Spain's post-war experience may well be regarded as an example of the effects of very rapid economic transformation on a fragile socio-political basis which on several occasions during the period endangered the process of economic expansion. The 1950s witnessed a period of rapid growth under extremely *dirigiste* conditions, which probably succeeded in taking the Spanish economy out of its very depressed post-war state and on to a new development path. This process, however, reached its natural limit towards the end of the decade and the very crude, autarkic methods resulting from the prevailing fascist ideology had to give way to a liberalization programme and the introduction of new men and new approaches. These provided the starting-point for the period of spectacular growth which followed. It must be noted, however, that the essence of the regime was maintained intact and that the liberalization measures adopted in 1959-60 did not really have any follow-up. Economic success, on the contrary, provided the regime with a precious asset whereby to justify political immobility.

That there was economic success in the 1960s is undeniable. Growth was rapid and standards of living rose considerably. Productivity increases were high and were encouraged by a pattern of low interest rates which favoured capital-intensive investment. And the liberalization measures of 1959-60 transformed a hitherto semi-autarkic country into a rather open economy in a matter of a few years. As a result, the decade witnessed a rapid increase in foreign trade, large capital inflows incorporating important technological improvements, a spectacular increase in incoming foreign travel, providing not only foreign exchange but a considerable cultural impact, and a surge of emigration which was also an important source of foreign exchange and an escape valve for excess active population.

Yet the process was self-destructive. Economic growth made the system far more complex and, consequently, more difficult to handle without recourse to new mechanisms. It also made the population less inclined to accept the authoritarian regime which ensured the coherence of the system. Thus, as the 1970s began, it was becoming increasingly clear that important reforms had to be made if Spain were to consolidate her economic development. The pressures to liberalize the financial system, reform the fiscal system, and establish free collective bargaining became widespread at the technical level, but the political implications of such changes were too great and the regime refused to consider them.

In addition, a number of structural problems had also emerged. The public sector, for instance, had remained relatively underdeveloped throughout the 1960s. Moreover, its activities had been concentrated on fostering production rather than promoting education and welfare. This, together with the inevitable side-effects of rapid growth, implied a number of negative counterparts to the picture of rising productivity and incomes. The distribution of output and employment was increasingly concentrated in three relatively small areas of Spain, leaving entire regions in a state of underdevelopment. Urbanization created large problems which remained unresolved not only because of the insufficiency of public sector resources as a result of an archaic and unjust fiscal system, but also because the use of such resources as were available was so centralized that local authorities never accounted for even 10 per cent of total public expenditure. These shortcomings — insufficiency of resources and excessive centralization — also applied to other social infrastructures and particularly to education, possibly the sector most neglected by the regime. This aggravated no doubt the change in social values inevitable in such a rapid growth experience, leaving a profoundly unsettled situation as traditional values were not replaced by a new stable pattern.

The experience of the first two years following the oil crisis, which were also the last two years of Franco's life, were indicative of these various difficulties. The Spanish working class simply refused to share the costs of the crisis, the regime was no longer able to impose those costs, and Spanish entrepreneurs were unprepared to negotiate a reasonable sharing. The eighteen months of transition after Franco's death were inevitably chaotic, and the new democratic regime began under the worst auspices on the economic front. It did achieve some success on inflation and the balance of payments, at the expense, however, of sharp increases in unemployment in a country that still has a rapidly growing population of working age and where productivity increases have remained high. Moreover, the crisis had been so prolonged that the financial situation of many firms was very fragile at the end of the decade and, even worse, entrepreneurial confidence was at its lowest. As a result, productive investment decreased considerably and was mainly directed towards labour-saving rather than output-expanding facilities.

The achievements of the new regime were more important on the institutional side. On the labour relations front, the whole corporatist system was replaced by labour and employer unions. On the fiscal front, a new reform package was approved and began to be applied in 1980. More generally, a number of liberalization measures were taken, and it can be safely said that Spanish economic institutions were more adapted to new challenges towards the end of the 1970s than at the time of the first oil crisis.

As the 1980s began Spain looked like a country lacking confidence in itself. Yet, the pause in growth and the rationalization effort that the crisis had imposed had probably placed its economy in a better position for dealing with future challenges than had been the case in the past. Its new democratic institutions were coping adequately with difficult problems, the worst of which was no doubt the Basque secessionist attempt. But time was running short, because with unemployment rising at 2 percentage points per annum the social and economic burden was rising.

There were hopeful signs, however. The trend towards a decline in the share of profits in national income had been arrested. Productivity was rising at a steady 4 per cent per annum and most wage settlements were being made at rates below the cost of living increase. This was harsh but inevitable if an adequate level of capital accumulation was to be restored. Liberalization of the financial sector was encouraging savings, while renewed attempts at a social contract held out the possibility of a restoration of confidence. In addition, the chances of a recovery Italian-style in the uncontrolled sector of the economy were not insignificant. Spain may well discover in the 1980s the advantages of economic freedom, after having tasted the advantages of political freedom.

Bibliography

A number of surveys exist in English of Spanish economic developments. A longer-run perspective is provided by J. Fontana and J. Nadal, 'Spain, 1914–1970', in C.M. Cipolla (ed.), *The Fontana Economic History of Europe*, Vol. 6, Glasgow 1976. C.W. Anderson, *The Political Economy of Modern Spain*, Madison, Wisconsin 1970, discusses the 1950s and 1960s, while A. Wright, *The Spanish Economy, 1959–1976*, London 1977, and E.N. Baklanoff, *The Economic Transformation of Spain and Portugal*, New York 1978, bring the story up to the end of the Franco regime. Finally, a very detailed survey of the economy at the beginning of the 1960s is provided by IBRD, *The Economic Development of Spain*, Baltimore 1963.

Among the better works in Spanish one could list H. París Eguilaz, *Renta nacional, inversiones y consumo en España*, Madrid 1960; L. Gámir Casares, *Política económica de España*, Madrid 1972; J. Ros Hombravella *et al.*, *Capitalismo español: de la autarquía a la estabilización (1939–1959)*, Madrid 1973; J. Jané Solá, *Política económica española*, Madrid 1977; R. Tamámes, *Estructura económica de España*, Madrid 1977.

In addition, the following periodical publications are worth consulting for background information and statistical data: Confederación española de cajas de ahorro, *Papeles de economía española* (in particular Nos. 3, 5, 7, and 8); Banco de España, *Informe anual*; Banco de Bilbao, *Informe económico*; Instituto nacional de estadística, *La renta española y su distribución*; as well as the OECD's annual *Economic Surveys*.

20

Benelux[*]

WILLY VAN RIJCKEGHEM[**]

Introduction

Probably not since the 'golden' seventeenth century had the Benelux countries experienced a period of broad economic and social progress such as during the twenty-five years which followed World War II. From 1948 to 1973 annual growth was as high as 4½ to 5 per cent. Figures for the years 1870 to 1938 suggest that over that period the area's output growth rate (excluding war years) averaged some 2 to 2¼ per cent per annum.[1]

Taking advantage of the post-war trend towards trade liberalization and European economic integration, Belgium, the Netherlands, and Luxembourg vigorously strove to overcome the limitations inherent in their small size, first by establishing the Benelux customs union, and later by joining the EEC. Their economic opportunities were greatly enhanced by their strategic location at the economic centre of gravity of Western Europe, which attracted important flows of foreign investment, concentrated particularly round the ports of Rotterdam and Antwerp (which provide direct access to the area formed by Northern France, the Lorraine, and the Ruhr and Rhine regions in Germany).

Given their proximity and close contacts (further reinforced by the customs union), it is not surprising that the development of the three economies over the period should have been similar. In all three, per caput GDP had, by 1979, reached $10,000, and industrial productivity and wages were among the highest in the world. The shares of both agricultural and industrial employment in the labour force in the late 1970s (close to 5 and 35 per cent respectively) were somewhat below the average for North Western Europe, and in both Belgium and the Netherlands, the decline in the agricultural population had been very similar (the share in total employment falling by roughly 10 percentage points between 1950 and 1979) – and so had been the rise in tertiary employment (20 percentage points in Belgium, 17 in the Netherlands). A further important characteristic shared by the three economies was the rapidly rising weight of the public sector in total output – though starting-points differed, tax revenues as a percentage of GDP rose by almost exactly the same amount in the twenty-five years to the end of the 1970s (some 18 percentage points) in both Belgium and the Netherlands (Table 20.1).

[*] As for other country chapters, editorial policy has imposed the use of internationally standardized statistics which at times differ from national concepts and figures.

[**] Free University of Brussels (VUB). Several friends and colleagues, in particular at the Centre of Econometrics and Management Science at the Free University of Brussels, have assisted with their advice and criticism. The Benelux Secretariat in Brussels was particularly helpful in providing data and documentation.
[1] See Ch. 1.

TABLE 20.1. *Longer-term trends, 1948–1979*

	1948–60	1960–73	1973–79
	average annual percentage changes		
GDP			
Belgium	3.1	5.0	2.3
Netherlands	4.8	5.0	2.5
Luxembourg	2.9[a]	4.3	1.0
Inflation[b]			
Belgium	1.3	3.6	8.4
Netherlands	3.9	4.9	7.2
Luxembourg	1.1	3.2	7.4
	1955–57	1962–64	1969–71	1977–79
	in per cent of GDP at current prices			
Tax revenues				
Belgium	(25.4)	(29.7)	35.7	43.9
Netherlands	(29.2)	(32.6)	40.2	46.9
Luxembourg	(27.9)	(29.2)	32.1	48.5
Exports of goods and services				
Belgium	39.2	42.3	50.7	55.9
Netherlands	48.4	47.0	46.8	49.7
Luxembourg	80.4	75.8	84.1	80.5

[a] 1953–60
[b] Consumer prices
Sources: OECD, *National Accounts of OECD Countries, 1950–1979*; OECD, *Revenue Statistics, 1965–1980*, OECD, *Public Expenditure Trends*, Paris 1978; IMF, *International Financial Statistics* (1967/68 and 1980 Yearbooks); Union économique Benelux, *Benelux, 1948–1974*, Brussels 1975.

But there were also major differences. All the Benelux countries had tradition-ally been very open economies. But while the importance of foreign trade rose sharply in Belgium, to reach Dutch levels, it remained relatively constant in the other two countries at rates, admittedly, well above those of any other European economy. And while growth was rapid by pre-war standards, a rather sharp divergence emerged in the earlier part of the period when Belgium clearly lagged behind. Indeed, in the 1950s, Belgium was one of the slowest-growing Euro-pean economies – comparable with the United Kingdom and Ireland. Perform-ance converged in the 1960s. The post-1973 period could have been expected however to show a repetition of the earlier divergent trends given that the Netherlands were in a much more favourable position than Belgium on account of their natural gas reserves. Yet, surprisingly perhaps, similar trends continued – growth was virtually the same and inflation differences seemed small.

This chapter analyses post-war developments by looking at three major sub-periods:

(i) The years 1948–60, which can be regarded as the learning period of economic integration and which were marked by the establishment and consolidation of the Benelux customs union. The section discusses divergent growth performance and puts forward a number of explana-tions – a major one being important differences in economic policies;

(ii) The period 1960–73, which covers the heyday of the EEC during which the Benelux countries reaped the benefits of European economic integration. An issue which receives particular attention is the contribution of foreign investment in stimulating growth (but also 'productivity inflation') and in creating a dualistic structure in several industrial sectors;

(iii) The period 1973–9, during which the Benelux countries made rather hesitant adjustments to the sharply increased price of energy and the changes in the world economy. The discussion covers the so-called 'Dutch disease', as well as the constraints (both domestic and international) which were imposed on policy-makers during the period.

The chapter concludes with a brief summary and overview.

I. The Learning Period of Economic Integration – The Benelux Union, 1948–1960

The Benelux customs union was the first example of regional economic integration achieved in Western Europe after World War II.[2] The foundations of the union were established by the London Convention of 1944, but the immediate reconstruction problems of the Netherlands in the post-war period delayed its effective start until 1948. In one bold move, all tariffs on inter-country trade were immediately removed, and a common external tariff was adopted. This was soon to be followed by the removal of all quantitative restrictions (except on agricultural commodities), by the liberalization of capital flows, the free movement of salaried workers, and the establishment of a common commercial policy with respect to third countries.[3] In 1958 a new treaty transformed the customs union into an economic union, which became effective in 1960. By then, however, most of the original impetus of trade liberalization had already been spent, and was overtaken by the dynamic forces released by the start of the EEC in 1958.

Rapid growth in the Netherlands – contributing factors

At the start of the customs union, Belgium and Luxembourg were far more industrialized than the Netherlands, which, historically, had been more oriented towards agriculture and trade. In 1948, the share of industrial employment in Belgium amounted to 46 per cent, compared with 37 per cent in the Netherlands. Agriculture accounted for 12 per cent of the labour force in Belgium but 16 per cent in Holland.[4] The formation of the customs union contributed in

---

[2] J.E. Meade, 'Benelux: The Formation of the Common Customs', *Economica*, August 1956. Belgium and Luxembourg had already established an economic union after World War I (the so-called Belgium-Luxembourg Economic Union, or BLEU), and had achieved near-perfect integration in the trade and monetary fields, especially after monetary union, involving a single central bank for both countries, had been established in 1935. The BLEU continued to operate within Benelux, just as the latter was to continue to operate within the EEC after 1958.

[3] For a chronological account of the successive Benelux agreements, see J.E. Meade, 'Negotiations for Benelux: An Annotated Chronicle, 1943–56', *Princeton Studies in International Finance*, No. 6, 1957.

[4] For a comparison of long-term trends in the structure of economic activity in Belgium and the Netherlands, see S. Kuznets, *Modern Economic Growth*, London 1966, pp. 106–7.

several ways to the accelerated industrialization of the Netherlands after 1948. On the one hand, by excluding the agricultural sector from free inter-country trade, the customs union steered the Netherlands away from an area in which it enjoyed a clear absolute and relative advantage. On the other hand, it created an opportunity for the Netherlands to take advantage of its substantially lower wage level, allowing it to compete successfully in almost all branches of manufacturing, but particularly in labour-intensive products. This competitive edge was reflected in the trade statistics which indicate that between 1948 and 1953 the Netherlands was able to increase its share in total BLEU imports from 8 to 14 per cent, whereas the corresponding share of the BLEU in Dutch imports only rose from 15 to 17 per cent. The trade balance between the BLEU and the Netherlands, still very lopsided in 1948, was thus almost in equilibrium in 1953. Indeed, in that year, some voluntary restrictions on the part of Dutch exporters were required to avoid a crisis in the Benelux household.

In a detailed analysis of Benelux intra-bloc trade, Verdoorn estimated that the formation of the customs union might have accounted for (at most) 65 per cent of the improvement of the Dutch share in total BLEU imports. He also suggested that the price component of this increase was more important than the volume component since the customs union tended to foster mutual trade in products where the value added was relatively high.[5] Another important conclusion, which foreshadowed the results obtained by Balassa fourteen years later for the EEC, was that specialization seemed to occur *within* rather than between trade categories.[6] Finally, it appeared that Dutch exporters, who were operating at full capacity, did not use their cost advantage to lower prices, but instead maximized profits by adjusting to the relatively higher Belgian price level, as represented by BLEU export prices.

It was remarkable that in spite of high export prices and high profits in the exporting sectors, the Netherlands managed to maintain its wage advantage throughout the 1950s. Even in a customs union, the process of wage equalization is apparently a slow one (Fig. 20.1). In this particular instance, the process was delayed by the famous system of Dutch incomes policy.[7]

In the initial stages of the policy the trade unions exercised great restraint in the interest of post-war recovery, and bargained primarily for cost-of-living

---

[5] P.J. Verdoorn, 'The Intra-Block Trade of Benelux', in E.A.G. Robinson (ed.), *Economic Consequences of the Size of Nations*, London 1960.

[6] B. Balassa, 'Trade Creation and Trade Diversion in the European Common Market: An Appraisal of the Evidence', *The Manchester School*, June 1974.

[7] The institutional set-up of this system has often been described in the literature, so that it is here relegated to a footnote. In a nutshell, the system involved three levels of intervention: *first*, the Minister of Economic Affairs, who issued general directives for overall wage increases in the economy, and who also made the final decision; *second*, the Board of Mediators, which approved the collective bargaining results, or which fixed the wage levels when no collective agreement was reached; *third*, the Foundation of Labour, composed of representatives of trade unions, of industry, commerce, and agriculture, who had to be consulted by the Board of Mediators; *finally*, the Social and Economic Council, a tripartite body, which also consulted with the Foundation and advised the government whether to permit the wage increases or not. For an evaluation of this system in its early setting, see B. Zoeteweij, 'National Wage Policy: The Experience of the Netherlands', *International Labour Review*, February 1955; see also J.G. Abert, *Economic Policy and Planning in the Netherlands, 1950-1965*, New Haven 1969.

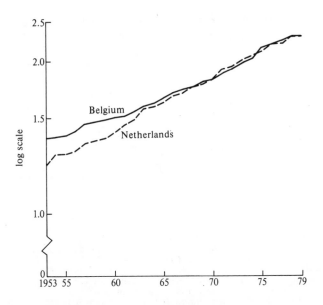

FIG. 20.1. *Gross average hourly wage of workers in industry* (in logs of Belgian francs)
Source: adapted and updated from E.D.J. Kruijtbosch, 'L'expérience acquise par plus de trente ans d'intégration économique dans le cadre du Benelux', *Revue d'inté-gration européenne*, No. 1, 1980, with the help of data in Banque Nationale de Belgique, *Bulletin mensuel*, and Eurostat, *Social Statistics* (various issues).

adjustments in order to prevent a decline in real wages. In 1951, during the Korean War boom, when the terms of trade of the Netherlands deteriorated, the unions even accepted a 5 per cent cut in real wages. From 1954 onwards, increases in wages were linked to the development of per caput national income in money terms, in order to prevent a further drop in the share of wages in national income. This new policy contributed to the slow convergence of wage levels in the Netherlands and in Belgium. In the latter country, by contrast, government interference in the process of wage formation was not tolerated either by the trade unions or by the employers' federations. The only form of government intervention was the introduction, in 1952, of a system ·linking wages and social transfer payments to the consumer price index. As a result, wage negotiations were from then on concerned with real wages rather than with nominal wages.

The Netherlands' low relative wage level helped to bring about high profits and an investment ratio which, in current prices, reached 24 per cent for the period 1948–60 as compared to only 18 per cent for Belgium. In constant prices, however, this gap nearly disappears in view of different relative price movements (Table 20.2). It might seem that the high investment ratio in the Netherlands was due to post-war reconstruction, and in particular to the am-bitious housing programme designed to accommodate a rapidly rising population. In fact, however, even when investment in housing is deducted from overall capital formation, the six percentage points gap between the (current price)

TABLE 20.2. *Major macroeconomic indicators, 1948-1960*

	Belgium	Netherlands	Luxembourg[a]	OECD Europe[b]
	average annual percentage changes			
GDP	3.1	4.8	2.9	4.8
Labour productivity[c]	2.7	3.6	2.7	(3.9)
Inflation[d]	1.3	3.9	1.1	3.5
	percentages			
Investment ratio[e]	(19.9)	20.2[b]	..	(19)
Unemployment rate[f]	6½	2	–	..

[a] 1953-60
[b] 1950-60
[c] GDP per employed
[d] Consumer prices
[e] Gross fixed investment in per cent of GDP at constant prices
[f] In per cent of the labour force; figures not strictly comparable across countries
Sources: OECD, *National Accounts of OECD Countries, 1950-1979* and *1950-1968*;
OECD, *Manpower Statistics, 1950-1962*; IMF, *International Financial Statistics* (1967/68 and 1980 Yearbooks); Union économique Benelux, *Benelux, 1948-1974*, Brussels 1975; 'La comptabilité nationale de la Belgique, 1946-1960', *Cahiers économiques de Bruxelles*, October 1961.

investment ratios remains, with the Netherlands at 18 per cent and Belgium at 12 per cent.[8] Among the industrialized nations, only the United Kingdom had a lower investment ratio than Belgium.[9]

This was not the only similarity between the two precursors of the 'Industrial Revolution'. The overall lacklustre performance of the Belgian economy reminded observers of the British scene in a number of ways, while the post-war recovery of the Netherlands was, in contrast, not unlike that which was taking place in neighbouring Germany. GDP grew at the vigorous pace of nearly 5 per cent per annum in the Netherlands, whereas the rate of growth barely exceeded 3 per cent in Belgium and Luxembourg. The growth rates of labour productivity display a similar pattern, in accordance with Verdoorn's hypothesis which links the growth rate of productivity to the growth rate of output.[10] Inflation also exhibits a positive relationship with GDP growth, and the familiar inverse relationship with unemployment rates is confirmed, at least for the two larger countries. On the other hand, and somewhat surprisingly, the degree of cyclical instability was similar in Belgium and the Netherlands. In both countries, the average absolute deviation of annual GDP growth rates from their respective averages amounted to some 50 per cent of the latter. This suggests that the

[8] This may seem surprising since during this period the Netherlands built twice as many houses as Belgium. But unit costs turned out to be much lower, largely because the average volume of housing constructed in the Netherlands was 40 per cent below that in Belgium; see Union économique Benelux, *Benelux 1948-1974*, Brussels 1975, p. 31.

[9] M. Gilbert and Associates, *Comparative National Products and Price Levels*, OEEC, Paris 1958. This study indicates, however, that the Belgian investment ratio may have been biased downwards because of low relative prices of capital goods.

[10] P.J. Verdoorn, 'On an Empirical Law Governing the Productivity of Labour', *Econometrica*, April 1951.

celebrated short-term demand management policies elaborated by the prestigious Dutch Central Planning Bureau, and based on the world's first operational econometric models, could not assure greater stability in the Netherlands than in Belgium, where no such models or policies were used. Though this does not detract from the value of the Dutch approach, it serves as a reminder that instability is inherent in the degree of openness of these economies, since it is difficult to offset external shocks by compensating measures. The models probably helped to pinpoint the strategic importance of the wage level, which indeed was treated as the major policy variable. Budgetary and monetary policy were probably less crucial. The former was on the whole expansionary, but public borrowing was restricted to the amount that could be financed in the capital marked 'without causing disturbance'. The main objective of monetary policy seems to have been to prevent money supply from becoming excessive in relation to transactions. This was done by systematically pursuing a targeted liquidity coefficient.[11]

The relative stagnation of Belgium − alternative hypotheses

Success is always easier to explain than an indifferent performance, and while the rapid growth of the Netherlands requires no particular effort of elucidation, the relative stagnation of Belgium (and at the same time of Luxembourg) has presented a greater challenge to economists. However, due to a relative shortage of reliable statistics, it was not until the end of the 1950s that they began to question the performance of the country as compared to the rest of continental Europe. Several hypotheses were then advanced to explain this slower growth. Among the most important were the following:

(i) Kindleberger's thesis which emphasized the role of labour supply;
(ii) The Rosselle−Waelbroeck hypothesis, which focused on the unfavourable commodity composition of Belgian exports;
(iii) Lamfalussy's explanation in terms of 'defensive' investment.

The central thesis of *Kindleberger*, which is discussed in greater detail elsewhere in this book, is that the major factor shaping the remarkable growth of Europe since 1950 was the availability of an abundant labour supply.[12] At first sight, the Benelux countries seem to fit this hypothesis: the active population grew at an annual rate of 1 per cent in the Netherlands, whereas it grew at only 0.2 per cent in Belgium, and remained stationary in Luxembourg. This would appear consistent with the differences in GDP growth rates in the three countries, and also with the fact that employment rose in the Netherlands whereas it remained constant in Luxembourg. Unfortunately, however, it is not consistent with excess labour supply in Belgium, where the unemployment rate reached an average of 6½ per cent for the period under consideration. Moreover, looking at Belgium from the important regional angle, it is clear that demographic growth

[11] See Ch. 11 above for a discussion of this early move to targets, and E. den Dunnen, 'Postwar Monetary Policy', *De Economist*, No. 1, 1979, for a more general survey of Dutch monetary policies.
[12] C.P. Kindleberger, *Europe's Postwar Growth*, Cambridge, Mass. 1967; see also Ch. 1 above.

in Flanders was not unlike that in the Netherlands, whereas its GDP growth rate was not higher than the Belgian average.[13] In fact, 70 per cent of all unemployment was concentrated in Flanders, where the unemployment rate reached 14 per cent. Whereas it could be argued that demographic factors account for the economic stagnation of Wallonia and of neighbouring Luxembourg, it seems impossible to do so for Flanders. Without disputing the possible validity of the Kindleberger hypothesis in the longer run and for a wider spectrum of countries, it does not seem able to account for the differences in economic performance within the Benelux during the 1950s.[14]

Moving from supply-side explanations to more demand-oriented ones, *Rosselle and Waelbroeck* set out, within the framework of Kindleberger's 'luck and flexibility' approach, to test the hypothesis that the commodity composition of BLEU exports was biased towards intermediate products with stagnating prospects (steel, glass, cement, textiles, etc.).[15] This had been a frequently voiced complaint during the 1950s. For this purpose the authors compared the actual expansion of exports with the increase which might have been expected on the basis of constant shares of world trade, determined by each country's initial commodity composition of exports (Table 20.3).

TABLE 20.3. *Actual and theoretical Benelux exports*
(indices: actual exports 1951–53 = 100)

	1958 exports	
	actual	theoretical[a]
BLEU[b]	121	135
Netherlands	156	135
Eight major industrial countries	141	141

[a] Based on constant shares for thirty product categories
[b] BLEU foreign trade statistics do not differentiate between Belgium and Luxembourg
Source: E. Rosselle and J. Waelbroeck, 'La position de la Belgique vis-à-vis de ses concurrents du Marché Commun, essai de diagnostic économétrique', *Cahiers économiques de Bruxelles*, January 1961.

The comparison shows that 'luck', as determined by the initial composition, was slightly unfavourable to both the BLEU and the Netherlands, since on the basis of the original structure their exports could have been expected to increase by 35 per cent as compared to 41 per cent for the eight major industrial exporters taken together. But whereas the Netherlands clearly succeeded in overcoming this structural handicap by superior 'flexibility' (probably due to a competitive wage level) and increased its actual exports by 56 per cent, the

[13] Growth rates of regional product can be found in G. Chaput and R. de Falleur, 'La production et l'investissement des regions flamandes, wallonne et bruxelloise', *Cahiers économiques de Bruxelles*, April 1961.

[14] The labour reserve of Flanders was to provide the basis for the region's economic expansion during the 1960s, but this is a different story, which will be discussed in the following section.

[15] E. Rosselle and J. Waelbroeck, 'La position de la Belgique vis-à-vis de ses concurrents du Marché Commun, essai de diagnostic économétrique', *Cahiers économiques de Bruxelles*, January 1961.

BLEU underperformed by falling short of its theoretical level. To be fair, it must be pointed out that the base period was unfavourable to the BLEU, since it covered the years of the Korean War boom when BLEU exports were artificially high because of high demand for steel. Similarly, the terminal year was also unfavourable, since it was a year of international recession. But even if one accepts these objections, the results reflect the cyclical vulnerability of BLEU exports, due to their concentration in semi-manufactures. It is worth recalling in this context that at least one school of thought at the time argued that BLEU specialization in standardized products was healthy from an economic viewpoint.[16] Lacking a sufficiently large industrial market, Belgian firms should specialize in standardized products to benefit from economies of scale. While this argument may have been valid for the interwar period, it was more difficult to accept after twelve years of Benelux integration and in a period of extensive liberalization of world trade. In any case, the Rosselle–Waelbroeck results clearly illustrate the difference in dynamism between the Belgian and Dutch economies, but do not really explain it. For this one must turn to the Lamfalussy thesis.

The major effort at interpretation of slow Belgian growth during the 1950s was undertaken by *Lamfalussy*.[17] His study was still handicapped by a lack of reliable statistics, but his insights profited from his professional involvement with the Belgian financial establishment. His starting-point was provided by the observation that the greater part of investment outlays during the 1950s was directed towards stagnating industries (coal-mining, steel, railway equipment, textiles). In order to explain this phenomenon, he developed the concept of *defensive investment*, which aims at lowering costs as a protective device when competition from abroad is active and profits are squeezed. He showed, theoretically, that *net* defensive investment using minor inventions as a form of rationalization might even appear profitable to entrepreneurs with a relatively short time horizon. What was particularly striking about this type of investment was its pervasive character throughout the economy: according to Lamfalussy more than 50 per cent of Belgian output was coming from industries relying on defensive investment. This prevented capital from flowing from declining (or stagnating) industries to expanding industries, and thus slowed down the country's overall growth.

The most immediate corollary to defensive investment was, therefore, the stability of the structure of industry. This was confirmed in an independent study of sectoral productivity growth in which it was shown that changes in output structure made only an insignificant contribution to the overall growth rate of productivity.[18] The results also indicated that some of the highest

---

[16] J. Drèze, 'Quelques réflexions sereines sur l'adaptation de l'industrie belge au Marché Commun Européen', *Comptes rendus des travaux de la Société Royale d'Economie Politique*, No. 275, December 1960. Drèze's argument echoes that of L. Duquesne de la Vinelle who wrote that Belgium's industrial orientation was determined by the country's geographical situation and size and stated that 'If the pattern of Belgian industry is not as perfect as it might be, the size of the nation is largely responsible.' cf. his 'Study of the Efficiency of a Small Nation' in Robinson (ed.), *Economic Consequences*, p. 88.

[17] A. Lamfalussy, *Investment and Growth in Mature Economies*, London 1961.

[18] J. Defay, 'La productivité du travail de 1948 à 1958', *Cahiers économiques de Bruxelles*, January 1961.

productivity growth rates were achieved in stagnating or declining industries, where productivity growth was indeed essential for survival, such as textiles, leather, or wood and furniture (all of which were able to increase productivity at rates of 6 to 6½ per cent per annum). As a result, overall productivity growth in Belgium was still respectable (2.7 per cent per annum) and was obtained with a smaller investment effort than in the Netherlands.

Although Lamfalussy correctly diagnosed the Belgian *malaise* of the 1950s, he did not identify its deeper causes. Though he suggested three possible ones — the type of entrepreneurial personality common to Belgium, low profits, and government subsidies to declining industries — none of these seems particularly convincing. More radical observers have pointed out the lack of dynamism of the large financial holding companies whose assets were largely concentrated in the sectors where defensive investment took place. The fact that these same companies were at the time still actively engaged in the (then) Belgian Congo, which became independent only in 1960, may provide a clue to the puzzle. Indeed, the Netherlands, which had reluctantly divested itself of its Indonesian colony in 1949, had been able to concentrate on its own development problems much earlier than Belgium.

None of the preceding hypotheses, taken separately, accounts sufficiently for the deflationary climate, so typical of the 1950s, for which government policies must ultimately be held responsible. Successive Belgian governments of the period attached greater weight to a strong currency and to price stability than to full employment.[19] A key role in explaining sluggish Belgian growth must be assigned to this policy stance and, in particular, to a usually neglected factor — the differential devaluation of 1949 when the Netherlands and several other European countries went all the way with the 30 per cent United Kingdom devaluation relative to the dollar, whereas the BLEU devalued by only 12 per cent. While this helped to restore the Dutch trade balance, it was also the straw which broke the back of post-war expansion in Belgium. The Korean War boom of 1950–1 was able to mask this weakness temporarily, but soon afterwards the Belgian economy fell into a lethargic state from which it only intermittently awoke. Thus, signs of revival appeared in 1955–6, but these were soon cut short for fear of inflation. Since Belgian exporters were (and are) generally price takers on the world market,[20] the burden of adjustment fell to a large extent on profits. Low profits encouraged in turn the defensive investment policies described by Lamfalussy.

Rather than admitting their mistake, the Belgian authorities made 'the defence of the Belgian franc' their battle-cry in the 1950s. While the Netherlands was using incomes policies to keep costs under control, the politically much weaker Belgian governments relied on high unemployment to achieve wage moderation. This strategy partially succeeded, in the sense that nominal wages rose more slowly in Belgium than in the Netherlands. However, due to substantially

---

[19] For a detailed analysis of economic policy during this period, see L. Morrissens, 'Economic Policy in Belgium, 1949–1961' in E.S. Kirschen and Associates, *Economic Policy in Our Time*, Vol. 3, Amsterdam 1964.

[20] Rosselle and Waelbroeck ('La position de la Belgique', p. 132) point out that, except in 1951, Belgian export prices were always lower than those of European competitors.

more rapid productivity growth, labour costs per unit of output fell in the Netherlands, whereas they remained constant in Belgium. Deflation, therefore, hardly improved Belgium's competitive position, but worsened the trade-off between inflation and unemployment.

Budgetary policy displayed the same attitude of cautiousness and fear of inflation. Hansen judges Belgian policy as follows: 'With more expansive budgets during the fifties . . . Belgium might have reached full employment earlier', and 'Belgian Governments have always given a high priority to price stability and the cautious budget policies of the fifties were partly due to concern about price developments.'[21] The differences in budgetary policy between Belgium and the Netherlands are illustrated in Table 20.4. In the Netherlands current government expenditures increased from 25 to 28 per cent of GDP between the first and

TABLE 20.4. *Selected government transactions, 1950–1960*
(in per cent of GDP at current prices)

	Belgium		Netherlands		Luxembourg	
	1950–55	1955–60	1950–55	1955–60	1950–55	1955–60
Tax revenue	23.8	25.2	29.4	29.6	30.1	29.3
Current expenditure	25.2	26.2	24.8	27.8	25.6	26.0
Investment	(3.1)	(2.5)	3.6	6.2	..	..
General government net lending	(−3.7)	(−4.1)	4.7	−1.7	..	..

Sources: OECD, *National Accounts of OECD Countries, 1950–1968, 1953–1969*, and *1950–1979*; 'La comptabilité nationale de la Belgique, 1948–1960', *Cahiers économiques de Bruxelles*, October 1961.

second half of the decade, whereas in Belgium they remained nearly constant. The difference is even more pronounced for public investment. At the same time, the tax pressure was hardly changed in the Netherlands, but rose in Belgium. Whereas the Dutch budget moved from substantial surplus to small deficit, Belgium maintained a moderate deficit throughout the period, due to its relatively low tax burden. By the end of the decade, and especially after the serious recession of 1958, a reaction occurred in government circles under the pressure of economists and politicians who were clamouring for more vigorous policies to promote economic growth. The result was the passing of the so-called 'Laws of Economic Expansion' in 1959 and the creation of a Programming Bureau (after the example of the Dutch Central Planning Bureau). One should also mention the economic blueprint for the 1960s produced by the Fifth Congress of Flemish Economists, which set as a target a growth rate of more than four per cent.

Thus Belgium was bracing itself for the challenges posed by the integration of

[21] B. Hansen, *Fiscal Policy in Seven Countries, 1955–1965*, OECD, Paris 1969, pp. 110–11, 125; see also W. Snyder, 'Measuring the Effects of Belgian Budget Policies, 1955–65', *Cahiers économiques de Bruxelles*, No. 44, 1969.

Benelux in the European Common Market, established in 1958. The customs union had prepared the Benelux countries rather well for the wider Common Market they were to enter. It had helped to establish a new industrial base in the Netherlands, and had brought home the lessons of economic competition to Belgium and Luxembourg by forcing them, however reluctantly, to eliminate their least efficient enterprises.

II. The Benefits of European Economic Integration, 1960–1973

Foreign investment and trade performance

The creation of the EEC provided the Benelux countries with a golden opportunity. Their location in the economic centre of Europe proved extremely attractive to foreign investors, especially North American multinationals that did not want to be excluded from the fast-growing EEC market. Factors which particularly favoured the Benelux area were:

(i) Central location and good communications – this applied especially to the growth poles around Rotterdam and Antwerp;[22]

(ii) Reserves of well-trained manpower – this applied particularly to Flanders, which had accumulated a substantial labour force reserve during the 1950s;

(iii) Tax incentives and favourable credit terms – the Belgian 'Economic Expansion Laws', which had been passed at the end of the 1950s in order to stimulate investment by domestic firms, provided incentives which proved particularly attractive to foreign investors, who in the end turned out to be the major beneficiaries.

By the end of 1972, the cumulative total of American direct investment in the manufacturing sector of the Benelux countries amounted to $2.3 billion (excluding oil refineries), of which $1.2 billion went to the BLEU and $1.1 billion to the Netherlands. The Benelux total represented at the time nearly one-quarter of all American investment in the six original EEC countries.[23] The contribution of foreign investment is even more striking when it is seen relative to the size of the recipient economies. Unfortunately, few published data are available for the Netherlands, but the Belgian case is well documented.[24] A study by the Belgian National Bank shows that during the period 1960–7 a total of more than 300 new foreign firms were established in Belgium, of which more than half were American. For the manufacturing sector *alone*, foreign investment accounted for one-third of total gross investment and for *half* of net investment between 1960

[22] J. Paelinck and J. van Overbeke, 'Forces économiques, flux et transport et infrastructure dans l'Europe des Six. Un essai de synthèse', *Recherches économiques de Louvain*, No. 6, 1962.

[23] D. van den Bulcke, *Investment and Divestment Policies of Multinational Corporations in Europe*, London 1979, p. 25.

[24] See especially the October 1970 issue of the *Bulletin* of the Belgian National Bank, the annual reports on foreign investment by the Ministry of Economic Affairs, the study by D. van den Bulcke, *De buitenlandse ondernemingen in de Belgische industrie* (Foreign Enterprise in Belgian Industry), Gent 1971, and the OECD, *Economic Survey of Belgium, 1972*.

and 1972. Investment was concentrated in metal transforming (40 per cent), oil refining (20 per cent), and chemical industries (15 per cent). The importance of foreign investment is also reflected in an upward shift of the overall investment ratio of the respective economies and in an acceleration of GDP growth rates (Table 20.5).

TABLE 20.5. *Major macroeconomic indicators, 1960–1973*

	Belgium	Netherlands	Luxembourg	OECD Europe
	average annual percentage changes			
GDP	5.0	5.0	4.3	4.8
Labour productivity[a]	4.2	4.1	3.1	4.4
Inflation[b]	3.6	4.9	3.2	4.6
	percentages			
Investment ratio[c]	23.0	24.0	29.4	23.2
Unemployment rate[d]	2.3	1.1	–	2.7[e]

[a] GDP per employed
[b] Consumer prices
[c] Gross fixed investment in per cent of GDP at constant prices
[d] In per cent of the labour force; figures not strictly comparable across countries
[e] 1965–73; average of eleven countries (representing some 80 per cent of the European labour force) for which comparable figures are available

Sources: OECD, *National Accounts of OECD Countries, 1950–1979*; OECD, *Labour Force Statistics, 1960–1971* and *1967–1978*; OECD, *Economic Outlook*, July 1981; IMF, *International Financial Statistics* (1980 Yearbook); EEC, *European Economy*, November 1980.

Foreign investment was primarily export-oriented and provided an element of 'flexibility' which was especially needed by the BLEU countries to overcome the structural handicap with which they had been saddled during the 1950s. In the course of the 1960s, BLEU exports did in fact seem to respond better to the opportunities offered by the Common Market than the Netherlands. This is confirmed by an interesting study which showed that in the two major French and German markets, the import allocation elasticity for BLEU products (between 1959 and 1967) was well above that for Dutch exports.[25] The study also showed that trade diversion had taken place in the Common Market as a whole, but not within the Benelux customs union, suggesting that the integration effects there had been exhausted in the 1950s.

All this suggests that the EEC did represent less of a dynamic force in the development of the Dutch economy than for the BLEU. This is confirmed in an econometric study which found a positive 'Common Market effect' only in the initial years (from the first quarter of 1959 to the second quarter of 1961), when the existence of the EEC may have added an extra 5 per cent to the growth rate of Dutch exports.[26] The satisfactory performance of BLEU exports

[25] A.P. Barten, 'An Import Allocation Model for the Common Market', *Cahiers économiques de Bruxelles*, No. 50, 1971.
[26] W. Driehuis, *Fluctuations and Growth in a Near Full-Employment Economy*, Rotterdam 1972, p. 90.

was also confirmed in a repeat study of the earlier Rosselle–Waelbroeck article.[27] The results indicated that, contrary to what had happened during the 1950s, the BLEU now performed better than the original composition of its exports would have led one to expect. The structure of its exports, however, did not change fundamentally and remained specialized in the traditional sectors of iron and steel, textiles and machinery. The Netherlands, on the contrary, made a breakthrough in the chemical and electrical equipment sectors. Though both countries exported mostly to the same regional markets, the commodity structure of their exports became complementary.[28]

Mounting problems

Whereas the driving forces of the expansion of the BLEU countries during this period were certainly foreign investment and exports, the development of the Dutch economy was led by private and public consumption. Dutch consumers clearly felt that they had done enough belt-tightening during the 1950s, and began to press for higher incomes. In the process, the system of incomes policy began to crumble.[29] Already in 1959 the adoption of sectoral productivity growth rates as a criterion for wage changes had created the possibility of differentiated pay settlements between industries or enterprises. This marked a fundamental departure from previous policy, which prescribed uniform wage increases for all sectors. It also paved the way for *productivity inflation* during the 1960s, when the competitive manufacturing sector with its high productivity growth acted as a wage leader, and transmitted its wage increases to the rest of the economy (the so-called sheltered sectors), where they caused inflation. In this context, it is of interest to point out that the growth rate of real wages for the Dutch economy as a whole corresponded exactly to the growth rate of productivity in the manufacturing sector alone (6.5 per cent per annum between 1960 and 1973). This represented a clear break with the previous period, when the growth rate of real wages had been only 3 per cent per annum. In Belgium, on the contrary, where the growth rate of productivity in the manufacturing sector was slower (4.6 per cent), the growth rate of real wages for the whole economy was also lower (5 per cent). This goes a long way to explain the differences in inflation rates which the two countries experienced during the 1960s.[30]

The tightening labour market also contributed to the breakdown of Dutch incomes policies. At the end of the 1950s, the unemployment rate had already come down to 1.5 per cent. In 1961, the working week was shortened by 6 per cent, which put further pressure on the labour market. The unemployment

[27] M. Gerard and H. Glejser, 'Quelques changements fondamentaux dans les relations économiques extérieures depuis 1960', *mimeo*, Namur 1978.

[28] P. de Grauwe, 'Determinanten van de exportprestatie van België en Nederland' (The Determinants of Export Performance in Belgium and in the Netherlands), *Tijdschrift voor Economie*, No. 1, 1971.

[29] For a description of the different steps in the breakdown of the incomes policy during the 1960s, see OECD, *Inflation, the Present Problem*, Paris 1970, pp. 86–8, and Abert, *Economic Policy*, pp. 85–97.

[30] W. van Rijckeghem and G. Maynard, 'Why Inflation Rates Differ: A Critical Examination of the Structural Hypothesis', in H. Frisch (ed.), *Inflation in Small Countries*, Berlin 1976.

rate declined to a historical low of 0.8 per cent in 1964. Nominal wages exploded in the autumn of 1963, rose by 15 per cent in 1964, and by another 11 per cent in 1965. By then, Dutch wages had almost caught up with the Belgian wage level, and by the end of the period, in 1973, they were marginally higher (see Fig. 20.1).

In the euphoric climate of the 1960s, the implications of this development were not immediately realized. With the benefit of hindsight, however, it is clear that the roots of some of the Dutch problems in the 1970s must be sought here. This was indeed the thesis of den Hartog and Tjan who, in a pioneering study of the period 1959–73 used a vintage capital model to demonstrate that the increase in real labour costs had led to early scrapping of the older vintages of Dutch production capacity.[31] According to their estimates, the age of the oldest vintage in use declined from forty-five to seventeen years between 1960 and 1973, while the average age of all vintages in use fell from 10.1 to 7.5 years. Until 1964, this development was mainly due to the technological obsolescence of equipment; after that, economic obsolescence became predominant. This did not lead immediately to higher unemployment because of the earlier situation of excess demand for labour. But the quadrupling of unemployment between 1965 and 1972 was, according to them, closely linked to the effects of high wages on the capital stock.

The results of this study caused a commotion in Dutch academic circles, and were followed by a flurry of econometric activity. The dust of the debate had not yet settled at the time of writing, but it was becoming clear that the model had not stood up very well to the criticism to which it had been subjected.[32] A major flaw of the model was that it predicted very poorly for the years preceding the period for which its parameters had been estimated. For the 1950s, when real wages were below the equilibrium level, the model predicted the creation of 1.2 million additional jobs, whereas the actual increase was only 370,000.[33] This strongly suggested that the model was too sensitive to changes in real wages, and tended to explain a loss of jobs in the 1960s and early 1970s which had never been created in the first place. Another criticism was that the model assumed perfect competition on the demand side – an acceptable hypothesis, perhaps, for the competitive sector facing the world market, but not for the sheltered sector, nor for the economy as a whole. Coupled with the earlier observation on productivity inflation, this suggests a reformulation of the model in the context of a dual economy, where the growth rate of productivity in the advanced internationally competitive sector pushes up wages, which then spill over to the rest of the economy, where they either cause unemployment in the traditional competitive sector, or inflation in the sheltered one.[34]

[31] H. den Hartog and H.S. Tjan, 'Investments, Wages, Prices and Demand for Labour', *De Economist*, Nos. 1–2, 1976.

[32] The debate is summarized in an excellent unpublished paper (brought to the author's attention by Professor A. Merkies) by H. Zeelenberg of the Free University of Amsterdam: 'Lonen en werkgelegenheid. Een studie over het jaargangenmodel van den Hartog en Tjan' (Wages and Employment: A Study of the den Hartog and Tjan Vintage Model), 1978.

[33] R.A. de Klerk, H.B.M. van der Laan, and K.B.D. Thio, 'Unemployment in the Netherlands: A Criticism of the den Hartog-Tjan Vintage Model', *Cambridge Journal of Economics*, September 1977.

[34] A well-known case of a dual economy where high wages imposed by foreign invest-

The large-scale implantation of foreign enterprises during the 1960s may have contributed to the creation of such a dualistic structure. A foreign-owned, technologically advanced, and capital-intensive sector coexisted with the traditional (but also competitive) industries, which reacted to the wage leadership of the advanced sector by defensive investment, but also by reductions in employment. To an extent, the same phenomenon was also at work in Belgium, but with less extreme consequences. A model similar to the one just discussed applied to the Belgian manufacturing sector suggested a drop in the age of the oldest vintage from thirty years in 1960 to twenty-five years in 1973 – a much less dramatic fall, related to the slower growth in real wages.[35]

Policies

In the absence of effective incomes policies, general economic policy failed to keep accelerating inflation under control. In the Netherlands, inflation was only briefly checked by a revaluation of the guilder by 5 per cent in 1961 (following the DM). Belgium tried to dampen the inflationary spiral by a rather elaborate system of price controls based on a thorough screening of price increase applications.[36] The controls were often aimed at products which were represented in the consumer price index, to which wages were automatically linked. This concern may have been excessive, since several studies covering this period have shown that changes in nominal wages were determined primarily by factors other than consumer prices, whose movement mainly provided a floor for negotiated wage increases.[37]

Except in Luxembourg, where inflation remained very low, the public sector was a net contributor to buoyant final demand. This was mainly due to the very rapid growth of current expenditures. The tax burden rose correspondingly, but this had sometimes inflationary consequences as well, both directly as was the case when VAT was introduced in the Netherlands in 1969, and possibly indirectly, in the form of increased wage–push on the part of workers conscious of increasing erosion of their post-tax earnings. Whereas previously in the Netherlands tax revenues had sometimes been able to cover both current and investment expenditures, this was no longer the case in the 1960s (Table 20.6). Belgium, which had made a serious effort to reduce its long-standing deficit in the early 1960s, relaxed again in later years.

---

ment led to a decline in employment for the economy as a whole is Puerto Rico; cf. W. van Rijckeghem, 'An Econometric Model for a Dual Economy: The Case of Puerto-Rico', *Tijdschrift voor Sociale Wetenschappen*, No. 4, 1969. The implications for inflation of this phenomenon are discussed in G. Maynard and W. van Rijckeghem, *A World of Inflation*, London 1976, pp. 62–4.

[35] M. Vandoorne and W. Meeusen, 'The Clay-Clay Vintage Model as an Approach to the Problem of Structural Unemployment in Belgian Manufacturing', State University Centre, Antwerp, 'Working paper', December 1979.

[36] M. van Hecke, 'Benelux', in OECD, *Regional Trade Union Seminar on Prices Policy*, Paris 1974.

[37] H. Glejser, 'Un modèle trimestriel partiel des prix, des salaires et de l'emploi en Belgique', *Cahiers économiques de Bruxelles*, No. 35, 1967; P. Ghikour, 'Les performances du moùcle trimestriel des prix, des salaires et de l'emploi "EOLE" élaboré par Glejser', *Cahiers économiques de Bruxelles*, No. 44, 1969; A. Kervyn and V. Staes, 'Les salaires, les prix et l'index', *Recherches économiques de Louvain*, No. 2, 1975.

TABLE 20.6. *Selected government transactions, 1960-73*
(in per cent of GDP at current prices)

	Belgium		Netherlands		Luxembourg	
	1960-66	1967-73	1960-66	1967-63	1960-66	1967-63
Tax revenue	29.0	34.5	33.3	41.0	31.2	32.5
Current expenditure	28.9	33.8	32.4	40.7	28.2	30.9
Investment	2.5	3.5	4.6	4.6	4.6	4.1
General government net lending	(−1.5)	(−2.1)	(−0.7)	(−0.2)	(2.8)	(1.1)

Sources: OECD, *National Accounts of OECD Countries, 1953-1969, 1961-1972, 1960-1977,* and *1961-1978*; EEC, *European Economy,* November 1980.

Monetary policy during this period was essentially restrictive. The rapid rise in nominal wages had led to increased demand for credit from the private sector. Both in Belgium and the Netherlands, the authorities had to resort regularly to quantitative credit restrictions, especially during the boom period from 1963 to 1967.[38] They were thus able to prevent additional inflationary forces emanating from easy money conditions.

III. The Energy Crisis and its Aftermath, 1973-1979

As was the case for the rest of Europe, the development of the Benelux countries during the OPEC-dominated later 1970s was characterized by a marked slow-down in the growth rates of GDP as well as by higher rates of inflation and of unemployment (Table 20.7). For an analysis of this period, one still lacks the necessary perspective to judge the relative importance of external and internal factors in explaining the rather unsatisfactory performance. While many commentators have emphasized national factors (e.g. the so-called 'Dutch disease'), one cannot fail to be struck by the similarity in the statistical record between the Benelux on the one hand and the rest of Europe on the other. Unless policy-making was deficient everywhere (a hypothesis which should not be dismissed altogether), this suggests that the Benelux countries adhered to a collective equilibrium pattern upon which they found it hard to improve despite quite different national characteristics, initial conditions, economic policies, and, in particular, energy endowments.

Luck and flexibility

In the early rounds of the energy crisis, the Benelux countries took the blow of the oil embargo and the ensuing price increases rather well. Both 'luck' and 'flexibility', but now in a wider sense, played a role in how each country weathered the crisis. At first, 'luck' seemed to be on the side of the Netherlands, which was almost energy self-sufficient, and which could have offset the terms of trade deterioration due to the oil price rise by a corresponding increase in the price of natural gas, the production of which is state-controlled. In fact, the Dutch

[38] J. Finet, 'Monetary Policy in Belgium', and E. den Dunnen, 'Monetary Policy in the Netherlands', in K. Holbik (ed.), *Monetary Policy in Twelve Industrial Countries*, Federal Reserve Bank of Boston, Boston 1973.

TABLE 20.7. *Major macroeconomic indicators, 1973–1979*

	Belgium	Netherlands	Luxembourg	OECD Europe
	average annual percentage changes			
GDP	2.3	2.5	1.0	2.4
Labour productivity[a]	2.3	2.3	0.2	2.2
Inflation[b]	8.4	7.2	7.4	10.9
	percentages[c]			
Investment ratio[d]	21.9	20.8	27.0	21.5
Unemployment rate[e]	6.5	4.0	0.6	4.6[f]

[a] GDP per employed
[b] Consumer prices
[c] 1974–79
[d] Gross fixed investment in per cent of GDP at constant prices
[e] In per cent of the labour force
[f] Average of eleven countries (representing some 80 per cent of the European labour force) for which comparable figures are available
Sources: OECD, *National Accounts of OECD Countries, 1950–1979*; OECD, *Labour Force Statistics, 1968–1979*; OECD, *Economic Outlook*, July 1981; IMF, *International Financial Statistics* (1980 Yearbook); EEC, *European Economy*, November 1980.

authorities delayed this measure, partly because of long-term export contracts, and partly because of their desire to cushion the inflationary impact of high energy prices on domestic consumers. This policy was also motivated by the fact that *before* the oil crisis, inflation had already reached the alarming 8 per cent level. Through its conservative energy pricing, the Dutch government succeeded in moderating the acceleration in inflation in 1974–5 to barely 2 percentage points as against a European average of 4½ percentage points. In the BLEU, on the other hand, where the inflation rate had been lower in the early 1970s, but where dependence on imported energy was above 80 per cent, the increase in oil prices had to be passed on entirely, and inflation, between 1972–3 and 1974–5, accelerated from some 6 to nearly 13 per cent in Belgium and from 5½ to 10 per cent in Luxembourg. During the later years of the decade the price levels in Belgium and the Netherlands converged again, as the Netherlands gradually adjusted its price for natural gas to that of oil, and Belgium got inflation under control.

Even if, by past standards, Benelux inflation in these years was clearly high, in relative terms the area's prices had, between 1973 and 1979, risen by approximately 20 per cent *less* than those of their competitors (Table 20.8). A major factor in this achievement was undoubtedly the gradual effective appreciation of their exchange rates, which attained 18 per cent for the Belgian franc and 23 per cent for the guilder. As a result, the relative competitive position of the two countries changed little over the period. The somewhat larger appreciation of the guilder than of the Belgian franc can be ascribed to the Netherlands' stronger current account position, in its turn due to the country's more favourable energy balance. In the course of the decade, however, the Dutch current surplus was gradually eroded, while the BLEU's deficit rose (Table 20.9). The continuing

TABLE 20.8. *Relative prices and competitiveness*
(indices: 1972 Q1 = 100)

	Relative prices[a]		Effective exchange rate		Relative competitiveness[b]	
	BLEU	Netherlands	BLEU	Netherlands	BLEU	Netherlands
1973	95.2	98.5	102.0	103.3	97.1	101.8
1974	93.5	90.0	103.9	109.1	97.1	98.2
1975	92.0	88.4	105.5	111.9	97.1	98.9
1976	88.7	87.8	107.7	115.0	95.5	101.0
1977	85.5	86.3	114.3	121.7	97.7	105.0
1978	81.9	83.9	118.5	125.4	97.1	105.2
1979	78.3	79.1	120.3	127.5	94.2	100.9

[a] Wholesale prices of manufactures
[b] Product of first and second columns
Source: EEC, *European Economy*, November 1979 and July 1980.

appreciation of both currencies seemed, therefore, progressively less justified. It was mainly inspired by the desire of the monetary authorities to follow the DM, Germany being their major trading partner in the EEC.

TABLE 20.9. *Current balance*
($ billion)

	BLEU	Netherlands
1973	1.2	2.4
1974	0.6	2.2
1975	0.3	2.0
1976	–	2.7
1977	−1.0	0.6
1978	−0.9	−1.4
1979	−3.2	−2.3

Source: OECD, *Economic Outlook*, July 1981.

The deterioration in the current accounts varied in size and in composition across the three countries. Between 1973 and 1979 the Dutch balance on goods and services (on a national accounts basis) worsened by an amount equivalent to 3.9 per cent of GDP, the Belgian one by 4.4 per cent, and the Luxembourg one by 12.4 per cent. The deterioration in the Netherlands was mainly due to terms of trade changes, that in Luxembourg mainly to volume changes, whereas the Belgian worsening was about equally divided between movements in relative prices and volumes. This implies, curiously enough, that the terms of trade loss was greater for the Netherlands than for Belgium, *despite* a much more favourable energy endowment and a larger appreciation of the guilder. One could conclude, therefore, that whereas 'luck' was on the side of the Dutch, Belgium showed greater flexibility by a better adaptation of export prices to changed international circumstances.

This more 'aggressive' pricing policy may, however, have implied some loss in competitiveness, and, indeed, Belgian exports performed less well than Dutch exports over this period. Their share in world exports of manufactures declined from 5.6 per cent in 1970–2 to 5.3 per cent in 1977–9, while the Dutch share remained unchanged at 4.3 per cent. An interesting study published by the EEC sheds some light on the continuing transformations (Table 20.10). The decline of the BLEU's overall share in the 1970s is entirely due to the category of intermediate products, its major area of specialization. This decline could be related

TABLE 20.10. *Share of Benelux countries in OECD exports of selected commodity groups*
(percentages)

	BLEU			Netherlands		
	1963	1970	1977	1963	1970	1977
Main technology- intensive products	3.0	3.2	3.4	6.7	5.3	5.1
Main investment goods	2.2	2.4	2.5	2.8	3.3	3.5
Main intermediate goods	10.5	10.4	8.4	3.9	4.8	5.5
Total	5.9	5.9	5.0	4.0	4.3	4.6

Source: EEC, *European Economy*, November 1979.

to the energy-intensiveness of some of these products (steel, glass, etc.). It is striking that this is an area where the Netherlands was able to improve its position, thus strengthening the hypothesis that these developments were related to the energy situation. In the area of technology-intensive products, the two economies also moved in opposite directions, but in this instance it was Belgium that was able to reinforce its position while the Netherlands lost ground. It is also worth noting that most of the changes in market shares were in fact a continuation of trends which were already apparent between 1963 and 1970. Although the energy crisis may have accelerated some developments, it would be excessive to blame it for everything.

The internal adjustment to the terms of trade loss also differed between the two countries. One indication of whether the terms of trade change induced by the oil crisis had particularly disruptive effects on internal equilibrium is provided by a comparison between the growth of actual real wages and the real wage growth that would have been warranted, assuming a constant profit share, by the growth in labour productivity *adjusted* for the income loss implicit in the terms of trade deterioration. OECD calculations suggest that in both countries this warranted real wage increased by some 17 per cent between 1972 and 1978, the greater terms of trade loss in the Netherlands having been almost exactly offset by a somewhat faster growth rate in productivity. But whereas in the Netherlands the rise in real wages (close to 18 per cent over the same period) was in accordance with the income 'norm', this was far from being the case in Belgium, where for a while real wages continued to rise at the same rate as before the oil crisis, and where over the 1972–8 period as a whole they rose by 30 per cent.

Partly as a consequence, the growth of real unit labour costs in the economy accelerated in Belgium (from 1.2 per cent per annum in the years 1960–72 to 1.5 per cent in the period 1973–9), whereas it slowed down quite sharply in the Netherlands (from 1.5 to 0.5 per cent). Given this upward momentum in unit labour costs and the deterioration in the terms of trade, the burden of adjustment fell on non-wage income, especially on profits. This was particularly evident in Belgium, where after-tax corporate profits fell to a mere 3 per cent of national income.

The component of final demand which was affected most by this development was business fixed capital formation, especially in the industrial sector. In Belgium and Luxembourg, private investment was virtually stagnant after 1973. In the Netherlands, it declined for three consecutive years (1974–6), but showed some modest pick-up subsequently, suggesting that the earlier shortfall had been due more to the effects of the world recession of 1974–5 on exports, and hence on profits and investment, than to the rise in real wages, which may even have acted as a stabilizer. The blame for the decline in private investment has sometimes been laid on multinational companies and their so-called disinvestment policies. The data seem to indicate, however, that while foreign investment did decline in this period, the behaviour of established multinational enterprises did not differ significantly from that of domestic firms.[39]

A 'Dutch disease'?

The relatively modest performance of the Netherlands in this period, in which its natural gas reserves could have imparted a favourable stimulus to the economy, has at times, and perhaps somewhat hastily, been diagnosed as a 'Dutch disease'.[40] One paradoxical hypothesis which has been advanced to explain Dutch problems in the latter 1970s is that the Netherlands performed poorly *because* of its natural gas endowments, which generated a surplus on current account and exerted upward pressure on the guilder. This, in turn, weakened the competitive position of, and squeezed profits in, the export and the import competing sectors.

Table 20.8 above has shown, however, that increases in the effective exchange rate were largely offset by declines in relative prices, and did not affect the relative competitive position of the Netherlands (with a possible exception in 1977–8). In any event, if there was deterioration, it was never of sufficient magnitude to explain a 'Dutch disease'. It was also seen that real wage increases were roughly in accordance with the national income norm, and that unit wage costs rose only slightly. If ever there was any 'disease', it must therefore have started before the energy crisis, in the late 1960s and early 1970s, as suggested, for instance, by the vintage models of den Hartog and Tjan. The main reason for the post-1973 deceleration of economic growth is to be found in the decline in export demand which occurred during the 1974–5 world recession. This recession affected all three Benelux economies, independently of their energy endowments. After all, of the three, the Netherlands was best able to maintain its share in total OECD exports, and to increase its share in energy-intensive intermediate products.

Did the natural gas windfall make no difference? It certainly did, most obviously for the Dutch government, which saw the proceeds from the sale of natural gas rise from 4 to 12 per cent of total government receipts between 1973

[39] van den Bulcke, *Investment and Divestment*, p. 55.
[40] See, for instance, OECD, *Economic Survey of the Netherlands, 1978*, pp. 34–40.

and 1977 and was thus able to continue to finance the ambitious social programmes which it had started in the 1960s. Between 1974 and 1977, domestic
final demand increased by 11½ per cent in real terms in the Netherlands, as compared to 7 per cent in Belgium. Even during the 1975 recession, when output
dropped, final demand increased by 1½ per cent in the Netherlands. The impact
of the crisis on the living standards of the Dutch population was therefore
probably much less than anywhere else in Europe.

A question that could be raised is whether it would not have been preferable
for the government to use its revenues to stimulate investment or to reduce
taxes. This might have moderated wage demands and might have improved the
future competitiveness of the corporate sector. Given the unfavourable external
environment, it is, however, uncertain whether this alternative would have made
a great difference. In any event, it appears that the Dutch government at the
time did not have the political flexibility to pursue such an alternative because
the decisions to expand the social services sector had already been taken before
the energy crisis.

Crisis and response

The preceding point about political flexibility raises an issue about the room for
manœuvre available to policy-makers in dealing with the repercussions of the
crisis. The trend towards European economic integration had been extremely
beneficial, but it had also further increased the degree of openness of the Benelux
economies and had introduced institutional restrictions on certain areas of
economic policy. At the same time, various economic interest groups had
organized themselves both at the national and at the European level, and had
become centres of economic power determined to preserve their acquired
positions. The climate of solidarity and co-operation, which had been characteristic of the post-war reconstruction period (particularly in the Netherlands),
had gradually given way to an atmosphere of mutual distrust created by constant haggling over purely notional gains. Traditional regional and cultural
differences, which had been exacerbated by the economic decline of certain
areas (particularly in Belgium), had become a constraint on national policy
initiatives. Increased political instability found its expression in short-lived
governments and frequent changes in the direction of economic policy. Finally,
the rapid growth of the public sector and the corresponding tax burden had
become a source of resentment and weariness among the general public, and
had led to scepticism about the ability of the government to deal adequately
with the effects of the crisis.

The nature of the crisis itself, which combined elements of cost inflation
with deflation of effective demand, was also confusing for policy-makers who
had become used to seeing inflation and unemployment as rival evils, not as
mutually reinforcing components of stagflation. Nor was the economics profession particularly helpful in suggesting policies to deal with the crisis, being
in the midst of revising its long-held views on the proper role of fiscal and
monetary policies. The fallout effects of radical monetarism in the United
States had contaminated economic thinking in Europe as well. The validity of
traditional econometric models and their use in the preparation of economic
policy were increasingly questioned, and new models were not accepted easily
either.

The immediate preoccupation of the authorities after the first oil crisis had been to contain the inflationary impact of increased energy costs. In the Netherlands (as was seen above) this was achieved by delaying the increase in natural gas prices and by allowing the currency to appreciate. The Belgian authorities were tempted to suspend wage indexation to limit the inflationary spiral, but in the face of determined union resistance they decided to strengthen their policy of price controls and to restrict effective demand. Public investments were postponed and a deflationary budget was adopted at the end of 1974, which resulted in a reduction of the central government deficit equivalent to 1 per cent of GDP. Monetary policy was tightened even more sharply – by using quantitative restrictions, credit expansion to the private sector in 1974 was limited to 11 per cent, while GDP at current prices was expanding at 17½ per cent. This measure, taken in conjunction with the reduction of the public deficit, contributed, together with world-wide deflation, in precipitating the economy into the 1975 recession. Belgian policy was thus destabilizing, and the belated realization of this in the course of 1975, followed by a reversal of fiscal and monetary policy, was to no avail (Table 20.11).

TABLE 20.11. *Selected economic policy indicators*
(in per cent of GDP at current prices)

	General government net lending			Credit to private sector	
	Belgium	Netherlands	Luxembourg	Belgium	Netherlands
1973	−3.1	1.1	3.5	0.20	0.18
1974	−2.5	−0.1	5.1	0.20	0.21
1975	−4.4	−2.7	1.2	0.20	0.22
1976	−5.4	−2.4	1.6	0.21	0.23
1977	−5.6	−1.4	2.1	0.23	0.27
1978	−6.0	−2.2	(3.2)	0.25	0.30
1979	−7.2	−3.1	(1.0)	0.27	0.34

Sources: Institut national de la statistique, *Annuaire statistique de la Belgique, 1979*; OECD, *National Accounts of OECD Countries, 1962-1979*, and *Economic Survey of the Netherlands* (various issues); EEC, *European Economy*, November 1980.

In the Netherlands, both fiscal and monetary policy were more relaxed at this early stage: the public deficit rose by 1.2 per cent of GDP and credit to the private sector was increased more rapidly than the growth of nominal incomes. It is therefore somewhat surprising that in their study of Dutch stabilization policy, Buiter and Owen should conclude that this policy had been destabilizing just before *and* after the OPEC crisis.[41] The only country which tried to implement a truly anti-cyclical policy (and then only in 1975) was Luxembourg, but the effectiveness of this policy was seriously constrained by the smallness of the economy.

In general, the degree of deficit spending was limited by the financial situation in which the public sector found itself before the OPEC crisis. Whereas

[41] W.F. Buiter and R.F. Owen, 'How Successful has Stabilisation Policy been in the Netherlands? A Neo-Keynesian Perspective', *De Economist*, No. 1, 1979.

Luxembourg enjoyed in 1972-3 a comfortable budget surplus, and the Netherlands were in rough balance, Belgium was already facing a large deficit equivalent to 3 per cent of GDP – a deficit which had become a structural characteristic of Belgian public finances in the 1960s. This limited the scope for an anti-cyclical budgetary policy in the event of a downturn.

The fact that during the ensuing years the budget deficit rose nevertheless must be seen primarily as a passive response to the rise in unemployment. There is a remarkable parallelism between the evolution of unemployment in each country and that of the public deficit. Luxembourg, which has a Swiss-type labour market in which foreign workers act as a buffer, had almost no registered unemployment, and maintained a budget surplus. In the Netherlands, where the unemployment rate was stabilized at 4 per cent after an upward jump in 1975, the deficit was also stabilized. Only in Belgium, where unemployment continued to climb (from 3 per cent in 1973 to 5 per cent in 1975 and nearly 9 per cent in 1979), did the deficit also go on rising, to reach 7.2 per cent of GDP by the end of the decade. The existence of a close relationship is supported by a calculation of the full-employment (central government) budget balance which found that the adjusted deficit had remained at a relatively constant level equivalent to 2 per cent of full-employment GDP in the years 1974-8 as against an actual deficit of 5½ per cent.[42]

This raises the question of why unemployment rose so much faster in Belgium than in the Netherlands after 1975. It is true that the growth rate of GDP was somewhat slower in Belgium, but productivity also advanced more slowly, so that the net impact was about the same. The answer must therefore lie on the supply side. In comparing the evolution of unemployment among men and women, one observes that whereas the male unemployment rate was at a comparable level in Belgium and in the Netherlands (just over 3 per cent in 1977 according to the EEC's *Labour Force Sample Surveys*), there was a large difference for women (3.3 per cent in the Netherlands, but 10.9 per cent in Belgium). Female participation rates have always been higher in Belgium than in the Netherlands,[43] but their relatively rapid increase after 1973 may have been stimulated by liberal regulations for unemployment compensation.[44]

The combination of relatively large budget deficits and relatively tight monetary policies, at least in Belgium and in the Netherlands, may have contributed to the relatively high level of interest rates that were recorded in the later 1970s (Table 20.12). Whereas in many European countries, high interest rates were justified by high actual and expected inflation rates, in the Benelux

[42] W. van Rijckeghem and P. Bekx, 'The Belgian Full-Employment Budget Deficit in the Seventies', *Tijdschrift voor Economie en Management*, No. 3, 1979.

[43] R. Leroy, *Essai sur la population active. Théories économiques récentes et analyse régionale de l'emploi féminin*, Louvain 1968.

[44] H. Glejser, J. Vuchelen, and M. Gerard, 'The Effect of Unemployment Benefits on Unemployment Rates: General Remarks and Analysis of the Belgian Case', in H.G. Grubel and M. Walker (eds.), *The Unemployment Insurance System*, Vancouver 1978. See also M.P. Verlaeten, 'Influence des allocations de chômage sur le taux de chômage', Ministry of Economic Affairs, *mimeo*, Brussels 1978. The last author however finds a rather low 0.6 elasticity of female unemployment with respect to unemployment benefits deflated by the wage level. This is insufficient to explain the observed increase in female unemployment.

TABLE 20.12. *Long-term interest rates*[a]
(percentages)

	Belgium		Netherlands	
	nominal	'real'[b]	nominal	'real'[b]
1973	7.4	0.7	7.8	1.0
1974	8.7	−6.5	9.7	−1.3
1975	8.5	−2.4	8.3	−2.1
1976	9.1	1.2	8.5	−0.6
1977	8.8	2.3	7.5	1.2
1978	8.5	3.8	7.3	1.1
1979	9.5	4.7	8.4	1.2

[a] Government bond yields
[b] Nominal interest rate less percentage change in implicit gross fixed investment deflator
Sources: IMF, *International Financial Statistics* (1980 Yearbook); OECD, *National Accounts of OECD Countries, 1950–1979.*

countries, which had succeeded in reducing inflation to more moderate levels by the end of the 1970s, high nominal rates also implied high real rates (a rough proxy for which is shown in Table 20.12). These were, in turn, invoked as a cause of low investment, and the public sector was at times blamed for 'crowding out' private expenditures. In point of fact, however, it would seem that the international interest rate escalation was probably a much more important influence.

Since the formation of the European 'snake' in 1972, the discount rate had been used with increasing frequency to protect the exchange rates of participating countries. For some time, the Benelux countries even formed a 'tapeworm' within the 'snake' which forced the Belgian franc to follow the more robust guilder. Every attack against the 'snake' coincided with a crisis for the Belgian franc, and each time the National Bank avoided devaluation by raising its discount rate. In 1976, as the economy was recovering, the discount rate increased in three consecutive steps from 6 to 9 per cent, thus setting the scene for a new contraction in 1977. Having successfully weathered these consecutive crises, the Belgian franc found itself substantially appreciated by the end of the 1970s, but at the cost of very high interest rates. The Netherlands, with an inherently stronger currency, were able to maintain a lower interest rate for some time. However, the gradual move into current account deficit weakened the guilder, and by 1978 the discount rate had been raised in several steps from 4 to 6.5 per cent, with a marginal rate attached to it, which at one point reached 12 per cent. During 1979, the first year of operation of the EMS, the Belgian franc remained chronically weak, neither of the two Benelux currencies was able to follow the small 2 per cent upward realignment of the DM, and by the end of the year the discount rates stood at the record levels of 10½ per cent in Belgium and 9½ per cent in the Netherlands.

Faced with increasing constraints on the use of the traditional instruments of demand management and at the same time subjected to rising pressures because of deteriorating labour markets and/or profit conditions, the Benelux authorities, not unlike those in other European countries, reacted by resorting to a number of special selective measures. The labour market side received a lot of attention, partly because of the high budgetary costs of unemployment. Belgium, which faced the more severe problems, took several active and imaginative steps. The measures included an ingenious scheme for voluntary early retirement, the compulsory recruitment by firms of a number of young trainees, increases in temporary public sector employment, and a marginal employment subsidy granted for new jobs created as a result of a voluntary reduction of working time to thirty-eight hours per week in 1979. In the Netherlands, the major measure directed at the labour market was a substantial increase in retirement benefits and accident compensation, to stimulate voluntary withdrawals from the labour market. An imaginative proposal to institute 'creative' leaves of absence was studied by a government committee, but had not been implemented by the end of the decade.[45]

The rise in unemployment would have been even worse had it not been for large-scale government subsidies and loan guarantees to enterprises which had found themselves in financial difficulties. The global cost of these interventions was not known, but was certainly substantial. In Belgium, for instance, almost the whole steel industry had to be bailed out following the huge losses incurred during the 1975 recession. The textile industry insisted on receiving a similar generous treatment. Pressure on the EEC resulted in additional measures of protection at an additional cost to consumers. The Netherlands established a 'Restructuring Company' to act as an intermediary between restructuring sectors applying for funds and the government, and a new investment law was passed providing subsidies corresponding to as much as 1 per cent of GDP for a period of four years to support new investment designed to create jobs, save energy, or promote regional development.

Whether these various and often *ad hoc* measures will succeed is a matter of debate. On the labour market side, reductions in hours worked could well stimulate productivity growth rather than employment creation, while selective wage subsidies often only result in jobs being displaced elsewhere in the economy. On the enterprise side the various subsidies and grants absorb savings which might have been better applied to more dynamic sectors. Indeed, at the very end of the period under review, signs were appearing that these initial and inevitably dispersed and even confused attempts at tampering with the effects of the crisis were being progressively replaced by a more coherent, if perhaps also less generous, outlook on economic policies.

Conclusions

As was the case for most other European countries, the Benelux experienced a period of unprecedented growth during the quarter of a century between 1948 and 1973. In this period, per caput income more than doubled in Belgium and Luxembourg, and tripled in the Netherlands. The faster relative growth of the Netherlands must be seen as part of a catching-up process, since this country started off with a per caput income of only two-thirds that of its Benelux

[45] L. Emmerij and J. Clobus, *Volledige werkgelegenheid door creatief verlof: naar een maatschappij van de vrije keuze* (Full Employment through Leisure Leave: Towards a Free Choice Society), Deventer 1978.

partners, but ended the period with an almost identical level. The preceding survey has indicated that, while the three Benelux countries faced a similar international environment during this period, their response to the opportunities it offered was not the same, and varied from one decade to the next.

The difference in economic performance was most pronounced during the first sub-period, between 1948 and 1960, when most of the catching-up by the Netherlands took place. This process was facilitated by the creation of the Benelux customs union and a 30 per cent devaluation of the guilder in 1949. In these years, the Netherlands established a firm industrial base through a very high investment ratio, which was financed by abundant profits made possible by a policy of low and centrally controlled wages. At the same time, Belgium and Luxembourg, which had devalued by only 12 per cent and were handicapped by a relatively high wage level, improved their industrial structure only marginally and relied on defensive investment in a highly conservative policy environment which used deflation and unemployment to keep wage costs from rising too rapidly.

In the course of the 1960s, the external climate was improved by the process of European economic integration, during which the Benelux countries became more dependent on their German neighbour. They benefited from a considerable inflow of American investment and technology, which contributed to the modernization of their industrial structure, but also introduced a dualistic element in wage formation, which contributed to inflationary pressures. These were further strengthened by tensions on the labour market, consequent upon the achievement of full employment (particularly in the Netherlands where the centralized wage policy collapsed), and by imported inflation after 1968.

After 1973, the increase in oil prices added to the inflationary fire and gradually worsened the countries' trade balances, partly because of deteriorating terms of trade and partly because of the accompanying slowdown in the rise of world trade in which the Benelux countries had increasing difficulty in maintaining their share. Stabilization policies were largely passive and automatic. Monetary policy was mainly used to protect the currencies, which may have become overvalued in a probably misguided attempt to follow the German mark. High and rising unemployment and the budget deficits became the most visible and intractable problems of the 1970s.

As the decade drew to a close with a repetition of the increase in oil prices and the associated prospect of further stagflation and increasing unemployment during the 1980s, the question quite naturally arises to what extent the postwar period was unique in the sense that it was based on low energy costs. Associated with this is the further issue of whether a renewed period of economic progress will be possible before a new cheap and environmentally acceptable energy source becomes available. Although it is always dangerous to try to explain developments in terms of a single factor, the experience of the Benelux throws some light on this question.

In the early 1950s, the region was almost self-sufficient in terms of energy because of its abundant coal reserves, which supplied close to 90 per cent of total energy needs. Mining conditions were such, however, that coal was becoming too expensive, and certainly could not have served as a vehicle for further rapid industrialization. Coal was therefore overtaken by oil, which was both cheaper and more convenient and had more forward linkages with the chemical sector. It was of major significance that the substitution of coal by oil took place much more swiftly in the Netherlands than in Belgium, where the process was obstructed by a coalition of affected interest groups. By 1960, for instance, oil accounted already for half of total primary energy consumption in the Netherlands, but for only 30 per cent in Belgium. The resistance to technical change, which was characteristic of the Belgian economy during the 1950s, thus also found a reflection in the energy sector. One of the more visible consequences of this lack of dynamism was the relative stagnation of the port of Antwerp when compared to the expansion of Rotterdam, which became not only the principal port of entry for oil imports but also the major growth pole in the Benelux area.

This imbalance was corrected during the 1960s, largely through the inflow of foreign capital, which created a new growth pole around Antwerp. By 1973, oil accounted for 58 per cent of Belgium's energy requirements, whereas its share in the Netherlands had declined somewhat to 45 per cent. The reason was that in the mean time another significant change had taken place in the Netherlands, through the exploitation of vast natural gas reservoirs. In 1973, natural gas accounted for 50 per cent of Dutch energy consumption, and for only 17 per cent in Belgium, although the latter was rapidly becoming a major importer of Dutch gas. The gas resources had no visible impact on the growth rate of the Dutch economy, which was already operating at full capacity, but they affected the structure of output in favour of energy-intensive sectors. They may also have encouraged wage increases in the public sector as well as a high level of public consumption, particularly in the field of social expenditures.

The role of energy supply after the 1973 oil crisis is still a matter of debate. One might have expected a better performance of the Dutch economy on the basis of its energy situation, but this was not the case. The presence of indigenous supplies probably stimulated the appreciation of the guilder and helped to keep down the rate of inflation, but it also discouraged traditional exports. It is ironical that at the end of the 1970s the Dutch government decided to keep its gas reserves underground so as to preserve them for future generations, while developing nuclear energy instead, an option which had already been chosen in Belgium. The lesson of the 1970s may, therefore, be that the possession of energy resources does not by itself assure the well-being of the nations which are blessed with them.

Bibliography

Considering the substantial contributions by economists from the Benelux region to the economic literature, it is somewhat surprising that they have produced relatively little by way of economic surveys of the post-war period. The best introduction to the recent economic history of the region is probably that by J. de Vries, 'Benelux, 1920–1970', in C.M. Cipolla (ed.), *The Fontana Economic History of Europe*, Vol. 6, Glasgow 1976. The book by A. Lamfalussy, *Investment and Growth in Mature Economies: The Case of Belgium*, London 1961, covers the post-war period up to 1960. Partial surveys can be found as country chapters in collections of essays, such as those edited by E.A.G. Robinson, *Economic Consequences of the Size of Nations*, London 1960; E.S. Kirschen and Associates, *Economic Policy in Our Time*, Amsterdam 1964; K. Holbik (ed.), *Monetary Policy in Twelve Industrial Countries*, Boston 1973; and G.R.

Denton and J.J.N. Cooper, *The European Economy beyond the Crisis: From Stabilisation to Structural Change*, Bruges 1977.

On specific topics, the following references may be useful. On *population and labour force*: H.G. Moore (ed.), *Population and Family in the Low Countries*, Leiden 1979; R. Leroy, *Essai sur la population active*, Louvain 1968. On *growth and fluctuations*: W. Driehus, *Fluctuations and Growth in a Near Full Employment Economy*, Rotterdam 1972; J.J. van Duijn, 'Dating Postwar Business Cycles in the Netherlands: 1948–76', *De Economist*, No. 1, 1979; Proceedings of the 12th Congress of Flemish Economists, *Conjunctuurtheorie en conjunctuurpolitiek* (Business Cycle Theory and Policy), Gent 1975. On *inflation*: W. Driehuis and P. de Wolff, 'A Sectoral Wage-Price Model for the Netherlands Economy', in H. Frisch (ed.), *Inflation in Small Countries*, Berlin 1976. For a monetarist viewpoint see: P. Korteweg, 'The Economics of Inflation and Output Fluctuations in the Netherlands, 1954–75: A Test of Some Implications of the Dominant Impulse-cum-Rational Expectations Hypothesis', in K. Brunner and A.H. Meltzer (eds.), *The Problem of Inflation*, Carnegie-Rochester Conference Series on Public Policy, Vol. 8, 1978.

On *competitiveness and the balance of payments*: J. Homard, X. Ghymers, and F.G. Prades, 'Evolution de la compétitivité sectorielle des principales économies industrialisées selon l'indicateur synthétique de l'IRES', *Bulletin de l'IRES*, Nos. 39–40, 1977. On *labour markets and unemployment*: H. den Hartog and H.S. Tjan, 'Investments, Wages, Prices and Demand for Labour', *De Economist*, Nos. 1–2, 1976; S.K. Kuipers and F.H. Buddenberg, 'Unemployment on Account of Market Imperfection in the Netherlands since the Second World War', *De Economist*, No. 3, 1978; R.S.G. Lenderink and J.C. Siebrand, *A Disequilibrium Analysis of the Labour Market*, Rotterdam 1976; R. de Falleur, 'Le Travail', in *Proceedings of the 3rd Congress of Belgian Francophone Economists*, Namur 1978.

On *budgetary policy*: W. Snyder, 'Measuring the Effects of Belgian Budget Policies, 1955–65', *Cahiers économiques de Bruxelles*, No. 44, 1969; M. Dombrechts, 'On the Effectiveness of Stabilization Policy in Belgium', *Tijdschrift voor Economie en Management*, No. 4, 1979; W.H. Buiter and R.F. Owen, 'How Successful has Stabilisation Policy been in the Netherlands? A Neo-Keynesian Perspective', *De Economist*, No. 1, 1979. On *monetary policy*: E. den Dunnen, 'Postwar Monetary Policy', *De Economist*, No. 1, 1979, H. Bosman, 'De monetaire politiek in Nederland' (Monetary Policy in the Netherlands) and J. Vuchelen, 'Monetaire politiek in de jaren zeventig in Belgie' (Belgian Monetary Policy in the 1970s), both in *Maandschrift Economie*, No. 9, 1980. On *income distribution and incomes policy*: J.G. Abert, *Economic Policy and Planning in the Netherlands, 1950–1965*, New Haven 1969; J. Tinbergen, *Income Distribution – Analysis and Policies*, Amsterdam 1975; Proceedings of the 14th Congress of Flemish Economists, *Inkomens en vermogensverdeling* (Income and Wealth Distribution), Brussels 1979. On *exchange rate policy*: P. de Grauwe and C. Holvoet, 'On the Effectiveness of a Devaluation in the EC-Countries', *Tijdschrift voor Economie en Management*, No. 1, 1978; H. Verwilst, 'The Determinants of the Exchange Rates in the BLEU', *Tijdschrift voor Economie*, No. 4, 1975.

21

Scandinavia*

PALLE SCHELDE ANDERSEN AND JOHNNY ÅKERHOLM**

Introduction

An analysis of post-war developments in the four Scandinavian countries is difficult to do comprehensively in one single chapter. Even though the four countries share a number of important common features, there are also significant differences regarding structures, cyclical developments, and longer-term trends. Hence the text will, inevitably, have to be somewhat selective. As its major subject-matter it chooses this juxtaposition of differences and similarities, and as major themes it considers three issues which tackle both common trends and divergences in inter-country performance.

First, it looks at the divergent growth paths of the period. These are particularly marked in the later 1970s, and reflect the different vulnerabilities of the four economies to changes in foreign prices and world trade conditions (Table 21.1). But divergences also appear in earlier years (for instance Denmark's relatively sluggish performance in the early 1950s, or Finland's rapid growth

TABLE 21.1. *Longer-term trends*
(average annual percentage changes)

	1950–60	1960–70	1970–79
GDP			
Denmark	3.2	4.7	2.9
Finland	4.9	4.8	3.3
Norway	3.5	4.3	4.4[a]
Sweden	3.4	4.6	2.0
OECD Europe	4.8	4.9	3.1
Inflation[b]			
Denmark	3.2	5.9	9.6
Finland	4.8	5.0	11.2
Norway	4.5	4.5	8.1
Sweden	4.7	4.0	8.7
OECD Europe	3.5	3.8	9.6

[a] 3.5 per cent excluding oil and shipping sectors
[b] Consumer prices

Sources: OECD, *National Accounts of OECD Countries, 1950-1979*; IMF, *International Financial Statistics* (1980 Yearbook).

* As for other country chapters, editorial policy has imposed the use of internationally standardized statistics which at times differ from national concepts and figures.

** Department of Economics and Statistics, OECD, and Monetary Policy Department, Bank of Finland, respectively. The views expressed are those of the authors and do not necessarily reflect those of either the OECD or the Bank of Finland.

throughout the period to the mid-1970s), and these reflect underlying differences in economic structures, in the orientation of policies, and in the reaction patterns of economic agents.

Secondly, it argues that due to a relatively high inflation rate and various structural changes which accompanied the rapid growth in the 1960s, and which in some of the countries reflected a worsening disequilibrium situation, developments in the 1970s would have been different from those of the two previous decades even in the absence of disrupting external events.

Thirdly, it considers the implications of dependence on the rest of the world for macroeconomic policies in small and open economies in the light of the experience of the later 1970s. This dependence was brought sharply into focus after the first oil crisis, when all four countries, at least temporarily, were forced to de-emphasize the full employment target. However, with hindsight, it may also be invoked in assessing the growth performance of the 1950s and 1960s.

Although a periodization according to decades is to some extent an arbitrary disaggregation of a continuous process and is not equally relevant for all four countries, a major distinction is made between the 1950-70 period and the 1970s. Following a brief description of major similarities and differences, Section II looks at growth, cycles, and structural changes in the 1950s and 1960s, and then attempts to identify the major sources of growth, distinguishing between supply and demand factors and giving particular attention to changes in trends between the two decades. This part concludes with a discussion of those features – notably inflation and balance of payments problems – which might explain why the four countries were in markedly different positions at the onset of the world recession of the 1970s. This theme is further pursued in the third section, which discusses the 1970-9 period, emphasizing the diverging growth patterns both between the four countries and in relation to earlier trends. The Conclusions attempt to assess the overall growth performance and the related changes in inflation and financial balances.

I. Some Characteristic Features of the Scandinavian Economies

Similarities

When looking at the four Scandinavian countries as a group and trying to distinguish them from most other European economies, it is natural to point to three common features: a high degree of international exposure, a large public sector, and a high priority attached to the full employment target.

Like all small economies the Scandinavian countries are dependent on and exposed to international developments. (This is particularly true in Norway, where in the late 1970s more than 40 per cent of total output was exported, while the corresponding share for the other three countries was between one-quarter and one-third (Table 21.2).) The importance of foreign trade increased considerably over the post-war period, reflecting the liberalization of world trade as well as a rising international division of labour. External dependence has, in fact, been larger than suggested by average foreign trade shares, as certain features tend to accentuate the influence of international trends. Particularly in Norway, but during certain periods also in Finland and Sweden, the deflationary

TABLE 21.2. *Share of exports*[a] *in output*
(in per cent of GDP at current prices)

	1950–52	1959–61	1969–71	1977–79
Denmark	30.6	32.0	28.0	28.3
Finland	24.0	22.0	25.2	31.0
Norway	42.3	40.5	41.3	42.2
Sweden	24.8	22.3	24.0	28.7
OECD Europe	19.3	20.1	22.7	27.9

[a] Goods and services

Source: OECD, *National Accounts of OECD Countries, 1950–1979.*

impact of weakening exports has been aggravated by a deterioration in the terms of trade so that national income declined relative to domestic output.[1] There is also evidence that the inflationary impact of an improvement in export conditions has gone beyond its direct effects on total demand and money supply, as wage claims in the exposed sectors have tended to escalate in periods of accelerating export prices.[2] And given a high degree of wage emulation, this has quickly spread to the sheltered sectors. Moreover, since imports weigh heavily in domestic expenditure, and wages are also highly sensitive to changes in consumer prices, it may be argued that the Scandinavian countries have been even more exposed to world inflation trends than to swings in the international business cycle.

All four Scandinavian countries have also experienced a marked rise in the public sector's share of total output, reflecting an increasing absorption of resources as well as an above-average rise in the public expenditure deflator. Since public sector spending was relatively high already at the beginning of the 1950s and the development in real expenditure has been accompanied by an even sharper rise in transfer payments, another feature of the Scandinavian countries has been their very high average and marginal tax rates.

In Sweden, the public sector's revenue share in GDP had increased to 51 per cent by the late 1970s (Table 21.3), and the average tax rate, which had doubled over the last twenty-five years, was probably the highest in the world. Denmark and Norway also ranked among the countries with high average tax rates, although public sector growth had been less spectacular than in Sweden. By contrast, in Finland the rise in the public sector had been comparatively slow, and by the late 1970s the average tax rate was close to the Western European average.

A third feature which sets the Scandinavian economies apart from most other countries has been the very active pursuit of full employment and high growth rates. Certainly the weights attached to these targets (or to the constraints imposed by other developments), as well as the reliance on different policy

---

[1] In all three countries raw materials constitute a relatively large share of exports, and in the case of Norway, the sensitivity to international price trends is magnified by the shipping sector, which through most of the period accounted for 20 to 25 per cent of total export earnings.

[2] This process has been most pronounced in Norway and Sweden, while in Denmark sheltered sectors have usually been wage leaders. In Finland, wages appear to react to export price changes with a lag.

TABLE 21.3. *Share of taxation*[a] *in output*
(in per cent of GDP at current prices)

	1955–57	1962–64	1969–71	1977–79
Denmark	(25.1)	(28.4)	39.8	42.8
Finland[b]	(31.5)	(28.3)	32.3	37.0
Norway	(29.0)	(33.1)	40.2	46.6
Sweden	(26.6)	(32.7)	41.1	50.8
OECD Europe	(25.4)	(28.0)	31.5	36.9

[a] General government tax revenues
[b] Excluding contributions to some pension funds which in the other countries are considered part of taxation; in the late 1970s these would have boosted the output share by some 5 to 6 per cent of GDP

Sources: OECD, *Revenue Statistics of OECD Member Countries, 1965–1980*, and *Public Expenditure Trends*, Paris 1978.

instruments, have varied over time and between countries. Generally, however, full employment has been the primary goal, and ambitions with respect to the achievable level of employment have increased, notably during the 1960s. Low inflation has been a secondary target, with anti-inflationary measures being adopted only when the rate of inflation exceeded certain thresholds, usually perceived in relation to foreign price trends. And balance-of-payments considerations have mainly been seen as a constraint on the potential for achieving full employment, although in certain periods this has had the same policy implications as specific balance of payments targets. It needs to be stressed, however, that this broad characterization of policy aims overlooks important differences between the 1950–73 period and the years following the 1974–5 recession. Thus, in all four countries, balance of payments and inflation considerations gained in importance during the latter period.

The various characteristics mentioned above have produced another set of features, which also distinguish the Scandinavian countries from other economies. In view of the large shares of imports and taxes, short-run expenditure multipliers have been relatively low, probably falling within a range of 1¼–1½, with Sweden and Finland at the upper end and Norway at the lower end. And due to the high priority attached to the full employment target, the rate of inflation has tended to exceed that of OECD Europe while external balances have generally been in deficit. As a result, a spontaneous change in private or foreign demand has quickly lost its momentum unless supported by international developments or by the governments. And as regards the latter, balance of payments constraints have usually forced the authorities to further 'break' the momentum of an autonomous strengthening of domestic demand while, for the same reasons, a decline in foreign demand has not always been counterbalanced by expansionary measures.

Differences

At the same time, it is also important to point out that the Scandinavian countries cannot be dealt with as one homogeneous area. While all four countries have benefited from a highly skilled and well-educated labour force and a smooth redistribution of employment in favour of high-productivity sectors, as well as a comparatively high and rising capital–labour ratio, there are significant differences as regards factor endowments which in turn explain a wide variation in output structures. Thus Finland, Norway, and Sweden are net exporters of raw materials (metals, pulp, forestry products, and – after 1977 in Norway – oil and gas), while Denmark has to import virtually all raw materials. On the other hand, Denmark has been – and continues to be – an important net exporter of agricultural products, whereas the other three countries are either net importers or are just self-sufficient owing to heavy subsidy payments to the agricultural sector.

There have also been important differences with respect to some of the features discussed above. This is particularly so as regards the *impact of* international trends. In both Norway and Sweden, for instance, exports have tended to lead domestic business cycles, but the presence of sizeable built-in stabilizers has dampened the impact of foreign trends on domestic demand and output. Thus, in Norway, fluctuations in the exported volume of goods and services have been importantly influenced by changes in the position of the shipping sector, which has a rather small influence on the domestic economy. Moreover, sharp fluctuations in exports of raw materials and semi-manufactured goods have been largely offset by corresponding changes in inventories or imports, and thus affected current production relatively little. In Sweden, which has traditionally produced a broader range of goods, the direct effect of exports has been more modest and subject to longer lags, as various sectors have been affected at different stages of the international business cycle. In addition, changes in export volumes have (except for the later 1970s) been largely matched by changes in import volumes. According to Lindbeck[3] this behaviour can be expected if growth is export-led and the difference between overall propensities to save and invest is small relative to the import propensity. In such circumstances, the induced rise in imports will be very close to the original rise in exports.

In Finland, the domestic repercussions of changes in exports have probably been more pronounced, reflecting the special and partly underdeveloped structure of the economy. Due to the large element of raw materials in exports, prices and volumes have tended to move in the same direction and export earnings have fluctuated sharply. Moreover, given the dominant position of the domestically based forest products, the import content of exports is significantly lower than in the other countries, while fluctuations in the forest industry are rapidly reflected in the whole domestic economy. In Denmark, finally, changes in the foreign balance in real terms have in some years significantly affected the growth pattern, but these shifts seem to have originated at home, while international repercussions have largely been felt in the form of terms of trade changes. This has been mainly due to the high – though declining – export share of agricultural products, and to the need to import virtually all raw materials, implying that the elasticity of imports with respect to domestic demand has been much higher than the elasticity of exports with respect to foreign demand. As a result, the Danish economy was frequently unable to take part in international upturns, as a large share of its exports was unaffected and the terms of trade tended

---

[3] A. Lindbeck, 'Theories and Problems in Swedish Economic Policy in the Post-War Period', *American Economic Review*, June 1968.

to deteriorate;[4] equally, however, it was spared the worst consequences of international slowdowns.

Within the broad characterization of policies given above, there have also been significant differences, both as regards the priorities attached to the different targets and the types of policies implemented. Thus, Norway has pursued the full employment target most persistently. Although the economy suffered severely during World War II, full employment was re-established by the end of the 1940s, and for most of the following thirty years the rate of unemployment has been below 2 per cent. While the scope for policy manœuvres has generally been constrained by balance of payments considerations, the authorities have usually preferred to finance current deficits by capital imports rather than to eliminate them by restraining domestic demand. The inflation target has been pursued by a broad range of incomes policies, and Norway has gone further than most other countries in institutionalizing wage and income negotiations and solving distributional issues within a macroeconomic framework. The government has frequently resorted to temporary price freezes and has influenced fixed investment through credit controls.

Swedish economic policy, though pursuing similar aims, has more consciously tried to control cyclical fluctuations by combining selective and general measures. The counter-cyclical power of fiscal policy had already been recognized in the 1930s, and the novel features of policies during the period under review have mainly been the development of selective instruments for stabilizing business fixed investment and reducing or preventing imbalances in the labour market. Selectivity has also been a characteristic feature of monetary policy, as the authorities have attempted to influence not only the total volume of credits, but also its distribution. Though the openness of the economy has naturally affected the room for manœuvre, balance of payments problems have only on a few occasions led to a change in the orientation of policies. And unlike the other three countries, the Swedish authorities have not applied incomes policies in a formal sense, though centralized bargaining and close co-operation between the government and the labour market parties have frequently produced results which in the other countries were achieved through more formal arrangements.

In both Denmark and Finland, on the other hand, balance of payments considerations have frequently been in conflict with the full employment target. In Denmark this has led to a typical 'stop-go' policy approach. For most of the 1950s, and again in the later 1970s, a precarious external position imposed the need for restrictive policies, resulting in very high unemployment rates compared with the other three countries. In the 1960s and early 1970s the employment target was more rigorously pursued, though periodically restrictive measures had to be taken as the economy tended to overheat and the external deficit grew to an unmanageable size. Monetary policy has generally been applied to ensure a capital inflow sufficiently large to finance the current deficit, and, in contrast

---

[4] The underlying reasons for the insensitivity of exports to international upturns changed during the period under review. In the 1950s it was mainly due to the large share of agricultural exports and a manufacturing sector mainly selling on the home market. In the 1960s, when the share of agricultural products was much smaller, the manufacturing sector frequently encountered difficulties in attracting resources in a generally full employment economy.

to the other three countries, domestic interest rates have exceeded international rates by a large margin. Incomes policies have been resorted to, while selective measures have played only a relatively minor role.

In Finland, the full employment target and the external position have also been in frequent conflict, and these considerations have largely guided policies. High growth rates were pursued by devaluation (1957, 1967, 1977–8), and measures favouring retained profits in order to stimulate the business sector. At the same time, interest rates were kept down by administrative measures, while efforts were made to direct the flow of loanable funds towards the manufacturing sector. But these policies, in combination with rapid structural changes within the economy, have entailed high inflation despite frequent attempts to shift the Phillips-curve by the use of incomes policies. This has tended to erode the competitive position, and from time to time restrictive demand management policies have been resorted to, resulting in temporary increases in unemployment.

Turning to the use of policy instruments, there are some similarities at a very aggregate level (e.g. the use of indirect taxes and government expenditures for short-term stabilization purposes, that of income taxes and transfer payments for longer-term aims, or that of credit supply rather than of money supply as the principal indicator and instrument of monetary policy). None the less, there are marked differences in actual implementation, particularly on the monetary policy side, reflecting institutional factors as well as the perceived role of monetary policy within general demand management.[5] Denmark has chosen a 'high interest rate option', and the stance of monetary policy has mainly been determined by balance of payments considerations, while stabilization of the domestic economy was only undertaken when domestic credit market conditions were consistent with international trends. For the period 1950–70 the long-term bond rate was the principal instrument, but for certain years interest rate policies were supplemented by quantitative controls on either mortgage loans or private bank lending.

In the other three countries the stance of monetary policy has been mainly determined by domestic considerations, and the principal channel for achieving credit supply targets has been the lending ability of the private banking sector. However, the regulation of private bank lending has differed quite considerably between them:

(i) In Finland the authorities have relied almost entirely on controlling commercial bank lending, which accounts for a major part of the credit market in the almost total absence of traditional financial markets. During the post-war period, the banks have been in constant debt to the Bank of Finland, and the main policy instrument has been regulation

[5] In assessing the appropriateness of monetary policy in small and open economies, it is frequently necessary to take account of the dual nature of such economies. Thus, a policy stance compatible with aggregate supply and demand may be too restrictive for the exposed sectors, while a policy more closely adapted to the conditions of the exposed sectors is likely to lead to excess demand in the sheltered sectors. As a result, actual monetary policy has usually involved a mixture of general measures such as interest rate variations, or open market operations and selective measures, or direct controls which are more easily adaptable to specific sectoral conditions.

of the conditions at which banks could borrow at the central bank. Interest rates have been kept within a very narrow band, and most often well below the equilibrium rate;

(ii) In Norway, policies have been based on an assumed close relationship between bank lending and primary reserves, and changes in reserve requirements have been the most important instrument. Until the late 1970s an additional feature has been a policy of very low interest rates, creating a permanent excess demand for loans, and a tight regulation of the overall credit supply through state bank lending;[6]

(iii) In Sweden (as in Norway), changes in primary reserves and reserve requirements have been the principal instruments in regulating overall credit supply. Over time, interest rate variations have become more frequent, but various selective measures favouring priority sectors have also gained in importance, partly reflecting the increased share in total lending of the National Pension Fund.

II. The 1950s and 1960s

Over these two decades growth in the Scandinavian countries (outside Finland) was somewhat below that achieved in OECD Europe, but well above pre-war averages.[7] It was, moreover, accompanied by full employment and relative price stability. Within this favourable environment there were, however, different trends and changes in trends which may require explanation. The following appear particularly interesting:

(i) The difference in behaviour in the 1950s between Denmark and Finland – the latter grew very rapidly, the former slowly and out of line with international trends, notably until 1957–8;

(ii) The generalized acceleration in growth which took place from the 1950s to the 1960s in Denmark, Norway, and Sweden;

(iii) The virtual absence of cyclical fluctuations and the continuous full employment achieved by Norway and Sweden;

(iv) The possibility that performance in all four countries was beginning to deteriorate as the period neared its end.

In the absence of econometric models it will not be possible to give very precise answers to these various questions, and the analysis will be largely qualitative in nature. The first subsection describes growth trends and cyclical movements, the second and third supply and demand factors respectively, while the fourth looks at whether the observed patterns were consistent with longer-run equilibrium conditions by analysing the inflation performance and shifts in external and internal financial balances.

[6] In both Norway and Finland the monetary authorities have also influenced the lending activity of private banks through directives as to the allocation of funds. External conditions have played only a minor role, and capital flows were subject to control throughout the period under review.

[7] See Table 1.1.

Growth, cycles, and structural change

During the 1950s, and with the exception of Finland, growth rates were 1¼–1½ percentage points below those of OECD Europe, though measured on a per caput basis the differences were smaller. During the 1960s average growth rates were in line with those recorded in other European countries, and the acceleration compared with the 1950s was particularly pronounced in Denmark and Sweden. For the period as a whole the sharpest increases were recorded in the late 1950s and early 1960s, while towards the end of the 1960s growth rates tended to fall, though the degree of deceleration varied from country to country.

With respect to cyclical developments, the 1950s were a period of quite pronounced fluctuations in Denmark and Finland, and both countries experienced years of falling or stagnating output. In Norway and Sweden, developments were much more stable, with average year-to-year variations in the rate of growth amounting to only 1 per cent. There was also a distinct difference in the respective roles of domestic and external factors. Thus Finland, Norway, and Sweden largely followed the international business cycles, with strong upturns in 1950–1 and 1953–7 and slowdowns in 1952–3 and 1957–8. The latter was the most severe recession of the 1950s as unfavourable external developments combined with weakening domestic demand to bring output well below potential. In Denmark, on the other hand, the cycle was almost the reverse of that observed internationally. A marked terms-of-trade deterioration during the Korean War led to a sharp fall in domestic demand. Over the following two years of relatively weak international trends, total output recovered strongly, while during the international boom years of 1953–4 restrictive policies reduced the average growth rate to less than 2 per cent. And finally, towards the end of 1957 and throughout 1958, when most other countries experienced a marked weakening of growth, Denmark saw a sharp cyclical upturn which lasted for almost five years.

During the 1960s cyclical movements were smaller (Fig. 21.1). Though both Denmark (1963) and Finland (1967–8) encountered recessions, and the growth pattern was considerably more unstable than that of OECD Europe, the downturns were brief and the output path smoother than in the previous decade. Cyclical fluctuations were almost absent in Norway and Sweden, where the absolute gap between actual and potential output averaged barely ½–¾ per cent through the decade.

In all four countries resource-shifts out of the primary sector contributed to growth in both decades. This shift was most pronounced in Finland (where at the start of the period the primary sector accounted for close to 50 per cent of total employment and where inter-sectoral productivity differences were wide)[8] – and may have been a major reason for the country's above-average growth rate. In Sweden, on the other hand, the primary sector produced less than 10 per cent of total output at the start of the period, and shifts of resources mainly took the form of movements within sectors and between regions. While the *overall* contribution to growth of such changes is, of course, unmeasurable,

---

[8] In 1960 output per employed person in the primary sector was only one-third of that recorded in manufacturing and construction.

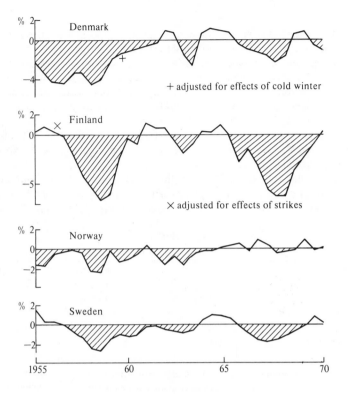

FIG. 21.1. *Indicators of cyclical fluctuations* (gap between actual and potential output in per cent of potential GDP)
Source: OECD, 'The Measurement of Domestic Cyclical Fluctuations', *OECD Economic Outlook – Occasional Studies*, July 1973.

the *direct* impact can be calculated, on the basis of some simplifying assumptions. According to OECD estimates[9] sectoral shifts accounted for 38 per cent of overall growth in Finland between 1955 and 1968, while for Denmark and Norway the corresponding figures were 24 and 23 per cent. Studies for Sweden suggest that the productivity gains from resource reallocation were somewhat smaller, particularly when the calculations also include the rising share of the public sector.[10]

[9] OECD, *The Growth of Output, 1960–1980*, OECD, Paris 1970.
[10] Results vary, depending on period and disaggregation, between 3 and 12 to 15 per cent. The former estimate, for the years 1946–65, is by Y. Aaberg, *Produktion och produktivitet i Sverige, 1861–1965* (Production and Productivity in Sweden), Industriens Utredningsinstitut, Stockholm 1969; the latter, for the 1950s, is by G.R. Österberg, 'An Empirical Study of Labour Reallocation Gains in Sweden between 1950 and 1960', *Ekonomisk Tidskrift*, No. 2, 1965.

Supply factors

In analysing long-term growth trends it is natural to start with the supply side. While developments in total demand determine the actual rates of growth, the scope for increasing demand will ultimately depend on the availability of resources. On the other hand, it is, of course, difficult to distinguish clearly between the impact of demand and supply factors. Thus, an expansionary demand management policy may generate an acceleration in actual as well as potential productivity increases. And, perhaps of even greater importance in small open economies, the interaction of supply and demand will affect the allocation of resources which may either ease or tighten the constraints on achieving potential output.

Reflecting the low birth rates of the 1930s, none of the four countries benefited from a particularly rapid expansion of labour supply in the 1950s (with Norway experiencing almost no increase at all) (Table 21.4). There was a

TABLE 21.4. *Growth of labour force*
(average annual percentage changes)

	1950–60	1960–70	1970–79
Denmark	0.6	1.3	1.3
Finland	(0.7)	0.3	0.6
Norway	0.2	0.7	1.9[a]
Sweden	0.6	0.9	1.0
OECD Europe	0.7	0.3	0.7

[a] 1972–79

Sources: OECD, *Manpower Statistics* and *Labour Force Statistics* (various issues).

sharp acceleration in the following decade (at least outside Finland), but a major share of the recorded growth can be attributed to higher participation rates for women,[11] which probably accentuated the downward trend in average hours worked and may also have reduced overall mobility due to a growing number of households with more than one breadwinner.

These aggregate figures tend, however, to understate the contribution of labour force developments to overall growth. As noted earlier, the outflow of labour from the primary sector increased overall labour productivity. Moreover, even though regional differences exist and the geographical mobility of the labour force has been constrained by housing shortages, the process of matching supply with demand worked rather smoothly. While this was helped by active labour market policies (particularly in Sweden), labour migration also served to contain losses of potential output due to frictional or structural unemployment. Thus there was a net flow of some 140,000 persons from Finland to Sweden during the 1960s,[12] and there are indications that this tended to reduce labour market imbalances in both countries.

---

[11] By the early 1970s female participation rates ranged from 50 to 60 per cent in all four countries and were the highest in Western Europe.

[12] Almost half of the outflow took place in 1969–70, when the Finnish labour force

TABLE 21.5. *Gross fixed capital formation*

	Investment ratio[a]			
	1950–52	1959–61	1969–71	1977–79
Denmark	(16.1)	(20.4)	25.5	22.3
Finland	(24.3)	(29.7)	28.4	24.5
Norway	26.5	27.2	28.4	30.3[b]
Sweden	16.7	20.7	21.8	19.5
OECD Europe	(16.9)	(21.4)	23.6	21.0

	Growth of investment[c]		
	1950–60	1960–70	1970–79
Denmark	5.3	7.3	0.8
Finland	7.6	4.3	0.9
Norway	3.1	5.1	3.6[d]
Sweden	5.6	5.1	0.5
OECD Europe	7.1	6.0	1.7

[a] Gross fixed investment in per cent of GDP at constant prices
[b] 25.6 per cent excluding oil sector
[c] Average annual percentage changes
[d] 2.4 per cent excluding oil sector
Sources: OECD, *National Accounts of OECD Countries, 1950–1979* and *1950–1968*.

On the capital side, Table 21.5 suggests that the share of output devoted to investment has been rather higher in Scandinavia than in most other European countries, and particularly so in Finland and Norway. While this could, in principle, have been favourable to growth, allowance must also be made for differences in capital–output ratios and in the composition of aggregate investment.[13]

Tentative estimates of capital–output ratios for the four countries[14] suggest

---

actually declined; despite some net returns during the early 1970s, more than 100,000 Finns (equivalent to 5 per cent of the Finnish and 2½ per cent of the Swedish labour forces) were at work in Sweden by the end of 1977.

[13] A comparison of (constant price) investment ratios and average GDP growth rates gives the following picture for the 1950–79 period as a whole:

	Investment ratio	GDP growth
Denmark	22.3	3.6
Finland	27.8	4.4
Norway	29.6	4.1
Sweden	20.6	3.4
OECD Europe	21.7	4.3

[14] Measured at constant prices and excluding residential buildings and the public sector, the following estimates were obtained for capital–output ratios:

	1950	1960	1970
Denmark	0.8	1.2	1.4
Finland	..	3.2	3.2
Norway	2.0	2.3	2.5
Sweden	2.3	2.4	2.4

These calculations were largely confirmed by H. Koskenkylä and K. Pekonen, 'Where are Finland's Excessive Investments?', *Unitas*, No. 2, 1976.

that these were relatively high in Norway and, particularly Finland (reflecting the importance of 'heavy' industries and shipping), and largely 'offset' the effect of high investment shares. In both countries, the rate of growth of the capital stock was of the order of 4½ to 5 per cent per annum and comparatively stable between the two decades. In Sweden, the growth rate was more moderate (3½ to 4 per cent per annum for both decades), partly due to a low investment share relative to the capital–output ratio and partly as the result of a high and rising proportion of residential construction in aggregate investment. By contrast, in Denmark the capital–output ratio was relatively low due to the high output shares of agriculture and 'light' industries. This meant that despite the comparatively low levels of investment, Denmark experienced the fastest growth in the capital stock as well as a clear acceleration between the 1950s and the 1960s (from 5¾ to 6¾ per cent per annum).

However, aggregate data for the capital stock provide only a partial impression of the contribution of investment. First, with depreciations accounting for 40 to 50 per cent of gross investment (lowest in Denmark and highest in Sweden), changes in the age structure of the capital stock could have a significant effect on growth potentials. This may have been of particular importance in Sweden were the share of depreciations increased considerably between the 1950s and the 1960s, suggesting that capital-deepening contributed to the acceleration in output and productivity. Second, since technical progress is partly embodied in new investment, it is reasonable to assume that the contribution of capital was higher than implied by changes in the capital stock and that the very high productivity increases during the early and mid-1960s may have largely reflected the preceding boom in manufacturing investment.

Third, there were important changes in the composition and sectoral distribution of capital formation. Thus, the investment share of manufacturing, which weighs heavily in an assessment of export potentials, tended to peak during the late 1950s and early 1960s, while over the second half of the latter decade sheltered sectors accounted for a rapidly rising share of total fixed investment. This process was most pronounced in Denmark and Sweden, where the investment booms in the manufacturing sector were relatively short-lived, while the service sectors experienced sharp rises in investment. In Finland and Norway the deceleration in manufacturing capital formation was much less pronounced, although there was some acceleration in the growth of service sector investment and residential construction.

All in all, it seems reasonable to conclude that supply factors were no more than permissive. In Denmark, Norway, and Sweden there was some acceleration in labour force growth between the 1950s and the 1960s, but the 'stimulus' to growth may have been partly offset by changes in the composition of the labour force which reduced aggregate labour productivity and the degree of mobility. As regards the contribution of gross capital formation, measurement problems preclude the derivation of firmer conclusions, particularly when changes in the age and sectoral structure of the capital stock are also taken into account. Indeed, if it is assumed, following Denison,[15] that factors are remunerated according to their marginal productivity, and average factor shares are applied

[15] E.F. Denison, *Why Growth Rates Differ*, Brookings Institution, Washington 1967.

in assessing the growth contribution of each productive factor, most of the acceleration from the 1950s to the 1960s is 'explained' by a residual component. While it hardly needs emphasizing that such calculations are highly tentative and arbitrary, they do suggest that the most important reasons for changes in growth patterns are to be found on the demand side.

Demand factors

Looking at the contribution to growth from the demand side is not as straightforward. The channels of transmission are many and their theoretical underpinnings are not always firmly based. This discussion will privilege two sets of 'exogenous' forces – those emanating from the external side and those stemming from the role of economic policies.

Owing to the openness of the Scandinavian countries, the impact of external changes is not confined to shifts in the volume of exports but also involves fluctuations in foreign prices and changes in international capital market conditions. Moreover, there are several ways in which external trends can influence the growth pattern, both directly and indirectly:

(i) The 'classical' case of export-led growth, where an autonomous rise in exports directly raises the level of activity and generates a sustained increase in all demand components;

(ii) An improvement in the terms of trade, which raises national income relative to output and stimulates domestic demand;

(iii) A stable development in export volumes and/or foreign prices which, by reducing uncertainties relating to the balance of payments outlook, may remove constraints on faster growth;

(iv) Greater availability of foreign loans and/or greater willingness to finance current deficits by capital imports.

There is little doubt that these latter two indirect effects contributed to the faster growth of the 1960s. The relatively stable development in foreign prices (compared with the turbulent early 1950s and what was to come later) is likely to have reduced uncertainties. And at the same time the rapid growth in international money and capital markets allowed the authorities to pursue more expansionary policies, as short-run balance of payments deficits could be financed rather easily.

With respect to the direct effects, Norway probably comes closest to the case of export-led growth, as exports contributed more than 50 per cent to the growth of GDP in the 1960s. In addition, terms of trade changes had a positive effect on national income, while in the 1950s foreign trade prices had not only reduced national income somewhat (Table 21.6), but also shown significant year-to-year fluctuations. Although domestic demand also increased at a faster rate and imports accelerated sharply as a result, the improvements in exports and the terms of trade were sufficiently large to reduce the current deficit compared with the earlier decade. In Sweden, higher exports were also a major factor behind the more buoyant trend of the 1960s. The average rate of growth more than doubled, and the foreign balance in real terms provided a positive contribution, compared with a 'loss' of 0.3 per cent of GDP on average for the previous decade. Unlike in Norway, however, the terms of trade were unfavourable,[16] and this more than offset the improvement in trade volumes, so that the external balance showed a net deterioration.

TABLE 21.6. *Changes in terms of trade*[a]
(average annual percentage changes)

	1950–55	1955–60	1960–65	1965–70	1970–73	1973–79
Denmark	0.6	0.5	0.9	0.6	0.4	−2.3
Finland	4.8	−2.1	1.4	−0.9	−0.4	−1.1
Norway	0.2	−0.9	0.8	1.7	−0.5	−1.5
Sweden	1.7	0.1	−1.1	0.3	−0.5	−1.8
OECD Europe	0.2	−	0.5	0.4	−0.3	−1.4

[a] Derived from implicit deflators for exports and imports of goods and services
Sources: OECD, *National Accounts of OECD Countries, 1950–1979* and *1950–1968*.

In the cases of Denmark and Finland, it is more difficult to assess the net influence of external changes since a number of special factors of crucial importance were at work in the 1950s and affected the growth pattern very differently in the two countries. In Finland, the very large terms of trade improvement in 1951 (export prices rose by 80 per cent, import prices by 'only' 32 per cent) was probably one of the most important factors behind the rapid growth of the early 1950s, as the authorities did not neutralize its influence on domestic output and demand. In addition, the high reparation payments for war damage, which still in 1949 accounted for some 4 per cent of GDP, were mainly concentrated on metal products and stimulated a rapid expansion of the metal sector. A third feature of this period was the maintenance of import controls which indirectly may also have helped domestic growth. It was only in 1957, in connection with a 28 per cent devaluation of the markka, that imports were freed from the license system.

Denmark, by contrast, suffered a substantial terms of trade loss in 1950–1 and the low level of foreign exchange reserves was an overriding constraint on policies through most of the decade. Thus, the combination of slow growth in export earnings (reflecting the large share of agricultural products in exports and the widespread tendency to protect domestic food production in other countries), or very low capital imports (partly due to difficult international borrowing conditions but also reflecting the official policy of repaying earlier debts), and of an underdeveloped industrial structure (which was heavily dependent on imports of raw materials) narrowed the scope for a faster expansion of the industrial sectors and for a less restrictive policy stance. However, in the course of the 1950s, the Danish economy saw a progressive removal of its main structural weakness, i.e. the commodity composition of exports. Helped by the devaluation of 1949 (which entailed some undervaluation of the Danish currency) and by a relatively moderate increase in unit labour costs,[17] the

---

[16] The commodity composition of Swedish exports and imports normally prevents very large changes in the terms of trade, and the deterioration recorded during the 1960s was mainly due to a very slow increase of export prices.
[17] The outflow of labour from the agricultural sector occurred before the manufacturing sector was quite ready to absorb it and probably had a dampening effect on wage trends.

underlying competitive position gradually improved and by 1957 manufactured goods accounted for 38 per cent of total exports compared with only 27 per cent in 1950. And the more favourable competitive position, combined with a number of specific factors (such as a marked improvement in the terms of trade, new depreciation rules, special credit arrangements favouring manufacturing investment, relaxation of the restrictions against foreign borrowing), implied that the industrial sector was ready for 'take-off' when the overall business climate improved in the late 1950s.[18]

Turning to the impact of economic policies, as a starting-point it may be useful to distinguish between:

(i) Direct effects emanating from the development in public spending on goods and services, but partly also including movements in those private demand components which are most sensitive to changes in policy instruments (residential construction and to a lesser degree business fixed investment and private consumption);

(ii) Indirect effects reflecting the generally high level of demand and the extent to which this influenced productivity gains and structural changes. Under this heading one might also include possible effects on business and consumer confidence stemming from the firm commitment to the full employment target and the success of anti-recession policies.

As regards the direct effects, all four countries experienced a marked acceleration in the rate of growth of public spending. This impulse was particularly strong in Denmark, where the increase attained almost 8 per cent on average for the 1960s, and least pronounced in Finland (Table 21.7). Though increased spending was accompanied by a sharp rise in taxation, the figures shown in the table suggest that higher taxes only partially offset the expansionary effect of higher expenditures. Thus, and with the exception of Sweden, the financial surplus of the public sector fell relative to GDP between the 1950s and 1960s. According to the balanced budget multiplier an unchanged financial surplus would have implied an expansionary effect, and even in Sweden the budgetary impact is likely to have been positive as the rise in net public saving can largely be ascribed to the National Pension Fund, which used almost its entire surplus in financing residential construction.

The impression that expansionary effects were strong is reinforced by the behaviour of some other demand components. The widespread acceleration in residential construction between the two decades, for instance, would seem to suggest that stimulating or at least permissive policies were present.[19] In both Norway and Sweden, relaxation of quantitative controls on building permits

[18] Another important feature was that from early on manufacturing exports were spread over a very wide range of products. This was clearly an important reason why Denmark was hardly affected by the 1958 recession.

[19] In all four countries the housing market had been characterized by excess demand throughout the 1950–70 period, implying that permissive policies or stimulatory measures have had a large and immediate effect, while contractionary policies influenced construction activity with a considerable time-lag.

TABLE 21.7. *Indicators of policy effects*

	Public spending[a]		Public net saving[b]	
	1950–60	1960–70	1950–60	1960–70
Denmark	4.4	7.9	2.2	1.5
Finland	3.9	5.1	4.8	3.0
Norway	4.8	6.6	4.1	3.5
Sweden	4.6	6.0	1.9	4.0

[a] Average annual percentage changes in general government total public expenditure
[b] In per cent of GDP at current prices
Source: OECD, *National Accounts of OECD Countries* (various issues).

and favourable financing conditions (low interest rates and preferential treatment in terms of credit availability) promoted house-building. Quantitative controls were rarely applied in Denmark, and the unusually sharp rise in residential investment in the 1960s was mainly the result of a rapid growth in household income, and expectations of large capital gains. Also, the more active use of interest rate policies combined with rising marginal tax rates and the full deduction of interest payments in taxable income may have provided an additional incentive.

It is more difficult to identify the policy effects on private investment. None the less, counter-cyclical policies, particularly in Norway and Sweden, probably had a stabilizing influence, and business fixed investment in Norway may have been further stimulated by very low interest rates and by the high priority attached to investment as opposed to household spending in determining overall credit supply and its distribution. In Sweden, the use of investment funds is generally regarded as having contributed to the unusually stable behaviour of investment and to a faster growth of total capital spending.[20]

Low interest rates are likely to have favourably influenced investment in Finland as well, but, otherwise, this demand element was highly volatile, reflecting a tax system which, though designed to promote investment, contains (in marked contrast to the Swedish counter-cyclical system) a number of built-in destabilizers. With favourable depreciation rules and few other policy instruments to even out fluctuations in business profits, the corporate sector was highly

[20] Since 1958, the Swedish authorities have relied on an investment funds system — as opposed to an earlier system of investment taxes — in which firms were allowed to set aside 40 per cent of profits and deduct such reserves in the calculation of taxable profits. Provided that the funds are used during a period — usually a cyclical downturn — stipulated by the authorities, the use of funds for investment purposes is also exempt from profit taxation, and a further 10 per cent tax deduction is allowed. Since only 46 per cent of the funds set aside have to be deposited in blocked accounts with the central bank, the immediate advantage to the firms is a gain of liquidity. Moreover, while the investment funds system may be characterized as a tax-free appropriation for future investment, and was mainly designed to change the timing of investment, it is also likely to have increased the level of expenditure. Effectively, the system is similar to accelerated depreciation or loans at very favourable interest rates and implies a more than 100 per cent depreciation allowance. For further discussion see A. Lindbeck, 'Some Fiscal and Monetary Policy Experiments in Sweden' in Federal Reserve Bank of Boston, *Credit Allocation Techniques and Monetary Policy*, Boston 1973, pp. 188–94.

motivated to invest during periods of rapidly increasing cash-flow. As a result, manufacturing investment rose strongly following the raw material boom in the early 1950s and in the wake of the 1957 and 1967 devaluations, but stagnated or even declined in periods of recession. In Denmark, finally, policy effects may have been least favourable. Though specific measures helped the acceleration in investment which took place in the late 1950s and early 1960s, the general orientation of policies may have exerted an inhibiting influence in the longer run. Thus the high interest option adopted by the authorities, combined with excess demand for housing, tended to produce a bias against business fixed investment, as firms were either 'crowded out' of the domestic credit market or reluctant to take foreign loans because of exchange risks.

Finally, as regards househould spending and saving, the impact of policies on long-term growth is mainly dependent on the extent to which they produce a stable consumption pattern and a development in the savings rate which is consistent with investment requirements. On both counts, policies were least favourable in Denmark, as the expansionary policy stance, combined with a shift of income distribution in favour of wage and salary earners, tended to further increase the already high output share of private consumption. In addition, the rather erratic changes in household spending can to some extent be ascribed to a particularly destabilizing feature of the income tax system[21] and to announcement effects in connection with major policy changes. Nor was private consumption a stabilizing element in Finland, where year-to-year fluctuations in household savings have been very pronounced. By contrast, in both Norway and Sweden the savings rate was relatively high and private consumption has been a stabilizing element. There was only a small acceleration between the 1950s and the 1960s and deviations from the longer-term trend were well below those of total output.[22]

Apart from the direct and indirect demand effects of the generally more expansionary stance in the 1960s, policies may also have contributed to a faster growth of output by stimulating productivity gains. When the level of demand is high relative to potential output, the shift of resources between, as well as within, different sectors tends to accelerate and existing resources are generally used more intensively. Moreover, in such conditions, aggregate productivity increases have a large endogenous component in the sense that excess demand pressures accompanied by accelerating wage increases eliminate the least efficient firms and thus raise the overall level of productivity gains. The latter effect may be particularly pronounced in small and open economies in which output prices are often determined on world markets. Indications of this process

---

[21] For most of the period, taxes paid in year t were based on taxable income of year $t-1$, and in calculating taxable income for year $t-1$ taxes paid in that year (i.e. levied on income of year $t-2$) were deductible. Hence, in the event of a strong nominal income rise in year t, most of the increase would be retained as disposable income. In year $t+1$, the tax burden would rise considerably, to be followed by a sharp rise in deductions in year $t+2$.

[22] It should be mentioned, though, that following a decade of rough stability around an 8 to 9 per cent level, Sweden's savings ratio fell to only 5 per cent of household disposable income in the late 1960s. This shift can be partly ascribed to the introduction of the National Pension Fund, which eliminated one important motive for saving, and redistributed a financial surplus from the private to the public sector.

are found in all four countries, though most visibly in Denmark and Sweden.

Summarizing the argument so far, it would appear that policies were clearly an important explanatory variable for the various trends selected at the beginning of this section, though external forces and special influences also played a role. Thus, the divergent performances of Denmark and Finland in the 1950s seem largely attributable to the upsurge in raw material prices which necessitated a restrictive policy in the former country, but allowed a more permissive stance in the latter. Moreover, the relaxation of the structural constraint on Danish growth (the unfavourable composition of exports) which took place through the 1950s would seem to have been largely generated from the supply side, although the relaxation of policies which intervened at the turn of the decade may also have helped the acceleration in growth which occurred. In the other two countries, this acceleration seems to have owed more to external demand and price trends, particularly in Norway, while the role of supply factors has been of only secondary importance.

Turning to the divergent cyclical experiences, foreign trade, and especially terms of trade, changes were clearly important, but economic policies would seem to have also had a large influence. Norway and Sweden actively used both general and selective measures to control demand fluctuations and to minimize unemployment. Their success in this, as noted above, was outstanding. Denmark and Finland, on the other hand, seemed somewhat less preoccupied by the extent of cyclical swings in activity. In the 1950s Denmark was worried about the balance of payments and accepted lower growth at times, while Finland was more concerned with growth, and let the currency devalue on two occasions. In addition both countries were inhibited by tax systems which inherently destabilized either household or corporate incomes. Even in these two countries, however, the development of activity was a good deal smoother than in the interwar years, and full employment was largely maintained, at least in the 1960s.

It is this latter factor which suggests that an even more indirect policy effect may have been at work in all the four countries. The commitment to full employment and the large degree of success achieved in avoiding marked cyclical fluctuations may have strengthened business and consumer confidence. However, since the business sector was less favourably placed in the competition for scarce resources, this sort of reaction tended to affect spending patterns rather than output potentials. Hence, while helping to remove slack and create a sustainable growth path, it carried the risk of also generating inflationary pressures and/or balance of payments difficulties. Indeed, the idea cannot be excluded that some of the problems which the four countries encountered during the second half of the 1960s were in part related to 'over-confident' spending behaviour, as total demand tended to rise faster than total output. This had important consequences for inflation and financial balances which in turn influenced output potential in the 1970s.

Growth, inflation, and financial balances

As mentioned earlier, a characteristic feature of the Scandinavian economies has been a relatively high rate of inflation. This was particularly apparent in the second half of the 1960s when in all four countries inflation rates were well above the average for OECD Europe (Table 21.8). There are a number of reasons for this 'inflation proneness'. One of them may well have been the high priority attached to the full employment target since in empirically estimated wage equations an important factor in all four countries seems to have been the degree of excess demand pressure in the labour market.

TABLE 21.8. *Selected inflation indicators*
(average annual percentage changes)

	1950–55	1955–60	1960–65	1965–70	1970–73	1973–79
Hourly earnings						
in manufacturing						
Denmark	7.5	6.4	10.2	11.2	14.0	14.1
Finland[a]	9.5	6.9	8.3	8.9	14.2	14.1
Norway	8.8	6.1	7.2	9.0	10.5	12.6
Sweden	10.8	6.0	8.3	8.9	10.3	11.1
Consumer prices						
Denmark	4.0	2.4	5.1	6.7	7.2	10.7
Finland	3.0	6.7	5.2	4.7	8.2	12.7
Norway	6.3	2.8	4.1	4.9	6.9	8.7
Sweden	5.7	3.6	3.7	4.4	6.7	9.8
OECD Europe	3.9	3.1	3.6	3.8	7.0	10.9

[a] Average earnings

Sources; OECD, *Main Economic Indicators* (various issues); IMF, *International Financial Statistics* (1980 Yearbook); Central Statistical Office of Finland, *Bulletin of Statistics* (various issues).

Apart from the commitment to full employment, policies may have aggravated the inflation performance in several other ways. First, the use of indirect taxes as the principal short-term instrument in dampening demand led to a faster rise in consumer prices. Second, there are indications of tax–push effects stemming from the longer-run rise in direct tax rates.[23] Third, while high growth rates generally helped to solve income distribution issues in a non-inflationary way, attempts at creating a more even wage distribution tended to push up nominal wage gains as pay increases for low-income workers often went beyond what the market could bear and subsequent excess demand for skilled workers led to higher wage drift.[24] Fourth, stop-go policies — most pronounced in Denmark and Finland — were at least in part responsible for an uneven growth pattern, which may also have imparted an upward bias to inflation.

Finally, and perhaps most importantly, the Scandinavian economies are

[23] Wage claims based on real disposable income targets were presented in Sweden as early as the mid-1960s and have since gained in importance in all four countries, though least explicitly in Denmark. Hence, while the rising average and marginal tax rates served partly to offset the direct demand effect of higher public expenditure, an inflationary effect came through the income formation process. For all four countries the coefficient of nominal wage gains with respect to the rate of change in consumer prices appears to be close to unity, even though there are large differences in the use of formal indexation schemes.

[24] In all four countries the trade unions have argued for a 'solidaristic' wage policy, and some policy measures, such as minimum wages and equal pay for men and women, have also had an equalizing effect on the pay structure.

highly sensitive to international price trends. Import prices explain a large part of the development in consumer prices which, in turn, have a significant influence on changes in nominal wages. Moreover, wage developments are quite sensitive to changes in export prices, as higher profits are reflected in wage claims, so that improvements as well as deteriorations in the terms of trade tend to increase cost pressures. In these circumstances, the acceleration in world inflation in the later 1960s was quickly transmitted into higher domestic prices.

While it would be difficult to isolate and quantify these various causes of price and wage increases, the inflation process had important structural implications which are most clearly seen within the framework of the Scandinavian theory of inflation.[25] According to this hypothesis, prices in the traded goods — or exposed — sectors are determined on the world market, and (on the assumption of unchanged factor shares) the 'room for wage increases' in these sectors will depend on price and productivity increases. With wages in the sheltered sectors following the trend set by the exposed industries, domestic prices will rise faster than international prices to the extent that productivity gains are below those of the exposed sectors. And the overall price rise will be determined by the increase in international prices, the shares of the two sectors in total output, and the differential rates of productivity gains.

Should wage gains in the exposed sectors exceed the 'room for wage increases' and the exchange rate remain unchanged, profit shares will decline and the competitive position deteriorate, with a subsequent worsening of the external balance. While in the short run deviations are bound to occur, departures from the equilibrium path over an extended period of time imply a situation of underlying disequilibrium, which sooner or later poses a threat to growth potentials.

Indications of such departures became increasingly evident in the Scandinavian countries in the course of the 1960s. In Denmark, the inflation rate had already exceeded that of other European countries by a large margin during the first half of the 1960s, and even though a further acceleration from the first to the second half of the decade was accompanied by a widening of profit margins, the higher productivity gains (Table 21.9) were to a large extent caused by wage cost pressures, and the share of profits declined. Moreover, the fact that output prices in the manufacturing sector increased considerably faster than in the other three countries and exceeded export prices for OECD Europe by an even larger margin suggests that a rising share of manufacturing output was sold on the home market rather than exported.

In Sweden there are some indications of a similar disequilibrium, but it seems to have started later than in Denmark, never to have gone quite so far, and differed somewhat in nature. Thus, for the first half of the 1960s the average rate of inflation was no higher than that of other European countries, and the foreign account was largely in balance. Starting in 1965, however, inflation rose above the European average, profits were squeezed, the share of manufacturing investment fell, and the foreign balance went into deficit. Even though average

---

[25] See O. Aukrust, 'Inflation in the Open Economy: A Norwegian Model', in L.B. Krause and W.S. Salant (eds.), *Worldwide Inflation*, Brookings Institution, Washington 1977; G. Edgren, K.-O. Faxén, and C.-E. Odhner, *Wage Formation and the Economy*, London 1973.

TABLE 21.9. *Growth of productivity, unit labour costs,
and prices[a] in manufacturing*
(average annual percentage changes)

	1950–55	1955–60	1960–65	1965–70	1970–73	1973–79
Denmark						
Output per hour	2.4	3.7	6.2	8.0	7.2	(3.3)
Unit labour costs	5.1	2.7	4.0	3.0	6.3	(10.5)
Prices	3.8	3.6	4.3	4.4	6.4	(11.0)
Finland						
Output per hour	4.8	3.2	4.8	4.5	4.3	3.1
Unit labour costs	4.8	3.8	4.9	4.2	11.1	12.9
Prices	6.3	4.6	2.8	6.7	8.8	12.7
Norway						
Output per hour	1.7[b]	4.1[b]	4.5	5.2	5.7	1.7
Unit labour costs	7.0[b]	2.0[b]	2.6	3.6	4.5	10.6
Prices	2.3	1.3	3.5	5.9	6.7	9.2
Sweden						
Output per hour	4.4	5.9	7.4	6.9	6.9	4.7
Unit labour costs	6.1	0.1	0.8	1.8	3.1	6.9
Prices	5.3	2.3	1.4	2.3	5.9	10.1

[a] Implicit deflator for value added

[b] For 1950–60, data on hours worked are not available; the figures shown are for output
per person

Sources: OECD, *National Accounts of OECD Countries* and *Main Economic Indicators*
(various issues); and Central Statistical Office of Finland, *National Accounts*
(various issues).

profit margins seem to have fallen only little between the first and second halves
of the 1960s, this may understate the extent of the problem. Thus, the growth
of industrial output decelerated sharply in the second half, and there are clear
signs of a rise in the endogenous component of productivity gains as the number
of close-downs in manufacturing nearly doubled. Moreover, with export prices
rising considerably less fast than output prices for total manufacturing, exporting
firms are likely to have felt a particularly severe profit squeeze.

In Finland, signs of a disequilibrium process were as clear as in Denmark and
Sweden, but the timing was different, mainly as a result of measures taken to
reverse the process. During the early and mid-1960s, a sharp acceleration in
labour costs occurred at a time when export prices were depressed or actually
fell in some years. Since the higher cost pressures were only partially offset by
an acceleration in productivity, profit margins were squeezed in the open sector
and the competitive position deteriorated. However, in 1967 the markka was devalued by almost 25 per cent and owing to a subsequent tight incomes policy
the 1968–70 period saw a significant slowdown in domestic cost and price
developments. With a simultaneous revival of productivity gains in the open
sector, profits increased sharply and market share gains were recorded both at
home and abroad.

In Norway, the price performance deteriorated relatively little during the

1960s. Although for the second half consumer prices rose 1 percentage point faster than the European average, this reflected the introduction of a value added tax rather than rising wage costs. In fact, towards the end of the 1960s, when a weaker investment trend led to some easing of excess demand pressure in the labour market, nominal wage gains fell significantly. Furthermore, since unit labour costs rose less fast than output prices and the deceleration in output growth was only moderate, the reduction in the aggregate profit share was limited. Another difference in relation to Denmark and Sweden was that cost pressures and loss of market shares were concentrated in the import-competing industries, whereas in the export and sheltered sectors profit margins were largely maintained.

When these wage and price trends are interpreted within the long-term equilibrium framework of the Scandinavian theory of inflation, it is not surprising that the inflation performance was paralleled by movements in the external account. In both Denmark and Sweden, rising cost pressures were accompanied by − and largely caused − a deterioration in the current balance of payments during the 1960s. On the other hand, in Finland and Norway lower price and wage increases together with, respectively, policy measures and a marked slowdown in investment, generated current surpluses at the very end of the decade. Moreover, these changes in external accounts were accompanied by very different movements in domestic financial balances (Table 21.10).

In Denmark and Sweden the financial deficit of the private sector increased sharply from the 1950s to the 1960s, with a clear widening during the second half of the latter decade. In both countries this can be related to three major factors:

TABLE 21.10. *Financial balances*
(in per cent of gross factor income)

	1951–55	1955–60	1960–65	1965–70
Denmark				
Private sector	−2.9	−2.2	−3.9	−4.9
Public sector	2.5	2.6	1.9	1.9
External balance	−0.4	0.4	−2.0	−3.0
Finland				
Private sector	−4.2	−3.9	−5.1	−4.9
Public sector	6.3	4.2	3.5	3.5
External balance	2.1	0.3	−1.6	−1.4
Norway				
Private sector	−7.3	−6.6	−6.7	−5.0
Public sector	4.7	4.6	3.7	3.8
External balance	−2.7	−2.0	−3.0	−1.2
Sweden				
Private sector	−1.7	−2.2	−3.8	−5.7
Public sector	2.4	1.9	3.8	5.0
External balance	0.7	−0.3	−	−0.7

Source: OECD, *National Accounts of OECD Countries* (various issues).

(i) A marked shift in income distribution in favour of wage and salary earners (Table 21.11), accentuated by a decline in the saving propensity of households;

(ii) A rapid rise in residential construction which, because of low down-payment requirements and long amortization periods, lowered total savings relative to investment;

(iii) A decline in the self-financing ratio of non-residential investment, notably in manufacturing. In fact, given the buoyant demand conditions and the apparent decline in the relative price of capital during the 1960s, the squeeze on profits was probably not accompanied by a decline in investment incentives,[26] so that business fixed investment may have been 'crowded out' for lack of either external or internal funds.

TABLE 21.11. *Share of employee compensation in output*
(in per cent of GDP at current prices)

	1950–52	1959–61	1969–71	1977–79
Denmark	48.3	49.7	54.1	54.0
Finland	48.4	45.8	51.5	56.2
Norway	(43.5)[a]	(49.6)	53.9	57.4
Sweden	50.2	53.5	60.6	66.3

[a] 1951–52

Sources: OECD, *National Accounts of OECD Countries, 1950–1979* and *1950–1968*.

In Norway and Finland it is more difficult to detect a clear trend and, as noted earlier, both countries moved into a surplus position on the external account towards the end of the period under review. With the public sectors in continuous surplus, most of the fluctuations on the external account can be related to private sector saving and investment, or more specifically to the corporate sectors. In Norway, the longer-run trends were dominated by short-run changes in the profit position of the shipping sector, and in Finland the forest industries played a similar role. It is also interesting to note that a rise in corporate saving usually, with some lag, increased investment even more, so that the financial deficit tended to widen immediately after periods of high profits. In both countries this pattern was clearly evident in the early 1970s, as the simultaneous improvement in the profit position and the external account towards the end of the 1960s was succeeded by an investment boom which significantly increased the financial deficit of the private sector and reversed the position on the balance of payments.

All in all, it appears that by the end of the 1960s all four countries were in largely the same position as far as the 'real side' (growth rates and level of employment) was concerned; there were large differences on the 'nominal side'

[26] During the 1960s wages in both countries rose faster than output prices, while real interest rates remained low or even turned negative in certain years. Given the very stable developments at home as well as abroad, it is reasonable to assume that perception of risks declined during the period under review, and that this led to a fall in both the *ex-ante* price of capital relative to wages and in the required minimum profitability of investments.

(inflation and financial balances), suggesting that the growth path had not in all cases been a balanced one. In Denmark and Sweden the process of growth seems to have been accompanied by greater disequilibrium; in Finland, similar signs had appeared in the mid-1960s, but a wide range of policy measures had — at least temporarily — rectified the situation; and in Norway some imbalances were present but never took on very large or serious proportions. These 'accompanying' trends came to play a very important role in the 1970s, partly as a result of policy measures taken to correct the situation, and partly through the way in which the four economies were affected by external events.

III. The 1970s

Like most other European countries, Denmark, Finland, and Sweden experienced a significant slowdown in growth (and acceleration in inflation) during the 1970s (Table 21.12). In Norway, on the other hand, there was hardly any deceleration, and even excluding the oil and shipping sectors the slowdown was

TABLE 21.12. *Major macroeconomic indicators*

	1970–73			1973–79		
	GDP[a]	Inflation[ab]	Unemployment[c]	GDP[a]	Inflation[ab]	Unemployment[cd]
Denmark	4.3	7.2	(1.0)	2.1	10.7	(4.8)
Finland	5.3	8.2	2.2	2.3	12.7	4.6
Norway	4.6	6.9	1.6	4.4[e]	8.7	1.8
Sweden	2.3	6.7	2.3	1.8	9.8	1.9
OECD Europe	4.6	7.0	2.9[f]	2.4	10.9	4.6[f]

[a] Average annual percentage changes
[b] Consumer prices
[c] In per cent of the labour force
[d] 1974–79
[e] 3.1 per cent excluding oil sector
[f] Average of eleven countries (representing some 80 per cent of the European labour force) for which comparable figures are available

Sources: OECD, *National Accounts of OECD Countries, 1950–1979*; OECD, *Economic Outlook*, July 1981; IMF, *International Financial Statistics* (1980 Yearbook); EEC, *European Economy*, November 1980.

only moderate. Developments in these years differed both between countries and between the early and later parts of the period, with the differences largely reflecting variations in the degree to which inflation and balance of payments developments were felt as a constraint on growth.

The early 1970s

While Norwegian developments in the years 1970-3 were relatively smooth, this was not the case for the other three countries. Sweden had entered the period in an unbalanced position, but was able partly to rectify it; Denmark was similarly unbalanced at the outset and possibly even more so by the time the oil crisis broke out; and Finland managed to undo many of the achievements of the late 1960s.

In Sweden, a set of restrictive policy measures was implemented in 1970-1 in order to reduce inflation and improve the balance of payments, the latter mainly through encouraging a faster rate of growth in the manufacturing sector. Largely as a result of this more restrictive stance, 1970-3 was a period of unusually slow growth in which some of the earlier imbalances were significantly reduced. The rate of inflation fell below the European average, investment in manufacturing picked up markedly, and there was a sharp improvement in the balance of payments. Hence, when the first oil price shock occurred and most other countries moved into a phase of very low or negative growth, Sweden was in a position to take expansionary measures and the rise in output accelerated to 4 per cent in 1974.

The Finnish economy entered the 1970s in less of a state of disequilibrium than it had experienced during most of the previous two decades. The external sector, which had been a constant problem since the liberalization of trade, was more or less in balance, the competitive position was strong, the rate of inflation was well below the OECD average, and, reflecting fast growth of production as well as large emigration to Sweden, the unemployment rate had been brought down to 2 per cent. However, the income distribution shift towards profits in the exposed sector led to inflationary pressures as soon as utilization rates increased. And as policies used the room provided by the external balance to keep up employment, these forces continued to gather momentum. For the period 1970-3 the inflation rate exceeded the European average by more than 1 percentage point[27] and the current balance moved back into deficit. Nevertheless, as in Sweden, the authorities reacted to the oil price rise by adopting an expansionary policy stance. Since the measures taken were mainly aimed at bolstering investment and producing the additional capacity required to pay for an expected structural deterioration in the terms of trade, investment demand increased rapidly, and despite declining export volumes, total output grew by almost 3½ per cent in 1974.

In Denmark, the early 1970s were also a period of rapid growth, led by private consumption and particularly residential investment, while public spending — reflecting the influence of growing tax-payer resistance — slowed down sharply. The balance of payments showed some improvement in 1971-2, but this was mainly the result of a temporary import surcharge; when this was removed in 1973, the deficit rose to 2 per cent of GDP despite a sizeable terms-of-trade gain following EEC membership. Since, moreover, the rate of inflation had increased further relative to international trends, the Danish economy was in a weak position to resist the repercussions of the oil price rise and the subsequent world recession. In fact, the imbalances of the later 1960s appear to have grown larger during the period 1970-3, and when international events brought this sharply into focus, the authorities were forced to meet the situation early on with restrictive measures. As a result, output fell in 1974 and the rate of unemployment started to rise towards levels which had not been experienced since the early 1950s.

---

[27] The comprehensive income policies, which had been very successful after the 1967 devaluation, proved to be insufficient in a situation characterized by excess demand pressures.

TABLE 21.13. Growth in nominal wages[a] and in 'real wage gap'[b]
(indices: 1972 = 100)

	1973	1974	1975	1976	1977	1978	1979	1973–79[c]
Denmark								
Nominal wages	114.1	135.7	155.5	169.7	184.5	195.8	213.4	11.4
'Real wage gap'	100.3	107.8	111.1	105.5	103.4	101.0	100.7	0.1
Finland								
Nominal wages	115.0	138.7	170.7	195.9	211.0	226.3	252.0	14.1
'Real wage gap'	97.6	99.8	103.0	102.3	96.2	93.3	92.4	−1.1
Norway								
Nominal wages	112.2	128.2	147.1	162.4	178.6	192.5	199.4	10.4
'Real wage gap'	99.2	100.4	103.4	105.5	106.7	104.5	96.5	−0.5
Sweden								
Nominal wages	106.3	116.2	131.6	148.1	162.1	175.4	189.3	9.5
'Real wage gap'	96.0	95.6	95.3	95.7	98.6	96.0	95.4	−0.7

[a] Compensation of employees per dependent employee
[b] Nominal wages deflated by implicit deflator for private consumption less GDP per employed adjusted for changes in the terms of trade
[c] Average annual percentage changes
Sources: OECD, *National Accounts of OECD Countries*, and *Labour Force Statistics* (various issues).

The later 1970s

As in other European countries, the 1973-9 period was characterized by slow growth, high unemployment, sharp deteriorations on external account and in public sector balances, and strong inflationary pressures. It was also a period in which policy-makers faced the dilemma of adopting an appropriate response to external events and had to make an explicit choice regarding the role of exchange rate policies in general demand management. In view of the differences in initial positions and in the degree of exposure to external trends, it is difficult to evaluate the growth performance over this period, let alone the prospects for the 1980s following the second oil price shock. Moreover, even though all four countries were eventually forced to introduce a more restrictive policy stance, an important feature of the period was the unusually wide range of measures adopted, the effects of which can only be ascertained over the medium term. Since, however, the most important problem would seem to have been the downward adjustment of real income aspirations to the less favourable growth prospects, the following analysis will focus on this process, emphasizing the role of policies and the extent to which rigidities generated inflationary pressures and imbalances.

As can be seen from Table 21.13, the level of real wages was, by 1979, more or less in line in all the four countries with that warranted by the growth of labour productivity *adjusted* for the income loss implicit in the terms of trade deterioration. The preceding years had, however, seen very marked differences in the adjustment pattern and in the extent to which policies had influenced the process. Finland, for instance, in some sense inflated its way out of the adjustment problem in 1974-5. At a time when most other countries faced a severe recession, the economy went into a situation of severe overheating helped by a surge in export prices which had eliminated the terms of trade deterioration by the end of 1974. But this process of reducing real wage gains through higher price increases led to a marked deterioration in international competitiveness (Fig. 21.2) – thus revealing the fragility of the earlier correction of imbalances – and the external deficit rose to almost 8 per cent of GDP in 1975. The subsequent shift in policies had an unusually sharp and almost instantaneous impact on output and employment as several self-correcting forces were at work. First, earlier high investment levels had added large amounts to capacity, which in conditions of weak external and internal demand became idle, while the balance sheets of the corporate sector weakened significantly. Second, since labour hoarding had been widespread until the end of 1975, restrictive policies and the decline in domestic demand generated a sharp rise in unemployment. The response of the balance of payments and the rate of inflation came with a somewhat longer lag but was equally pronounced. Influenced by the growing degree of slack and the nature of the policy measures taken (including income tax reductions as compensation for a moderation in nominal wage gains and lower payroll taxes), the rate of inflation fell to well below the average for OECD Europe in 1978-9, and the balance of payments, reflecting the changed cyclical position as well as an improvement in international competitiveness, moved into surplus. In fact, when export conditions improved in 1979 the authorities were able to relax the restrictive policy stance and the ground was laid for a new upward spurt in activity and a possible repetition of the cycle.

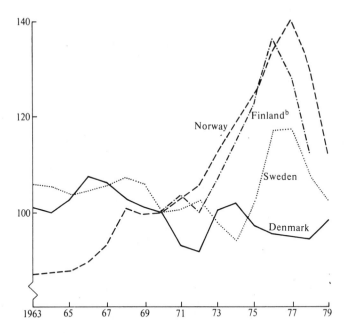

FIG. 21.2. *Indicators of international competitiveness* (relative unit current costs in common currency[a]; indices: 1970 = 100)
[a] Calculated as a weighted average of unit labour costs and raw-material prices and measured in relation to the current cost position of the most important trading parterns
[b] Data not available for the whole period
Sources: OECD, 'The International Competitiveness of Selected OECD Countries', *OECD Economic Outlook – Occasional Studies*, July 1978, and *Economic Outlook*, December 1980.

In Denmark the restrictive policy stance introduced after the oil price rise was maintained through most of this period, as the precarious balance of payments position left virtually no room for policy manœuvres. Due to the sharp rise in the rate of unemployment, wage drift initially declined and nominal wage gains were further reduced through a tight incomes policy and modifications of the indexation system. As a result, the rate of inflation fell to below the European average, and since productivity gains remained high — reflecting a relatively low degree of labour hoarding as well as the policy of not supporting inefficient firms – international competitiveness improved (despite the effective appreciation of the currency through membership of the European 'snake'). Nevertheless, the 'real wage gap' was eliminated only in 1979, while the improvement in the trade balance was more than offset by mounting interest payments. Hence, the basic problem of correcting the foreign imbalance was not resolved, and towards the end of the period there were signs of built-up wage pressures — probably reflecting reactions to the squeeze of wage differentials imposed by three consecutive contractual wage agreements legislated by parliament – as wage drift started to accelerate despite widespread and increasing labour market slack.

Initially Norway and Sweden followed policies similar to those of Finland — general demand stimulus, employment-supporting measures,[28] and, in addition, selective policies in favour of weak industries. And in both countries the results were similar — relatively high growth rates and virtually full employment, but a marked deterioration in international competitiveness, reflecting some acceleration in nominal wage increases, a sharp decline in productivity gains, and an effective appreciation due to the 'hard currency option' initially adopted by the authorities. Moreover, the longer-run flexibility of the two economies in responding to sudden changes in demand may well also have diminished. There were differences, on the other hand, regarding the extent of the imbalances and the nature and timing of the stabilization measures subsequently adopted.

In Sweden, real wages moved in line with the virtually flat trend in real national income, and nominal wage increases were comparatively moderate. Nevertheless, since the moderation was partly due to compensatory income tax reductions which, in turn, were financed by higher payroll taxes, wage costs rose considerably faster than earnings and the improvement in international competitiveness achieved during 1970-4 was quickly eliminated. When policies were shifted towards restriction in 1977, output fell by 2½ per cent (the steepest fall of the entire 1950-79 period) and, due to a simultaneous depreciation and reductions in social charges and payroll taxes, the deterioration in competitiveness was sharply reversed. There were, though, also indications of growing social unrest, pointing to suppressed inflationary pressures and the risk of a renewed widening of imbalances.

Signs of imbalance have also appeared in the late 1970s in Norway, which well into the decade had been characterized by high and stable growth. At one point (1976-7) the external deficit grew to 13 per cent of GDP, and even though this was influenced by special factors such as large imports of investment goods for the oil sector, a slump in net freight earnings, and stagnating exports of raw materials, it was also indicative of surging consumer goods imports and of difficulties in maintaining export market shares for manufactures. Indeed, it would appear that real income aspirations had been adjusted upwards in the light of prospective revenues for the oil sector, so that even if realized real wages did not exceed the 'warranted' growth rate, this implied rising cost pressures for the traditional sectors. The deterioration in competitiveness was the sharpest in Scandinavia and led to the adoption in 1977-8 of a wide set of policy measures, including a depreciation, a reduction in the expansionary stance of fiscal policy, a more active use of interest rate policies, and a complete price and wage freeze lasting until the end of 1979. As a result, the rate of output growth as well as inflation decelerated, but given the temporary nature of some of the measures taken, it is uncertain whether a permanent improvement had been achieved.

[28] In both countries, the authorities relied on subsidies to inventory formation, granted on the condition that firms did not reduce employment during the period when the subsidy was received. In Norway large tax reductions were also granted in an attempt to hold down nominal wage gains. Overall, fiscal policy is estimated to have stimulated real output growth by as much as 15 per cent during the period 1974-7. Labour market measures were used most extensively in Sweden, and by 1977-8, 4 to 4½ per cent of the labour force was enrolled in public relief work and training schemes, with an additional 2 to 2½ per cent estimated to have been 'underemployed' within the private sector.

By the end of the decade all the four countries had taken important policy measures to correct imbalances induced by either external events or past internal developments. However, while some success was achieved in terms of reversing unfavourable trends, the durability of the corrections remained uncertain, with obviously important implications for prospective developments in the 1980s.

Conclusions

Following a long period of high growth, all four countries in the 1970s found the full employment target to be in increasing conflict with other major aims of economic policy, in particular inflation and external balance. The severeness of the problems and the extent to which they reflected states of underlying disequilibrium certainly varied from country to country, being most apparent in Denmark and least in Norway. Though this alone makes it difficult to generalize, it would seem obvious that some of the difficulties stemmed from world recession and from the problems small and open economies encounter when they either try to isolate themselves from international trends or are forced to subject domestic growth and employment targets to external constraints. However, there are also indications that in some of the countries the problems of the 1970s reflected growing disequilibrium, whose origin is to be found in the earlier period. Though policies had achieved a high degree of success during the 1950s and 1960s – and probably more than could reasonably have been expected at the outset – the employment and growth targets may have been too ambitious relative to the balance of payments and inflation constraints.

It could thus be argued that in all four countries the growth path had been accompanied – either as a permanent feature or as a trend over an extended period of time – by internal changes which implied certain risks for a continuation of high growth. In particular, the financial position of the business sector tended to worsen, at least in some of the countries, while household saving rates either stagnated or fell. Since a strong expansion of public sector spending combined with some hesitancy to raise taxes correspondingly made it difficult to create a sufficiently large public sector surplus, all four countries experienced a tendency towards aggregate demand exceeding aggregate supply, with consequent deteriorations in the current external account and high rates of wage and price increases. Moreover, while surging imports served to dampen the inflationary effect of excess demand pressures, the high degree of exposure to international price trends meant that the sharp movements in export and import prices later in the 1970s tended to accentuate inflation and inflationary expectations.

The observed developments in financial balances and inflation may be interpreted and analysed within the framework of the Scandinavian model of inflation. Even though this hypothesis is not equally relevant for explaining inflation in all four countries, it implies certain longer-run conditions which must be satisfied if economic growth is not to be constrained by balance of payments developments. Thus, when long-run wage gains in the exposed sectors exceed the 'room for wage increases', as determined by productivity and export price developments, the growth path will sooner or later be 'broken' by an unsustainably high external deficit, as the exposed industries lose their competitiveness and resources are increasingly absorbed by the sheltered sectors.

From this point of view, Finland, Norway, and Sweden obtained a favourable start in the early 1950s, as the 1949 devaluation *vis-à-vis* the dollar, combined with the boom in commodity prices, considerably widened the 'room for wage increases' in the exposed sectors. In the case of Norway and Sweden, the devaluations no doubt led to a considerable undervaluation of the currency, so that despite relatively high nominal wage gains during the 1950s and the early 1960s the exposed sectors remained competitive, though apparently more so in Norway than in Sweden. In Finland, the wage gains in both the 1950s and the 1960s did exceed the 'room for wage increases', thus threatening the continuation of high growth, but large devaluations in 1957 and 1967 and accompanying incomes policy measures went a long way towards restoring international competitiveness.

In Denmark, on the other hand, the direct benefits of the 1949 devaluation were much smaller due to the low share of manufactured exports, though later in the 1950s an apparent undervaluation of the currency encouraged more rapid industrial development, with wage gains remaining well within the boundaries determined by export prices and productivity gains. However, with excess demand pressures in the labour market during most of the 1960s, the sheltered sectors — mainly construction and the public sector — became wage leaders, so that the exposed industries experienced additional cost pressures with only limited possibilities for raising prices. As a result, they were faced in Denmark — and to a smaller extent in the other countries as well — with a deteriorating competitive position both with regard to maintaining market shares abroad and attracting resources at home.

The effects on growth potentials of this deterioration in export competitiveness, whether it took the form of excess cost pressures or of longer-term shifts of resources into the sheltered sectors, were aggravated by the international recession. Although it is difficult to draw a sharp distinction between the role of exogenous and endogenous factors — and equally difficult to separate cyclical from structural influences — in the situation of the 1970s, the growth experience of the four countries clearly illustrates that high and sustainable growth rates could only be achieved if a certain balance was maintained between exposed and sheltered sectors. Imbalances may appear in various ways, with excessive cost increases being the most visible one, but with shifts in financial balances and related changes in investment patterns being equally important as far as longer-term growth potentials are concerned. And imbalances can have various causes, such as a too rapid growth in public sector spending and/or excess demand pressures and high wage and price increases as a result.

This points to a risk that the high growth rates of the 1950s and the 1960s would have come to an end even in the absence of external shocks. However, it also raises the question of whether timely policy measures could have corrected the imbalances and resurrected favourable growth patterns, and, in particular, whether a more active use of exchange rate policies would have been appropriate. Considering the openness of the Scandinavian countries, it might be argued that a policy aimed at achieving a higher level of employment than in the most important trading partners cannot be continued unless supported by a depreciation of the currency, since otherwise the competitive position and the balance of payments are bound to deteriorate. On the other hand, given the high degree of exposure to external price changes, it might also be argued that exchange rate depreciations are unlikely to provide a durable solution as their main effect will be an aggravation of the wage–price spiral.

The experience of the four countries, particularly in the 1970s, clearly underlines this dilemma regarding the role of exchange rate policies in general demand management. Thus the Finnish devaluations and subsequent domestic policy measures in 1957 and 1967 reversed earlier disequilibrium trends with only a small loss of output, and the Finnish and Swedish devaluations in the later 1970s also appear to have been successful, although the loss of output was now much higher. At the same time, the experience also suggests that it is very difficult to make a devaluation 'stick' once policies are relaxed, and there is always the risk that a process of frequent devaluations gets built into inflationary expectations and thereby loses even its initial effectiveness. In this context, the Swedish policy measures of 1970 provide an example of a successful reversal of earlier unfavourable trends without resort to exchange rate changes and with only a moderate slowdown in growth. And the history of Norway until the mid-1970s illustrates that with a high degree of social consensus and an appropriate combination of demand management and incomes policies it is possible to achieve both high and stable growth even for a small and extremely open economy. On the other hand, Denmark's experience during the 1970s shows that exclusive reliance on restrictive demand management and incomes policies can be very costly in terms of lost output, although the lack of social consensus might also have reduced the effectiveness of a more flexible exchange rate policy.

Against this background it would seem that Norway is most favourably placed as regards growth prospects for the 1980s. In addition, with large energy resources and a likely rising trend for real energy prices, the main problem may well be one of absorbing oil revenues without raising real income aspirations too rapidly and thereby complicating the necessary adjustment of the domestic sectors. Finland also seems to have come through the 1970s without any major imbalances and is less exposed to real oil price changes because of a large proportion of foreign trade with the Eastern bloc. Sweden, on the other hand, is likely to suffer from future increases in real energy prices, and a higher growth path may be conditional on a reduction in the public sector and a restoration of social consensus. Finally, Denmark would appear to be least favourably placed. By 1979 the foreign debt had increased to 20 per cent of GDP (compared with only 1 per cent in 1960), and being almost totally dependent on imported energy Denmark is highly exposed to increases in the real price of oil. Moreover, a smooth transfer of resources from sheltered to exposed sectors in conditions of weak world demand will require a certain degree of consensus regarding the distribution of real incomes, which so far has proved difficult to achieve.

Bibliography

Probably reflecting the relatively favourable growth performance of the Scandinavian countries, there are rather few contributions analysing longer-term growth trends, while there is a rich literature on specific issues (such as inflation and balance of payments problems) and on short-term stabilization policies.

Surveys dealing with parts of the post-war period may be found in: Y. Aaberg, *Produktion och produktivitet i Sverige, 1861–1965* (Production and Productivity in Sweden, 1861–1965), Industriens Utredningsinstitut, Stockholm 1969; E. Dahmen, 'Equilibrium and Development Problems in the Swedish Economy', *Skandinaviska Enskilda Banken Quarterly Review (SEBQR)* 1977; J.H. Gelting, 'Denmark, Norway and Sweden', in M. Bronfenbrenner (ed.), *Is the Business Cycle Obsolete?*, New York 1969; J.H. Gelting, 'Recent Trends in Economic Thought in Denmark', *American Economic Review*, June 1964; S.A. Hansen, '100 aars økonomisk vaekst' (100 Years of Economic Growth) *Nationaløkonomisk Tidsskrift (NT)*, Nos. 5–6, 1972; P. Korpinen and N. Lundgren, 'Finland's Economy: An Outline of a Structural Analysis', *SEBQR*, 1971; A. Lindbeck, 'Theories and Problems in Swedish Economic Policy in the Post-War Period', *American Economic Review*, June 1968; H. Olsson, 'Development Tendencies in Swedish Industry', *SEBQR*, 1971; Statistisk Sentralbyrå, *The Norwegian Post-War Economy*, Oslo 1965.

The following contributions emphasize *stabilization policy*: J.H. Gelting, 'Om finans- og creditpolitikkens effektivitet' (The Efficiency of Fiscal and Monetary Policy), *NT*, 1979, and 'National Autonomy of Stabilisation Policy', in A. Ando, R.J. Herring, and R.C. Marston (eds.), *International Aspects of Stabilisation Policies*, Federal Reserve Bank of Boston, Boston 1974; A. Lindbeck, 'Some Fiscal and Monetary Policy Experiments in Sweden', in Federal Reserve Bank of Boston, *Credit Allocation Techniques and Monetary Policy*, Boston 1973; id., *Swedish Economic Policy*, London 1975; id., 'Business Cycles, Politics, and International Economic Dependence', *SEBQR*, 1975; O. Lindgren and E. Lundberg, 'Sweden's Economy in an International Perspective', *SEBQR*, 1971; E. Lundberg and A. Olseni, 'A Dilemma for Monetary Policy', *SEBQR*, 1971; E. Lundberg (ed.), *Svensk finanspolitik i teori och praktik* (Swedish Fiscal Policy in Theory and Practice), Stockholm 1971.

A discussion of *inflation problems* and particularly the Scandinavian theory of inflation can be found in: O. Aukrust, 'Inflation in the Open Economy: A Norwegian Model', in L.B. Krause and W.S. Salant (eds.), *Worldwide Inflation*, Brookings Institution, Washington 1977.

Balance of payments issues are addressed in: J.H. Gelting, 'Betalingsbalancen 1872–1972' (The Balance of Payments 1872–1972), *NT*, Nos. 5–6, 1972; T. Sukselainen, 'Finnish Export Performance in 1961–1972. A Constant-Market-Shares Approach', *Suomen Pankki A: 36*, Helsinki 1974.

Labour market questions and policies are taken up in the following contributions: E. Brehmer and M.R. Bradford, 'Incomes and Labour Market Policies in Sweden, 1945–70', *IMF Staff Papers*, March 1974; G.R. Österberg, 'An Empirical Study of Labour Reallocation Gains in Sweden between 1950 and 1960', *Ekonomisk Tidskrift*, No. 2, 1965; R. Wiman, 'Työvoiman kansainvälisen muuttoliikkeen mekanismi' (The Mechanism of International Labour Migration), *ETLA B9*, Helsinki 1975 (English summary).

Industrial developments and the determination of *investment* are discussed in: V. Bergström, 'Industriell utveckling, industriens kapitalbildning och finanspolitiken' (Industrial Development, Capital Formation in Industry and Fiscal Policy), in Lundberg, *Svensk finanspolitik*; D.M. Jaffee, 'Capital Market Structure, Housing Policy and Monetary Policy: Sweden and the United States', *SEBQR*, 1974; H. Koskenkylä and K. Pekonen, 'Where are Finland's Excessive Investments?', *Unitas*, No. 2, 1976.

Finally, *consumption, saving, and public sector trends* are analysed in: T. Backelin, 'Konsumtion och sparende' (Consumption and Saving), in Lundberg,

Svensk finanspolitik; F. Ettlin, 'Swedish Private Consumption and Saving During Two Decades', *SEBQR*, 1976; P.N. Rasmussen, 'Den offentlige sektor gennem 100 aar' (The Public Sector over 100 years), *NT*, Nos. 5–6, 1972.

Names Index

Subject Index